Dorothy Binger

ORGANIZATIONAL BEHAVIOR

OVERVIEW OF CONTENTS

MANAGEMENT AND ORGANIZATIONAL BEHAVIOR

1. Understanding the Job of Managing

2. Studying Organizational Behavior

INDIVIDUAL BEHAVIOR

3. Satisfying Human Needs

4. Learning and Reinforcing

5. Understanding the Perceptual Process

6. Understanding the Motivational Process

SUPERVISORY BEHAVIOR

11. Understanding the Leadership Process

12. Developing Leadership Skills

13. Acquiring and Using Power in Organizations

14. Managing Reward Systems

INTERPERSONAL AND GROUP BEHAVIOR

7. Understanding Interpersonal Dynamics

8. Improving Communication Effectiveness

9. Understanding Group Dynamics

10. Dealing with Intergroup Conflicts

ENVIRONMENTAL ADAPTATION

15. Task Design—Matching Jobs to People

16. Designing Organizational Structure

17. Making Managerial Decisions

18. Managing Organizational Change

ORGANIZATIONAL EFFECTIVENESS

19. Developing Effective Organizations

APPENDIX

Developing Careers in Organizations

Micro-organizational analysis

Macro-organizational analysis

ORGANIZATIONAL BEHAVIOR
DEVELOPING MANAGERIAL SKILLS

Kae H. Chung
Wichita State University

Leon C. Megginson
University of South Alabama

HARPER & ROW, PUBLISHERS, New York
Cambridge, Hagerstown, Philadelphia, San Francisco,
London, Mexico City, São Paulo, Sydney

1817

Sponsoring Editors: John A. Woods/Arthur P. Sotak
Project Editor: Nora Helfgott
Designer: Karen Emerson
Assistant Production Manager: Marian Hartsough
Senior Production Manager: Kewal K. Sharma
Compositor: Com Com
Printer and Binder: R. R. Donnelley & Sons Company
Illustrator: John Foster
Cover design: T. R. Funderburk

ORGANIZATIONAL BEHAVIOR: DEVELOPING MANAGERIAL SKILLS

Library of Congress Cataloging in Publication Data

Chung, Kae H
　Organizational behavior.

　Includes index.
　1. Organizational behavior. 2. Management.
I. Megginson, Leon C., joint author. II. Title.
HD58.7.C49 658.3 80-27252
ISBN 0-06-041299-2

CONTENTS

A NOTE TO STUDENTS

The title of this book, *Organizational Behavior: Developing Managerial Skills,* was chosen quite deliberately. The text is for students of organizational behavior—the first or second course in the management curriculum—and it is, therefore, about the behavior of organizations. Perhaps that sounds redundant. We want to emphasize, however, the idea that this course is not just one you have to take to get a degree in business. It is a course about the real world and ways to deal with it successfully. Specifically, it is about the real world of formal organizations, especially business organizations. It is psychology and sociology in action. Understanding organizations and your place in them will help you to better manage one.

This brings us to our subtitle, *Developing Managerial Skills.* This book is written for you as managers and potential managers of organizations. By understanding the behavior of individuals, groups, and the total organization within its environment as they all interact to survive, you can help enhance the survival possibilities. How well you do that will directly affect your personal success in that organization. So besides explaining behavior, we suggest methods for putting observed patterns of behavior into context so you can act in a way that will be congruent with the reality of the situation. These analytical methods and the examples we have included of the resultant managerial acts are the managerial skills of our title. Be aware of them as you read, and know that the information in this text is not an end in itself but a means toward being successful in your chosen field.

What follows is the preface. Consider reading it. It describes what is in the book: its organization, goals, and features. In other words, it, too, is a means to help you understand something—this book. Finally, we say best wishes in your study of organizational behavior.

PREFACE

There are many books currently available on organizational behavior (OB). Why, then, would anyone want to write another book on the same subject? The answer is that we feel this book is different from the others because it integrates various viable theories and relates them to practices. Most books in the field basically present theories and concepts for the purpose of understanding how and why people behave the way they do in organizations. Our book goes beyond this step; it tells students what they can do with the theories and concepts they learn.

The Objectives of the Book

As we wrote this book, we had three objectives in mind. First, we attempted to develop a set of conceptual schemes that can help managers understand the complexity of organizational behavior. Second, we wished to provide a set of heuristic tools that can guide managerial behavior. Third, we wanted to make the book interesting and thought provoking. To these ends, we have used the following approaches: (1) integrative, (2) developmental, (3) theme-oriented, (4) contingency, and (5) action-oriented.

The material *integrates* both micro and macro aspects of organizational behavior. The systems view of an organization, presented in Chapter 2, links the behavior at the micro level (e.g., individual, group, and supervisory) to the behavior at the macro level (e.g., structure, technology, and environment). These micro and macro behaviors are then linked to a firm's organizational effectiveness. This book, however, has a definite micro slant, but so does the subject matter of organizational behavior.

A *developmental approach* was taken in organizing the content of the book. The text begins with an overview of managerial work and provides a framework for studying organizational behavior. The core of the material is organized in such a way that it moves from the micro behavior to the macro. This approach is based on the idea that an understanding of individual and group behavior is essential to the understanding of complex organizational behavior. In addition, it can be argued that managers need to manage their own personal affairs and interpersonal relationships before they can effectively manage complex organizations.

The book takes a *theme-oriented* approach. Instead of grouping the theories and concepts together, by themselves, they are identified with the behavior they describe. No attempt is made to present an exhaustive review of theories and research findings. Instead, the material focuses on the development of *workable* theories in considerable depth before moving on to the presentation of action guidelines. We believe this uncluttered theoretical path facilitates the learning process and, we hope, a mastery of the subject matter. Instructors may add some theoretical complexity if they desire.

The book takes a *contingency approach*. Rather than suggesting one best way of managing people, or a set of universal management principles, it assumes that some theories and managerial practices are useful under certain conditions but not under others. Therefore, it specifies particular conditions under which a certain theory or practice can be used effectively. This approach also provides a means of judging the appropriateness of certain managerial practices for different people in varying situations.

The book is *action-oriented*. We have done three things to achieve this end. First, a set of theme-oriented and workable theories are translated into on-the-job managerial behaviors so that they will be useful to future managers. Second, each chapter has one or two "vignettes" that are introduced to bring a concept, theory, or issue to life. These vignettes show how some concepts can be applied. Third, each chapter ends with a set of questions, key concepts and words, and short cases or learning exercises. These materials will stimulate class discussion and learning experience.

In summary, the overriding theme of this book is a *heuristic approach*. The book attempts to present a set of conceptual schemes and action guidelines that can be used as "heuristic tools" or "walking sticks" to help managers understand and deal with complex managerial behaviors. This heuristic approach should enable managers to reduce the complexity of organizational behavior to a manageable level. Rather than suggest any solutions to a manager's problems, it aims to develop the manager's capacity to understand and solve his or her own problems.

Organization and Content

The book is divided into six parts: (1) understanding the managerial roles, (2) individual behavior, (3) interpersonal and group behavior, (4) supervisory behavior, (5) environmental adaptation, and (6) organizational effectiveness.

Part I is an introduction to organizational behavior. It consists of two chapters. Chapter 1 is designed to provide an understanding of the nature of managerial work. It identifies what managers do on their jobs and discusses what they can do to improve their performance. Chapter 2 presents a conceptual framework for studying organizational behavior and its implication for improving managerial effectiveness. A contingency model is presented in this chapter.

Part II presents a conceptual framework for studying individual behavior. It discusses some of the major determinants of behavior. Chapter 3 identifies the internal causes of behavior—human needs—and the process of satisfying these needs. It raises the question of what people want from their jobs. Chapter 4 deals with the external causes of behavior. It presents the reinforcement theory, which explains how behavior is learned and manipulated. Chapter 5 presents the perceptual view of behavior and deals with individual differences in perceiving and responding. A theory of attitudes is discussed in this chapter. The expectancy theory of motivation is presented in Chapter 6. This theory integrates those three theories presented in Chapters 3, 4, and 5.

Part III deals with interpersonal and group behavior. Chapter 7 focuses on interpersonal behavior that occurs between two individuals. It is directed toward developing interpersonal sensitivity. Chapter 8 focuses on interpersonal communication. It studies the sources of communication problems and the ways to overcome barriers to effective communication. Chapter 9 deals with dynamics within groups. It proposes several group process techniques for improving group effectiveness. Chapter 10 deals with dynamics between groups. It identifies sources of group conflict and proposes ways of promoting group cooperation.

Part IV covers supervisory behavior—leadership and motivation. Chapter 11 presents several theories of leadership. It suggests that leadership effectiveness increases when leadership style matches the situational demands—tasks and subordinates. Chapter 12 focuses on leadership development. It provides methods of changing leadership styles and situational factors. Chapter 13 suggests that managers need to acquire power. Chapter 14 presents methods of evaluating and rewarding employee performance.

Part V deals with various ways of dealing with the environmental forces—technological, market, labor, political, and economic conditions. Chapter 15 proposes a way of enriching jobs and suggests that jobs need to be redesigned to adjust to the changing needs of employees and technological changes. Chapter 16 discusses ways of designing organizational structure. It indicates that structure needs to be designed to meet the information processing requirements created by the internal and external environments. Chapter 17 is primarily concerned with managerial decision making under uncertainty. It also stresses the need for using creative decision processes. Chapter 18 discusses the characteristics of environmental changes and proposes ways of coping with these changes.

Part VI consists of an integrating chapter. It summarizes major theories, concepts, and suggestions presented in the book in three different but interrelated perspectives: theoretical, developmental, and managerial. It argues that organizational effectiveness increases when (1) organizational components, internal as well as external, are congruent, (2) the organization has the capacity to make timely responses to environmental changes, and (3) managers have the capacities to deal with day-to-day managerial responsibilities.

Acknowledgments

So many people were involved in completing this book that we can only recognize a few of them. We wish to acknowledge the contributions of our colleagues at different universities who reviewed the manuscript at various stages. .

We are specially indebted to Elmore R. Alexander, III, Memphis State University; William R. Allen, University of Rhode Island; John Close, University of Wisconsin, Eau Claire; Edward J. Conlon, Georgia Institute of Technology; H. Kirk Downey, Oklahoma State University; Cynthia V. Fukami, State University of New York at Buffalo; Janice Glab, Southeastern Louisiana University; William W. McKelvey, University of California at Los Angeles; Bonita H. Melcher, University of Akron; Richard M. Steers, University of Oregon; David D. Van Fleet, Texas A & M University; Michael C. White, Texas Tech University; and Allen L. Wilkins, Brigham Young University.

In addition, we would like to thank our colleagues at Wichita State and South Alabama: George Beason, Fred Fraft, Gerald Graham, Donald Mosley, Joe Paolillo, Terrell Pike, Bob Ross, Carl Nielsen, Art Sweney, and Curt Wood. These individuals knowingly, or unknowingly, served as our sounding boards. We would also like to acknowledge the assistance of secretaries, typists, graduate assistants, and others who helped us with researching, editing, and typing. They are Julie Amon, Suzanne Barnhill, Jane Beltz, John Chung, Ed Griffith, Cammy Holler, Ruth Johnson, Stephanie Lisowski, Marjorie Nielsen, Parry Pendry, Victoria Rehm, Dennis Szalla, Phillip Turnquist, and Joclaire Waldorf. We would also like to express our appreciation to Nora Helfgott, Kathy Whalen, and the staff of Harper & Row for their guidance and technical assistance throughout this project.

Finally, our families paid the price for this book to be written.

Without the help of these people, the book would not have come to life. Although they all made definite contributions toward improving the content, any limitations or shortcomings are ours.

Kae H. Chung
Leon C. Megginson

MANAGEMENT AND ORGANIZATIONAL BEHAVIOR

1. Understanding the Job of Managing

2. Studying Organizational Behavior

Micro-organizational analysis

Macro-organizational analysis

INDIVIDUAL BEHAVIOR

3. Satisfying Human Needs

4. Learning and Reinforcing

5. Understanding the Perceptual Process

6. Understanding the Motivational Process

SUPERVISORY BEHAVIOR

11. Understanding the Leadership Process

12. Developing Leadership Skills

13. Acquiring and Using Power in Organizations

14. Managing Reward Systems

INTERPERSONAL AND GROUP BEHAVIOR

7. Understanding Interpersonal Dynamics

8. Improving Communication Effectiveness

9. Understanding Group Dynamics

10. Dealing with Intergroup Conflicts

ENVIRONMENTAL ADAPTATION

15. Task Design – Matching Jobs to People

16. Designing Organizational Structure

17. Making Managerial Decisions

18. Managing Organizational Change

ORGANIZATIONAL EFFECTIVENESS

19. Developing Effective Organizations

APPENDIX

Developing Careers in Organizations

MANAGEMENT AND OB

*P*art I is designed to provide some understanding of the nature of managerial jobs. It emphasizes the importance of studying organizational behavior in pursuing managerial careers. Chapter 1 identifies various managerial roles, such as interpersonal, informational, and decision-making, and studies how managers perform these roles. Chapter 2 presents a conceptual framework for studying organizational behavior and a contingency model to go by. The managerial roles in Chapter 1 and the organizational components of the contingency model provide the basis for developing the contents of the book.

LEARNING OBJECTIVES

1. To understand the nature of managerial jobs.
2. To present and compare two views of managing—normative and descriptive.
3. To become aware of the skills needed to perform managerial activities.

CHAPTER OUTLINE

The Normative View of Managing

The Planning Function
The Organizing Function
The Coordinating Function
The Control Function
Evaluating the Normative View

The Descriptive View of Managing

Personal Activities
Interactional Activities
Administrative Activities
Technical Activities
Variation in Managerial Activities

The Nature of Managerial Work

The Hectic Pace of Work
Heavy Reliance on Oral Communication
The Reactive Nature of Managerial Work
The Political Reality of Managerial Work
Evaluating the Descriptive View
Managerial Implication

Summary and Conclusion

1 UNDERSTANDING THE JOB OF MANAGING

The manager's activities are characterized by brevity, variety, and fragmentation. The vast majority are of brief duration, on the order of seconds for foremen and minutes for chief executives. A great variety of activities are performed, but with no obvious patterns. The trivial are interspersed with the consequential so that the manager must shift moods quickly and frequently.

HENRY MINTZBERG, THE NATURE OF MANAGERIAL WORK[1]

Managers play an important role in organizations. Although all members of an organization are responsible for its success, managers usually play a more important role than others because of their positions. They are formally granted authority to manage their organizational units and are responsible for producing efficient results. They serve as doorkeepers to control organizational membership. It is they who decide which projects are on and which ones are not, and they allocate resources accordingly. Because what they do is closely related to organizational effectiveness, students in management and organizational behavior need to study managerial roles and search for ways of improving their effectiveness.

This chapter is primarily concerned with identifying what managers do—managerial roles. There are two different views of managing—normative and descriptive. The *normative view* specifies what managers are supposed to do in the process of managing; the *descriptive view* describes what managers actually do on their jobs. These two views give us some understanding of managerial roles, and from this understanding we can draw a set of implications for improving managerial effectiveness.

THE NORMATIVE VIEW OF MANAGING

> *The normative view of managing defines management as the process of getting the job done. Managerial effectiveness is said to increase when organizational activities are more efficiently planned, organized, coordinated, and controlled.* [2]

When an organization introduces a new product, service, or program, it undertakes a series of actions, activities, or operations that will lead to a desired objective. This process involves planning, organizing, coordinating, and controlling functions.* Any organization must decide what it wants to achieve and how to achieve it (planning); must assemble the human, physical, and financial resources, arrange them into a productive pattern, decide what activities are needed to achieve objectives, and assign responsibility for the necessary activities to various work groups or members (organizing); must communicate with, motivate, and lead employees and coordinate their activities (coordinating); and must see that employees have performed their jobs correctly (controlling).

The following example shows how a manager performs these managerial functions according to the prescriptions of the normative view. The manager's actions contain the elements of planning, organizing, coordinating, and controlling.

> *Mr. Ron Engelberg was a project manager in charge of developing a new computer model at XYZ Computer Manufacturing Company. The objective of this model was to improve the performance of an existing medium-sized computer and reduce its costs. The group felt the objective could be achieved by improving the computing capacity and time.*
>
> *The project was planned for completion in 18 months. It involved the following steps: (1) doing an engineering feasibility study, (2) designing the product, and (3) testing the product. Once completed, the product would go to the production department. Mr. Engelberg prepared a PERT (Program Evaluation Review Technique) chart to lay out the sequence of activities and to monitor the project's progress.*
>
> *The project group was divided into three technical sections: software, logic development (hardware), and packaging. After re-*

---

* *Although writers and speakers use different terminology, we believe that the terms we use best describe these essential and basic functions.*

cruiting 39 engineers and technicians to staff these technical sections, Mr. Engelberg appointed a system coordinator to integrate the activities of the technical groups. The project manager's primary responsibility was to supervise the activities of technical managers and the coordinator.

In addition to monitoring the project, Mr. Engelberg was responsible for handling the personnel matters of his project members. He interacted with functional department managers to request the transfer of project members. He also coordinated the project with the managers in the production and sales departments.

This situation illustrates the process by which a project is carried out. Although the managerial functions are not clearly discernible and separable, the manager performs all of the four major functions. Reducing the computer size, improving the computing capacity, and preparing the PERT chart are part of the *planning function.* (PERT is a planning method frequently mentioned in production and management science textbooks.) Creating the project group and identifying the sequence of operations involve the *organizing function.* Giving instructions and supervising the group's activities involve the *coordinating function.* Finally, monitoring the progress of the project involves the *control function.* The essence of these managerial functions is presented and evaluated in the following sections.

The Planning Function

The planning function can be defined as (1) *deciding the objectives of an organization and its subunits* and (2) *determining the means of achieving them.* The need for planning derives from the fact that organizations are goal-seeking entities; planning is a tool for identifying these goals and finding ways of achieving them. If organizational activities are properly planned and communicated, they give employees a sense of direction that can reduce confusion and random behavior.

Planning is a prerequisite to other managerial functions. It produces budgets, policies, procedures, and schedules that guide organizational activities. Without them, organizational members would respond to their job demands randomly and reactively. Planning also allows managers to coordinate the activities of organizational members toward the predetermined goals. Planning is required to perform the control function; it provides a basis for monitoring actual progress.

Although planning is an important managerial function, it is a difficult tool to apply and, consequently, is often misused. First, planning assumes that the future can be predicted with some accuracy. This assumption is reasonable in stable industries (e.g., foods, beverages, and utilities), but not in most cyclical and volatile industries (e.g., aerospace, communications, electronics, and defense). The limitations of planning will be elaborated on later.

Second, many organizations misuse the planning function. All too often, sales and profits specified in the plan become management's commitment to the stockholders and the financial community. Once made, this commitment becomes the criterion for gauging management performance. Consequently, the plan takes on a life of its own, and managers stick to it even if a need for modification arises.[3]

To overcome these limitations, planning should be flexible and adaptive enough to reflect the changes in internal and external environments. A set of alternative plans should be established or some criteria set up for abandoning existing plans. U.S. foreign policy makers seem to use such an adaptive planning approach. When a policy dealing with other nations does not serve the national interest, they either modify it or abandon it.

The Organizing Function

The organizing function can be defined as: (1) *grouping organizational activities in some logical fashion, (2) structuring the relationships among the group members, and (3) defining working relationships among work groups.* An organization can be divided by functions, products, regions, or projects. The functional form of organizational structure is commonly used in many organizations. This structure typically contains production, sales, accounting, personnel, and research functions. The rationale for dividing organizational activities is to provide task specialization and a system of management. Figure 1.1 shows how a university is divided and structured.

Organizational structure defines working relationships among the divided parts. It can be formal or informal. The formal structure defines

FIGURE 1.1
The Union State University Organizational Chart.

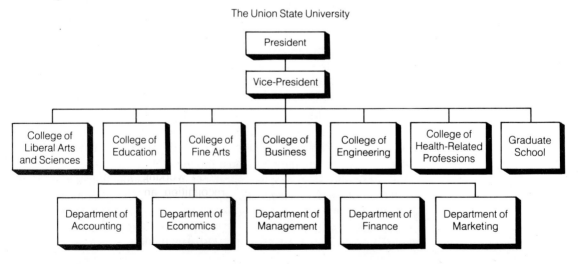

The Union State University

task assignments, authority and responsibility relationships, and formal communication systems. Within the formal structure, informal relationships exist among individual members and between groups. Informal relationships are naturally formed to meet employee needs not well satisfied by the formal structure. These relationships can satisfy socialization needs and facilitate informal communication flow.

An organization's structure can either promote or restrain desirable interactions among work groups. Many jobs in an industrial society demand a high degree of interaction among functional groups. Rigid organizational structure can hinder the natural flow of information among them. In order to facilitate the needed information flow, management can form a flexible organizational structure, such as a project group composed of various functional specialists. This issue will be discussed further in Chapter 16.

While the planning function is primarily concerned with *what* the organization and its subunits *wish* to accomplish, the organizing function is concerned with *who* is responsible for *doing* what. The organizing function facilitates the process by which the planned activities are carried out. This function is also closely related to the coordinating function. Organizational structure provides a communication network through which information is processed within and outside of the organization. In essence, structure provides a system by which group activities are coordinated.

The Coordinating Function

The coordinating function can be defined as *a process of motivating, leading, and communicating with* employees for the purpose of achieving organizational goals. Since organizational activities are performed by many individuals, their efforts need to be coordinated. Most managers spend a greater portion of their time and energy performing this function than any other. Once plans are established and activities organized, the remaining task is to get them carried out. This responsibility is greater at lower levels of management than at higher levels where the plans are usually originated.

Motivation is very important because it is related to employee satisfaction and job performance. People join and work in organizations to satisfy their needs; organizations, in turn, need people to carry out the activities required to achieve organizational goals. Motivation involves *finding the incentives that can satisfy the needs of employees and cause them to work toward the organizational goals.* These incentives or rewards include pay, job security, good working conditions, appropriate supervision, friendly co-workers, recognition, an interesting job, and professional growth.

Leadership may be defined as *the ability to influence the behavior of other people in a certain direction.* The manager's ability to influence organization members is an important element of management. A manager is given the formal *right* to lead (authority), but often does not have the *ability* to lead (leadership). Since the formal positions they hold do not guarantee the ability to lead, managers must acquire leadership ability through expertise, personal charm, or other means.

Communication is defined as *the transmission of information to— and from—all levels of an organization.* Communication is the nerve system of the organization. Most managers spend a great deal of time communicating with other people because it is a major means of performing other functions. Information is transmitted to managers so they can make appropriate decisions; organizational tasks are assigned through communication; instructions are communicated to workers; and performance feedback is given to workers in the form of oral or written communication. Since communication is so pervasive in organizations, managers must learn to communicate effectively.

The Control Function

The control function is needed to ensure that the organization has achieved the desired goals. It can be defined as *the process of seeing whether organizational activities are achieved as planned.* Controlling involves the following four steps:

1.   Establishing performance standards

2.   Measuring actual performance

3.   Comparing actual performance against standards

4.   Taking corrective actions

Performance standards are the yardsticks against which actual performance is measured. In order to make the first step effective, management may set the standards to be attainable, specific, and accepted by the workers. Standards need to be attainable for workers to feel that they can achieve. Standards also need to be specific in order to avoid any confusion regarding what and how performance is going to be measured. In addition, when standards are accepted as reasonable, workers are likely to take them seriously. Unaccepted standards can be a source of employee dissatisfaction.

The second step is to *measure actual performance.* This task can be done periodically to monitor performance progress or at the end of a performance period to evaluate its accomplishment. Actual performance is then *compared against the predetermined standards.* If performance matches standards, managers can assume they are achieving the expected results. If it does not, they need to *take corrective actions.* A corrective action may involve a change in one or more aspects of organizational operations, or it may involve a change in the standards.

Evaluating the Normative View

The normative view of management was first set forth by Henri Fayol, the managing director of a large coal mining company in France, in the early part of the twentieth century.[4] Since then, it has been widely accepted by many management scholars and practitioners. Its popularity is attested to by the fact that many management textbooks are written following the order of the management functions suggested in the normative view, and by the fact that many practicing managers see these functions as a guideline for structuring their activities.

Strengths of the Normative View.   The major strengths of this view are theoretical and practical. From a theoretical standpoint, the normative view presents a useful overview of management. It captures the complexity of managerial work in a simple and logical way. Without such a conceptual framework, it would be difficult to understand or describe what managers do—or what they are supposed to do.

From a practical standpoint, the normative view can help managers improve their effectiveness. Although there is no concrete evidence that managers who follow this view perform better than those who do not, the former can probably utilize their resources in a more concerted and orderly manner than the latter. For example, one study reported that managers who planned, organized, and executed their activities efficiently produced more positive results than those who had poor work habits.[5] When activities are poorly planned and organized, managers tend to spend more time and energy in the implementation process.

Limitations of the Normative View.   There are several limitations related to this view. First, the normative view does not tell what managers actually do on their jobs. It describes managerial functions in an abstract, general way; it does not describe the specific activities or behaviors associated with carrying out each function. For example, when managers say they are planning, they are, in reality, interacting with other people to communicate their perceptions of future events. In other words, interactional and conceptual activities constitute the core of the planning function.

Second, although planning and organizing are important functions that managers need to perform, most managers spend a great deal of their time on activities related to the coordinating and controlling functions. These latter functions involve many activities concerned with personal, interpersonal, group, and organizational problems. Because there are so many activities to perform in a given day, most managers find little time for reflective planning and organizing. Managerial education should reflect this reality by giving more attention to the study of the coordinating and controlling functions.

Finally, the normative view assumes that the managerial job is composed of activities or projects that have relatively fixed life spans. When a project has a starting point and an ending point, it can be planned, organized, coordinated, and controlled. But when a manager performs open-ended activities that do not have clear starting and ending points, the activities cannot be managed as easily as this view suggests. Since most of what managers do is open-ended, the normative view is often inadequate for explaining the nature of managerial work.

 # THE DESCRIPTIVE VIEW OF MANAGING

> *The descriptive view of managing focuses on the activities that managers perform. These activities are: (1) personal, (2) interactional, (3) administrative, and (4) technical.*

What do managers do? If you ask managers this question, they will probably say that they plan, organize, coordinate, and control organizational activities. But if you watch what they actually do on their jobs, you will see that they probably spend most of their time attending meetings, talking on the telephone, or touring the organization's property. These activities may seem unrelated to the managerial functions, but they are in fact the means by which they perform the functions. The following example gives some idea about what managers do on their jobs.[6]

Mike Feldon was the general manager of a computer manufacturing plant. The plant was responsible for producing small and medium-sized computers for a nationally known computer manufacturer. Although it was a subsidiary, it had its own sales, production, research, and other functional departments. It also had several project groups responsible for developing and promoting new computer models.

Mr. Feldon woke up around 7:00 A.M. and left for the plant about 7:40. The plant was located about 10 miles from home, and the drive usually took him about 20 minutes. On the way he had an opportunity to think about what he had scheduled for the day. On this particular day, he remembered that he had to attend at least three scheduled meetings: (1) the morning conference at 9:30 A.M., (2) the Chamber of Commerce meeting at noon, and (3) a conference with the personnel manager at 2:00 P.M. He also remembered that he had to be home in time to go to his son's Little League game at 7:00 that evening.

When he entered his office around 8:05, his secretary told him that a project manager had called to notify him of a possible delay in the project due to a threatened trucking strike. The strike might delay the delivery of circuit boards. He called the project manager and asked him to develop a contingency plan to deal with delivery if the strike materialized. The project manager promised a status report and contingency plan within two days.

Around 8:30 A.M., his secretary brought in the previous day's status report. It had been prepared by the Management Information System (MIS) specialists, and showed that an order was behind schedule. He called the production supervisor, who told him the order had been rescheduled to take care of a rush order and assured him there was no real problem.

He usually took a tour of the plant around 9:00, but he decided to do it this morning around 8:45. He asked the plant supervisors about the types and volumes of orders they were running, how they were meeting the schedules, and whether they were having any problems with employees or supplies. One supervisor mentioned a problem with a couple of employees not showing up for work. Mr. Feldon told the supervisor to call the production department manager and to notify the personnel department to prepare a reprimand for them.

When he returned to his office at 9:05, a pile of mail was waiting for him. Since much of it was insignificant, he spent only about 10 minutes going through it. Of the two dozen letters he received, he responded to only three. Some of the mail was sent on to departmental and project managers either for their responses or for reference.

As he was about to leave for the morning conference, he was waylaid by an employee who complained that she had been bypassed for promotion because of her sex. He promised to talk to her boss and listen to her case. Because of this interruption, he was late for the meeting, but everyone seemed to be still engaged in light conversation. The meeting was a weekly conference, and department heads and project directors discussed major issues of the week there. The particular issues discussed this morning included (1) a pending sales contract with a computer user, (2) the upcoming labor contract with the electrical workers' union, and (3) a brief mention of the potential delay of a project.

The meeting broke up around 10:40, but Mr. Feldon detained the product assurance manager to chat with him about the sex discrimination charge. They spent about 15 minutes discussing the matter and its potential ramifications.

When he returned to his office around 11:00, a couple of phone calls were awaiting him. He returned one call but did not *respond to the other. He enjoyed about five minutes of rest before calling his stockbroker to get the latest quotations on his stocks. He then left for the luncheon meeting around 11:30.*

This example provides a glimpse of what managers do and indicates the characteristics of managerial work. Feldon engaged in a number of activities during the morning, including ones that were (1) personal, (2) interactional, (3) administrative, and (4) technical (see Figure 1.2). These activities are related to the managerial functions: Managers achieve the latter by performing the former. By focusing on these activities, managers can identify the managerial skills needed to perform the activities effectively; this in turn leads to a successful execution of managerial functions.

Personal Activities

In the example, Mike Feldon performed several personal activities: managing his own time, calling the stockbroker, eating his lunch, and attending

FIGURE 1.2
The Core of a Manager's Activities.

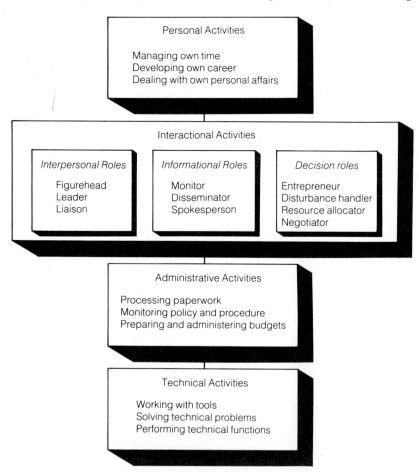

the baseball game. Attending the Chamber of Commerce meeting can be classified as an organizational function since he represents the company. But if he participates in the Chamber's activities to satisfy his own social conscience, he is performing a personal activity.

We often think of managers as part of an organization, and we ignore their personal interests, families, and social life. Doing so, however, distorts the real picture of managers. Managers bring their own perceptions, goals, ideals, values, and practices into their organizations, and these personal elements influence what they do on their jobs. Because their personal goals are sometimes different from organizational objectives, those goals might even work against the interests of the organizations. For example, some managers increase their power at the expense of other managers and thereby reduce the effectiveness of the others.

Managing one's personal affairs is an important factor in being an effective manager. When we are free from constant worry and strife in our personal lives, we can devote ourselves more effectively to our jobs. As Confucius said: Those who can manage themselves and their families can manage large organizations and even a country. A study by Vaillant suggests that individuals who are successful tend to better harmonize their careers with their personal life. In his study of Harvard graduates of 1942–1944, he found that those who were successful had much better relationships with their spouses and children, socialized more with friends, and had more time for public-spirited activities than their unsuccessful counterparts.[7]

Many people, however, achieve their career goals at the expense of their personal, family, and social lives. People who spend more time at work than with family may indeed do better on their jobs.[8] But they may lose the emotional support needed to cope with the pressure and stress resulting from the jobs. Personal hobbies and interests, intimate family relationships, and enjoyable social interactions can all provide these emotional supports. Although organizational demands are responsible for creating the stresses and anxieties, individuals are responsible for coping with them. Therefore, individuals need to develop a well-rounded pattern of activities that satisfy a variety of life demands in order to cope with job-related stresses.

Interactional Activities

Managers spend considerable time and energy interacting with other people—subordinates, peers, superiors, customers, unions, and community leaders. You may have noticed that Mike Feldon interacted directly with at least two dozen individuals in the course of the morning and probably interacted with another dozen or more in the afternoon, individually or in groups, in person or on the phone. It is no wonder, then, that many writers define management as *getting things done through* people.[9]

Studies suggest that managers spend about 80 percent of their time interacting with other people. For example, Mintzberg found that a group of chief executives spent 78 percent of their time attending meetings, talking on the telephone, and touring their plants.[10] Lawler and his associates reported that a sample of middle managers devoted 80 percent of their time to verbal communication.[11] Jennings reported a figure of 78 percent for another group of middle managers.[12] Pearse reported a similar finding.[13]

With whom do these managers spend their time? The chief executives studied by Mintzberg spent 48 percent of their contact hours with subordinates, individually or collectively; 20 percent with clients, suppliers, and professional associates; 16 percent with peers; 7 percent with the board of directors; and 8 percent with independent outsiders.[14] This finding is similar to the findings of Stewart.[15] Her research was conducted with a sample of British senior and middle managers. Combining the findings of these two researchers, we can draw a profile of managerial interactions with other people. Figure 1.3 shows such a profile, indicating the diversity of interactional activities and the proportion of time allocated to each interaction.

Interactional activities serve interpersonal, informational, and decision-making roles.[16] Because managers are charged with the responsibility of managing organizational units, they become *figureheads, leaders,* and *liaisons,* which are *interpersonal roles.* They participate in ceremonial activities such as attending Chamber of Commerce meetings (as Mike

FIGURE   1.3
The Manager's Interactions with Others.

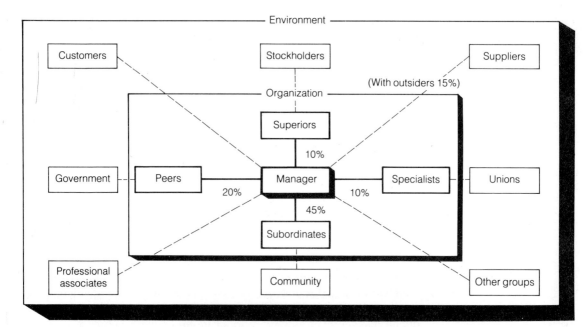

Feldon did in the example), manage their own work groups, and serve as liaison between their own work units and other organizational units.

Managers also interact with others for the purpose of *collecting* and *disseminating information—informational roles.* By maintaining a network of personal contacts, they can collect the information needed to perform their jobs and pass it on to their subordinates. They collect and disseminate information for the purpose of *making right decisions—decision-making roles.* For example, Mike Feldon collected information to make decisions related to resource allocation, labor contract negotiation, employee grievance, and business contracts.

Administrative Activities

A small portion of a manager's time is spent in performing administrative duties. These include processing paperwork, preparing and administering budgets, monitoring policies and procedures, and handling personnel matters. Although they spend a relatively small portion of their time performing them, managers complain that too much time is wasted on such activities.[17] Nevertheless, these are the activities that separate managers from nonmanagers. Other employees perform personal, interpersonal, and technical activities, but they do not perform administrative activities.

The demand and pressure for increased administrative activities comes from the external environment. As a society becomes more legalistic and prone to litigation, it places a heavy burden on managers and increases the need for administrative activities. For example, a growing number of employees are suing their employers because of health problems allegedly originating in hazardous working conditions. Also on the rise are suits alleging discrimination or reverse discrimination in the workplace.[18]

Added to this is the increasing number of laws, regulations, and court decisions that managers must know about, understand, and comply with. For example, equal employment opportunity laws—such as the Civil Rights Act of 1964, the Age Discrimination in Employment Act of 1967, and the Vocational Rehabilitation Act of 1973—require that managers develop Affirmative Action Plans (AAPs), explain how they comply with the action guidelines, and keep voluminous and detailed records. It takes a great deal of time and paperwork to comply with these federal laws or guidelines and others, such as the Environmental Protection Acts (EPA), Occupational Safety and Health Act (OSHA), and Employee Retirement and Income Security Act (ERISA).

Managers in line functions such as production and sales usually delegate most of their paperwork to administrative assistants, secretaries, and/or to managers in staff functions such as personnel, accounting, and legal departments. However, they must be aware of these laws and guidelines and comply with them, because any failure or any suspicion of noncompliance is very costly. For example, Mike Feldon and the product assurance manager in our example had to spend a considerable amount of their time preparing a hearing on the sex discrimination case brought against them by a female employee. If the case was not resolved at the local level, it might go through the federal district court all the way to the U.S. Supreme Court.

Technical Activities

Managers may occasionally perform technical activities that involve the use of tools, technical knowledge, and job skills to solve technical problems. The amount of time managers spend in performing such activities decreases as they move up the organizational ladder. However, effective managers will have an adequate knowledge of the technical activities they supervise. For example, when serving as a production manager, a person is primarily required to know the production function. But when that person becomes the general manager, he or she should be knowledgeable about all phases of the technical functions of the organization. Such knowledge is necessary if managers are to communicate with, coordinate the activities of, and assist people in various technical functions.

Technical activities are especially important to junior managers because they tend to be hired on the basis of their technical competence and are initially assigned to technical functions. Many organizations prefer to hire people at the entry level to perform specific technical functions, and then promote them to managerial positions on the basis of their managerial potential. Some specialists, then, gradually become generalists as they move up in the organizational hierarchy. Because of their technical background, however, they often get involved in technical activities and may become personally interested, especially in favorite projects.

Variation in Managerial Activities

Do all managers perform all these activities in the same way? Managers do perform all of these activities, but they will place varying emphases on different ones. These variations result from the differences in the function they serve, in the organizational hierarchy, and in the organizational type.

Functional Variation. When organizational activities are divided into various functions, such as production, sales, and research, differences in managerial behavior result.[19] For example, sales managers spend more time dealing with clients and training sales personnel, production managers spend more time in scheduling, providing maintenance, and solving technical problems. Sales managers heavily rely on their interpersonal skills to perform their jobs, while production managers rely on administrative and technical skills to do theirs. Managers in accounting, engineering, and research are more concerned with technical activities.

Hierarchical Variation. In general, as managers progress upward through the organizational hierarchy, their involvement in technical activities decreases, but the importance of their informational and decision-related activities increases. Administrative activities are important for all managers, but managers at lower levels are more likely to be involved in detailed paperwork than those higher up. Also, interpersonal activities are important to managers at all levels, but those at higher levels are more likely to be engaged in peer-to-peer relationships with people outside their organizations, while those at lower levels are engaged in superior-subordinate relationships.

Organizational Variation. Organization type also influences managerial behavior. For example, managers in service industries like banking and the hotel industry are more likely to be involved in interpersonal activities than those in manufacturing. The size of an organization also affects the kinds of activities performed by managers. In small organizations the manager's jobs are less specialized; so the manager needs to be familiar with all aspects of the operation. In addition, the manager needs to be more creative in producing goods and services than the manager in large organizations.

One implication of these activity variations is that organizations should not try to hire managers with all the same personal and managerial qualifications. Instead they need managers of different types, with varying backgrounds. Fortunately, people differ in their personal and managerial qualifications. For example, managers who are analytical thinkers are better suited to such systematic tasks as production, logistics, and financial analysis. Those who are intuitive thinkers are more suitable for such jobs as advertising and personnel managers.[20]

THE NATURE OF MANAGERIAL WORK

Managerial activities are characterized by brevity, variety, fragmentation, reactiveness, oral communication, and political inclination. Managers are doers rather than reflective planners and have to cope with a constant parade of challenges and surprises.

How do managers deal with their managerial activities? Do they handle these activities in the orderly, structured, and logical manner that the normative view of managing describes? Or do they handle their day-to-day activities in a more unstructured, illogical, and haphazard way?

On the basis of the Mintzberg study, McCall concluded that the manager's activities are characterized by (1) a hectic pace, (2) oral communication, (3) reactive behavior, and (4) political inclinations.[21] What are the implications of each of these for your study of management?

The Hectic Pace of Managerial Work

The normative view of managing assumes that managers have (1) a relatively small number of activities to perform in a given day and (2) enough time to be analytical and reflective in making decisions. But the reality is far different from these assumptions. There are too many activities to perform in the time available for doing them, and the work pace of managers becomes hectic at best and chaotic at worst.

Pace Due to Volume of Work.   In order to understand the hectic pace of managerial work, we need to examine the volume of managerial activities. Several years ago, a study of foremen's work found that the typical foreman engaged in an average of 583 activities a day.[22] Most of these activities lasted less than a minute; only a few lasted more than two minutes. As they were loaded with pressing problems, foremen handled them in a "fire-fighting" fashion and had very little time to relax and think. We believe these findings apply to today's supervisors as well; perhaps their pace is even more hectic.

Mintzberg's study of chief executives yielded similar findings. The executives studied engaged in at least 50 distinct activities per day, and half of these lasted less than nine minutes.[23] Only a tenth of these activities lasted more than an hour. Thus, the activity duration is somewhat longer for chief executives than for supervisors, but the executive's work pace is still a hectic one because the activities usually occur in a random and unrelenting fashion.

Reasons for Large Work Volume.   There are several reasons for this great number of activities. First, the managerial job is composed of an array of activities that demand the manager's attention. It takes a considerable amount of time to maintain a complex network of interpersonal contacts, to process a large amount of incoming and outgoing information, and to attend to all the formal and informal meetings.

Second, the managerial job is an open-ended one. Unlike other professionals, who deal with concrete work units, managers perform few activities that have terminal points. For example, engineers start and end their projects, professors face new quarters or semesters with new students, and lawyers undertake cases and bring them to trial. But few managerial activities have starting or ending points. Since managers are responsible for what happens to their organizations but rarely have specified work assignments, there is a tendency for them to become involved in numerous activities, voluntarily or involuntarily.

Finally, many phases of the managerial job cannot easily be delegated. Since they are responsible for the outcome even when activities are delegated to others, managers want to maintain control over these activities. Further, overseeing the work of others is time-consuming; so managers often find it more practical to do the jobs themselves.

Heavy Reliance on Oral Communication

Managers interact with other people to collect and disseminate information, and much of this information arrives and departs orally. Why do managers prefer oral to written communication?

First, oral communication is action-oriented and it occurs on a real-time basis. Written communication, on the other hand, is slow and time-consuming, and it tends to be formal and less personal. Since written words are often kept on file, the writer has to be careful in choosing them.

Second, written communication rarely brings any up-to-date or confidential information. Confidential information, gossip, and personal secrets travel through oral communication. Such information tends to be more interesting, real, and valuable than those transmitted through written communication.

Finally, oral communication satisfies one of the most basic human needs—social interaction. Such interaction occurs through oral communication, not written communication. In addition, oral communication is a means of maintaining close interpersonal contacts, especially among individuals who are well acquainted with each other.

The Reactive Nature of Managerial Work

The hectic pace of managerial work can be reduced somewhat if managers plan, organize, and control their activities. Realizing this, time management specialists emphasize the need for planning, strict deadlines, and tight control of meetings.[24] However, managers usually do not plan activities in advance; instead, they tend to react to various situations as they arise.

Why do managers not plan their activities? There are two reasons for inadequate planning. First, some people dislike planning because it involves discipline. Also, since things often do not turn out as planned, people are discouraged from planning. When people are faced with a variety of activities to perform in a limited time span, they tend to pay closer attention to the things that are current and tangible than to the things that are remote and intangible.

Second, planning assumes that managers have control over their internal and external environments. But many things that managers react to are not under their control and do not occur in a predictable fashion.[25] Changes in variables such as economic conditions, political leadership, and market conditions frequently affect the validity and reliability of planning.

Further, the successful execution of planning activities depends on the predictability of internal resources, both human and nonhuman. Yet these resources do not always behave as planners wish them to. People often disregard the goals and procedures imposed on them, machines break down unexpectedly, and raw materials do not arrive on schedule. As these uncontrollable and unexpected things continuously occur, managers become more reactive problem solvers than reflective plan executers.

The Political Reality of Managerial Work

The essence of interpersonal activities reflects the political reality of managerial work. Managers spend considerable time with people within and outside of their organizations in order to maintain a network of interpersonal contacts. These contacts are created and maintained in order to give and receive information and favors.

Through such a network managers can collect current and crucial information not available through other means. Anyone who is engaged in competition with others (for promotion, power, or market share) will know how important such information can be.

Also through this network managers gain the favors and support they need to perform their jobs effectively. Research has revealed little about how such contacts are created and maintained, but effective managers know their importance and use them to further their careers and do their jobs effectively. Many technically competent individuals fail to progress in their professional and managerial careers because they do not have the right contacts to "pull strings" for them.

Finally, the need for political activity also comes from the outside. Managers at all levels, especially those in the upper levels, spend much of their time as spokespersons for their organizations. As society demands more from their organizations than just efficiency, managers have to engage in public relations activities in order to sell or defend what they do. As outside demands on organizations—for pollution control, consumer protection, equal employment opportunity, and social responsibility—increase, the political activities of managers increase proportionately.

Evaluating the Descriptive View

The descriptive view of managing provides a clearer description of what managers actually do on their jobs than the normative view. The latter provides an overview of the managerial process and can describe managerial work when it involves a simple and structured task. However, when the task involves complex and unstructured activities, the normative view is incapable of such description. In contrast, the descriptive view of managing identifies a number of activities that managers undertake in the process of performing managerial functions. By focusing on these activities, we can identify the managerial skills that can enhance managerial effectiveness.

The descriptive view realistically describes what managers actually do on their jobs, but it does not tell us whether or not what they do is good or bad. We tried to understand why managers behave in a hectic and reactive manner. There are many good reasons, but at the same time it is possible that they behave in such a manner because of poor management. For example, they may have more employee complaints because they treat employees unfairly. Or they may behave frenetically because they are not able to differentiate the relative importance of various activitives and thus react to them indiscriminately.

Managerial Implication

From the descriptive view we can draw an implication for improving managerial effectiveness: that is, managers need to have a set of managerial skills to deal with day-to-day managerial activities effectively. The needed skills are interactional, conceptual, administrative, and technical.[26]

1. **Interactional skills.**   These include interpersonal, communication, conflict resolution, leadership, motivation, and group process skills. Such skills are needed (1) to create and maintain a network of personal contacts, (2) to communicate with others effectively, (3) to develop effective work groups, (4) to handle interpersonal and group conflicts effectively, (5) to lead and motivate employees to perform, and (6) to promote a sense of fairness and equity in reward systems. Since interactional activities are of prime importance in managerial work, a major portion of this book is devoted to them. Parts II, III, and IV are devoted to an understanding of interactional activities and to the development of interactional skills.

2. **Conceptual skills.**   These include analytical, decision-making, resource allocation, and organizational skills. They are needed (1) to collect and analyze information from the internal and external environment, (2) to understand the meaning of environmental changes, (3) to reflect these meanings in designing jobs and structure, (4) to make appropriate managerial decisions, and (5) to bring about necessary organizational changes. Parts I and V are devoted to the development of conceptual skills.

3. **Administrative skills.**   The term *administrative skill* is often used in conjunction with the normative view of managing—that is, with planning, organizing, coordinating, and controlling skills. In a narrow sense, however, these skills involve the abilities (1) to develop and follow plans, policies, and procedures effectively, (2) to process paperwork in an orderly and timely manner, and (3) to manage

expenditures within a budget. Having interpersonal and conceptual skills will facilitate the mastery of administrative skills.

4. **Technical skills.**   These skills involve the ability to use the knowledge, tools, experiences, and techniques of a specific discipline, such as accounting, engineering, production, law, psychology, or chemistry to solve technical problems. Although the amount of time managers spend performing technical activities decreases as they move up the organizational ladder, they still need some knowledge of the function(s) they supervise.

SUMMARY AND CONCLUSION

This chapter presents two views of managing—the normative and the descriptive. The normative view defines management as the process of getting the job done through planning, organizing, coordinating, and controlling. It provides an overview of the managerial process, but it fails to describe what managers actually do on their jobs. It is abstract and often removed from the real world of managing.

The descriptive view of managing describes what managers actually do on their jobs. It identifies a set of specific activities that managers perform in the process of managing: interpersonal, informational, decision-making, administrative, and technical activities. This view is more complex, however, than the normative view, and it lacks a normative direction. It does not tell whether what managers do is good or bad. Consequently, it does not help managers improve their managerial effectiveness.

In order to overcome the limitations of both views of managing, this book attempts to find a "happy medium" that combines the strengths of both. This approach adds a normative orientation to the descriptive view. More specifically, it attempts to identify a set of theories and appropriate skills that can help managers perform their managerial activities more effectively.

KEY CONCEPTS AND WORDS

Conceptual skill
Hectic pace of work
Managerial process
Controlling
Informational role
Normative view of
  managing

Coordinating
Interpersonal role
Organizing
Decision role
Interpersonal skill
Planning
Managerial functions

Descriptive view of
  managing
Political behavior
Reactive behavior

Questions For Review And Discussion

1. a. What do you expect to get out of this course?
   b. What do you think the job of managing is?

2. a. What is the essence of the normative view of managing?
   b. What are the strong and the weak points of this view?

3. a. What is the essence of the descriptive view of managing?
   b. What are the strong and the weak points of this view?

4. In what way is the descriptive view complementary or contradictory to the normative view of managing?

5. Why do managers often behave in the hectic and reactive manner noted by the descriptive view of managing?

6. How important is office politics in organizations?

7. a. Do you agree with the normative view or the descriptive view of managing? Explain.
   b. As a manager would you behave according to the normative view or the descriptive view? Explain.

EXERCISES

EXERCISE 1.1. UNDERSTANDING THE JOB OF MANAGING

Managers perform a great variety of activities on their jobs. These activities can range from simple telephone calls to major investment decisions. They can also vary in relative importance and the time they consume. This exercise is designed to help you gain some first-hand knowledge of managerial work.

The Procedure

1. Find a manager (supervisor, plant manager, office supervisor, general manager, personnel manager, production manager, or the like) whose job primarily involves supervising the work of other people. Then arrange an interview to obtain information regarding that person's job.

2. Ask the manager to identify the activities that he or she considers important and those that are time-consuming. The following managerial job survey chart can be a guide.

3. Prepare a managerial job profile by compiling your findings and those of other students. The average scores for the relative importance and the time consumption of each item can be the basis of the profile. Rankings can be made from these average scores.

4. Make comparisons among managers in different functional groups and in different hierarchical levels.

5. Discuss the implications of these findings for improving managerial performance and for managerial education.

The Managerial Job Questionnaire

Instructions: The following items concern the activities you perform as a manager. This survey is to identify the relative importance you attach to various managerial activities and the amount of time per week you devote to each activity or role. Enter an appropriate number for each activity on the basis of a 5-point scale, with *1* representing *least important* or *least time-consuming* and *5* representing *most important* or *most time-consuming.*

Managerial Activities	Importance	Time Consumed
Interpersonal Roles *Figurehead:* Activities involving ceremonial, social, or legal duties (dinners, luncheons, signing contracts, civic affairs, etc.)		
Leader: Motivating, guiding, and developing subordinates (staffing, training, and rewarding employees)		
Liaison: Maintaining contacts with people outside of your chain of command (staff meetings, lunches with peers, customers, and suppliers)		
Informational Roles *Monitor:* Seeking and obtaining information through verbal and written communication media (meetings, memos, reports, telephone calls)		
Disseminator: Transmitting information to subordinates (through meetings, memos, briefings, and telephone calls)		
Spokesperson: Transmitting information to people outside the work group (speaking to groups, reporting to outsiders, and briefing stockholders)		

Managerial Activities	Importance	Time Consumed
Decision Roles *Entrepreneur:* Searching for business opportunities and planning new activities for performance improvement (new venture, new product, and planning)		
Disturbance Handler: Taking corrective actions on problems or pressures (labor strikes, material shortages, and personal conflict resolutions)		
Resource Allocator: Deciding which organizational units get what resources and how much (budgeting, capital expenditure decisions, and personnel assignment)		
Negotiator: Negotiating with employees, customers, suppliers, and unions (sales negotiations, labor contract negotiations, and salary negotiations)		
Administrative Activities: Processing paperwork, budgetary administration, and monitoring rules and regulations		
Technical Activities: Solving technical problems, supervising the technical work, and working with tools and equipment		
Organizing Activities: Organizing or reorganizing group activities, reassigning tasks, and defining authority and responsibility relationships		

EXERCISE 1.2. STUDYING WORK HABITS OF MANAGERS

Managers differ greatly in their work habits. Some are well organized; others are disorganized. Some perform many activities and accomplish much, while others accomplish very little. This exercise is designed to help you find out if there are any significant differences in the work habits of these two types of managers that may cause their effectiveness or ineffectiveness.

The Procedure

1. Find two managers or group of managers who behave differently in their jobs.

2. For a period of time you consider "adequate," study their work habits—their working hours and selection of activities, how they budget their time, and so on. The managerial job survey prepared in Exercise 1.1 can be used as a guide.

3. List the work habits of the effective managers on the left side of a sheet of paper and those of the ineffective managers on the right side.

4. Discuss the implications of this exercise for improving managerial effectiveness. Are there certain personal qualities, habits, or skills that cause managers to be either effective or ineffective? Can these be taught—or learned?

Footnotes

1. Henry Mintzberg, *The Nature of Managerial Work* (New York: Harper & Row, 1973), p. 171.

2. See J. A. F. Stoner, *Management* (Englewood Cliffs, NJ: Prentice-Hall, 1978), pp. 17–20.

3. R. N. Paul, N. B. Donavan, and F. W. Taylor, "The Reality Gap in Strategic Planning," *Harvard Business Review,* May–June 1978, 124–130.

4. Henri Fayol, *General and Industrial Management* (London: Pitman & Sons, 1949).

5. J. P. Campbell, M. D. Dunnette, E. E. Lawler, and K. E. Weick, *Managerial Behavior, Performance, and Effectiveness* (New York: McGraw-Hill, 1970), pp. 78–83.

6. The idea for studying managerial roles is derived from R. P. Pearse, *Manager to Manager* (New York: American Management Association, 1974); Mintzberg, *Managerial Work,* pp. 54–99; and H. J. Reitz, Behavior in Organizations (Homewood, Ill.: Irwin, 1977), pp. 3–11.

7. G. E. Vaillant, "The Climb to Maturity," *Psychology Today,* September 1977, 34–49; also see F. Bartolome and P. A. L. Evans, "Profes-

sional Lives Versus Private Lives—Shifting Patterns of Managerial Commitment," *Organizational Dynamics,* Spring 1979, 3–29.

8. See D. W. Bray, R. J. Campbell, and D. L. Grant, *Formative Years in Business* (New York: Wiley, 1974).

9. See, for example, L. R. Sayles, *Managerial Mind* (New York: McGraw-Hill, 1964), p. 33.

10. Mintzberg, *Managerial Work,* p. 38.

11. E. E. Lawler, L. W. Porter, and A. S. Tannenbaum, "Managers' Attitudes Toward Interaction Episodes," *Journal of Applied Psychology,* 1968, **52,** 432–439.

12. E. E. Jennings, *The Mobile Manager* (Ann Arbor: University of Michigan Bureau of Industrial Relations, 1967).

13. Pearse, *Manager to Manager,* pp. 19–21.

14. Mintzberg, *Managerial Work,* p. 46.

15. Rosemary Stewart, *Managers and Their Jobs* (London: Macmillan, 1967).

16. Mintzberg, *Managerial Work,* pp. 54–99.

17. Pearse, *Manager to Manager,* pp. 19–21.

18. David F. Pike, "Why Everybody Is Suing Everybody," *U.S. News & World Report,* December 4, 1978, 50–54.

19. Mintzberg, *Managerial Work,* pp. 174–186; and L. D. Alexander, "The Effect Level in the Hierarchy and Functional Area Have on the Extent Mintzberg's Roles Are Required by Managerial Jobs," *Academy of Management Proceedings '79,* 39th Annual Meeting, Atlanta, Georgia, August 8–11, 1979, pp. 186–189.

20. J. L. McKenney and P. G. W. Keen, "How Managers' Minds Work," *Harvard Business Review,* May–June 1974, 79–90.

21. M. W. McCall, "Leaders and Leadership: Of Substance and Shadow," in *Perspectives on Behavior in Organizations* ed. J. R. Hackman, E. E. Lawler, and L. W. Porter (New York: McGraw-Hill, 1977), pp. 375–386.

22. R. H. Guest, "Of Time and the Foreman," *Personnel,* May 1956, 478–486.

23. Mintzberg, *Managerial Work,* pp. 31–35.

24. Roy Rowan, "Keeping the Clock from Running Out," *Fortune,* November 1978, 76–79.

25. Paul, Donavan, and Taylor, "The Reality Gap," pp. 126–127.

26. See R. L. Katz, "Skills of an Effective Administrator," *Harvard Business Review,* September–December 1974, 90–102.

LEARNING OBJECTIVES

1. To become familiar with the systems view of organizations.
2. To develop the diagnostic skills of studying human behavior in organizations—*organizational behavior.*
3. To know how to use the diagnostic information for improving managerial effectiveness.
4. To understand the purpose of studying organizational behavior.

CHAPTER

2 STUDYING ORGANIZATIONAL BEHAVIOR

Other things being equal, the greater the total degree of congruence or fit between the various components, the more effective will be organizational behavior at multiple levels. Effective organizational behavior is defined as behavior which leads to higher levels of goal attainment, utilization of resources, and adaptation.

David A. Nadler and Michael Tushman, A Diagnostic Model for Organizational Behavior[1]

As we saw in Chapter 1, the world in which managers operate is very complex. Not only do they interact with other people at interpersonal, intragroup, and intergroup levels, but they also interact with nonhuman elements such as tasks, organizational structure, and operational procedures. Unless managers know what goes on around them, they may react indiscriminately to all the internal and external pressures. This chapter presents a conceptual framework for studying organizational behavior that can help managers analyze various organizational components to see how they affect such behavior. More specifically, it (1) presents the *systems view* of organizations and (2) discusses how this view can be applied in studying organizational behavior and in managing complex organizations—the *contingency approach* to management.

THE SYSTEMS VIEW OF ORGANIZATIONS

> *The systems view defines an organization as a sociotechnical system composed of individuals, groups, tasks, and managerial controls. It studies both the relationships among these components and their impact on human behavior and organizational performance.*

An organization comes into being when two or more people interact with each other to achieve their goals. When a person invites a friend over for coffee, they create an informal organization. When people start a business venture, they create a formal organization. Organizations exist in a variety of forms—small and large, informal and formal, contractual and noncontractual. They also have a variety of organizational goals—economic, cultural, social, governmental, political, and religious. Whatever differences there may be, however, organizations have the following properties:

1. Organizations have *several goals* that their members strive to achieve.
2. Organizations are composed of *human and nonhuman components* (that is, individuals, groups, tasks, and control systems).
3. These organizational components *interact* with each other to achieve organizational goals.
4. Organizations interact with their *environments*—competitors, technology, raw materials, political environment, and economic conditions.

Organizational Goals

People organize, join, and remain in organizations to satisfy their needs—economic, social, and psychological (see Chapter 3). Satisfying these needs becomes the individual goal. Chester I. Barnard recognized the limitations people have in satisfying their needs.[2] People are limited in their ability to satisfy their own needs because environmental constraints such as weather, physical distance, and limited resources impose restrictions on their freedom. By joining organizations, however, they are able to cope with the constraints and even make use of them for their own benefit. Thus the ultimate limitation of individuals in obtaining their goals is a function not of their own individual physical strength or intelligence but of their ability to use organizational endeavors to benefit themselves.

Although people organize and maintain organizations to meet their own personal goals, the organizations, once created, take on their own goals. These may be distinct from the personal goals of the members. Individual members contribute their efforts to attain these organizational goals, however, because they view such effort as a means of achieving their personal goals. For example, students pay tuition and study because they perceive these acts to be the means of obtaining education and desirable jobs. Carpenters build houses for the builders who want to make profits because they view it as a way of earning a living.

In a complex organization, the goals of individual members and their organization are so diverse that one person's goals may seem unrelated to the goals of other members and of the organization. For example, a university is a complex organization composed of thousands of individuals—students, professors, secretaries, administrators, coaches, food service personnel, maintenance people, and so forth. Each group has a unique set of goals distinct from the goals of others. Some are highly compatible, however, while others are unrelated. The goals of students and professors, for example, may be different, but they are highly complementary and are directly related to the organizational goal of education. The goals of service and maintenance personnel are unrelated to the goals of students and professors, but they make it possible to attain the educational goal. Thus, people with seemingly unrelated goals can work together to meet personal as well as organizational goals.

The survival of an organization depends largely on its ability to satisfy both individual and organizational goals. If an organization does not meet the needs of its members, the members are not likely to contribute to its goals. If the members do not achieve the organizational goals, however, the organizations cannot continue to provide them with the means to satisfy their personal needs—pay, job security, supervisory training, and interesting jobs.

In order to achieve their own goals in organizations, managers must perform two types of managerial functions—task and maintenance. The *task function* concerns the attainment of organizational goals (such as market standing, innovation, productivity, resources, profitability, managerial development, employee performance, and public responsibility).[3] The *maintenance function* concerns satisfying the members' personal needs.

Organizational Components

An organization is composed of human and nonhuman components—individuals, groups, tasks, and management controls.[4] *Individuals* are the members of the organization. *Social groups* are small groups of people who interact closely with each other within the organization. *Tasks* are the activities performed by the organizational members. *Management controls* are the various control systems designed to influence the behavior of organizational members. Figure 2.1 shows the major contents of each component.

Individual Component.   The study of the individual component involves studying differences in individual characteristics and examining how these differences affect behavior. People in organizations differ in a number of ways. First, they differ in their needs and in the way they satisfy them. A person has a variety of needs to satisfy, and these needs often conflict. A student may need to study but may be unable to decide which subject to study first, or he or she may have to choose between studying and going to a ball game or a movie. The student has to resolve this conflict by doing one thing at a time. A person plays a variety of roles in our society, and often these roles conflict.

People differ in how they deal with such conflicts. Some people emphasize certain needs and roles at the expense of others; other people try to harmonize the variety of demands in their lives by maintaining a balance among them. In order to understand why people behave differently in organizations, we have to understand the differences in their needs, life goals, and values.

Individual differences also stem from differences in education, job experience, and professional interests. Some people are more suited for analytical work, while others are more adept at creative work. Some prefer

FIGURE 2.1
Major Dimensions of
Organizational
Components.

Individuals	Work Groups	Task	Managerial Controls
Demographic factors	*Interpersonal behavior*	*General factors*	*Leadership factors*
Age	Mutual attraction	Task goals	Leader behavior
Sex	Interpersonal skill	Complexity	Position power
Education	Interpersonal communication	Interdependency	Informal power
Social backgrounds		Programmability	Situation
Individual behavior	*Intragroup behavior*	*Motivational factors*	*Motivational tools*
Needs and goals	Group goals	Task variety	Task design
Personality	Group norms	Ability utilization	Performance measurement
Learning	Cohesiveness	Feedback	Reward systems
Perception	Individual roles	Autonomy	
Attitude	Group process	Meaningfulness	
Ability	Organizational climate	Work module	*Environmental adaptation*
			Technology
	Intergroup behavior		Structural design
			Decision making
	Cooperation		Organizational change
	Coordination		Organizational development
	Conflict		
	Competition		

to work with other people; others prefer to work with things or ideas. People, thus, respond differently to the same organizational situation. For example, some people prefer complex tasks; others despise them. Some prefer close supervision; others prefer more general oversight. These individual differences have important implications for the career planning, selection, placement, and training of organizational members.

Group Component.   When individuals interact with each other over a period of time, social groupings emerge. A large organization is composed of small groups—the basic work units that carry out most organizational tasks. From a managerial standpoint, the study of group behavior is important because organizations achieve their goals through group efforts. Therefore, managers must understand how groups function in organizations. Interaction theorists argue that when employees develop favorable sentiments toward each other as a result of task-related interactions, they increase their performance level.[5] The major dimensions of the group component are interpersonal, intragroup, and intergroup behaviors.

Interpersonal behavior deals with interactions that take place between individuals. It is primarily concerned with the reasons why people are attracted to each other, the patterns of their interactions, and how and why some relationships prosper while others fail. Understanding these issues can help individuals increase interpersonal sensitivity and help them develop mutually reinforcing relationships.

Intragroup behavior involves interaction between a person and the group he or she belongs to. Since a person with certain characteristics interacts with a group with its own unique characteristics (which is often called "syntality"), there must be congruence or fit between them to make their relationship productive. Group norms, cohesiveness, group process, and organizational climate are elements in any study of group behavior.

Intergroup behavior refers to interactions between smaller groups within larger organizations. In complex organizations, members are divided into various functional and project groups; each group performs tasks that contribute to the attainment of overall organizational goals. Most of these tasks require the various work groups to interact to a high degree. Overall goals are accomplished through the joint effort of groups. Yet managers often find it difficult to integrate group activities. Conflict and competition between work groups, for example, often hinder needed cooperation. The study of intergroup behavior can help managers understand the causes of such intergroup conflict and help them develop a set of conflict resolution strategies.

Task Component.   This component concerns the characteristics of the tasks performed by individuals or work groups. Typically, organizational activities are assigned to work groups on the basis of functional specialization—such as production, sales, research, personnel, and finance. These functionalized tasks differ in a number of ways. They vary in their departmental objectives, technical complexity, programmability, interdependency, autonomy, and feedback. Also, some tasks are simple and easy to perform, others are complex and difficult to accomplish. The former can be programmed and standardized easily, but the latter require constant revision in the hopes of improving performance.

The degree of interdependency required to perform different tasks also varies. Some jobs can be performed independently, but others require a high degree of interaction among and between work group members. For example, traveling sales representatives can perform their jobs independently, but engineers in project groups depend greatly on one another.

Autonomy, performance feedback, and meaningfulness are other important dimensions of the task component. Some tasks provide employees with a great deal of autonomy, feedback, and a sense of worth; other tasks provide very little. These task differences influence the way the tasks are designed and managed.

Managerial Controls Component. Various managerial mechanisms can influence the behavior of organization members. Major ones are motivational tools, leadership practices, and structural arrangements. Motivational tools include goal-setting systems, performance measurements, reward and punishment systems, and task assignments. Leadership practices may involve leadership behaviors ranging from authoritarian to participative to free rein. Structural arrangements deal with organizational structure, organizational formality, and the organizational decision process.

Just as the attributes of tasks, individuals, and social groupings differ, so do the characteristics of managerial controls. People respond differently to different managerial techniques. For example, some people function better in a highly structured environment; others function poorly under such an arrangement. Since no one tool is best for all situations, managers need to choose a set of managerial tools suitable to them and their particular situation. Or they may modify other organizational components, through job redesign or personnel change, to suit their managerial styles. Such a managerial strategy is called the *contingency approach;* this is elaborated on in a later section.

Organization As an Open System

An organization does not exist in a vacuum; it exists in a larger environment. It receives inputs from the environment, transforms them into outputs, and sends these outputs back into the environment (see Figure 2.2).[6] *Inputs* include capital, labor, technology, raw materials, customer demands, competition, and so forth. These inputs are influenced by a variety

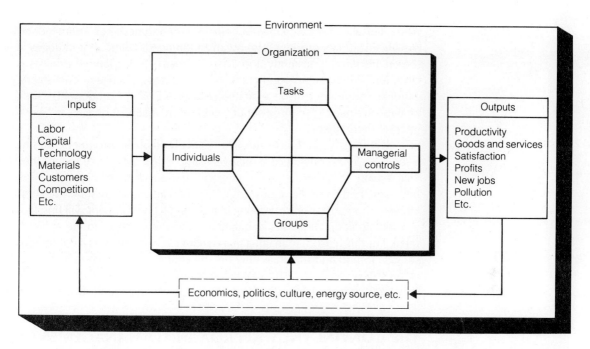

FIGURE 2.2
An Organization As an
Open System.

of environmental forces—econopolitical, sociocultural, and technostructural factors, for instance. The *transformations* of inputs result from the interaction of individuals, groups, tasks, and managerial controls. *Outputs* include organizational productivity (goods and services), employee satisfaction, profits, new jobs, pollution, and so forth. These outputs in turn influence the environmental forces, which, then, further influence the configuration of organizational input.

Managerial Responsibilities

In the systems view, managers have two main responsibilities. The first responsibility is to transform inputs into outputs. The nature of outputs depends on how the organizational components interact with each other in the transformation process. If there exist mutually reinforcing relationships between these components, the organization is likely to perform effectively. For example, if a complex task is performed by employees with the needed expertise, a reinforcing relationship exists between the two components. When such a compatible relationship exists between a pair of organizational components, there is an *organizational fit* or a *match*. A main responsibility of managers is to maintain organizational fits between pairs of various organizational components.

The second major responsibility is to maintain a fit between the organization and its environment. Because an organization is an open system, whatever happens in the environment affects its internal components. For example, a change in consumer preferences has an impact on the organization's product. The organization needs to monitor changes in the environment constantly and adapt to them. This adaptive process is complex. When an environmental change causes a change in one organizational component, it necessitates changes in other components. Such changes are needed to bring about a new set of organizational fits between internal components.

If an organization operates in a relatively stable environment, finding a set of organizational fits is a relatively simple task. And once found, they will remain effective for a considerable period of time. Firms in food, beverage, and container industries are in such an environmental category. However, organizations operating in a dynamic environment will find that a workable fit quickly loses its balance with rapid changes in the environment. For this reason, managing in a dynamic environment is a continuous struggle to find and maintain new organizational fits. Managers may react to pressures for change by making short-term adjustments or long-term structural changes to find and maintain new organizational fits.

 ## THE CONTINGENCY APPROACH TO MANAGEMENT

> *The contingency view of managing defines management as a process of finding and maintaining organizational fits among various organizational components. Since managerial jobs differ from one situation to another, managers need to find combinations of organizational fits suitable to particular situations.*

When a manager moves to a new position in the same organization or to a similar position in another one, he or she faces a new challenge and must make a few adjustments. As the nature of the job and its skill requirements are about the same, however, the adjustment period will probably be brief, and after a few months, the manager should be as effective as before. If the manager moves to a job that is very different from the previous one, though, he or she may need to make many and varied adjustments before mastering the new job. The following example describes such a major change.

> *When we first met Ron Engelberg, he was a senior engineer with a computer manufacturing company and frequently assumed the project managership for the company. As he became known as a capable engineering administrator, the general manager and the*

president kept an eye on him for possible promotion. Recently, a vacancy was created by the transfer of the former plant manager to headquarters, and Mr. Engelberg was appointed to his position.

Within a few days of his appointment, he began to see a considerable difference in the job demands made on a project manager as opposed to a plant manager. As a project manager, he had dealt with professional personnel such as engineers and computer programmers. Now he had to deal with people with a variety of job, educational, and social backgrounds. These included production workers, plant supervisors, project directors, functional managers, union officials, suppliers, customers, and government officials.

He became acutely aware that the nature of the two jobs was different. The job of managing an engineering project was highly structured and could be neatly planned, organized, and executed. Although some unexpected problems would arise, most of them were only temporary and few hindered the project's progress. But the new job was different. It did not consist of a set of neat, well-defined projects. While some manufacturing projects could be planned, organized, and executed, most of the problems occurred randomly and unexpectedly.

Mr. Engelberg responded to the job demands as they arose, and his work pace became very hectic and chaotic. As the pressures got on his nerves, he began to wonder if he was approaching his job correctly. As he wondered how all the things happening around him were related, he began to search for a better, more systematic way to understand and approach the job.

This example illustrates the contingency approach to managing. Because the job of project manager is different from that of plant manager, and because the organizational components he had to deal with had changed, Mr. Engelberg's managerial behavior also had to change. The problem was that he was not sure if his approach was effective.

His managerial effectiveness would increase if his approach were based on a systems analysis of his job situation. Managers can use the information obtained from such analysis—the analysis of organizational components—to improve their managerial performance. They can use the systems concept for analyzing organizational components and the contingency concept to improve their managerial effectiveness. Although the two terms *systems concept* and *contingency concept* can be used interchangeably, each has a different connotation. The former implies an analytical or diagnostic aspect; the latter implies an applied perspective. The entire process of diagnosing organizational components and finding workable fits among them involves the following steps:

1. Analyzing organizational components
2. Analyzing organizational fits
3. Finding the sources of misfits
4. Finding organizational fits[7]

Analyzing Organizational Components

Since organizational components with which managers interact vary in different managerial situations, the nature of these components need to be studied and understood. Some managers are primarily concerned with small projects, others with major divisions or the entire organization. The nature of organizational components differs depending on how the target system or situation is defined, so the unit of analysis must be clearly specified. Once the unit of analysis or system is defined, the manager can study the four key organizational components of the system under consideration. The systems view, discussed earlier, can be a guide for analyzing these components (see Figure 2.1). The analyst should concentrate, however, on dimensions considered important in the particular situation.

Analyzing Organizational Fits

Understanding the characteristics of organizational components is important, but to make such understanding useful, one must also understand the dynamic relationships that exist among the organizational components. The relationships can be either congruent or incongruent. When all pairs of components are matched and congruent, the organization is likely to function effectively. When they are mismatched and thus incongruent, the organization functions less effectively.

Since it is difficult to study the numerous and complex relationships among organizational components simultaneously, we will look at one pair of relationships at a time.

Individual-Organization.   This linkage primarily concerns the reciprocal relationships among individuals and their organizations. Individuals have needs and goals—economic, social, and professional—that they expect to satisfy in an organization. Likewise, organizations expect from their employees a fair day's work, compliance, loyalty, and high performance. When the expectations of both are met, an organizational fit exists between the individual and the organization. Such a fit is often called the *psychological contract.* [8] It is psychological because the expectations are unwritten but important to the relationship. This linkage has some implications for hiring and placing individuals in organizations.

Individual-Task.   This linkage concerns a person's relationship to his or her job. The individual-task fit occurs when the employee is well suited to his or her task assignment. As tasks differ in their motivational characteristics and skill requirements, so do individuals in their attributes and job qualifications. Unless individuals and their jobs are matched, both are less likely to achieve their goals satisfactorily.[9] If individuals are either under-qualified or overqualified for their jobs, they are likely to experience anxiety and frustration. Matching jobs with people, or people with jobs, is therefore an important motivational principle; it has implications for employee selection, training, placement, and job design.

Individual-Work Group. The individual-group fit is achieved when an individual is able to interact effectively with other people in the group. People work in groups because it is required or can satisfy their needs. As people differ in their characteristics, so groups differ in group norms and group goals. If individuals are to function effectively, their characteristics must be compatible, therefore, with those of the group.[10] How well individuals meet their needs through group participation depends on the degree of compatibility (the individual-group fit) and the effectiveness of their interpersonal skills. Managers especially need to have a temperament that is suitable to the characteristics of their group members.

Task-Work Group. Groups can either facilitate or hinder task performance. As tasks differ in their interdependency requirement, so groups differ in their cohesiveness. Tasks requiring a high degree of interaction can be performed better by cohesive work groups, whereas independent tasks can be performed well by individuals acting independently.[11] Although competition can increase performance in an independent task situation, it is usually detrimental to task performance requiring cooperation. The same observation can be applied to intergroup relations. Depending on the interactional requirement between work groups, the strategies for competition and cooperation must be properly balanced. The task-group linkage is significant in designing reward systems, organizational structure, and decision processes.

Task-Organization. This linkage involves the way management (1) structures organizational tasks and (2) measures their performance. Degree of task structure is related to employee motivation: An overstructured task tends to reduce its intrinsic motivational value. Consequently, the need for task structure for standardization has to be balanced with the needs of employees. As performance measurement, management can vary the methods of measuring task performance according to the nature of the task.[12] Some tasks are quantifiable (for example, sales volume, production units, and costs); others are subject to qualitative judgment (for example, initiative, work quality, cooperation, and leadership). Also, depending on the interactional requirement of the tasks, performance can be measured individually or collectively. While individual measurement encourages competition, group measurement encourages cooperation. The task-management linkage is important in designing tasks, performance measurements, and reward systems.

Organization-Work Group.   This linkage is primarily concerned with (1) whether the goals and norms of work groups are consistent with those of the formal organization, and (2) whether organizational structure provides the necessary coordination among work groups. Since social relationships have a strong impact on employee behavior, their norms and goals will significantly affect the performance of a work group. For example, if the group accepts the organizational goals as its own, its members will be motivated to seek high productivity.[13] The way the organization structures the task, the group composition, and the group process also have a significant effect on group performance.[14] A heavy emphasis on individual differences in ability and contribution, for example, often destroys harmonious work group behavior. This linkage has an implication for designing tasks, structure, and group processes.

Organization-Environment.   When all pairs of organizational components are highly congruent, the organization is likely to function effectively in transforming inputs into desirable outputs. But internal consistency alone cannot enable an organization to survive in a dynamically changing environment. Unless it has the capacity to adapt to, or cause, changes in the environment, the organization cannot long survive.[15] It must maintain both internal and external consistency.

Both reactive and proactive strategies can be used to maintain such overall organizational fits. Reactive strategies involve passive adaptation to environmental constraints such as limited resources, governmental regulations, consumer preferences, and environmentalists' demands. Proactive strategies involve the entrepreneurial activities of studying situational opportunities and bringing about changes in the environment. Powerful and innovative companies, such as AT&T, General Motors, and IBM, and small innovative entrepreneurs frequently rely on proactive strategies to change the world around them, but most organizations rely on reactive strategies to survive in the constantly changing environment.

Finding the Sources of Misfits

The analysis of organizational fits will produce information about sources of organizational problems. The analyst may relate any dysfunctional behaviors in the system to certain organizational misfits. For example, employees may feel frustration due to a misfit between their jobs and their qualifications, or due to a misfit between their qualifications and managerial practices. Although one or two misfits may not reveal the sources of organizational problems clearly, overall fit analyses will give some ideas about the most pressing problems in the system.

Finding Organizational Fits

Once the sources of organizational misfits are identified, the manager can take appropriate action. If any critical misfit reduces organizational effectiveness, the manager must take a corrective action. The following example illustrates how the information obtained from analysis can be used to solve a problem.

> *Ms. Leftvich was recently appointed general manager of a large department store. In order to get acquainted with the employees, she walked through the store whenever it was feasible. One day, as she was passing the credit department, she heard the credit manager arguing with a home appliance salesman. Since this was the second time she had heard such an argument, Ms. Leftvich thought the matter deserved her attention, so she went into the credit office and asked for an explanation.*
>
> *The salesman explained that a customer wanted to buy a vacuum cleaner on credit, but the credit manager would not approve the request. The credit manager replied that the customer was new in town and had no credit records. The salesman replied that the customer's secure employment would reduce the credit risk. The credit manager replied that she was the person to make such credit judgments. Ms. Leftvich promised to look into the credit extension procedure and returned to her office.*

The general manager's intuitive judgment could lead to a number of conclusions about the cause of the conflict. She might see it as a personality conflict, a procedural deficiency, or a goal conflict. Without a proper analysis of the relevant organizational components, however, it would be difficult to avoid such an inconclusive judgment. Analysis might reveal that the task of selling the merchandise on credit required a joint effort of the sales and credit departments. If so, management should encourage cooperation rather than competition. The analysis might further reveal that management had been rewarding the managers on the basis of their departmental performance. That is, the sales manager was rewarded for high sales, while the credit manager was rewarded for avoiding collection problems. Such a competitive reward system would cause conflict between the two managers.

Once the specific cause of the conflict had been identified, Ms. Leftvich could take a specific course of action to minimize the problem. She could, for example, do away with the competitive reward system or make the sales managers share the credit risk. A noncompetitive reward system, such as a companywide performance bonus plan, might encourage cooperation among the various operating departments.

Evaluating the Contingency Approach

The contingency approach to management, which is based on the systems view of organizations, is an important organizational theory and a viable management tool. There has been growing acceptance of this theory in management literature, and it is expected to be more influential in the future.

Strengths. There are several reasons for the growing acceptance of contingency theory. First, it provides a conceptual framework within which managers can systematically study the characteristics of and relationships among key organizational components. Such study could show how the relationships among organizational components are related to specific behaviors in an organization. As managers develop the conceptual capacity to use systems analysis, they will be able to digest the bits and pieces of information they receive and draw a comprehensive and meaningful picture of their managerial world.

There are many theoretical frameworks that can help managers understand the world around them. As we will see in all the later chapters, however, most of these theories deal with subsystems or individual components of an organization. As such, they are useful tools for understanding parts of the organization rather than overall organizational behavior. Thus, they can be called "partial theories" or "short or mid-range theories," whereas the contingency theory can be called a "comprehensive or long-range organizational theory." Remember, however, that all these theories can be complementary to each other in studying complex organizational problems.

Second, the contingency theory provides a meaningful linkage between theory and practice. The information obtained from such analysis is a reliable basis for selecting a set of managerial tools and for taking specific managerial actions. Unlike traditional management theories, which suggest one "best way" of managing, contingency theory suggests a set of alternative actions that might be applicable to particular situations. And since managerial activities differ from one situation to another, the ways to manage them need to be differentiated.

Finally, contingency theory provides a basis for introducing changes into organizations. Managers operate in a constantly changing environment that necessitates compatible changes in organizational components. Contingency theory, which is capable of explaining the dynamic process of organizational change, provides information about what changes should occur in order to keep a dynamic or a moving equilibrium (that is, finding new levels of workable fits between various organizational components) in a constantly changing environment.

Limitations.   Contingency theory also has some drawbacks. First, it is more complex than other theories, as it involves more organizational and environmental variables, both short and medium range. Even a simple managerial situation involves analyzing a number of organizational components, each of which has several dimensions. Added to this complexity is the manager's lack of time to do such analysis. And as they have no time or patience to be reflective and analytical, managers may avoid using such a complex tool.

Second, the contingency theory hypothesizes that the greater the total degree of congruence between various pairs of organizational components, the more effective will be organizational behavior at multiple levels.[16] There is some indication that overall organizational fits can improve organizational effectiveness,[17] but no concrete research evidence exists to prove the hypothesis. Because of its theoretical complexity, there is even doubt as to whether or not the theory can be empirically tested.

Third, the theory is criticized for suggesting a reactive rather than a proactive strategy in coping with environmental demands. Wooton, for example, argued that since managers have a considerable amount of power in our society, they should be able to provide a sense of purpose and direction through their innovative and creative efforts in coping with problems in a complex and sometimes directionless society. He contends that the contingency theory fails to deal with such a proactive strategy.[18]

Finally, while the analysis of organizational fits provides managers with knowledge of the misfits that need correction, it does not provide the managerial skills needed to correct these misfits. Managers who apply the contingency approach should already possess the managerial skills needed to bring about changes in organizational components. For example, if the analysis indicates that the task needs to be coordinated, the manager should have the leadership skill to increase coordination. If the task requires negotiating between work groups, the manager should have the negotiating skills.

 ## WHAT IS ORGANIZATIONAL BEHAVIOR?

> *Organizational behavior is the study of organizational components, their interactions, and their impact on human behavior and organizational performance. Such study can benefit from various behavioral and social sciences.*

Organizational behavior is an academic discipline that studies the dynamic relationships existing among various organizational components and their impact on how people behave in their organizations. This definition differs from the conventional one, which puts primary emphasis on the human side of an organization—on attitudes, perceptions, motivation, group dynamics, and leadership.[19] By broadly defining the scope of organizational behavior, however, one can study the impact of nonhuman elements (such as technology, structure, and the environment) on human behavior in organizations in addition to the material covered in the conventional organizational behavior (OB) textbook.

Why Organizational Behavior

Organizational behavior is more than just a behavioral science. If students were interested in the study of human behavior merely to understand human interactions, they could simply study psychology, sociology, and cultural anthropology, and business schools could omit courses in organizational behavior. This latter would be particularly regrettable, for business schools do a better job than others of accommodating the technical and structural elements in the study of human behavior in work organizations.[20] The study of organizational behavior is different from the core behavioral sciences in that, while the former uses an interdisciplinary approach, the latter use an intradisciplinary approach to study human behavior. In addition, organizational behavior accommodates not only the core behavioral sciences but also other applied sciences.

Another difference is that organizational behavior has an applied orientation. The purpose of any science is to enhance knowledge in the field, and students often study the subject for the sake of understanding it. This is undoubtedly a purpose of studying organizational behavior. However, a more popular reason is that the reader is interested in pursuing a career in work organizations and wants to know how these theories and concepts can be applied in predicting and managing human behavior in organizations.

Related Fields of Study

Since organizational behavior takes an interdisciplinary approach, it can benefit from the study of several behavioral and social sciences—psychology, social psychology, sociology, cultural anthropology, economics, and political science. As shown in Figure 2.3, psychology is more closely related to our understanding of individual and group behavior at the microlevel of analysis, while the other disciplines have contributed to the study of organizational behavior at the macrolevel.

Psychology. Psychology is the study of human behavior. Several branches of psychology provide theoretical foundations for studying human behavior in organizations. *Individual psychology* deals with indi-

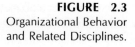

FIGURE 2.3
Organizational Behavior
and Related Disciplines.

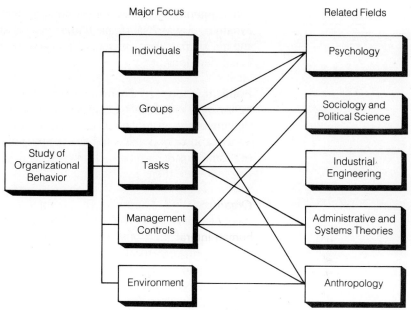

vidual behavior; it explains why people behave the way they do. To this end, the psychologist studies the causes of behavior in terms of needs, learning experiences, and perceptions. *Social psychology* deals with individual behavior as it relates to that of other individuals. It focuses on intragroup behavior—the process by which individuals and their groups influence and modify each other's behavior.

Sociology.   Sociology studies human behavior in groups. The sociologist studies the behavior of small groups and the impact of small groups on the organization. The sociologist is also interested in studying the effects of leadership and organizational structure on organizational effectiveness. The study of bureaucracy is a major contribution of sociology to organizational behavior.

Cultural Anthropology.   Cultural anthropology attempts to explain human behavior in a cultural context. It examines how sociocultural institutions such as the family, the church, the community, and the culture influence the behavior of people in a given society. As it focuses on a society or a culture, it compares the behavior of people in different cultural settings. It explains how people from different cultural settings behave differently to satisfy their needs and behave differently in dealing with other people in organizations.

Economics.   Economics is a social science that studies human behavior in the process of producing goods and services and of earning and consuming incomes. It encompasses human interactions involved in allocating resources toward satisfying human needs as fully as possible. It helps explain human motivation and the way people and their organizations make decisions.

Political Science.   Political science is a social science that studies the behavior of individuals and groups in a political environment. The contributions of this discipline to the study of organizational behavior include understanding of political behaviors in organizations, such as "office politics" and group coalition, conflict resolution, and the way organizations can influence their environments.

Administrative Theory.   The administrative theories developed by Henry Fayol and Max Weber can help managers structure their jobs at the macrolevel of their organizations. Fayol provided the normative process of structuring organizational activities in the order of planning, organizing, coordinating, and controlling.[21] Weber provided a bureaucratic model that stresses the principle of task specialization, a system of hierarchical structure, a system of rules and regulations, and the importance of professionalism.[22]

General Systems Theory.   General systems theory helps us see an organization as a system composed of interrelated parts.[23] The systems view of organizations presented in this chapter is based on this general systems theory. It helps us to see the dynamic relationships existing among various organizational components and between an organization and its environment.

In addition to these related fields of study, organizational theory can benefit from other applied sciences, such as industrial engineering, management science, and public administration. Industrial engineering has an implication for task design; management science provides a tool for making decisions; and public administration is related to organizational behavior in managing public and political institutions.

SUMMARY AND CONCLUSION

Managers operating in a complex world need to have a set of conceptual schemes to analyze and understand what goes on around them. The systems view of organizations is such a scheme. It enables managers to look at the dynamic relationships existing among various organizational components and that existing between the organization and its environment. It sees the organization as a sociotechnical system composed of human and nonhuman components. These components interact with each other in the process of transforming organizational input into output. The systems view argues that organizational effectiveness increases when congruence exists between various pairs of organizational components.

Systems analysis can reveal the unique characteristics and problems of a particular managerial situation. This information can then be used in selecting managerial tools suitable to the situation. Since the selection of managerial tools is contingent upon the nature of the situation, this managerial strategy is known as the contingency approach to management or contingency management. The terms *systems view or analysis* and *contingency approach* represent two sides of the same coin. The former has an analytical connotation, however, while the latter has an applied perspective. When the two terms are jointly used, the concept can be called *contingency theory.*

Contingency theory is a comprehensive organizational theory dealing with a variety of organizational and environmental variables. In this sense, it is a long-range theory. It can be applied to the study of subunits of an organization at the microlevel. Established contingency theories dealing with various subsystems will be discussed throughout this book. Although it is difficult to use such an analytical approach, the contingency view can help managers improve their managerial effectiveness.

KEY CONCEPTS AND WORDS

Organizational behavior
Systems view of organization
Contingency approach
Open system
Task function
Maintenance function

Individual behavior
Interpersonal behavior
Intragroup behavior
Intergroup behavior
Task component
Group component
Management control
Organizational fit

Transformation process
Psychological contract
Short-range theory
Psychology
Sociology
Administrative theory

Questions for Review and Discussion

1. Why do managers need a conceptual framework for studying behavior in organizations?
2. a. What is an organization?
   b. Is a mob an organization? Explain why or why not.
3. a. What is the systems view of organizations?
   b. What are the reasons for using the systems view?

4. a. What is the contingency approach to management?
    b. How is it different from the management approach that advocates "one best way" of managing?

5. "Organizational effectiveness increases when congruence exists among organizational components." Do you agree with this statement or not? Explain.

6. This chapter defines an organization as an "open system" and management as a "transformation process" by which organizational inputs are converted into outputs. What are the implications of these definitions for managers?

7. a. What is organizational behavior?
    b. Why do we study organizational behavior?
    c. How is it different from psychology, sociology, and anthropology?

CASE AND EXERCISE

CASE 2.1. A & J PLASTICS

This case will give students an opportunity to use the systems view of organizations to understand what goes on in an organization. By analyzing the characteristics of tasks, individuals, groups, and management controls, they should be able to predict the performance of the organization.

The Situation

A & J Plastics is a small plastic manufacturing company located in a midwestern city. It produces a variety of plastic products, including garbage cans, liquid containers, and helmets. The company produces these products on a job-order basis. Competition is very intense, and customer orders are unstable.

The production methods used involve molding or casting. Chemical compounds, known as synthetic resins, are melted before they are poured into a mold. Once molded or casted, they are taken out of the mold for cooling. The work is done manually and does not require much training. No more than one day is spent instructing new employees.

The company is nonunionized, and its labor force fluctuates between 5 and 20 people, depending on the size of customer orders. The workers in the plant can be categorized into two groups: long-term service and transient-type. Three long-term service employees have been with the company for more than two years. The transient-type employees are either part-time workers or people who were temporarily laid off elsewhere.

Because of seniority and pressure from management, the long-term service employees initiate the work pace and put pressure on other employees for productivity. The three employees are paid much better than the transient-type employees, who are paid minimum wages. Working conditions are considered poor.

Discussion Questions

1. Do you feel that the company is meeting its profit objective? Explain your prediction.
2. Do you feel the worker productivity is high or low? Explain why.
3. Are there workable fits among organizational components—tasks, individuals, groups, and management controls?
4. Can the company survive in a tight labor market? Explain why or why not.

EXERCISE 2.1. ANALYZING BEHAVIOR IN ORGANIZATIONS

This exercise is designed to give you an opportunity to analyze an organization in terms of the systems view. Since it may be your first attempt to analyze an organization at a macrolevel, it may be difficult for you. You may be overwhelmed by the view's complexities. Indeed, any attempt to find important relationships between organizational components is a difficult task. Hence your analysis may not be complete at this point in your study. As you progress during the term, though, you will gain a better insight into the systems view and will find it useful.

The Procedure

1. Find an organization or a group with which you are familiar—one with a specific set of tasks to perform. A typing pool, gas station, restaurant, engineering project, university academic department, or city department can be the target of your study.
2. Analyze the organization or group you have selected in terms of the systems view. You may follow these action steps:
   a. Identify the target organization or work group.
   b. Identify the goals of the organization.
   c. Define the task(s) of the organization.
   d. Analyze the characteristics of the task.
   e. Study the characteristics of the people.
   f. Study the characteristics of the social groupings.
   g. Study the characteristics of the managerial systems—reward systems, leadership styles, organizational structure, and so forth.
   h. Analyze the organizational fit between pairs of organizational components.
3. Identify the areas of organizational misfit, if any.
4. Recommend a specific course of action to be taken to correct the misfit(s).

Footnotes

1. D. A. Nadler and M. L. Tushman, "A Diagnostic Model for Organizational Behavior," in *Perspectives on Behavior in Organizations,* ed. J. R. Hackman, E. E. Lawler, and L. W. Porter (New York: McGraw-Hill, 1977), p. 94.

2. C. I. Barnard, *The Functions of the Executive* (Cambridge, MA: Harvard University Press, 1938), pp. 23–37.

3. Peter Drucker, *The Practice of Management* (New York: Harper & Row, 1954), p. 63.

4. Nadler and Tushman, "A Diagnostic Model," pp. 90–93.

5. G. C. Homans, *The Human Group* (New York: Harcourt Brace Jovanovich, 1950); G. C. Homans, "Social Behavior As Exchange," *American Journal of Sociology,* May 1958, 597–606.

6. The discussion and the figure are derived from H. M. Carlisle, *Situational Management* (New York: AMACOM, 1973), pp. 18–33; and Nadler and Tushman, "A Diagnostic Model," pp. 86–90.

7. Nadler and Tushman, "A Diagnostic Model," pp. 94–97.

8. Roosevelt Thomas, "Managing the Psychological Contract," in *Organizational Behavior and Administration* ed. P. R. Lawrence, L. B. Barnes, and J. W. Lorsch (Homewood, IL: Irwin, 1976), pp. 465–480.

9. J. P. Wanous, "Who Wants Job Enrichment?" in *Perspectives on Behavior,* ed. Hackman, Lawler, and Porter, pp. 257–263.

10. D. Cartwright and A. Zander, *Group Dynamics: Research and Theory* (New York: Harper & Row, 1968); and Theodore Levitt, "The Managerial Merry-Go-Round," *Harvard Business Review,* July-August 1974, 120–128.

11. See D. M. Herold, "Improving the Performance Effectiveness of Groups Through a Task-Contingency Selection of Intervention Strategies," *Academy of Management Review,* April 1978, 315–325.

12. Michael Keeley, "A Contingency Framework for Performance Evaluation," *Academy of Management Review,* July 1978, 428–438.

13. F. J. Roethlisberger and W. J. Dickson, *Management and the Worker* (Cambridge, MA: Harvard University Press, 1939); and Stanley F. Seashore, *Group Cohesiveness in the Industrial Work Group* (Ann Arbor: Institute for Social Research, University of Michigan, 1954).

14. See J. R. Hackman and C. G. Morris, "Improving Group Performance Effectiveness," in *Perspectives on Behavior,* ed. Hackman, Lawler, and Porter, pp. 343–358; and L. R. Hoffman, "Applying Experimental Research on Group Problem Solving to Organizations," *The Journal of Applied Behavioral Science,* 1979, **15,** 375–391.

15. R. E. Miles, C. C. Snow, A. Meyer, and H. Coleman, "Organizational Strategy, Structure, and Process," *Academy of Management Review,* July 1978, 546–562; and Mariann Jelinek, "Technology, Or-

ganizations, and Contingency,'' *Academy of Management Review,* January 1977, 17–26.

16. See L. W. Mealiea and Dennis Lee, ''An Alternative to Macro-Micro Contingency Theories: An Integrative Model,'' *Academy of Management Review,* July 1979, 333–345.

17. See J. W. Lorsch, ''Making Behavioral Science More Useful,'' *Harvard Business Review,* March-April 1979, 171–180; and Mealiea and Lee, ''Alternative to Macro-Micro,'' 336–341.

18. L. M. Wooton, ''The Mixed Blessing of Contingency Management,'' *Academy of Management Review,* July 1977, 431–441.

19. See W. C. Hamner and D. W. Organ, *Organizational Behavior* (Dallas: Business Publications, 1978); and H. J. Reitz, *Behavior in Organizations* (Homewood, IL: Irwin, 1977).

20. C. C. Pinder, ''Concerning the Application of Human Motivation Theories in Organizational Settings,'' *Academy of Management Review,* July 1977, 393.

21. Henri Fayol, *General and Industrial Management* (London: Pitman & Sons, 1949).

22. Max Weber, *The Theory of Social and Economic Organization* (New York: Free Press, 1964).

23. K. E. Boulding, ''General Systems Theory: The Skeleton of Science,'' *Management Science,* April 1956, 197–208.

MANAGEMENT AND ORGANIZATIONAL BEHAVIOR

1. Understanding the Job of Managing

2. Studying Organizational Behavior

INDIVIDUAL BEHAVIOR

3. Satisfying Human Needs

4. Learning and Reinforcing

5. Understanding the Perceptual Process

6. Understanding the Motivational Process

SUPERVISORY BEHAVIOR

11. Understanding the Leadership Process

12. Developing Leadership Skills

13. Acquiring and Using Power in Organizations

14. Managing Reward Systems

INTERPERSONAL AND GROUP BEHAVIOR

7. Understanding Interpersonal Dynamics

8. Improving Communication Effectiveness

9. Understanding Group Dynamics

10. Dealing with Intergroup Conflicts

ENVIRONMENTAL ADAPTATION

15. Task Design—Matching Jobs to People

16. Designing Organizational Structure

17. Making Managerial Decisions

18. Managing Organizational Change

Micro-organizational analysis

Macro-organizational analysis

ORGANIZATIONAL EFFECTIVENESS

19. Developing Effective Organizations

APPENDIX

Developing Careers in Organizations

INDIVIDUAL BEHAVIOR

Traditionally, the study of individual behavior has focused on three major questions: (1) What energizes behavior? (2) How can one influence the behavior of other people? (3) Why do people differ in their responses to the same stimulus? The first question has led to the development of needs theory of behavior. The second question has paved the way for developing the reinforcement theory. And the third question relates to the development of the perceptual theory of behavior. These three theories are complementary and thus are integrated into a theoretical framework called expectancy theory. Expectancy theory explains the motivational process in organizations. These four theories of behavior are discussed in Chapters 3, 4, 5, and 6 respectively.

LEARNING OBJECTIVES

1. To understand the role of human needs in energizing behavior.
2. To know what employees want from their jobs.
3. To find ways of satisfying employee needs.
4. To learn to deal with the problem of need dissatisfaction.

CHAPTER OUTLINE

Types of Human Needs

Existence Needs
Relatedness Needs
Growth-Oriented Needs
Need Satisfaction and Human Maturity

Satisfying Needs in Organizations

Extent of Need Satisfaction
What Employees Want from Their Jobs
Organizational Constraints

Personality and Need Satisfaction

Adjusted Extraverts
Adjusted Introverts
Anxious Extraverts
Anxious Introverts

Dealing with Need Dissatisfaction

Stress and Anxiety
Frustration and Invigoration
Psychological and Physical Withdrawal
Psychological Defense Mechanisms

Evaluation of the Needs Theory

Summary and Conclusion

3 SATISFYING HUMAN NEEDS

The laws of human psychology and of nonhuman nature are in some respects the same, but are in some respects utterly different. The fact that humans live in the natural world does not mean that their rules and laws need to be the same. The human being, living in the real world, certainly has to make concessions to it, but this in itself is not a denial of the fact that the human being has intrinsic laws, which are not those of natural reality.

Abraham H. Maslow, Motivation and Personality[1]

People have a multitude of needs, and satisfying those needs is their lifelong objective. Studying human needs is important for understanding organizational behavior, because it explains the internal causes of behavior. The term *need* is defined as an internal stimulus that can cause a person to act. Needs theory occupies an important position in organizational behavior because it partly explains the causes of employee behavior in organizations.

Why should managers study the needs theory of behavior? To answer this question, we may list the following points:

1. In order to manage, direct, and coordinate human behavior in organizations, we need to predict it.

2. In order to predict behavior, we must understand the causal relationships involved.

3. In order to comprehend these relationships, we must do sufficient meaningful research to generate hypotheses that can be tested under controlled conditions.[2]

Managers should be able to understand the characteristics of human needs so they can predict what their subordinates want from them. While managers do not have direct control over their employees' needs, they can influence employees' behavior by applying organizational rewards and incentives that help satisfy those needs. Such knowledge also helps managers understand their own motives and define their own personal goals. This chapter discusses (1) types of human needs, (2) need satisfaction in organizations, and (3) personality and need satisfaction.

TYPES OF HUMAN NEEDS

> *The needs theory emphasizes the importance of human needs as major determinants of behavior. These needs can be classified into three major categories: (1) existence, (2) relatedness, and (3) growth. The ultimate goal for most people is to satisfy these needs; this, in turn, leads to self-actualization.*

There are several ways of classifying human needs. For example, Maslow classified them into five basic categories in order of importance: (1) biological, (2) safety, (3) socialization, (4) self-esteem, and (5) self-actualization.[3] According to him, lower-order needs (such as hunger and thirst) must be satisfied before higher-order needs (like autonomy and growth) emerge as a motivator of behavior. Lower-order needs can be easily satisfied and thus their motivational importance is easily reduced, but higher-order needs are insatiable and the task of satisfying them can increase their motivational importance.[4] An implication of this theory is that management should appeal to these higher-order needs for continuous work motivation.

Although Maslow's need hierarchy theory is popular in management literature, it has not been empirically supported. Several studies that sought to validate the theory found no support.[5] These studies found instead that once biological and safety needs are reasonably satisfied, all other needs can be important motivators of behavior, even though some needs may be stronger than others. For example, while a feeling of security is essential to self-actualization, self-esteem may not be. These studies suggest a two-level theory of needs rather than the five-level theory suggested by Maslow.

Alderfer and Chung, however, classify human needs into three major categories: (1) existence, (2) relatedness, and (3) growth.[6] This three-level theory is called the *ERG theory.* As we shall see later, Maslow's five basic needs and McClelland's three motives (affiliation, power, and achievement)[7] can all be incorporated into this three-level classification.

There are several reasons for this three-level classification. First, although it is possible that socialization, self-esteem, and self-actualization needs all become important once lower-order needs are gratified, the satisfaction of socialization needs (relatedness) is more critical to most people than that of growth needs (autonomy, competence, and self-actualization). For example, Lynch relates loneliness to a variety of illnesses including heart disease, cancer, and mental disorder.[8]

Second, the satisfaction of relatedness needs seems to be a prerequisite for satisfying the growth needs in organizational settings. Managerial programs designed to satisfy growth needs (for example, employee participation, job enrichment, and management-by-objectives) often fail to produce positive results when people are not satisfied with relatedness needs.[9] These programs require a high level of trust and openness, and positive emotional ties among organizational members. The absence of relatedness need satisfaction hinders the development of such an organizational climate.

Finally, the ERG theory does not assert that one group of needs must be satisfied before another group emerges as motivators. Although most people may satisfy their needs in the order of existence, relatedness, and growth needs, other people may not follow such a progression. Differences in education, family upbringing, and cultural backgrounds can cause people to put varying emphases on different needs. For example, individualistic people who place a heavy emphasis on success in life may have never considered the importance of socialization need satisfaction.

The main basis for the three-level classification is the similarity of needs existing in each category. Existence needs are vital to our survival and can be satisfied by such external factors as foods, water, air, and money. Relatedness needs are satisfied by interacting with other people, and growth needs can be satisfied by performing interesting tasks. The following sections examine the major contents of the ERG theory (see Figure 3.1).

Existence Needs

At the lowest level of the hierarchy are the existence needs—those that are necessary for our survival. Satisfying these needs is vital to the continuous function of the human organism and, consequently, to the organization. The deprivation of these needs means poor health and a threat to existence. The needs are universal because all people have to satisfy them to survive. They can be subclassified as (1) physiological, (2) safety, and (3) security needs.

Physiological Needs.   Physiological needs are biological stimuli: respiration, elimination, hunger, thirst, fatigue, sex, and other biological disequilibriums. When one or more of these needs is unsatisfied, an in-

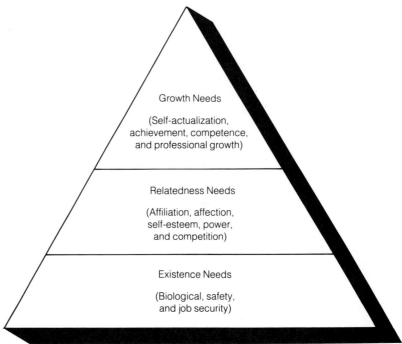

FIGURE   3.1
The Three-Level Needs Hierarchy.

Growth Needs

(Self-actualization,
achievement, competence,
and professional growth)

Relatedness Needs

(Affiliation, affection,
self-esteem, power,
and competition)

Existence Needs

(Biological, safety,
and job security)

ternal stimulus causes our system to pursue certain courses of action in an effort to regain the state of equilibrium. The organism operates on the *homeostatic principle;* that is, it activates behavior in response to a state of disequilibrium and ceases to act when a state of equilibrium is reached. Since most people in industrial societies are reasonably able to satisfy these needs, they are less important as motivators in organizations.

Safety Needs.   Safety needs result from the desire to protect ourselves from physical dangers and threats—accidents, fire, and assault. People are afraid of unsafe environments and tend to avoid physical danger or threat. Like biological needs, safety needs are vital to the preservation of our physical and mental well-being.

Security Needs.   While the safety needs are an immediate response to the physical presence of external threat, security needs are aroused as people fear possible dangerous conditions in the future. People do not feel secure in a fast-moving, technological society where nothing seems to remain constant—thus, security is one of our major concerns. Our apprehensions manifest themselves in monetary savings, insurance programs, pension programs, and in seeking secure jobs.

Relatedness Needs

Relation-oriented needs reflect our desire to interact with others for the purpose of socializing, affiliating, competing, or influencing. We satisfy these needs by interacting with other people, for they are our primary means of doing so. We exchange feelings and emotions, which are the basic units of interaction. There are two kinds of relatedness needs: (1) socialization needs and (2) self-esteem or egotistic needs.

Socialization Needs.   Socialization needs include affiliation and affectional needs, which can be satisfied by sharing feelings and emotions with others. *Affiliation needs* derive from our gregarious nature. We are social creatures who need to be with other people, and who feel more secure in the presence of others. Some form of social contact is necessary for the normal physical and psychological development and maintenance of human beings. Total isolation is virtually intolerable for most of us, even if our physiological needs are fully satisfied.[10] We also have a tendency to seek out others to relieve the stress and anxiety generated by uncertainty.[11] Furthermore, socialization is a means of achieving personal and group goals that would otherwise be difficult or impossible to achieve effectively.

Affectional needs involve more intensive socialization than affiliation needs. While affiliation needs are met by being with others, affectional needs can be satisfied only by an exchange of love, affection, and/or friendship. Affectional needs are derived from the desire to be accepted, liked, and loved by others. As we better satisfy our existence needs, satisfying relation-oriented needs becomes increasingly important. Yet we find it increasingly difficult to satisfy affectional needs in modern societies where interpersonal relationships are becoming legalistic, impersonal, and even antagonistic. As we become concerned with the quality of life in organizations, satisfying our affectional needs takes on added importance in the study of organizational behavior.

Self-Esteem Needs.   The self-esteem needs include power and competitive motives, which involve our ego-satisfaction. *Power motives* involve our desire to have an influence on other people. According to McClelland, there are two kinds of power: (1) negative, personalized power and (2) positive, socialized power.[12] The negative power motive is the desire to gain and use power for personal benefits, while the positive power is the desire to gain and use power for the benefit of other people. One's personal interest is secondary to the interests of other people in exercising the positive power.

Competitive motives are deeply embedded in our lives and are a leading force in our striving for high performance. We compete with others for scarce resources and limited power positions; winners get more at the expense of losers. We compare our economic and power possessions with others as a basis for determining self-esteem and status. "Keeping up with the Joneses" is an important motivator! It is ironic that while we tend to be unconcerned about strangers, we become very concerned if our neighbors or colleagues are doing better than we are. This motivates us to overcome our deficiency and do better than they.

There are three kinds of competitive motive: (1) competing against other people, (2) striving against performance standards, and (3) contending with our own past performance. Competing with other people is a part of our relatedness needs, while competing against certain performance standards is part of our growth-oriented needs.

Growth-Oriented Needs

Growth-oriented needs reflect the desire to be competent, achieving, independent, and self-actualizing. While the satisfaction of existence and relatedness needs is achieved through materials or people outside of the individual, the satisfaction of growth needs can be achieved through working. Thus, the work system or task design has great potential for increasing work motivation—appealing to higher-order needs.

Competence Needs.   Competence refers to the ability to manipulate one's own environment and get what one wants. Its energy source lies in the central nervous system, which motivates the organism to search for an optimal level of stimulus and to conquer it. Behavior aroused to satisfy the competence or mastery need is called *effectance motivation.*[13] Effectance is the capacity to generate satisfaction internally with no need for an extrinsic source of need satisfaction. For example, ordinary people enjoy playing games and sports because these activities are intrinsically stimulating. They do not play for monetary reward as professionals do. By engaging in challenging activities such as ski jumping, parachuting, research projects, and political campaigns, they can experience a sense of excitement and a feeling of mastery over their environment.

Achievement Needs.   The desire to achieve what one wants to accomplish is one of the strongest motivators of high performance. According to McClelland, the need for achievement plays an important role in individual success, particularly in entrepreneurial settings.[14] McClelland found that successful executives in countries as diverse as the United States, Italy, India, and Mexico, when tested on their need for achievement, generally scored higher than comparably educated people in other professions. A person with a high achievement need tends to seek a high degree of personal responsibility, set realistic goals, take moderate risks, use performance feedback, and actively search for achievement opportunities.

Independence Needs.   The desire to be independent is a sign of maturity—of liberation from our childhood dependency on other people, such as our family or peer group. People who have the ability to "stand on their own two feet" and yet acknowledge their need to depend on others have reached human maturity. Independent individuals are psychologically healthy, in the sense that they are free of need deprivation, are usually economically and emotionally secure, and are able to make independent judgments. Harrell and Alpert asserted that some MBA (Masters in Business Administration) candidates have a high need for autonomy, and for some managerial positions, having the autonomy need is essential in getting the job done.[15]

The Self-Actualizing Need.   The highest-order need that stimulates us to excel is probably the desire to realize our potential and become what we are capable of becoming. This need is situated at the pinnacle of the needs hierarchy and becomes important when other needs are reasonably well satisfied. People who are motivated by this need are in general economically, psychologically, and professionally secure and independent, so they are able to pursue self-actualization as their life goal. As with the behavior for satisfying any growth need, self-actualizing behavior is intrinsically motivated: People work for the sheer enjoyment of doing and accomplishing something worthwhile.

Need Satisfaction and Human Maturity

Need satisfaction is essential for our survival and growth. Therefore, we can function as mature individuals only when we are able to satisfy our needs continuously. Adequate satisfaction of existence needs, especially during childhood, produces a healthy, stable, and assured adolescent. Similarly, an abundance of love and affection during childhood and adolescence tends to produce an autonomous individual who can fully develop into an emotionally, physically, and psychologically fully functioning adult.

A major consequence of satisfying existence and relatedness needs is freedom from motivational compulsion. Freedom from worry about potential need deprivation, according to Maslow, is the major ingredient in psychological health.[16] Psychologically healthy and mature individuals feel free to pursue various activities that lead to self-actualization. These activities may include artistic expression, invention, craftsmanship, professionalism, statesmanship, and superb job performance. Self-actualizing individuals enjoy these activities in their own right, with or without extrinsic rewards such as money, fame, power, or status.

SATISFYING NEEDS IN ORGANIZATIONS

> *People can satisfy their lower-order needs better than higher-order needs. Higher-order needs are more important to managers than lower-order needs.*

To what extent are people satisfied with their needs? Maslow has categorically stated that typical adults in our society have satisfied about 85 percent of their biological needs, 70 percent of safety needs, 50 percent of socialization needs, 40 percent of self-esteem needs, and 10 percent of self-actualization needs.[17] Although there are no empirical data to support this assertion, people do apparently satisfy their lower-order needs better than the higher-order ones. For example, several studies have found that managers satisfied their lower-order needs better than their higher-order needs, and that higher-order needs were clearly more important to them.[18] Figure 3.2 shows the relationship between the relative importance of various needs and the extent to which these needs are satisfied. The gap between the two constitutes motivational force. (See Exercise 3.1 for measuring motivational strength.)

Extent of Need Satisfaction

The following observations offer several underlying reasons why people can satisfy their lower-order needs better than their higher-order needs.

Existence Needs Relatively Well Satisfied.   Most people in our society have reasonably satisfied their existence needs. Many socioeconomic programs such as social security, the minimum wage, worker's compensation, unemployment compensation, and "welfare" help people satisfy their existence needs. Concern for the energy shortage, inflation, and crime in the streets increases their importance, but they are not the prime movers of our behavior in organizations. Most adults in the work force have secure jobs and enjoy good retirement prospects.

Diminishing Opportunities to Satisfy Relatedness Needs.   While people's existence needs are better satisfied, satisfying relatedness needs is becoming increasingly important. People have become more concerned with the quality of life in their organizations, and satisfying these needs takes on added importance in human management. Yet increasing social mobility makes it difficult to develop deep and stable relationships with particular employers, co-workers, and others in the community. Further-

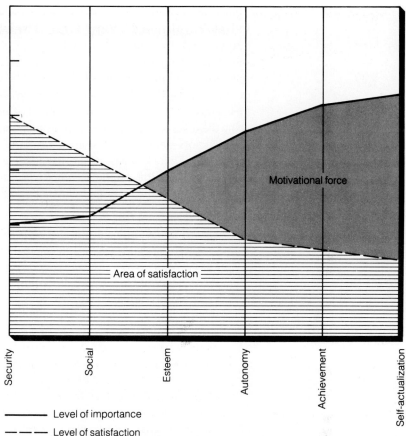

Level of importance
Level of satisfaction

more, as our society becomes increasingly legalistic and impersonal, opportunities for satisfying relatedness needs diminish. In Maslow's view, frustration of socialization and self-esteem needs is the most critical source of psychological maladjustment in our society.

Growth Needs Difficult to Satisfy.   Finally, satisfying the highest-order needs is a difficult task. Since the satisfaction of these needs depends on the prior satisfaction of other needs, they become the most difficult needs to satisfy. In order to satisfy higher-order needs, people should be reasonably well satisfied with existence and relatedness needs and have the opportunity to engage in challenging and interesting tasks. Yet many people seem to find it difficult to meet such requirements. Thus, only a small proportion of people are reasonably well satisfied with growth needs. The extent to which people satisfy their needs in organizational settings will be examined further in the following section.

What Employees Want from Their Jobs

Knowing what employees want from their jobs is the first step toward satisfying employees' needs. Such information is useful in designing or selecting appropriate rewards and work systems. Although this seems simple and reasonable, managers often do a poor job of identifying what their employees want from their jobs. For example, managers often assume the relative importance of what their employees want—usually monetary factors—and use this as a primary inducement for motivating employees. Unfortunately, what managers assume may not be what employees want. If this happens, employees are less likely to satisfy their needs. The following example illustrates such a problem.

> *Ron Engelberg had been on the job as plant manager for about six months. Although he was not directly involved with engineering projects, he had close contacts with them for informational and consultation purposes. He recently learned that project groups were experiencing some problems of employee turnover. Some valuable employees had left the company for better jobs elsewhere.*
>
> *With the suggestion of a consultant, he undertook a survey. Twenty-six employees in two project groups were asked to rank what they wanted from their jobs in order of relative importance —pay, job security, and autonomy, for example. Most of these employees had college degrees in engineering, business administration, computer science, or other related fields. The two supervisors in the groups were then asked to rank the relative importance of the same factors from their employees' perspectives—that is, what they thought the employees wanted from their jobs.*
>
> *The survey results are reported in Figure 3.3. What managers thought their employees wanted from their jobs was substantially different from what the employees actually wanted. The employees rated intrinsic factors (challenging work, professional recognition, and autonomy) as the most important; pay and relatedness factors as the second most important; and other factors (physical working conditions and fringe benefits) as least important. On the other hand, the managers ranked pay and relatedness factors as something the employees wanted most, and the intrinsic factors were ranked second.*

This survey indicated that while college-educated employees (some with masters' degrees) wanted to satisfy higher-order needs, managers assumed that extrinsic factors such as pay and supervision were the most important motivators for these employees. Note that what managers con-

FIGURE 3.3
The Relative Importance of
Job-Related Factors.

Job-Related Factors	Employees	Supervisors
Job security	7	2
Good pay	4	3
Professional recognition	2	5
Fair supervisory treatment	8	1
Autonomy and freedom	3	7
Interaction opportunity	5	6
Challenging work (The nature of work)	1	4
Physical environment	10	10
Fringe benefits	9	9
Power and influence	6	8

sidered to be important to employees were those factors over which they had some control. They might have considered such intrinsic factors as job challenge and professional recognition as important to employees, but they might have lacked control over such factors. Such an incongruence existing between employees and their managers could have contributed to employee job dissatisfaction.

There are several ways managers can identify what their employees want. A simple way is to judge intuitively. The problem with this approach, however, is that what managers think employees want is often different from what employees want for themselves. The above survey demonstrates this point.

The second method is to rely on research findings. The studies mentioned earlier indicated that managers at high-levels are more concerned with satisfying growth needs than those at lower levels. However, we should not automatically assume that pay and job security are not important for high-level managers, or that a challenging job is not important to operational workers. In fact, there is some evidence that young blue-collar workers rate the importance of job challenge and advancement highly.[19]

The third method is to ask employees what they want from their jobs. As demonstrated in the survey, managers can be wrong in guessing the needs of employees. So one can use survey instruments, such as that in the exercise at the end of this chapter, to obtain information on employee needs. This information can be used in designing or selecting appropriate reward and work systems.

Organizational Constraints

Knowing what employees want is one thing, but satisfying them is another. Management may know that employees want better pay, but it may lack the capacity or the desire to improve pay. Managers may want to improve their relationships with employees, but they may not know how. Managers may know that employees want to have more autonomy and control in the work environment, but they may be afraid to share their power because they fear losing control.

In describing a model of man, Argyris pointed out that human beings move from an immature to a mature state.[20] As infants, we depend on others for survival, but we become increasingly independent of others as maturity develops and we become more active in satisfying our own needs. However, organizations impose various constraints that prevent their members from expressing and satisfying their personal needs. Organizations are interested in order and predictability; thus, they structure the jobs and control the behavior of organization members. These organizational demands are at odds with the needs of maturing individuals for autonomy, creativity, and self-actualization.

The usual organizational model, which emphasizes control, predictability, and structure, encourages immature behavioral responses from employees—passivity, dependence, and subordination. When employees are encouraged to be immature, the organization cannot expect them to be creative and develop their fullest capacities. Conflict exists between organizations and their members in that, while the former need control and reliability, the latter need the opportunity to be creative and independent.

If organizations are to develop their human resources to the fullest possible extent, organization members must be given the opportunity to satisfy their own needs and to grow psychologically. Various organizational and job enrichment programs are suggested as remedies, and these programs will be fully discussed in Chapters 15 and 16.

PERSONALITY AND NEED SATISFACTION

> *People differ in the ways they satisfy needs. Some people are aggressive; others are restrained. Differences in personality influence the way people satisfy their needs.*

Personality describes a set of traits that people possess. These traits are usually manifested in the manner by which people satisfy their needs.

In this context, *personality* can be defined as "the dynamic organization within the individual of those psycho-physical systems that determine his unique adjustments to his environment."[21] More specifically, one's personality determines how he or she will act or react in a given situation.

People describe human personality in many ways—type, trait, body type, and psychoanalysis. The most frequently used personality description, however, is based on two psychological dimensions: (1) introversion-extraversion and (2) emotionality or neuroticism. The first dimension deals with a person's inward or outward orientation, the second with one's level of anxiety and emotionality.

The effects of personality on behavior can be best understood when the two dimensions are considered jointly. For example, neurotic individuals will display different patterns of behavior, depending on whether they are introverts or extraverts. Neurotic extraverts are likely to behave aggressively, but neurotic introverts may act nonassertively. Based on the writings of Cattell, Eysenck, Maddi, and others, we made an attempt to draw the profiles of four personality types (see Figure 3.4).[22]

Adjusted Extraverts

These individuals are extraverted and have a low level of anxiety. Their personality traits can be described as adaptable, assertive, carefree, easygoing, gregarious, outgoing, sociable, stable, lively, warm, and so

FIGURE 3.4
The Profile of Personality.

High Anxiety

Introversion				Extraversion
Anxious	Shy	Aggressive	Excitable	
Fearful	Moody	Hyperactive	Impulsive	
Nervous	Reserved	Irritable	Talkative	
Sober	Suspicious	Restless	Touchy	
Unsociable	Cold	Temperamental	Tense	
Calm	Gentle	Assertive	Active	
Considerate	Passive	Carefree	Easygoing	
Even tempered	Meek	Gregarious	Lively	
Relaxed	Reliable	Joyful	Outgoing	
Thoughtful	Composed	Sociable	Warm	

Low Anxiety

forth. These characteristics enable them to better satisfy their needs in an interaction-oriented society like ours. Since they can easily socialize and maintain interpersonal contacts, they are able to draw on the resources of other people to help satisfy their needs. They are more likely to prefer job situations requiring a high degree of social interaction—sales, personnel, and politics.

A problem with this type of personality may be that it is not a favorable trait for task performances requiring concentration and persistence—such as scholastic achievement, scientific research, and precision workmanship.[23] Adjusted extraverts may be better contented with what they do and have, but such a contentment can mean lack of motivation for accomplishment. March and Simon pointed out that satisfaction reduces search behavior, that is, motivation.[24] An old cliché, "the nice guy finishes the job last," seems to support this point.

Adjusted Introverts

These individuals are introverted and have a low level of anxiety. Their traits can be described as calm, composed, controlled, gentle, relaxed, even-tempered, meek, passive, stable, and considerate. Because of these characteristics, they should be able to maintain satisfactory interpersonal relationships with others. They are likely to prefer job situations that provide peace and stability.

A problem with this personality may be that they lack motivation to achieve high goals. As in the case of adjusted extraversion, a lower level of anxiety is associated with low motivation. Since they are contented with the status quo, these people are less likely to press themselves and others for a high level of achievement.

Anxious Extraverts

Neurotic extraverts are high on both extraversion and neuroticism. Their personality traits can be described as aggressive, excitable, hyperactive, impulsive, restless, talkative, temperamental, tense, touchy, and so forth. Because of these characteristics, they may act impatiently in gratifying their needs and demand their need satisfaction in an inappropriate and irritating manner. They may get what they want, but often at the expense of other people. Eysenck found that a common profile of criminals is high on both neuroticism and extraversion.[25] A high level of anxiety is generally disruptive of performance.

A redeeming feature of this personality is that they can destroy the status quo that inhibits innovation in organizations. Their discontentment can cause them and other people to search for new ideas or products, or cause some changes in ineffective managerial practices. When their aggressive impulse is directed to positive causes, such as accomplishing difficult tasks, they can be the prime moving forces.

Anxious Introverts

These individuals are introverted and have a high level of anxiety. Their traits can be described as aloof, anxious, cold, fearful, reserved, shy, unstable, moody, sober, and so forth. Shyness is an overt manifestation of neurotic introversion. A study by Zimbardo and his associates reported that more than 40 percent of college and high school students responding to the survey considered themselves shy.[26] Many people overcome their shyness eventually, but this seems to be a problem for many. Because of such characteristics, these people are less likely to be successful in creating and maintaining interpersonal contacts. Consequently, they tend to prefer jobs requiring fewer interpersonal contacts.

A redeeming feature of this personality is that it helps people to develop the capacity to be self-sufficient. Since they are relatively unsuccessful in drawing on the resources of other people, they have to learn to be self-sufficient in order to meet their needs. Introverts with a moderate level of anxiety can be very productive in jobs requiring concentration, persistence, and hard work.[27] Remember, however, that extremely high anxiety can be disruptive of performance.

DEALING WITH NEED DISSATISFACTION

> *Prolonged need dissatisfaction leads to a number of undesirable behaviors—frustration, anxiety, stress, withdrawal, low morale, and low productivity. People differ in how they deal with these problems.*

If our existence needs are not satisfied, the result is obvious; our physical health deteriorates. If relatedness needs are not satisfied, we become psychologically alienated and depressed. If our growth needs are not satisfied, assuming that we have them, we may feel stagnated and become apathetic. Although reaction to need deprivation may vary with different individuals and different types of need, there is a general progression of behaviors that accompanies the problem of dissatisfaction (see Figure 3.5).[28] It involves:

1. Stress and anxiety
2. Frustration
3. Invigoration

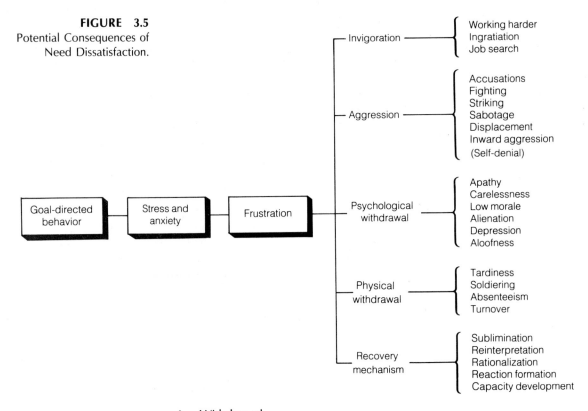

FIGURE 3.5
Potential Consequences of
Need Dissatisfaction.

4. Withdrawal

5. Coping behaviors

Stress and Anxiety

Stress is the mental and physical strain that people feel when they pursue a need satisfaction. It is normal in the sense that it is associated with goal-directed behavior. It prepares our mind and body to pursue activities leading to need satisfaction. Selye argued that stress is a part of living and that it can be conducive to personal growth, development, and mental health.[29] However, stress becomes dysfunctional when it is excessive and prolonged. Such stress is said to be related to health problems, such as insomnia, asthma, ulcers, and heart disease.[30]

Anxiety is an emotional response to stress; it shows how we handle stress. Since it is an emotional response, it is more personal to an individual than stress. For example, even if two people face the same stressful situation, such as taking a test, they may experience different levels of stress due to differences in their emotional responses. Neurotic individuals will experience more severe stress than normal people.

Frustration and Invigoration

Stress and anxiety will be reduced if our needs are consummated. If these needs are not satisfied for an extended period of time, we experience frustration. *Frustration* refers to the mental state of being disappointed. When we are frustrated, our behavior undergoes some changes. Healthy and rational individuals often behave irrationally, and their behavior becomes less predictable. Since their usual manner of behavior does not produce positive results, they try other behavior as a way of coping with frustration. Such behavior includes invigoration and aggression.

Invigoration refers to an increase in activities in response to frustration. When people are frustrated, they have a tendency to perceive the blocked goal to be more attractive and important than ever before.[31] So they tend to act with increased vigor, hoping that this will lead to the desired outcomes. For example, an employee who is dissatisfied with a pay increase or promotion may suddenly work harder, try to ingratiate himself with the boss, or search for other employment.

Since such reactionary behaviors are usually less well planned and executed, they tend to produce less than desirable outcomes. When this happens, the frustrated individual may turn to *aggression.* Aggression can be externally or internally directed. Accusations, fights, strikes, and sabotage are forms of external aggression. When aggression cannot be directed at the frustration-causing agent, it is often directed at others who are less threatening. For example, an unhappy employee, rather than express his hostility toward his supervisor, may become hostile toward his wife or children at home. Such aggression is called *displacement.*

Aggression can also be directed toward the self. When we are unable to satisfy a particular need, we may prohibit ourselves from satisfying other needs. For example, the employee who has been denied a pay increase or promotion may feel that he does not deserve having a good meal or a good time. This is called *self-denial.* When aggression is directed inwardly, a person may appear calm and even-tempered, but the unrelieved frustration can cause emotional turmoil internally.

Psychological and Physical Withdrawal

If invigoration and/or aggression do not produce long-term positive results, people may psychologically or physically withdraw themselves from performing problem-solving behaviors. In organizational settings, psychological withdrawal takes the form of apathy, indifference, carelessness, low morale, and alienation. People who withdraw psychologically may perform their jobs with a minimum level of interest or effort; they are physically present, but mentally absent. Dissatisfaction may also lead to physical withdrawal by removing oneself from the frustrating situation. It takes the form of tardiness, absenteeism, or turnover. When the problem of withdrawal persists, it can be called *depression.*

Psychological Defense Mechanisms

Most people have a natural capacity to recover from frustration. A number of coping behaviors are employed in the recovery process. Some coping behaviors are constructive, while others are destructive. For example, invigoration is constructive behavior, but aggression and withdrawal are not. A study by Vaillant suggests that people use constructive coping behaviors to deal with painful problems in their lives, and that nobody is totally exempt from such problems.[32] Following are several constructive and less harmful *psychological defense mechanisms.*

Sublimation.   Sublimation refers to the process of discharging an unfulfilled desire or need. This desire may be socially unacceptable or simply blocked by external constraints. Under such circumstances, we tend to direct our energy into a socially more acceptable behavior or find a substitute desire to gratify. Vigorous physical activities can be a substitute for interpersonal aggression. Athletes sublimate their aggressive impulse in contact sports such as boxing and football, while viewers discharge their aggression and frustration by watching these sports. Some people sublimate their unfulfilled desires through business, politics, or other professional endeavors.

Rationalization.   Rationalization is the process of creating an acceptable reason for an unacceptable behavior. We rationalize our unsatisfactory behaviors to alleviate the feeling of guilt or uneasiness associated with these behaviors. When we are not able to meet a target date for completing a project, we may rationalize it by saying that more time is needed to produce a high-quality project. Rationalization is an unconscious process; it should not be confused with consciously making up an excuse. It is not an effective mechanism for solving problems, but it does help people cope with their inadequacies.

Reaction Formation.   Reaction formation is a way of warding off an unacceptable feeling by stressing exactly the opposite of what we really want. For example, an employee really wants a promotion but fears it may go to someone else. In order to forestall the possible embarrassment of not being promoted, the person may tell other people that he or she does not want the promotion. Like rationalization, reaction formation is not an effective way of dealing with our problems, but it helps us cope with our inadequacies—at least temporarily. Also, it does so without hurting other people.

Reinterpretation.   When a desired need is unattainable, we may reinterpret the value of this goal to us or look at it in a different light. As a result, we may revise our aspiration level downward or find a substitute goal. An executive who wanted to be president of a corporation may accept the vice-presidency as a substitute. (Might that not be the reason why some people who run for the presidency of the United States often accept the vice-presidency when they fail to obtain the top job?) This adjustment of goals can help us to deal with feelings of failure.

Whether or not one recovers from frustration and withdrawal depends on one's ability to cope with frustrating situations. Such psychological defense mechanisms as those just described can help us constructively cope with these situations. There are other psychological mechanisms, but they tend to be dysfunctional for solving problems in the sense that they not only deprive the frustrated person of the ability to solve his or her problems but also hurt other people in the process.

In addition to using constructive defense mechanisms, the frustrated person should increase the use of technical and interpersonal skills to deal with problems. When people are skillful in performing their tasks and solving their problems, they will not be so frustrated and consequently will not have to rely on psychological defense mechanisms to such a degree to cope with the challenges of life. If frustration is caused by external barriers such as excessive rules and regulations, lack of organizational resources, or lack of direction, the barriers should be removed, you should remove yourself from them, or you must learn to live with them.

EVALUATION OF THE NEEDS THEORY

> *The needs theory emphasizes the importance of internal causes of behavior and stresses the role of autonomous individuals in determining their own destiny. However, this theory is difficult to test empirically because of its introspective nature.*

The needs theory of behavior is well accepted and popular among management scholars and practitioners. It is particularly popular among the managerial class because most managers prefer to think of themselves and others as self-actualizing individuals rather than as creatures controlled by external manipulation.

Strengths. The main strength of this theory lies in the description of self-actualizing people, who are constantly striving to reach their fullest potentials. This description depicts human behavior and struggle as never ceasing while human beings are alive. Satisfaction of their needs is not only the means but also the goal of existence.

This theory also emphasizes the importance of the *internal locus of control.* People who believe that their actions influence what they have are said to have this internal locus of control. Studies suggest that people with this belief tend to rely on their own resources to tackle their problems, and to engage actively in goal-oriented activities.[33] People with an external locus of control, however, tend to be passive in dealing with challenges and problems in their lives and even blame others for their failures.

Limitations. This theory has a number of limitations, both theoretical and practical. From a theoretical standpoint, it has two limitations. First, the concept of needs is introspective in nature and so cannot be objectively tested. It is hard to know what needs are, when people have them, and how one need differs from another. Because of this problem, Salancik and Pfeffer argue against the usefulness of the needs theory.[34] In response to their criticism, however, Alderfer points out that needs do exist within us and are basic to human functioning.[35] Properties of needs are studied by the survey method.

Second, although a behavior is energized by an internal stimulus such as hunger and thirst, its direction is controlled by the external factor that satisfies or denies the need. So it can be said that the needs theory alone cannot explain human behavior. It is only a partial theory of behavior.

From a practical standpoint, the theory also has two limitations. First, it explains the internal causes of behavior, but it does not explain how people satisfy their needs. Anyone who wants to know how people satisfy their needs must look elsewhere to find the answer. Second, from a managerial standpoint, managers do not have direct control over the needs of employees. In order to influence the behavior of employees, they need to control the means of satisfying employee needs—reward systems. However, knowing what employees want from their jobs will help them design and select appropriate rewards and work systems.

 ## SUMMARY AND CONCLUSION

This chapter has presented the needs theory, which emphasizes the importance of human needs as behavioral determinants. According to this theory, behavior is energized by internal stimuli or needs. These needs are classified into three major categories: (1) existence, (2) relatedness, and (3) growth. Satisfaction of existence needs is vital to our survival; these needs are satisfied by external means such as food, water, shelter, and money. Relatedness needs are the desires to relate to other people through socializing, group activities, and competing. Growth needs are the desires to be competent, achieving, and self-actualizing. These needs can be satisfied through working.

A number of barriers prevent people from satisfying their needs. These barriers can be internal or external. Internal constraints involve our mental and physical limitations; external constraints involve societal and organizational ones—structure, rules, and moral standards. People differ in how they satisfy their needs and deal with these constraints. Some people behave assertively, others behave nonassertively.

People use psychological defense mechanisms to cope with need dissatisfaction. Some defense mechanisms are constructive, others are not. Constructive ones include sublimation, reinterpretation, reaction formation, and rationalization. Destructive ones include aggression, displacement, self-denial, and withdrawal. People have the capacity to recover from the state of frustration by using constructive coping behaviors and by increasing problem-solving capacities.

Knowing what employees want and how they satisfy their needs is important for managers in designing and selecting reward systems (including work systems), because these systems are a means of satisfying employee needs. Managers do not have direct control over employee needs, but they can influence employee behavior by manipulating the reward systems. The principles of managing reward systems will be discussed in the next chapter.

KEY CONCEPTS AND WORDS

ERG theory	*Effectance*	*Frustration*
Maslow's need	*motivation*	*Invigoration*
hierarchy	*Personality*	*Psychological defense*
Achievement	*Extraversion*	*mechanism*
motive	*Introversion*	*Sublimation*
Existence needs	*Neuroticism*	*Rationalization*
Relatedness needs	*Homeostatic*	*Locus of control*
Growth needs	*principle*	

Questions for Review and Discussion

1. a. What are the major themes of the needs theory of behavior?
   b. Why should managers study this theory?

2. a. What is the three-level (ERG) theory?
   b. How is it different from Maslow's hierarchy of needs?

3. Why is it more difficult to satisfy higher-order needs than lower-order needs?

4. a. What is personality?
   b. How does it influence behavior?
   c. Is personality a good predictor of performance on jobs?

5. Would adjusted extraverts or anxious introverts be more likely to thrive on solving complex tasks?

6. a. What happens when people are unable to satisfy their needs?
   b. Describe the patterns of behavior associated with need dissatisfaction.

7. a. Explain how people recover from frustration.
   b. What are some constructive psychological defense mechanisms?

CASE AND EXERCISES

CASE 3.1. GENERAL MOTORS' VEGA PLANT*

The labor problem at GM's Vega plant was well publicized because of its unique nature. Unlike many other labor problems, which focus on economic issues, the problem at the Vega plant was associated with work systems. The workers stuck against the assembly lines. This case illustrates the importance of knowing what employees want from their jobs and satisfying those wants.

The Situation

GM's Vega plant was built in Lordstown, Ohio, in 1970. It was considered the assembly line of the future, and was designed to make work easier and faster. Because the line moved fast, workers had only 35 seconds to finish their tasks.

Workers on the line were young, and they lacked discipline and respect for authority. They did not like the assembly operation and began to sabotage it. Cars began coming down the line with engine parts stacked on top of the motor block. Other cars had slashed electrical cables.

*Information for this case was taken from Terry Ryan, Associated Press, September 2, 1974.

The union struck the plant in 1972. The strike centered around the work system rather than around pay. When the strike ended, nothing had changed. The workers feared that the extended strike might cause the company to move the production line out of Lordstown.

Few workers were willing to go out on strike a second time. But they expressed job dissatisfaction in different ways. They missed work more and complained more. The absenteeism rate increased from about 8 percent in 1971 to about 12 percent in 1974. The number of grievances increased from 6,000 before the 1972 strike to 16,000 in 1974.

Discussion Questions

1. What do you see as the major causes of the employees' complaints?
2. Do you think GM would have the same problem if the plant was located in Detroit? Explain why or why not.
3. What did the employees want from their jobs?
4. If you were the plant manager, what would you propose to deal with the problem?

EXERCISE 3.1. IDENTIFYING EMPLOYEE NEEDS

This exercise provides a diagnostic tool for identifying the dominant needs of employees and the extent to which they are able to satisfy those needs. The information obtained from this study can reveal the motivational force of employees, and such information can be used in designing or selecting reward and work systems.

The Procedure

1. Conduct a need strength survey. Ask about ten employees in a work group to respond.
2. Prepare a motivational strength profile by finding the average scores for the *actual* and the *desired* levels of need satisfaction. The difference between the two levels can be considered the motivational force.
3. Discuss the implication of the survey finding to managing people in organizations.
4. Make comparisons between various occupational groups (such as accountants, engineers, lawyers, physicians, professors, government administrators, production workers, and so forth).

The Need Strength Survey

Instructions: Each of the following items concerns what you may want from your jobs. Place an A in the column that indicates the degree to which you can currently satisfy your wants and an I in the column that indicates the degree to which you realistically desire or want to satisfy your wants.

Items	Very Little 1 2 3		Very Much 4 5
1. Pay is satisfactory.			
2. I have job security.			
3. Safety need is satisfied.			
4. Co-workers are friendly.			
5. My supervisor is supportive.			
6. I have some influence on others.			
7. I hold a prestigious job.			
8. My work is recognized by others.			
9. I am my own boss on my job.			
10. My job gives me a sense of accomplishment.			
11. My job requires my own unique abilities and skills.			
12. My job fulfills my life dreams.			

EXERCISE 3.2. WHAT DO PEOPLE WANT FROM THEIR JOBS?

This exercise gives an opportunity to collect information on what people want from their jobs. It can reveal the nature of employees' needs and what their organizations can do to satisfy these needs.

The Procedure

1. Conduct a survey measuring the relative importance of job-related factors (see the survey form). The student may ask about ten employees in a work group what they want from their jobs.

2. Find the ranking of importance for the group.

3. Ask the supervisor of the work group to rank the relative importance of job-related factors from his or her subordinates' perspectives.

4. Compare the relative ranking of the employees with that of the supervisor. Explain any congruency or incongruency between the two.

The Job-Related Factor Survey

Instruction: The following items concern what you may want from your jobs. Rank them in the order of importance to you—one being the most important and ten being the least important.

_____ Job security
_____ Good pay
_____ Professional recognition
_____ Fair supervisory treatment
_____ Autonomy and freedom

_____ Interaction opportunity
_____ Challenging work (the nature of work)
_____ Physical environment
_____ Fringe benefits
_____ Power and influence

Footnotes

1. A. H. Maslow, *Motivation and Personality* (New York: Harper & Row, 1970), p. 7.

2. See Karen Arnold, "An Investigation of the Applicability of Maslow's Need Hierarchy Theory and the Porter-Lawler Model of Motivation" (Ph.D. dissertation, Louisiana State University, 1979), p. 1.

3. Maslow, *Motivation and Personality* (New York: Harper & Row, 1954).

4. Maslow, *Motivation and Personality,* 1970; and M. A. Wahba and L. G. Bridwell, "Maslow Reconsidered: A Review of Research on the Need Hierarchy Theory," *Organizational Behavior and Human Performance,* 1976, **15,** 212–240.

5. E. E. Lawler and J. L. Suttle, "A Casual Correlational Test of the Need Hierarchy Concept," *Organizational Behavior and Human Performance,* 1972, **7,** 265–287; K. H. Roberts, G. H. Walter, and R. E. Miles, "A Factor Analytic Study of Job Satisfaction Items Designed to Measure Maslow Need Categories," *Personnel Psychology,* 1971, **24,** 205–220; and E. W. Mathes and L. L. Edwards, "An Empirical Test of Maslow's Theory of Motivation," *Journal of Humanistic Psychology,* 1978, **18,** 75–77.

6. C. P. Alderfer, "An Empirical Test of New Theory of Human Needs," *Organizational Behavior and Human Performance,* 1969, **4,** 142–175; C. P. Alderfer, *Human Needs in Organizational Settings* (New York: Free Press, 1972); Kae H. Chung, *Motivational Theories and Practices* (Columbus, Ohio: Grid, 1977); and Y. Yinon, A. Bizman, and M. Goldberg, "Effect of Relative Magnitude of Reward and Type of Need on Satisfaction," *Journal of Applied Psychology,* 1976, **16,** 325–328.

7. D. C. McClelland, "The Two Faces of Power," *Journal of International Affairs* 1970, **24,** 29–47; and D. C. McClelland and D. H. Burnham, "Power Is the Great Motivator," *Harvard Business Review,* March–April 1976, 100–110.

8. J. J. Lynch, *The Broken Heart: The Medical Consequences of Loneliness* (New York: Basic Books, 1977).

9. See D. Sirota and A. D. Wolfson, "Pragmatic Approach to People Problems," *Harvard Business Review,* January–February 1973, 120–128.

10. Bernard Berelson and Gary A. Steiner, *Human Behavior* (New York: Harcourt Brace Jovanovich, 1964), p. 252.

11. Stanley Schachter, *The Psychology of Affiliation* (Stanford, CA: Stanford University Press, 1959), pp. 6–8.

12. McClelland, "Two Faces of Power," pp. 29–47.

13. R. W. White, "Motivation Reconsidered: The Concept of Competence," *Psychological Review,* 1959, **66,** 297–334.

14. D. C. McClelland, "Business Drive and National Achievement," *Harvard Business Review* 1962, **40,** 99–112; and David C. McClelland, "That Urge to Achieve," *Think Magazine,* November–December 1966, 19–23.

15. T. W. Harrell and Bernard Alpert, "The Need for Autonomy Among Managers," *Academy of Management Review,* April 1979, 259–268.

16. A. H. Maslow, *The Farther Reaches of Human Nature* (New York: Viking Press, 1962), pp. 41–53; and A. H. Maslow *Toward a Psychology of Being* (New York: Van Nostrand, 1962).

17. Maslow, *Motivation and Personality,* 1954, p. 54.

18. L. W. Porter, *Organizational Patterns of Managerial Job Attitudes* (New York: American Foundation for Management Research, 1964); C. Altimus and R. Tersine, "Chronological Age and Job Satisfaction: The Young Blue-Collar Worker," *Academy of Management Journal,* 1973, **11,** 53–66; and L. W. Porter, "Job Attitudes in Management: II, Perceived Importance of Needs As a Function of Job Level," *Journal of Applied Psychology,* 1963, **47,** 141–148.

19. Daniel Yankovich, "Youth Attitude Toward Work," *Business and Society,* Autumn 1974, 46–47.

20. Chris Argyris, *Personality and Organization* (New York: Harper & Row, 1957), pp. 20–53.

21. G. W. Allport, *Personality: A Psychological Interpretation* (New York: Holt, Rinehart & Winston, 1937), p. 48.

22. R. B. Cattell, *The Scientific Analysis of Personality* (Chicago: Aldine, 1965); H. J. Eysenck, *The Structure of Human Personality* (London: Methuen, 1953); and S. R. Maddi, *Personality Theories* (Homewood, IL: Irwin-Dorsey, 1968).

23. R. B. Cattell and H. W. Eber, *Sixteen Personality Factor Questionnaire—The Manual* (Champaign, IL: Institute for Personality and Ability Testing, 1962), pp. 21–22.

24. J. G. March and H. A. Simon, *Organizations* (New York: Wiley, 1958), p. 49.

25. H. J. Eysenck, *Crime and Personality* (London: Routledge and Kegan Paul, 1977), pp. 38–61.

26. P. G. Zimbardo, P. A. Pilkonis, and R. M. Norwood, "The Social Disease Called Shyness," *Psychology Today,* May 1975, 69–72.

27. Cattell and Eber, *Sixteen Personality Factors,* pp. 21–22.

28. E. Klinger, "Consequences of Commitment to Disengagement from Incentives," *Psychological Review,* 1975, **82,** 1–21.

29. Hans Selye, *The Stress of Life* (New York: McGraw-Hill, 1956).

30. C. G. Weiman, "A Study of Occupational Stressor and the Incidence of Disease Risk," *Journal of Occupational Medicine,* February 1977, 119–122; and M. T. Matteson and J. M. Ivancevich, "Organizational Stressors and Heart Disease: A Research Model," *Academy of Management Review,* July 1979, 347–358.

31. R. Adamson, "Contrast Effects and Reinforcement," in *Adaptation Level,* ed. M. H. Appley (New York: Academic Press, 1971); and J. W. Brehm, *Responses to Loss of Freedom* (Morristown, NJ: General Learning Press, 1972).

32. G. E. Vaillant, "The Climb to Maturity: How the Best and the Brightest Came of Age," *Psychology Today,* September 1977, 34–49.

33. T. R. Mitchell, C. M. Smyser, and S. E. Weed, "Locus of Control: Supervision and Work Satisfaction," *Academy of Management Journal,* September 1975, 623–631; J. B. Rotter, "External Control and Internal Control," *Psychology Today,* June 1971, 28–33; and E. J. Phares, *Locus of Control* (Morristown, NJ: General Learning Press, 1973).

34. G. R. Salancik and Jeffrey Pfeffer, "An Examination of Need-Satisfaction Model of Job Attitudes," *Administrative Science Quarterly,* September 1977, 427–456.

35. C. P. Alderfer, "A Critique of Salancik and Pfeffer's Examination of Need-Satisfaction Theories," *Administrative Science Quarterly,* December 1977, 658–669.

LEARNING AND REINFORCING

When a person changes his physical or social environment "intentionally"—that is, in order to change human behavior, possibly including his own—he plays two roles: one as a controller, as the designer of a controlling culture, and another as the controlled, as the product of a culture. There is nothing inconsistent about this; it follows from the nature of the evolution of a culture, with or without intentional design.

B. F. Skinner, Beyond Freedom and Dignity[1]

The "carrot and stick" approach—using a combination of reward and punishment—is widely used to control and influence other people. In organizations, rewards such as pay increases, promotions, and "pats on the back" are offered to employees to promote high performance and institutional loyalty, while punishments such as demotion, pay decreases or penalties, and reprimands are used to discourage low performance and insubordination. Although this approach has been used throughout history, it has not until recently emerged as a science with principles and rules. Without a systematic effort to specify the relationships between behaviors and their consequences, the target behaviors that need reinforcing cannot be clearly identified and reinforced.

This chapter presents a set of principles by which managers can influence the behavior of employees. These principles can be used to design organizational reward systems that can effectively satisfy employee needs and increase their performance. More specifically, the chapter discusses (1) learning and reinforcement, (2) types of reinforcement strategy, (3) schedules of reinforcement, and (4) rules for applying operant conditioning.

LEARNING AND REINFORCEMENT

> *According to the learning theory, most behaviors are acquired through learning. Rewarded behaviors are learned and repeated; unrewarded behaviors are discontinued. Operant conditioning plays an important role in organizational learning.*

Most human behaviors are learned behaviors. Except for a few automatic physiological responses, such as heartbeat, respiration, adrenalin secretion, knee-jerking reflex, and pupil contraction in the eyes, most behaviors are acquired through learning. People learn new behaviors throughout their lives. Knowledge, language, skills, attitudes, and values are learned, and so are organizational activities, such as job performance, loyalty, and supervisory behavior. Learning is important because it permeates all aspects of behavior in organizations.

What is learning? *Learning* is defined as a relatively permanent change in behavior that results from practice and rewarding experience.[2] People learn a behavior by observing how others behave or by a cognitive process. Such a behavior cannot be maintained permanently, however, unless it is practiced and rewarded. The different types of learning processes are discussed later in this chapter.

Reinforcement plays an important role in learning. A behavior is learned and maintained because it is rewarded; if it is not rewarded, it will be discontinued. *Reinforcement* is the process by which an external reinforcer or reward produces and maintains a behavior. The ability to produce and maintain a behavior through reinforcement is an important managerial tool for influencing the behavior of organizational members.

As indicated in Chapter 3, managers do not have direct control over the behavior of employees, but they can influence employee behavior by manipulating organizational rewards that satisfy employee needs. It is, therefore, important for managers to learn the reinforcement principles that can be used in managing organizational reward systems. The following example illustrates the importance of knowing and applying such principles.

> *Fred was an interviewer in the personnel department of a large city government. Six people were primarily responsible for interviewing prospective employees before referring them to other departments. Since the department served a large number of departments, there was a constant flow of job applicants.*

Fred was a conscientious worker who was able to handle more job applicants than other employees. Yet, while he was with the department, he never received a higher pay increase than the others. He had been with the department for about 18 months when he began to wonder whether or not hard work would pay off.

Annoyed with this situation, he talked to a co-worker who informed him that uniform pay increases had been the policy of the department for some time. The co-worker added that even a habitually tardy employee, who just happened to be a personal friend of the supervisor, received the same pay increase as everyone else.

This story may sound familiar to some of you. Under this situation, people are discouraged to exert an extra effort. Since the reward system does not reinforce productive behavior, such behavior cannot be learned and maintained. Productive people will either reduce their performance level or leave the situation. (A word of caution, however: Competitive reward systems are not desirable for all situations. When a task is performed by group rather than individual efforts, a competitive reward system can be detrimental.)

In this section our discussion focuses on the process of learning and reinforcement. There are basically two ways by which a behavior can be learned—behavioral and cognitive. *Behavioral learning* involves an active stimulus-response association (S-R), and *cognitive learning* involves a thought process in finding the S-R association. In other words, the former requires actual experience with behavioral consequences (reward or punishment), while the latter is a mental exercise. For example, students can learn theories and concepts of management in classes (cognitive learning), and they can gain practical experiences through behavioral learning.

Behavioral Learning Processes

Two kinds of behavior are evoked by the S-R association: respondent and operant. *Respondent behavior* is evoked by a prior stimulus. It commonly occurs as a reflex, such as knee-jerking in response to a tap or salivating in response to foods placed on the tongue. Such responses are automatic reflexes, so people do not consciously learn them. But people can be conditioned to evoke such responses through conditioning. *Operant behavior* is a voluntary behavior emitted to produce desirable consequences. Such behavior is called "operant" because it operates on the environment, in contrast to behavior that responds to an existing stimulus.

The process of learning respondent behavior is different from that of learning operant behavior. The former process is called *classical conditioning,* and the latter process is called *operant conditioning.* (The term *conditioning* refers to the process of teaching a subject to associate a specific response with a particular stimulus.) These two types of learning processes can be traced to Thorndike's laws of learning: (1) the law of exercise and (2) the law of effect.[3]

The *law of exercise* states that a behavior can be learned by repetitive association between a stimulus and a response; this is called *S-R association*. This repetition or practice is the core of classical conditioning. The *law of effect* states that the S-R association is strengthened by rewarding experiences. In other words, rewarded behaviors will be repeated, while unrewarded behaviors will be discouraged. The rewarding experience is the core of operant conditioning.

Classical Conditioning.   The work of Pavlov demonstrated the classical conditioning process.[4] In his experiments, dogs learned to salivate at the ringing of a bell. To teach this behavior, Pavlov first presented food to the dog, whereupon the dog salivated. Since the food automatically caused salivation, it was an *unconditioned stimulus,* and the salivation was an *unconditioned response.* Pavlov subsequently introduced the sound of a bell each time food was given to the dog, and the dog eventually learned to salivate in response to the bell even when there was no food. The ringing of the bell was a *conditioned stimulus* and the salivation a *conditioned response.* In this example, the dog learned to produce a respondent behavior. Figure 4.1 illustrates the classical conditioning process.

Classical conditioning has some implication in organizational settings. Many neutral stimuli, such as a pat on the back, a stern face, or a status symbol, can evoke certain responses through their association with other stimuli. For example, people learn to dislike stern faces because such expressions are associated with anger that produces unpleasant emotions. People respond to certain status symbols such as uniforms, badges, and flags, because they are associated with authority and power.

Operant Conditioning.   In classical conditioning, subjects are essentially passive: They merely react or respond to a presented stimulus. In

FIGURE   4.1
The Classical Conditioning Process.

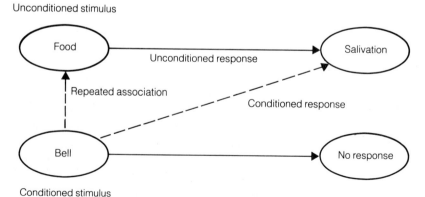

operant conditioning, however, individuals actively operate and work on the environment to produce desirable consequences—receiving rewards or avoiding punishment. For example, students may study hard to obtain satisfactory grades; workers may work hard to obtain a pay raise or promotion. Such proactive operant behaviors are common in organizations, and they are either reinforced or discouraged by their consequences. If these behaviors are rewarded, they will be repeated, otherwise, they will be discontinued.

B. F. Skinner, who identified the key elements of operant conditioning, suggested that it can be used to model and determine people's behavior.[5] This has important implications for managing people in organizations. Since behavior can be controlled by its consequences, management can influence employee behavior by manipulating the reward systems. Management can promote desirable behaviors by rewarding them and discourage undesirable behaviors by not rewarding them. At the same time, employees can control the behavior of managers by presenting or withholding the behaviors desired by them. They can condition management to grant them a certain type of reward by exhibiting the behavior desired by management only when this incentive is present.

Cognitive Learning Processes

Cognitive learning processes can be divided into (1) observational learning and (2) cognitive learning. These two learning processes recognize the importance of both external factors (rewards and punishments) and internal factors (cognition and perception). Since both processes have behavioral and cognitive aspects, they are often called *cognitive behaviorism.* (The term *learning* is synonymous with *conditioning,* except that it implies the use of mental processes.)

Observational Learning.   Learning can take place as a result of observing a model's behavior. One can learn a behavior by watching the behavior of another person and appraising the consequences of that behavior.[6] The learner imitates the observed behavior that produces positive consequences but is discouraged from repeating the behavior that produces negative consequences. Observational learning is different from classical and operant conditioning processes in that it does not require an overt response, and it does not produce direct consequences to the learner. For example, when employees see that another employee is rewarded for high performance, they learn the positive relationship between performance and rewards without actually being rewarded themselves.

Observational learning plays an important role in altering behaviors in organizations because it is convenient and inexpensive. If management wants to encourage high productivity by granting promotions, it may promote a few selected employees who have performed outstandingly. This practice will convey to other employees the message that they can expect to be promoted only if they too exhibit high performance. These other employees do not have to receive actual promotions to learn the importance of performance in obtaining one. However, if a learned behavior is to be maintained, it has to be rewarded eventually.

Cognitive Learning. Most of the learning that takes place in the classroom is cognitive learning. Students learn the concepts and theories of a certain subject, and, without rewarding experiences (operant conditioning) or practice (classical conditioning), they become aware of behaviors that will lead to desirable consequences. The emphasis is on cognition of, or knowing, how events and objects are related to each other, and how specific behaviors are related to specific consequences. Competence, or how well the person actually performs the task, is of secondary concern.

Cognitive learning does not automatically produce desirable behaviors or skills. These behaviors and skills must be acquired through practice and reward. Whether these behaviors will be performed again depends largely on the consequence experienced by the learner. However, cognitive learning is important because it increases the chance that the learner will do the right thing the first time, without going through a lengthy operant conditioning process. In other words, it minimizes the need for tedious and frustrating trial-and-error experiences.

Evaluating the Learning Theory

People learn new behaviors through one or more of the four learning processes: classical conditioning, operant conditioning, observation, and cognition. However, operant conditioning is the most influential tool for managing people in organizations. First, most behaviors in organizations are operant behaviors aimed at producing desirable consequences while avoiding undesirable ones. Since operant behaviors are controlled by their consequences, management can use the operant conditioning process to control and influence the behavior of employees by manipulating its reward system. Furthermore, operant conditioning is the necessary element for both observational and cognitive learning processes. In order to learn a behavior by observation, a person must observe other people being rewarded. And a behavior acquired at the cognitive level cannot be sustained unless it is reinforced by rewarding experiences.

TYPES OF REINFORCEMENT STRATEGY

Four types of reinforcement strategy can be used to influence behavior: (1) positive reinforcement, (2) negative reinforcement, (3) extinction, and (4) punishment. The former two are used to promote desirable behaviors; the latter two are used to discourage undesirable behavior.

Four types of reinforcement strategy can be used by management to influence the behavior of employees: (1) positive reinforcement, (2) negative reinforcement (or removal of punishment), (3) extinction, and (4) punishment. The first two are used to promote desirable behaviors, the last two to discourage undesirable behaviors. The strategy of changing behavior by adjusting the environment is called *behavior modification.*[7] Figure 4.2 shows the types of reinforcement strategy, with their objectives and some examples of each.

FIGURE 4.2
Types of Reinforcement Strategies.

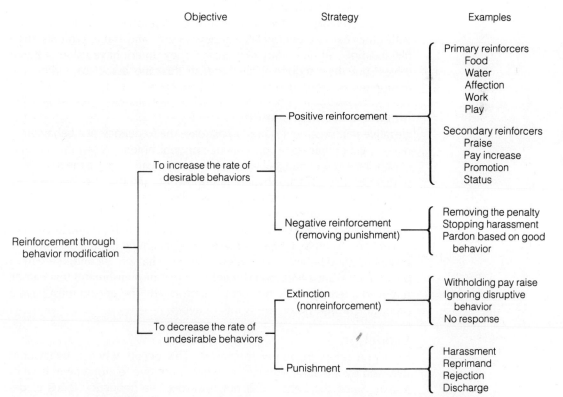

Positive Reinforcement

Positive reinforcement is used to increase the frequency or extent of desirable behaviors. A reward that follows a behavior is called a *positive reinforcer* and is capable of increasing the frequency of that behavior. However, not all rewards are positive reinforcers. If a reward does not increase the frequency of the behavior it follows, it is not a reinforcer.

For a reward to become an effective reinforcer, it must meet at least two conditions. First, the reward must be contingent upon the rate or extent of performance. If the reward is not contingent upon performance, it cannot strengthen the motivational power of the incentive. Second, the reward must be matched with the need or desire of the performer. If it is not, it will not be valued by the person and consequently will not reinforce the person's behavior.

There are two kinds of positive reinforcers: (1) primary, or unconditioned, and (2) secondary, or conditioned. A *primary reinforcer* innately satisfies a person's needs and directly reinforces the behavior that it follows. For example, food and water are the primary reinforcers that satisfy hunger and thirst needs. Cuddling can be a primary social reinforcer that satisfies affectional needs. Work and play can be primary reinforcers that satisfy a person's competence need.

A *secondary reinforcer* is a conditioned reinforcer that is associated with other existing reinforcers. Money, praise, and status symbols are a few examples of secondary reinforcers. They do not have value of themselves, but they acquire value because they are associated with such reinforcers as food, affection, and pay increase.

Negative Reinforcement

Negative reinforcement is used to increase the frequency of a behavior by removing an unpleasant consequence or punishment. When the removal of punishment is contingent upon a behavior, it can increase the frequency of that behavior. The removal of punishment or the threat of punishment, rather than presentation of a reward, is called *negative reinforcement.* To be effective, it requires two conditions. First, the removal of a punishment or an aversive stimulus must be contingent upon the behavior to be reinforced. For example, when the release of a prisoner is contingent upon the prisoner's good behavior, it reinforces good behavior. Second, there must be an unpleasant event (punishment or threat of punishment) that can be removed after a specific behavior is performed. The person must have a predicament that he or she wants to avoid.

Extinction

Extinction refers to nonreinforcement. This occurs when a behavior is followed by a neutral stimulus, or when a positive reinforcement is withdrawn. Since the behavior is not rewarded, its frequency tends to decrease, and it may eventually disappear. In everyday life, one exercises extinction by ignoring the behavior of others. If a teacher ignores a disruptive student, the student may drop the attention-getting behavior.

Since extinction does not involve the direct application of an aversive consequence (punishment), it can be considered less painful than an actual punishment. In some cases, however, it can be as cruel as an actual punishment. For example, if an employee receives no pay increase, while everyone else is getting one, the experience can be as painful as a slap in the face. In addition, like punishment, extinction does not promote desirable behaviors. When a desirable behavior is not rewarded (through extinction), it is discouraged. For example, when an employee's extra effort, such as working through the lunch hour, is not recognized, he or she may soon revert to "standard" performance.

Punishment

Punishment involves the presentation of an unpleasant consequence after a behavior is performed. A threat of punishment is also a form of punishment. People do things to avoid punishment. Students study to avoid failing grades. Workers are punctual and maintain a favorable attendance record to avoid criticism from supervisors. People can learn avoidance behavior through past experience with a certain punishment or by observing other people being punished for a particular behavior. This kind of learning is called *avoidance learning,* and it is closely related to an act of punishment.

Punishment or the threat of punishment is used by organizations to discourage undesirable behaviors. It is a popular form of control because it usually produces its objective; that is, it reduces the annoying behavior of others. For example, a supervisor may admonish a secretary for tying up the phone. If the secretary gets off the phone, the supervisor's objective has succeeded.

However, punishment is not effective in producing long-term desirable effects on behavior. Also, it has a number of undesirable side effects.[8] For example:

1. The frequency of undesirable behavior is reduced only when the punishing agent is present. Once the agent is removed, the undesirable behavior usually reappears. ("When the cat's away, the mice will play.")

2. Punishment reduces the frequency of an undesirable behavior, but it does not promote a desirable behavior. For example, yelling at the children may stop their noise temporarily, but it does not help them engage in productive behaviors.

3. Punishment only frustrates those punished if they are not capable of improving their behavior. Helping people increase their problem-solving ability should be more beneficial.

4.   Punishment leads to antagonism toward the punishing agent, which can be detrimental to a manager who wants to develop supportive relationships with subordinates.

5.   Punishment often reinforces an undesirable behavior instead of reducing it. If a manager pays attention to a subordinate when the employee has done something wrong, the employee may continue to exhibit undesirable behaviors to attract the supervisor's attention.

Combined Strategies

Reinforcement strategies may be combined in two ways to produce desired behaviors. First, positive reinforcement may be combined with punishment. Positive reinforcement increases the attraction power of a positive incentive, while punishment or the threat of punishment increases the repellent power of a negative incentive. When they are arranged in such a way that a positive incentive leads employees to perform satisfactorily, while a negative incentive threatens or drives them to do so, the resultant force will be substantially greater than either force by itself. This strategy is commonly called the "carrot and stick" approach to motivation and is often used by managers.

Another method is to combine positive reinforcement with extinction. This strategy is recommended when one wants to weaken an undesirable behavior but still avoid the undesirable side effects of punishment. Ideally, extinction weakens the undesirable behavior while positive reinforcement strengthens the desirable behavior. Under this strategy, then, undesirable behaviors are systematically deprived of reinforcement, while desirable behaviors are heavily reinforced.

 SCHEDULING AND ADMINISTERING REINFORCEMENT

> *Reinforcers can be scheduled and administered in several ways, including (1) continuous, (2) intermittent, and (3) partial reinforcement schedules.*

Reinforcement schedules specify the timing of reinforcement. Generally, reinforcement should be applied as soon as a target behavior—a behavior that needs to be encouraged or discouraged—is exhibited. The specific timing and frequency of reinforcement, however, should be based on the magnitude of the reinforcer, the type of behavior exhibited, and the degree of satiation. The schedules of reinforcement, as shown in

Figure 4.3, can be differentiated reflecting the differences of these factors.

Continuous Reinforcement

Under a continuous reinforcement schedule, each time a correct response is emitted, it is followed by a reinforcer. Performance tends to increase while it is reinforced. But when the reinforcement is removed, performance decreases rapidly. This schedule follows the principle of immediate reinforcement; it strengthens the instrumental relationship between a behavior and a reinforcer. Therefore, it can be used in teaching a behavior at an early stage of learning. Correct behaviors are reinforced immediately, while incorrect behaviors are not rewarded and thus are discouraged. This schedule is used in programmed learning, or "teaching machines."

The problem with continuous reinforcement is that it can produce a *satiation effect,* which reduces the incentive value of a reinforcer. For example, if employees are paid each time they produce something, or every hour, they may lose interest in monetary incentives. In addition, it is administratively impractical. Once a behavior is learned, therefore, it can be maintained by intermittent reinforcement.

FIGURE 4.3
Schedules of
Reinforcement.

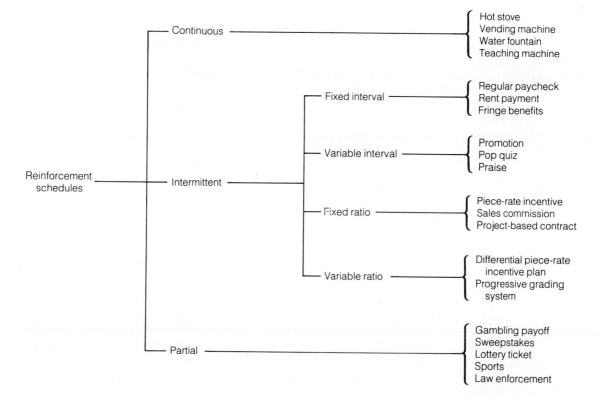

Intermittent Reinforcement

Intermittent schedules are commonly used in administering organizational rewards. Pay, praise, promotion, award, and recognition are the prime examples of intermittent reinforcements. Organizations use intermittent schedules to manage their reward systems because it is almost impossible to reinforce desirable behaviors each time they occur. There are four ways of arranging intermittent schedules: (1) fixed-interval, (2) variable-interval, (3) fixed-ratio, and (4) variable-interval.

Fixed-Interval Schedule.   An interval schedule is based on the amount of time that passes before a behavior is rewarded. If a fixed amount of time has to pass before reinforcement is administered, it is called a *fixed-interval schedule.* Most pay systems in organizations are on a fixed-interval basis. Workers are paid hourly, weekly, or monthly for the time they spend on their jobs. Since pay is tied to time interval, rather than productivity, this method is less effective as a motivational tool.

Variable-Interval Schedule.   Under this schedule, reinforcement is administered after a certain amount of time has elapsed, but the time interval is not fixed. Pop quizzes, promotions, and sales contests follow this type of schedule. Since the timing of reinforcers under this system is unpredictable, people tend to expect reinforcement during extinction. For this reason, variable reinforcement schedules are said to be more effective in maintaining behavior than fixed schedules.[9]

Fixed-Ratio Schedule.   Under this schedule, a fixed quantity or a fixed rate of a reinforcer is delivered only after a fixed number of desired responses have been performed. A real estate sales commission and a project-based contract are examples of the fixed-ratio schedule. A fixed-ratio schedule can increase the cause-effect relationship between a behavior and its consequences. Performance under a fixed schedule is usually higher than that obtained under an interval schedule. For example, workers generally produce more under a piece-rate system than under an hourly rate system.[10]

Variable-Ratio Schedule.   Under this schedule, the reinforcer is delivered after a certain number of desired responses have been performed, but the amount of reinforcement varies. A differential piece-rate pay method is an example of a variable-ratio schedule. In order to encourage high productivity, management can apply lower piece rates up to a certain production level and then increase the piece rate for higher production (say 12 cents per piece for the first 100 units produced, then 15 cents per piece for all above that).

Partial Reinforcement (Variable Schedules)

When the amount of reinforcement and/or its time interval varies to an extreme degree, it can be called *partial reinforcement*. This is nothing more than an extreme case of a variable-ratio or a variable-interval schedule. It is constrained by neither reinforcement amount nor timing. It reinforces a limited number of operant behaviors at an irregular rate or time interval. Payoff schedules adopted by gambling establishments, lotteries, and promotional sweepstakes are prime examples of partial reinforcement.

Why are we interested in studying partial reinforcement? There are two reasons. First, partial reinforcement is said to be more effective in maintaining a high level of performance than the other schedules—continuous, fixed-ratio, and fixed-interval. A study by Yukl, Wexley, and Seymore reported that subjects under two partial reinforcement schedules performed better than those under a continuous schedule.[11] One implication of this is that a behavior can be acquired through a continuous schedule and maintained through a partial schedule.

Second, partial reinforcement tends to produce greater resistance to extinction than other schedules.[12] Since reinforcement and extinction are mixed, people expect reinforcement during the period of extinction. Furthermore, people tend to increase the rate of their activities when they fail to receive the desired outcomes in an earlier period of extinction. When they receive some reinforcement at the end of an extinction period, it helps to maintain the expectation of future reinforcement. Such an expectation, in turn, helps maintain a high level of performance.

Partial reinforcement is well accepted and used in gambling institutions and in promotional campaigns, but not in managing regular reward systems such as pay systems. What are the reasons for this? Partial reinforcement is an effective motivational tool when (1) the total size of the reward is relatively small and (2) the required effort or investment is insignificant.

If a small-sized reward, such as a sweepstake fund, is distributed to a large number of recipients, the average size of the reward will be too small to elicit any response. If the reward is distributed on a partial reinforcement schedule, however, the average size becomes more attractive to recipients. The required effort or investment has to be relatively insignificant also. If a significant amount of effort or investment is required, people tend to prefer that payoffs be distributed on a regular reinforcement schedule. For example, Yukl and Latham found that, in an industrial setting that required substantial physical effort, productivity was higher under a regular schedule than under a partial schedule.[13]

SOME GUIDELINES FOR BEHAVIOR MODIFICATION

Several guidelines need to be observed when modifying human behavior through operant conditioning. These rules specify the contingency relationships between behaviors and their consequences—that is, rewards and punishments.

Much interest is currently being shown in *behavior modification,* which is the process of changing human behavior through rewards and punishments applied according to the principles of operant conditioning. Proponents of behavioral theory indicate that the effectiveness of reward systems in organizations can be substantially increased if managers follow the principles of operant conditioning.[14] And a number of organizations have implemented a variety of reinforcement programs involving the use of operant conditioning techniques. These organizations claim that the programs have improved employee satisfaction and job performance.[15] The organizations include Emery Air Freight, AT&T, IBM, American Can, General Electric, Michigan Bell, Donnelly Mirrow, Standard Oil of Ohio, Maytag, Zenith, and Weyerhauser. The following episode illustrates how Emery Air Freight has successfully used a positive reinforcement program.[16] Emery was one of the pioneers in applying such programs.

Emery Air Freight is a large air-freight company. Truck drivers pick up shipments and deliver them to cargo loading docks where they are routed to appropriate flights. Each dock handles shipments for a particular destination.

Management believed that if small shipments intended for the same destination were shipped together, the company could save a considerable amount in shipping costs, since large containers were charged at lower rates. So management began encouraging employees to use large, standardized containers. The company initially believed that larger containers were used about 90 percent of the time.

However, E. J. Feeney, a vice-president, questioned this optimistic usage estimate and undertook the following actions. First, he conducted a performance audit. The audit team found that large containers were actually used only about 45 percent of the time. It also revealed some areas where improvement would have a positive impact on the company's profits. Second, management established realistic performance goals for using large containers. The goals were defined in measurable terms, and the employees were encouraged to help set them. Third, employees were given the opportunity to measure their own performance. Thus, workers could monitor their own container usage.

Finally, increases in performance were positively reinforced. Frequent praise and recognition were given at the outset; then, a variable-ratio schedule was followed. Reinforcement schedules were manipulated to facilitate the learning process and maintain the learned behavior.

After the initial success of the positive reinforcement program, Emery expanded it to other operations wherever it could be applied. By 1976 the entire work force was affected by this program. Previously, only praise and recognition had been used as reinforcers; now other reinforcers such as special time off, invitations to business luncheons, and special task assignments were also used.

We can draw up some guidelines for applying positive reinforcement programs from the experience of Emery Air Freight. The following guidelines can be used to enhance the effectiveness of such programs.

Defining the Target Behavior

The first step in behavior modification is for management to define the behavior it wants to influence. Usually, the *target behavior* is the one that has the greatest impact on organizational goals. It can be attendance, customer service, cooperative behavior, or skill training. Failure to identify or specify the target behavior or performance often leads managers to reinforce unintended behaviors. That is, they mistakenly reward one behavior while hoping for another behavior to occur.[17] For example, managers usually want their employees to work closely together; yet they often use highly competitive reward systems that discourage cooperation to motivate those employees. To avoid the folly of rewarding wrong behavior, managers should clearly define (at least in their own minds) the target behavior or performance they want to reinforce.

Setting Performance Goals

The target behavior needs to be translated into specific performance goals, such as increasing profits, expanding the market share, reducing costs, or reducing absenteeism. If possible, these goals should be expressed in quantifiable terms—for example, increasing profits by 10 percent or reducing turnover by 3 percent. Not all performance goals, however, can be quantified. A manager's interpersonal competence cannot be quantified.

Such a behavior can be evaluated only qualitatively. Managers who are obsessed with quantifiable goals often overlook the importance of qualitative areas of managerial performance. Because of the problem of defining performance goals, however, behavior modification does not work well in reinforcing qualitative behaviors.[18]

Measuring Performance Progress

Performance measurement can serve two purposes. First, it provides employees with feedback on their performance progress. If they know they are doing well, it reinforces their behavior; if they are not, they can take corrective actions. Studies suggest that workers with performance feedback outperform workers without it.[19] High performers seem to use it for setting new goals. When performance goals are clearly defined, workers can measure their own performance against the goals. Greller and Herold point out that internally generated performance feedback is more meaningful to workers than externally generated feedback, because the former is more direct and immediate than the latter.[20]

Second, it relates performance to rewards. If the behavior is to be continued, it must be reinforced. Thus, good performance needs to be recognized and rewarded. In the absence of internally generated feedback, supervisors can evaluate the performance of their employees and use this information to give employees some form of recognition or correct undesirable behaviors.

Rewarding Good Performance

A system of rewards is a means of recognizing the valuable contributions of organizational members, and it can stimulate high performance. Since most people perceive rewards as a measure of their contributions, the rewards need to be commensurate with performance. Failure to tie rewards to performance is a major reason why some reward systems do not produce positive outcomes.

If a reward is to have maximum effect, it must be applied immediately after the instrumental behavior is performed. When the reward is delayed for a long period of time, the performer may find difficulty relating it to the specific instrumental behavior. For example, when employees are given annual bonuses, they may not know what specific behaviors are rewarded. It is thus important to reinforce a behavior in a timely manner. This suggestion does not mean that reinforcement should be given frequently, however. As pointed out earlier, frequent reinforcement can lead to a satiation effect that reduces the incentive value of a reinforcer.

Using Punishment Sparingly

Although punishment is not an effective means of promoting desirable behaviors, it can be used to discourage undesirable behaviors. However, since punishment can produce undesirable side effects, such as revenge, one must be cautious in applying it. The following guidelines can reduce such side effects:[21]

1. Punishment should be directed to the specific behavior rather than to the person. If it is directed at the person, it becomes revenge and punishes all the person's behaviors, both desirable and undesirable. Such punishment not only produces resentment against the punishing agent but also discourages desirable behaviors.

2. Punishment should be commensurate with the severity of an undesirable behavior. Underpunishment will not deter the behavior; overpunishment may deter the behavior but may unnecessarily produce undesirable side effects.

3. Punishment should quickly follow the undesirable behavior. Timely administration of punishment increases the contingency relationship between the behavior and its consequences. This is called the "hot stove rule" since punishment is applied as quickly and impersonally as a hot stove burns the unwary.

4. If possible, punishment should be administered by an agent other than the rewarder. Politicians use "hatchet men" to perform unpleasant political tasks, and managers use committees or rules to punish their employees. This practice displaces the feeling of resentment toward the punishing agent.

5. Punishment should be accompanied by suggestions for improving the behavior. If the punished person has no knowledge of why he or she is punished, or no ability to correct his or her behavior, punishment will only frustrate the person further. So it is essential for management to help employees deal with their problems more effectively.

EVALUATION OF THE REINFORCEMENT THEORY

> *The reinforcement theory presents specific operant principles by which managers can control and influence the behavior of employees. Its major limitation is that it ignores the importance of internal causes of behavior—that is, needs and perceptions.*

Like other theories of human behavior, the reinforcement theory has advantages as well as limitations. Understanding these strengths and limitations is essential for the proper application of this theory in organizational settings.

Strengths.   The reinforcement theory has several advantages, both theoretical and practical, over the needs theory of behavior. First, since this theory deals with observable behaviors, its theories can be experimentally tested. A great number of empirical studies on the effects of various reinforcers on both animal and human behavior have been done. This large volume of research gives credence to the assertion that the behavioristic view is a science.

Second, reinforcement theory presents a set of tools by which people can learn new behaviors and skills. The learning theory based on this approach has been used in teaching humans and animals to acquire new skills needed to satisfy their needs more effectively.

Third, this view gives managers a set of managerial tools with which they can effectively control and influence employee behavior. Although managers cannot change employees' internal states (needs and perceptions), they can exercise indirect control by manipulating organizational rewards that satisfy individual needs.

Finally, managers do not need a formal education in psychology or psychiatry in order to use the principles of reinforcement or behavior modification in organizational settings. The basic principles of reinforcement theory are simple to understand and apply; thus, managers can become effective users of behavior modification.

Limitations.   The reinforcement theory has been criticized by many scholars on moral, theoretical, and practical grounds. First, critics argue that the use of behavior modification on human beings is unethical, inhumane, and dictatorial.[22] Through behavior modification people are manipulated and molded into another person's concept of the ideal. Argyris argues that the purpose of behavioral science should be to help individuals achieve their own personal growth and freedom rather than to shape them according to the controller's ideal.[23] One reaction to this criticism may be that operant behavior is a voluntary behavior; it is not imposed on someone against his or her will.

Second, from a theoretical standpoint, the theory ignores the importance of the internal causes of behavior. Since internal causes cannot be observed, behaviorists act as if they do not exist. They seem to ignore the fact that people respond to external factors to satisfy their needs. The differences in needs and strengths determine the incentive value of a particular reinforcer. Unless this reinforcer appeals to a person's needs, it will have little influence on his or her behavior.

Third, the use of behavior modification is limited to specific situations in which employees depend heavily on the particular organization for their reinforcement. When individuals depend on one source of reinforcement, it can have a strong influence on their behavior. In reality, however, most people face a variety of competing reinforcers from different sources, including family, social groups, and other organizations. This situation reduces the influence of reinforcers offered by a particular organization.[24]

Finally, behavior modification is also limited to job situations in which the target behavior can be clearly defined. In many job situations, people cannot define what the desired behavior should be. For example, we do not know what constitutes good leadership or good teaching. We do have some ideas, but these ideas vary. When a target behavior cannot be defined, reinforcement cannot be carried out in a coherent manner.

The criticisms cited do not imply that the behavioristic view is wrong—rather that, like all other theories of human behavior, it is imperfect since it does not cover and explain all aspects of human behavior. However, it is one of the more viable theories for explaining human behavior. And since our behavior is influenced by external factors, understanding reinforcement theory can help managers design and administer reward systems.

SUMMARY AND CONCLUSION

This chapter has presented the *reinforcement theory,* which emphasizes the role of the environment in determining behavior. According to this view, all behaviors except a few automatic responses are acquired through learning. Behavior is learned through classical and operant conditioning processes. *Classical conditioning* emphasizes the importance of repetitive association between stimulus and response, whereas *operant conditioning* emphasizes the importance of rewarding experiences as a way of reinforcing desired behaviors.

Four reinforcement strategies can be used to influence behavior: (1) *positive reinforcement,* (2) *negative reinforcement,* (3) *extinction,* and (4) *punishment.* The first two are used to promote desirable behaviors, the last two to discourage undesirable behaviors. In organizations *behavior modification,* or *reinforcement programs,* call for maximum use of positive reinforcement and minimum use of punishment. Punishment is discouraged because it is an ineffective means of changing behavior, and it produces numerous undesirable side effects. It should be used only when it is necessary to deter specific undesirable behaviors.

The major strength of the behavioristic view is that it provides managers with practical managerial tools with which they can try to control and influence the behavior of their employees. A number of operant conditioning principles are listed in this chapter, including those related to the amount of the reward, the timing of reinforcement, performance feedback, target behaviors, performance goals, the incentive value of the reward, and the use of punishment.

KEY CONCEPTS AND WORDS

Learning
Reinforcement
Classical conditioning
Operant conditioning
Observational
  learning
Cognitive learning
Conditioned
  response

S-R association
Positive
  reinforcement
Cognitive
  behaviorism
Negative
  reinforcement
Punishment
Extinction

Primary reinforcer
Secondary reinforcer
Continuous schedule
Intermittent schedule
Partial reinforcement
Behavior
  modification
Target behavior

Questions for Review and Discussion

1. a. What is the relationship between learning and reinforcement?
   b. How does the reinforcement theory explain behavior?

2. a. What is classical conditioning?
   b. What is operant conditioning?
   c. What is the difference between them?

3. a. What is observational learning?
   b. What is cognitive learning?
   c. How do these learning processes differ from the classical and operant conditioning processes?

4. "Continuous reinforcement is more effective in teaching a new behavior than intermittent or partial reinforcement." Defend or refute this statement.

5. "Partial reinforcement is said to be more effective in maintaining a high level of performance than other reinforcement schedules, such as continuous, fixed-ratio, and fixed-interval." Defend or refute this statement.

6. Can you use the reinforcement strategies and principles presented in the chapter to increase productivity in the garment industry? Explain why or why not. If your answer is yes, describe how you would set up such a reinforcement system.

7. Some people criticize the application of the reinforcement theory—behavior modification—to organizations as unethical. How would you respond to this criticism?

 ## CASES

CASE 4.1. GREAT OUTDOOR EQUIPMENT

This case allows you to apply some of the reinforcement strategies and principles you have learned in solving an absenteeism problem in a company. This case can be handled as an exercise.

The Situation

Great Outdoor Equipment produces camping equipment and sporting goods, relying on mass production systems that use assembly line operations. The company employs approximately 2000 employees, most of whom are transients doing temporary work until they find permanent employment elsewhere or meet temporary financial needs. Most production workers last less than two years. Although the turnover rate is high, management is unconcerned because farm workers, students, and housewives provide a constant flow of new labor.

However, management is concerned with the problem of absenteeism because this disrupts the technically sequential assembly operations. The absenteeism rate runs around 10 percent or more every day. To reduce absenteeism, the company undertook a partial reinforcement system. The employees with perfect attendance records were randomly rewarded in cash on monthly and yearly bases. Scheduled days off, such as holidays and paid vacations, were not counted as absences. Each month throughout the year, ten employees with perfect attendance records in that month were selected by drawings to receive a prize of $25. At the end of the year, six employees with perfect annual attendance records were selected by drawings and awarded $500 each.

Management claims that the absenteeism rate was reduced by an average 2.3 percentage points during the period of the partial reinforcement. However, this achievement is less than originally expected. In this exercise, consider these questions: (1) If you were the manager, would you continue to use the system? (2) How would you improve the effectiveness of the reinforcement system?

The Procedure

1. Divide yourselves into small groups.

2. Each group will prepare an action plan consisting of recommendations to deal with the absenteeism problem. The plan should include a positive reinforcement program.

3. Debate the pros and cons of each plan as it is presented.

CASE 4.2. THE AMERICAN NATIONAL BANK

Like the previous case, this one lends itself to the application of a positive reinforcement program. It can be discussed as a case or can be handled as an exercise.

The Situation

A few years ago, the American National Bank opened a branch office in a fairly affluent residential area of a medium-sized city. The branch basically handles checking and savings accounts. Business volume has increased considerably since its opening. Initially, the branch started with two drive-in windows, but now it has five. On normal weekdays, it usually opens three windows with two or three tellers. However, on any given "big bank business day" (such as Friday, Saturday, and paydays), all five drive-in ramps are served by four or five tellers. Even with a full-capacity service, however, automobiles wait in line for five to ten minutes before being served.

Because of this increase in business volume, it is becoming increasingly difficult to provide personalized service to customers, and many tellers find it difficult to balance their transactions at the end of busy days. Most tellers have experienced such a problem at one time or another. Ninety percent of the tellers have at least a high school education. In order to minimize the risk of cashing bad checks, the tellers are required to check the customer's account balance or to obtain permission from a bank officer before completing a transaction.

Faced with an increase in customer complaints, balancing errors, and risk potential, the bank has invited a management consultant to help solve the problems. As a consultant, you are pondering the possibility of introducing a reinforcement program. You are told that the branch's service facility cannot be expanded because of limited space. However, personnel can be added, if necessary.

The Procedure

1.   Divide yourselves into small groups.
2.   Each group will prepare an action plan involving a positive reinforcement program.
3.   Debate each group's plan as it is presented.
4.   Discuss some of the problems positive reinforcement programs face in this particular case.

Footnotes

1.   B. F. Skinner, *Beyond Freedom and Dignity* (New York: Knopf, 1972), p. 207.
2.   Fred Luthans, *Organizational Behavior* (New York: McGraw-Hill, 1973), p. 362.
3.   E. L. Thorndike, *Animal Intelligence* (New York: Macmillan, 1911).
4.   I. P. Pavlov, *Conditioned Reflexes* (New York: Oxford University Press [Clarendon Press], 1927).
5.   B. F. Skinner, *Science and Human Behavior* (New York: Macmillan, 1953).
6.   A. Bandura, *Principles of Behavior Modification* (New York: Holt, Rinehart and Winston, 1969).
7.   Fred Luthans and Robert Kreitner, *Organizational Behavior Modification* (Glenview, IL: Scott, Foresman, 1975).
8.   See K. H. Chung, *Motivational Theories and Practices* (Columbus, OH: Grid, 1977), p. 65; and W. R. Nord, "Beyond the Teaching Machine: The Neglected Area of Operant Conditioning in the Theory and Practice of Management," *Organizational Behavior and Human Performance,* 1969, **4,** 375–401.
9.   G. S. Reynolds, *A Primer of Operant Conditioning* (Glenview, IL: Scott, Foresman, 1968); and G. A. Yukl, K. N. Wexley, and J. D. Seymore, "Effectiveness of Pay Incentives Under Variable-Ratio and

Continuous Reinforcement Schedules," *Journal of Applied Psychology*, 1972, **56,** 19–23.

10. E. E. Lawler, *Motivation in Work Organizations* (Monterey, CA: Brooks/Cole, 1973), pp. 114–121.

11. Yukl, Wexley, and Seymore, "Effectiveness of Pay Incentives."

12. J. L. Williams, *Operant Learning: Procedures for Changing Behavior* (Monterey, CA: Brooks/Cole, 1973).

13. G. A. Yukl and G. P. Latham, "Consequences of Reinforcement Schedules and Incentive Magnitudes for Employee Performance: Problems Encountered in an Industrial Setting," *Journal of Applied Psychology*, 1975, **60,** 294–298.

14. Nord, "Beyond the Teaching Machine"; and Luthans and Kreitner, *Organizational Behavior Modification*, pp. 60–66.

15. H. W. Babb and D. G. Kopp, "Application of Behavior Modification in Organizations: A Review and Critique," *Academy of Management Review*, 1978, **3,** 281–292; and W. C. Hamner and D. W. Organ, *Organizational Behavior* (Dallas: Business Publications, 1978), pp. 242–258.

16. E. J. Feeney, "At Emery Air Freight: Positive Reinforcement Boosts Performance," *Organizational Dynamics*, 1978, **1,** 41–50; and Hamner and Organ, *Organizational Behavior*, pp. 249–253.

17. Steven Kerr, "On the Folly of Rewarding A, While Hoping for B," *Academy of Management Journal*, 1975, **18,** 769–783.

18. Babb and Kopp, "Application of Behavior Modification," 288–290; and Steven Kerr, "Overcoming the Dysfunctions of MBO," *Management by Objectives*, 1976, **5,** 13–19.

19. G. P. Latham and S. B. Kinne, "Improving Job Performance Through Training in Goal Setting," *Journal of Applied Psychology*, 1974, **59,** 1874–1891; R. M. Steers, "Factors Affecting Job Attitudes in a Goal-Setting Environment," *Academy of Management Journal*, 1976, **19,** 6–16.

20. M. M. Greller and D. M. Herold, "Source of Feedback: A Preliminary Investigation," *Organizational Behavior and Human Performance*, 1975, **13,** 244–256.

21. See R. D. Arvey and J. M. Ivancevich, "Punishment in Organizations: A Review, Propositions, and Research Suggestions," *Academy of Management Review*, January 1980, 123–132.

22. Babb and Kopp, "Application of Behavior Modification," pp. 286–290.

23. Chris Argyris, *"Beyond Freedom and Dignity,* by B. F. Skinner: A Review Essay," *Harvard Educational Review,* 1971, **41,** 550–567.

24. S. F. Jablonsky and D. L. DeVries, "Operant Conditioning Principles Extrapolated to the Theory of Management," *Organizational Behavior and Human Performance,* 1972, **7,** 340–358.

LEARNING OBJECTIVES

1. To understand the perceptual process in organizations.
2. To know how perception influences our attitudes and behavior.
3. To acquire a set of perceptual skills.

CHAPTER OUTLINE

The Nature of Perception

What Is Perception?
Why Should Managers Study Perception?
The Perceptual Process

Perceptual Mechanisms

Perceptual Selection
Perceptual Organization
Perceptual Interpretation
Interpretative Tendencies

Factors Influencing Perception

External Factors
Internal Factors

How Perception Affects Behavior

What Is an Attitude?
Functions of Attitude
Attitudinal Influences on Behavior
Attitudinal Influences on Perception

Developing Perceptual Skills

Perceiving Oneself Accurately
Developing an Empathic Skill
Beware of Perceptual Distortion
Managing Impressions

Evaluation of Perceptual Theory

Summary and Conclusion

5 UNDERSTANDING THE PERCEPTUAL PROCESS

*B*eauty is altogether in the eye of the beholder.

Lew Wallace, The Prince of India

*P*eople do not behave according to the facts as *others* see them. They behave according to the facts as *they* see them. What governs behavior from the point of view of the individual himself are his unique perceptions of himself and the world in which he lives, the meanings things have for him.

Arthur Combs and Donald Snygg, Individual Behavior [1]

People perceive things differently and behave accordingly. The world is not the same for different people because they receive differing perceptual inputs, use different perceptual frames of reference, and attach different meanings to the perceived objects or events. Differences in perception become more evident when the perceived world is not clearly discernible. Lack of clarity leads people to perceive only those things that are relevant to them. The perceived world is a subjective world, but it is the only world the perceiver actually experiences.

We are interested in studying the concept of perception because it influences our behavior. We react to the perceived world as we see it. Understanding how it works will help us understand our own behavior and that of others. In organizational settings, people react to others and make job-related decisions based on how they perceive what is going on in the work environment. This chapter focuses on the perceptual process in organizational settings. It discusses (1) the nature of perception, (2) the perceptual process, (3) factors affecting perception, (4) how perception affects behavior, and (5) developing perceptual skills.

 ## THE NATURE OF PERCEPTION

> *Perception is defined as the process by which people select, organize, and interpret the sensory information they receive into a meaningful mental picture. People often perceive things differently and behave accordingly.*

What is perception? How does it affect behavior? Why should managers understand the concept of perception? How can one study perception? These are some of the questions that will be discussed in this section. Answering these questions will help us understand how perception influences our behavior in organizations.

What Is Perception?

We all see that the sun rises in the east and sets in the west, but in reality it never rises or sets. We may notice that "eye witnesses" often "see" a crime scene differently from each other and testify accordingly. These perceptual phenomena illustrate that the perceived world is not the real world, and yet this is the world we know and we react to it accordingly. The perceived world has the feel of reality. So strong is this feeling that we seldom question what we see. In fact, when other people do not perceive things as we do, we often conclude that they are either unreasonable or wrong.

Perception can be defined as the process by which we see ourselves and the things around us and attach particular meanings to what we see. People perceive things differently and attach different meanings to the perceived objects or events. And because of these differences, people act differently. The following episode illustrates such perceptual differences and their impact on behavior.

> *Joan Sanchez was a new insurance clerk. After her first day at work, she returned home and described her experience on the job to her husband: "It was a long day. I didn't like it. The girls were unfriendly. When I walked into the office, they stared at me as if I were a strange creature. Only one girl in the whole office came up*

to me to say 'hello' and ask me to join her at lunch. The boss showed me around and introduced me to the office employees. The girls were giggly and had no manners. I will hate going back there tomorrow."

Ernest Betz, another new insurance clerk, responded to the same situation quite differently: "I like the job. The people are very friendly. When I walked into the office, they greeted me with smiles on their faces. One guy even came over to say 'hello' and asked me to join him at lunch. They are a bunch of lively and nice people that I'll enjoy working with. I think I can get along well with them."

Joan and Ernest perceived the same situation differently. Of course, it is possible that the office employees did react differently toward the two—because of their differences in appearance. Ernest might be an amiable person, while Joan is a moody one. It is also possible that the employees reacted in the same way, but that the two new employees perceived the situation differently and reacted accordingly. These perceptual differences might have been caused by differences in their personalities, attitudes, and self-concepts. Joan might have been anxious and unsure of herself, so she might have perceived the situation in a less favorable light. Ernest, however, could be an assured and self-confident person, so he tended to see things favorably. In short, the characteristics of the perceiver as well as the perceived affect the way people view the world around them.

Despite the fact that we see things differently, the perceived world is not a chaotic world. It is an orderly world in which the perceiver draws an interpretive meaning from the perceived object or event. The same object or event may look unclear or meaningless to some, but it is meaningful, genuine, and real to those of us who perceive it. Since perception is formed in an orderly manner, it can be studied systematically. If we want to understand how perception influences behavior, we can study the perceptual process, which involves the selection, organization, and interpretation of the perceived world.[2] This point is discussed later in the chapter.

Why Should Managers Study Perception?

Managers often make decisions on the basis of common sense and observations. Some examples of common sense and observations are:

1. Big organizations dehumanize employees.
2. People are generally lazy, so you have to control them.
3. Happy workers are productive workers.
4. People are emotional.

5. Good leaders are always firm but fair.

6. First impressions are the lasting impressions.

7. Big organizations are successful organizations.

These statements may be true sometimes but not always. Yet managers who hold such beliefs develop certain theories about management, and they act accordingly. These beliefs are based on their perceptions, which are often distorted; and any managerial theories based on such beliefs are also likely to be distorted.

Managers can improve their perceptual accuracy if they become conscious of how perceptions are formed and can be distorted. Instead of jumping to conclusions, managers must think before they make judgments. Understanding the perceptual process can be useful in this effort.

The Perceptual Process

Studying the perceptual process involves knowing how perceptions form and how they influence attitude and behavior. Figure 5.1 illustrates the perceptual process as a system. It shows how objects, events, and people in the environment are received into our perceptual field, and how these perceptual inputs are selected, organized, and interpreted into some meaningful form. The perceptual process involves the following elements:

FIGURE 5.1
The Perceptual Process As a System.

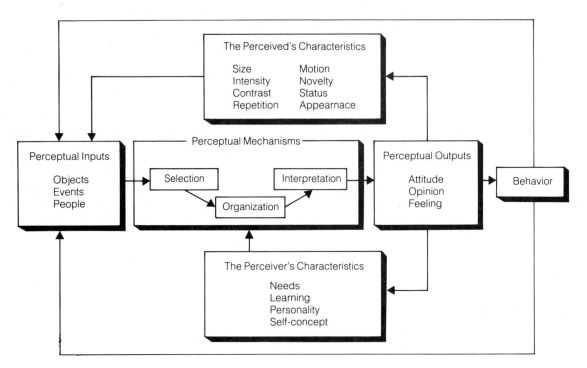

1. **Reception.** Perceptual inputs are received through our sensory mechanisms; that is, objects, events, and people in the environment enter our perceptual field through our senses of sight, hearing, touch, smell, and taste.

2. **Processing.** These inputs are processed by perceptual mechanisms; that is, they are selected, organized, and interpreted to give meaning to the perceiver.

3. **Influences.** These mechanisms are affected by both internal and external factors. Internal factors are the characteristics of the perceiver—needs, learning acquired from past experience, self-concept, and personality. External factors are the characteristics of the perceived—size, intensity, contrast, repetition, motion, novelty, status, and appearance.

4. **Output.** Perceptual outputs are attitudes, opinions, and feelings. These outputs not only determine the perceiver's behavior but also influence the way the perceptual inputs will be perceived in the future.

5. **Reaction.** The perceiver's behavior generates responses from the perceived. These responses constitute a new set of inputs that will be processed to provide new meanings to the perceived.

The core elements of this perceptual process model are discussed throughout this chapter. Guidelines for developing perceptual skills will be drawn from this discussion.

PERCEPTUAL MECHANISMS

> *Perceptual inputs—objects, events, and people in the environment—are processed by the perceptual mechanisms—selection, organization, and interpretation—to give meaningful and useful information (or meaning) to the perceiver.*

We do not see things as they really are. Instead, the things we perceive are selected, organized, and interpreted to give us useful information or meaning that may satisfy our needs. The first mechanism we use in this information processing is *perceptual selection*—we selectively perceive only those stimuli that are considered relevant for our purposes. The second mechanism is *perceptual organization,* which involves organizing the perceived inputs into a meaningful form. The last mechanism is *per-*

ceptual interpretation, which draws some useful meaning from the perceived events or objects.

Perceptual Selection

A well-known nursery rhyme goes, "Pussy cat, pussy cat, where have you
been? / I've been to London to visit the Queen. / Pussy cat, pussy cat,
what did you do there? / I frightened a little mouse under her chair." This
doggerel illustrates the point that we see the things that are important to
us. To the cat a little mouse is more relevant than the Queen. Out of the
thousands of names listed in a new telephone directory, we look up our
own names first. Out of a hundred children playing in the playground,
parents see their own children before others enter into their perceptual
field. The tendency to perceive what we want to see is called *selective
perception.* This tendency involves two psychological principles: figure-
ground and perceptual relevancy.

Figure-Ground Relationship.   When we look at objects or events in a
perceptual field, we find that not all objects or events enter our awareness
with equal clarity. Some perceptual inputs stand out as salient factors in
a meaningful picture, while others disappear as insignificant into the background. The tendency to perceive the salient factors in a picture against
insignificant factors in the background is called the *figure-ground principle.* For example, the printed words on this page are the *figure,* and the
white space around the words is the *ground.*

The figure-ground principle operates in all perceptual inputs. Some
inputs are always more important than others to the perceiver. The stars
in the sky stand out more clearly than the dark space. A book on a desk
stands out as a figure, while the desk is the background. However, the
figure-ground relationship is not clear in all perceptual instances. It can
change as the perceiver changes his or her attention or perspective. For
example, in the picture in Figure 5.2, we can see either a fancy wine glass
or the profiles of two people facing each other. Either one can be the figure
or the ground, but not both at the same time: When one is the figure, the
other must be the ground.

The figure-ground principle also operates in organizations. A manager may select some employee qualities, such as creativity and initiative,
as important, but ignore other qualities, such as dependability and reliability, which are then perceived as unimportant. Creativity and initiative are
the figure, while dependability and reliability are the ground. If the manager wishes to reward employees for the latter qualities, the figure-ground
relationship is simply reversed.

Perceptual Relevancy.   People selectively perceive things that are relevant to their needs, wishes, or desires. Leavitt points out that people

FIGURE   5.2
The Figure-Ground
Principle.

perceive things that are pleasing to them, ignore what is mildly disturbing, and pay attention to what are considered a threat to them.[3] In organizational settings, managers are attuned to favorable information that makes them look good, ignore mildly disturbing facts, and pay close attention to threatening information.

An object or event acquires meaning only when it is closely related to the perceiver. We may hear that a war is going on in a village in Africa, but we do not pay much attention to it unless we happen to have a friend who is a missionary or Peace Corps worker there. However, if we hear the loud crash of an automobile accident near our home, we will give it our full attention. The more closely an event is related to us, the greater will be its effect on our perception. The same event can be relevant to one person but not to another.

Perceptual Organization

The second perceptual mechanism is perceptual organization. Selected perceptual inputs are organized to provide a meaningful picture to the perceiver. The perceived inputs do not exist as bits and pieces of information or isolated stimuli. They are organized into complete objects, events, or mental pictures. The process by which these perceived inputs are organized into "meaningful pictures" is called the *gestalt process*. There are several mechanisms by which people organize perceived objects or events, including grouping, closure, and simplification.

Grouping.   Grouping refers to the tendency to group things or people on the basis of *proximity* or *similarity*. Things that are closer to each other, or that share similar characteristics, are perceived to be the same and are treated alike. People are grouped in the same way—this is the basis on which individuals are stereotyped. Regardless of their individual differences, people are often judged by the group to which they belong or the company they keep.

Closure. People have a tendency to fill in missing information. When they are presented with a set of stimuli that is not complete, they fill in the missing parts. For example, Figure 5.3 is perceived as a circle rather than a series of broken lines. In organizations, people are faced with incomplete messages, and they usually fill in the missing information in order to make sense out of them. For example, managers usually do not have complete information on which to judge their employees, and yet they fill in missing information and make personnel decisions.

Simplification. This principle is the opposite of the closure principle. Rather than adding informational inputs, the perceiver subtracts less salient informational items. When people are overloaded with information, they tend to simplify it to make it understandable. For example, when people are encountered with complex social or political issues, such as abortion, taxation, and social welfare, they tend to organize and simplify them in accordance with their own beliefs without considering relevant points.

Perceptual Interpretation

The third perceptual mechanism is the interpretation of perceived events and objects. People interpret the meaning of the perceived world in order to make it useful to their purposes. Unless they did this, the perceived world would be meaningless. The process of perceptual interpretation has the following characteristics:

FIGURE 5.3
The Gestalt Principle of
Enclosure.

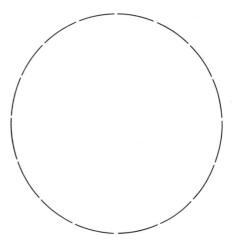

1. **It is a subjective process.**   Since perceptual interpretation serves the perceiver, it is highly subjective. The more important the perceived world is to the perceiver, the greater the influence subjective elements (emotions, feelings, and bias) have on the interpretation process. Thus, a person who is ordinarily rational may suddenly become highly emotional when the issue is related to his or her own job, family, or reputation.

2. **It is a judgmental process.**   The perceived world is usually expressed in judgmental terms—right or wrong, good or bad, beautiful or ugly, meaningful or meaningless. An object or event that is perceived in a favorable light is pleasing to the perceiver, while an object or event that is perceived negatively causes the perceiver to act defensively.

3. **It can be easily distorted.**   Since informational inputs are added to or subtracted from the perceived world, it is usually different from the real world. The perceiver actively molds the real world to suit his or her needs. And when the perceiver is confronted with unpleasant objects or events, he or she may distort their meaning or deny their existence entirely.

Interpretative Tendencies

Several factors influence perceptual interpretation in social and organizational settings. These include the halo effect, stereotyping, impression and inference, and attribution.

Halo Effect.   This is the process of using a single favorable trait of a person to judge all the individual's other traits. (When the process involves an unfavorable trait, it is sometimes called the "horn effect.") For example, Mason Haire reported that well-liked Army officers were judged more intelligent than those who were disliked, even though tests revealed they had the same intelligence.[4] This halo effect has an important implication for evaluating employees. Those employees with some favorable characteristics will be rated highly on other characteristics also. For example, managers tend to rate highly individuals who have value systems similar to their own.[5] This tendency can result in situations in which managers reward their employees on the basis of their likes or dislikes rather than on job performance.

Stereotyping.   Stereotyping, as noted earlier, is the tendency to judge other people on the basis of the characteristics (real or imagined) of groups to which they belong. For example, Americans are stereotyped as materialistic and ambitious, Japanese as industrious, blacks as musical and athletic, Irish as quick-tempered, and Italians as passionate.[6] Although one particular trait may more likely be found among members of one racial or social group than another, it is not fair to assume that all members of the group share the same trait. Yet we tend to do this all the time. Stereotyping helps us simplify the complexity of the perceived world. However, it is a major source of perceptual distortion. It causes us to misjudge other people, and is a common source of social and racial bias.

Impression and Inference. People frequently judge other people on limited information. If we see a person staggering out of a bar, we infer that the person is drunk. If we see a person smile, we conclude that he or she is happy. Thus, we may say that the first person is a drinker and the second happy-go-lucky. In judging other people, we tend to use first impressions as the basis for forming opinions. We tend to place more importance on information we received early than on more recent information. Unless the first impression is greatly contradicted by information received later, it tends to last longer.[7]

Attribution. In judging the action of another person, we tend to evaluate the causes of the action. If the action is perceived as intentional and directed toward a particular person, we will have a strong feeling toward the perpetrator of the behavior. If, however, the action is unintentionally or unconsciously carried out by the individual, we tend to judge him or her less critically or favorably. This theory indicates that the intensity of perceptual judgment is based on whether another person's action is directly attributable to him or her.[8] The more directly the action is attributable to the behaver, the greater the intensity of perceptual judgment will be.

For example, when an employee's productivity increases as a result of his or her initiative, management is more likely to acknowledge it than when it is increased as a result of a newly installed machine. When a high-status employee puts in overtime, he or she will be seen as doing it for the good of the organization. However, if a low-status employee puts in overtime, he or she will be seen as doing it for the money or in order to finish work that should have been completed earlier. A behavior can be judged favorably or unfavorably depending on its attribution.

FACTORS INFLUENCING PERCEPTION

External and internal factors cause us to see the same perceived object or person differently. External factors include the size, intensity, contrast, repetition, motion, novelty, status, and appearance of the perceived. Internal factors include the needs and motives, past experience, self-concept, and personality of the perceiver.

A number of external and internal factors influence perceptual selection, organization, and interpretation. Both types of factors affect all phases of perception, but external factors tend to have more influence on the selection phase, while internal factors have more influence on the interpretive phase.

External Factors

External factors of perception are the characteristics of the perceived object or person. These characteristics include size, intensity, contrast, repetition, motion, novelty, status, and appearance. (The first six characteristics are inaminate in nature, while the last two represent social characteristics). Knowing how these characteristics influence our perception has some implications for understanding and influencing human behavior. For example, managers may manipulate the size and intensity of rewards to influence employee behavior.

Size.   The larger the size of the perceived stimulus, the more likely it is to be perceived. A tall person in a crowd is noticed first; a word typed in capital letters is more readily noticed than other words on a page. Size establishes dominance and thus enhances perceptual selection.

Intensity.   Intensity accentuates the perceived stimulus. The more intense the stimulus, the more likely it is to be perceived. The loudness of a sound, the brightness of a light, and the underlining of a sentence intensify the message of the perceived stimulus.

Contrast.   The stimulus that stands out against a background or that is different from other stimuli is easily perceived. When a desirable behavior is compared with an undesirable behavior, the value of the former is easy to detect. A black dot on a blank sheet of paper is more readily noticed than the white space.

Repetition.   A repeated stimulus is more likely to be perceived than an unrepeated one. Awareness of a stimulus increases when it is repeated. This is why a radio or TV commercial is repeated. Repetition aids perceivers by reminding them of the existence of the stimulus.

Motion.   A moving object is more likely to be perceived than a stationary one. A moving car is more easily noticed than parked cars in a parking lot. A flashing neon sign is more easily noticed on the street than nonflashing ones.

Novelty.   A novel stimulus appearing in a familiar setting attracts the perceiver's attention. A familiar stimulus appearing in a novel surrounding also attracts the perceiver's attention. This concept is similar to that of contrast.

Status.   The social status of the perceived person influences perceptual judgment. Generally, a high-status person exerts a stronger impact on perception than a low-status person. For example, if we are introduced to the president and to the janitor of a company, we are more likely to remember the name of the president than that of the janitor.

Appearance.   The appearance of the perceived influences perceptual judgment. If a person acts, dresses, and talks like a lawyer, people perceive him or her to be a lawyer. Impostors use this concept to con other people into believing them. People also use it to impress other people favorably.

Internal Factors

Internal factors in perception are the characteristics of the perceiver. The perceiver has a tendency to use himself or herself as a basis for perceiving others. Several internal factors influence perception: needs and motives, past experience, self-concept, and personality.

Needs and Motives.   Our needs play an important role in perception. A hungry person is more sensitive to food than a person who has just eaten. A frustrated person tends to overestimate the value of money more than a less frustrated person.[9] Studies suggest that when pictures of individuals in relatively ambiguous social settings are shown to people, they perceive different things in the same pictures.[10] People with strong achievement needs tend to perceive the people in the pictures as successful in business or the professions; those with strong power motives tend to see them as people who have control or power over others; and people who have affiliation needs tend to perceive them as people who are socializing.

Past Experience.   Past experience or learning influences perception by creating a readiness to perceive an object or a person in a certain way. It teaches the perceiver to attend to certain characteristics of the perceived —and the perceiver remembers this knowledge whenever he or she encounters the perceived. If we have had a good relationship with another person, these experiences affect the way we perceive the other, even if he or she changes. Past experience with a task affects the way we perceive its difficulty and our chance of accomplishing it. Successful experiences enhance our perception of our own capacity. Failure erodes self-confidence.

Self-Concept.   Our self-concept is the way we perceive ourselves. It is the basic frame of reference we use in perceiving things and people around us. The perceptual world is organized around the perceived self. It may not be our real self, but, as it is the only self we know, we use it as our basis for perceiving others. For example, if we perceive ourselves as incompetent, the world around us is likely to be perceived as threatening. We are, therefore, unlikely to venture out and try to conquer our environment. Self-concept is also related to our level of aspiration. If we perceive ourselves as competent, we will set and strive to achieve high performance goals; otherwise, we will set and achieve lower goals.

Personality.   Personality affects the way people perceive others. Optimistic individuals see things in favorable terms, pessimistic individuals, in negative terms. Between these two extremes are individuals who can see things more accurately and objectively.[11] Carl Rogers indicates that individuals who perceive themselves realistically can function effectively without being defensive about their shortcomings. They are fully aware of their faults as well as their virtues.[12]

Several researchers have summarized the effects of personality on perception as follows:[13]

1.   Secure individuals tend to perceive others as warm rather than cold.

2.   Thoughtful individuals are less likely to perceive things in black and white or to express extreme judgments of others.

3.   Persons who accept themselves tend to perceive others more favorably than those who reject themselves.

4.   Self-accepting individuals perceive themselves as liked, wanted, and accepted by others.

5. People tend to perceive others more accurately when their characteristics are similar to those of the perceived rather than when the characteristics are not similar.

 ## HOW PERCEPTION AFFECTS BEHAVIOR

> *People develop attitudes toward what they have perceived. These attitudes are perceptual outcomes; they influence the perceiver's behavior and how he or she will perceive things in the future.*

What is an attitude? How is it formulated and maintained? How does it affect behavior? What is the relationship between attitude and future perceiving?

What Is an Attitude?

An *attitude* can be defined as a set of beliefs, feelings, and opinions that people hold toward the perceived world. An attitude reflects a person's readiness to respond to the perceived object or person. It is acquired as a result of perceptual interpretation. If we perceive people to be aloof, we may develop a less favorable attitude toward them.

As perception is affected by the internal and external characteristics of the perceiver, so is attitude. The perceiver's own needs, past experiences, self-concepts, and personality, as well as his or her environment, influence the formation of attitudes. Once an attitude is formed, it remains an integral part of a person's personality. It not only influences the perceiver's current behavior but also affects the way he or she will perceive in the future.

Functions of Attitude

Why do we hold onto certain attitudes toward the perceived? It is because these attitudes help us respond to the perceived in a meaningful way. Katz has pointed out that attitudes serve four major functions: (1) utilitarian, (2) ego-defense, (3) value-expressive, and (4) knowledge.[14]

Utilitarian Function. Attitudes are formed and maintained to help us satisfy our needs. For example, some people have a high regard for themselves, and this attitude satisfies their self-esteem needs. Attitudes are maintained or adjusted to maximize perceived rewards or minimize the perceived penalties in the external environment. If we are successful in achieving our goals or rewards, we are likely to attach a high value to them.

Conversely, if we fail to achieve our goals, we may attempt to lower their perceived value. In order to change utilitarian attitudes, we must either change our needs or find a better way to satisfy them. For example, if we are no longer motivated by self-esteem needs, we do not need to have an unnecessarily high regard for ourselves.

Ego-Defense Function. People often form and maintain certain attitudes to protect their own psychological well-being. When they feel they are threatened, they use a variety of psychological defense mechanisms to deal with this threat (see Chapter 3). For example, workers may feel threatened by the employment or advancement of minority or female workers in their organization. These threatened workers may develop prejudices against the new workers. They may develop an attitude that such newcomers are less qualified, and they might mistreat these workers. Such an ego-defensive attitude is formed and used to cope with a feeling of guilt or threat. Unless this feeling is removed, this kind of attitude will remain unchanged.

Value-Expressive Function. Our attitudes reflect our value systems. And our value-expressive attitudes are closely related to our self-concept. If we view ourselves as "liberal," we may favor government spending and control, deficit financing, minimum wage laws, and generous welfare payments, while expressing opinions against war, nuclear energy, the death penalty, and racial discrimination. If we view ourselves as "conservative," we may favor strong defense programs, free enterprise, decentralized government authority, and restrained fiscal policy, while objecting to expensive social programs, excessive government control, and reverse discrimination. These attitudes will remain unchanged until we feel dissatisfied with our value system and acquire a new set of values.

Knowledge Function. Attitude is often substituted for knowledge. In the absence of knowledge, we use our attitude to organize and make sense out of the perceived object or person. For example, people who are not familiar with nuclear energy may develop an attitude that it is dangerous and should not be used as an energy source. Stereotyping is another example. In the absence of knowledge about a particular person, we may use a stereotyped attitude for judging the person. Attitudes like these do not change unless we gain more knowledge about the perceived object or person.

Why should managers know about these attitudinal functions? Such knowledge can serve two purposes. First, it helps us understand and predict how a certain person is likely to behave. For example, if a person is "prejudiced" against another, he or she is less likely to be fair in judging the other person. Moreover, this knowledge helps us see why the person has developed such an attitude. Second, it can help us change the attitude of another person. We can do this by changing the conditions that sustain the attitude. For example, we can change people with low self-images by helping them increase their ability to solve their problems, or by providing them with positive feedback on what they accomplish. A study by Gergen suggests that people who receive favorable reactions from others, regardless of what they do, tend to accept the positive evaluation as true.[15]

Attitudinal Influences on Behavior

Attitudes influence behavior, but their influences on a particular behavior cannot be easily determined. For example, a study by Vroom reported that employees' attitudes toward their jobs were unrelated to actual job performance, but they were related to resignations.[16] In other words, employees who were satisfied with their jobs were not necessarily higher performers, but those who were dissatisfied tended to leave. A possible explanation is that job performance is a function of a number of variables such as ability, motivation, and expectations, but the decision to leave is largely determined by whether or not one likes the job.

Actions are not always consistent with attitudes. Since attitude is only one of many factors that influence behavior, it often does not lead to any specific action.[17] For example, a manager may dislike certain people in minority groups, but he or she may nevertheless treat them fairly and pleasantly in the office. This inconsistency occurs because these people do not allow their attitudes to interfere with their professional judgment, or because their social norms prohibit an overt expression of prejudice. However, these attitudes or feelings may manifest themselves in other behavior. For example, the manager may treat the minority workers fairly on the job but not invite them to social gatherings.

Although the impacts of attitude on behavior are not clearly discernible, the following theories help us understand the direction of attitudinal influences.

Cognitive Dissonance.   According to this theory, people seek consistency between their attitudes, beliefs, and feelings, and their behavior. If there is any inconsistency, they feel uncomfortable. This feeling of inconsistency is called *cognitive dissonance.* When people experience such an uncomfortable feeling, they are motivated to rectify the situation by modifying the cognitive elements or behaviors that cause the dissonance.[18] For example, if an employee perceives that he or she is underpaid in comparison with other employees, the employee may work more slowly in order to reduce the cognitive dissonance.[19]

Self-Fulfilling Prophecy.   The *self-fulfilling prophecy* is the process by which we try to convert our attitudes, beliefs, and expectations into reality. If we predict that something is going to happen, we will try very hard to make it happen. For example, if we feel that we are competent, we will undertake challenging tasks. Consequently, we gain experience and skills that make us more competent, so that we accomplish even more. However, if we have a negative attitude toward ourselves, we will not provide ourselves with the chance to become competent.

Attitudinal Influences on Perception

Perceptual outcomes are derived from past experiences and perceptions, but they also influence the way we perceive perceptual inputs. Such sayings as "Beauty is altogether in the eye of the beholder" and "One person's trash is another person's treasure" emphasize the importance of attitudes in perceiving the world around us. If our attitudes are positive, things will look brighter to us than if they are negative.

It is often difficult to tell which comes first, attitudes or perceptions. Generally, past experiences and perceptions influence our attitudes, but it is also true that our attitudes influence how we perceive things around us. The sayings "We believe what we see" and "We see what we believe" illustrate the difficulty in describing the casual relationship between attitudes and perceptions.[20]

Because of mutual influences, we expect to experience congruency between what we perceive and what we believe. However, there are occasions when our beliefs are contradicted by our perceptions. For example, we may feel that we are very capable. But when we find ourselves unable to perform a task as well as we expected, we may feel disappointed.

DEVELOPING PERCEPTUAL SKILLS

> *We can develop or improve our perceptual skills by (1) having an accurate perception of ourselves, (2) emphasizing a positive attitude, (3) empathizing with others, (4) being aware of perceptual distortions, and (5) creating a favorable image of ourselves.*

Understanding how our perceptions are formed and can be distorted can help us develop perceptual skills. These skills involve perceiving things or persons accurately and projecting a favorable image of ourselves to others. The following discussion provides several guidelines for improving perceptual skills.

Perceiving Oneself Accurately

Knowing oneself is important in developing the ability to deal with reality. When we correctly recognize our strengths and limitations, we should be able to utilize the strengths and correct any deficiencies. Some people may not use their own strengths, however, because they do not know if they have them. Maslow pointed out that self-actualizing individuals have more accurate perceptions about themselves than those who are not self-actualizing.[21] These individuals rely on their own personal strengths to deal with their environment without being defensive about their own shortcomings. Self-acceptance and positive self-regard can help us overcome our shortcomings through the self-fulfilling prophecy. When we have a positive attitude toward ourselves, we are more likely to pursue actions that may lead to further self-improvement.

Developing an Empathic Skill

If we want to understand another person better, we need to use that person's frame of reference rather than our own. The ability to put ourselves in another person's shoes is important for improving interpersonal understanding. However, it is not easy to be empathic. In order to empathize with another person, we may have to abandon our own perceptual frame of reference and see the world from that person's perspective. We often say that "I know *exactly* how you feel." The truth is that we usually do not know how others feel exactly.

Although it is a difficult skill to learn, we can improve our ability to empathize with others by making an extra effort to see and understand the thought processes of others from their standpoint without being defensive or judgmental. This does not mean that we have to agree with another person's attitudes, judgments, or opinions. Rather, it means we must be willing to put ourselves in another person's place. This thought is well expressed by the Indian prayer: "Lord, grant that I may not criticize my neighbor until I have walked a mile in his moccasins."

Beware of Perceptual Distortion

One important lesson to learn about perception is that the perceived world is not necessarily the real world. This lesson is especially important in evaluating other people. Managers can be misled by people who deliberately emphasize performance criteria that accentuate their own performance, while minimizing other areas of performance that are important but that do not accentuate their own contributions. Or managers can easily and unconsciously develop biased attitudes toward certain employees and treat them unfairly. When such a possibility of perceptual distortion exists, managers should make a conscious effort to evaluate their own perceptual judgment.

Managing Impressions

People often judge another person on how they perceive him or her. In social settings, how we appear to others is more important than what we actually are. This is because how we appear to others is what they know about us. Therefore, we must try to show ourselves in a positive light in social settings. This does not mean we have to distort ourselves to impress others. Such an attempt would be dishonest—the stock-in-trade of confidence men.[22] However, creating and presenting an honest image of ourselves to others is considered a requirement for socialization. In order to manage impressions, people must be conscious of how they appear to others. They may ask others to provide such information or use videotapes to examine their own behavior. Some politicians even take acting lessons to improve their images in the public's eyes.

EVALUATION OF PERCEPTUAL THEORY

> *Perception theory provides the personal frame of reference through which we see ourselves and others. It helps us understand how and why people see things as they do and behave as they do. Its major limitation is that it is difficult to describe one's own frame of reference accurately, let alone anyone else's.*

The perceptual view of behavior presents a theoretical framework for understanding the personal frames of reference or perceptual mechanisms that people use in perceiving themselves and the world around them. It does not present a normative framework to show how people ought to behave. Rather, perception theory presents a descriptive, conceptual framework for understanding how and why people perceive and behave as they do.

Although the perceptual view does not present us with a normative conceptual framework, we can use it, from a practical standpoint, to enhance our personality and to understand and more effectively evaluate other people's behavior.

Perception theory has limitations similar to those of the needs theory. First, the concept of perception is subjective in nature; its effects on behavior cannot be experimentally tested. The theory is derived by a deductive rather than an inductive reasoning process. Second, in order to fully understand and utilize another individual's personal frame of reference, we must have an intimate knowledge of the other person. But people seldom have such knowledge about others, especially in complex organizations. Third, although we cannot directly influence another person's perceptual mechanisms, we can do so indirectly by manipulating the external factors. The reinforcement theory, however, not the perceptual view, provides the tools to do this. Finally, the perceptual theory assumes that "if a person does not see an object or event, it does not exist." But such an argument seems too extreme—an object or event can exist, even if a person may not perceive it.

SUMMARY AND CONCLUSION

This chapter has presented the perceptual view of behavior, which explains human behavior from the behaver's perspective. This *personal frame of reference* is useful for understanding how and why people perceive and behave as they do. The theory does not present a normative framework for telling people what their life's goals should be or how they should behave, but it does help us develop our conceptual skills for understanding the underlying reasons behind actions.

A person's perceptual world is a subjective world. Objects, events, and people in the environment are *selected, organized,* and *interpreted* through the perceiver's subjective perceptual organs in order to provide him or her with specific meanings. The meanings derived from perception are reflected in a person's *attitudes* toward the perceived world. These attitudes not only determine the perceiver's behavior but also his or her future perception.

This view has some implications for personal and managerial development, interpersonal understanding, and personal evaluation. It suggests that people learn to perceive themselves more accurately but still have positive regard for themselves. Fully functioning individuals are very much aware of their own strengths and limitations without being defensive about their shortcomings. The perceptual view also suggests that one use empathy to understand the other person's behavior. This empathic skill can minimize the possibility of perceptual distortion in evaluating another person.

KEY CONCEPTS AND WORDS

Perceptual process	*Perceptual*	*Selective perception*
Self-concept	*mechanism*	*Attitude*
Figure-ground	*Gestalt process*	*Impression*
relationship	*Utilitarian function*	*management*
Halo effect	*Ego-defense function*	*Cognitive dissonance*
Distortion	*Value-expressive*	*Self-fulfilling*
Perceptual selection	*function*	*prophecy*
Perceptual	*Knowledge function*	*Personal frame of*
organization	*Stereotyping*	*reference*
Perceptual	*Inference*	*Empathy*
interpretation	*Attribution theory*	

Questions for Review and Discussion

1. Why is it important to understand the perceptual process and influences in organizational settings?

2. Why are some people better judges of people than others?

3. How do the following perceptual mechanisms influence our behavior in organizational settings?
   a. Selective perception
   b. Figure-ground principle
   c. Gestalt principle
   d. Halo effect
   e. Stereotyping

4. a. How does our self-concept affect our perception?
   b. How does our personality affect our perception?

5. a. What is an attitude?
   b. To what extent does a person's attitudes influence his or her behavior?

6. Many companies, as well as opinion survey agencies, conduct attitude surveys among their own employees or the public. Why are they interested in taking such surveys?

7. How do the following two concepts influence our behavior?
   a. Cognitive dissonance
   b. Self-fulfilling prophecy

EXERCISES

EXERCISE 5.1. PERCEIVING THINGS OBJECTIVELY

We have a tendency to take sides on an issue and perceive things from this lopsided perspective. This exercise is designed to give you an opportunity to look at an issue from the opposite side. Its purpose is to help you perceive an issue or object more objectively.

The Procedure

1. Take a side, either individually or as a group, on an issue (such as military draft, military spending, high taxes, price and wage controls, and social programs).

2. After the issue and its positions are selected, study the issue from the opposite side's perspective.

3. Present your findings to the class and discuss whether or not your attitude toward the issue has changed.

4. After this, you, and the class, should be able to prepare a list of the pros and cons of the selected issue more objectively than before.

EXERCISE 5.2 USING ANOTHER PERSON'S FRAMEWORK

To perceive the world as another person does is to have empathy. Empathy requires the perceiver to abandon his or her own personal frame of reference. This exercise is designed to help you practice the empathic skill.

The Procedure

1. Assume you are a counselor or friend who wants to understand and help another person. Read each of the situations that follow and write down your response to each, using your empathic skill.

2. When everyone has finished the assignment, the class should review a few responses to see if the participants used the empathic skill. The following example illustrates an empathic response.
   Example: "Steve, you know John in the personnel department. He repeatedly interrupted me and the other group members at the staff meeting yesterday. He acted like he knew it all, reducing the effectiveness of other group members. If he does it again at the next meeting, I don't know what I'll do."
   Empathic response: "John is monopolizing the meetings. It sounds as if you are frustrated because you don't know what to do about it."
   Nonempathic responses: "I know how you feel. He does that all the time." "Maybe you guys don't take any stand on it. Show him that you are the boss." "If he does that again, why don't you tell him to shut up." "If I were you, I would ask him to shut up."

The Situations

1. A co-worker stops by your office and tells you that she is upset because she has received less than the average pay increase for next year. She thinks she is being discriminated against because she does not ingratiate herself with the boss as others do.
    Your response: _____
    _____

2. "I thought that coming here would help my career. The boss promised that I would have opportunities to undertake challenging tasks and prove myself. But so far that promise has not been realized. I still have this crummy job, and I will never get a decent job assignment or a promotion in this place."
    Your response: _____
    _____

3. "I have been with this company for almost six years, but I don't really know anybody well. I try to be friendly to other people, but they don't seem to care. I just don't understand why I can't make friends. Maybe something is wrong with me, but I don't know what it is. Mary, what can I do to make friends?"
    Your response: _____
    _____

4. "I have an employee who has been bugging me for some time. Whatever I do, he always finds something to complain about. The other day, I called him in and told him that I did not appreciate his behavior. You know what? He charged me with favoring those employees who ingratiate themselves with me. What would you have done in that situation?"
    Your response: _____
    _____

Footnotes

1. Arthur Combs and Donald Snygg, *Individual Behavior* (New York: Harper & Row, 1959), p. 17.

2. C. R. Rogers, *Client-Centered Therapy* (Boston: Houghton Mifflin, 1965).

3. H. J. Leavitt, *Managerial Psychology* (Chicago: University of Chicago Press, 1972).

4. Mason Haire, "Role-Perception in Labor-Management Relations: An Experimental Approach," *Industrial and Labor Relations Review,* 1955, **8**, 204–216.

5. G. H. Labovitz, "In Defense of Subjective Executive Appraisal," *Academy of Management Journal,* 1969, **12,** 293–307.

6. P. F. Secord, C. W. Backman, and D. R. Slavitt, *Understanding Social Life: An Introduction to Social Psychology* (New York: McGraw-Hill, 1976), pp. 88–105.

7. C. A. Dailey, "The Effect of Premature Conclusion upon the Acquisition of Understanding of a Person," *Journal of Psychology,* 1952, **33,** 133–152.

8. E. E. Jones and R. E. Nisbett, *The Actor and the Observer: Divergent Perceptions of the Causes of Behavior* (New York: General Learning, 1971).

9. P. D. Knott, "Effects of Frustration and Magnitude of Reward in Selective Attention, Size Estimation, and Verbal Evaluation," *Journal of Personality,* 1971, **39,** 378–390.

10. J. W. Atkinson, *Motives in Fantasy, Action, and Society* (New York: Van Nostrand, 1958); and D. C. McClelland, *The Achieving Society* (New York: Van Nostrand, 1961).

11. A. H. Maslow, *The Farther Reaches of Human Nature* (New York: Viking Press, 1972), pp. 41–53.

12. C. R. Rogers, *On Becoming a Person* (Boston: Houghton Mifflin, 1961).

13. T. W. Costello and S. S. Zalkind, *Psychology in Administration* (Englewood Cliffs, NJ: Prentice-Hall, 1963), pp. 45–46; and D. E. Hamachek, *Encounters with the Self* (New York: Holt, Rinehart and Winston, 1971).

14. Daniel Katz, "The Functional Approach to the Study of Attitudes," *Public Opinion Quarterly,* 1960, **24,** 163–204.

15. Kenneth Gergen, *The Concept of Self* (New York: Holt, Rinehart and Winston, 1971).

16. V. H. Vroom, *Work and Motivation* (New York: Wiley, 1964), pp. 175–187.

17. Icek Ajzen and Martin Fishbein, "Attitude—Behavior Relations: A Theoretical Analysis and Review of Empirical Research," *Psychological Review,* 1977, **84,** 888–918.

18. B. J. Calder and M. Ross, *Attitudes: Theories and Issues* (Morristown, NJ: General Learning Press, 1976).

19. J. S. Adams, "Toward an Understanding of Inequity," *Journal of Abnormal and Social Psychology,* 1963, **67,** 422–436; and M. R. Carrell and J. E. Dittrich, "Equity Theory: The Recent Literature, Methodological Consideration and New Directions," *Academy of Management Review,* April 1978, 202–210.

20. A. G. Athos and J. J. Gabarro, *Interpersonal Behavior* (Englewood Cliffs, NJ: Prentice-Hall, 1978), p. 147.

21. Maslow, *The Farther Reaches,* pp. 41–53.

22. Mark Snyder, "Self-Monitoring of Expressive Behavior," *Journal of Personality and Social Psychology,* 1974, **30,** 526–537; and Mark Snyder, "The Many Me's of the Self-Monitor," *Psychology Today,* March 1980, 33–40.

UNDERSTANDING THE MOTIVATIONAL PROCESS

The contributions of personal efforts which constitute the energies of organizations are yielded by individuals because of incentives. The egotistical motives of self-preservation and self-satisfaction are dominating forces; on the whole, organizations can exist only when consistent with the satisfaction of these motives, unless, alternatively, they can change these motives.

Chester I. Barnard, The Functions of the Executive[1]

People join and work in organizations to satisfy their needs. They are attracted to organizations that have the means of satisfying their needs. These means are called incentives or rewards; organizations use them to induce people to contribute their efforts toward achieving organizational goals. The continued existence of an organization depends on its ability to attract and motivate people to achieve these personal and organizational goals.

This chapter focuses on understanding the motivational process in organizations. It presents a comprehensive motivational model that identifies major determinants of behavior and explains the relationships among them. In addition, this model explains how people make motivational decisions and how their motivation is related to employee satisfaction and job performance. Motivational principles are then drawn from this process model.

THE CONCEPT OF MOTIVATION

Motivation is defined as goal-directed behavior. It concerns the level of effort one exerts in pursuing a goal. Managers are concerned with this concept because it is closely related to employee satisfaction and job performance.

If managers are asked to list the problems they face, the problem of motivating employees is likely to be near the top. Employee motivation is a major concern of managers as well as scholars because motivation is closely related to the success of an individual, an organization, and a society. Through motivational efforts, people achieve their personal, organizational, and societal goals. In an age of high labor costs and limited natural resources, the effective utilization of human resources is a key to solving many organizational and economic problems.

Yet, motivating employees is becoming increasingly complex and difficult. As people become better educated and economically more independent, the traditional means of motivation—formal authority and financial incentives—become less effective. In addition, the ever-increasing constraints placed on organizations further erode the power of managers to motivate employees. Within these constraints, however, managers still have the responsibility of motivating their employees toward the attainment of organizational goals. To meet this responsibility, they should understand how and why people are motivated to work in organizations and be equipped with a set of principles that can be applied to employee motivation.

What Motivates People?

Why are some employees better motivated than others? Employee motivation is difficult to understand because it involves a variety of individual and organizational factors. The individual factors include needs, goals, attitudes, and abilities; the organizational factors include pay, job security, co-workers, supervision, praise, and the job itself.

A number of theories have been developed to explain employee motivation in organizations. These theories can be divided into two major categories: (1) content and (2) process. Content theories include the needs theory and the reinforcement theory, presented in Chapters 3 and 4, respectively. The needs theory indicates that human behavior is energized by internal stimuli—needs; the reinforcement theory explains how behavior can be controlled by its consequences—reward and punishment.

While content theories are primarily concerned with the internal and external causes of behavior (needs and incentives), process theories attempt to explain the process by which people make motivational choices. The perceptual theory, presented in Chapter 5, can help explain why people differ in their motivational choices. The process theories included in this chapter are the expectancy theory, the equity theory, and the discrepancy theory. These theories are discussed throughout the chapter.

The Motivational Process in Organizations

Before we examine the process theories, let's examine a conceptual model that describes the process by which various motivational determinants influence work motivation, which in turn is related to employee satisfaction and performance. This conceptual model is composed of three parts: motivational inputs, motivational decisions, and motivational outcomes (see Figure 6.1).[2]

The first part of the model identifies a set of motivational determinants. These key variables can be described as:

1. **Employee needs.**   People have a set of needs they want to satisfy: (a) existence (biological and safety), (b) relatedness (affection, companionship, and influence), and (c) growth (achievement and self-actualization).[3] These internal stimuli energize behavior.

2. **Organizational incentives.**   Organizations have a set of rewards that can satisfy employee needs. These include: (a) substantive rewards (pay, job security, and physical working conditions), (b) interactive rewards (co-workers, supervision, praises, and recognition), and (3) intrinsic rewards (accomplishment, challenge, and responsi-

FIGURE   6.1
The Motivational Process
in Organizations.

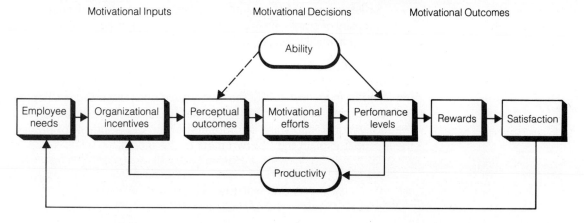

bility).[4] These organizational factors influence the direction of behavior.

3. **Perceptual outcomes.** People develop a set of perceptions regarding: (a) the value of organizational rewards, (b) the relationship between performance and rewards, and (c) the likelihood that their efforts may result in task performance.

The second part of the model explains the process by which people make motivational choices or decisions. This process describes the motivational efforts involved in deciding to perform effectively. The specific element involved is:

4. **Motivational efforts.** If they have the ability and authority, people make motivational decisions based on how they perceive the value of rewards, the instrumental relationship between performance and rewards, and the likelihood of task accomplishment.[5] Generally, positive perceptions lead to high motivation.

The last part of the model explains the outcomes of employee motivation. It shows the relationships among motivation, performance, rewards, employee satisfaction, and organizational productivity. These key variables can be described as:

5. **Performance levels.** Performance is a function of ability and motivation.[6] Ability determines what a person *can* do, while motivation determines what the person *will* do. Employee job performance influences organizational productivity, which in turn affects the levels of organizational rewards.

6. **Rewards.** Performance may be either rewarded or not rewarded. Equitable rewards lead to employee satisfaction; inequitable rewards or no rewards lead to dissatisfaction.[7]

7. **Satisfaction.** The amount of satisfaction modifies the type and intensity of employee needs. This modified need structure influences the individual's future behavior.

This conceptual model identifies a number of factors influencing employee motivation, satisfaction, and performance. Since the motivational inputs in the first part of the model have been discussed in Chapters 3, 4, and 5, this chapter focuses on the last two parts. Note, however, that the motivational inputs are incorporated in the development of process theories that explain the last two parts of the model.

THE EXPECTANCY THEORY OF MOTIVATION

> *Expectancy theory explains the process by which people make motivational choices. According to this theory, people make motivational choices based on how they perceive (1) the value of rewards, (2) the instrumental relationship between performance and rewards, and (3) the chance of getting the job done.*

The expectancy theory starts with the assumption that people are rational beings who want to maximize their gains in their goal-directed endeavors. Therefore, when they are faced with a number of behavioral options leading to need satisfaction, they will evaluate the potential outcomes of these options and select the one that promises an optimal result.[8] In evaluating these behavioral options, a rational person will analyze (1) the value of the rewards that the organization offers (valence), (2) the relationship between performance and rewards (instrumentality), and (3) the perceived chance of accomplishing the required task (expectancy). The tendency to act (motivation) is said to be a function of the valence *(V),* the instrumentality *(I),* and the expectancy *(E).*[9] Using the initials of these three variables, expectancy theory is often called the *VIE theory.* Each of these key elements of expectancy theory is discussed in this section.

Valence of Rewards

Valence is a subjective value attached to an incentive or reward. People attach a valence to an incentive because they believe it satisfies some of their needs. Since it is subjective, people differ in the value they attach to a given incentive. For example, one person may attach a high value to promotion, while another person may avoid it. The former may like it because it brings money and power, while the latter dislikes it because it means more responsibility or the headaches of dealing with other people's problems.

Also since it is subjective, managers have little control over the valences their employees attach to organizational incentives. However, managers can influence the valence of incentives by *matching rewards to employee needs.* Valence usually increases when (1) an employee has strong needs, (2) the incentive matches one or more needs, and (3) the size of the incentive is large enough to satisfy the aroused needs. For example, an employee will probably attach a high valence to money if (1) he or she has a strong economic need, (2) money is used as an incentive, and (3) the size of the monetary incentive is sufficiently attractive.

Performance-Reward Instrumentality

Instrumentality refers to the relationship between performance and reward. People ask, "Will I be rewarded if I perform the job well?" If the answer is affirmative, they will be motivated to exert an effort and increase the level of task performance. If the answer is negative, their motivational efforts will be reduced. As with valence, the measures of instrumentality can be positive or negative. If people perceive that their performance is generally rewarded, the perceived instrumentality will be positive. If they perceive that performance does not make any difference to their rewards, or if poor performers are rewarded as much as or more than high performers, the instrumentality will be low.

Since perceived instrumentality is a subjective judgment, managers do not have direct control over it. But they can positively influence their subordinates' perception of the instrumental relationship by *matching rewards to performance* and by communicating this fact effectively to the subordinates. For example, managers can improve instrumentality by using performance-contingent pay systems such as piece rates, merit rates, or performance bonuses, and by managing such systems fairly.

Effort-Performance Expectancy

Expectancy is the belief that effort leads to performance. It is a subjective feeling that people attach to the likelihood of accomplishing a task. They may ask, "Can I perform and accomplish the task goal?" "How much effort would the task require?" If they feel there is a close relationship between their effort and task accomplishment, expectancy will be favorable. However, if the task is too simple or too complex relative to their ability, then they may feel that their effort is not related to task performance.

Like other motivational concepts, expectancy is subjective; people attach varying expectancies to an outcome. A task may seem simple to some but not to others. A person's ability and personality influence his or her effort-performance expectancy. Competent and secure individuals tend to perceive expectancy more positively than incompetent and pessimistic individuals.

Managers have no direct control over how their employees perceive the chance of achieving an outcome or task, but they can influence the employee's expectancies positively by *matching people to jobs*. When people are matched with jobs, employees can utilize their job skills and energies effectively. Consequently, effort-performance expectancy will be increased.

The Motivational Decision Process

People make motivational decisions based on how they perceive the valence, instrumentality, and expectancy of performing a task. The level of motivational effort will be high if they perceive that (a) they can effectively perform the task, (b) their performance will be equitably rewarded, and (c) the rewards can satisfy their needs.

The following example illustrates a thought process involving a motivational decision (see Figure 6.2). The values in the figure are computed by considering the level of motivation as a multiplicative function of valence, instrumentality, and expectancy.

> *John Dow is an office employee with a strong need for power and status. He thinks he can satisfy this need by receiving an impending promotion, so he attaches a high valence to promotion. He thinks he can obtain the promotion by doing good work and by engaging in some office politics. Although both good work and office politics are important in obtaining the promotion, he feels the former contributes a little bit more than the latter.*
>
> *John is a likable person and is very capable in dealing with people. He is confident that he can please the supervisor as well as other people who might be involved in the promotion decision process. As to doing good work, he is not so sure about his chance of performing the job satisfactorily. He thinks he can do an adequate job, but it may not be an impressive one.*
>
> *Faced with these two behavioral options, he would probably prefer to engage in office politics than in doing good work. In fact, note from the figure that the motivational value of engaging in office politics is 2.99 and that of doing good work is 2.56. These numbers imply that he will indeed exert more energy in office politics than in performing the task.*

Evaluation of Expectancy Theory

Expectancy theory is one of the most ambitious theories ever developed in the area of organizational behavior. Unlike content theories of behavior, which focus on one dimension of motivation, the expectancy theory accommodates a number of motivational determinants in its theoretical framework. It considers employee needs, organizational rewards, and task performance, as well as their contingency relationships in particular work situations.

Is the theory valid? Although it emerges as an important theory of motivation, it has not been fully tested empirically. It is complex, and thus its validity is difficult to test in its entirety. Most studies that have attempted

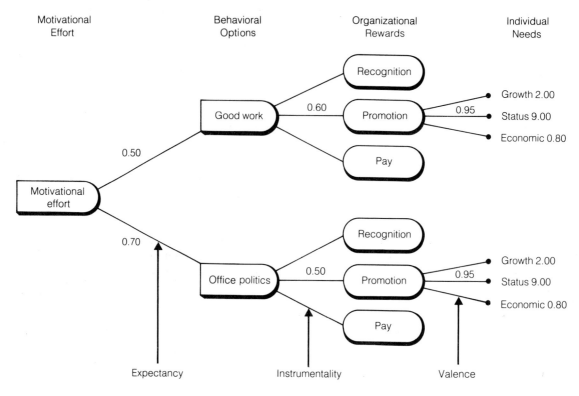

Motivation (good work) = 0.50 × 0.60 × 0.95 × 9.0 = 2.56
Motivation (politics) = 0.70 × 0.50 × 0.95 × 9.0 = 2.94

FIGURE 6.2
The Motivational Decision
Process.

to test its validity have been only marginally successful.[10] Some critics even argue that the theory has only limited use because it tends to be valid only in situations where the effort-performance and the performance-reward linkages are clearly perceived by the employees.[11] Since many individuals in organizations are rewarded on the bases of seniority, education, job requirements, and positions rather than on their actual performance, the theory tends to be idealistic. However, this criticism does not invalidate the theory. Rather, it supports it by explaining why people in many organizations are not well motivated in performing their jobs.

The expectancy theory is intended as a predictive theory of motivation, but it cannot be used as a predictive measurement because of the problem of test validity. However, it can be used as a heuristic decision tool to guide managers in dealing with the complexity of employee motivations in organizations. Motivational principles can be drawn from the theory, and these principles can be used to guide managers in designing organizational reward and work systems.

DEVELOPING MOTIVATIONAL PRINCIPLES

> *Managers can improve the valence, instrumentality, and expectancy employees place in their job situations by (1) matching rewards to needs, (2) matching rewards to performance, and (3) matching jobs to employees.*

As pointed out earlier, the strength of expectancy theory lies in the fact that it accommodates three theories of individual behavior (needs, reinforcement, and perception) and that it can be operationalized. In this section we will derive a set of motivational principles from expectancy theory and explain how these principles can be applied in organizational settings.

Matching Rewards to Employee Needs

By matching rewards to needs, management can increase not only the valence of rewards but also the level of employee satisfaction. How can management match rewards to needs? There are a few things that managers can do:

1. **Figure out what employees want.** It was suggested in Chapter 3 that managers ask their employees what kinds of rewards they prefer. This information can be used to select appropriate rewards. Remember that people want different things from their jobs, and that matching rewards to these needs increases the valence of the rewards.

2. **Find people who value rewards.** The match between rewards and needs can be achieved by finding people who may value what the organization can offer. Some organizations are limited in their ability to offer a variety of rewards. In this case the organization needs to attract people who can be motivated by what it can offer. For example, if the only things a company can offer is money, it should hire people who are striving for economic need satisfaction.

Matching Rewards to Performance

By relating organizational rewards to job performance, management can increase the chances of attaining both individual and organizational goals. This strategy favorably affects the performance-reward instrumentality. There are several things that managers can do in this effort.

1. **Use performance-contingent reward systems.**   As pointed out earlier, some reward systems lack motivational value because they are not tied to performance. Annual bonuses and fringe benefits are often not tied to performance; they are usually given to employees instead for maintaining organizational membership. Incentive pay and merit pay systems are examples of relating rewards to performance.

2. **Maintain equity in reward systems.**   Matching rewards to performance also means that the amount of reward should be commensurate with task complexity, labor availability, prevailing wage level, and amount of responsibility. When there are no objective performance criteria, managers need to be cautious in evaluating the performance of their employees. This issue will be further discussed in Chapter 14.

3. **Communicate performance-reward contingencies.**   It does not matter whether or not rewards are actually tied to performance. Unless the performance-reward contingencies are clearly communicated to employees and perceived by employees as such, the reward systems cannot have a strong impact on employee motivation. Performance feedback, followed by reinforcement, is essential in maintaining a high level of performance.

Matching Jobs to Employees

Matching the technical, physical, and psychological requirements of the job to the employee's qualifications enhances the effort-performance expectancy. If the job is either too simple or too complex, the employee may not feel that his or her effort has been effectively utilized in the task performance. The matching process involves the following actions.

1. **Design the job to suit employee needs.**   People want different levels of job challenge. Some employees may prefer complex and challenging jobs; others may prefer simple tasks. Task complexity needs to be differentiated to reflect the technical and psychological qualifications of employees. The process of matching jobs to people is the main theme of Chapter 15.

2. **Match employees to jobs.**   The match between jobs and people can also be achieved by hiring people who will fit the jobs. When it is economically and technically impractical to redesign jobs, it makes more sense to fit employees to jobs than the other way around.

3. **Improve employee job skills.**   Another way of fitting people to jobs is by training. When employees are underqualified to perform

their jobs, training can help them find a better fit. Training also enhances effort-performance expectancy.

4. **Set challenging but attainable goals.**   Set performance goals that are challenging but attainable. If the task goals are either too high or too low, employees are not likely to feel that their efforts are related to task performance. When the task goals are challenging but attainable, they are more likely to perceive the relationship between effort and task accomplishment.[12]

This discussion demonstrates how motivational principles can be applied in managing organizational reward and work systems. Since the task of managing such systems is the major responsibility of managers, it is discussed further in Chapters 14 and 15. In the remainder of this chapter, we will examine the relationships between motivation, performance, rewards, and satisfaction.

WHAT CAUSES PERFORMANCE AND SATISFACTION

Performance is a function of ability and motivation. An employee's satisfaction increases when he or she is able to perform the job effectively, when performance is equitably rewarded, and when the rewards match the employee's needs.

Does high motivation lead to high performance? Are satisfied workers productive workers? What are the relationships between satisfaction and performance? Many managers want to believe that highly motivated employees are better performers, and that satisfied workers are productive workers. Yet there are many cases where motivated workers consume their energies and organizational resources endlessly without achieving noticeable performance, and where satisfied workers, contented with what they have, are not motivated to produce. In this section, we identify the determinants of performance and satisfaction and investigate relationships between them.

Determinants of Performance

Motivation is said to be the key to high performance, but motivation alone cannot increase job performance. Unless one has the necessary job skills and knowledge (ability), one cannot achieve high performance. Workers, then, must possess *both ability and motivation* in order to achieve high job performance. It is therefore hypothesized that performance *(P)* is a multiplication function of ability *(A)* and motivation *(M)*: $P = f(A \times M)$.[13] According to this formula, performance increases when both ability and motivation increase; it declines when either ability or motivation decreases.

Motivational Effect on Performance.   Increasing motivation affects performance, but its effect is not always direct and positive. At a given level of ability, performance usually increases when motivation increases from a low level, and it reaches an optimum level with a moderate increase of motivation. But, at an extreme level of motivation, performance starts to decline. An example is the classic case of a person who tries too hard to accomplish a goal. When people are overanxious about something, their anxiety often impairs proper mental and physical functioning. For example, students who are anxious to get an A grade might study all night without rest and thus be unable to perform well on the examination in the morning. They might then panic and find that their minds have gone blank.

The *Yerkes-Dodson law* explains the inverted-U relationship between motivation and performance. As shown in Figure 6.3, increased motivation improves performance up to a point, but beyond that, it depresses performance.[14] There are several reasons why high motivation can have a detrimental effect on performance.

First, increased motivation produces anxiety that can be functional for solving problems up to a point, but beyond that level it becomes a hindrance to performance. A high level of anxiety produces such in-

FIGURE   6.3
The Effects of Ability and Motivation on Job Performance.

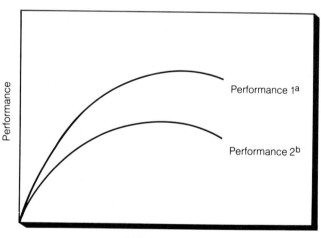

Performance 1a

Performance 2b

Performance

Ability and motivation

aResult of increasing both ability and motivation.

bResult of increasing ability or motivation only.

voluntary responses as insomnia, emotional stress, and other psychosomatic reactions that interfere with performance. As indicated in Chapter 3, prolonged stress and anxiety can even impair mental and physical health.

Second, under conditions of high stress and anxiety, people tend to rely on unproductive defense mechanisms such as aggression, rationalization, and regression to deal with their emotional problems. Such defense mechanisms may help reduce the level of anxiety, but they do not help solve the problems effectively. Effective solutions to organizational problems require reflective analysis and careful selection of problem-solving tools.

Finally, overmotivated individuals may be so preoccupied with a limited set of valued outcomes or goals that they overlook the importance of other behaviors. For example, task-oriented managers may be so preoccupied with task performance that they ignore the social needs of their employees. Consequently, they may lose the support of subordinates who might be very helpful in achieving task goals.

Ability as Performance Moderator.   Ability moderates the effect of motivation on performance. At a given level of motivation, performance can increase with increased ability (see Figure 6.3). When ability is low, increased motivation does not improve performance. But when ability is high, motivation can cause high performance.[15] As long as motivation increases with a person's capacity, it enhances performance.

An increase in ability without an increase in motivation, however, can have a detrimental effect on performance. When an employee is overqualified for a job, there will be a negative impact on motivation. If a job is so simple that it does not require the worker's skills, it will not provide the person with intrinsic motivation. Unless the job effectively utilizes newly acquired ability, an increase in ability may be useless.

Determinants of Satisfaction

What is job satisfaction? What causes job satisfaction? How is job satisfaction related to job performance? *Job satisfaction* generally means the degree to which employees satisfy their needs in organizations. If they are able to satisfy their needs reasonably well, they are said to be satisfied. Managers are concerned with job satisfaction because it affects employees' attitudes toward their jobs, co-workers, superiors, and management; and these, in turn, affect their job performance. However, there is no inherent relationship between satisfaction and performance. In some cases, job satisfaction is achieved as a direct result of performance. In other cases, employee satisfaction can be achieved independently of job performance.

Performance Causes Satisfaction. Performance can produce either intrinsic or extrinsic rewards.[16] *Intrinsic rewards* are the outcomes derived from task performance, such as challenge, excitement, task accomplishment, and a sense of doing something worthwhile. These rewards satisfy employee needs for achievement, competence, and self-actualization. Since these rewards are derived directly from task performance, the linkage between satisfaction and performance is direct.

Extrinsic rewards are the rewards given to employees by management—pay, benefits, job security, praise, and recognition, for instance. If rewards are based on the employee's performance, performance can cause satisfaction. However, since rewards can be given to workers independently of their performance, performance does not necessarily lead to satisfaction. Lower performers may be better rewarded and more satisfied than higher performers.

Equity Causes Satisfaction. The degree of employee satisfaction with extrinsic rewards depends on how employees perceive the equity of the reward system. If they perceive that they are fairly treated, they will be satisfied; otherwise, they will be unhappy, even if they are rewarded. According to this view, level of *perceived equity* determines the level of satisfaction. Two theories are based on perceived equity: discrepancy theory and equity theory.

Discrepancy theory states that perceived equity is determined by the balance between what people feel they should receive and what they actually receive.[17] If the actual reward level is equal to the expected level, they will be satisfied. Any imbalance or discrepancy between the two reward levels, however, can cause dissatisfaction.

People set their expected level of rewards on the basis of what they bring to their jobs—education, training, job skills, seniority, performance, and other qualifications. These personal and professional qualifications are called *inputs.* The actual reward level is determined by what they receive from their jobs—pay, job security, praise, promotion, position, recognition, and other rewards. These organizational rewards are called *outcomes.* Some people determine perceived equity by comparing their own inputs with their outcomes. As long as their outcomes or rewards are perceived as equitable compared to their inputs or qualifications, they will be satisfied regardless of what other people receive.

Equity theory involves social comparisons of input-outcome ratios, as shown in Figure 6.4. People tend to compare their own inputs and outcomes with those of other people, who are called the *referent persons.* If the *focal person's* input-outcome ratio is equal to those of the referent others, the focal person will perceive the reward system as equitable and be satisfied. If the person's ratio is smaller than those of others, however,

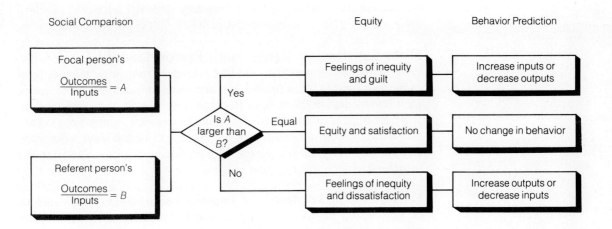

FIGURE 6.4
Equity Theory and
Behavior Prediction.

dissatisfaction will result. If the person's ratio is larger than those of others, he will have feelings of inequity or guilt.

How do people deal with feelings of dissatisfaction or inequity? Individuals who feel underrewarded will probably try to increase their outcomes (rewards) or reduce their inputs (performance), while those who feel overrewarded will do the opposite.[18] For example, an employee who feels underpaid is likely to demand a higher wage under an hourly-rate pay system or increase his or her production quantity to increase wages under a piece-rate incentive system. If these efforts prove unsuccessful, the person will reduce his or her performance—either qualitatively or quantitatively.

Reward Causes Satisfaction.   Satisfaction is ultimately a function of rewards. If employees are given rewards that satisfy their needs, they will be satisfied with their jobs. As long as the rewards match the employee's needs and are large enough to satisfy these aroused needs, rewards can cause satisfaction. However, as indicated earlier, since some rewards can be given to workers independently of their performance, satisfaction can be unrelated to job performance.

Cherrington and his associates report a case where rewards caused satisfaction, but satisfaction was inversely related to job performance.[19] Their study reports that, regardless of performance, individuals who were well rewarded expressed satisfaction, while those who were poorly rewarded expressed dissatisfaction. When poor performers were rewarded, they expressed satisfaction but continued to perform poorly. When high performers were poorly rewarded, they expressed dissatisfaction, and their performance subsequently declined. When rewards were contingent upon performance, however, their performance was significantly higher than when rewards were not related to performance.

Does Satisfaction Cause High Performance?

Early human relationists believed that employee morale determines level of performance.[20] Since people join and work in organizations to satisfy their needs, organizations have to satisfy these needs to induce them to work for organizational goals. According to this view, employee satisfaction is an antecedent condition to high productivity; the view reflects the popular belief that satisfied workers are productive workers. This view has been well accepted for several reasons.

Factors Causing Satisfaction to Improve Performance.   At least four factors related satisfaction to performance. First, managers believe that satisfied workers have positive attitudes toward their jobs, co-workers, and superiors, and that these positive attitudes positively affect their performance. When workers are satisfied with what they receive from the organization, they are likely to express their gratitude in high productivity and institutional loyalty. It is also easier for managers to work with satisfied workers than with dissatisfied workers.

Second, satisfied workers are likely to show up for work more regularly and stay on their jobs longer than dissatisfied workers. Job satisfaction is a key factor in maintaining low rates of absenteeism and turnover.[21] As absenteeism and turnover account for a major portion of labor costs, job satisfaction can be helpful in reducing these costs.

Third, job satisfaction tends to improve the mental and physical health of organization members.[22] Healthy organization members can use their energies for productive endeavors. When workers are dissatisfied with their jobs, however, they become less committed to their work. Chronic dissatisfaction with work can cause such stress-related health problems as hypertension, coronary disease, and nervous disorders.

Finally, some managers feel morally responsible for providing employees with job satisfaction. Most workers spend a major part of their waking hours in work organizations. It is important, therefore, for workers to maintain a satisfying work life if they are to function as productive members of society. If they are not happy with their jobs, not only their personal lives, but also their families and eventually society will be adversely affected.

Factors Keeping Satisfaction from Improving Performance.   Although job satisfaction is a major concern of managers, it may not directly cause high performance. There are several reasons for this conclusion. First, satisfaction reduces search behavior—that is, motivation. Satisfied needs are not motivators of behavior. Unless satisfaction activates other unfulfilled needs, it only depresses motivational effort. Second, when extrinsic rewards are given to workers independently of performance, poor performers who are rewarded may be satisfied but find no reason to increase performance. Finally, employee activities that lead to high morale are often in conflict with productive endeavors. For example, employees may be so busy socializing on the job that they do not have time to perform their jobs adequately.

RELATIONSHIPS BETWEEN SATISFACTION AND PERFORMANCE

> *Managers may want to believe that satisfaction leads to high performance. However, there is no inherent relationships between the two.*

As we have seen, there is no inherent relationship between employee satisfaction and job performance. The relationship between the two can be manifested in four possible combinations, as shown in Figure 6-5: (1) satisfaction is high, but performance is low, (2) satisfaction is low, but performance is high, (3) both satisfaction and performance are high, and (4) both satisfaction and performance are low.

High Satisfaction with Low Performance
You may sometimes notice people who are happy-go-lucky but do not produce. These people may have achieved certain levels of success or

FIGURE 6.5
Relationships Between
Satisfaction and
Performance.

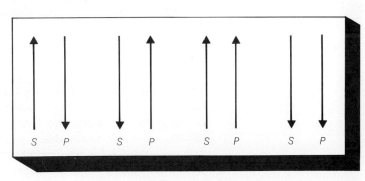

S = satisfaction   P = performance

do not have the desire to achieve more than what they have. When people get what they want from their jobs (for example, job security or a respectable professional standing), they may search for life fulfillment outside of work organizations. They may spend more time with their hobbies, their families, or social causes. This can be a healthy adjustment for individuals, but it reduces their performance contribution to their organizations.

The combination of high satisfaction with low performance is likely to be seen in organizations where employees are overprotected. For example, federal government employees are reasonably well paid, and their pay increases tend to be based on seniority rather than performance. Also, even if federal employees are found to be incompetent, it takes a lengthy litigation process (often lasting three years) to fire them.[23] By and large, the Civil Service System tends to protect incompetent employees whose needs are satisfied but who find no pressure for high productivity. This was a reason why the Civil Service Reform Act of 1978 was promulgated.

Low Satisfaction with High Performance

Can a dissatisfied worker really be a productive worker? Yes, it happens frequently. The HEW (Health, Education, and Welfare) report *Work in America* indicates that more than three out of four blue-collar workers would not choose the same line of work if they had the option—mainly because of lack of job satisfaction.[24] However, these workers perform their jobs well—even though they may dislike them—as long as they consider the jobs to be their means of supporting themselves and their families.

People are motivated to remove discontent from their lives and to satisfy unfulfilled needs. As Oscar Wilde said, "Discontent is the first step toward progress." Anticipated need satisfaction is what motivates people to strive. Although chronic dissatisfaction with work impairs people's psychological ability to cope with discontent, temporary dissatisfaction, if it can be removed, can be a motivator. As long as they perceive their performance as a means of removing discontent, people will increase their performance level.

High Satisfaction and High Performance

Meeting the demands of both employees and their organizations is a major challenge for managers. This goal can be achieved, however, when employees are continuously able to satisfy their needs while meeting organizational goals. This is possible when need satisfaction is contingent upon job performance. If employees are striving for economic need satisfaction, tying monetary rewards to performance can increase both satisfaction and performance. If they strive for higher-order need satisfaction, providing them with challenging jobs can produce the desired result.

Both job satisfaction and performance are expected to be high among managerial, scientific, and professional people. Since their jobs are interesting and challenging and require high degrees of job skill and knowledge, these individuals are likely to be motivated to produce. Their performance not only results in intrinsic job satisfaction but also yields extrinsic rewards. Reward differentiation between high and low performers is usually higher among professional personnel than among nonprofessional employees.

Low Satisfaction with Low Performance

This is the most disappointing situation for both employees and employers, but it occurs in many organizations. Employees are dissatisfied with what they receive from their employers, who, in turn, are unhappy with the performance of their employees. Such an impoverished situation occurs (1) when employers do not adequately reward employees or (2) when employees do not perform well enough to justify rewards. The first case can be corrected when management begins to reward employees adequately and equitably; the second case can be corrected by replacing or training employees. Failure to correct the situation will lead to the eventual failure of an organization.

Chronic job dissatisfaction causes a number of behavioral problems in organizations. Dissatisfaction with pay may cause people to leave the organization or discourage them from showing up for work. Lack of social reinforcement causes people to withdraw their commitment to work groups. Dissatisfaction with the job itself increases workers' apathy and indifference toward their work. All these dysfunctional behaviors can cause poor job performance.

Achieving High Satisfaction and Performance

Although it is possible for management to achieve organizational goals at the expense of individual goals, the continuous survival of an organization depends on its ability to satisfy both individual and organizational goals. What conditions are needed to achieve both satisfaction and high performance? If employees seek to satisfy economic needs, a pay rate commensurate with their performance is sufficient for high productivity. However, if they are striving to satisfy higher-order needs, the following conditions are needed:

1. Jobs must be matched to employee qualifications. When this condition prevails, employees' motivational efforts will be effectively utilized and will result in task accomplishment (see Chapter 15).

2. Employees' performance must be followed by such extrinsic rewards as pay increase, praise, and promotion. They must be rewarded equitably according to their contributions to performance (see Chapter 14).

3. The rewards employees receive must satisfy their needs. In order to achieve this end, the rewards should be compatible with these needs (see Chapter 3).

Notice that conditions for achieving high satisfaction and performance are also related to the three decision variables—valence, instrumentality, and expectancy. As Figure 6.6 shows, matching employees to their jobs is likely to enhance the effort-performance expectancy. Matching rewards to performance improves the performance-reward instrumentality. Matching rewards to employees then increases the valence of organizational rewards. In essence, the way the reward and work systems are designed and managed influences, to a large extent, the way organizational members behave.

SUMMARY AND CONCLUSION

This chapter (1) presents a comprehensive model of motivation, (2) shows how motivational decisions are made, (3) proposes a set of motivational principles, and (4) discusses the relationship between satisfaction and performance. The motivational process model accommodates a variety of motivational determinants, that is, needs, incentives, and perceptions. And need, incentive, and perceptual theories of motivation are integrated into the framework of the expectancy theory.

Expectancy theory explains how motivational decisions are made.

FIGURE 6.6
The Effects of Performance and Satisfaction on Motivation.

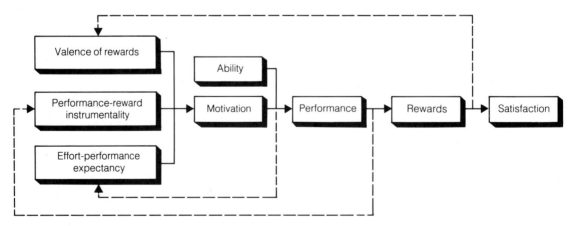

People make motivational decisions based on how they perceive the relationships between (1) their needs and organizational rewards—*valence,* (2) their performance and rewards—*instrumentality,* and (3) their efforts and task performance—*expectancy.* Generally, work motivation increases when they perceive these relationships favorably.

A set of motivational principles can be derived from the expectancy theory. The valence, instrumentality, and expectancy of performing a task can be improved by adopting the following three principles:

1.   Match rewards to employee needs (valence).
2.   Match rewards to performance (instrumentality).
3.   Match jobs to employees (expectancy).

Performance can cause satisfaction and vice versa. However, there is no inherent relationship between satisfaction and performance. Some rewards can be given to workers independently of their performance. When employees are rewarded independently of their performance, lower performers may be satisfied while higher performers are not. Both satisfaction and performance can be achieved when management adopts the proposed motivational principles in managing organizational rewards.

KEY CONCEPTS AND WORDS

Expectancy theory	*Valence*	*Motivational choice*
VIE theory	*Instrumentality*	*Motivational*
Content theory of	*Expectancy*	*principle*
motivation	*Yerkes-Dodson law*	*Job satisfaction*
Process theory of	*Discrepancy theory*	
motivation	*Equity theory*	

Questions for Review and Discussion

1.   If someone asked you to explain why and how people are motivated to work in organizations, how would you respond? Outline your responses.

2.   a.   What are the major determinants of motivation?
     b.   Explain how they are related to, and influence, motivational behavior in organizations.

3.   a.   Explain the expectancy theory of motivation.
     b.   How is it different from the need, incentive, and perceptual theories of behavior?

4. Define the following concepts and explain how management can influence them in a positive way.
   a. Valence of rewards
   b. Performance-reward instrumentality
   c. Effort-performance expectancy

5. a. Are satisfied workers productive workers? Defend your answer.
   b. What are the possible relationships between satisfaction and performance?
   c. What are the necessary conditions under which satisfaction and performance can both be high?

6. "There is no inherent relationship between satisfaction and performance. Yet managers are very much concerned about employee satisfaction." Explain why.

7. "The nation's productivity has been increasing over the years. However, the rate of increase in recent years has fallen behind that of previous decades and that of other industrial nations."
   a. What is productivity?
   b. Study the current trend in the nation's productivity growth.
   c. To what extent does employee motivation contribute to slow productivity growth?
   d. What are some other factors that contribute to the slow growth in productivity?

 EXERCISES

EXERCISE 6.1. IDENTIFYING MOTIVATIONAL PROBLEMS

The following situations describe the motivational problems of individual employees and of organizations as a whole. Identify the causes of these problems by using the basic concepts of expectancy theory: valence, instrumentality, and expectancy.

The Situations

1. Marie Brown is an engineer who has been with the company for the past fifteen years. She is interested in a managerial post. Most engineers in managerial positions had some administrative experience as project coordinators and directors before they were advanced. Although Marie knows she needs administrative experience, she refuses to take the responsibility of being a project director. She complains that there are too many hassles in coordinating the activities of various functions.

2. The Starlite TV Manufacturing Company is using a performance bonus system to boost employee productivity. Quarterly bonuses are paid to work groups that exceed quarterly performance goals. Initially, the employee

response to this incentive system was favorable, and at least half of the work groups exceeded the performance goals. However, as time passed, more supervisors complained that their employees were exhibiting low morale and motivation.

3. Last year, the White Motor Company used a sales contest to motivate salespeople to increase their sales volume. Two salespeople were selected from each regional sales office for grand prizes. The first prize was an automobile; the second prize was a company-paid vacation in Hawaii. Since the first year's reaction was very good, the company has decided to continue the program. Yet regional sales managers indicate that their salespeople are not as excited as they were the first year. As a matter of fact, few are even talking about the contest.

4. The Excell Corporation is an engineering company that designs and constructs industrial facilities. Its main line of business involves oil refinery and coal-gasification facilities. Because of energy shortages around the world, the demand for company services has increased substantially in recent years. To meet the increased demand, the company recently hired a large number of engineers just out of school and some from other companies. The main attraction is financial: The corporation offers higher-than-average pay and fringe benefits. But although it attracts a large number of engineers, few stay more than two years. The president wonders why these employees continue to leave the company.

The Procedure

1. Discuss each of the situations, using various motivational theories presented in this book, such as needs theory, reinforcement theory, expectancy theory, and equity theory.

2. Indicate the theory that best describes the problems in each situation.

3. Present potential remedies for each situation.

EXERCISE 6.2. CONDUCTING A MOTIVATIONAL SURVEY

This exercise is designed to show students how the expectancy model of motivation can be used to predict employee work motivation. Since this kind of exercise requires a considerable amount of time and effort, it should be used as a semester project.

The Procedure

1. Conduct a survey among a group of employees using the following questionnaire.

2. Find the average scores for the valence, instrumentality, and expectancy of each item. Multiply these to arrive at the predictive motivation measure.

3. Obtain the performance ratings of your subjects from the company. (It will be difficult to obtain these ratings unless your study is endorsed by the supervisor.)

4. Find the coefficient of correlation between the predictive motivation measures and the performance ratings. The size of the coefficient will tell the predictability of the expectancy model.

The Motivational Survey Questionnaire

Instructions: The following items measure your assessment of your job situation. Respond to each item by checking the column that best describes your judgment.

Items	Measurement Scales				
The Valence of Rewards: How important is each of the following incentives to you?	Not Important 1	2	Somewhat 3	4	Very Important 5
1. Amount of pay					
2. Amount of job security					
3. Fringe benefits					
4. Chances to work with others					
5. Friendly co-workers					
6. Supportive superiors					
7. Respect you receive from others					
8. Chances for promotion					
9. Amount of autonomy on your job					
10. Chances to learn new things					
11. Chances to use your skills					
The Performance-Reward Instrumentality: How likely is it that each of the items stated below will be realized if you perform your job well?	Unlikely 1	2	Somewhat 3	4	Most Likely 5
1. You will get a pay raise.					
2. You will have more job security.					
3. You will get more fringe benefits.					
4. Other people want to work with you.					
5. Co-workers will be friendly to you.					
6. You will get support from superiors.					
7. You will be respected by others.					
8. You will be promoted.					
9. You will have more freedom.					
10. You will be given challenging jobs.					

	Unlikely	Somewhat		Most Likely
	1	2	3	4	5
11. You will have more opportunities to develop and use your skills.				

The Effort-Performance Expectancy: Do you agree or disagree with the following statements?	Strongly Disagree	Somewhat		Strongly Agree
	1	2	3	4	5
1. You have the necessary job skills.				
2. The job requires your job skills.				
3. You need to exert extra effort to do the job well.				

Footnotes

1. Chester I. Barnard, *The Functions of the Executive* (Cambridge, MA: Harvard University Press, 1938), p. 137.

2. K. H. Chung, *Motivational Theories and Practices* (Columbus, OH: Grid, 1977), pp. 7–10.

3. C. P. Alderfer, *Human Needs in Organizational Settings* (New York: Free Press, 1972).

4. Chung, *Motivational Theories and Practices,* pp. 73–82.

5. V. H. Vroom, *Work and Motivation* (New York: Wiley, 1964), pp. 14–19.

6. Ibid., p. 203.

7. J. S. Adams, "Toward an Understanding of Inequity," *Journal of Abnormal and Social Psychology,* 1963, **67,** 422–436.

8. E. E. Lawler, *Motivation in Work Organizations* (Monterey, CA: Brooks/Cole, 1973), pp. 49–60.

9. Vroom, *Work and Motivation,* pp. 17–18.

10. R. E. Kopelman and P. H. Thompson, "Boundary Conditions for Expectancy Theory Predictions of Work Motivation and Job Performance," *Academy of Management Journal,* June 1976, 237–258; T. R. Mitchell, "Expectancy Models of Job Satisfaction,

Occupational Reference and Effort: A Theoretical, Methodological and Empirical Appraisal," *Psychological Bulletin,* 1974, **81,** 1053–1077; and J. P. Campbell and R. D. Pritchard, "Research Evidence Pertaining to Expectancy-Instrumentality-Valence Theory," in *Motivation and Work Behavior,* ed. R. M. Steers and L. W. Porter (New York: McGraw-Hill, 1979), pp. 229–246.

11. R. J. House, H. J. Shapiro, and M. A. Wahba, "Expectancy Theory as Predictor of Work Behavior and Attitudes: A Re-evaluation of Empirical Evidence," *Decision Sciences,* January 1974, 481–506.

12. See J. W. Atkinson, *An Introduction to Motivation* (New York: Van Nostrand, 1964), pp. 241–268.

13. Vroom, *Work and Motivation,* pp. 192–210.

14. R. M. Yerkes and J. D. Dodson, "The Relation of Strength of Stimulus to Rapidity of Habit Formation," *Journal of Comparative and Neurological Psychology,* 1908, **8,** 459–482.

15. E. E. Lawler, "Ability as a Moderator of the Relationship between Job Attitudes and Job Performance," *Personnel Psychology,* 1966, **19,** 153–164.

16. B. M. Staw, *Intrinsic and Extrinsic Motivation* (Morristown, NJ: General Learning Press, 1976).

17. Lawler, *Motivation in Work Organizations,* pp. 66–69.

18. Adams, "Toward an Understanding of Inequity"; and M. R. Carrell and J. E. Dittrich, "Equity Theory: The Recent Literature, Methodological Consideration, and New Direction," *Academy of Management Review,* April 1978, 202–210.

19. D. J. Cherrington, H. J. Reitz, and W. E. Scott, "Effects of Reward and Contingent Reinforcement on Satisfaction and Task Performance," *Journal of Applied Psychology,* 1971, **55,** 531–536.

20. Elton Mayo, *The Social Problems of an Industrial Civilization* (Boston: Division of Research, Harvard Business School, 1945); and F. J. Roethlisberger and W. J. Dickson, *Management and the Worker* (Cambridge, MA: Harvard University Press, 1939).

21. L. W. Porter and R. M. Steers, "Organization, Work, and Personal Factors in Employee Turnover and Absenteeism," *Psychological Bulletin,* 1973, **80,** 151–176.

22. Harry Levinson, *Executive Stress* (New York: New American Library, 1975), pp. 12–30.

23. A. K. Campbell, ''Civil Service: Is Management Reform Possible?'' *Personnel Administrator,* June 1978, 33–37.

24. United States, Department of Health, Education, and Welfare, *Work in America* (Cambridge, MA: Harvard University Press, 1973), p. 16.

MANAGEMENT AND ORGANIZATIONAL BEHAVIOR

1. Understanding the Job of Managing

2. Studying Organizational Behavior

INDIVIDUAL BEHAVIOR

3. Satisfying Human Needs

4. Learning and Reinforcing

5. Understanding the Perceptual Process

6. Understanding the Motivational Process

SUPERVISORY BEHAVIOR

11. Understanding the Leadership Process

12. Developing Leadership Skills

13. Acquiring and Using Power in Organizations

14. Managing Reward Systems

INTERPERSONAL AND GROUP BEHAVIOR

7. Understanding Interpersonal Dynamics

8. Improving Communication Effectiveness

9. Understanding Group Dynamics

10. Dealing with Intergroup Conflicts

ENVIRONMENTAL ADAPTATION

15. Task Design—Matching Jobs to People

16. Designing Organizational Structure

17. Making Managerial Decisions

18. Managing Organizational Change

Micro-organizational analysis

Macro-organizational analysis

ORGANIZATIONAL EFFECTIVENESS

19. Developing Effective Organizations

APPENDIX

Developing Careers in Organizations

INTERPERSONAL AND GROUP BEHAVIOR

People in organizations spend a great deal of their time interacting with others in interpersonal and group settings. How well other people support them in accomplishing their personal and task goals depends largely on how successful they are in generating and maintaining helpful relationships with other people in organizations. Part III is primarily concerned with studying human behavior at interpersonal and group levels.

Chapter 7 focuses on behavior that occurs between two individuals. It investigates the way in which two people create and maintain mutually helping relationships. Chapter 8 deals with interpersonal communication. It studies the sources of communication problems and the way to overcome them. Chapter 9 deals with group dynamics. It studies a number of ways groups can be effectively utilized to solve organizational problems. Chapter 10 concerns intergroup behavior. It identifies sources of group conflict and studies ways of promoting intergroup cooperation.

LEARNING OBJECTIVES

1. To understand how an interpersonal relationship is created, developed, and maintained.
2. To know how people differ in their interpersonal styles.
3. To develop a set of interpersonal skills.

CHAPTER OUTLINE

The Importance of Interpersonal Competence
Effect of Interpersonal Competence
Quality of Dyadic Relationships

Developing Interpersonal Relationships
Forming First Impressions
Developing Mutual Expectations
Honoring Psychological Contracts
Developing Trust and Influence

Analyzing Interpersonal Styles
The Johari Window
Modes of Interpersonal Style

Developing Interpersonal Skills
Increasing Interpersonal Awareness
Taking Interpersonal Risks
Developing Cooperative Relationships
Resolving Interpersonal Problems

Summary and Conclusion

7 UNDERSTANDING INTERPERSONAL DYNAMICS

Because man is a social animal, most of his happiness and fulfillment rests upon his ability to relate effectively to other humans. In addition, the foundations of all civilizations rest upon man's ability to cooperate with other humans and to coordinate his actions with theirs. . . . There is no way to overemphasize the importance of interpersonal skills in our lives.

David W. Johnson, Reaching Out[1]

Most human experiences involve interactions with other human beings. People interact with each other to satisfy their needs. They interact with other people as business partners, superiors, subordinates, friends and/or lovers. Of these relationships, some flourish, grow richer, and expand, while others remain dormant, wither, and eventually die. Understanding how and why such relationships are created and maintained—or stagnate and dissolve—can help us develop and improve our own relationships with other people.

Basic to human interactions are the personal relationships that occur between two individuals. Knowing how these relationships are developed and maintained can help us understand the interactions occurring at group, intergroup, and organizational levels. Thus, this chapter focuses on the processes involved in creating, developing, and maintaining interpersonal relationships. It discusses (1) the importance of interpersonal competence, (2) the process of developing helping relationships, (3) the modes of interpersonal relationships, and (4) the ways of improving interpersonal skills.

THE IMPORTANCE OF INTERPERSONAL COMPETENCE

> *Interpersonal competence refers to the degree to which individuals are aware of their impact on others and of the impact of others on them, and to their ability to engage in mutually helpful relationships. It enables organizational members to achieve their personal and task goals.*

In Chapter 1, we saw that managers spend a considerable amount of their time interacting with other people in and out of their organizations, including their superiors, subordinates, peers, clients, interest groups, and the general public. These interactions involve (1) hierarchical relationships that take place between superiors and subordinates in dealing with task-related roles and (2) universal human interactions that take place between individuals regardless of their hierarchical roles. While the hierarchical relationships can be maintained by organizational structure, rules and regulations, and other forms of control, the universal human interactions are maintained by interpersonal competence. The ability to maintain effective personal relationships with others can help managers maintain effective hierarchical relationships. This ability is often said to be the key to performing the coordination function, that is, leadership, motivation, and communication.

Effect of Interpersonal Competence

What are the effects of interpersonal competence on managerial behavior? In studying the effect of interpersonal competence on organizational effectiveness, Argyris has pointed out that lack of interpersonal competence in a manager leads to an increase in conformity, mistrust, and dependence among his or her work group members. These kinds of responses reduce communication effectiveness, increase defensive interpersonal norms, and increase organizational rigidity—all of which tend to reduce organizational effectiveness. In order to become more effective, Argyris has suggested, a manager should allow his or her subordinates to challenge each other's ideas, to generate valid information, to encourage search behavior, and to increase internal commitment (see Figure 7.1).[2]

Interpersonally incompetent managers create an organizational climate in which their members act defensively to protect their own interests. These members learn what is or is not acceptable behavior within existing organizational norms and behave accordingly. Since organizational learn-

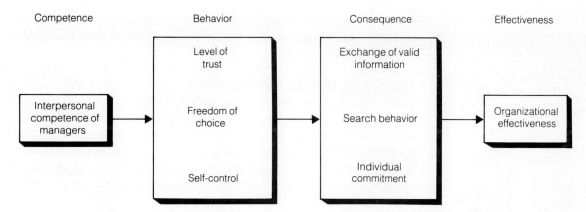

Competence	Behavior	Consequence	Effectiveness

Interpersonal competence of managers → Level of trust / Freedom of choice / Self-control → Exchange of valid information / Search behavior / Individual commitment → Organizational effectiveness

FIGURE   7.1
The Effect of Interpersonal Competence on Organizational Effectiveness.

ing is confined by existing norms, Argyris and Schon have termed it *single-loop learning,* and they have indicated that it can be detrimental to organizational effectiveness, as demonstrated in the following example:[3]

> *A multibillion dollar corporation has decided that Product X was a failure and should be disbanded. The total loss amounted to more than $100 million. At least five middle managers—plant and marketing—knew about the problem, but failed to correctly communicate it to top management for a period of six years.*
>
> *There were several reasons for this problem. First, the middle managers felt that they could solve the problem without alarming top management. More importantly, however, they knew that in their company bad news would not be received well by the upper level managers. They also knew that the top management was very enthusiastic about the new product.*
>
> *The middle managers, therefore, spent much time composing memos that would communicate the realities without shocking top management. Small doses of bad news were released with some promises of improvement—a common mode of interlevel communication. The result was that top management failed to recognize the gravity of the problem until it became too late to reverse its direction.*

This kind of problem could have been avoided if managers at all levels of the organization had developed the capacity to confront each other on task-related problems without fearing repercussions. Interpersonally competent managers would have allowed their subordinates to challenge their views and to question the organization's norms, policies, rules, and objectives. When these kinds of behaviors are tolerated, people are likely to discover problems and commit themselves to their solution. In such an organization, learning is not confined by existing norms and policies, as in a single loop. Since norms and policies are open to challenge, people become freer to search for alternative ways to solve organizational problems outside of the single loop. Argyris and Schon have termed this kind of behavior *double-loop learning.*[4]

Quality of Dyadic Relationships

Graen and his associates are more explicit in stressing the importance of interpersonal relationships between superiors and subordinates. They argue that the quality of these relationships determines the quality of working life of the subordinates. "In-group" managers are on favorable terms with their bosses and are better able to command organizational resources than "out-group" managers who are on less favorable terms with their bosses.[5]

These scholars see organizational units as systems of vertical dyads connected by linking-pin personnel—managers. Each reporting relationship between a subordinate and a superior is represented by a separate dyad. Managers in upper-level positions do not treat their subordinate managers equally. They tend to favor those who have developed "in-group" relationships with them. In a longitudinal study involving 60 managerial dyads, such differential treatment was found to be the rule rather than exception.[6] Managers who were able to maintain favorable relationships with their bosses (1) were more involved in the managerial decision processes, (2) behaved more in accordance with their bosses' wishes, (3) received more resources, (4) experienced fewer employee problems, and (5) were more satisfied with various aspects of their jobs.

How do managers develop "in-group" relationships with their superiors? Jacobs argues that these managers develop exchange relationships with their superiors.[7] In other words, these managers help their superiors achieve taks-related goals, and then they expect their superiors to help them achieve their goals. Both parties develop a set of expectations that they expect the other to satisfy. These expectations must be met if the dyadic relationship is to continue. If the expectations cannot be met, one of three things can occur: (1) the relationship will terminate, (2) the parties may change their expectations, or (3) compliance may be forced. Jacobs argues that such a use of power and coercion hinders the development and maintenance of favorable exchange relationships.

In view of the importance of interpersonal competence, managers as well as would-be managers need to acquire the interpersonal skills necessary to achieve personal and task goals in organizations. These skills involve knowing the dynamics of one's interaction with others and being able to communicate effectively with others. Having and understanding these skills may not guarantee successful human relations, but it can increase one's interpersonal sensitivity and help a manager take appropriate action to improve relationships.

DEVELOPING INTERPERSONAL RELATIONSHIPS

A successful interpersonal relationship develops over a period of time. It goes through the following stages of development: (1) initial impression, (2) development of expectations, (3) negotiation of expectations, (4) development of psychological contract, and (5) maintenance of the contract.

The development of successful working relationships takes time. No one can cultivate such a relationship with another person without going through a painstaking socialization process that is evolutionary and usually takes months or years to develop. As Figure 7.2 suggests, the development of a working relationship occurs in the following sequence:

1. The initial contact produces a set of *impressions* and attitudes in each toward the other. A favorable mutual impression is needed to develop a long-term relationship.

2. A positive impression opens the door for a long-term working relationship. When this occurs, the interacting parties develop a set of *expectations* regarding their roles, performance, and relationships.

3. Any differences in initial expectations will be consciously or unconsciously negotiated, resulting in a *psychological contract*—a set of mutually agreeable expectations.

4. The interacting parties should make continuous attempts to meet each other's expectations. Failure to carry out this psychological contract will probably terminate the relationship.

FIGURE 7.2
A Model for Developing
Interpersonal Relationships.

5. Mutual *trust and influence* develop as a result of meeting the psychological contract, and these ensure the continuous existence of the relationship.

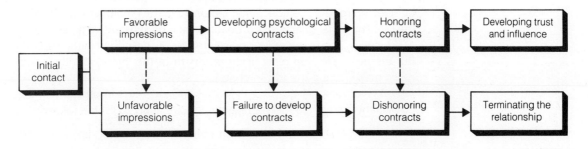

Forming First Impressions

It is often said that first impressions are lasting impressions. Back in the 1950s, Harold Kelly studied the effect of first impressions on behavior.[8] He told a large class of undergraduate students that they would have a visiting lecturer for the day, and that they would be asked to evaluate the lecturer at the end of the class. He then passed out a brief biographical note about the person to help students form their first impressions. Half the class received a note describing the lecturer as being "rather a warm person," while the rest received a note describing the person to be "rather a cold person." After the class had read the printed notes, the lecturer arrived and led the class discussion for about 20 minutes. Although everyone witnessed the same man at the same time, the manner in which students responded to him differed between the two groups. The students who had been told the lecturer was warm rated him to be more informal, sociable, good-natured, and humorous than those who had been told he was cold. Some 56 percent of the students in the first category actually interacted with the lecturer in the discussion, while only 32 percent in the second group participated.

A similar study by Dailey found that first impressions tend to be lasting and inaccurate.[9] First impressions are lasting because they influence the way in which people see subsequent data about the perceived object or person. Whether or not first impressions are correct, they influence our behavior. It is, therefore, important for us to make favorable impressions on other people in our socialization processes. Initial impressions do not guarantee long-term relationships, but they are essential for entering into enduring relationships with others. A study conducted by Gabarro found that when new chief executives interact with their subordinates for the first time, they size up the situation and set the tone for the way their relationship will develop. Much of the groundwork for their relationships with others are laid at this stage.[10]

This stage of socialization has a significant implication for those who are looking for jobs. When an organization searches for a new manager, it will probably contact between 10 to 30 potential candidates. Of these, it will probably interview between three and five people, but only one will be selected for the position. What factors help the employer narrow down the list? The initial selection is probably based on substantive qualities such as education, job experience, and references, as described in the resumés. But the next selection most likely results from the impression the candidates make during the job interview.

What personal qualities help make a good first impression? Image consultants and personnel representatives are likely to list the following:[11]

1. **Poise.**   One should maintain composure by being diplomatic and personable, for nervousness disturbs one's poise.

2. **Articulateness.**   One should speak naturally and fluently, use proper language, and add deep tones to the voice to create an impression of maturity and intelligence.

3. **Conservative dress.**   Conservative suits for men and good-quality dresses in classic styles for women are appropriate for a business engagement such as a job interview. Extremes in fashion should be avoided.

4. **Positive attitude.**   Without being a naive optimist, one should show a positive outlook on life, for people generally prefer a prudent optimist to a pessimist.

5. **Knowledgeability.**   Learning something about the organization and its products, services, and people before an interview demonstrates one's interest and intelligence.

6. **Thoughtfulness.**   One should be alert and responsive, yet weigh each question before responding. A hasty response can be seen as indicative of immaturity or lack of intelligence.

7. **Self-confidence.**   In order to make other people have confidence in him or her, the person needs to appear self-confident. An erect posture, head held high, and an assertive tone of voice can help show self-confidence.

Developing Mutual Expectations

When people are mutually impressed, they are more likely to enter into a long-term relationship. When this happens, they develop certain expectations about each other. In work organizations, these expectations may include organizational roles, performance, job competence, trust, and interpersonal influence. Managers may expect new employees to be competent, productive, reliable, and loyal and to conform to organizational norms. New employees, on the other hand, expect their superiors to be friendly, fair, supportive, and considerate of their needs.

Many of these expectations are unwritten and unspoken. Thomas points out that people usually do not have clear ideas about what they expect from other people or from organizations, especially at the beginning of a relationship.[12] Initial expectations are usually very general and tend to be unrealistic. Unrealistic expectations often develop because people promise more than they can deliver at the initial stage in order to impress the other party. For example, the personnel representative promises a new recruit a challenging task assignment within a few months, or the new recruit pretends to be an expert in a technical area in which he or she is really only a learner.

Participants must go beyond the stage of establishing general expectations in order to determine whether or not the relationship is satisfactory. Unless they work out more realistic expectations, the relationship becomes superficial and less meaningful. Without knowing what the other specifically expects, a participant may not be able to commit himself or herself to the relationship. The process of working out mutual expectations involves a series of exchanges and adjustments to each other's expectations.

Participants also want to know what the other party expects from them. For example, new employees may want to know what their roles are and where they stand in relation to their superiors. "How much do I have to produce?" "To what extent should I be loyal to him?" "Will I get a promotion?" "Can I rely on her?" "Is he honest with me?" These are some of the questions that have to be answered in order to develop mutual contracts.

A set of mutual expectations that is worked out and understood by the participants is called a *psychological contract;* it governs the relationship between them in day-to-day interactions.[13] Although this contract is neither formally stated nor legally binding, it serves as the basis for evaluating the quality of the relationship. Unless the participants continuously honor this contract, the relationship will falter and eventually fail.

Honoring Psychological Contracts

An effective interpersonal or work relationship cannot develop and be maintained unless the participants are willing to honor their psychological contracts. Honoring contracts means that the parties to them are committed to the affiliation. Each party expects the other to be faithful in the relationship, not to take arbitrary actions, and to be honest with him or her. There will, of course, be times when some of these expectations cannot be fully satisfied. But when this happens, each party must be reassured that the other is acting in good faith.

What do people expect from others in working relationships? Gabarro reports that the executives in his study expected three things from their colleagues: *reliable character, professional competence,* and *good judgment.*[14] The character-based expectations include:

1. **Integrity:** maintaining honesty in the relationship (in the personal and moral sense).
2. **Motive:** having good intentions and acting in good faith.
3. **Consistency:** showing consistency in behavior.
4. **Openness:** leveling and being honest with another person.
5. **Discretion:** maintaining confidences.

The competence-based expectations include:

1. **Technical competence:** having the ability to perform the assigned task.
2. **Interpersonal competence:** being able to maintain effective interpersonal relationships.

The judgment-based expectations include:

1. **Business sense:** making good business judgments.
2. **Interpersonal judgment:** making an accurate perceptual judgment of other people.

In general, people expect their colleagues to be honest, good-natured, reliable, predictable, trustworthy, competent, and intelligent in working relationships. It is difficult to meet all these expectations at all times, but participants should usually be able to satisfy them.

Each of us has a minimum acceptable level of satisfaction. If the actual fulfillment of expectations is below that level, the situation will be viewed as a violation of the contract. When this happens, the affected member will send out signals of dissatisfaction in the form of joking, complaining, or showing anger. If these signals are received and honored by the other person, the relationship can be restored, or the contract can be renegotiated. Otherwise, the association will suffer chronic discontent, strife, alienation, and eventual termination.

Developing Trust and Influence

The result of meeting the psychological contract is an increased level of trust and influence. When the parties to the contract are able to meet their mutual expectations, the relationship produces mutual trust and favorable sentiment. The more satisfactory the association becomes, the greater the influence the parties have on each other. Since the relationship is fulfilling, the participants will continuously rely on it to satisfy their needs. This dependency permits them to exert influence on each other. As Kotter points out, to the extent that we depend on another person, we allow ourselves to be influenced by that other.[15]

Trust is the key to maintaining a meaningful relationship. Trust is having faith that another person is capable of honoring the psychological contract. When a mother leaves her baby with a babysitter, she trusts that the babysitter will take care of the baby. When an employer hires an employee, the former trusts the latter to carry out the assigned task. In order to trust another person, we must have faith in that person. The level of trust increases when the other person has met the psychological contract.

The increased level of *influence* enhances each participant's ability to affect the behavior and thinking of the other. When a person is able to influence others, the person becomes more effective in performing a task. The person's effectiveness is especially increased when the task requires a high degree of interaction with other people, for the influential person is capable of enlisting the necessary support and cooperation from others.

ANALYZING INTERPERSONAL STYLES

> *Interpersonal styles range from highly unproductive to very productive. Effective styles are characterized by openness in relationships; ineffective styles are characterized by a lack of openness.*

The quality of interpersonal relationships is largely affected by the way the participants relate to each other—that is, their interpersonal styles. This interpersonal style determines how closely and effectively participants will engage in the association. In order to develop a close and binding relationship, participants must expose themselves to each other so they can really get to know each other. Unless they know each other well, they cannot develop a trusting relationship. This section presents a conceptual framework for studying a variety of interpersonal styles.

The Johari Window

The Johari Window is a conceptual model for studying interpersonal styles; it was developed by Joe Luft and Harry Ingham (the name *Johari* combines their first names).[16] It is a schematic model that shows how people expose themselves to others and receive feedback from others in their interpersonal relationships. As shown Figure 7.3, the Johari Window has four parts: public, private, blind, and hidden. The public area is the part of us, the window, that is known to the self and others. The private area is known to the self, but not to others. The blind area is known to others, but not to the self. The hidden area is known neither to the self nor to others.

The implication of this model is that, as the participants in a relationship expose themselves to each other and receive feedback from each other, the public area expands. The larger the public area, the greater the chance for participants to make correct perceptual judgments about each other. This accurate perceptual judgment helps them to develop realistic mutual expectations. Meeting these expectations increases their level of trust and influence, and it helps them maintain a mutually satisfying relationship. When the participants mutually expand the public area, there is a reduction of facade, defensive behavior, and "games playing."

Self-Disclosure.   The public area can be expanded by means of self-disclosure and feedback. Self-disclosure means revealing oneself to another person and sharing one's own feelings, emotions, facts, and knowledge with that individual. A close relationship develops between

FIGURE 7.3
The Johari Window. (After
*Group Processes: An
Introduction to Group
Dynamics* by Joseph Luft,
by permission of Mayfield
Publishing Co., copyright
© 1963, 1970 by Joseph
Luft.)

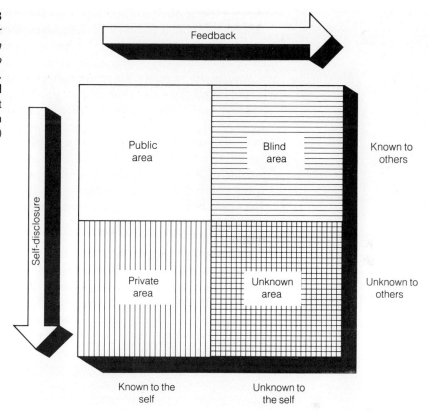

individuals as they become acquainted and become more open about
themselves. The relationship can flourish only when the participants are
willing to share their feelings, emotions, and other relevant information.
Self-disclosure is an act of showing respect for, and sharing intimacy with,
another person. Such an act requires trust in another person and is likely
to encourage the other person to follow suit.

When we disclose ourselves to another, we are taking the risk of
being rejected or misinterpreted. The other person may use the information revealed for the wrong purpose. So self-disclosure should be undertaken cautiously and gradually. Unless one is confident that the other can
handle such a trusting relationship, the first may be wise to refrain from
self-disclosure. However, unless someone takes the risk and initiates self-
disclosure, the relationship will not develop.

Obtaining Feedback.   If we want to know how other people see us, we
should seek feedback from them. Feedback reduces the blind area and
helps us increase our self-awareness, since we often do not know how

others view us. We can guess how they see us by their reactions, but these reactions are often not clear. Unless we receive feedback as to how they see us, or what kinds of effects our behaviors have on them, we are likely to be blind to their feelings and reactions.

The effectiveness of our own behavior depends largely on our awareness of what goes on in our relationships with other people. In order to improve our interpersonal effectiveness, we should be aware of the consequences of our behavior to others and see if these consequences match our intentions. Such interpersonal sensitivity can be increased only when we are able to obtain genuine feedback from others. Ron Engelberg, whom we met in Chapter 2, was unsure of how his role as the plant manager was being perceived by his subordinates. To gain some feedback on his performance, he expressed his concerns to a trusted friend. This is the essence of disclosure and feedback.

Modes of Interpersonal Style

In order to maintain an effective interpersonal relationship, participants should make proper use of both the self-disclosure and feedback processes. Often, participants favor one or the other of the two processes and consequently fail to increase the public area in the Johari Window. This imbalance tends to create disruptive tensions between them. Depending on how participants employ the self-disclosure and feedback processes, their interpersonal styles may differ considerably and yield differences in their interpersonal effectiveness.[17] Figure 7.4 shows four personality types characterized by different interpersonal styles: the *loner,* the *exhibitionist,* the *gamesman,* and the *open-minded person.*

The Loner. This interpersonal style is characterized by an absence of self-disclosure and feedback. Loners do not expose themselves, and so other people do not know much about them; that is, their private area is large. The absence of feedback from others makes their blind area large, too, for they do not know how others see them. The hidden area will be the largest, however. People like this are likely to be detached, withdrawn, and uncommunicative. They may be found in some formal organizations in which members are interested in protecting themselves by avoiding personal disclosure and involvement.

Since they are uncommunicative, it is difficult to establish any meaningful relationship with them. They will be viewed by others as aloof, cold, and indifferent; so other people will hesitate to approach them. The loner style is particularly troublesome in organizations because it is difficult to work with such people. The style not only stifles the potential of the person involved, but also frustrates other people's energies.

The Exhibitionist. This style is characterized by a great deal of talking but little listening. The exhibitionist exposes a lot but receives little feed-

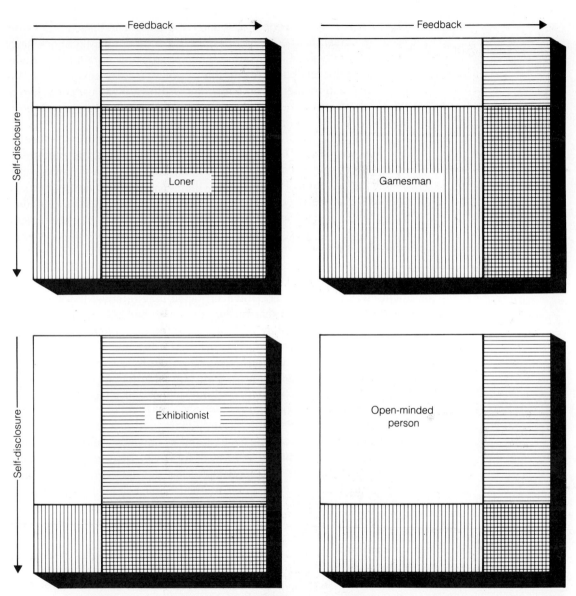

FIGURE 7.4 Interpersonal Style and Communication. (After Jay Hall, "Communication Revisited," © 1973 by the Regents of the University of California, reprinted from California Management Review, **XV,** 3, 60, by permission of the Regents.)

back. The net result is that the private area is reduced and the blind area expanded. Consequently, other people know about the person, but the person does not know how others see him or her. People who use this style may feel self-confident about their opinions and are likely to demand compliance from others. A hierarchical organizational structure may encourage the use of this style for managers, for they need to be assertive, self-confident, and directive. They tend to talk to others, but not listen to others, especially their subordinates or peers.

This is also an ineffective style because it does not utilize inputs from other people. When people encounter someone who talks but does not listen, they feel that he or she does not respect them. Furthermore, since they feel the person is not interested in listening, they refrain from providing meaningful feedback. Again, this absence of feedback increases the blind area, and the person no longer knows how others feel about him or her. Thus, the person is likely to be less effective in dealing with other people.

The Gamesman.   The opposite of the exhibitionist is the gamesman, who is successful in collecting information from others while giving little, if anything, in return. The net result is that while the blind area is reduced, the private area expands. People use this style for two reasons. First, they reveal very little of themselves because they fear others may take advantage of their inadequacies and vulnerabilities. Second, they obtain knowledge about other people in order to influence and manipulate them.

The gamesman may be regarded as a good listener. The gamesman is receptive to feedback from other people, and they are likely to expose themselves to him or her. However, when they discover that they have engaged in a one-sided relationship, they may become suspicious of the gamesman's behavior and eventually withdraw from the relationship. The gamesman often uses a facade to cover his or her true identity, as well as feelings, values, and opinions. Once this facade is removed, the likely result is a reciprocal withdrawal of trust by other parties. When this happens, the gamesman's behavior becomes an ineffective interpersonal style.

The Open-Minded Person.   The open-minded person uses both self-disclosure and feedback effectively. Candor, openness, and interpersonal sensitivity are the dominant features of this style. The person who uses it tends to be competent, secure, flexible, and socially extroverted.[18] Since the person feels self-confident and secure, he or she is not afraid of self-disclosure and becomes less defensive about feedback from others. The net result is that the people in this relationship know more about themselves and others.

Which style is most effective in managerial situations? A study by Hall found that managers who were highly concerned with both production and people tended to be more open-minded than others.[19] They tended to be expressive and sensitive to the feelings of others, for example. Managers who were production-oriented, however, tended to be more self-disclosing than receptive to feedback. They were more inclined, for instance, to give orders and instructions than to receive feedback. Managers who were people-oriented tended to prefer feedback over self-disclosure. Since they were concerned with the feelings of other people, they were sensitive to what others thought of them. Blake and Mouton argue that this combination of production and people-oriented leadership styles is more effective than other styles.[20] (The effect of leadership style on performance is discussed further in Chapters 11 and 12 on leadership.)

The open-minded interpersonal style is, thus, associated with an effective managerial style. However, the research evidence on this has so far been scanty, and there are many situations in which self-disclosure and feedback are inappropriate and not practiced. Selection of interpersonal style depends on personality, the characteristics of people with whom one interacts, and the organizational norms under which the person operates.

DEVELOPING INTERPERSONAL SKILLS

> *In order to enter into and maintain an effective interpersonal relationship, one must acquire certain basic skills. These include (1) interpersonal sensitivity, (2) ability to know and trust other people, (3) ability to develop helping relationships, and (4) ability to resolve interpersonal problems.*

How we relate to another person reflects our own personality. Some people have more desire to maintain intimate relationships; others are relatively insensitive. But the ability to create, develop, and maintain such relationships is not inborn. More often than not, this ability involves the way a person listens, questions, cares, and responds to others.

Increasing Interpersonal Awareness

The first major skill involved in interpersonal competence is the ability to know what is involved in an interpersonal relationship. If we know how our relationships are working out, and what effects our behaviors have on others, we should be able to take appropriate actions either to further enrich the affiliation or to correct any potential problems. Many valuable associations in families, schools, and work organizations falter and eventually fail because participants are not aware of what goes on in the relationship.

Although some people may take abrupt unilateral actions, things rarely happen suddenly in interpersonal relationships. As indicated earlier, the afflicted party usually sends out signals indicating dissatisfaction or the desire to renegotiate the psychological contract before taking harmful action. These signals can range from a harmless joking remark to an active complaint or sabotage. In working relationships, the signals can be an absence of warm greetings, failure to be promoted, a lower than average pay increase, or not being assigned to meaningful tasks.

Interpersonal awareness can be increased in several ways. When you feel that something is wrong with a relationship, but the problem area cannot be identified, you may take one of the following actions:

1. Ask the other party how the relationship is working out for him or her. Take the initiative in expressing your concerns and feelings and listen to the answer, which may not be satisfactory, but at least opens the door for improvement.

2. Ask yourself whether you are fulfilling the psychological contract. Take an inventory of your perceptions of mutual expectations and see if each of you is meeting these expectations. Reflect your perceptions in your behaviors or communicate them to your partner.

Taking Interpersonal Risks

Nothing really happens in a relationship until the participants learn to trust each other. However, trusting another person is not simple because it involves risk. Unlike other interpersonal skills, such as interpersonal awareness and empathic skill, it requires a response from the other person. If the other person behaves in such a manner that it violates one's trust in him or her, the relationship cannot continue. However, we do not know if we can trust another person until such an opportunity arises. There are a few things a person can do to create and maintain a trusting relationship:

1. Take the initiative in self-disclosure. This can set the tone for developing and maintaining a trusting relationship.

2. Accept another person's self-disclosure. Appreciate the other person for taking the initiative and risking being rejected.

3. Reciprocate another's initiative with your own self-disclosure. Failure to do so will be interpreted by the other person as a lack of interest.

4. Remember that the self-fulfilling prophecy works in an interpersonal relationship. An initial assumption about a person has a way of proving itself.

Developing Cooperative Relationships

A relationship will be maintained and will prosper only when it satisfies the participants' needs and expectations. In a mutually helping relationship, the participants tend to cooperate rather than compete in sharing limited resources or rewards. In work organizations, people compete for limited resources—pay increases, promotions, and recognition. Depending on how they deal with such conflicting situations, people can develop either mutually helping or competing relationships. Those who want to develop mutually helping relationships with others should make an effort to cooperate rather than compete in such a situation. The following example illustrates the effects of the two kinds of behavioral strategy:

John and James are sales managers, and both are considered the best in the company. Their jobs, selling the company's products to industrial users, can be structured so that they work either jointly or independently.

The company recently announced a sales contest that pays $5,000 for the top salesperson or team. Since it is a major contest and also decides the future relationship between John and James, the two want to be very careful in deciding their strategies. They know that if they work together, they can almost certainly win the contest, but they will have to divide the prize.

If they compete, they fear they will both lose the contest to others because they have a tendency to sabotage each other. Also, there is a slight chance (say 20 percent) that one party will deceive the other into believing he is cooperating but will in fact be competing to obtain the entire prize for himself. If this happened, it would damage the relationship permanently. Figure 7.5 shows the potential payoffs.

Since neither knows exactly how the other will behave in the contest, each has to consider all these possibilities in computing the expected payoffs for both strategies. The expected payoffs are defined here as the arithmetic means of potential payoffs for different strategies; they are found as follows:

For cooperating: (2,500 × .80) + (−5,000 × .20) = $1,000

For competing: (5,000 × .20) + (−5,000 × .80) = −$3,000

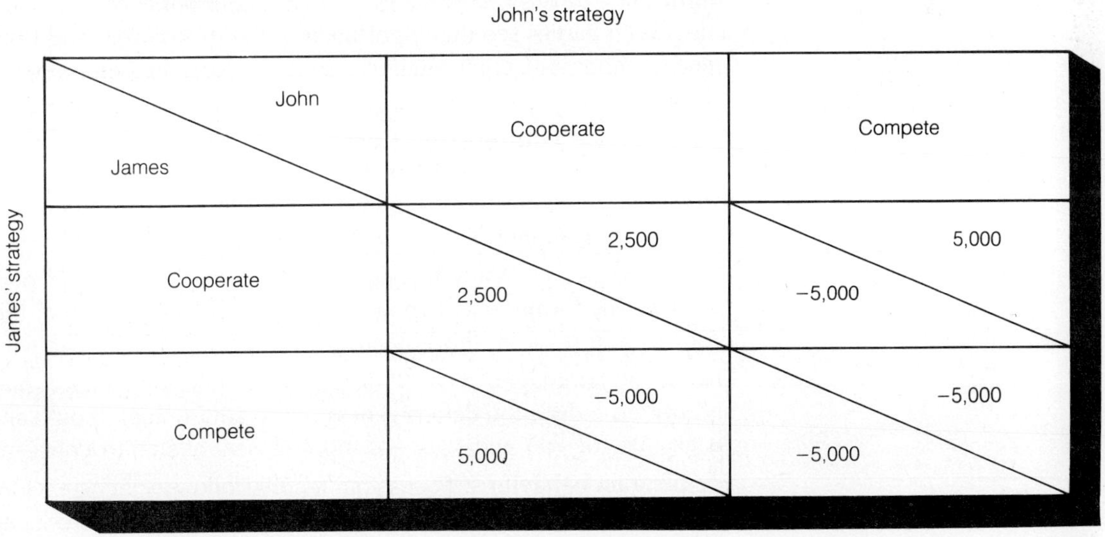

FIGURE 7.5
A Payoff Matrix for Cooperation and Competition.

Faced with these two behavioral alternatives, John and James will probably choose the cooperative strategy—the non-zero-sum game. Even

John's strategy

James	John	Cooperate	Compete
Cooperate		2,500 / 2,500	5,000 / −5,000
Compete		−5,000 / 5,000	−5,000 / −5,000

James' strategy

if it involved only a small reward in the short run, this strategy would foster a long-term helping and trusting relationship. Whether they will actually choose this strategy, however, depends largely on the level of trust they have developed in the past. The more trusting they have become, the more likely it is that they will engage in helping relationships. In the absence of such mutual trust, they are more likely to engage in competitive relationships.

Resolving Interpersonal Problems

A close interpersonal relationship is maintained by building trust, acceptance, and supportiveness. But there are times when one party may become angry with the other for failing to meet the psychological contract. When this occurs, the first party should constructively confront the second. How well the two handle such an interpersonal problem will indicate the depth of the relationship. In a shallow relationship, one party may ignore the destructive behavior of another; in a mature relationship, however, both parties should engage in constructive confrontation in order to improve the quality of the relationship.

Constructive confrontation is defined as a deliberate attempt to help another person examine the consequences of his or her behavior.[21] It is not intended to criticize, but rather to express concern and help the person behave in a constructive manner. It involves providing feedback that is useful and unthreatening to the confrontee. Threatening feedback produces defensive behavior and aggravates the situation further. The effectiveness of confrontation can be improved by observing the following principles:

1. **Importance of the relationship:** Do not confront another person unless both parties see the importance of the relationship and truly value it. Otherwise, confrontation may turn into, or be perceived as, criticism.

2. **Ability of the confrontee:** Confront another person only when you perceive that he or she has the ability to act on your feedback. If the confrontee cannot change his or her behavior, confrontation can lead to frustration.

3. **Use of empathy:** View the problem from the confrontee's perspective. The former may even change his or her perception of the problem as a result of this empathy.

4. **Use of "I" language:** Use "I" language, such as the words *I, me,* and *my,* to reduce the defensiveness of the confrontee. "You" language—use of *you* and *your*—is more closely related to criticism.

5. **Focusing on behavior:** Focus your feedback on specific behaviors rather than on the person. A person-directed feedback produces

defensive behavior and resentment. We can change our behavior, but not ourselves.

6. **Use of descriptive statements:** Describe how you see and feel about the situation. Evaluating it in judgmental statements can easily evoke defensive behavior because such statements can be interpreted as criticism.

7. **Exploring alternative behaviors:** Instead of suggesting any specific solution to the problem, help the person explore various means of overcoming it.

8. **Selection of time:** Since timing is important for an effective confrontation, select a time when the confrontee is relaxed and more open to receiving feedback without being defensive.

9. **Importance of privacy:** Confront the person in private. Open confrontation will be considered a personal attack rather than a helpful encounter.

10. **Use of nonverbal behavior:** Use nonverbal behavior, which is as important as verbal behavior, to express yourself to others. Eye contact, appropriate tone of voice, and correct posture can all add to the effectiveness of confrontation.

 ## SUMMARY AND CONCLUSION

Interpersonal behavior is basic to all kinds of behavior in organizations. The reasons why two people enter into a relationship, and why some relationships prosper while others falter, also explain why social groups are formed and maintained. The complementary needs and styles of individuals become the basis for creating interpersonal or group relationships. These relationships will continue and prosper as long as the participants meet their needs and the expectations of the other members.

Patterns of interpersonal style differ among individuals. Some people are able to maintain close associations with others, but other individuals shy away from such relationships. People who maintain close relationships with others tend to be highly self-disclosing and are receptive to feedback from others. They feel relatively more secure and confident about themselves than non-self-disclosing individuals. Some people tend to avoid self-disclosure altogether because they are afraid of being rejected or misinterpreted.

Interpersonal competence is a key to managerial effectiveness. The ability to create, develop, and maintain effective relationships with others is the most important requirement for becoming an effective manager. This ability involves (1) knowing what goes on in a relationship, (2) learning to trust others, (3) developing mutually helpful relationships, and (4) learning to deal with interpersonal problems. These skills can be developed by acquiring knowledge related to interpersonal dynamics and by practicing the skills suggested in the chapter.

KEY CONCEPTS AND WORDS

Interpersonal competence	*Trust*	*Double-loop learning*
Interpersonal sensitivity	*Influence*	*Johari Window*
Psychological contract	*In-group*	*Self-disclosure*
	Out-group	*Confrontation*
	Vertical dyad	
	Single-loop learning	

Questions for Review and Discussion

1. a. Why are people attracted to each other? What are the bases for interpersonal attraction?
    b. Do we have to be the same in order to like each other?

2. a. How does an interpersonal relationship develop? Is it an evolutionary or a revolutionary process?
    b. Describe the process by which such a relationship develops.

3. a. What is a psychological contract?
    b. Explain how such a contract is established and maintained.

4. a. How important is trust in maintaining a relationship?
    b. Explain how it is developed and maintained.

5. a. What is the Johari Window?
    b. What are the implications of this window for developing effective relationships?

6. a. Describe the four interpersonal styles discussed in the chapter.
    b. Explain how each of these styles affects a person's managerial style.

7. a. Can we develop interpersonal skills?
    b. What are some basic skills that we need to acquire in order to function as effective managers?

EXERCISES

EXERCISE 7.1. CONSTRUCTING A PSYCHOLOGICAL CONTRACT

When a person establishes a relationship with another, he or she expects something from the other, and at the same time feels obligated to meet the other person's expectations. This reciprocal relationship is the basis for the development of a psychological contract between the two. Sometimes the participants feel that the relationship is not working well but they are not sure why. At this point, one or both participants should reflect on the relationship and determine the source(s) of the problem. This exercise is designed to help you identify potential problem areas in a relationship.

The Procedure

1. Divide yourselves into small groups.

2. Select a person with whom you would like to develop a closer relationship in a work-related environment.

3. Make a list of the things that you want most from this person. After you have done this, make a list of the things that this person may want from you.

	Your expectations		Other person's expectations
a.	_____	a.	_____
b.	_____	b.	_____
c.	_____	c.	_____
d.	_____	d.	_____
e.	_____	e.	_____

4. Compare what you want from the other person with what you think the other person wants from you, and answer the following questions:
   a. What are the basis for mutual attraction?
   b. How well can or do you meet the other person's expectations?
   c. How well does the other person meet your expectations?
   d. If the relationship is not satisfactory, what do you think is the cause?

5. Discuss your analysis with other members of your group. Discuss how and why the relationship is or is not working. Discuss how the relationship can be improved.

EXERCISE 7.2. IDENTIFYING INTERPERSONAL STYLE

We differ in the ways we relate to other people. Some people are open in expressing themselves and in receiving feedback from other people; other individuals are restrained in their interpersonal interactions. This exercise is designed to help you see how you relate to others.

The Procedure

1. Divide yourselves into small groups of three or four.
2. Respond individually to the following interpersonal style survey.
3. Prepare the interpersonal style on the Johari Window chart.
4. Share your interpersonal style profile with other members of your group.
5. As a group discuss the following questions:
   a. Do the group members agree with other members' assessments of their own interpersonal style?
   b. If any of the members' interpersonal styles is less than satisfactory, what can be done to make it more desirable?

Interpersonal Style Survey

Instructions: Each of the following items measures the way you relate to other people. Respond to each item by placing an X in the column that indicates the way you are now.

Item	Very Little 1	2	Somewhat 3	4	Very Much 5
1. Do you usually reveal yourself to other people?					
2. Do you express your feelings to others easily?					
3. Do you usually trust others?					
4. Do you think other people are willing to listen to you?					
5. Do you like yourself?					
6. Do you listen to others?					
7. Do you feel comfortable when others talk to you about your behavior?					

The Johari Window Profile

Instructions: The first five items in the interpersonal style survey reflect how ready you are to disclose yourself. Add the scores on these items and divide the total by five to arrive at the self-disclosure index. The last five items reflect your capacity to receive feedback from others. Add the scores on these items and divide the total by five to arrive at the feedback index. Chart the self-disclosure and feedback indexes on the Johari Window profile (see Figure 7.6).

EXERCISE 7.3. CONSTRUCTIVE CONFRONTATION EXERCISE

This exercise is designed to give you an opportunity to engage in constructive confrontation. This confrontation is intended to help another person see the nega-

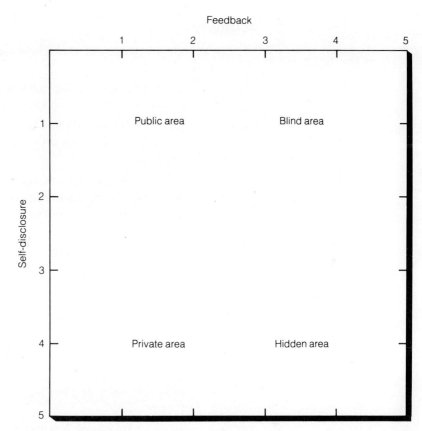

FIGURE   7.6
The Johari Window Profile.

tive consequences of his or her behavior and to improve a relationship; you are not seeking revenge on someone who has hurt you.

The Situation

One of your staff members keeps interrupting you at staff meetings and often snipes at you by charging that you are not solving some of the difficult problems you have in your department. You could aggressively or assertively ask the person to "can it," but you want to handle it in a more professional way. Since you consider the employee a valuable member of the department, you want to help the person change his or her behavior.

The Procedure

1.   Select two persons from the class to play the roles of the confronter and the confrontee.
2.   Let the persons play the roles for about five minutes.
3.   After the role-play, discuss with the class how well the confronter handled the situation.
4.   If the class feels that the situation was not properly handled, make a list of suggested ways to improve the effectiveness of the confrontation.

Footnotes

1. D. W. Johnson, *Reaching Out* (Englewood Cliffs, NJ: Prentice-Hall, 1972), p. 1.

2. Chris Argyris, *Interpersonal Competence and Organizational Effectiveness* (Homewood, IL: Irwin-Dorsey, 1962), pp. 38–50.

3. Chris Argyris and D. A. Schon, *Organizational Learning* (Reading, MA: Addison-Wesley, 1978), pp. 1–2, 18–20.

4. Ibid., pp. 20–26.

5. George Graen, J. F. Cashman, Steven Ginsburg, and William Schiemann, "Effects of Linking-pin Quality on the Quality of Working Life of Lower Participants," *Administrative Science Quarterly,* September 1977, 491–504.

6. Fred Dansereau, George Graen, and W. J. Haga, "A Vertical Dyad Linkage Approach to Leadership in Formal Organizations," *Organizational Behavior and Human Performance,* 1975, **13,** 46–78.

7. T. O. Jacobs, *Leadership and Exchange in Formal Organizations* (Alexandria, VA: Human Resources Research Organization, 1970).

8. H. H. Kelly, "The Warm-Cold Variable in the First Impressions of Persons," *Journal of Personality,* 1950, **18,** 431–439.

9. C. A. Dailey, "The Effects of Premature Conclusion upon the Acquisition of Understanding of a Person," *Journal of Psychology,* 1952, **33,** 133–152.

10. John Gabarro, "Socialization at the Top–How CEOs and Subordinates Evolve Interpersonal Contacts," *Organizational Dynamics,* Winter 1979, 3–23.

11. J. A. Thompson, "The Image Doctors: A Guide to the Personal Packaging Consultants," *MBA,* September 1977, 23–30.

12. Roosevelt Thomas, "Managing the Psychological Contract," in *Organizational Behavior and Administration,* ed. P. R. Lawrence, L. B. Barnes, and J. W. Lorsch (Homewood, IL: Irwin, 1976), pp. 466–467.

13. Ibid., pp. 466–469.

14. J. J. Gabarro, "The Development of Trust, Influence, and Expectations," in *Interpersonal Behavior,* ed. A. G. Athos and J. J. Gabarro (Englewood Cliffs, NJ: Prentice-Hall, 1978), pp. 270–276; also see M. B. Parlee and the Editors of *Psychology Today,* "The Friendship Bond," *Psychology Today,* October 1979, pp. 43–54.

15. J. P. Kotter, "Power, Dependence, and Effective Management," *Harvard Business Review,* July–August 1977, 125–136.

16. Joseph Luft, *Group Processes: An Introduction to Group Dynamics* (Palo Alto, CA: National Press Books, 1970).

17. Jay Hall, "Communication Revisited," *California Management Review,* Spring 1973, 57–67.

18. D. E. Hamachek, *Encounters with the Self* (New York: Holt, Rinehart and Winston, 1971).

19. Hall, "Communication Revisited," pp. 62–65.

20. R. R. Blake and J. S. Mouton, *The New Managerial Grid* (Houston: Gulf Publishing, 1978).

21. Johnson, *Reaching Out,* pp. 159–163.

IMPROVING COMMUNICATION EFFECTIVENESS

Seldom do we allow ourselves to function with reasonable guess about how we are being read, and almost never is there an opportunity to engage someone else candidly and talk about one another's *interpretation* of what has been said. But an important aspect of real-world learning, learning the lessons of our actual experience, depends on such communication.

Samuel A. Culbert, "The Real World and the Management Classroom,"
California Management Review[1]

Most human progress has been made through cooperative efforts resulting from communication. People interact with each other by means of communication, which, in its various forms, permeates all aspects of our organizational lives, including family, church, school, business, and government. Organizations cannot function effectively without effective communication at all levels—interpersonal, intragroup, and intergroup—for ideas are exchanged in order to perform tasks, and feelings are shared to show likes and dislikes. Yet many organizations are plagued by communication problems, especially those arising from interpersonal communication between individuals in face-to-face encounters.

This chapter focuses on the core of organizational communication —interpersonal communication. It describes the basic elements involved in the communication process, identifies various barriers to effective communication, and suggests ways of improving communication skills and enhancing the effectiveness of communication in general. Forms of communication associated with other kinds of organizational behavior will be discussed in later chapters on groups, leadership, and organizational structure.

COMMUNICATIONS IN ORGANIZATIONS

> *The term* communication *refers to the process by which information is exchanged between individuals. It can be intentional or unintentional. This chapter is concerned with intentional communication.*

Managers spend a great deal of their time interacting with other people, and communication is the primary means of these interactions. We are concerned with communication because it is a means of exchanging ideas and information needed to perform organizational tasks. A number of studies have shown that effective communication is closely related to job performance in various work situations and to the satisfaction of communicational participants.[2] Yet, understanding the process by which information is exchanged is a complex task because a variety of factors influence its effectiveness. In this section, we are primarily concerned with the communication process and types of communication in organizations.

The Communication Process Model

The communication process model presented in Figure 8.1 shows the process by which messages are exchanged between people. This model identifies eight basic elements in the communication process: the sender, encoding, the message, the medium, the receiver, decoding, feedback, and noise.[3] These elements jointly determine the quantity and quality of communication.

FIGURE   8.1
The Communication Process Model.

The Sender.   The sender is the person who has a message to communicate. The characteristics of the sender influence the communication pro-

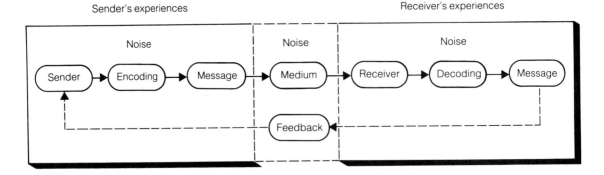

cess. The sender's attitudes, credibility, and other attributes influence the way he or she perceives and interprets the objects or events to be communicated. The sender's personality also influences the manner in which the message is transmitted. For example, a sensitive person will look at the communication process from the receiver's perspective; an insensitive person will be primarily concerned with his or her own needs.

Encoding.   Encoding refers to the process of formulating ideas, thoughts, and feelings about objects and events and transforming them into some form of message—such as words, symbols, charts, or gestures. The connection between the objects that the sender wants to communicate and the words used is indirect, as it is moderated by the thought process.[4] The way the sender perceives, organizes, and interprets the objects can distort the encoding process. The study of the relationship between words and reality (objects) is called *general semantics,* and the problems associated with semantics will be discussed later.

The Message.   The outcome of the encoding process is a message, either verbal or nonverbal. A verbal message is referred to as language, and it is the form of message most frequently used in organizations. Nonverbal messages take the form of facial expression, body posture, tone of voice, eye contact, touching, gesture, and spatial distance. Nonverbal messages can affect the effectiveness of a verbal message by distorting or reinforcing it.

The Medium.   The medium is the carrier of the message. A variety of means—face-to-face conversations, telephone conversations, group conferences, written reports, charts, and memos—are employed to carry the messages. The objective of communication often determines the type of medium used. For example, face-to-face or telephone conversation is usually used when the communicators want to discuss informal, private, or confidential matters. A group conference may be used to exchange ideas or to arrive at group decisions. Written media are used to deal with business matters that require formality and a written record.

The Receiver.   The receiver is the recipient of the message. (A receiver becomes a sender when he or she responds to the sender's message.) The characteristics of the receiver, such as knowledge about the message, relationship with the sender, and personality can influence the way the messages are received and interpreted. If the receiver does not understand or share the perspective of the sender's message, he or she may not decode it as the sender had intended. For example, if the receiver has a positive relationship with the sender, the sender's messages are likely to be interpreted as having positive meanings. Also, thoughtful receivers are more likely to listen attentively than inconsiderate ones.

Decoding.   Decoding is the thought process by which the received message is translated into ideas, thoughts, and feelings. The messages received are interpreted into things or events that convey some meaning to the receiver. The effectiveness of the decoding depends on the receiver's comprehension of the message and the receiver's relationship with the sender. Once the received message is decoded, the receiver can respond to the sender—that is, provide feedback.

Feedback.   Feedback is the response of the receiver to the message. It allows the sender to determine whether or not the message has been received and interpreted correctly. Studies indicate that two-way communication produces a more accurate exchange of messages than one-way communication.[5] The two-way process permits the communicators to check the accuracy of their communication and take corrective action if the messages have not been received correctly.

Noise.   Noise is any factor in the communication process that changes the intended message. The sender's attitudes, assumptions, and perceptions can affect the encoding process adversely. The receiver's attitudes toward the sender and the message can also distort the decoding process. Noise can also occur in the medium. Environmental sounds such as static, traffic, and poor-quality sound systems can interfere with the transmission of a message. To a large extent, quality of communication depends on the degree to which these noises are controlled.

The elements discussed in this section may individually or jointly determine the quality of communication, for they provide many opportunities for communication to be distorted. To achieve communication goals, communicators should understand various causes of ineffective communication and attempt to overcome these problems. These barriers to effective communication are further discussed in a later section.

Types of Interpersonal Communication

Managers engage in a variety of interpersonal relationships in their organizations, and these relationships are reflected in their interpersonal communications. These communication relationships include (1) downward, (2) upward, (3) lateral, (4) diagonal, and (5) external relationships (see Figure 8.2). Understanding the varying characteristics of these communications helps us understand areas of communication problems and ways of dealing with them.

Downward Communication.   Downward communication is the communication flow from superiors to subordinates. The primary purpose of this type of communication is to convey job-related information to em-

FIGURE   8.2
Interpersonal
Communications in an
Organization.

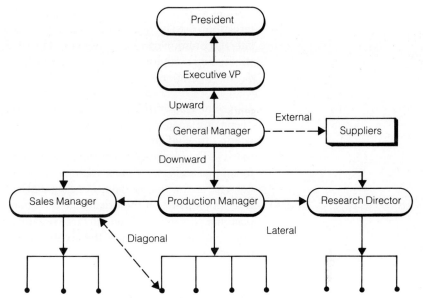

ployees at lower levels. Employees need these informational inputs to carry out their jobs and meet the expectations of their superiors. An absence of these inputs can create role ambiguity, stress, and anxiety among the employees.[6] The most common forms of downward communication are dyadic conversations, group meetings, budgets, operational procedures, official memos, employee handbooks, and company publications. Downward communication is often characterized by high levels of exposure with low levels of feedback. Several studies indicate that less information is passed upward by subordinates than is passed either laterally or downward.[7] Employees may enjoy interacting more with superiors than with subordinates, but they often withhold unfavorable information.

Upward Communication.   Upward communication refers to communication from subordinates to superiors. Management often uses suggestion boxes, open-door policies, and "gripe sessions" to encourage upward communication.[8] These methods, however, do not produce positive results unless the employees feel confident that their superiors are genuinely interested in their messages. As indicated earlier, the trust the sender has in the receiver often dictates the quality and quantity of communication. Subordinates tend to hesitate to communicate unfavorable information upward because of fear of repercussion.

Lateral Communication.   Lateral communication takes place among and between peers and is needed to achieve cooperation among group members and between work groups. Technology can influence the amount of cooperation needed among and between peers. For example, tasks that require high degrees of interaction necessitate a great deal of lateral communication. However, lateral communication is often restrained by competitive reward systems that encourage competition rather than cooperation.

Diagonal Communication. Diagonal communication takes place between a manager and the members of other work groups. A manager needs this kind of communication to interact with employees in other managers' jurisdictions regarding his or her particular function—that is, functional authority. For example, a controller interacts with plant personnel who deal with cost data. The diagonal communication network usually does not appear on the organizational chart, but a substantial number of diagonal contacts are found in large organizations.[9] Diagonal communication is often hindered by the existence of in-group languages and by differences in work group goals.

External Communication. External communication occurs between managers and people outside the organization. Managers interact with clients, suppliers, government officials, professional associates, and other interest groups to link the organization to the external environment. Unlike internal communications which can, to some extent, be maintained by authority and responsibility relationships, external communications are usually maintained through interpersonal skills and business interests. Because they are a primary means of maintaining contact with the external world, some managers are encouraged to create and maintain a broad range of external contacts. When managers have greater contact with the external environment, internal communications are also increased because external communication brings business opportunities that must be distributed to all organization levels.[10]

Interpersonal and Organizational Communication

Managers engage in two kinds of communication: interpersonal and organizational. *Interpersonal communication* is the process by which two people or a small group of people exchange information. *Organizational communication* is the process by which managers collect and disseminate information from and to a large number of people in and out of the organization. Although we can make this distinction, we need to understand that most organizational communications are carried out through interpersonal communication. Top management communicates with a small group of upper-level managers in a dyadic or a small group setting, and these managers do the same with their immediate subordinates. Managers seldom address important messages to a large group of employees except for informational and ceremonial purposes.

Because most vital information is channeled through interpersonal communication, managers need to be sensitive to the kinds of relationships they maintain with their superiors and subordinates. As pointed out in Chapter 7, Graen and his associates argue that the quality of dyad relationships determines the quality of working life of subordinate managers.[11] When a manager is able to maintain "in-group" relationships with his or her superiors and subordinates, the quality and quantity of communication can increase.

BARRIERS TO EFFECTIVE COMMUNICATION

Effective interpersonal communication is achieved only when the sender obtains the intended response(s) from the receiver. There are, however, a number of barriers to effective communication that are caused by various elements in the communication process.

When we say we "have a communication problem" or "cannot communicate," one of two things is implied. One possibility is that the receiver has not understood the sender's message because the message was incorrectly communicated. Second, the message may have been communicated correctly, but the receiver did not give the expected response. The second case is more difficult to deal with than the first because it involves interpersonal problems in addition to communication problems. Therefore, both interpersonal and communication problems must be adequately dealt with in order to achieve communication goals.

Effective vs. Good Communication

Tagiuri presents a useful distinction between "effective" and "good" communication.[12] Communication is called *good* if the receiver correctly understands the sender's message, and it can be called *effective* if the sender obtains the expected response from the receiver. While effective communication requires good communication, good communication does not ensure effective communication. When a manager tells an employee to increase productivity by 10 percent, the employee may clearly understand the message but fail to comply with the manager's wish. In this case, the communication can be said to be good but not effective.

The distinction between good and effective communication is important because, while it is relatively easy to achieve good communication, effective communication involves other aspects of behavior such as motivation, leadership, persuasion, and power. Many communication problems originate from difficulties in interpersonal relationships. Athos and Gabarro point out several instances in which interpersonal problems can severely impair effective communication—political infighting and power struggles, personality conflicts, and conflicting goals.[13] When these situations occur, each party understands the other party's intentions quite well, but they tend not to comply with each other's wishes.

Even if the communicators do not experience serious interpersonal problems, communication problems can arise when the receiver does not understand the meaning of the sender's message (poor communication) because of differences in attitudes and perceptions. Athos and Gabarro give the following example to illustrate how perceptual and attitudinal differences can cause communication problems and eventually lead to interpersonal difficulties.[14]

> *Steve Watson, a regional manager in charge of four sales districts, was known by his colleagues and superiors as an effective sales manager. Whenever there was a need for a capable manager, his name was brought up as a candidate. He reported to Tom Elly, vice-president for sales. Tom was asked by the marketing vice-president to recommend someone to head up the marketing services department, which employed about 400 people and provided various marketing services to sales. Because of a lack of leadership, this department had become unresponsive to the sales department's needs and had developed a poor image. It was known as the place to which ineffective salespeople were transferred. In order to improve the department's effectiveness, management decided to hire a manager like Steve Watson.*
>
> *After consultation with the marketing vice-president, Tom recommended Steve for the position. Tom called upon Steve, explained the situation, and recommended that he accept the position. Tom also indicated that the position was one level higher than regional sales manager. To Tom's surprise, Steve indicated that he was not interested in the transfer.*
>
> *Despite additional efforts by Tom and the marketing vice-president, Steve remained unconvinced and even avoided Tom. About a month later, Tom received a call from Steve's area manager saying that he had resigned to take a position with a competitor. Tom later learned that he had left because he had concluded that his career with the company was finished when he was offered a transfer to the discredited department.*

Note from this example that the sender's positive intention does not produce an affirmative result unless it is properly interpreted by the receiver. Furthermore, even if the transfer had been interpreted as a positive recommendation, Steve might not have accepted it unless it were some-thing he wanted. But at least this understanding might have prevented his resigning. In order to avoid such unfortunate incidents, managers need to understand various sources of communication problems and learn to deal with them. Communication barriers can be grouped into three categories: sender-related, receiver-related, and others (see Figure 8.3).

Sender-Related Barriers

The sender is responsible for defining the communication goal; encoding ideas, thoughts, and feelings into messages that can be understood by the receiver; and creating a favorable communication climate. When this responsibility is not appropriately discharged, communication is bound to be ineffective. The following communication barriers are usually caused by, or related to, the sender.

Communication Goals.   There should be some goal or objective in communication. This goal provides the sender with the basis for formulat-ing messages. Lack of such a goal can lead to formulation of incoherent messages.

FIGURE   8.3
Strategies for Dealing with
Communication Barriers.

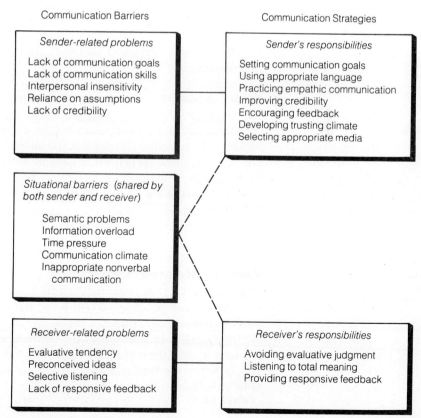

Communication Barriers

Communication Strategies

Sender-related problems

Lack of communication goals
Lack of communication skills
Interpersonal insensitivity
Reliance on assumptions
Lack of credibility

Sender's responsibilities

Setting communication goals
Using appropriate language
Practicing empathic communication
Improving credibility
Encouraging feedback
Developing trusting climate
Selecting appropriate media

Situational barriers (shared by both sender and receiver)

Semantic problems
Information overload
Time pressure
Communication climate
Inappropriate nonverbal
    communication

Receiver-related problems

Evaluative tendency
Preconceived ideas
Selective listening
Lack of responsive feedback

Receiver's responsibilities

Avoiding evaluative judgment
Listening to total meaning
Providing responsive feedback

Communication Skills. Incorrect word usage, grammatical errors, poor delivery of messages, incorrect spelling or pronunciation, and poorly organized sentences or speech make it difficult for the receiver to understand the sender's message. Some of these problems may be attributable to inadequate education and training.

Interpersonal Sensitivity. Some people have the necessary verbal skills but are unable to achieve their communication goals because they lack interpersonal sensitivity. They may convey the messages clearly and correctly to others but fail to produce intended results because their messages do not motivate the receivers to respond positively. Insensitive individuals may use language that is offensive to others, or they may be indifferent to the needs and feelings of other people.

Frame of Reference. As pointed out in Chapter 5, people often perceive the same thing differently but *assume* that other people perceive it the same way they do. Failure to recognize other people's frame of reference is one of the most common causes of miscommunication. When communicators use different frames of reference, they cannot achieve "common understanding" in their communicating. In the previous illustration, for example, Steve and Tom were clearly using different frameworks or assumptions.

Sender Credibility. Sender credibility refers to the attitude the receiver has toward the reliability or trustworthiness of the sender's message. Johnson points out several dimensions that affect the credibility of the sender, including (1) expertise, (2) reliability, (3) intention, (4) warmth, (5) dynamic characteristics, and (6) general reputation.[15] Thus, the amount of faith put in the message will depend largely on how the receiver evaluates the sender. The more the receiver trusts the source of information, the greater will be the receiver's willingness to listen to the sender's message.[16] The sender's credibility will be challenged when the words do not match his or her actions.

Receiver-Related Barriers

The receiver is just as responsible as the sender for effective communication—which can be achieved only when the receiver is responsive to the sender's message and provides the sender with feedback. If the receiver fails to do this, poor and ineffective communication results. Evaluating the sender instead of the message, preconceived ideas, selective listening, and lack of responsive feedback are some of the major communication problems attributable to the receiver.

Evaluative Tendency. Rogers and Roethlisberger consider the tendency to evaluate the sender to be the most important single barrier to effective communication.[17] After making a judgment about the sender or the sender's message, the receiver cannot perceive the message effectively. The message's meaning will be distorted in one way or another; the message cannot be registered in the mind of the receiver objectively because this judgment stands in the way. When a receiver thinks, "I don't like that person" or "I don't like what that person is saying," it is difficult to hear the rest of the message correctly.

Preconceived Ideas. The interpretation or reception of the message can be influenced by the receiver's preconceived opinions about the idea or thought. When this happens, the receiver tends to make a snap judgment about what is being said. These preconceived ideas or assumptions are the frame of reference through which the receiver receives, organizes, and interprets the message. Since the message is interpreted from the receiver's point of view, with little or no consideration of the sender's viewpoint, the intended meaning of the message may be completely lost.

Selective Listening. We have a tendency to hear what we want to hear and "tune out" what we do not want to hear. As with selective perception (discussed in Chapter 5), we tend to be receptive to messages that satisfy our needs or coincide with our beliefs. But we tend to deny, reject, or distort messages that are threatening or in conflict with our existing beliefs.[18] Thus, people become defensive when they are criticized by others, and so upward communication becomes biased toward favorable information. Criticism is a threat to a person's ego, and upper-level management wants to hear that everything is going well in the organization.

Lack of Responsive Feedback. Nonresponse, or an inappropriate response, discourages the message sender. A nonresponse usually implies that the receiver is not interested in the sender or the sender's message, and it is difficult to communicate with such a person. An inappropriate response, or one that is unexpected by the sender, hurts the sender's ego or feelings. For example, when a person asks for the time, and the receiver responds with a comment like "Why don't you buy a watch?" the communication can quickly terminate.

Situational Barriers

Several communication barriers are attributable to factors other than the sender or receiver—the message and the medium, for example. These include semantic problems, information overload, time pressure, communication climate, and nonverbal communication.

Semantic Problems.   Words mean different things to different people. Unless the words used are understood and interpreted the same way by both sender and receiver, effective communication cannot take place. This is especially true when the sender uses highly abstract or technical terms with vague meanings. Many of the words or phrases used in management and organizational behavior fall into this category. For example, when top management talks about "exercising leadership," it may mean setting specific goals for the company. But employees may interpret it as meaning imposing strict control over their behavior, or as management's interest in their activities.

Information Overload.   Poor communication often results from information overload. When receivers are bombarded with more messages than they can handle, communication effectiveness is reduced. The increasing complexity of our lives results in an increasing number of messages from various sources. Because of this information overload, a given receiver cannot accommodate a heavy load of messages from a particular sender. Therefore, the sender should not impose too much information on the receiver at one time.

Time Pressure.   Time pressure can cause poor communication by preventing management from providing adequate information to people. Faced with the need to maintain a large number of contacts with a variety of individuals, managers may not have sufficient time to provide adequate information to them all. As a result, the manager's communications may become relatively superficial, and this superficiality can adversely affect interpersonal relationships.

Communication Climate.   The climate in which communication takes place influences its effectiveness. If communication takes place in an organization with a high degree of trust and openness, it is more likely to produce a positive response. If a message is incomplete, the receivers are likely to fill in the missing part with favorable interpretations. Conversely, if communication takes place in a climate where distrust prevails, even a well-intended message can be negatively distorted. For example, when a manager talks about a cost-saving program to reduce expenses, it may be interpreted as meaning that employees will be laid off or major research and development programs cut back.

Nonverbal Communication.   Inappropriate use of nonverbal messages can hinder effective communication. In face-to-face communication, we use both verbal and nonverbal language. When these two types of language are synchronized, communication is effective; when they are contradictory, effectiveness decreases. For example, a person may be saying, "I am happy," but if he or she is frowning and tense and avoids eye contact, the listener can hardly see him or her as happy. In addition, the sender's mannerisms, such as hand twitching, foot tapping, or stuttering, may distract the receiver's attention.

 ## OVERCOMING BARRIERS TO COMMUNICATION

> *Many of the barriers to communication can be circumvented by developing an awareness that such barriers exist and by overcoming the psychological factors that distort the messages. Both the sender and the receiver are responsible for taking corrective steps.*

With all these barriers to communication, it is no wonder that we have communication problems in organizations. However, by knowing what may go wrong in the communication process, we should be able to take corrective actions. The following suggestions should help improve the effectiveness of interpersonal and organizational communication.

Sending Messages Effectively

Senders can do several things to increase the likelihood that their messages will be more accurately understood. These include setting communication goals, using appropriate messages, using empathy, improving credibility, encouraging feedback, developing a trusting climate, and selecting appropriate media.

1. **Setting communication goals.**   Before communicating, we should know what the message is to accomplish. Is the purpose to disseminate or obtain information, to change another person's attitudes, or to unload one's frustrations on other people? Depending on the purpose, the modes of communication should vary. If the purpose is to disseminate information, a well-organized talk or written communication may achieve the goal adequately. If the message is intended to help others change their attitudes or opinions, a more skillful and empathic communication is needed.

2. **Using appropriate language.**   The sender must clarify and organize ideas clearly and put them into appropriate messages—oral, written, and/or body language. Appropriate language does not mean simplistic wording; rather, it means words, gestures, or other symbols that receivers can understand and with which they can identify.

Verbal messages can be synchronized with nonverbal language; certain messages can be repeated to stress some points.

3. **Practicing empathic communication.** The sender must understand the receiver's frame of reference (assumptions, attitudes, and beliefs) to understand how the message will be received and interpreted. This form of communication is known as *empathic communication;* it requires the communicators to place themselves in each other's frame of reference. Empathic communication can solve many of the communication problems discussed earlier. In order to increase this skill, communicators should not *assume* that they understand another person's point of view and also should suspend any premature judgments until they clearly do understand the other person's viewpoint.

4. **Improving sender credibility.** Sender credibility can be increased when the sender gains expertise in the topic under discussion. Specific information related to the topic increases the sender's credibility. It is also important that the sender's actions support the message. Many politicians lose their credibility by failing to fulfill their campaign promises. The problem of loss of sender credibility is also illustrated by parents' frequent admonitions to their children to "Do as I say, not as I do." This problem can be corrected only by matching deeds to words—"practicing what you preach."

5. **Encouraging feedback.** Effective communication is achieved only when the sender receives the appropriate feedback from the receiver. Feedback tells the sender if the message has been transmitted to the receiver as intended. Two-way communication and sensitivity to nonverbal messages can increase the feedback process. But, unless the receiver perceives that the feedback is genuinely accepted and respected, it will not be very meaningful.

6. **Developing a trusting climate.** Effective communication cannot take place unless the communicators trust each other. If they fear that the other person may misuse or abuse the information they disclose, they will hesitate to disclose it, or they may withhold any appropriate feedback. It is important to create a trusting climate before any genuine communication is attempted. When a climate hinders effective communication, it is no longer a communication problem but an interpersonal problem.

7. **Selecting appropriate media.** Managers can rely on a variety of media when exchanging information. The selection of a medium depends on the communication purpose. After surveying managers' communication methods, Level has proposed the following guidelines for selecting communication media:[19]

a. **Oral communication only.**   This medium is desirable for discussing employee problems such as tardiness, work deficiency, and interpersonal disputes. It is not desirable for communicating company directives, instructions, policy changes, and information of a general nature.

b. **Written communication only.**   This medium is desirable for communicating information of a general nature and information requiring future action. It is not desirable for communicating information requiring immediate action or for discussing employee and interpersonal problems.

c. **Oral communication, then written communication.**   The managers in the survey felt that this method is effective in most communication situations. This method is especially desirable for communicating information requiring immediate action, company directives, job-related instructions, and policy changes.

d. **Written communication, then oral communication.**   The managers did not view this as a frequently used method of communication.

Listening to Messages Attentively

The receiver can improve communication effectiveness by listening to the sender's messages attentively. Effectiveness, to a large extent, depends on how well the receiver listens and reacts to the sender. Attentive listening improves the quality and effectiveness of communication, poor listening hampers the interactional process. Rogers and Farson have suggested the following actions for improving one's listening habit:[20]

1. **Avoiding evaluative judgment.**   Premature judgments prevent the receiver from listening to the total meaning of the sender's message and make the sender defensive. When we know we are being evaluated or judged, we tend to "put our best foot forward" in an effort to please others. Thus, when we feel we cannot perform satisfactorily, we tend to withdraw from communicating. A positive evaluation can be as destructive as a negative evaluation: It can be seen as a superficial response. Therefore, the receiver should try to create a climate that fosters acceptance, trust, and understanding.

2. **Listening to total meaning.**   A receiver can create a climate of trust and understanding by listening actively and attentively to the *total* meaning of the sender's message. A message contains both *content* and *feeling* components, and the receiver should be attuned to both of these components in order to fully understand the meaning of the message. In many cases content is far less important than the feeling that underlies it. For example, an employee may say,

"Next time you ask me to do this, please give me some advance warning." The content indicates that the employee needs more lead time, but the feeling component may indicate anger or resentment about having to meet a target date on short notice. The manager must recognize this feeling to understand the employee's message. The feeling component is usually expressed in nonverbal language such as the tone of voice, facial expression, and other bodily expressions. All of these must be observed in listening for the total meaning of the message.

3. **Providing responsive feedback.** By "responsive feedback" we mean a response indicating the receiver's understanding of what the sender is saying, how the sender feels about the problem or issue, and how the sender reacts to the problem.[21] When an employee asks, "Don't you think job performance should count more than seniority in promotion?" the manager's understanding response may be, "Do you feel that your performance was not counted in considering your promotion?" This response may not be satisfactory to the employee, but it is better than saying, "Are you charging me with not considering your job performance?" or "Your job performance doesn't count." The purpose of sending responsive feedback is to engage in a constructive dialogue without creating a defensive atmosphere and to achieve a common ground in communication.

Active listening conveys the message that the listener is interested in the speaker as a person and in what the speaker feels and has to say. This message is very real and very effective in conveying the listener's feeling and respect toward the speaker. This kind of listening behavior stimulates the other person to act in a similar manner. One can cultivate this listening skill by prefacing any response with a paraphrase or restatement of what the sender has said. The restatement should not be expressed in the listener's own words, but it should be accurate enough to satisfy the speaker (see Exercise 8.2 for examples).

 ## TRANSACTIONAL ANALYSIS IN COMMUNICATION

> *Transactional analysis is a technique for examining an interaction between two individuals—interpersonal communication. It is a way of identifying the nature of interpersonal interaction to see if it is appropriate or inappropriate.*

Transactional analysis (TA) was introduced by Eric Berne and popularized by Thomas Harris in the 1960s.[22] While it was originally used as a group psychotherapeutic tool, it has been moving into corporations as an integrative part of their training programs.[23] Many organizations whose business involves extensive interaction with people—airlines, banks, retail service organizations, and telephone companies, for example—have found it helpful. It is popular because it is simple to understand and yet provides a tool for analyzing and understanding complexity in interpersonal relationships and for improving the quality of interpersonal relationships. Transactional analysis starts with a structural analysis.

Structural Analysis

Transactional analysis starts with the proposition that an individual has three ego states that characterize his or her personality: the Parent, the Adult, and the Child.

The *Parent ego state* represents the part of a person's personality that is authoritative, dogmatic, overprotective, and righteous. These characteristics are usually learned from one's actual parents or other adults who guided one's early life experiences. Its overt expressions are mostly *opinionated.*

The *Adult ego state* represents the mature, rational, and objective part of a person's personality. These characteristics are acquired as one matures into adolescence and adulthood. This ego state helps one to think and process *information* logically before acting. It is aimed at exchanging ideas.

The *Child ego state* represents the childish, dependent, and immature part of a person's personality. These characteristics grow out of one's childhood experiences. Behaviors that are influenced by this ego state are laden with *emotions* and *feelings.*

Transactional Analysis

Transactional analysis studies the ego states involved in an interaction between two individuals. Depending on the kinds of ego states involved, the interaction can be either complementary or noncomplementary. As shown in Figure 8.4, a *complementary transaction* has parallel lines of communication. A *noncomplementary transaction* has lines that are crossed.

Complementary Transactions.   Complementary transactions occur when the receiver responds to the sender's message in a predictable manner. For example, if a person in the Parent ego state interacts with a person in the Child ego state, both are acting in a predictable manner. This Parent-Child relationship can be seen in the following interaction:

FIGURE 8.4
Complementary Versus
Noncomplementary
Transaction.

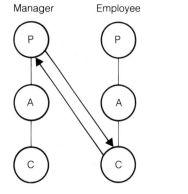

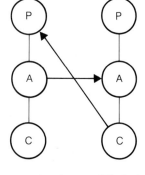

Manager   Employee

"I will take care   "I really appreciate   "Can you complete the   "What's the matter?
of you."   your consideration."   project by the weekend?"   Do you think I am
                                                                goofing off?"

Manager: I will take care of you.

Employee: I really appreciate your consideration.

The most common forms of complementary transaction are Parent-Parent, Parent-Adult, Parent-Child, Child-Child, and Adult-Adult transactions. Since these transactions meet the needs and expectations of the communicators, their interactions will continue. However, the ideal transaction is the Adult-Adult transaction because it enables organization members to communicate in a mature manner, exchanging information needed to perform assigned tasks. An example is found in the following:

Manager: Can you complete the project by this weekend?

Employee: Yes, it can be completed by Friday.

Other types of complementary transaction allow the communicators to interact continuously, but they are not always desirable. For example, the Parent-Child transaction is the dominant form of interaction in the doctor-patient relationship or in the parent-child relationship. The dependency of a weaker person on the helping person is inevitable in such relationships. However, the Parent-Child transaction is considered undesirable in work organizations because it often produces negative consequences. Such a relationship usually exists between authoritarian bosses and submissive subordinates. It is considered undesirable by many because it undermines the maturity and independence of the subordinates.

Crossed Transactions.   The crossed or noncomplementary transaction is found when a person with a certain frame of reference (such as Adult-Adult) addresses another person, who responds with a different frame of reference (such as Parent-Child or Child-Parent). Since the receiver's response is not what was expected by the sender and does not satisfy the sender's needs, the sender sooner or later withdraws from interaction with the receiver. An example of a crossed transaction can be found in the following interchange:

Manager: Can you complete the project by this weekend?

Employee: What's the matter? Do you think I'm goofing off?

The most common forms of crossed transaction are the conflicts of Adult-Adult with Parent-Child, Adult-Adult with Child-Parent, Parent-Child with Adult-Adult, and Child-Parent with Adult-Adult. When these kinds of crossed transactions occur, the communicators should be aware of communication difficulties and modify their behaviors. In order to keep the crossed transaction open, each must respond to the other's dominant ego state before they engage in transactions on an Adult-Adult level. This means that each communicator should be sensitive to the Parent or Child ego state of the other if this ego state would hinder their interaction (see Exercise 8.3 for an example).

Evaluation of Transactional Analysis

Transactional analysis is a simple concept to understand and to apply. Unlike other management tools—such as sensitivity training and team building, which require considerable time and skill to use—TA offers a very simple and yet effective tool for changing some dysfunctional aspects of interpersonal behaviors. Since it aims at reducing inappropriate and unproductive interactions between individuals, it can, to some extent, reduce unnecessary ill feelings and defensive behaviors among organization members. Thus, they should be able to engage in more productive communications that will enhance the quality of their interactions.

This tool, however, has two major drawbacks. First, the TA concept can be seen as an amateurish attempt at psychology without sound foundation in scientific investigation.[24] Although it can be practiced easily in our daily encounters with other people, it does not lend itself to rigorous scientific research because the results of TA-trained behavior are difficult to measure. Second, this tool does not offer the empathic skill that is essential for understanding another person's viewpoint. As the introductory quotation indicates, without such empathic skill, one cannot achieve "oneness or commonness" in communicating with others.

SUMMARY AND CONCLUSION

Managers spend most of their time interacting with other people, and they exchange information and coordinate their activities through communication. Therefore, people in organizations should try to communicate with each other more effectively in order to achieve organizational goals. Yet there are many opportunities for them not to communicate or to miscommunicate. These communication problems often contribute to interpersonal difficulties, which in turn hinder joint efforts in organizations.

Communication problems can arise from a number of sources—the sender, the message, the encoding process, the medium, the receiver, the decoding process, feedback, and noise. But the sender and the receiver of the message are primarily responsible for controlling these sources of problems and for achieving their communication goals.

The sender is responsible for sending a message that can be understood and accepted by the receiver. To achieve this goal, the sender must be sensitive to the needs of the receiver and should encode and transmit the message from the receiver's perspective.

The receiver is as responsible as the sender for achieving effective communication. Communication often fails because the receiver prematurely evaluates and judges the sender's characteristics and message. When this happens, the receiver does not listen for the total meaning of the sender's message. Active listening with empathic understanding is the key to improving the effectiveness of interpersonal communication. It not only allows the receiver to listen for the total meaning of the message, but it also fosters a communication climate in which the sender and the receiver can trust each other and openly engage in genuine communication without being defensive. In essence, empathy is the key to effective communication and to the development of mutually satisfying interpersonal relationships.

KEY CONCEPTS AND WORDS

Communication process model	*Lateral communication*	*Communication goal*
Encoding	*Diagonal communication*	*Sender credibility*
Decoding	*Communication climate*	*Semantics*
Feedback	*Good communication*	*Selective listening*
Noise	*Effective communication*	*Responsive feedback*
Downward communication		*Empathic communication*
Upward communication		*Transactional analysis*
		Complementary transaction

Questions for Review and Discussion

1. a.   Outline the communication process between you and a friend you frequently communicate with.
   b.   What specific elements in the process cause some problems in your communication?

2. a.   Identify a few individuals with whom you most frequently communicate.
   b.   What characteristics or factors lead you to communicate with them rather than with others?

3. a.   Identify a few individuals you have difficulty communicating with.
   b.   What causes such difficulty?

4. a.   What are the differences between "good communication" and "effective communication"?
   b.   Recall an incident when you had good communication without achieving effective communication.

5. a.   What is empathic communication?
   b.   Give some examples of empathic communication.

6. a.   What is transactional analysis (TA)?
   b.   Explain how TA can help to improve interpersonal communication.

7. a.   Identify some communication problems you have or had in upward or downward communications. These experiences can be drawn from your class or from job situations.
   b.   What factors have contributed to such problems?
   c.   What can you or the other person do to improve such communications?

 EXERCISES

EXERCISE 8.1. AN EMPATHIC COMMUNICATION EXERCISE

The example on page 198 indicates how the different assumptions, perceptions, and feelings communicators have on a subject under discussion can cause communication problems and interpersonal difficulties. This exercise is presented to help you analyze these differences and to see whether an understanding of them can help achieve communication effectiveness. This exercise involves two parts: cognitive understanding and role-playing.

Cognitive Understanding

Read the example on page 198 carefully and answer the following questions:

1. What were Tom's assumptions, perceptions, and/or feelings about the situation and Steve when he recommended Steve for the marketing services position?
2. What were Steve's assumptions, perceptions, and/or feelings about the situation and Tom when he learned that he had been recommended for the marketing services position?
3. What were the major causes of their communication breakdown?
4. Could they have avoided such an unhappy failure? If so, how? If not, why not?

Role-Playing

After the class finishes discussing these questions, engage in role-play to see if you can improve the situation. You may use the following procedure for this exercise.

1. Two students should be selected to play the roles of Tom and Steve.
2. Tom calls Steve for a chat regarding the recommendation. They spend about five to ten minutes role-playing.
3. The rest of you make observations on the role players.
4. You then discuss how well Tom and Steve have achieved their communication goals. You may want to discuss what the role players have done right or wrong.

EXERCISE 8.2. AN ACTIVE LISTENING EXERCISE

Active listening occurs when the receiver intends—and attempts—to understand the total meaning of the sender's message. It can be achieved by rephrasing or restating the sender's message in the receiver's own words and by communicating the receiver's perception of the sender's feelings. This exercise is designed to help you learn and practice your active listening skills.

The Procedure

1. Divide yourselves into small groups of five or six.
2. Each group discusses the importance of interpersonal communication in work organizations.
3. All members can speak their opinions or feelings, but only after first restating their understanding of the previous speaker's message—verbal, nonverbal, or feeling—to the speaker's satisfaction. An active listening response may start with an opening phrase like:
   "I hear you saying that . . . "
   "Do I understand that you . . . "
   "It seems to me that you . . . "
   "I have a feeling that you . . . "

4. The groups spend about ten minutes on this exercise. Afterwards, the class evaluates the exercise to see if it has improved the effectiveness of their communication.

EXERCISE 8.3. TRANSACTIONAL ANALYSIS IN ACTION

Complementary transactions help communicators engage in continuous dialogues while crossed transactions hinder continuous interactions. In order to keep transaction open, communicators must be sensitive to the ego states of other people and respond to them appropriately, that is, through complementary responses. This exercise demonstrates a way of reestablishing complementary transactions at an Adult-Adult level.

The Situation

Assume that you are an office manager who needs a report typed and mailed by the end of the day. When you ask your secretary to type it for you, this is what happens:

> Office Manager: Could you have this report done for me by 4:30? I need to mail it before 5:00.
>
> Secretary: I can't just drop everything and type that report. If you need to have something typed, why don't you give me some lead time?

The Procedure

1. Identify the ego states that the manager and the secretary are relying on in this transaction. Show this transaction on a transactional analysis diagram.

2. Which of the following responses could most appropriately be used to keep their transactions on a complementary path?
   a. "Listen, you are my secretary. If I need something done right away, you should be willing to drop everything and do it for me."
   b. "I don't care how you feel. You are only my secretary. You just do as I say."
   c. "I am sorry. You are right. I should have gotten this report to you earlier, but I really need to have it typed before the day is over. I would appreciate it if you could type it for me."
   d. "I can see why you are so upset. I know you have a lot of things to do, and they all seem to be urgent."

3. Explain why you have selected a certain response and indicate the potential consequences of other responses. Identifying the ego states of the manager and the secretary will help you in answering this question.

Footnotes

1. S. A. Culbert, "The Real World and the Management Classroom," *California Management Review,* Summer 1977, 67–68.

2. C. A. O'Reilly, "Superiors and Peers as Information Sources, Work Group Supportiveness, and Individual Decision-Making Performance," *Journal of Applied Psychology,* 1977, **62,** 632–635; C. A. O'Reilly and K. H. Roberts, "Task Group Structure, Communication and Effectiveness in Three Organizations," *Journal of Applied Psychology,* 1977, **62,** 674–681; and K. H. Roberts and C. A. O'Reilly, "Some Correlations of Communication Roles in Organizations," *Academy of Management Journal,* 1979, **22,** 42–57.

3. D. K. Berlo, *The Process of Communication* (New York: Holt, Rinehart and Winston, 1960), pp. 23–38.

4. S. I. Hayakawa, *Language in Thought and Action* (New York: Harcourt Brace Jovanovich, 1964).

5. W. V. Haney, "A Comparative Study of Unilateral and Bilateral Communication," *Academy of Management Journal,* June 1964, 128–136.

6. J. M. Ivancevich and J. H. Donnelly, "A Study of Role Clarity and Need for Clarity in Three Occupational Groups," *Academy of Management Journal,* March 1974, 28–36.

7. S. B. Bacharach and Michael Aiken, "Communication in Administrative Bureaucracies," *Academy of Management Journal,* September 1977, 365–376; C. A. O'Reilly and K. H. Roberts, "Information Filteration in Organizations: Three Experiments," *Organizational Behavior and Human Performance,* 1974, **11,** 253–265; and C. A. O'Reilly, "The Intentional Distortion of Information in Organizational Communication: A Laboratory and Field Approach," *Human Relations,* 1978, **31,** 173–193.

8. V. G. Reuter, "Suggestion Systems: Utilization, Evaluation, and Implementation," *California Management Review,* Spring 1977, 78–89.

9. A. K. Wickesberg, "Communications Networks in the Business Organization Structure," *Academy of Management Journal,* September 1968, 253–262.

10. Bacharach and Aiken, "Communication in Administrative Bureaucracies," pp. 375–376.

11. George Graen, J. F. Cashman, Steven Ginsburg, and William Schiemann, "Effects of Linking-pin Quality on the Quality of Working Life of Lower Participants," *Administrative Science Quarterly,* September 1977, 491–504.

12. Renato Tagiuri, "A Note on Communication," 4-475-013, Intercollegiate Case Clearing House, 1972.

13. A. G. Athos and J. J. Gabarro, *Interpersonal Behavior* (Englewood Cliffs, NJ: Prentice-Hall, 1978), p. 51.

14. Ibid., pp. 52–54.

15. D. W. Johnson, *Reaching Out* (Englewood Cliffs, NJ: Prentice-Hall, 1972), pp. 66–67.

16. C. D. Fisher, D. R. Ilgen, and W. D. Hoyer, "Source Credibility, Information Favorability, and Job Offer Acceptance," *Academy of Management Journal,* March 1979, 94–103; and C. A. O'Reilly and K. H. Roberts, "Relationships Among Components of Credibility and Communication Behaviors in Work Units," *Journal of Applied Psychology,* 1976, **61,** 99–102.

17. C. R. Rogers and F. J. Roethlisberger, "Barriers and Gateways to Communication," *Harvard Business Review,* July–August 1952, 23–34.

18. L. Larwood and W. Whittaker, "Managerial Myopia; Self-serving Biases in Organizational Planning," *Journal of Applied Psychology,* 1977, **30,** 194–198.

19. Dale Level, "Communication Effectiveness: Method and Situation," *Journal of Business Communication,* Fall 1972, 19–25.

20. C. R. Rogers and R. E. Farson, "Active Listening," in *Organizational Psychology,* ed. D. A. Kolb, I. M. Rubin, and J. M. McIntyre (Englewood Cliffs, NJ: Prentice-Hall, 1979), pp. 168–180.

21. Johnson, *Reaching Out,* pp. 124–125.

22. Eric Berne, *Games People Play* (New York: Grove Press, 1964); and T. A. Harris, *I'm OK—You're OK* (New York: Harper & Row, 1969).

23. H. M. F. Rush and P. S. McGrath, "Transactional Analysis in Corporate Training: A Theory of Interpersonal Relations Becomes a Tool for Personal Development," *The Conference Board Record,* July 1973; J. H. Morrison and J. J. O'Hearne, *Practical Transactional Analysis in Management* (Reading, MA: Addison-Wesley, 1977); and Dorothy Jongeward and Philip Seyer, *Choosing Success: Transactional Analysis on the Job* (New York: Wiley, 1978).

24. D. D. Bowen and Raghu Nath, "Transactional Analysis in OD: Applications within the NTL Model," *Academy of Management Review,* January 1978, 79–89.

LEARNING OBJECTIVES

1. To understand how and why small groups are formed and maintained in organizations.
2. To learn how a group forms its characteristics.
3. To understand the effects of groups on individual behavior and group performance—*group dynamics.*
4. To increase the skills of developing effective work groups.

CHAPTER OUTLINE

The Nature of Small Groups

What Is a Small Group?
Types of Small Groups
How Can Small Groups Help Us?

Group Formation and Development

Group Attraction
Structural Formation
Individual Roles
Group Norms
Group Maturity

Factors Influencing Group Dynamics

Task Characteristics
Member Characteristics
Group Composition
Structural Factors
Group Decision Processes

Improving Group Effectiveness

Technically-Socially Complex Tasks
Technically Complex Tasks
Socially Complex Tasks
Socially-Technically Uncomplicated Tasks

Summary and Conclusion

UNDERSTANDING GROUP DYNAMICS

The effective formation of a group, and its continued development, require time and patience. It requires active effort on the part of the leader to produce an atmosphere of trust and the involvement of group members in the functioning of the group. . . . By indicating through word and action the necessary group task and maintenance roles, a leader can encourage members to assume these roles whenever appropriate.

Leland P. Bradford, Group Development[1]

People are social beings, and they form, join, and work in groups to satisfy their needs. Groups not only satisfy needs for affiliation, affection, and emotional support, but also help members achieve other goals such as training, recognition, and task performance. From an organizational standpoint, small groups are an integral part of organizational reality. An organization is composed of many groups, and most of its activities are carried out by groups. In this sense, small groups in organizations are intermediaries serving the needs of both individuals and their organizations. Depending on how they are organized and managed, they can or cannot effectively meet these needs.

In this chapter we examine the effects of groups on individual behavior and group performance—that is, *group dynamics*—and discuss how these dynamics can improve group effectiveness. We discuss (1) the nature of groups, (2) the developmental process of groups, (3) various factors influencing group dynamics, and (4) managerial implications for developing effective work groups.

THE NATURE OF SMALL GROUPS

> *Small groups are formed and maintained to serve the needs of organizations and their members—maintenance and task functions. Depending on the function they serve, groups can be termed either formal (task) or informal (social).*

What is a small group? How is it different from a large group or organization? Why are we interested in small groups? These are some of the questions that will be discussed in this section. Because group behavior is so complex, it is impossible to discuss here every aspect of groups. For this reason, we focus our attention on some salient points of small groups and their influence on behavior. We begin by defining the meaning, types, and functions of small groups.

What Is a Small Group?

The term *small group* means different things to different people, but it is defined here as:

> *A collection of two or more individuals who (1) interact with each other on a face-to-face basis, (2) maintain a pattern of interdependent relationships, and (3) are aware of one another as a group member.[2]*

A small group can be differentiated from a large group (like a department or division) or a large organization on these three points. First, people in a small group can regularly interact with each other face to face, but people in a large department or organization cannot. Second, people in a small group may feel mutually interdependent, but the feeling of psychological interdependence reduces as group size increases. Finally, people in a large group do not recognize other members as part of the small groups to which they belong. Two people may work in the same organization, but they often do not know each other or have enough contacts to perceive themselves as a group.

Large groups and organizations are not included in the study of group dynamics because they have a relatively small impact on behavior on a psychological level. The impact of large groups on behavior is indirect and can be studied independently of small group dynamics. In this chapter we are most interested in the small groups formed to achieve organizational and personal goals.

Types of Small Groups

There are basically two types of small groups in organizations: formal and informal. Although it is possible for a group to be both formal and informal, an informal group is usually smaller because some members of the formal group may not participate in informal group gatherings. Figure 9.1 shows the typology of groups in organizations.

Formal Groups.   Formal groups are those created by management to accomplish specific tasks. In this regard, they are often called *task groups.* Formal groups serve a variety of functions—managerial, production, sales, project, engineering, and so forth. Not all formal groups are included in the study of group dynamics. Some are so large that they conform to the definition of an organization rather than a small group. When they are large, they can be called "departments," "divisions," or "organizations."

Informal Groups.   Informal groups are the social groupings that exist in organizations to satisfy the needs of members that are not adequately met by formal groups. These groups include coffee groups, recreational teams, bridge clubs, and other social cliques. A formal group can be informal, but when it fails to meet members' needs, several informal groups can be formed within it.

    The relationship between formal and informal groups can be mutually reinforcing or competing. A study by Allen found that engineers in the study developed informal groups based on their task-related activities.[3] As they interacted more with each other on technical matters, they socialized more as friends. Allen also found that frequency of interaction was closely related to physical proximity of the engineers' offices. Moreover, engineers

FIGURE   9.1
The Typology of Groups in
an Organization.

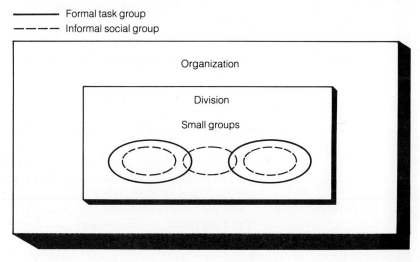

who were socially active with others were technically well informed and thus became more effective on their jobs.

Not all informal groups are supportive of formal groups or organizations, however. Some groups are deliberately formed to work against management. According to Sayles, two types of informal groups are active in resisting coercive efforts by management—erratic groups and strategic groups.[4] *Erratic groups* often protest against management, but they do so in a disorganized and erratic manner. Because their efforts are disorganized, they usually do not have a strong influence on management. *Strategic groups* are well organized and disciplined in pursuing their goals against management. Because they are well organized, they tend to be more successful than erratic groups in forcing management to listen to their views. These groups are more likely to occupy leadership positions in the union.

The following example illustrates how an informal group can work against the interest of a formal organization.

> *Art Boswell, treasurer of a large, independent insurance firm, set up an incentive system for the 50-odd typists in the main office. At the end of each day, each employee's output would be determined, and the highest producer would find a dozen red roses on her desk the next morning.*
>
> *Production immediately increased as most of the typists competed to earn the coveted reward. However, after about two weeks, Art noticed that output began slipping. After it had declined below the prereward level, he talked to a couple of the older, long-service employees to find out what had gone awry.*
>
> *At first, he learned, the roses had been sought after, not only for their intrinsic desirability but also as a symbol of achievement. Soon, however, some of the slower, less capable typists began to make disparaging remarks such as "Rate buster!" to the one with the roses, and some even refused to speak to her or go to lunch or have coffee with her.*
>
> *The program was thereupon dropped, and production returned to "normal."*

How Can Small Groups Help Us?

Small groups can help us in a number of ways. While formal groups help management achieve its goals, informal groups help the members achieve their personal goals. Small groups serve two kinds of functions in organizations: task and maintenance.[5]

Task Functions.   Task functions are the group activities performed to achieve organizational goals. They include:

1. Working on a *complex and independent task* that is too complex for an individual to perform and that cannot be easily broken down into independent tasks.

2. Generating *new ideas or creative solutions* to solve problems that require inputs from a number of people.

3. Serving *liaison or coordinating functions* among several work groups whose work is to some extent interdependent.

4. Facilitating the *implementation of complex decisions.* A group composed of representatives from various work groups can coordinate activities of these interrelated groups.

5. Serving as a *vehicle for training new employees.* Groups teach new members methods of operations and group norms.

This list is not exhaustive. The importance of groups in organizations cannot be overemphasized because most organizational activities are carried out by groups. Since jobs in organizations are becoming more complex and interdependent, the use of groups in performing task functions will become increasingly important.

Maintenance Functions.   Organizational members bring with them a variety of needs, and groups can satisfy many of them. The aspects of group activity that help organizational members satisfy their needs are called *maintenance functions.* They include the following:

1. Fulfilling members' *needs for social interaction,* including the needs for affiliation, friendship, support, and love.

2. Providing a *sense of identity and self-esteem.* People identify themselves by the groups they belong to.

3. Reducing *anxiety and uncertainty.* By talking over and sharing their concerns with other members in the group, people can reduce their anxiety and sense of powerlessness.

4. Helping group members *solve their own personal problems.* Group members help each other in dealing with personal problems such as sickness and boredom, and provide emotional support.

In essence, groups are important in organizations because they have the potential to satisfy both organizational and individual goals. A work group can function effectively if it can perform both the task and maintenance functions. In order to create and maintain an effective work group, we need to know how a group is formed, developed, and maintained.

GROUP FORMATION AND DEVELOPMENT

Groups go through forming, structuring, and maturing stages of development. Groups are formed to satisfy some goal; relationships among members are shaped; and the groups develop and maintain the capacity to sustain their existence.

Small groups are formed and developed through several stages. People are attracted to each other to form groups. Once formed, working relationships develop within groups. Some groups grow and mature; others become stagnant. Figure 9.2 shows the stages of group development.

Group Attraction

Shaw points out the following reasons why people join groups: (1) interpersonal attraction, (2) group goals, (3) group activities, (4) social interaction, and (5) groups as a means to an end.[6] Physical proximity and group synergy are other reasons.

Interpersonal Attraction. By far the most important reason for joining a group is because one person is attracted to another. There are three bases for interpersonal attraction: similarity, complementary difference, and task competence. First, the old proverb, "Birds of a feather flock together," is generally true in our social life. We like to be with people who are like us,

FIGURE 9.2
The Process of Group Formation and Development.

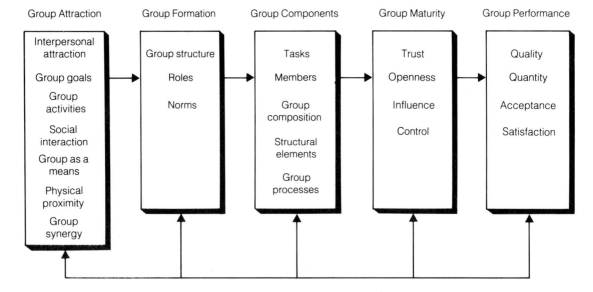

Group Attraction	Group Formation	Group Components	Group Maturity	Group Performance
Interpersonal attraction	Group structure	Tasks	Trust	Quality
Group goals	Roles	Members	Openness	Quantity
Group activities	Norms	Group composition	Influence	Acceptance
Social interaction		Structural elements	Control	Satisfaction
Group as a means		Group processes		
Physical proximity				
Group synergy				

who have similar social, educational, ethnic, and economic backgrounds —rather than be with strangers. Second, the old saying, "Opposites attract," is also true in our social life. People who have complementary differences can form a coalition for mutual need satisfaction. The relationships between male and female in marriage, buyers and sellers in economic exchange, and dominant bosses and submissive employees are examples of such complementary differences. Finally, technical competence is an important source of attraction in work-oriented relationships. You may hear a comment like, "I don't care about his personality, but he is the best production man I have in the company."

Group Goals.   Groups are formed to achieve certain goals such as carrying out an engineering project, socializing during lunch hours, or sabotaging management. If these goals coincide with a person's own goals, that person is likely to join the group. For example, people join activist groups like environmentalists or consumer protection groups because they agree with the group goals.

Group Activities.   People can be attracted to a group simply because they like its activities, whether they agree with the group goals or not. For example, college students join a fraternity or sorority, not necessarily because they agree with the group's ideals, but because they enjoy the social activities.

Social Interaction.   The desire to belong to and be part of a group often leads to group formation. People often congregate for no apparent reason other than fellowship. The intensity of this socialization need is shown by the existence of so many social and fraternal organizations. In addition, many civic, political, and work groups exist to provide people with interactional opportunities.

Group Membership as a Means to an End.   A person may join a group in order to achieve some goal external to the group. For example, an executive may join a country club, not because he or she agrees with the club's purpose or enjoys its activities, but because it provides an opportunity to meet important clients.

Physical Proximity.   Individuals who are physically close tend to interact with each other. These interactions often result in some type of group formation. If the members enjoy each other's company, they may undertake various social or task-oriented activities to sustain the group.

Group Synergy.   Most work groups are formed in organizations because management believes that groups can perform better than individuals. *Group synergy* is the outcome of joint effort by group members; it is believed to be greater than the sum of individual efforts. Whether or not groups are better than individuals in solving organizational problems is debatable, however, because group effectiveness depends on the nature of the problem, group composition, and the group process used. (This point is discussed again later in this chapter.)

Structural Formation

When two or more individuals begin to interact for the first time, individual differences in group participation become apparent. Some people are more active than others in the group process. Some are listened to by group members, while others are ignored. These individual differences provide a basis for structuring relationships among the members.

Group structure refers to the patterns of status relationships existing among members. These status differences permit the group structure to be hierarchically arranged, and such a hierarchical structure permits high-status individuals to control lower-status members.

Another important dimension of group structure is the communication network established. This network shows how information is processed within the group and who controls the communication flow. Some networks allow group members to communicate openly with each other, while other networks restrict the pattern of communication. Types of communication in groups are discussed later in this chapter.

Individual Roles

A *role* is defined as a set of behaviors expected of a member who occupies a particular position in a group. Most group members play the role of either *leader* or *follower* within the group structure. Each group has expectations as to how a member should behave. In addition, certain members are expected to play other roles, such as *expert, group facilitator,* or *trouble-shooter.*

Individual roles can be viewed from several different perspectives: expected, perceived, and enacted.[7] The *expected role* is what other people expect from a person. The *perceived role* is how the person thinks he or she should behave. The *enacted role* is the behavior the person actually performs. Role conflicts can occur as a result of differences among these three roles. For example, the group expects a person to be a task expert, but he or she may perceive the expected role to be that of formal leader. When the person attempts to be the leader, then, the group may resist it.

Group members play several enacted roles—*task-oriented, relation-oriented,* and *self-oriented.* The following list of enacted roles was developed in conjunction with the group development effort at the National Training Laboratory.[8]

Task-Oriented Roles.   These roles are directly related to the performance of group tasks. Task-oriented roles facilitate and coordinate problem-solving activities. Examples of these roles are:

1. **Initiator:**   offers new ideas, solutions, or perspectives regarding the group tasks or problems.

2. **Information giver:**   offers facts or generalizations relevant to group tasks.

3. **Information seeker:**   asks for information relevant to group tasks.

4. **Elaborator:**   elaborates and clarifies ideas and suggestions previously made.

5. **Coordinator:**   relates various ideas and suggestions, and coordinates the activities of group members.

6. **Evaluator:**   evaluates the relevance and practicality of various suggestions.

Relation-Oriented Roles.   These roles are performed to ease the stress and anxiety felt by group members and to build group loyalty. Some examples of relation-oriented roles are:

1. **Encourager:**   encourages others to express themselves better and accepts their contributions.

2. **Harmonizer:**   mediates the differences between other members.

3. **Expediter:**   expedites the group process by facilitating the flow of communication.

4. **Standard setter:**   expresses and applies standards for evaluating the quality of the group process.

5. **Group observer:**   observes the group functioning and provides feedback to other group members.

6. **Follower:**   passively goes along with the group.

Self-Oriented Roles.   These roles are performed by some members to satisfy personal needs. But performing these roles may disrupt the group process by increasing the stress and anxiety of group members.

1. **Aggressor:**   antagonizes other members by belittling their acts, egos, and values.

2. **Blocker:**   tends to oppose the ideas, opinions, and suggestions of others for the sake of opposition.

3. **Recognition seeker:**   tries to call the attention of other members to self.

4. **Dominator:**   attempts to dominate the group process and assert authority over others.

5. **Interest pleader:**   represents special interest groups such as feminists, environmentalists, or stockholders.

There are two reasons why managers should know about these roles. First, while task- and relation-oriented roles can help the group function effectively, self-oriented roles can be disruptive of group functioning. Anyone who can effectively perform the two positive roles can have a strong and positive influence on the group process. Second, as a group leader, the manager needs to identify the members who play self-oriented roles. The manager may try to satisfy the concerns of such members if possible, but if a satisfactory result is not achieved, the manager may discourage these individuals by not responding to their self-serving roles. Extinction can reduce such behaviors.

Group Norms

Group norms are a set of beliefs, feelings, and attitudes commonly shared by group members. While roles are closely related to particular position holders, norms are more generally applied to all members. Group norms have the following characteristics:[9]

1. **They represent the characteristics of the group.**   Just as an individual shows his or her characteristics through personality, so a group does through its norms. Such norms are often called *group syntality;* they show the degree to which relationships among members are structured and the members adhere to the group norms.

2. **They are related to behaviors considered important by most group members.**   Norms develop because group members want to have a set of behavioral guidelines regarding important aspects of their group life. These norms become the basis for their own behaviors in the group.

3. **They provide a basis for predicting the behavior of others.** Since norms are generally accepted by members, knowing them provides a clue as to how other members are likely to behave. For example, if a group norm promotes open communication, it encourages group members to express their concerns without fearing rejection.

4. **They are a basis for controlling and regulating the behavior of the group members.**   Some degree of uniformity of action is necessary if the group is to survive and achieve its goals in an orderly manner. Group norms serve such a guiding function.

5. **They are applied to all members but not uniformly.**   Some members are permitted to deviate from group norms to the extent to

which they have contributed to the group goals. This helps explain why high-status members are freer to deviate from the group's norms than low-status members.

Norms serve three functions in groups—predictive, control, and relational. First, norms provide a basis for understanding the behavior of others and for deciding one's own behavior. Second, norms regulate the behavior of members. They have a binding force because they are backed by group members. When someone violates a norm, other members are likely to exercise sanctions ranging from a casual remark to physical abuse. Finally, some norms define relationships among roles. For example, while high-status members are expected to play leadership roles, low-status members are prohibited from doing so.

Group Maturity

Some groups grow, mature, and become effective in achieving their task and maintenance goals. Their members feel proud of the group and what it is achieving, they enjoy doing things with the group, and the group plays an important part in their lives. In contrast, other groups stagnate and fail to meet their task and maintenance goals.

What make mature groups different from immature ones? They differ in four group dimensions: mutual trust, genuine communication, mutual influence, and self-control.[10] As shown in Figure 9.3, trust is the pacemaker variable in group maturity, for all other variables depend on it. To the extent that trust develops, people are able to (1) exchange relevant information needed to solve group problems, (2) allow others to influence them concerning goals and procedures, and (3) develop group goals that are congruent with individual goals.

In investigating the effects of trust on group effectiveness, Zand found that high-trust groups were significantly different from low-trust groups in the clarification of group goals, the quality of information exchanged, the scope of search behavior for solutions, and the commitment of members to implement solutions.[11] In the study, groups of business executives were given the same factual information about a major business policy problem. Half the groups were briefed to expect trusting behavior from other members, while the other half were led to expect distrusting behavior.

In both trusting and distrusting groups, the members were concerned

FIGURE 9.3
The Dynamics of Group Maturity. (After D. E. Zand, "Trust and Managerial Problem Solving," *Administrative Science Quarterly,* 1972, **17,** 232. Used with permission.)

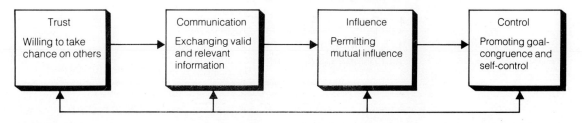

| Trust | Communication | Influence | Control |
| Willing to take chance on others | Exchanging valid and relevant information | Permitting mutual influence | Promoting goal-congruence and self-control |

with the problem itself and with the way they related to each other in their groups, that is, with task and maintenance functions. However, in low-trust groups, interpersonal relationships reacted to and distorted the perceptions of the problem. Much energy and creativity was diverted from finding realistic solutions, and the members engaged in self-serving behaviors rather than task-oriented behaviors. In contrast, high-trust groups exhibited less interpersonal uncertainty, and problems were solved more effectively. This finding coincides with the description of mature groups by Bennis and Shepard,[12] where:

1. Individual differences are accepted, without being judged good or bad.

2. Conflict exists but is over substantive rather than emotional issues.

3. Consensus is reached as a result of rational discussion rather than through a compulsive attempt at unanimity.

4. Members are aware of their own involvement in the group process.

5. Members show greater personal interest in each other and allow themselves to be influenced by each other.

Except for a few intimate social groups such as family and cliques, most small groups probably have not reached the maturity stage. People generally neither completely trust nor entirely distrust others in their work organizations but tend to be cautious about what they do and say. There is a significant difference between what they say in the group and what they say outside of the group. They tend to suspect the motives of other people who want to exert influence over them, and they resist any manipulative attempt by others. In many cases, work group members do not work out their own group goals and control systems; group goals and control systems are often imposed externally by management or group structure. This group immaturity partially explains why many work groups function less than effectively and efficiently. The following section examines various group dimensions that can facilitate or hinder the group maturing process.

FACTORS INFLUENCING GROUP DYNAMICS

> *The effect of groups on behavior is called group dynamics.* The components that influence group dynamics include task characteristics, membership quality, group composition, structural influence, and decision processes.

When you attend group meetings, you find that some groups are lively and get a lot of things done. Other groups are dull and do not get much done. What makes one group different from another? A number of factors influence the characteristics of groups and their performance. Among the important factors are (1) task characteristics, (2) group membership, (3) group composition, (4) group structure, and (5) decision process.

Task Characteristics

Tasks differ in their technical and social complexity. As shown in Figure 9.4, tasks can be classified into four major categories—simple, technically complex, socially complex, and technically-socially complex.[13]

The first category includes tasks that are simple and repetitive and require little technical or social interdependence. Such tasks can easily be performed independently by individuals. Examples are unit production tasks, record-keeping functions, and routine maintenance functions.

In the second category are tasks that are highly complex but do not require social interaction. These tasks usually involve a sequence of activities that cannot easily be divided into separate parts and do not lead to specific solutions. Such tasks require the concentration of an individual or a few individuals throughout various stages of problem solving. Research and writing projects are examples.

The third category involves tasks that are technically simple, but whose performance requires people with diverse information. For example, allocating resources is technically a simple task, but it is socially complex because people in various work groups must be satisfied with the allocations.

The last category involves tasks that are technically as well as socially complex. These tasks require people with specialized skills and knowledge who can work closely together. For example, developing a major weapons

FIGURE 9.4
The Nature of Task Demands. (After D. M. Herold, ''Improving the Performance Effectiveness of Groups Through a Task-Contingent Selection of Intervention Strategies,'' *Academy of Management Review,* April 1978, p. 317. Used with permission.)

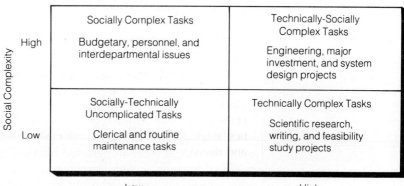

system or conducting a space program requires such technical and social complexity. No one person has all the information or skills needed to complete such a project.

The analysis of task characteristics provides some insight into the question of whether or not groups should be used and who should be selected to perform the task. Since these questions are important issues in group dynamics, they are fully discussed later in the chapter.

Member Characteristics

The characteristics of group members influence group effectiveness. Among the important characteristics are ability, personality, and prior commitment.

Ability.   The specific skills, knowledge, and experience that group members contribute to a task affect group effectiveness. Capable individuals are more likely to be active in the group process and are less conforming in groups than less capable people.[14] As tasks increase in complexity, so does the need to examine a variety of alternative solutions.

Personality.   Two personality dimensions seem to play an important role in group functioning—extroversion and authoritarianism. Extroverted, dominant, and socially aggressive people influence the group process by being active participants, but their dominance may inhibit the expression of other members.[15] Authoritarian individuals conform to group norms more than nonauthoritarian individuals. When authoritarianism is combined with a need for social approval, the individual is more likely to agree with the opinions expressed by other members.[16]

Prior Commitment.   Members already committed to a particular solution tend to argue forcefully for their favored solution, to avoid other alternatives, to make group consensus difficult, and to become dissatisfied when their suggestions are rejected.[17] Such commitment can occur when the members have a strong personal interest in the group decision.

Group Composition

The composition of group members and the ways they relate to each other have a significant impact on group performance. Among the important dimensions of group composition are membership diversity, group cohesiveness, and group conformity.

Membership Diversity.   Membership diversity refers to the degree to which members differ in personal background. Some groups are composed of individuals with homogeneous or similar backgrounds, while other groups are composed of members with heterogeneous or differing backgrounds. Homogeneous work groups may perform simple tasks requiring a high degree of cooperation better than heterogeneous groups. In such situations, groups with heterogeneous backgrounds might cause strains in social relationships.[18]

But heterogeneous groups are likely to perform better than homogeneous groups when a task is complex and requires a high degree of technical interdependence. Groups composed of people with diverse technical backgrounds should be able to provide the information needed to solve complex problems. Among heterogeneous groups, however, socially trained groups are likely to perform better than untrained groups. Trained groups can better handle social strains caused by people with diverse backgrounds.

Group Cohesiveness.   Group cohesiveness occurs when members of a group are attracted to each other and to the group. When this happens, group members are likely to interact better and engage in more activities together. Consequently, cohesive groups are more likely to be productive than noncohesive groups. However, the degree to which the cohesiveness of a group contributes to its productivity depends on the group's production norms. If group norms are compatible with organizational goals, the cohesive group can be highly productive.[19] If the group develops antimanagement norms, group cohesiveness can be detrimental to performance.

The following generalizations can be made about cohesive groups:

1. When tasks require a high degree of interaction among group members, cohesive work groups can facilitate the needed interaction.

2. When group norms are compatible with organizational norms, management can rely on the group to manage group activities.

3. Groups exercise social controls that reduce the need for close supervision. Supervisors can devote their time and resources to more important activities.

4. Management can rely on cohesive work groups to satisfy the employee's needs for autonomy and control. Cohesive groups allow their members to have influence on each other and on the group process.

Group Conformity.   Conformity refers to the behavior of individuals who adhere to the group's wishes. Pressure to accept group norms usually results in conformity. Asch demonstrated how simple it is for people to conform to group norms. In the control groups, subjects were asked to match a line on a card with one of three lines shown on another card. The task was so simple that most subjects in the control group matched the two lines without mistakes. In the experimental groups, the researcher instructed all but one member of each group to give an incorrect answer. The uninformed subjects, faced with the unanimous choice of other members, often gave the same incorrect answer.[20] In another experiment Milgram discovered that, under social pressure, subjects administered greater electric shocks to other subjects than they would have given on their own initiative.[21]

Conformity to group norms tends to be higher in cohesive work groups, for the more cohesive they are, the greater is the influence they have on their members' behavior. However, group cohesiveness does not automatically lead to high conformity. As pointed out earlier, members of mature groups are allowed to be different in their behavior and thought, and yet they can be highly committed to each other.

Like group cohesiveness, conforming behavior can be either positively or negatively related to group performance. If the group develops productive norms, conformity can be desirable. But if the group develops unproductive norms, conformity can be detrimental to group performance. The potential danger of group cohesiveness was shown in the Kennedy administration's planning of the Cuban invasion in 1961. The close-knit group of presidential advisors, including Dean Rusk, Robert McNamara, Robert Kennedy, Arthur Schlesinger, and others, developed what is known as "groupthink."[22] This phenomenon forces group members to think and behave homogeneously. In the Cuban incident, it prevented the presidential advisors from questioning the invasion plan. If anyone had a doubt about the plan, he was discouraged by the others in the name of solidarity and unanimity.

Structural Factors

Several structural factors influence group performance. Two important ones are size and communication network.

Group Size.   Group performance tends to increase with increasing size up to a certain point; then it tends to stagnate.[23] A group with three to five members seems to be ideal for solving simple problems, while a group of five to seven seems to be more appropriate for solving complex problems. This group size is large enough to provide diversity but small enough to encourage interaction.

As the size of the group increases, the potential sources of information increase. But the increased size can produce several undesirable side effects. First, it reduces the opportunity to participate in group activities. Second, there is a tendency for cliques or factions to form in larger groups. Finally, people tend not to work as hard in larger groups because their contribution to group productivity is less discernible; also, they often like to see other people carry their work load. This phenomenon, which detracts from the benefits of teamwork, is called "social loafing," or "the

Ringlemann effect." Ringelmann, a German psychologist, asked workers to pull as hard as they could on a rope, first alone and then with other people. He found that group performance increased with an increase in group size, but the average productivity per member declined as more people were added (see Figure 9.5).[24]

The degree to which the size of the group is related to group effectiveness depends on the nature of the problem or task.[25] If the quality of the group decision is of primary importance, it is useful to include a large number of members so that many inputs are available. But, if the degree of consensus or acceptance is of primary importance, it is useful to have a smaller group so that each member's concerns and opinions are fully considered. When both quality and acceptance are important, about five members seems most appropriate.

Communication Network.   A communication network is the flow of information between, and interaction patterns among, group members. The most common communication networks are the unilateral, Y, wheel, circle, and all-channel. Figure 9.6 shows the information flow within a

FIGURE   9.5
Ringelmann Effect on
Group Performance.

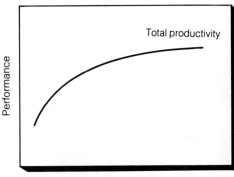

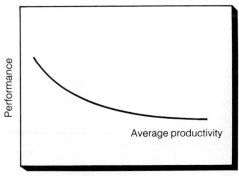

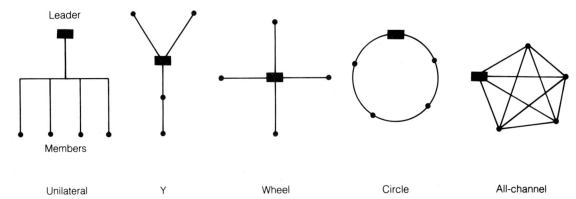

Unilateral   Y   Wheel   Circle   All-channel

FIGURE 9.6
Communication Networks
in Small Groups.

group. The selection of a network depends on the communication objective.[26]

The *unilateral network* sends messages downward by managers to subordinates. It is suitable when the manager has information that the subordinates lack and need. In the *wheel network* and the *Y network,* information is channeled through the manager, who thus has a high degree of control over its flow. Managers who are concerned with predictability and control are likely to use such networks. The *circle network* can be used to relay messages, but the manager may find it less controllable.

In the *all-channel network,* group members communicate with each other with little supervisory control. It is suitable for dealing with complex tasks that require a high degree of interaction among experts. A participative manager is likely to use this network to encourage employee interaction among and between group members. The manager may find it less controllable, but his or her subordinates may find it satisfying.

Group Decision Processes

Groups differ in the way they solve problems and make decisions. These decision processes can be classified into four categories: interacting, nominal, Delphi, and creative.

Interacting Group Process.   This process is the most frequently used method in group decision making. It is designed to obtain information and ideas from interacting group members and to make certain decisions. It is called the "interacting group process," because its decisions are mostly contributed by the interacting members. Research findings indicate that it is suitable for evaluating ideas and for reaching group decisions.[27] It is less suitable for generating ideas because interacting group members have a tendency to inhibit the contributions of nominal group members who do not participate in group discussions.

The group process can be either structured or unstructured, but it can accomplish more if it is structured. A decision process may involve the following steps:

1. **Define the problem.** Diagnose and define the problem or task.
2. **Select group members.** Identify and select group members whose qualifications match the task characteristics.
3. **Select a decision process.** Adopt an appropriate decision process, based on the nature of the group.
4. **Gather and analyze information.** Collect, exchange, and analyze relevant information.
5. **Develop alternatives.** Develop feasible alternative solutions based on available information.
6. **Evaluate the alternatives.** Analyze the pros and cons of each alternative.
7. **Select the best alternative.** On the basis of the above evaluation, choose the best alternative.
8. **Implement the decision.** Carry out the alternative selected.
9. **Follow up the implementation.** Evaluate the outcomes of the decision to determine its effectiveness.

Nominal Group Process. The nominal group process is a technique for soliciting ideas from nominal groups members. It is called the "nominal group process," because it involves the participation of nominal (or noninteracting) group members. An underlying assumption is that noninteracting group members may have valuable ideas relevant to the problems but they do not express them. A round-robin approach is thus used to encourage these members to express their ideas, usually in writing. Delbecq and his associates argue that this method increases the number of ideas generated by the group.[28] They point out that the effectiveness of group decisions can be increased if the process follows these steps:

1. Use the nominal group technique for fact finding and idea generation.
2. Use the interacting group discussion for information synthesis, idea evaluation, and consensus generation.
3. Use the nominal group technique for the final decision.

The Delphi Technique. This technique is a method of soliciting expert opinions without the members being involved in a group discussion.[29] The process operates as follows:

1. Each expert is provided with the problem.
2. Ideas are collected from the experts.

3. The collected ideas are compiled and distributed to the same experts for their evaluation.

4. A decision can be made by the majority rule. If a consensus is required, steps 3 and 4 are repeated as often as necessary.

Since this process is carried out anonymously, on a non-face-to-face basis, social influences on individual behavior (such as social inhibition and groupthink) will be minimized. It is a suitable method for generating high quality ideas, but it is time-consuming and lacks control over the behavior of the participants.

Creative Decision Process.   Groups can be used to stimulate the creativity of individual members. The process involves a nonstructured interacting group technique. Nonstructuredness and nonevaluation are stressed in a creative decision process to encourage the participants to express their ideas freely.[30] Once ideas are generated by this process, they can be evaluated for practical use through other decision processes. There are a variety of creativity producing techniques; among them are brainstorming, the Gordon technique, grid analysis, and the catalogue technique. Some of these techniques will be further discussed in Chapter 17.

Why should managers know about these decision processes? Groups are prominent in solving organizational problems, so managers must know about types of group processes and their intended purposes. The effectiveness of group decision making depends on the nature of the task, people, and social influence. The final selection of a decision process hinges on an analysis of these variables.

IMPROVING GROUP EFFECTIVENESS

> *Knowledge of group dynamics can be used to improve group effectiveness. Group effectiveness can be increased when there is a match among the task, the individuals, the group, and the structure.*

Are groups better than individuals in solving organizational problems? A great deal of research has been devoted to this question, but no definitive answer has yet been found. Earlier discussions in this chapter on group dynamics produced the following dichotomies:

1. **Group synergy vs. Ringelmann effect.**   Groups are often used to produce synergy, that is, a group effort greater than the sum of

individual efforts. But the Ringelmann effect—social loafing or free riders—also occurs in group endeavors. However, group synergy can be increased when the members have complementary differences and mutually reinforcing relationships.

2. **Divergent views vs. groupthink.** Groups are often used to produce divergent views and ideas for problem solving, but some groups experience "groupthink"—that is, they force their group members to think in a uniform direction. Groupthink can be avoided if different ideas are encouraged rather than suppressed.

3. **Group moderation vs. risky shift.** Groups tend to moderate the extreme views of their members, but some groups have a tendency to produce riskier decisions than an average individual. The tendency to produce a risky decision is called the "risky shift phenomenon."[31] This phenomenon occurs for three reasons: (1) the diffusion of responsibility, (2) the influence of a risky individual, and (3) the cultural value associated with risk taking.

These dichotomies are reflected in our proverbs. We often say that "two heads are better than one," and yet we also believe that "too many cooks spoil the broth." How can we deal with such a dichotomy? To be practical, we might ask, "When are two heads better than one?" or "How can we make two heads better than one?"

In the following sections we try to specify some contingencies that can help increase the effectiveness of groups. This attempt is based on the notion that group effectiveness increases when there is a fit between various group components.[32]

Technically-Socially Complex Tasks

Many jobs in organizations are technically as well as socially complex. Most developmental activities, such as weapons system development and major investment analysis, belong in this category. In this situation, groups can be better than individuals, but the following characteristics are needed for a group to be effective:

1. The group should stress both quality and acceptance of its solution as major goals.

2. The members should possess technical and interpersonal skills.

3. The group should be composed of people with various technical and functional backgrounds.

4. Prior socialization should occur to facilitate the interactional process.

5. The group should be small—about five to seven members—to produce valuable ideas.

6. The all-channel communication network should be used to facilitate information exchange.

7. *Interacting and nominal group processes* should be used to generate more and better ideas for decisions.

Technically Complex Tasks

Jobs that are technically complex require an individual's concentration throughout the various stages of completion, and can therefore be performed better by individuals than by groups.[33] Nevertheless, some people may choose to work in groups. Such groups need the following characteristics:

1. Since the group does not involve social complexity, the quality of its product should be the main concern.
2. Individuals involved should have technical competence and enduring personalities (persistence and ability to concentrate).
3. Both technical and social compatibilities are essential for maintaining intimate working relationships.
4. Prior socialization should occur in order to develop interpersonal relationships.
5. Groups should be small—two to three members at most.
6. The all-channel communication network should be used, as members need to interact on a face-to-face basis in an unstructured environment.
7. Since the group is small, there is no need to structure the decision process.

Socially Complex Tasks

Some jobs are technically simple but socially complex. Most managerial problems, such as budgetary, personnel, and interdepartmental problems, are in this category. Since such tasks require cooperation, coordination, or consensus between various functional or interest groups, group decision processes are more appropriate than individual decision making. To be effective, the group needs to possess the following characteristics:

1. The main concern of the group should be arriving at decisions that are acceptable to all parties involved.
2. Socially competent members, with interpersonal skills to deal with conflicts and negotiate differences, should facilitate the group process.
3. Functionally heterogeneous groups composed of people with diverse functional backgrounds should be used, but such a group may cause conflicts among members.
4. Prior socialization should occur but is not essential.

5. Group size should vary according to the number of concerned parties.

6. Both wheel and all-channel communication networks should be used to facilitate information exchange.

7. A structured group process such as parliamentary procedure or the nominal group process should facilitate decision making.

Socially-Technically Uncomplicated Tasks

Some jobs require little technical or social interdependence. Many production line jobs and clerical tasks in offices are in this category. Since the jobs can be performed independently, they do not require group involvement. If groups are used for these jobs, however, it is for their additive rather than synergetic effect. To be effective, such groups should possess the following characteristics:

1. Quality should be the group's goal, and group activities may increase the group's outputs.

2. Group activities should be undertaken only if the members are socially competent and can work well together.

3. Technical and social homogeneity should facilitate group interaction.

4. Prior socialization should increase compatibility among group members.

5. Groups should be smaller, for "social loafing" can increase as the size of the group increases.

6. A simple communication network, such as the wheel or Y channel should effectively serve the communication purpose.

7. The individual decision process should be used, as the task requires little technical and social interdependence and does not require group involvement.

Several themes run through these suggestions. First, the group must have technically and/or socially competent people who can perform the assigned tasks. The nature of the task determines the types of job skill needed. Second, the members need to know the process by which information is exchanged and analyzed, and by which the group decision is reached. Failure to define the decision process often leads to unproductive group experiences. Finally, it is necessary to create a group atmosphere in which the members are free to express their ideas and concerns. When the group lacks such an atmosphere, it can inhibit members' contributions to task-oriented behaviors.

SUMMARY AND CONCLUSION

Groups have a profound impact on our lives. They exist to satisfy most of our needs, especially existence and relatedness needs. Individuals, because of their limited capacity for self-sufficiency, must rely on other people to help them satisfy their needs. This interdependence provides the impetus for forming groups.

From an organizational standpoint, small groups play an important role. As jobs become increasingly complex, the cooperation and coordination of people who have diverse skills and knowledge is needed. This technical interdependence increases the need for groups.

Groups go through several stages of development: formation, structure, and maturity. People are attracted to groups for a variety of reasons, including social and economic reasons. Once groups are formed, members develop a pattern of relationships that guides their behavior through group norms and individual roles. Some groups grow and mature; other groups stagnate. Mature groups are characterized by the high level of trust, open communication, mutual influence, and commitment among group members.

Groups are not inherently better than individuals in solving organizational problems. Whether or not a group is superior depends on the nature of the task, the quality of the individuals involved, the characteristics of group composition, and management of group activities. The degree of technical and social complexity involved in the task determines the need for group involvement. Groups are suitable for performing tasks requiring a high level of sociotechnical interdependence, but individuals can better perform tasks requiring little interdependence.

KEY CONCEPTS AND WORDS

Group dynamics
Group synergy
Group structure
Individual role
Group norm
Group maturity
Group cohesiveness
Groupthink

Delphi technique
Group conformity
Communication network
Interacting group process
Nominal group process

Decision procedure
All-channel communication
Ringelmann effect
Risky shift phenomenon

Questions for Review and Discussion

1. People seem to have a love-hate relationship with groups. They may think that "two heads are better than one," but they also say that "a camel is a horse assembled by a committee." What are the reasons for this ambivalence toward groups?

2. a. Why do people join groups?
   b. What are the characteristics of a mature group?
   c. What causes a group to be mature or immature?

3. a. What is the difference between a role and a norm?
   b. What are the characteristics of roles?
   c. What are the characteristics of norms?

4. a. Are groups better than individuals in solving organizational problems? Explain.
   b. What causes some groups to be more effective than others?

5. What could President Kennedy have done to avoid the problem of "groupthink" in planning the Cuban invasion in 1961?

6. a. What is the interacting group decision process?
   b. What is the nominal group decision process?
   c. Under what conditions might a group use each of these decision processes?

7. Assume that your company is expanding its productive capacity. You are planning to form a committee to select a construction site for a new plant. Assume that your company distributes its products nationwide.
   a. What would be the characteristics of the committee's task?
   b. Who should be involved in the committee's activities?
   c. What kind of group process should be used in managing the committee's task?

EXERCISES

EXERCISE 9.1. SELECTING A DEPARTMENT HEAD

This exercise is designed to give you an opportunity to participate in a group process and/or observe group dynamics. You will be able to see the effects of certain group processes. This exercise can help you think of some ways to improve group effectiveness.

The Situation

You are appointed to a personnel committee in charge of selecting a manager for the department that provides administrative services to other departments. Before you begin interviewing candidates, you are asked to develop a list of the personal and professional qualifications the manager needs. This list will be used as the selection criteria.

The Procedure

1.   Select five to seven members to serve on the committee.
2.   Ask the committee to rank the items in the following list in their order of importance in selecting the department head.
3.   The students not on the committee should observe the group process. Some should observe the whole group, and others individual members. The observers can use observation guides A and B.
4.   The observers should provide feedback to the participants.
5.   The class should discuss how the committee might improve its performance.

Selection Criteria

_____ Strong institutional loyalty

_____ Ability to give clear instructions

_____ Ability to discipline subordinates

_____ Ability to make decisions under pressure

_____ Ability to communicate

_____ Stable personality

_____ High intelligence

_____ Ability to grasp the overall picture

_____ Ability to get along well with people

_____ Familiarity with office procedures

_____ Professional achievement

_____ Ability to develop subordinates

A. Group Process Observation Guide

Instructions: Observe the group behavior in the following dimensions. Prepare notes for feedback.

Group Behaviors	Description	Impact
Group Goal: Are group goals clearly defined?		
Decision Procedure: Is the decision procedure clearly defined?		

Group Behaviors	Description	Impact
Communication Network: What kind of communication network is used? Is it appropriate?		
Decision Making: What kind of decision process is used? Is it appropriate?		
Group Norm: Observe the degrees of cohesiveness, compatibility, and conformity.		
Group Composition: What kind of group is it?		
Other Behavior: Is there any behavior that influences the group process?		

B. Individual Role Observation Guide

Instructions: Observe one committee member. Tabulate (or note) behaviors that he or she exhibits as the group works.

Initiating Ideas: Initiates or clarifies ideas and issues.	*Confusing Issues:* Confuses others by bringing up irrelevant issues or by jumping to other issues.
Managing Conflicts: Explores, clarifies, and resolves conflicts and differences.	*Mismanaging Conflicts:* Avoids or suppresses conflicts, or creates "win-or-lose" situations.

Influencing Others: Appeases, reasons with, or persuades others.	*Forcing Others:* Gives orders or forces others to agree.
Supporting Others: Reinforces or helps others to express their opinions.	*Rejecting Others:* Deflates or antagonizes others.
Listening Attentively: Listens and responds to others' ideas and opinions.	*Showing Indifference:* Does not listen or brushes off others.
Showing Empathy: Shows the ability to see things from other people's viewpoint.	*Self-Serving Behavior:* Exhibits behavior that is self-serving.
Exhibiting Positive Nonverbal Behaviors: Pays attention to others, maintains eye contact, composure, and other signs.	*Exhibiting Negative Nonverbal Behaviors:* Tense facial expression, yawning, little eye contact, and other behaviors.

EXERCISE 9.2. IDENTIFYING ORGANIZATIONAL CLIMATE

Organizational climate refers to the psychological makeup of a group or organization. It is composed of members' perceptions of various group dimensions, including task structure, individual autonomy, managerial support, trust and openness, fairness in giving rewards, risk taking, conflict, and conformity. An understanding of the group climate is important because it influences employees' affective reactions to their jobs, co-workers, and management. In turn, these affective reactions influence employee job performance and satisfaction.[34] This exercise is aimed at helping you develop diagnostic skill in identifying the group climate.

The Procedure

1. Conduct a survey of the organizational climate of a work group or organization, using the questionnaire that follows. (Studying the learning climate of a class can be an interesting project.)

2. Collect the completed questionnaires and compute the group average for each dimension.

3. Prepare the organizational climate profile and show the "actual" and "ideal" scores and the gap between them on each dimension.

4. Discuss each dimension on which there is a large gap between the actual and the ideal. The discussion should include causes, effects, and remedies.

A. Organizational Climate Questionnaire

Instruction: Each of the following organizational dimensions concerns the characteristics of your group. Place an (A) in the column that describes your assessment of each dimension at the present time and an (I) on the column that shows where you would like that dimension to be.

Questionnaire Items	Not At All 1	Somewhat 2	3	Very Much 4	5
1. How much flexibility do you have in utilizing your time and resources?					
2. Does your group encourage you to use your own judgment and initiative?					
3. How much trust is there between you and your superiors?					
4. Do you feel free to discuss work-related problems with superiors?					
5. Are your superiors sympathetic to your problems?					
6. Are your co-workers friendly and supportive of one another?					
7. Are you treated fairly according to your contributions?					
8. Are employees recognized and rewarded for good work?					
9. Are your task goals clearly defined?					
10. Do you know how your activitie are related to group goals?					
11. Do employees feel free to disagree with superiors without fear of repercussions?					

Questionnaire Items	Not At All	Somewhat		Very Much
	1	2	3	4	5
12. Can employees do something new without fearing possible failure?					
13. Does your group emphasize high-quality performance?					
14. Is task accomplishment emphasized in your organization?					

B. Group Climate Profile

Instructions: The survey items can be classified into seven group climate dimensions: (1) autonomy and flexibility, (2) trust and openness, (3) warmth and support, (4) fairness and recognition, (5) goal clarity, (6) risk-taking behavior, and (7) concern for personal growth. Add the scores on the related survey items and divide the sum by 2 to arrive at the average actual and ideal scores for each dimension. The gap is the difference between the actual and ideal scores.

Climate Dimensions	Items	Actual	Ideal	Gap
Autonomy and flexibility	1,2			
Trust and openness	3,4			
Warmth and support	5,6			
Fairness and recognition	7,8			
Goal clarity	9,10			
Risk-taking behavior	11,12			
Personal growth	12,14			

Footnotes

1. L. P. Bradford, "Group Formation and Development," in *Group Development,* ed. L. P. Bradford (La Jolla, CA: University Associates, 1978), p. 8.

2. See Edgar Schein, *Organizational Psychology* (Englewood Cliffs, NJ: Prentice-Hall, 1980), p. 145.

3. T. J. Allen, *Managing the Flow of Technology* (Cambridge, MA: MIT Press, 1977).

4. L. R. Sayles, *Behavior of Industrial Work Groups* (New York: Wiley, 1958).

5. Schein, *Organizational Psychology,* pp. 149–153.

6.   M. E. Shaw, "An Overview of Small Group Behavior," in *Psychological Foundations of Organizational Behavior,* ed. B. M. Staw (Pacific Palisades, CA: Goodyear, 1977), pp. 360–364.

7.   Ibid., pp. 380–383.

8.   K. D. Benne and Paul Sheats, "Functional Roles of Group Members, *Journal of Social Issues,* 1948, **2,** 41–49.

9.   Cf. Shaw, "An Overview of Small Group Behavior," p. 384.

10.   J. R. Gibb and L. M. Gibb, "The Group as a Growing Organism," in *Group Development,* Bradford, pp. 104–116; and Dale E. Zand, "Trust and Managerial Problem Solving," *Administrative Science Quarterly,* 1972, **17,** 229–239.

11.   Zand, Ibid., pp. 235–239.

12.   W. G. Bennis and H. S. Shepard, "A Theory of Group Development," *Human Relations,* 1965, **9,** 417–457.

13.   D. M. Herold, "Improving the Performance Effectiveness of Groups Through a Task-Contingency Selection of Intervention Strategies," *Academy of Management Review,* April 1978, 315–325.

14.   F. DiVesta and L. Cox, "Some Dispositional Correlates of Conformity Behavior," *Journal of Experimental Psychology,* 1960, **52,** 259–268; and S. Milgram, "Group Pressure and Action Against a Person," *Journal of Abnormal and Social Psychology,* 1964, **69,** 137–143.

15.   L. R. Hoffman and M. M. Clark, "Participation and Influence in Problem-Solving Groups," in *The Group Problem-Solving Process,* ed. L. R. Hoffman (New York: Praeger, 1979).

16.   I. Steiner and H. Johnson, "Authoritarianism and Conformity," *Sociometry,* 1963, **26,** 21–34.

17.   L. R. Hoffman and R. O'Day, "The Process of Solving Reasoning and Value Problems," in *The Group Problem-Solving Process,* ed. L. P. Hoffman (New York: Praeger, 1979); and L. R. Hoffman, "Applying Experimental Research on Group Problem Solving to Organizations," *Journal of Applied Behavior Science,* 1979, **15,** 375–391.

18.   F. E. Fiedler and W. A. T. Meuwese, "Leader's Contribution to Task Performance in Cohesive and Uncohesive Groups," *Journal of Abnormal and Social Psychology,* 1963, **67,** 83–87.

19.   S. F. Seashore, *Group Cohesiveness in the Industrial Work Group* (Ann Arbor: Institute for Social Research, University of Michigan, 1954); and R. M. Stogdill, "Group Productivity, Drive, and Cohesiveness," *Organizational Behavior and Human Performance,* 1972, **8,** 26–46.

20. S. E. Asch, "Opinions and Social Pressures," *Scientific American,* November 1955, 31–35.

21. Milgram, "Group Pressure and Action Against a Person," pp. 137–143.

22. I. L. Janis, *Victims of Groupthink* (Boston: Houghton Mifflin, 1972).

23. I. D. Steiner, *Group Processes and Productivity* (New York: Academic Press, 1972); and R. M. Bray, N. L. Kerr, and R. S. Atkin, "Effects of Group Size, Problem Difficulty, and Sex on Group Performance and Member Reactions," *Journal of Personality and Social Psychology,* 1978, **36,** 1224–1240.

24. B. Latane, K. Williams, and S. Harkins, "Many Hands Make Light the Work: The Causes and Consequences of Social Loafing," *Journal of Personality and Social Psychology* 1979, **37,** 822–832.

25. L. L. Cummings, G. P. Huber, and Eugene Arendt, "Effects of Size and Spatial Arrangements on Group Decision Making," *Academy of Management Journal,* 1974, **17,** 460–475.

26. See H. J. Leavitt, "Some Effects of Certain Communication Patterns on Group Performance," *Journal of Abnormal and Social Psychology,* 1951, **46,** 38–50.

27. A. L. Delbecq, A. H. Van de Ven, and D. H. Gustafson, *Group Techniques for Program Planning* (Glenview, IL: Scott, Foresman, 1975); A. H. Van de Ven and A. L. Delbecq, "The Effectiveness of Nominal, Delphi, and Interacting Group Decision Making Processes," *Academy of Management Journal,* 1974, **17,** 605–621; also see F. C. Miner, "A Comparative Analysis of Three Diverse Group Decision Making Approaches," *Academy of Management Journal,* 1979, **22,** 81–93.

28. A. H. Van de Ven and A. L. Delbecq, "Nominal versus Interacting Group Processes for Committee Decision-Making Effectiveness," *Academy of Management Journal,* 1971, **14,** 203–212.

29. See N. Dalkey and O. Halmer, "An Experimental Application of the Delphi Method to the Use of Experts," *Management Science,* 1963, 458–467.

30. See Irvin Summers and D. E. White, "Creative Techniques: Toward Improvement of the Decision Process," *Academy of Management Review,* April 1976, 99–107.

31. M. A. Wallach, N. Kogan, and D. J. Bem, "Group Influence on Individual Risk Taking," *Journal of Abnormal and Social Psychology,* 1962, **65,** 75–86; and J. H. Davis, P. R. Laughlin, and S. S. Komorita, "The Social Psychology of Small Groups: Cooperative and Mixed Motive Interaction," *Annual Review of of Psychology,* 1976, **27,** 501–541.

32. See Herold, "Improving the Performance Effectiveness of Groups"; and S. A. Stumpf, D. E. Zand, and R. D. Freeman, "Designing Groups for Judgmental Decisions," *Academy of Management Review,* October 1979, 589–600.

33. M. E. Shaw and W. T. Penrod, "Does More Information Available to a Group Always Improve Group Performance?" *Sociometry,* 1962, **25,** 377–390; and B. Schoner and G. Rose, "Quality of Decision: Individual Versus Real and Synthetic Groups," *Journal of Applied Psychology,* 1974, **59,** 424–432.

34. E. E. Lawler, D. T. Hall, and G. R. Oldham, "Organizational Climate: Relationships to Structure, Process, and Performance," *Organizational Behavior and Human Performance* 1973, **9,** 126–146.

10 DEALING WITH INTERGROUP CONFLICTS

One of the important advantages of large complex organizations is that they are capable of coordinating the labor of many different groups of men, . . . A by-product of this condition, however, is that the groups involved . . . enjoy contrasting experiences which lead their members to view the world in different ways. Such differences can often lead to intergroup conflict.

Eric H. Neilsen, "Understanding and Managing Intergroup Conflict,"
Organizational Behavior and Administration[1]

An important task of management is to create an environment in which groups of people can cooperate with each other to achieve their goals. Yet one persistent problem in organizations is that work groups compete for limited resources, power, and status to the extent that their competition leads to disruption of cooperative endeavors. Once work groups are formed, they tend to develop their own group goals and norms. Since they are committed to these goals and norms, they often compete against each other and undermine the needed cooperation.

This chapter deals with the problem of organizational conflict, especially intergroup conflict. It presents a way of thinking about and coping with group conflict. More specifically, it discusses (1) the nature of conflict, (2) the sources of intergroup conflict, (3) conflict-handling behaviors, (4) consequences of intergroup conflict, and (5) managing intergroup conflict. Particular emphasis is placed on cooperation as a way of managing conflict.

THE NATURE OF CONFLICT

Conflict is the struggle between incompatible or opposing needs, wishes, ideas, interests, or people. Conflict arises when individuals or groups encounter goals that both parties cannot obtain satisfactorily.

We live in an age of conflict. Everyday we face a large number of conflicts. You may want to become a manager, doctor, lawyer, or engineer, but you must choose among these professions and select only one. In most organizations, the level and number of conflicts seem to be increasing. Employees are becoming more assertive in demanding their share of organizational rewards such as status, recognition, pay, benefits, and autonomy. Conflicts among groups are also increasing. As there are so many interest and pressure groups in organizations, it is difficult to find a sense of community and reach any kind of agreement among them.[2] Organizational tasks, as they become increasingly complex, demand cooperation between various functional and technical groups. This increased demand for task interdependence tends to foster group conflict.

In a complex organization, management faces conflicts with external forces. Government, unions, and other pressure groups impose increasing numbers of restrictions on managerial activities. Similar kinds of conflict are also found in the economy as a whole. The conflict between maintaining high employment while avoiding inflation is an age-old struggle. The demand for increased energy, protecting the environment, maintaining employment, and keeping prices reasonable is a common source of conflict today.

With increased conflict comes the increased need for and importance of conflict management. A recent survey reports that top and middle managers say they spend about 20 percent of their time dealing with some form of conflict.[3] Furthermore, they indicate that conflict management skills have become important for performing their jobs, and that they are interested in learning more about the tools.

Is Conflict Desirable or Undesirable?

Traditionally, conflict has been considered destructive and thus to be avoided at all costs. Conflict was, and still is, considered undesirable for the following reasons:[4]

1. Conflict produces stress and anxiety for those experiencing it. Since normal decision processes or activities are interrupted, it causes some level of discontent and frustration.

2. Conflict threatens harmony and unity within social groups such as the family, church, club, and school. People in these groups are taught that it is important to get along with others and avoid conflicts.

3. In many organizations, managers are evaluated and rewarded on the basis of how well they maintain peace and harmony in their work units. The absence of conflict is often considered a sign of managerial effectiveness.

Are these views valid? Although conflict can be painful and produce undesirable consequences, the absence of conflict can be dysfunctional to organizational effectiveness. As shown in Chapter 9, people often think and do things in groups in order to conform to group norms. Because of "groupthink," they think or say things—in the name of group loyalty and unity—that they don't really believe.[5]

A similar example is found in business organizations. For example, the failure of the Penn Central Railroad was attributable to this same tendency.[6] The board was composed of outside directors who met monthly to discuss the company's operations. Few questioned management's decisions, although several board members felt uneasy about some major managerial problems. Apathy and the desire to avoid conflict, however, allowed poor managerial decisions to be sustained.

The Value of Conflict

One view that is emerging is that conflict can be valuable in strengthening organizational performance. According to this view, conflict and discontent stimulate organizational change.[7] Without change, organizations will stagnate. Dissatisfaction with the status quo, concern about doing things better, and the desire to remove inadequacies provide impetus for change and improvement.

There is some empirical evidence that conflict can lead to managerial effectiveness. A study by Evan measured interpersonal and technical conflict in government and private laboratories engaged in basic and applied research projects. *Interpersonal conflict* involves personal dislikes or personality differences; *technical conflict* involves differences of opinion about task-related matters. The study reported a positive correlation between technical conflict and group performance in the government laboratory.[8] No significant relationships were found, however, in the private laboratory.

Another study also demonstrated that, among established groups, performance tended to improve more when there was some conflict among members than when there was no conflict.[9] In ad hoc groups, however, conflict did not produce a positive effect on performance. The established groups had developed mechanisms to deal with conflict effectively, while the ad hoc groups had not. Hoffman reports that groups with diverse personalities and technical backgrounds are more creative and innovative in solving problems than groups whose members have similar characteristics.[10]

Realistic View of Conflict

Although conflict can be valuable for organizational revival, not all conflicts are good for an organization. Conflict can be harmful to employee satisfaction and job performance if it becomes excessive and unmanageable. Unresolved conflicts can lead to job dissatisfaction, high absenteeism and turnover, prolonged disruption of activities, and lack of concerted effort by organization members.

A realistic view is that conflict can have either a positive or a negative impact on organizational performance depending on how it is managed.[11] To the extent that conflict results in better organizational performance, it is considered functional. Conflict may generate many diverse ideas related to task performance. It becomes dysfunctional when it is extremely disruptive and hinders the attainment of organizational goals. Two kinds of conflict can be considered dysfunctional: interpersonal and excessive conflict.

Interpersonal conflicts resulting from personality variables such as dislike, distrust, or prejudice usually hinder group performance. The study by Evan reported that, while technical conflict or disagreement was positively related to group performance in government laboratories, interpersonal conflict was not.[12] When interpersonal conflict occurs, people are more concerned with gaining advantages over others than with task performance.

Excessive conflict, no matter how valuable it may be, can be dysfunctional to organizational performance because it cannot be effectively managed. The resulting chaos can easily threaten organizational survival.

Model of Intergroup Conflict

Since the value of conflict is determined by how it is managed, managers should know its causes, progression, and consequences. The process model of conflict shown in Figure 10.1 depicts some potential causes and consequences of intergroup conflict. As the figure shows, intergroup conflict can be caused by a number of circumstances. Among them are task dependency, differing goals, dissimilar work orientation, competition for limited resources, and competitive reward systems. Once conflict has surfaced, it goes through certain stages covering a wide range of behaviors.

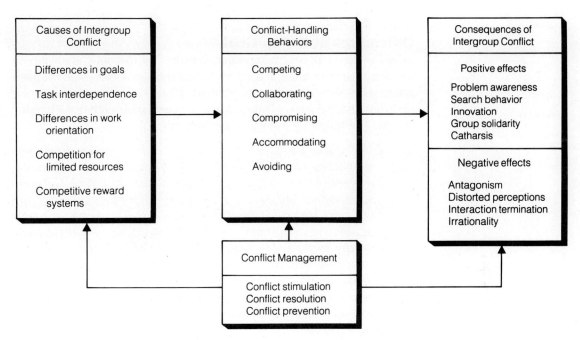

FIGURE   10.1
A Model of Intergroup
Conflict.

These include competing, collaborating, compromising, accommodating, and avoiding.

Changes can occur within groups and between groups as a result of conflict. Some changes have positive effects, others have negative effects. Understanding these key elements in the model will help managers determine an appropriate strategy for managing conflict. The remainder of this chapter deals with these elements.

SOURCES OF INTERGROUP CONFLICT

Groups differ in their tasks, goals, and concerns, which can cause conflict when the groups work together. Many conflicts are related to resource allocation and sharing.

The organizational factors that contribute to group conflict, as shown in Figure 10.1, include differences in group goals, task interdependence, differences in work environment, resource allocation, competitive reward systems, and interpersonal conflict.

Differences in Group Goals

When groups in an organization perform different functions, these groups develop their own goals and norms. Theoretically, achievement of these group goals should achieve overall organizational goals. However, we often find that the goals of one group are incompatible with those of other groups. The following example illustrates this point.

> The Outdoor Equipment Company produces camping equipment and sporting goods. The company is divided into three major departments—production, marketing, and administration (accounting, personnel, and finance). Since the major business season runs from early spring to about midsummer, the marketing manager wanted to have sufficient merchandise in stock during that period. In order to meet this seasonal market demand, the production department needed to gear up its production capacity during the spring months. But the production manager found it difficult to hire people only temporarily. The employment problem has become more acute in recent years because of a tight labor market in this region.
>
> To overcome this seasonal employment problem, the production department decided to employ people on a permanent basis. This policy helped to maintain a stable labor force in the company, but it created another problem. The controller complained that storage costs were becoming quite expensive. As the stock built up in the slack seasons, the company had to rely on external warehouses for storage. In addition, the company had to borrow money to maintain the production line during the slack seasons, and these financing costs imposed an additional burden.

This example shows several things about group goals. First, the departments have to interact with each other to achieve overall organizational goals. Second, each of the departments develops its own goals. Third, the goals of one group may conflict with those of other groups. Finally, one department often achieves its goals at the expense of other departments.

Differences in group goals can easily lead to group conflict. When the reward system is related to group performance rather than to overall organizational performance, it tends to create a win-lose situation. When this happens, groups compete against each other for better resource allocation and even seek to undermine the rival group's activities.

Task Interdependence

Task interdependence occurs when two or more groups interact with each other to accomplish their tasks. Three types of task interdependence often cause intergroup conflict—pooled, sequential, and reciprocal.[13] *Pooled interdependence* exists when two work groups may not directly interact with each other but are affected by each other's actions. For example, when one independent product group performs poorly, all other groups may suffer financially. This can happen when rewards are contingent upon collective performance.

Sequential interdependence occurs when one group's performance depends on another group's prior performance. In a construction project, for example, the excavating team must prepare the foundation before the carpenters can work on the building structure. Since the carpenters depend on the excavators, conflict between the groups can occur when the excavators' work is delayed.

Reciprocal interdependence occurs when two or more groups are mutually interdependent in accomplishing their tasks. For example, in developing and marketing a new product, three major departments (marketing, production, and research) depend on each other to perform their tasks. Information possessed by one department is needed by another department. For example, the research department needs market information from the marketing department, and marketing needs research to provide customer services. When one group is unable to meet the expectations of another group, intergroup conflict usually results.

Differences in Work Environment

People who spend many years performing a particular task tend to develop certain ways of thinking about and performing their jobs. They may differ in structuring their tasks, meeting deadlines, relating to others, and pursuing their career goals. Production tasks, for instance, tend to be highly structured and are performed in a relatively certain environment. Production employees are more concerned with day-to-day operations and short-term goals than with long-term goals. Interpersonal and leadership styles tend to be directive rather than permissive in the production department. Research tasks, on the other hand, tend to be unstructured, involve long-term goals, and require participative or permissive interpersonal styles. Sales tasks fall somewhere between the two.[14]

These differences in work orientation can cause intergroup conflicts. When people with different functional and technical backgrounds are forced to cooperate, they tend to view the task differently and are often unable to understand how others think and behave. Furthermore, the status differentiation between them can be another source of conflict. Usually, people in research groups are better educated and have a higher status than those in production and marketing groups. But managers in production and marketing may have more decision-making or position power than those in research.

Competition for Limited Resources

The fourth major source of conflict involves resource allocation. The sharing of limited resources by two or more groups can easily lead to group conflict. These resources may be tangible, such as materials, money, and facilities, or they can be intangible, such as power, status, and prestige. Whatever they are, they contribute to conflict when people perceive them as limited—and desirable.

People are concerned about resource allocation because resources are the means of achieving their goals, both task and personal. When reward systems are designed to tie organizational rewards to group performance, it is imperative that managers obtain more resources for their work groups. This is one reason why resource-allocation decisions are often based on the political behaviors of managers rather than on rational decision criteria such as optimizing profits and improving production efficiency.[15]

Competitive Reward Systems

Many managers seem to believe that performance can be increased by competition, and this belief is reflected in their reward systems. Competition can indeed increase the level of performance in job situations where tasks can be performed independently. However, when tasks require high levels of interdependence, competition can hurt cooperation among members and work groups. Reward systems based on departmental performance can cause intergroup conflict. For example, if the sales department is rewarded on the basis of sales volume, while the production department is rewarded for production cost saving, conflicts can arise between them. When production sets high production cost budgets, it can show some improvement in cost saving and thus be rewarded. But high production costs mean higher selling prices for the sales department, leading to lower sales volume.

Interpersonal Conflict

Intergroup conflict can occur not only for technical and structural reasons, but also for reasons of interpersonal incompatibility. When influential members of different groups are not able to get along with each other, it can lead to adversary relationships between the groups. When the group members know their influential members, especially leaders, have some conflict with members in the other group, they may limit their cooperative interactions with the conflicting group members in support of their own members. Moreover, influential members may intentionally provoke group conflict as a way of dealing with their own interpersonal problems. Strategies for dealing with interpersonal conflict were discussed previously in Chapter 7.

To summarize, intergroup conflicts are common in organizations. They are caused by various circumstances, many of which are derived from organizational characteristics such as division of labor, task specialization, interdependence, goal differentiation, and resource allocation. Resource-related conflicts seem to be the most critical, for they are directly related to attaining group goals and rewards. Depending on how these resources and rewards are distributed, the number of conflicts can be either increased or decreased.

 ## CONFLICT-HANDLING BEHAVIORS

> *People or groups can deal with conflict in a number of ways. Conflict-handling behaviors include competing, collaborating, compromising, avoiding, and accommodating.*

When people face a conflict situation, they can handle it in a number of ways. Depending on their intentions in a given conflict situation, their behaviors can range from full cooperation to outright confrontation. As shown in Figure 10.2, the two intentions that determine the type of conflict-handling behavior are assertion and cooperation. *Assertion* refers to an attempt to confront the other party; *cooperation* refers to an attempt to find an agreeable solution. Depending on the degree of each intention involved, one of five kinds of conflict-handling behaviors—competing, collaborating, compromising, avoiding, and accommodating—can be seen.[16]

Competing

Competition is characterized by high assertion and low cooperation. This is called a *zero-sum game*—one party wins at the expense of the other, and when one's win is added to the other's loss, the sum amounts to zero. The competing parties use weapons such as arguments, fights, and threats to achieve their goals. Competitive behavior can be useful when the other party is not willing to cooperate or compromise and when the issue is vital to one's survival.

FIGURE   10.2
The Modes of
Conflict-Handling
Behaviors. (After Thomas
Rubble and Kenneth
Thomas, ''Support for a
Two-Dimensional Model of
Conflict Behavior,''
*Organizational Behavior
and Human Performance,*
1976, **16,** 145. Used with
permission.)

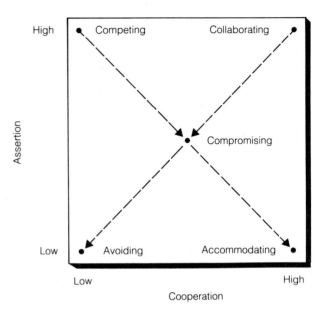

Collaborating

Collaboration involves considerable assertion and cooperation in an attempt to satisfy the needs of both parties. Collaboration is often called a *non-zero-sum game,* for both parties can win or lose at the same time. A major task of managing group conflict is to find a set of common goals that can be achieved by the competing parties and benefit them both.

Compromising

Compromise requires some assertion and some cooperation, for it searches for partial satisfaction for both parties. ''Splitting the difference,'' ''give and take,'' and ''horse trading'' are some behavioral examples. Compromise is necessary when the two parties find no ground for collaboration but want to avoid competition. It is also an expedient way of solving conflict.

Avoiding

Avoidance shows little assertion or cooperation, for it depends on moving away from the other party, or ignoring or withdrawing from the situation. It can be an appropriate behavior when the issue is trivial or when nothing can be gained by either competing or cooperating.

Accommodating

Accommodation requires high cooperation and low assertion, for it involves giving in to the other party or sacrificing one's own needs. One party may accommodate the other party's wishes for a number of reasons. First, the party may have no other choice. Second, the first party may find it more beneficial to give in to the other on certain issues rather than compete because the issues are important to the other party but insignificant to the accommodating party. Finally, when one party finds that it has been wrong, it may simply conform to the other party's assertion.

Practical Application

When people face conflict situations, they tend to assert themselves by trying to collaborate or compete. However, if they find that assertion produces less than satisfactory results, they may attempt to compromise. If agreement cannot be reached, they may either accommodate or avoid the other party.[17] In order to prevent undesirable group behaviors such as competition and avoidance, managers need to promote organizational strategies that encourage cooperation rather than competition. Before we discuss such strategies, however, we will examine the consequences of intergroup conflict.

CONSEQUENCES OF INTERGROUP CONFLICT

> *Although unresolved intergroup conflict may have a devastating effect on intergroup relationships, it can have a unifying effect on intragroup behavior.*

What happens to groups when their conflicts are not resolved? On the basis of research findings by Blake and Mouton, Schein has compiled a list of changes that can occur within and between conflicting groups.[18]

Changes Within Each Group

The changes that may occur within the groups involved are:

1. **Group cohesiveness increases.** The group becomes more closely knit; its members show greater loyalty.

2. **The group becomes task-oriented.** Group climate changes from informal to task-oriented in order to deal with the external threat.

3. **Leadership becomes more directive.** As the group becomes more task-oriented, the leader becomes more authoritarian.

4. **Organizational structure becomes more rigid.** Authority and responsibility relationships among and between members become more clearly defined.

5. **Group unity is stressed.** The group demands increasing loyalty and conformity from its members.

Changes Between Groups

Unresolved group conflicts cause the following changes in relationships between groups:

1. **Groups become antagonistic toward each other.** Each group sees the other as an enemy who interferes with its goal-oriented behavior. This is the psychology that promotes war.

2. **Perceptions are distorted.** Each group develops positive perceptions about its own group and negative perceptions toward the other. For example, Thomas and Pondy indicate that managers see themselves as cooperative in conflict situations but see others as competitive.[19]

3. **Communication ceases to exist.** When in conflict, members of one group avoid interaction with members of the other. If they are forced to interact, they tend to show hostility and aggression toward each other.

4. **Groups apply a double standard.** Each group clearly sees all the vicious acts of the other party while remaining completely blind to the same acts performed by their own group.

When one party perceives the other in negative terms, group conflict is harder to resolve. This negative attitude can result in a self-fulfilling prophecy in which (1) one party perceives the other party as hostile, and therefore (2) it takes defensive or hostile action, so that (3) the other party's hostility intensifies, (4) which confirms the first party's assumption. Examples of the self-fulfilling prophecy can be seen in many broken relationships between individuals, groups, and nations. The relationship between the United States and the Soviet Union and that between Arabs and Jews are evidence of this phenomenon.

Consequences of Winning or Losing

What happens to the winner? The winning group maintains high morale, becomes more cohesive, and tends to release its tensions. But the winner tends also to become complacent and may even lose some motivation to excel. Winning has confirmed the positive stereotype of the winners and the negative perception of the losers. There is, therefore, little reason to reevaluate the perceptions.

What happens to the loser? The losing group tends to deny or distort the reality of losing and to blame its failure on others. It may become even more aggressive in other directions. However, once the reality of defeat is accepted, the group tends to reevaluate its self-perceptions and stereotyping of others and engage in problem-solving behaviors. The acceptance of reality is an important step toward reorganizing the group's efforts and becoming effective in solving problems.

In most organizations, group conflicts usually do not lead to physical aggression or a complete win-or-lose situation. Except for labor–management conflicts, most group conflicts are not well known or publicly proclaimed. However, once conflicts do develop between groups, no matter how subtle they may be, the problems of perceptual distortion, reduced communication, and lack of cooperation can be easily seen. For example, many universities have recently been faced with the problem of declining enrollment. In order to protect their jobs, many departments and colleges revise their curricula so that their own and other students take more of their courses. These behaviors make it harder for the university to develop a coherent set of academic programs.

Positive Consequences of Conflict

So far, we have explored the negative side of intergroup conflict. Conflict may be painful to the people or groups involved, but it can also produce some positive outcomes for the organization. Some *potential* benefits of conflict are:

1. **Conflict clarifies the real issue.**   When people or groups express their concerns and differences, it helps sharpen the real issue involved in a problem. Without conflict, many organizational problems go unnoticed and remain unresolved.

2. **Conflict increases innovation.**   Conflict generates a greater diversity of ideas and viewpoints. Such a diversity can stimulate innovation in organizational practices.

3. **Intergroup conflict solidifies the group.**   When members of a group are faced with an external enemy, they tend to work together more closely to deal with it. A manager may use this new cohesion to reduce internal conflicts.

4. **Conflict serves as a catharsis.**   Conflict can provide an outlet through which organizational members can ventilate their feelings without damaging organizational functioning.

5. **Conflict resolution solidifies intergroup relationships.**   Once group conflict is successfully resolved, it can solidify the relationships between groups. "A good fight helps clear the air," and it may even make the groups feel closer to each other.

It should be noted that these benefits are possible but are not always achieved. If conflict stimulates diverse ideas, and if it is then resolved, it can have positive influences on organizational performance. However, unresolved conflicts can have detrimental effects on interpersonal, intergroup, and even intragroup relationships. Thus any effort to manage conflict must aim at promoting positive consequences while minimizing negative effects.

MANAGING INTERGROUP CONFLICT

Managing conflict is a major responsibility of managers. Conflict management involves both stimulating functional conflicts and resolving dysfunctional ones.

Recent developments in conflict management stress both conflict stimulation and conflict reduction techniques. As shown in Figure 10.3, conflict management attempts to maintain an optimal level of conflict at which differing ideas and viewpoints are fully considered but unproductive conflicts are discouraged. Since innovation and change are not encouraged at low levels of conflict, it might be desirable for management to stimulate some. Conversely, management should try to reduce high levels of conflict in order to avoid negative consequences.

FIGURE   10.3
Direction of Conflict Management.

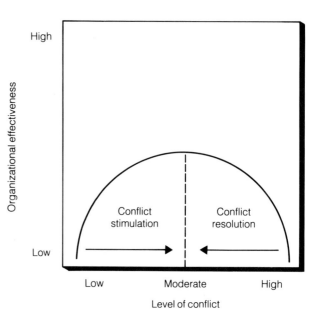

Stimulating Productive Conflicts

Robbins suggests the following as signs that conflict stimulation is needed:[20]

1. The organization is filled with "yes men."
2. Employees are afraid to admit ignorance.
3. Compromise is stressed in decision making.
4. Managers put too much emphasis on harmony and peace.
5. People are afraid of hurting the feelings of others.
6. Popularity is considered more important than technical competence.
7. People show great resistance to change.
8. New ideas are not forthcoming.
9. There is an unusually low rate of employee turnover.

Although one or two signs may not tell much, a number of them together can point up the need for conflict stimulation. Once the need is identified, management may adopt one or more of the following techniques to stimulate conflict.

1. **Use a nominal group process.** As shown in the preceding chapter, the nominal group process encourages members to generate diverse viewpoints.

2. **Encourage individualistic thinking.** Instead of relying on "yes men" for decision making, the group can be composed of people who freely express different viewpoints.

3. **Increase individual competition.** Management can recognize and reward individual or group differences in performance.

4. **Provide threatening information.** If there is any threatening information, such as a reduction in profits or the loss of a competitive edge in the market, tell the employees rather than trying to minimize its importance.

5. **Create role conflict.** Management can increase its expectations of employee performance. It can create a role conflict between perceived and enacted roles.

6. **Change the organizational structure.** Structural change often signals a need for change in behavior. It often involves transfer of organization members, job redefinition, and a new leadership structure.

These are only a few of the suggestions possible, but they give some idea of how management can create a desirable degree of conflict between individuals or groups.

Reducing Unproductive Conflicts

As pointed out earlier, the fundamental problems of intergroup conflicts are: (1) differences in goals, (2) the breakdown in interaction and communication, (3) distorted perceptions, and (4) antagonistic attitudes toward each other. Any effort to resolve group conflict, therefore, should address these problems. The strategies that can be employed are (1) locating a common enemy, (2) finding a superordinate goal, (3) individualizing the rival group, and (4) restructuring the organization.

Locating a Common Enemy.   The classical study by Sherif and Sherif illustrates how dysfunctional intergroup conflicts can be developed and subsequently resolved.[21] In the initial stages of the study, boys in a summer camp were divided into two groups, the "Bulldogs" and the "Red Devils." The groups were housed in different areas of the camp, and situations were arranged so that members of one group interfered with or frustrated the members of the other group. Competitive sports and harassments in the mess hall were enough to create hostility between the groups. Once the group conflict was created, the researchers formed an all-star baseball team out of the two rival groups. When this team played a game with a team from another camp, the attention of the whole camp shifted from their own conflict to defeating the rival camp. The implication is that the creation of an external enemy solidifies the relationships between groups within an organization.

Finding a Superordinate Goal.   This strategy is similar to finding a common enemy but may create a less intense emotional feeling. A *superordinate goal* is a goal that appeals to all of the parties involved and whose achievement requires their cooperation. For example, the Outdoor Equipment Company, mentioned earlier, could introduce a product line—such as home heating systems—that could produce business for the fall and winter seasons. This product line would occupy the functional departments throughout the year, so that there would be no need for departmental conflicts.

Individualizing the Rival Group.   Several studies indicate that the mere classification of people into different groups is sufficient to promote intergroup conflict and discrimination.[22] People develop biases against members of other groups because they are more depersonalized than members of their own group. Such an intergroup bias can be reduced by individualizing a rival group member. In an experiment, subjects were requested to invite a member of the rival group into their group sessions. The participation of the rival group member was found to be effective in reducing intergroup bias. When the member of the rival group is accepted as an individual, bias tends to be minimized.[23] Such individualization also tends to reduce intergroup stereotyping. An implication is that an exchange of membership can reduce intergroup conflict. When the exchanged member returns to his or her own group, the member is in a better position to communicate with the other group.

Restructuring the Organization.   Changing organizational structure is another way of reducing intergroup conflict. In order to facilitate cooperative efforts between groups, management can create coordinating bodies, such as the coordinating office or the project group. The *coordinating office* is a managerial group that moderates the differences between conflicting groups and integrates their activities. The person who occupies such an office (for example, general manager, executive vice-president, or president) needs to understand the differences in work orientation of the groups and possess formal and informal authority to moderate and coordinate. The *project group* is a work group composed of people from various functional groups created to perform a particular task. Since the project members are working on the same project, they may be able to reduce any goal conflict that exists between them. The structural influences on group and intergroup behavior will be further discussed in Chapter 16.

Third-Party Intervention

A third party can help conflicting parties resolve their differences.[24] The role of the third party, such as a consultant, is to provide an outlet by which the conflicting parties can assemble and search for solutions themselves. The interventionist guides the interaction process so that each party can listen to the other's frustrations and perceptions without engaging in argument or other behaviors that might escalate the conflict. Third-party intervention involves the following steps:

1.   The groups in conflict show a desire to resolve their conflicts. Mutual commitment to conflict resolution is essential to the success of this process.

2.   Each group is asked to prepare a list that describes the members' perceptions of the other group. This list may include a variety of things that bother the members or are considered important.

3.   Each group is asked to prepare another list describing the members' perceptions about themselves and the effects their behavior may have on the other group.

4. The groups are brought together to share the lists. This step is for information exchange only; it gives an opportunity to clarify some of the points raised by each group. It is not intended as a conflict resolution session.

5. The groups separate to react to the lists.

6. Each group lists, in order of importance, the issues or problems that need to be resolved.

7. The groups reassemble to agree on a common list of issues and problems they want to deal with.

8. The groups engage in problem-solving activities that may help resolve their differences.

9. As all differences cannot be resolved in one session, the groups develop action plans that can be carried out after the intervention session.

Preventing Unproductive Conflicts

As existing conflict is difficult to resolve, it is important to prevent unproductive intergroup conflicts from developing. Preventing such conflict is especially important for groups that need high levels of interaction. The greater the interdependence between them, the greater the undesirable consequences of group conflict on organizational performance.

Certain organizational characteristics encourage intergroup conflict. Division of labor, functional specialization, task dependence, limited resources, and performance appraisal are inevitable in most organizations, but they do contribute to intergroup conflict. Management, however, can do a number of things to minimize unnecessary conflicts between groups. The following suggestions can be used in minimizing intergroup conflicts.

Maintaining a Balanced Orientation.   Lawrence and Lorsch found that coordinators with high legitimate status, expertise in various functional areas, and personal attributes valued by different people could perform better than others because they were able to maintain a balanced approach to the demands of various work groups.[25] When coordinators lack such qualities, they lose a sense of balance and alienate certain groups while favoring others. An implication of this suggestion is that a coordinator such as a general manager or project director needs to have some training and experience in various functional areas.

Grouping Based on Task Interdependence.   Organizational activities are usually grouped along functional lines, such as production, sales, and research. People in these groups have similar technical backgrounds. But different groups have different backgrounds. When a task requires coordination between the groups, coordination is carried out by a high-level manager. A problem of this organizational design, however, is that it tends to foster intergroup conflict over resources and goals. Many of these conflicts can be avoided if people are grouped according to interaction requirements rather than occupational similarity. The rationale and strategy for various organizational designs are covered in Chapter 16.

Avoiding Unnecessary Zero-Sum Games.   Some managerial practices such as budgetary controls, cost and profit centers, and performance measurements intentionally or unintentionally promote competition among organization members and work groups. Performance responsibility on an individual or group basis increases competition between individuals or groups. Such competition promotes work motivation, but it also tends to destroy cooperation. Competition can be functional for those employees whose task performance can be accomplished independently, but it can be dysfunctional for those whose task performance involves interdependence. Competition should be deemphasized in task situations requiring a high level of interdependence.

Placing Emphasis on Superordinate Goals.   A major responsibility of top management is to create superordinate goals that appeal to all members and groups in the organization. Such goals tend to promote cooperation rather than competition. This approach may mean a change in managerial philosophy from that of pitting people or groups against each other to that of promoting collaboration. Some examples of superordinate goals are emphasizing competition against outsiders such as competitors, developing a companywide safety campaign, or instituting a profit-sharing plan for all employees.

SUMMARY AND CONCLUSION

Conflict is not inherently good or bad. It is good for the organization when it stimulates creativity and diversity in problem solving. But it can be bad if it does not help organizational goals. Unmanageable conflict often undermines cooperation, which is the fabric of an organization. Thus, the important task of management is to maintain an optimal level of functional conflict and to reduce dysfunctional conflict.

Intergroup conflict is caused by a number of circumstances. Among them are differences in group goals, task interdependence, differences in work orientation, competition for limited resources, and competitive reward systems. Division of labor, which is basic to organizational structure, also creates opportunities for intergroup conflict.

Groups differ in the ways they deal with conflict. They can use such behavioral strategies as collaboration, competition, compromise, accommodation, and avoidance. Collaboration and compromise are considered more positive than competition and avoidance. But all of these conflict-handling strategies can be useful in certain managerial situations.

There are a number of conflict-resolving strategies. Among them are (1) finding a common enemy, (2) finding a superordinate goal, (3) individualizing the rival group members, and (4) restructuring the organization. A combination of these strategies can be applied to reduce undesirable conflict. Management can also use the third-party intervention technique. This strategy differs from the others in that it does not try to resolve the conflict for the groups, but provides a forum where the groups can define and solve the problems themselves.

KEY CONCEPTS AND WORDS

Intergroup conflict	*Compromise*	*Pooled*
Rival group	*Avoidance*	* interdependence*
Task	*Accommodation*	*Sequential*
* interdependence*	*Conflict stimulation*	* interdependence*
Zero-sum game	*Third-party*	*Reciprocal*
Non-zero-sum game	* intervention*	* interdependence*
Collaboration	*Superordinate goal*	*Common enemy*

Questions for Review and Discussion

1. a.   What is conflict?
    b.   What causes intergroup conflict?

2. Traditionally, conflict has been thought undesirable and to be avoided. Explain why.

3. Some people feel that conflict is necessary for organizational vitality. Explain why.

4. What types of intergroup conflict do you think are most detrimental to organizational functioning?

5. a.   What is the difference between collaboration and compromise?
    b.   What strategy (or conflict-handling behavior) is likely to be used first? Explain why.

6. a.   What is a superordinate goal?
    b.   Give an example of how a superordinate goal can be effectively used to reduce intergroup conflict.

7. What happens to the relationships between groups when conflicts remain unresolved? Give some examples to support your answer.

8. Give some examples of managerial strategies that can help prevent intergroup conflicts.

 ## CASE AND EXERCISES

CASE 10.1. UNION STATE UNIVERSITY

This case is introduced to give students an opportunity to study the causes of intergroup conflict. You may analyze the kind of interdependence existing between work groups and see how this interdependence affects the behavior of organizational members.

The Situation

Since the mid-1970s, Union State University has been losing about 2 percent of its students each year. The current enrollment stands at 12,400 students (full-time equivalent). Among the important implications of this trend is the question of faculty staffing, tenure, and reduction. The university currently employs 703 faculty members. About 80 percent of them are primarily responsible for instruction, while the rest are responsible for other duties such as administration, research, and operating the library.

The governing agencies (the board of regents and the state legislature) have a policy that a state university should maintain a student-faculty ratio of 18 to 1. If the university fails to maintain this ratio for two consecutive years, faculty reduction occurs the following year. In order to maintain the required ratio, the university needs to have at least 12,650 students. If the university fails to attract 250 additional students in the coming academic year, it will have to discharge at least 14 faculty members. In view of the current enrollment trend, it is unlikely to attract that many students.

In order to deal with this problem, the administration has created a retrenchment committee charged with the task of formulating a faculty reduction plan. The committee is composed of eight faculty members—one from each of the colleges and one from the administration. The members are provided with a large volume of relevant data. Figure 10.4 shows the essence of these data.

If the enrollment decline were occurring uniformly throughout the colleges and departments, it would be much easier for the administration to allocate the losing positions. But the fact is that, while some colleges are losing students, others are steadily gaining them. Furthermore, the colleges with the decline in enrollment have more tenured faculty members (about 85 percent) than the colleges with growing enrollment (about 40 percent). If the positions are eliminated evenly, or if untenured faculty must be terminated first, the departments or colleges with rapid growth will be severely penalized.

The average number of credit hours taught by a faculty member varies from college to college. Faculty members in some colleges such as business and liberal arts teach more students than those in other colleges. (The average number of credit hours per faculty member can be found by dividing the total number of credit hours taught by a college by the total number of faculty mem-

Colleges and others	1978–1979 Academic year			1980–1981 Academic year			Percentage change in credit hours
	Students	Faculty	Total credit hours	Students	Faculty	Total credit hours	
Business	2,200	72	23,700	2,300	76	26,500	+12
Education	1,500	83	19,900	1,200	82	18,000	−10
Engineering	650	42	7,600	700	43	8,300	+9
Fine Arts	550	45	7,600	450	43	6,500	−14
Health related	500	56	6,200	550	58	6,800	+9
Liberal Arts and Sciences	3,400	275	82,800	2,900	269	73,200	−12
Others	4,100	135		4,300	132		
Total	12,900	708	147,800	12,400	703	139,300	−6

Note: Others include faculty and students in graduate school, continuing education, and university college. Other employees with faculty status who are serving in nonteaching functions are also included therein.

FIGURE   10.4
Student Enrollment and
Credit Hour Production.

bers in that college.) Differences in average number of credit hours stem from differences in teaching methods, the size of the faculty, and the number of students.

Discussion Questions

1. What kinds of interdependence are there between the colleges?
2. What might cause intergroup conflict?
3. Can you justify the differences in the number of students that a faculty teaches in different colleges?
4. If you were the administrator, how would handle the conflict? What are the bases for your action?

EXERCISE 10.1. UNION STATE UNIVERSITY

You may use Case 10.1 as the basis for an experiential learning process. Since you may have a cognitive understanding of the issue, you may try to resolve it experientially. This exercise will give you an opportunity to discover your own conflict-handling behavior, as well as those of others.

The Procedure

1. Eight of you may serve as the committee members. Each member will represent a certain college or the administration.

2. The committee is charged with deciding the following questions:
   a. How many positions should be eliminated from each college?
   b. Who should make the termination decisions?
   c. Should tenured faculty be removed?

3. The rest of you may observe the conflict-handling behaviors of the committee members, analyze the causes of conflict (if there is any), and see if any political coalition is emerging.

4. After the committee has spent about 30 minutes on the task, the class may discuss any issues related to intergroup conflict, political coalition, and conflict resolution.

EXERCISE 10.2. XYZ PAPER TOWER CONSTRUCTION

This exercise is designed to show you the effects of intergroup conflict on group behavior and to show how intergroup conflict can be resolved. The exercise can also be used with a discussion of task design, motivation, and reward systems.

The Situation

The XYZ Paper Tower Company constructs and markets paper towers in the international market. The tower is constructed of computer cards and tape. Since most customers want tall, strong, good-looking towers, management uses height, durability, and creativity as the criteria for judging the quality of prototype paper towers.

The Procedure

1. Divide yourselves into groups of five to seven members.

2. Each group should have Scotch tape and about 150 computer cards.

3. Each group has the task of constructing a prototype paper tower using the cards and tape. The group may not use any materials other than those provided and the surface on which the work is to be done. Each group has about 20 minutes to complete the task.

4. The instructor or a group of judges is to evaluate the performance of each group on the stated criteria. (The judges may use a ten-point scale for each performance criterion.) The judges announce their decision to the groups.

5. If the groups do not agree with the decision of the instructor or the judges, representatives from each group should resolve their differences. They have about seven minutes for this session.

6. If the group representatives cannot resolve the differences within seven minutes, no group will receive rewards. The instructor may then give them another three minutes to see if they can resolve the problem.

7. Discuss a number of issues or concepts that have been raised by the exercise. The discussion may involve such issues as division of labor, leadership, team spirit, competition, performance appraisal, coalition, and superordinate goals.

Footnotes

1. Eric H. Neilsen, "Understanding and Managing Intergroup Conflict," in *Organizational Behavior and Administration,* ed. P. R. Lawrence, L. B. Barnes, and J. W. Lorsch (Homewood, IL: Irwin, 1976), p. 291.

2. See Warren Bennis, "Leadership: A Beleaguered Species?" *Organizational Dynamics,* Summer 1976, 1–16.

3. K. W. Thomas and W. H. Schmidt, "A Survey of Managerial Interests with Respect to Conflict," *Academy of Management Journal,* 1976, **19,** 315–318.

4. See S. P. Robbins, "Conflict Management and Conflict Resolution Are Not Synonymous Terms," *California Management Review,* Winter 1978, 67–75.

5. I. L. Janis, *Victims of Groupthink* (Boston: Houghton Mifflin, 1972), pp. 15–40.

6. P. Binzen and J. R. Daughen, *Wreck of the Penn Central* (Boston: Little, Brown, 1971).

7. S. P. Robbins, *Managing Organizational Conflict* (Englewood Cliffs, NJ: Prentice-Hall, 1974), pp. 12–14.

8. W. M. Evan, "Conflict and Performance in R & D Organizations," *Industrial Management Review,* 1965, **7,** 37–45.

9. J. Hall and M. S. Williams, "A Comparison of Decision-Making Performance in Established and Ad Hoc Groups," *Journal of Personality and Social Psychology,* 1966, **3,** 214–222.

10. L. R. Hoffman, "Applying Experimental Research on Group Problem Solving to Organizations," *Journal of Applied Behavioral Science,* 1979, **15,** 375–391.

11. Robbins, *Managing Organizational Conflict,* pp. 12–14.

12. Evan, "Conflict and Performance."

13. See J. D. Thompson, *Organizations in Action* (New York: McGraw-Hill, 1966), pp. 54–55.

14. P. R. Lawrence and J. W. Lorsch, *Organization and Environment* (Boston: Graduate School of Business Administration, Harvard University, 1967); and J. W. Lorsch and P. R. Lawrence, "Organizing for Product Innovation," *Harvard Business Review,* January–February, 1965, 109–122.

15. Jeffrey Pfeffer, "Power and Resource Allocation in Organizations," in *Psychological Foundations of Organizational Behaviors,* ed B. M. Staw (Pacific Palisades, CA: Goodyear, 1977), pp. 278–301.

16. T. L. Rubble and K. W. Thomas, "Support for a Two-Dimensional Model of Conflict Behavior," *Organizational Behavior and Human Performance,* 1976, **16,** 143–155; and K. W. Thomas, "Toward Multi-Dimensional Values in Teaching: The Example of Conflict Behaviors," *Academy of Management Review,* July 1977, 484–490.

17. See C. B. Derr, "Managing Organizational Conflict," *California Management Review,* Winter 1978, 76–83.

18. E. H. Schein, *Organizational Psychology* (Englewood Cliffs, NJ: Prentice-Hall, 1980), pp. 172–176; and R. R. Blake and J. S. Mouton, "Reactions to Intergroup Competition under Win-Lose Conditions," *Management Science,* 1961, **7,** 420–435.

19. K. W. Thomas and L. R. Pondy, "Toward an 'Intent' Model of Conflict Management Among Principal Parties," *Human Relations,* 1977, **30,** 1089–1102.

20. Robbins, "Conflict Management," p. 71.

21. See M. Sherif and C. W. Sherif, *Groups in Harmony and Tension* (New York: Harper & Row, 1953).

22. V. L. Allen and D. A. Wilder, "Categorization, Belief Similarity, and Intergroup Discrimination," *Journal of Personality and Social Psychology,* 1975, **32,** 971–977; H. Tajfel and M. Billing, "Familarity and Categorization in Intergroup Behavior," *Journal of Experimental Social Psychology,* 1974, **10,** 159–170; and see M. B. Brewer, "In-Group Bias in the Minimal Intergroup Situation: A Cognitive-Motivational Analysis," *Psychological Bulletin,* 1979, **86,** 307–324.

23. D. A. Wilder, "Reduction in Intergroup Discrimination Through Individualization of the Out-Group," *Journal of Personality and Social Psychology,* 1978, **36,** 1361–1374.

24. Richard Beckhard, *Organizational Development* (Reading, MA: Addison-Wesley, 1969), pp. 33–35; E. H. Schein, *Process Consultation* (Reading, MA: Addison-Wesley, 1969), pp. 70–75; and R. R. Blake, H. Shepard, and J. S. Mouton, *Managing Intergroup Conflict in Industry* (Houston: Gulf Publishing, 1964).

25. Lawrence and Lorsch, *Organization and Environment,* chap. 3.

MANAGEMENT AND ORGANIZATIONAL BEHAVIOR

1. Understanding the Job of Managing

2. Studying Organizational Behavior

INDIVIDUAL BEHAVIOR

3. Satisfying Human Needs

4. Learning and Reinforcing

5. Understanding the Perceptual Process

6. Understanding the Motivational Process

SUPERVISORY BEHAVIOR

11. Understanding the Leadership Process

12. Developing Leadership Skills

13. Acquiring and Using Power in Organizations

14. Managing Reward Systems

INTERPERSONAL AND GROUP BEHAVIOR

7. Understanding Interpersonal Dynamics

8. Improving Communication Effectiveness

9. Understanding Group Dynamics

10. Dealing with Intergroup Conflicts

ENVIRONMENTAL ADAPTATION

15. Task Design—Matching Jobs to People

16. Designing Organizational Structure

17. Making Managerial Decisions

18. Managing Organizational Change

Micro-organizational analysis

Macro-organizational analysis

ORGANIZATIONAL EFFECTIVENESS

19. Developing Effective Organizations

APPENDIX

Developing Careers in Organizations

SUPERVISORY BEHAVIOR

Most managers spend a great deal of their time interacting with their subordinates. These interactions occur so managers can lead their subordinates toward achieving organizational goals. Leadership is the opposite of motivation in this goal-oriented process. While the analysis of motivation focuses on employee behavior, the analysis of leadership focuses on leader behavior. Part IV is primarily concerned with understanding the complex process of leadership, and it presents ways of helping managers and would-be managers become more effective leaders.

Chapter 11 reviews several major theories of leadership. These theories are then integrated into a leadership process model. Fiedler's contingency theory and the path–goal theory of leadership are reviewed in this chapter. Chapter 12 is primarily concerned with developing leadership skills. It presents a set of action guidelines for improving leadership effectiveness through leadership skill development. Chapter 13 contends that managers need power to influence their subordinates. It identifies various sources of managerial power and discusses ways of acquiring and using it. Chapter 14 is concerned with ways of measuring and rewarding employees' contributions to their organizations. Managing reward systems is an important part of supervisory behavior.

LEARNING OBJECTIVES

1. To understand the leadership process in organizations.
2. To learn how various personal and situational factors influence leadership effectiveness.
3. To learn a set of leadership principles or guidelines.

CHAPTER

11 UNDERSTANDING THE LEADERSHIP PROCESS

In the United States leadership is exercised by all kinds of people. The leader is not a man who dresses in a distinctive fashion, sits in impressive surroundings, and issues commands. . . . This diversity of leadership is a product of our pluralistic way of life, and is essential to the continuance of that way of life. . . . The varied leadership of our society must come to recognize that one of the great functions of leadership is to help a society to achieve the best that is in it.

John W. Gardner, Excellence[1]

Leadership is a fascinating subject to most people. It is intriguing because all people are affected by the actions of leaders and because most people, at one time or another, are placed in leadership positions—as parents, officers in organizations, or leaders in society. Without proper leadership, an organization or society drifts aimlessly and is eventually subjugated by another that exercises proper leadership. The quality of leadership often determines the success or failure of an organization.

Leadership is defined as the process of influencing other people toward accomplishing group tasks. It involves a complex set of interpersonal and organizational interactions. Leadership effectiveness increases when a leader's personal characteristics are compatible with the characteristics of the subordinates, group tasks, and other organizational influences. This chapter focuses on the relationships between the personal traits of leaders, leader behaviors, and situational factors. To this end, it reviews the trait, behavioral, and contingency theories of leadership.

MANAGEMENT AND LEADERSHIP

> *Leadership is a tool of management. Managers exercise leadership to influence employees to achieve organizational goals.*

Before various theories of leadership are reviewed, we will investigate the dynamics of leadership and its relationships to management. This section deals with the distinction between leadership and management.

Definitions of Managership and Leadership

The terms *management, managership,* and *leadership* are so closely related that the distinctions between them have become blurred. However, they can be defined in the following manner:

Management is a process of planning, organizing, coordinating, and controlling the activities of other people.

Managership is the authority to carry out these management functions.

Leadership is the process of influencing other people for the purpose of achieving shared goals.

Both managership and leadership are management tools with which managers can influence the behavior of employees to achieve organizational goals. The distinction between them can be made on the basis of the qualifications that managers have. Managers, by virtue of being in a managerial position, have managership, but they may not possess leadership or the ability to influence other people.

Attributes of Leaders

Only successful managers can have the attributes of both managership and leadership. The following attributes of leaders further point out the distinction between leadership and managership.

1. **Leaders have followers.** Not all managers are leaders. Managers have other people to supervise, but if these people are not willing to accept and follow the supervisory authority, the managers are not leaders. Subordinates may comply with the supervisory command out of fear, but such compliance is not a response to leadership. By the same token, not all leaders are managers. Some leaders may have followers, but if they lack the formal authority to manage, they are

not managers. For example, informal leaders in a work group are leaders, but they are not managers.

2. **Leaders have emotional appeal.** Zaleznik points out the differences in our expectations of the behavior of managers and of leaders.[2] Managers are expected to be rational decision makers and problem solvers. They are expected to use their analytical minds in the process of establishing and achieving organizational goals. Leaders, however, are expected to be charismatic people with great visions who can alter the mood of their followers and raise their hopes and expectations.

3. **Leaders meet the needs of followers.** Both managers and leaders are responsible for meeting the demands of the organization as well as the demands of its members. However, managers are expected to be more concerned with attaining organizational goals, while leaders are expected to be more concerned with meeting the needs of their followers. Managers cannot be good managers without meeting organizational goals. Likewise, leaders cannot be good leaders without satisfying their followers' needs.

Both Terms Used to Refer to Managers

Although we have made a distinction between managership and leadership, the two terms can be used interrelatedly, if not interchangeably. Both of them are important tools of management; managers can use them together in the process of managing employees. Managership gives managers the formal authority to manage the employees, while leadership gives them a means of securing voluntary compliance from the employees.

THE LEADERSHIP PROCESS MODEL

> *Leadership is a complex social phenomenon that is affected by a number of personal, interpersonal, and organizational factors, including (1) the personal traits of the leader, (2) the leader's behavior, and (3) situational factors—subordinates, tasks, and organizational practices.*

The leadership process model, shown in Figure 11.1, identifies a number of factors that affect leadership effectiveness. It describes the process by which a leader's personal traits and the various factors in the environment affect the selection of a particular leader behavior that, in turn, influences the behavior of work group members—in other words, it

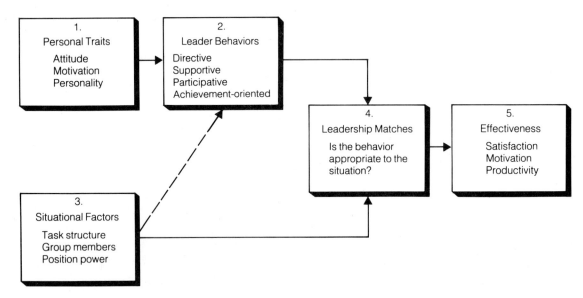

FIGURE 11.1
An Integrated Leadership Process Model.

describes leadership effectiveness. More specifically, the model contains the following leadership variables:

1. **Personal traits.** Managers have certain personal traits, such as attitude, motivation, and personality. These traits influence their behavior as leaders. For example, a manager who can trust other people is more likely to consult with his or her subordinates than a manager who does not.

2. **Leader behaviors.** Managers exhibit certain behavioral patterns in the course of managing other people. These leader behaviors reflect their own personal traits and the situational demands. Among the common leader behaviors are: (1) directive, (2) supportive, (3) participative, and (4) achievement-oriented behaviors.

3. **Situational factors.** Managers do not operate in a vacuum. The environment in which they operate influences their behavior. Environmental influences affecting leader behavior are called *situational factors.* Among the important situational factors are: (1) group tasks, (2) group members, and (3) organizational practices such as the formal authority granted to the manager.

4. **Leadership matches.** In order for managers to function effectively as leaders, they need to exhibit leader behavior that is suitable to their personal traits and the situational demands. If these are mismatched, they are not likely to function effectively. A leadership match can be realized by:
    a. Finding leadership situations that are suitable to the manager's personal traits and leader behaviors.

    b.   Modifying situational factors to suit them to the manager's traits and behaviors.

    c.   Increasing versatility of leadership styles to match varying situations.

5.   **Leadership effectiveness.**   The effectiveness of a leader behavior is expected to increase when there is a match between leadership styles and situations.[3] Leadership effectiveness can be measured by the degree to which the manager meets organizational goals (task function) and satisfies the needs of employees (maintenance function).

This model is an overview of the leadership process that occurs in organizations. It shows how leader behaviors interact with situational factors to determine leadership effectiveness. Several theories of leadership are closely related to the key variables identified in this process model. For example, *trait theories* are related to personal traits of leaders. *Behavioral theories* study the effects of leader behaviors on leadership effectiveness. *Contingency theories* examine the interactions between personal traits, leader behaviors, and situational factors.

TRAIT THEORIES OF LEADERSHIP

> *Trait theories of leadership focus on the individual characteristics of successful leaders. It is almost impossible, however, to find characteristics that make leaders successful in all situations.*

Most leadership theories before the mid-1950s were primarily concerned with discovering the personal traits of successful leaders. Trait theorists searched extensively for psychological, emotional, biographical, intellectual, and motivational characteristics that were associated with successful leaders or managers.

Findings of Trait Theorists

On the basis of a thorough review of the literature, Stogdill points out that successful leaders tend to have the following qualities:[4]

1.   A strong desire for task accomplishment.

2.   Persistent pursuit of goals.

3.   Creativity and intelligence used to solve problems.

4.   Initiative applied to social situations.

5. Self-assured personality.
6. Willingness to accept behavioral consequences.
7. Low susceptibility to interpersonal stress.
8. High tolerance for ambiguity.
9. Ability to influence other people.
10. Ability to structure social interactions.

A similar list of desirable traits was prepared by Ghiselli.[5] Except for the last two items, Ghiselli's list of traits is the same as Stogdill's list.

There has been little systematic study of the personal traits of unsuccessful leaders, but ineffective leadership is probably associated with certain personal characteristics such as poor temperament, inability to get along with others, and mental health problems such as aggression, depression, disorganization, paranoia, neurosis, and procrastination. In addition, some attitudinal factors seem to be associated with ineffective leadership. These include: (1) overconcern with morale, (2) failure to maintain an objective attitude, (3) lack of a sense of proportion, (4) practicing "polarization," or seeing things as either good or bad, (5) idealism in decision making, and (6) overeagerness to do the "right" thing.[6]

Absence of Universal Traits

Trait theorists searched for a list of personal characteristics that would make leaders effective in all situations, but they failed to produce such a list. Some traits, such as intelligence and appearance, seemed to be important in all leadership situations, but subsequent investigations yielded inconsistent results.[7] The problem is that a certain personal trait, though desirable in some situations, is not desirable in others. For example, although high intelligence may be desirable in dealing with professional personnel, it can be a disadvantage in dealing with uneducated workers.

Given the many situational factors that influence leadership effectiveness, it is doubtful whether research can produce a set of universally acceptable traits that would make leaders effective in all situations. Nevertheless, trait theorists can make a significant contribution to the study of leadership if they can identify a set of leadership traits associated with particular situations. For example, successful sales managers are outgoing, achievement-oriented, enthusiastic, and so forth.

BEHAVIORAL THEORIES OF LEADERSHIP

> *Behavioral theories of leadership attempt to find the effects of leader behaviors—such as structuring and consideration—on employee behaviors.*

Behavioral theories of leadership focus on the relationship between leader behaviors and employee reactions. Instead of trying to determine what successful leaders are, the researchers focus on what leaders actually do. This behavioral approach to leadership was popular until the mid-1960s. The two groups of researchers who were mainly responsible for pursuing the behavioral approach to leadership did studies at Ohio State University and the University of Michigan.

The Ohio State University Studies

The well-publicized Ohio State studies started shortly after World War II. The studies initially concentrated on leadership in military organizations.[8] Their primary objective was to identify the major dimensions of leadership and to investigate the effects of leader behavior on employee satisfaction and performance. From a list of leader behaviors (instruction, communication, production emphasis, task assignment, evaluation, fraternization, consultation, fair treatment, and so forth), the Ohio State group identified consideration and initiating structure as two major dimensions of leadership.

1. **Consideration** refers to leader behavior that can be characterized by friendliness, respect, supportiveness, openness, trust, and concern for the welfare of the employees.

2. **Initiating structure** refers to leader behavior that defines and organizes the group tasks, assigns the tasks to employees, and supervises their activities.

The findings of the Ohio State studies can be summarized as follows:

1. Initiating structure was positively related to employee performance but was also associated with such negative consequences as absenteeism and grievances.

2. Consideration was positively related to low absenteeism and grievances, but it was negatively or neutrally related to performance.

3. When both consideration and structure were high, both productivity and satisfaction tended to be high. But, in some cases, high productivity was accompanied by absenteeism and grievances.

These findings were challenged by other studies that failed to find evidence of the predictive relationships between leader behaviors and employee reactions.[9] These studies found that a number of situational factors (such as the nature of the task, the characteristics of the employees, and the organizational climate) interfered with the predictive relationships. For example, when job pressure is high, the relationship between initiating structure and performance is more positive than when the pressure is low. When the task is intrinsically motivating, the relationship between consideration and satisfaction is less positive, and the relationship between structure and satisfaction is less negative.[10]

The University of Michigan Studies

About the same time the Ohio State studies were being conducted, a group of researchers at the University of Michigan were investigating the leadership styles associated with high-performing and low-performing groups.[11] They found two distinctive styles of leadership that were similar to, but different from, the two leader behaviors of the Ohio State studies. They called the two styles *job-centered* and *employee-centered.*

1. The *job-centered leader* uses close supervision so employees perform their jobs according to specified procedures. This type of leader exercises formal authority to influence the behavior and performance of employees.

2. The *employee-centered leader* uses general supervision, delegation, and supportiveness in supervising employees. This kind of leader is concerned with employees' personal growth as well as task achievement.

The Michigan studies failed to find any consistent relationship between the use of one leadership style and managerial effectiveness. In studying the effects of leadership style on employee behaviors in two different industries (insurance and railroad), Katz and his associates found that a job-centered leadership style was effective in less structured job situations (such as railroad track crews) where the supervisor could provide some technical assistance and operational instructions. But it was dysfunctional in highly structured job situations (such as with insurance clerks), where the employees did not need any detailed supervision.[12]

In a later study, the researchers at the University of Michigan found that both job-centered and employee-centered leaders were able to increase productivity in clerical task situations.[13] They found, however, that employee satisfaction was higher in the employee-centered work groups than in the job-centered work groups. After interpreting these results Likert argued that employee-centered leadership is more effective than job-centered leadership.[14] This is because the former is concerned with the long-term productivity increase, while the latter is primarily short-term oriented. Likert further indicated, however, that employee-centered leadership correlates with a number of group and member characteristics, such as skilled group members, institutional loyalty, well-established working relationships, and supportive climate. It is doubtful whether employee-centered leadership can be effective without such characteristics.

The Managerial Grid®

Blake and Mouton developed a conceptual framework for studying leadership that was termed the *Managerial Grid.* Instead of dichotomizing the two dimensions of leadership, Blake and Mouton contended that managers should be concerned with both people and production in order to achieve effective performance results.[15]

The Managerial Grid is shown in Figure 11.2. The grid identifies five basic styles of leadership. The 9,1 leader is primarily concerned with

FIGURE 11.2
The Managerial Grid. (After Robert R. Blake and Jane S. Mouton, *The New Managerial Grid.* Houston: Gulf Publishing Co., copyright © 1978, p. 11. Used with permission.)

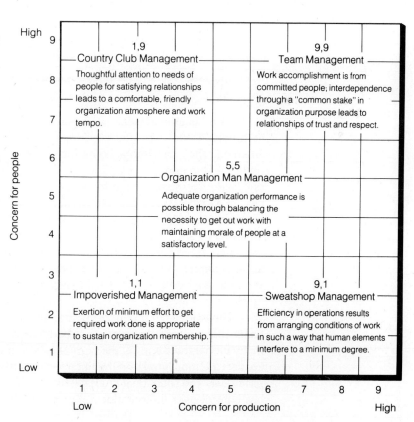

production and has little concern for people. This person wants to get the job done at all costs. The 1,9 leader is primarily concerned with people and has little concern for production. The 1,1 leader has little concern for either people or production. The 5,5 style reflects a moderate concern for both. The 9,9 leadership style is viewed as the ideal approach to leadership; it shows a maximum concern for both people and production.

Support for the Managerial Grid concept is available in the form of case analysis. Blake and Mouton state that organizations that have gone through Managerial Grid training have seen behavioral changes among their employees toward more cooperative working relationships and increases in productivity. The grid concept, however, has not been fully supported by other forms of research. For example, it cannot explain why productivity increases under production- or people-oriented leadership in some situations.

 ## FIEDLER'S CONTINGENCY THEORY OF LEADERSHIP

> *According to Fiedler, the leadership process is a function of the leader's motivational traits and situational factors, and its effectiveness increases when they are matched.*

As it became evident that behavioral theories were also inadequate to predict leadership effectiveness, contingency or situational theories emerged. They take into account the effects of various situational factors on leadership effectiveness. The major theme of these theories is that no one leadership style is good for all situations. The selection and effectiveness of a leadership style depends on the interaction of the personal traits of the leader, the characteristics of subordinates, and the situational factors. Mary Parker Follett, an early social scientist, called this the "law of the situation."[16] Two major situational theories of leadership are discussed in this chapter—Fiedler's contingency model and the path–goal theory. We examine Fiedler's model in this section and the path–goal theory in the next.

The leadership model developed by Fiedler and his associates contends that the effectiveness of a leader is a function of (1) his or her motivational traits and (2) the favorableness of the leadership situation.[17] Leaders are motivated by either interpersonal relations or task-goal accomplishment. The situational favorableness is the extent to which the leader has control over the situation.

Leader's Motivational Traits

Managers differ in their motivation on the job. Some managers (task-motivated) place primary emphasis on "getting the job done"; others (relation-motivated) are primarily concerned with "getting along with other people." Once these primary concerns are satisfied, the managers will place emphasis on other concerns. The psychological profiles of relation-motivated and task-motivated leaders are as follows:

1. **Relation-motivated leaders.** Although these leaders are concerned with doing a good job, they are even more concerned with maintaining good interpersonal relationships. As their self-esteem depends largely on how other people relate to them, they are quite sensitive to the needs and feelings of others. Even if they do not wish to work with certain people, they still respect their feelings. Because of their sensitivity to others, they can be effective in applying participative leader behavior.

2. **Task-motivated leaders.** As these leaders are primarily concerned with getting the job done, their self-esteem comes from accomplishing tangible goals. They put so much emphasis on task accomplishment that they tend to judge other people on the basis of whether or not they can work with them. If they can, they will consider them to be "good" people. When things are under control, they may become considerate and pay attention to the needs of employees. However, under unfavorable situations, they may become directive leaders.

The leader's motivational traits are measured by having him or her describe the characteristics of the least preferred co-worker (see Figure 11.3). This measurement is called the LPC (Least Preferred Co-worker) scale. According to Fiedler, leaders who describe the characteristics of the LPC in positive terms, such as pleasant and friendly, are considered to be relation-motivated; those who describe the LPC in negative terms, such as unpleasant and unfriendly, are considered to be task-motivated. In other words, leaders who rate other people on the basis of interpersonal relationships are considered to be relation-motivated. Those who rate others on the basis of task competence are considered to be task-motivated.

Situational Factors   Other major determinants of leadership effectiveness are the situational factors surrounding the leader. As shown in Figure 11.4, the leadership situation is composed of three major factors: (1) leader–member relations, (2) task structure, and (3) position power.

1. **Leader–member relations.** This factor shows the degree to which a leader maintains good relationships with his or her subordinates,

The LPC Scale

Think of the person with whom you can work least well. He or she may be someone you work with now or someone you knew in the past.

He or she does not have to be the person you like least well but should be the person with whom you had the most difficulty in getting a job done. Describe how this person appears to you.

Pleasant	8	7	6	5	4	3	2	1	Unpleasant
Friendly	8	7	6	5	4	3	2	1	Unfriendly
Rejecting	1	2	3	4	5	6	7	8	Accepting
Helpful	8	7	6	5	4	3	2	1	Frustrating
Unenthusiastic	1	2	3	4	5	6	7	8	Enthusiastic
Tense	1	2	3	4	5	6	7	8	Relaxed
Distant	1	2	3	4	5	6	7	8	Close
Cold	1	2	3	4	5	6	7	8	Warm
Cooperative	8	7	6	5	4	3	2	1	Uncooperative
Supportive	8	7	6	5	4	3	2	1	Hostile
Boring	1	2	3	4	5	6	7	8	Interesting
Quarrelsome	1	2	3	4	5	6	7	8	Harmonious
Self-assured	8	7	6	5	4	3	2	1	Hesitant
Efficient	8	7	6	5	4	3	2	1	Inefficient
Gloomy	1	2	3	4	5	6	7	8	Cheerful
Open	8	7	6	5	4	3	2	1	Guarded

FIGURE 11.3
The Least Preferred Co-worker (LPC) Scale. (After Fred E. Fiedler, *A Theory of Leadership Effectiveness.* New York: McGraw-Hill, 1967, p. 41. Used with permission.)

and the degree to which the subordinates are willing to comply with the leader's wishes. If the relationships are good and the subordinates have the necessary job skills, the situation is said to be favorable. (See the Leadership Situation Survey in Exercise 11.1.)

2. **Task structure.** This factor describes the degree to which the task has a well-defined goal, its methods of operation are clearly defined, its accomplishment can be easily measured, and it leads to a unique solution. When the task is well structured and the workers know what is to be done, the situation is said to be favorable to the leader.

3. **Position power.** This factor describes the extent to which the position enables the leader to gain compliance from his or her subor-

FIGURE   11.4
The Essence of Fiedler's
Contingency Theory.

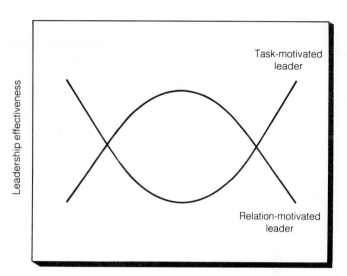

Situational favorableness

Situational Factors	High Control	Moderate Control	Low Control
Leader–member relations	Good	Neutral	Poor
Task structure	High	Medium	Low
Position power	Strong	Moderate	Weak

dinates. Position power comprises formal authority and reward power. The authority to reward, punish, and fire employees is included in position power. The more position power leaders have, the more favorable the situation is for them.

Overall situational favorableness is determined by the combination of these situational factors. A high-control situation occurs where the leader has good leader-member relations, highly structured tasks, and strong position power. A low-control situation exists when the leader has poor relationships with subordinates, unstructured tasks, and weak position power. Between these two situations exists a moderate-control situation.

Finding a Leadership Match

The contingency theory predicts that task-motivated leaders will perform better than relation-motivated leaders in high- or low-control situations, whereas relation-motivated leaders will do well in moderate-control situations. What are the reasons for this prediction? Figure 11.4 shows a leadership match between leader traits and situations.

High-Control Situation.   Since task performance is controlled in high-control situations, task-motivated leaders should be able to relax and even become considerate toward their subordinates. By doing so, they can meet the needs of both the organization and its members—task and maintenance functions. On the other hand, relation-motivated leaders, who pride themselves on being able to solve problems with interpersonal skills, do not find much challenge in this situation. Since their subordinates are willing to comply with their wishes, the managers do not have much opportunity to use their interpersonal abilities.

Moderate-Control Situation.   Relation-motivated leaders perform best in this situation because they are able to accomplish task goals by using their interpersonal skills. They are sensitive to the needs of group members, encourage others to participate in the group process, and incorporate different viewpoints in solving complex problems. On the other hand, task-motivated leaders are so engrossed in accomplishing the task that they are not able to deal patiently with interpersonal conflicts and pay little attention to the needs and feelings of their work group members.

Low-Control Situation.   In this situation, task-motivated leaders should be able to provide the direction that the employees want. When the situation is chaotic, people will be more concerned with direction and leadership than with interpersonal likes or dislikes. Although leaders may irritate subordinates at times by being directive, they can quickly achieve task-oriented goals by structuring and monitoring the group tasks. On the other hand, relation-motivated leaders are so concerned with interpersonal relationships that they feel uneasy about making decisions without consulting others. Their hesitation to make decisions can be seen as poor leadership.

Examples of Leadership Match

The following examples show how leaders' traits can be matched with job situations. In military organizations, task-motivated leaders are likely to perform better than relation-motivated leaders, since most situations are either very favorable or very unfavorable. In peacetime, military tasks tend to be highly structured and routinized, the officers have strong position power, and subordinates are expected to be submissive to them. In this highly favorable situation, the task-motivated officers can be considerate of the needs of their followers.

In wartime, however, the situation is usually characterized by unfavorable conditions, for tasks are not well defined and become chaotic at times. Subordinates may even resist orders, as happened during the Vietnam conflict. Under these unfavorable conditions, task-motivated officers should provide direction and exercise formal authority to control the behavior of their followers.

In collegial organizations such as university and professional associations, relation-motivated leaders can function more effectively than task-oriented leaders. For example, most teaching jobs in a university are not well structured, the professors tend to be highly individualistic, and tenure systems protect the teachers' academic freedom—and jobs. In this situation, administrators have to be skillful and relation-oriented in dealing with professors. They must be sensitive to the needs of the faculty to gain any cooperation.

Evaluation of the Contingency Model

Many studies have been conducted to test the validity of the contingency model. Although several of them have supported the model,[18] a significant number have questioned its validity.[19] In addition to this lack of research support, the model can also be criticized from theoretical perspectives.

Theoretical Limitations.   Three major criticisms are directed against the contingency model.

1.   Some scholars argue that the contingency model lacks a theoretical orientation.[20] Since it has been developed from research data rather than based on a theoretical scheme, it has a predictive power but lacks an explanatory power. It does not adequately explain how and why one particular leadership trait is more desirable than others in a particular situation.

2.   There is a question of what the LPC scale measures. It does not satisfactorily explain how and why leaders who describe least preferred co-workers in negative terms are considered to be task-motivated and those who describe them in positive terms are considered relation-motivated. Therefore, the theory generally lacks explanatory power.

3.   The model is based on the assumption that leaders do not change their motivational traits. Although it is true that a person's leadership style is stable in the short run, people have the capacity to change their motivational traits and leadership styles over a period of time. It is possible that people are more task-oriented in their earlier years but become more relation-oriented in their later years.

Reasons for Its Success.   Despite these criticisms, the contingency model has proven to be an important addition to the study of leadership, for two reasons. First, it accommodates a number of personal and situational factors in the study of leadership. Instead of suggesting one best leadership trait or style for all situations, it specifies various leadership situations in which a particular leadership trait or style can be effective. Second, it operationalizes the model into a set of actions that can be used to improve one's leadership effectiveness.

The following leadership principles can be drawn from this contingency model:

1. **Find leadership situations that suit leadership styles (traits and behaviors).**   Leaders can increase leadership effectiveness by being in situations that match their leadership styles. To this end, leaders must have an accurate perception of their own leadership styles and situational demands.

2. **Change situational factors to suit leadership styles.**   If leaders find themselves in situations that do not match their own leadership styles, they may attempt to modify the situational factors—leader–member relations, task structure, and position power. The methods of changing situational factors are presented in Chapter 12.

 ## PATH–GOAL THEORY OF LEADERSHIP

> *The path–goal leadership theory explains how and why certain leader behaviors are more effective than others in particular situations. It also specifies situational conditions under which each leadership style can be effectively used.*

The path–goal theory of leadership has its origin in the expectancy theory of motivation. As pointed out in Chapter 6, the expectancy theory of motivation specifies the path to goal attainment. More specifically, the theory indicates that people make motivational choices based on how they perceive (1) the valence of rewards, (2) the performance-reward instrumentality, and (3) the effort-performance expectancy. In other words, employees will be motivated to perform tasks if they perceive that (1) their efforts can result in task accomplishment (expectancy), (2) their performance leads to certain rewards (instrumentality), and (3) the rewards offered can satisfy their needs (valence).

According to the path–goal theory, leaders can influence the behavior of employees by helping to clarify the path to goal attainment.[21] The term *path–goal* is used because the theory focuses on how a leader influences employees' perceptions of the valence, instrumentality, and expectancy. A manager can become a path–goal leader by:

1. **Matching rewards to employee needs.** The manager should know what employees want from their jobs and try to satisfy these needs as much as possible.

2. **Matching rewards to performance.** The manager should try to reward employees on their performance, either individually or as a group, to encourage high performance.

3. **Matching jobs to people.** When employees' technical and psychological qualifications match the task requirements, the employees are likely to perceive that their efforts are well utilized in task performance.

To path–goal theorists, motivating employees is the same as leading them. However, they go further in terms of explaining why certain leader behaviors are more effective in particular situations. They argue that a leader's task is to compensate for something that is lacking in a leadership situation. For example, if the task is ambiguous and the employee wants clarity, the leader should be able to provide it.

House and Mitchell have investigated the relationships between four leadership behaviors (directive, supportive, participative, and achievement-oriented) and several situational factors, including employee and task characteristics (see Figure 11.5).[22] They seem to consider the situational factors as given, and ask how a leader can help employees achieve their goals within the situational constraints. In this section we review the characteristics of different leader behaviors and specify situational conditions under which a particular behavior can be effectively used.

FIGURE 11.5
The Essence of Path–Goal Theory.

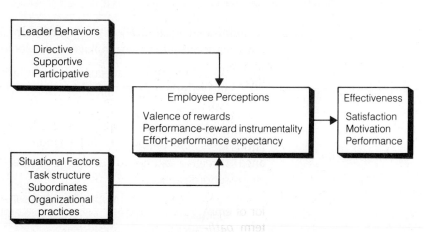

Directive Leader Behavior

Directive leader behavior is often called "boss-centered" leadership, "leader facilitation," "leader structure," or sometimes "instrumental leadership." The major characteristic of directive leadership is that the leader initiates the task structure of the subordinates' work and guides them to achieve their task goals.

Characteristics of Directive Leadership. Directive leadership can be manifested in many ways. Managers using directive leader behavior tend to:

1. Define the group's performance goals.
2. Assign responsibilities for individual performance.
3. Establish a well-defined chain of command.
4. Train employees to perform the tasks.
5. Provide the necessary information and instructions.
6. Use rewards and punishments to control employee behavior.
7. Define performance-reward relationships.

Directive leader behavior is positively correlated with employee satisfaction and job performance in some situations but is dysfunctional in others. When employees perceive that directive leader behavior benefits their need satisfaction and task accomplishment, it has a positive impact on these.

Conditions Favoring Directive Leadership. Directive leadership can have a positive impact on employee behavior in the following situations.[23]

1. When the job is so unstructured that task ambiguity creates tension and frustration for employees, supervisory efforts to structure the task are perceived as benefiting task accomplishment.
2. When subordinates expect their supervisor to be directive, directive leadership satisfies that expectation.
3. Directive leadership satisfies the dependency need of submissive subordinates.
4. When subordinates depend on the supervisor for information and technical support, the supervisor's coaching behavior is perceived as assisting task accomplishment.
5. When the supervisor has strong position power—the power backing of the organization—subordinates are more receptive to directive leadership.

Conversely, when tasks are highly structured and their path–goal relationships are clearly defined by the system, supervisory efforts to further structure the tasks or operational procedures are perceived as unnecessary. Also, self-directed employees with sufficient job knowledge and skills will perceive supervisory instructions and directions as excessive. In these situations, directive leadership adds no job or organizational dimensions that benefit employee need satisfaction and task performance.

Supportive Leader Behavior

Supportive leadership is often called "leader consideration," "people-oriented," or "employee-centered leadership." It is characterized by friendly, approachable, and considerate leader behavior. Such leader behavior can have a positive impact on employee satisfaction and job performance. It is helpful in satisfying socialization needs of employees and in improving cooperation between supervisor and subordinates.

Characteristics of Supportive Leadership. Managers who use supportive leader behavior tend to:

1. Show personal interest in subordinates.
2. Be friendly and approachable.
3. Provide ongoing personal consultations.
4. Encourage subordinates to express their feelings and concerns.
5. Strive for harmony in the work group.
6. Use rewards as a means of gaining support.
7. Use positive rewards rather than negative sanctions.

A number of studies have shown that supportive leadership is positively correlated with positive attitudes, satisfaction, and—in some cases—job performance of employees.[24] Supportive leader behavior not only satisfies the socialization needs of employees but also the expectancy that their efforts will be adequately and equitably rewarded.

Conditions Favoring Supportive Leadership. Supportive leadership can have a positive impact on employee behavior in the following situations:[25]

1. Supportive leadership is desirable when tasks are highly structured. A supportive leader can reduce the frustration resulting from routinized tasks that provide little intrinsic job satisfaction.
2. Workers with high socialization needs tend to react favorably to supportive leader behavior. Office parties, picnics, frequent coffee breaks, and "happy hours" help them satisfy socialization needs.

3. When the job requires a high degree of interaction among work group members, supportive leader behavior can foster the needed interactions, for it can promote a cooperative climate.

In some situations, however, supportive leadership can have a negative impact on employee behavior. When there is a feeling of uncertainty and frustration because tasks are not well structured, supportive leader behavior may not help employees achieve task goals. With low task structure, structuring leader behavior is of more help to workers than leader consideration. Any undue emphasis on supportive leader behavior that does not help task performance is seen as a sign of weakness and incompetence. Also, when a trusting relationship is lacking between managers and subordinates, the subordinates may take advantage of supportive leader behavior. They may no longer be afraid of being punished for poor performance and so may reduce their efforts. In general, supportive leader behavior is more closely related to employee satisfaction than to job performance.

Participative Leader Behavior

Participative leadership is often called "group management" or "team management" because the manager shares the responsibility of performing the task and maintenance functions with work group members. Participative leaders share information and power with their subordinates in decision-making and implementation processes.

Characteristics of Participative Leadership.   Although participation means different things to different people, we can identify certain common characteristics. Managers who use participative leadership tend to:

1. Allow group members to define their own performance goals.
2. Permit group members to structure their own jobs.
3. Negotiate differences or difficulties with subordinates.
4. Use employee participation as a means of communicating.
5. Allow group members to exercise control over their performance progress.
6. Use group-based reward systems rather than individual-based systems.
7. Share the group's successes and failures with subordinates.

Participative leader behavior has been recommended as a means of increasing employee motivation. However, the relationship between participative leadership and employee behavior is ambiguous and is often modified by the characteristics of both subordinates and tasks. For example, employees with little need for independence and achievement may not respond positively to participative leader behavior, for they perform better under directive leadership.

The amount of knowledge possessed by participants and the level of their intelligence also moderates the effectiveness of participative leadership. When participants lack the necessary information and intelligence, they have little to contribute to high-quality decisions.

Conditions Favoring Participative Leadership.   Participative leadership can have a positive impact on employee behavior in the following situations:[26]

1.   Participative leadership is most successful when the tasks are intrinsically motivating—interesting, challenging, and moderately structured.

2.   When the group tasks require a high degree of interaction among employees, participative leadership can increase the frequency and quality of the interactions, thus promoting cooperation.

3.   Workers with a strong need for independence and achievement are more receptive to participative leadership than dependent workers.

4.   Individuals whose goals are compatible with organizational or group goals are more receptive to participative leadership.

5.   Participants should have the necessary knowledge and information to make quality decisions. When they do not have such characteristics, directive leadership can be more productive than participative leadership.

6.   Participative leader behavior can be used when acceptance of decisions by employees is important in the implementation process.

Although participative leadership is widely recommended, many managers find it difficult to be participative. This style requires a high degree of trust between the manager and subordinates, and the manager should also have a high level of interpersonal competence. Unlike other leader behaviors, it requires interpersonal interactions between equals rather than between dominant and submissive individuals. Because it requires a high degree of interpersonal skill and sensitivity, relation-motivated leaders are likely to use it more effectively than task-motivated leaders. When task-motivated leaders use it, the employees may perceive it as manipulation or deceit.

Achievement-Oriented Leadership

Achievement-oriented leader behavior is a special case of the participative leader behavior. It emphasizes setting challenging goals, expects employees to perform at their fullest ability, and shows a high degree of confidence in employee ability to assume performance responsibility. The conditions under which this approach can be effectively used are the same as those conditions for participative behavior. However, this approach can be more effective for achievement-oriented individuals who are performing complex tasks.

Evaluation of Path–Goal Theory

As pointed out earlier, several studies on consideration and initiating structure provide some support for certain aspects of the path–goal theory. This support is mostly related to the moderating effect of task structure on the relationship between leader behavior and employee behavior.

Strengths of the Theory.   The major strength of this theory is its ability to explain how and why certain leadership styles can be effective in particular situations and not in others. Path–goal theory draws its explanatory power from the expectancy theory of motivation. That is, the leader influences employee behavior by strengthening employee perceptions of the motivational elements of valence, instrumentality, and expectancy. The clues to how managers can positively influence these motivational elements are found in the expectancy theory presented in Chapter 6.

Problems with the Theory.   A major problem with path–goal theory is that it is difficult to test successfully since it involves a complex set of variables. Just as expectancy theory is hard to test, so is testing the validity of path–goal theory. Another limitation is the assumption that leaders can change their behaviors to suit different leadership situations. It does not consider the effect of personal traits that may limit the selection of leader behaviors. Notice that the strength of the path–goal theory is the limitation of Fiedler's contingency theory, and vice versa. By integrating the two situational theories of leadership, as the leadership process model suggests, we can better explain the leadership phenomenon in organizations.

LEADERSHIP EFFECTIVENESS

> *The leader has an impact on organizational effectiveness. However, because there are so many factors influencing organizational performance, it is questionable whether one leader can make a major difference in the organization's performance.*

Behavioral scientists have devoted considerable resources, time, and effort to studying leadership, but there is still controversy over whether it has any significant impact on organizational performance. In this section we summarize some of the conflicting findings about leadership's influence on organizational performance.

Situational Influence

Two studies have demonstrated the significant impact of situational factors on organizational performance. A study by Lieberson and O'Conner reported that organizational performance, as measured by profits, sales, and profit margin, is mostly attributable to such situational factors as year (economic trend), industry, and company. Only a small portion of performance variance could be explained by leadership.[27] The organizational characteristics of a company, such as size, location, product, and reputation, are closely related to profits and sales (67.7 and 64.8 percents respectively). Leadership accounted for 8 percent of profits, 7 percent of sales, and 15 percent of profit margins.

Salancik and Pfeffer reported similar results.[28] In studying the effects of mayors on municipal budgets, they found that mayors had little effect on property tax revenue (5 percent), while the nature of the city had a significant effect (86 percent). Mayors, however, had some impact on the level of general debt (24 percent), although the city factor accounted for more than twice that.

Leadership Influence

Despite these discouraging reports that leadership makes little difference in organizational performance, the importance of leadership in organizational functioning cannot be ignored. It is doubtful whether an organization can function effectively without effective leadership, although it often appears that an organization or the country is running itself. But both have management systems that guide the behavior of their members. Employees will open a store in the morning and close it in the evening whether the manager is there or not. University classes are taught without the deans appearing to lead the faculty members.

Yet we also know that the course of our history has often been changed by leaders such as Bismarck, Churchill, Eisenhower, Henry Ford, the Founding Fathers, Ghandi, Martin Luther King, Jr., Lenin, Lincoln, Mao Tse-tung, and Truman. Some of them were history makers, while others—such as President Truman and Martin Luther King—became leaders because of the historical processes at work at the time. The greatness of leaders is measured by the degree to which they are able to change the situational factors in the environment or to use the environmental forces.

In organizations, effective leaders are people who have a strong impact on situational factors such as product, organizational structure, technology, and reputation. If these situational factors are considered a function of leadership, then leadership accounts for most organizational successes or failures.[29]

Leadership Constraints

Effective leaders can make a difference in organizational performance. However, the extent to which one leader can have a major impact on organizational effectiveness is limited by a number of personal, organizational, and environmental constraints. Among them are leadership inflexibility, the selection process, leadership fragmentation, pressure groups, and external factors, including governments.[30]

Leadership Inflexibility.   Most managers are limited in their leadership versatility. Job situations may require a variety of leadership behaviors or styles, but managers are often unable to adjust their leadership styles to match the situations. In addition, pressures to conform to the role expectations of other people may limit the use of certain leadership styles.

Selection Process.   The leader selection process often hinders the selection of the best qualified leader for a position. People have a tendency to rate favorably those individuals whom they perceive to be similar, and this personal like or dislike is likely to influence the selection process. An implication of this observation is that people who are mediocre are more likely to select mediocre individuals as their leaders.

Leadership Fragmentation.   In many organizations, leadership is divided among so many individuals that no one can have a strong impact on organizational performance. In government, for example, the governing responsibility is divided into the legislative, judicial, and executive branches. In each branch—especially the executive—responsibility is shared by an army of bureaucrats. Every president since Roosevelt has lamented his inability to make changes because of this fragmented authority. This situation exists also in other organizations.

Pressure Groups.   Gone are the days when managers made decisions and subordinates followed. There are now so many interest and pressure groups, inside and outside the organization, questioning and challenging managerial decisions, that many managers are very cautious about or even afraid of making decisions. These groups are consumerists, environmentalists, feminists, racial minorities, special interest groups, and government agencies, to name just a few. When managers are afraid of taking leadership roles, nothing much can happen in an organization.

External Factors.   Many environmental factors are beyond a leader's control. For example, production costs are largely determined by the prices of energy, raw materials, labor, and externally imposed standards. For example, all cars must have seat belts, which cost around $70 to $75 per car. Customer preference is another example, which is to a large extent a function of economic conditions and customer tastes. Consequently, leaders' successes or failures in many cases result from external circumstances beyond their control.

In conclusion, then, leadership is only one component affecting organizational performance and managerial effectiveness, and it should not be overemphasized at the expense of other managerial functions. Managers must plan, organize, and control various organizational activities in addition to performing the leadership function.

SUMMARY AND CONCLUSION

Leadership theories have developed in three phases: Trait theories came first, followed by behavioral theories, and then situational or contingency theories. The trait approach to leadership tried to identify universal traits of successful leaders. The behavioral approach focused on leader behaviors that might lead to successful performance. The situational approach tried to integrate the first two approaches.

Two situational leadership theories were presented in this chapter: Fiedler's contingency theory and the path–goal theory. Fiedler's contingency theory examines the relationships between the leader's motivational traits and the situational favorableness in which the leader operates. It predicts that task-motivated leaders perform better in favorable and unfavorable situations, whereas relation-motivated leaders perform better in moderately favorable situations. Path–goal theory specifies situational conditions under which particular leader behaviors (directive, supportive, and participative) can be effectively utilized.

The essence of situational leadership theories is that leadership effectiveness increases when leadership styles (trait and behavior) match the situation. A leadership match can be realized by adopting the following leadership principles:

1. Find a leadership situation that suits the leadership style.
2. Modify the situational factors to make them suitable to the leadership style.
3. Acquire a variety of leadership styles to adapt to varying situations.
4. Select an appropriate leadership style to match the situation.

KEY CONCEPTS AND WORDS

Leadership
Managership
Trait theory
Behavioral theory
Consideration
Initiating structure
Contingency theory of leadership
Path–goal theory of leadership

Leadership match
The Managerial Grid
Task-motivated leader
Relation-motivated leader
Task structure
Position power
Leader–member relations

Directive leader behavior
Supportive leader behavior
Participative leader behavior
Situational favorableness

Questions for Review and Discussion

1. a. What makes a leader different from a manager?
   b. What are the essential elements of leadership?
2. a. What are the major themes of trait theories?
   b. What are the major themes of behavioral theories?
   c. What are the major differences between the two?
3. a. What are the major themes of Fiedler's contingency model of leadership?
   b. What are the strong points of this model?
   c. What are its limitations?
4. a. What is the path–goal theory of leadership?
   b. What are the major themes of this theory?
   c. What are its strengths and limitations?
5. a. What are the similarities between Fiedler's contingency model and path–goal theory?

    b.   What are the dissimilarities?

    c.   How are they related? Are they complementary or competitive?

6.   How reasonable is it to expect a leader to change his or her leadership style to match various leadership situations?

7.   a.   What are some constraints that reduce the effectiveness of a leader?

    b.   How realistic is it to expect a leader to remove each of these constraints?

8.   At least two studies in the chapter suggest that leadership does not make much difference in organizational performance. What is your reaction to their argument?

EXERCISES

EXERCISE 11.1. STARLITE CHEMICAL CORPORATION

This exercise is designed to give you an opportunity to develop your diagnostic skill in finding a leadership situation where you can function effectively. To this end, you need to analyze your own leadership style and the leadership situation, and see if your style is compatible with the situational demands.

The Situation

The Starlite Chemical Corporation is looking for a marketing director to replace the previous one, who was fired for incompetence. The situation is less than desirable, as the competition is very keen. A continuous marketing campaign is needed just to sustain present sales volume. The major responsibility of the director is to ensure a continuous flow of creative marketing campaigns; this requires favorable leader–member relations. But because of the job pressure, there was a great deal of interpersonal conflict between the former director and the department members, and among the members themselves.

    The directorship provides the formal authority to hire and fire the employees, but it is often difficult to exercise this authority because the labor market has been tight, and it is difficult to recruit competent personnel. Also, it is suspected that if the director exercises negative sanctions against employees, it may build up further employee resentment.

    Management wants to hire someone who can take charge of the department and make it productive. You are a senior member in the department and are considered a candidate. You want the job, but you are wondering whether or not you are suited for it.

The Procedure

1.   Identify your own motivational style by responding to the LPC scale in Figure 11.3. To determine your LPC score, add the numbers you have checked in

the column. If your score is 64 or above, you are considered a relation-motivated leader. If your score is 57 or below, you are a task-motivated leader.

2. Identify the situational favorableness by using the leadership situation survey that follows. If you have two or fewer Y's for a situational dimension, it is considered unfavorable. Three and four Y's are considered moderately favorable. Five or more Y's are considered favorable.

3. See if your style is suitable to the situation. Use Figure 11.4 as a guide in finding a leadership match.

4. Discuss how much faith you will put in such an analysis. You may point out the pros and cons of this analysis.

Leadership Situation Survey

Instructions: Respond to the following questions with Y (yes) or N (no).

_____ 1. Are the group members supportive of the leader?

_____ 2. Is there a friendly atmosphere among workers?

_____ 3. Are they submissive and loyal to the leader?

_____ 4. Do they have the necessary job skills and knowledge?

_____ 5. Are their personal goals compatible with group goals?

_____ 6. Is their performance satisfactory?

_____ 7. Are group goals clearly defined?

_____ 8. Are operational procedures clearly established?

_____ 9. Is the task simplified so that anyone can perform it?

_____ 10. Is there a specific way to accomplish the task?

_____ 11. Is there one correct answer or solution to the problem?

_____ 12. Is it easy to check on whether or not the job was performed correctly?

_____ 13. Does the manager have a formal, official title?

_____ 14. Does the manager have the formal authority to evaluate employees' job performance?

_____ 15. Does the manager have the formal authority to hire and fire employees?

_____ 16. Does the manager have the formal authority to reward employees?

_____ 17. Does the manager receive strong support from his or her superior?

_____ 18. Does the manager have the necessary job skills?

Scoring: Count the Y's for each situational dimension.

_____ Leader-member dimension (1 through 6)

_____ Task dimension (7 through 12)

_____ Position power dimension (13 through 18)

EXERCISE 11.2. IDENTIFYING LEADERSHIP STYLES

This exercise is designed to help you identify your own leadership style (or leader behavior) and the styles of others. This exercise can be used in conjunction with other subjects such as organizational climate and group productivity.

The Procedure

1. Identify your own leadership style (or leader behavior) using the leadership style survey that follows.

2. See if there is any relationship between your leadership style and the organizational climate of your work group. (This step can be done if you are a manager.) The organizational climate survey can be obtained from Chapter 9.

3. You may study the relation between your leadership style or the leadership style of the manager you surveyed and the organizational climate of your work group or the manager's work group.

4. This exercise can be conducted in conjunction with other subjects such as group performance and employee satisfaction.

Leadership Style Survey

Instructions: Respond to each item with Y (yes) or N (no).

_____ 1. Do you define the group's task goals?

_____ 2. Do you show personal interest in employees?

_____ 3. Do you allow group members to set their task goals?

_____ 4. Do you tell employees what jobs should be done and how?

_____ 5. Are you friendly and approachable?

_____ 6. Do you allow group members to structure their own jobs?

_____ 7. Do you establish a clear chain of command?

_____ 8. Do you encourage employees to express their feelings and concerns?

_____ 9. Do you use employee participation as a means of communication?

_____ 10. Do you provide the necessary information and instruction?

_____ 11. Do you discourage conflict among group members?

_____ 12. Do you encourage teamwork rather than competition?

_____ 13. Do you tell employees how they will be rewarded?

_____ 14. Do you reward employees to make them happy?

_____ 15. Do you encourage employees to discuss any conflicts or problems with the supervisor?

_____ 16. Do you use rewards and punishments to control the employees?

_____ 17. Do you emphasize loyalty and interpersonal relations?

_____ 18. Do you share the group's success and failure with group members?

Scoring: Add the number of Y's for each leadership style.
_____ Directive leadership (1, 4, 7, 10, 13, 16)
_____ Supportive leadership (2, 5, 8, 11, 14, 17)
_____ Participative leadership (3, 6, 9, 12, 15, 18)

Footnotes

1. John W. Gardner, *Excellence* (New York: Harper & Row, 1961), pp. 123–124.

2. Abraham Zaleznik, "Managers and Leaders: Are They Different?" *Harvard Business Review,* May–June 1977, 67–68; and also see E. E. Berlew, "Leadership and Organizational Excitement," in *Organizational Psychology,* ed. D. A. Kolb, I. M. Rubin, and J. M. McIntyre (Englewood Cliffs, NJ: Prentice-Hall, 1979), pp. 343–356.

3. See Robert Tannenbaum and W. H. Schmidt, "How to Choose a Leadership Pattern," *Harvard Business Review,* May–June 1973, 162–180; and F. E. Fiedler and M. M. Chemers, *Leadership and Effective Management* (Glenview, IL: Scott, Foresman, 1974).

4. R. M. Stogdill, *Handbook of Leadership* (New York: Free Press, 1974), p. 81.

5. E. E. Ghiselli, *Exploration in Managerial Talent* (Pacific Palisades, CA: Goodyear, 1971).

6. L. C. Megginson, *Personnel: A Behavioral Approach to Administration,* rev. ed. (Homewood, IL: Irwin, 1972), pp. 528–532.

7. R. M. Stogdill, "Personal Factors Associated with Leadership: A Survey of the Literature," *Journal of Psychology,* January 1948, 35–71; and C. A. Gibb, "The Principles and Traits of Leadership," *Journal of Abnormal Psychology,* 1947, **42,** 267–284.

8. R. M. Stogdill and A. E. Coons, *Leader Behavior: Its Description and Measurement* (Columbus, OH: Bureau of Business Research, Ohio State University, 1957); E. A. Fleishman, E. F. Harris, and H. E. Burtt, *Leadership and Supervision in Industry* (Columbus, OH: Bureau of Business Research, Ohio State University, 1955); and E. A. Fleishman and D. R. Peters, "Interpersonal Values, Leadership Attitudes, and Managerial Success," *Personnel Psychology,* 1962, **15,** 127–145.

9. A. K. Korman, "Consideration, Initiating Structure, and Organizational Criteria: A Review," *Personnel Psychology,* 1966, **19,** 349–

361; and S. Kerr, C. A. Schriescheim, C. J. Murphy, and R. M. Stogdill, "Toward a Contingency Theory of Leadership Based upon the Consideration and Initiating Structure Literature," *Organizational Behavior and Human Performance,* 1974, **12,** 62–82.

10. Kerr, Schriescheim, Murphy, and Stogdill, "Toward a Contingency Theory."

11. D. Katz, N. M. Maccoby, G. Gurin, and L. Floor, *Productivity, Supervision, and Morale Among Railroad Workers* (Ann Arbor: Institute for Social Research, University of Michigan, 1951); and D. Katz, N. M. Maccoby, and N. Morse, *Productivity, Supervision, and Morale in an Office Situation* (Ann Arbor: Institute for Social Research, University of Michigan, 1950).

12. Katz, Maccoby, Gurin, and Floor, *Productivity, Supervision, and Morale,* pp. 33–34.

13. N. C. Morse and E. Reimer, "The Experimental Change of a Major Organizational Variable," *Journal of Abnormal and Social Psychology,* January 1956, 120–129.

14. Rensis Likert, *New Pattern of Management* (New York: McGraw-Hill, 1961), chapters 5 and 8.

15. R. R. Blake and J. S. Mouton, *The Managerial Grid* (Houston: Gulf Publishing, 1964); and R. R. Blake and J. S. Mouton, *The New Managerial Grid* (Houston: Gulf Publishing, 1978).

16. Mary Parker Follett, *Freedom and Co-ordination* (London: Management Publications Trust, 1949), pp. 47–60.

17. F. E. Fiedler, *A Theory of Leadership Effectiveness* (New York: McGraw-Hill, 1967).

18. M. J. Chemers and G. J. Skryzypek, "An Empirical Test of the Contingency Model of Leadership Effectiveness," *Journal of Personal and Social Psychology,* 1972, **24,** 172–177; F. E. Fiedler, "Validation and Extension of the Contingency Model of Leadership Effectiveness: A Review of Empirical Findings," *Psychological Bulletin,* 1971, **76,** 128–148; and L. S. Csoka and P. M. Bons, "Manipulating the Situation to Fit the Leader's Style: Two Validation Studies of LEADER MATCH," *Journal of Applied Psychology,* 1978, **63,** 295–300; and R. W. Rice, "Psychometric Properties of the Esteem for Least Preferred Coworker (LPC Scale)," *Academy of Management Review,* January 1978, 106–111.

19. B. Graen, K. Alvares, J. B. Orris, and J. A. Martella, "Contingency Model of Leadership Effectiveness: Antecedent and Evidential Results," *Psychological Bulletin,* 1970, **74,** 285–296; S. E. Ashour,

"The Contingency Model of Leadership Effectiveness: An Evaluation," *Organizational Behavior and Human Performance,* 1973, **9,** 339–355; and R. P. Vecchio, "An Empirical Investigation of the Validity of Fiedler's Model of Leadership Effectiveness," *Organizational Behavior and Human Performance,* 1977, **19,** 180–206.

20. Ashour, "The Contingency Model"; and C. A. Schriescheim and Steven Kerr, "Theories and Measures of Leadership: A Critical Appraisal of Current and Future Directions," in *Leadership: The Cutting Edge,* ed. J. G. Hunt and L. L. Larson (Carbondale: Southern Illinois University Press, 1977), pp. 9–45 and 51–56.

21. M. G. Evans, "The Effects of Supervisory Behavior and the Path Goal Relationship," *Organizational Behavior and Human Performance,* 1970, **5,** 277–298; and R. J. House, "A Path Goal Theory of Leadership Effectiveness," *Administrative Science Quarterly,* 1971, **16,** 321–338.

22. R. J. House and T. R. Mitchell, "Path–Goal Theory of Leadership," *Journal of Contemporary Business,* 1974, **5,** 81–97.

23. See House and Mitchell, "Path–Goal Theory," and Kerr, Schriescheim, Murphy, and Stogdill, "Toward a Contingency Theory."

24. H. K. Downey, J. E. Sheridan, and J. W. Slocum, "Analysis of Relationships Among Leader Behavior and Satisfaction: A Path–Goal Approach," *Academy of Management Journal,* 1975, **18,** 253–262; and Katz, Maccoby, and Morse, *Productivity, Supervision, and Morale.*

25. House and Mitchell, "Path–Goal Theory"; and J. E. Stinson and T. W. Johnson, "The Goal–Path Theory of Leadership: A Partial Test and Suggested Refinement," *Academy of Management Journal,* 1975, **18,** 242–252.

26. T. R. Mitchell, "Motivation and Participation: An Integration," *Academy of Management Journal,* 1973, **16,** 670–679; and House and Mitchell, "Path–Goal Theory."

27. S. Lieberson and J. F. O'Conner, "Leadership and Organizational Performance: A Study of Large Corporations," *American Sociological Review,* 1972, **37,** 117–130.

28. G. Salancik and J. Pfeffer, "Constraints on Administrative Discretion: The Limited Influence of Mayors on City Budgets," *Urban Affairs Quarterly,* 1977, **12,** 475–496.

29. Nan Weiner, "Situational and Leadership Influences on Organization Performance," *Academy of Management Proceedings—1978,* 38th Annual Meeting, San Francisco, California, August 1978, pp. 230–234.

30.   See Jeffrey Pfeffer, "The Ambiguity of Leadership," *Academy of Management Review,* January 1977, 104–112; and Warren Bennis, "Leadership: A Beleaguered Species?" *Organizational Dynamics,* Summer 1976, 1–16.

LEARNING OBJECTIVES

1. To learn how to modify a leadership situation to make it compatible to one's leadership traits and behaviors.
2. To learn how to develop positive exchange relationships with superiors and subordinates.
3. To learn to develop leadership versatility.
4. To know how to select an appropriate leader behavior.

CHAPTER OUTLINE

12 DEVELOPING LEADERSHIP SKILLS

Leadership training essentially is leadership experience compressed in time. We distill the experiences of others into rules and guidelines, and we simulate typical problems in leadership situations. We role-play them, or we discuss instances or cases in which problems or conflicts have occurred, so that the leader in training will vicariously experience some of these problems prior to meeting them in real life.

F. E. Fiedler and M. M. Chemers, Leadership and Effective Management[1]

Countless billions of dollars are spent each year by business, government, and other organizations to train managers to be more effective. These efforts have many names, such as supervisory training, executive development, and management development, but all of them are primarily concerned with improving leadership effectiveness—in increasing employee performance and improving interpersonal relations.

What skills will improve leadership effectiveness? Can these skills be developed or improved? What are the methods used to develop these skills? These are some of the questions that are discussed in this chapter.

Leadership effectiveness increases when a manager's leadership style matches the situational demands. There are several ways in which managers can find such a leadership match (see Figure 12.1). First, managers can seek leadership situations that are compatible with their own leadership styles—their own traits and behaviors. Second, managers may modify the situational factors to suit them to their own styles. Finally, managers may change their behaviors to match the situational factors. The first strategy was discussed in Chapter 11; this chapter focuses on the last two strategies.

MODIFYING SITUATIONAL FACTORS

> *When managers find themselves in situations that do not match their leader behaviors, they may change the situational factors to make them suitable. This strategy, however, is not a long-term solution to leadership deficiency.*

Some managers have acquired a variety of leader behaviors and become flexible in selecting the appropriate ones for different situations. But most inexperienced and nonversatile managers may find it difficult to be flexible. Levitt and Fiedler and his associates question whether managers can change leadership styles that were shaped at an early age and have been with them for most of their lives.[2] Because changing a style can be difficult, many managers may find it easier to change leadership situations than to change their behavior. Fiedler and his associates suggest that managers can change their leadership situation by modifying (1) leader–member relations, (2) task structure, and (3) position power.[3]

Modifying Leader–Member Relations

FIGURE 12.1
The Leadership Process and Change.

The relationship between leaders and their subordinates is perhaps the single most important relationship dimension determining a leader's effec-

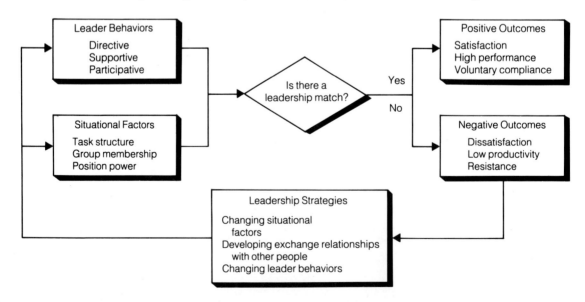

tiveness. From an intuitive standpoint, when a manager maintains a favorable relationship with employees, he or she will be better able to influence them on the job.

There are two things a manager can do to improve his or her relationship with employees. The first is to change the group membership by hiring more loyal subordinates, or by transferring out employees who cause problems. This is an effective method, but many managers may find it difficult because they lack either the power or the desire to carry out such changes.

The second is to improve the relationship with present subordinates by making a conscious effort to be more considerate of their needs and by increasing interpersonal sensitivity and skills. More specifically, managers can improve overall leader–member relations by:

1. Spending more time with subordinates informally.

2. Organizing some off-work social activities.

3. Increasing rewards for subordinates, such as pay increases, special bonuses, promotions, and more attractive jobs.

4. Increasing job-related interactions through use of an "open-door policy" and "gripe sessions."

5. Sharing information with subordinates.

Although most managers want to maintain favorable relationships with their subordinates, it is not always desirable in creating effective work groups. Having too close a personal relationship with subordinates makes it difficult to discipline them. Managers who are overconcerned with interpersonal relationships or with being accepted by subordinates may find themselves playing favorites and being indecisive. It is sometimes wiser for managers to maintain a psychological distance so they can exercise formal authority.

Modifying Task Structure

Since people differ as to the amount of task structure they prefer,[4] managers may wish to restructure the tasks and work procedures. If they want highly structured jobs, they may restructure their jobs by:

1. Requesting a clear job description from the superior.

2. Learning as much as possible about the job.

3. Obtaining further training.

4. Simplifying the tasks through job simplification.

5. Volunteering for structured tasks.

6. Avoiding unstructured tasks.

If managers want to structure subordinates' jobs, they can do so by:

1. Defining the group task goals.
2. Establishing operational guidelines and procedures.
3. Defining individual task responsibilities.
4. Preparing job descriptions.
5. Providing job training.
6. Simplifying the tasks.

This structuring behavior increases a manager's control over the situation, but high task structure is not necessarily desirable for everyone. As the situational favorableness increases, job challenge may decrease for some managers.

If managers want to reduce task structure, they can do so in several ways. They may (1) find a less structured job situation, (2) hire people who are less qualified to do the job, or (3) add more job content and responsibility to the existing job. These strategies will make the job less structured and provide managers with more challenge.

Modifying Position Power

Task-motivated leaders seem to require position power to exercise leadership. Since they lack interpersonal sensitivity and skills, they tend to rely on formal position power to compel compliance from subordinates.[5]

Increasing Position Power. If a situation requires strong position power, the manager may increase it by:

1. Acquiring formal power bases—such as being able to hire, fire, reward, and punish subordinates.
2. Gaining more support from superiors in exercising position power.
3. Showing willingness to exercise formal position power, especially coercion.
4. Controlling information flow by collecting, hoarding, and selectively disseminating vital information.
5. Removing other power holders through transfer or other means.

Decreasing Position Power. An increase in position power is desirable for some, but it can be cumbersome to others. Some situations demand that the manager rely on informal power bases (expertise, charisma, and association) rather than formal power bases (reward and coercion) to accomplish group tasks. For example, professional employees such as lawyers, engineers, and university professors tend to have more respect for supervisors who rely more on informal than on formal power. In fact, they may even perceive the use of formal position power as a sign of powerlessness.[6]

If a situation indicates the need for informal power, the manager can increase it by:

1. Gaining expertise in the field.
2. Developing interpersonal sensitivity and skills.
3. Maintaining a network of interpersonal and social contacts in and out of the organization.
4. Sharing information with subordinates.
5. Using a participative approach to decision making.
6. Exercising formal power unobtrusively.

Evaluating the Modification Strategy

Some managers are versatile in adapting their leader behavior to different situations, but others are not. Nonversatile managers may change situational factors to make them compatible to their own leadership styles. Such a strategy, however, has several limitations and should be used with caution.

First, the strategy does not increase leadership versatility. Managers lacking broad leadership styles cannot function effectively in job situations requiring leadership versatility. For example, a general manager or project manager has to deal with people with different personal and technical backgrounds, and these people may expect different kinds of leader behavior from the manager.

Second, the manager's ability to change situational factors is limited. Group tasks are usually structured by the company's operational policies or by task design engineers. It takes time to hire, fire, or transfer people in and out of the work group. The manager's position power is set by the company's managerial policies, and, to bring about a change, the manager must have considerable power. Yet acquiring and using such power requires a great amount of time and skill.

Finally, even if the manager were able to modify the situational factors, some people might resent being manipulated and might retaliate against the manipulator. As people tend not to respect manipulators, if a manager is known as a manipulator, it might ruin his or her career.[7] Furthermore, moving people into and out of work groups and manipulating position power can adversely affect the lives of some people and can cause them to resist.[8]

CHANGING LEADER BEHAVIORS

> *In order to adapt to different leadership situations, managers need to acquire a variety of leader behaviors. It may take time to learn a new leader behavior, but once acquired, it can add to leadership versatility.*

Fiedler's contingency theory of leadership assumes that leadership is something people are born with and that any attempt to change it is a futile exercise. If this assertion is true, any discussion on leadership beyond Fiedler's theory is useless. However, other theories of leadership do assume leadership versatility. It may be true that our behavioral options are to some extent limited by our personal traits (attitudes, beliefs, motivation, and personality), but it is also true that people have the capacity to learn and change their behaviors.

If managers are not able to change their behaviors, and adapt to changing leadership situations, their careers are doomed to fail. The situational factors that make up a leadership situation change constantly, and any change in these can cause a leadership mismatch that may lead to managerial ineffectiveness. Some managerial jobs, such as general manager and project manager, require a variety of leader behaviors to deal with people in various functional groups. The following episode illustrates the need for changing leader behavior.

> *Pat Jones, an engineer, was recently promoted to computer project manager of a computer manufacturing company. She joined the company upon graduation, with honors, from a state university about five years ago, and is respected by her colleagues as a competent engineer.*
>
> *As a task-motivated leader, Jones emphasizes getting the job done and becomes impatient when things are not moving as planned. She barely tolerates employee tardiness or any other performance delays. Although the project is relatively well organized, many unexpected problems need to be resolved. Some of these problems—such as labor market conditions, labor strikes, raw materials, and customer-induced specification changes—are beyond the control of the project group.*
>
> *In order to deal with the task ambiguity caused by these problems, Jones is becoming increasingly directive in demanding that project members develop a set of contingency plans. Several*

project members who are older and more experienced have been complaining that many of the problems could be dealt with as they occur, and that the contingency plans are unnecessary and even wasteful.

In analyzing the above situation, you may find it "moderately favorable." The project is moderately structured, the leader–member relations are moderate, and the manager's position power is also moderate. According to Fiedler's contingency theory, a relation-motivated manager should function better in such a situation than a task-motivated manager. Since relation-motivated managers would be sensitive to the needs of other people and skillful in dealing with them, those managers should be more successful in securing cooperation from them.

Faced with this leadership mismatch, what can Jones do to improve her effectiveness as a leader? There seem to be three choices. First, she can try to change the situational factors to make them suitable to her own leader behavior. Second, she can change her behavior to suit the situation. Finally, she can leave the position. The first strategy may appeal to her, because it does not require much change on her part. However, it is doubtful whether she has enough power to change situational factors like group membership and supervisory support. Furthermore, such a change may not serve the interest of the organization because it may create an adversary relationship with the other engineers.

She may best serve the company and herself if she changes her behavior as leader of a professional work group. A number of leadership training programs (the Managerial Grid and sensitivity training, for example) promise a drastic change in leader behavior. However, whether or not she can benefit from such a program is questionable. Such programs require a psychological readiness—openness, receptiveness, and lack of defensive behavior—on the part of the participant. When a manager is under pressure like Jones, it is doubtful whether he or she will be receptive to such programs.

The decision to adopt a particular method of behavioral change depends on (1) the perceived ability of the person to perform the new behavior, (2) the perceived relationship between the new behavior and its resultant outcomes, and (3) the attractiveness or valence of the outcomes.[9] In other words, unless the person views the suggested change as useful and something that he or she can perform, the method is not likely to be adopted. This is probably why training programs like those mentioned are not widely practiced.[10]

What choices does Pat Jones have? Before she attempts to learn an entirely new leadership style or tries to be manipulative, she needs to direct her attention to the relationships she has with her subordinates and her superiors. Instead of just asking them to meet her needs, she should try to meet others' needs first. Leadership is indeed an exchange process by which superiors and subordinates develop mutually helping relationships to meet their personal and task-oriented goals.[11] When such relationships are lacking, regardless of the leader behaviors employed, managerial effectiveness is unlikely to improve.

Once such exchange relationships are developed, the manager gains the power to modify situational factors. Furthermore, the manager may feel psychologically secure enough to try out new kinds of leader behaviors. In this regard, there are three things Jones can do to improve her leadership effectiveness: (1) become an "in-group" manager, (2) become a path–goal leader, and (3) become a versatile leader.

On Becoming an "In-Group" Manager

The vertical dyad linkage (VDL) theory provides some clues concerning how a manager can develop a positive relationship with his or her superior and how such a relationship can affect relationships with subordinates (see Chapter 7). According to this theory, managers behave differently toward different subordinates, depending on the exchange relationships the parties have developed with each other. The theory divides subordinates into two subgroups: (1) those who are members of the "in-group" and (2) those who are members of the "out-group." In-group managers are allowed to participate and exercise a great deal of latitude in decision-making processes; out-group managers are allowed little negotiating latitude.[12]

How do these in-group and out-group relationships affect a manager's relationships with his or her own subordinates? Subordinates' perceptions of their superiors differ depending on whether they work for in-group or out-group managers. As Figure 12.2 suggests, subordinates who work for in-group managers tend to express satisfaction with their superiors, whereas those working for out-group managers tend to express dissatisfaction.[13] Apparently, in-group managers, having established strong ties with their bosses, are better able to support the task accomplishment of their subordinates.

It was suggested in Chapter 7 that managers can develop "in-group" relationships with their bosses by meeting their bosses' expectations. For example, their bosses may expect them to be technically competent, reliable, and loyal. In return for meeting these expectations, their bosses can offer them negotiating latitude, influence in decision making, action support, resources for subordinates, and so forth. When such in-group relationships are developed, managers are more likely to be seen as effective leaders in the eyes of their own subordinates.

According to the vertical dyad theory, then, Pat Jones should be more sensitive to the needs and expectations of her superior. She seems to assume that all her superior wants from her is to meet project deadlines at all costs. Since this may be an erroneous assumption, she needs to find

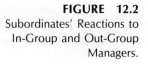

FIGURE   12.2
Subordinates' Reactions to In-Group and Out-Group Managers.

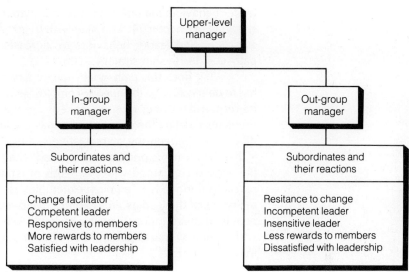

out what her superior expects from her and work out a way of meeting these expectations.

On Becoming a Path–Goal Leader

The path–goal leadership theory, discussed in Chapter 11, provides some clues concerning how a manager can develop a positive relationship with subordinates. The theory indicates that managers can be effective leaders if they help employees achieve their personal task-related goals. The main responsibility of a manager, according to the theory, is to compensate for something that is lacking in a leadership situation.[14] This something can be structuring the subordinates' jobs or meeting their needs for approval or support. To this end, the manager must be sensitive to the needs of employees and to what they want from their supervisor as they perform their jobs. The basic principles involved in this strategy are:

1. **To help employees accomplish task goals.**   This can be done by providing them with necessary instructions, training, resources, and supervisory supports.

2. **To help employees acquire desired rewards.**   This can be done by knowing what the employees want from their jobs and by making these rewards available to them.

3. **To help them know what it takes to obtain the rewards.**   The contingency relationships between rewards and performance need to be established and clearly communicated to employees.

A set of specific motivational principles and action guidelines associated with the path–goal theory is presented in Chapter 6. In addition, leader behaviors that are appropriate to different leadership situations are specified in Chapter 11. You may wish to go back and review these action guidelines and leader behaviors to increase your understanding of the path–goal leadership strategy.

What does this path–goal strategy mean to Pat Jones? It means she has to be sensitive to the needs of employees before she demands that they be responsive to her own needs. For example, if her subordinates have problems meeting the deadline, she may ask how she can help them. The difference between the manipulative strategy and the path–goal strategy is that the former is primarily concerned with the leader's needs, whereas the latter is concerned with the needs of employees. Because the leader reacts to the needs of employees, employees are more likely to react to the needs of the leaders. In Chapter 7 we discussed the process by which people in organizations develop mutually helping relationships. You may wish to review that chapter to get a better understanding of the developmental process.

On Becoming a Versatile Leader

Once they establish positive exchange relationships with other people, managers gain flexibility in using various leader behaviors. First, they gain the power and resources to modify situational factors. They obtain increased position power to grant or withhold rewards from their subordinates. They gain power to move people in and out of their work groups. Second, in-group managers may feel secure enough to experiment with new types of leader behavior. They may feel secure enough to share power and responsibility with their subordinates.

According to this concept, then, once she establishes in-group relationships with her superior, Pat Jones should become more versatile. She can then draw more resources and position power to modify the situational factors making up the leadership situation, or she can become more participative in dealing with subordinates. If she decides to become more participative, a number of things can happen in the learning process.

Changes in Managerial Attitudes. Managers have certain attitudes about people that seem to influence their leader behaviors. Some managers have task-motivated attitudes, so they become directive in dealing with subordinates. Other managers have relation-motivated attitudes that influence them to be more supportive. And still others believe they should cooperate with subordinates, so they become participative.

In order for managers to change their leader behavior, they must change their managerial attitudes. For example, Pat Jones relies primarily on directive leadership because she has task-motivated attitudes. These managerial attitudes reflect the idea that:

1. Managers are primarily responsible for achieving organizational goals.

2. Managers are to manage, and employees are to carry out their instructions.

3. Employees are primarily interested in satisfying their own personal needs.

4. Employee satisfaction is secondary to organizational productivity.

Whether Jones is or is not able to change these attitudes is up to her. However, once she establishes positive exchange relationships with other people, she is more likely to perceive that task attainment is a cooperative effort. This perception may enable her to develop cooperative attitudes. The following attitudes may help her behave in a participative manner:

1. Both managers and employees are responsible for achieving organizational goals.

2. Managers are responsible for meeting the needs of both the organization and its members.

3. Employees are capable of managing their own jobs.

4. Employees are as conscientious as managers in meeting their performance responsibilities.

Learning a New Leader Behavior.   Managers may want to behave in a certain way, but they may not know how. For these managers who want to expand their leadership versatility, leadership training programs are available. For example, Managerial Grid training, led by Blake and Mouton, can help managers identify their own leadership traits or behaviors and move toward the 9,9 style.[15] Other training groups are at the National Training Laboratory (NTL); these groups teach managers to be more participative.[16]

Training programs differ in their contents, but they have some characteristics in common. For example, they usually rely on *sensitivity training groups* in which the participants are encouraged to exhibit certain behaviors and provide feedback to each other's behaviors. They are often called *T-groups (training groups)* because the participants are able to learn about their effects on others and the effects others have on them through such group experiences. The theory is that once the participants become aware of their impact on others, and the impact of others on them, they are more likely to change their behaviors and become more productive. These training programs usually contain the following elements:

1. **Leadership Concepts.**   Participants learn major theories and concepts of leadership. These may include the various theories we have already discussed.

2. **Leadership Awareness.**   Participants become aware of their own leadership styles (traits and behaviors). The leadership style survey (Exercise 11.2) in Chapter 11 can be used to achieve this purpose.

3. **Learning Goals.**   Participants decide the target behavior they wish to learn. Assuming they are learning to be participative, the trainer may assign a simulated task calling for participative leader behavior.

4. **Learning Exercises.**   Participants demonstrate what they consider to be participative behaviors. They take turns playing the roles of leader and subordinates. The role players' behaviors are observed by the trainer and other observers (see Exercise 12.2).

5. **Observation Feedback.**   The observers provide feedback to the role players and discuss how they were perceived. The role players then react to the observers' comments.

6. **Aftermath Discussion.**   Participants review what they have learned in the training sessions and discuss potential problems in implementing their newly learned behavior.

While leadership training can be multidirectional, most training efforts, such as those by the National Training Laboratory and the Blake and Mouton Managerial Grid, focus on developing participative leadership. One reason for this focus may be that participative leadership is not widely used. It seems easier to be directive and/or supportive than participative when dealing with employees. Many organizations emphasize task accomplishment through close supervision, rational decision making, and task structuring. And, as most employee training is directed to task structuring behavior, there is less need to particularly develop it. At the same time, there is a lack of emphasis on supportive leader behavior. Management may not perceive it as an essential leader behavior that needs to be cultivated.

Participative leadership is sought after by some managers because they believe it to be an important tool for meeting the needs of both the organization and its members. Thus, leadership training is designed to prepare managers to be participative in solving organizational and employee problems in an open and unthreatening manner. In many decision situations, such as those involving resource allocation, personnel selection, and performance appraisal, people can easily become defensive because these decisions affect their stake in the organization. Effective managers deal with these issues openly and search for appropriate solutions. Ineffective managers, however, may avoid discussing unpopular issues, dominate the group process, monopolize the credit for success, and place the blame for failure on others.

Practicing a Newly Acquired Behavior

Learning a behavior is one thing, but practicing it is another. When a manager changes behavior suddenly, other people may not respond in a manner that reinforces the new behavior. Managers should expect such an initial reaction and prepare to deal with it. They cannot develop a desirable relationship independently of others. The development of such a relationship depends to some extent on the capacity of others to respond in an authentic manner.[17] Hence, the behavior of work group members must change along with that of the manager.

There are basically two ways of achieving behavioral changes in work groups: revolutionary and evolutionary. The *revolutionary* method employs group-oriented sensitivity training, that is, a *family T-group*.[18] In the family T-group, group members can improve their own behavior and that of others by discovering and removing barriers to effective group functioning. Since members develop new behavioral patterns together in the learning group, it is easier for them to carry those patterns over into their real organizational life.

The *evolutionary* method involves gradual changes in the behavior of both manager and subordinates. The manager gradually reduces the use of old behavioral patterns while introducing the new patterns. For example, a manager who has previously told employees what to do and has demanded their compliance can begin to discuss the nature of the instructions and listen attentively to employees' problems and suggestions. If formal meetings were previously held to discuss employees' work, informal gatherings to discuss mutual job concerns can be substituted.

Employee participation can take place in formal encounters or informally at coffee breaks, in locker rooms, or in social gatherings after work. This increased communication can generate more and better ideas for organizational problem solving. However, the quality of participation is determined not by when, where, and how employees participate but by the extent to which they feel they have influence in the decision-making process. Thus, managers who do not hold formal meetings but listen to employees in informal settings can have more authentic participation than those who hold frequent meetings but do not listen.

Evaluating the Behavior Change Strategy

Behavior change strategy does not categorize managers by their leadership styles. Rather, it assumes that managers can learn a variety of leader behaviors and choose the appropriate ones for particular situations. The manager may use directive leadership when employees desire task structuring or some direction. He or she may use participative leadership with in-group subordinates, and directive leadership with out-group subordinates. The degree of participation also can vary with the quality of leader–member relationships.

The theoretical position of this strategy is a departure from those of the theories discussed in Chapter 11, especially the behavioral and Fiedler's contingency theories. Those theories assume that managers have a fixed pattern of leader behavior that they apply to employees as a group. The leadership versatility theory discussed in this section, however, individualizes leader behavior.

Which theoretical position is correct? It is probably true that managers can learn and use a variety of leader behaviors. However, not all managers are capable of learning new leader behaviors, nor are they equally effective in utilizing them. Some are good at using participative leader behavior; others are effective in using directive leader behavior. The degree to which managers can effectively use different leader behaviors may depend on their experience and personal traits. So one theory does not repudiate the other theory.

HOW TO CHOOSE A LEADER BEHAVIOR

> *When managers have acquired a variety of leader behaviors, they become versatile and can adapt to varying leadership situations. The proposed leadership selection model can help a manager select an appropriate leader behavior.*

Once managers have acquired leadership versatility, they must: (1) study the characteristics of situational factors and (2) select an appropriate leader behavior. Vroom and Yetton propose a leadership selection model involving ten decision variables and eighteen leadership situations.[19] Although it is designed to select, and predict the outcomes of, a leader behavior, it has been criticized as unnecessarily complex and cumbersome.[20] Furthermore, this model is limited to information-sharing behaviors of managers in group decision situations. In this respect, their model is more of a group decision theory than a leadership theory.

We believe the complexity can be reduced without reducing predictive power. We also believe that a moderately complex model has a better chance of being applied than a complex one. Furthermore, the leadership selection model described in this section can be applied to leadership situations dealing with employees as a group and as individuals. The model has been developed in line with the research findings reported in Chapter 11 and this chapter.

The Leadership Selection Model

The leadership selection model, shown in Figure 12.3, describes the process by which the leader can select an appropriate leader behavior. The model contains six decision variables and nine leadership situations. The decision variables involved are task structure, leader–member relations, member quality, position power, leader quality, and time factor. The user may ask the following six questions relevant to these decision variables:

1.   Are the group tasks structured?

2.   Are the leader–member relations good?

3.   Do the group members have the necessary job knowledge?

4.   Does the manager have strong formal position power?

5.   Does the manager have the necessary job knowledge?

6.   Does the work group have sufficient time to deal with the task-related problems; is time a critical factor?

FIGURE   12.3
The Leadership Selection Model.

Only the nine leadership situations that are most likely to occur frequently in real life are considered in the model. When the model does

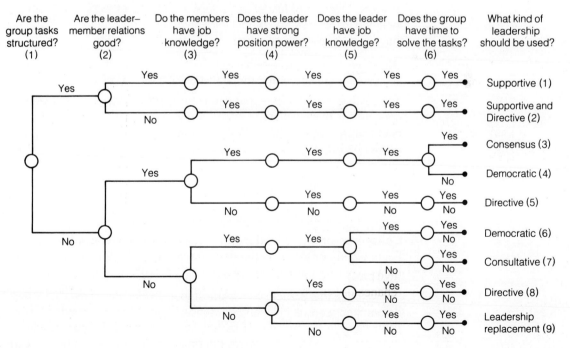

Are the group tasks structured? (1)	Are the leader–member relations good? (2)	Do the members have job knowledge? (3)	Does the leader have strong position power? (4)	Does the leader have job knowledge? (5)	Does the group have time to solve the tasks? (6)	What kind of leadership should be used?

not show a yes or a no choice, it means that the particular decision variable is not critical for selecting a leadership style at that point.

Several concessions were made in reducing the number of plausible leadership situations to nine. First, if the tasks are highly structured and simplified, both managers and their subordinates may have sufficient job knowledge to perform the assigned tasks. So job knowledge is not a critical decision factor for simplified jobs.

Second, most managers have some position power; so it is considered as a decision factor in the model only when the managers do not have it.

Third, most managers have job knowledge, which is gained through experience and training. Occasionally, however, some subordinates may have more job knowledge than their supervisors, especially in dealing with unstructured jobs. This special situation is considered in the model.

Finally, time is an important factor for solving unstructured task problems, but it becomes less important in dealing with structured problems. Structured problems are usually handled by following programmed solution manuals. By making these concessions, it was possible to eliminate from consideration a number of less plausible leadership situations.

Selecting a Leader Behavior

After identifying the situational characteristics, the manager can select one or a combination of leader behaviors. Five types of leader behaviors are included in this selection model: directive, supportive, democratic, consultative, and consensus-oriented.

Directive leadership—behavior characterized by defining, organizing, assigning, and supervising the activities of subordinates.

Supportive leadership—characterized by friendliness to employees and concern for their welfare.

Democratic leadership—involves employee participation, but the decisions are made by majority rule. It is used when decisions cannot be reached unanimously.

Consultative leadership—involves consulting employees, but managers make the final decision. It can be used when time is a critical factor or when employees do not wish to influence the decision.

Consensus-oriented leadership—behavior characterized by mutual influence and consensus in the decision process. It is time-consuming, but it can pay off in increased employee acceptance of the decision.

Notice that participative leadership is divided into three categories—democratic, consultative, and consensus. This division is needed because differences in the manner of participation can yield different results.

The following summarizes the situations in which a particular leader behavior can be effectively used. These summaries are keyed to the numbers in the right-most column of Figure 12.3. This figure can be seen as a decision tree for leadership selection.

1. **Supportive leadership** can be used in a situation in which (a) tasks are highly structured, (b) employees are loyal and have the necessary job knowledge, and (c) the manager has strong position power and job knowledge.

2. **A combination of supportive and directive leader behavior** is recommended in situations in which all the situational characteristics are the same as in (1) above, but the group members are not submissive. Directive leadership is needed to control them, but managers can improve the leader–member relationship by becoming supportive.

3. **Consensus-oriented leadership** can be used in a situation in which (a) the tasks are unstructured, (b) time is not a critical factor, (c) leader–member relations are favorable, and (d) both managers and subordinates have the necessary job knowledge.

4. & 6. **Democratic leadership** can be exercised in a situation in which all the situational characteristics are the same as in (3) except the time element. It can be used when there is no time for consensus-oriented participation. The same leadership style can be used in similar situations regardless of the favorableness of the leader–member relations.

5. & 8. **Directive leadership** is suggested in situations in which (a) the tasks are unstructured, (b) the employees do not have the necessary job knowledge, and (c) the manager has the necessary position power and job knowledge.

7. **Consultative leadership** can be used in a situation in which (a) the tasks are unstructured, (b) leader–member relations are not very favorable, and (c) group members may have more job knowledge than the manager.

9. This is a chaotic situation in which no one exercises leadership. Someone may replace the existing leadership and provide some direction to cope with the uncertain situation.

Evaluating the Selection Model

The selection model provides a systematic way of selecting an appropriate leader behavior to match a given situation. It analyzes situational characteristics and suggests a specific leader behavior to be employed. This model can be valuable to managers who are versatile in their selection of leadership behavior but who do not know what kind of behavior is appropriate in a given situation.

Since this model is derived from various contingency leadership theories already discussed, it should be as valid as its predecessors. The suggestions in the model are generally congruent with the research findings related to Fiedler's contingency theory and the path–goal theory.

SUMMARY AND CONCLUSION

An underlying theme of leadership theories is that leadership effectiveness increases when there is a match between leader behavior and the situation. There are basically three strategies that can be used to find such a match. First, managers can find situations that suit their leader behavior. Second, they may change their leader behavior to match situational demands. Third, managers can change the situational factors to match their style. These leadership strategies have the following advantages and disadvantages.

The first strategy is a simplistic and passive approach to leadership improvement. While managers can function effectively in situations that reinforce their behaviors, they do not develop new leader behaviors that can be used in other situations. Thus, they cannot function effectively if situational demands change.

The second strategy is an expedient method of reestablishing a leadership match. It involves changing the characteristics of situational factors —group members, group tasks, and position power, for example. An argument for this suggestion is that it is often easier to change situational factors than to change one's behavior. While it seems useful, this strategy is, however, somewhat limited to managers who have considerable power in an organization. Such power is needed to move people into and out of work groups and to reward and withhold rewards to employees.

The last strategy involves an active cultivation of leadership quality. This strategy allows managers to acquire new leader behaviors that can be used in various leadership situations. However, it is a complex and time-consuming strategy because it involves developing positive exchange relationships with other people and learning a new set of behaviors. Laboratory learning experience can help managers who wish to learn a new leader behavior. The development of positive relationships with other organizational members is essential for experimenting and maintaining a new leader behavior.

KEY CONCEPTS AND WORDS

*Situation
  modification
Leader–member
  relations
Task structure
Consensus-oriented
  leadership*

*Exchange relationship
In-group manager
Path–goal manager
Laboratory training
Family T-group
Consultative
  leadership*

*Democratic
  leadership
Leadership selection
  model
Versatile leader*

Questions for Review and Discussion

1. This chapter presents several approaches to improving leadership effectiveness.
   a. Identify these approaches and discuss the major theme of each approach.
   b. Discuss the strengths and limitations of each.

2. Some people suggest that leadership effectiveness can be improved by modifying the situational factors.
   a. What are the reasons for this suggestion?
   b. What are the situational factors to be modified?
   c. Give some examples of situational modification.

3. Why do some people believe that leadership training does not help managers improve their effectiveness?

4. It is suggested that managers should develop positive exchange relationships with their superiors to become effective leaders? Explain why.

5. What is a path–goal leader? How does one become a path–goal leader?

6. a. Explain the leadership selection model.
   b. How is it different from Fiedler's contingency model and the path–goal theory of leadership?
   c. How can it help managers?

7. On the basis of what you understand of the various ways of improving leadership effectiveness, which one do you prefer? Why?

EXERCISES

EXERCISE 12.1. MANAGING A NURSING STATION

Some managers are highly versatile in utilizing leader behaviors. These managers can adapt to various leadership situations. But, to be effective, they need to (1) assess the situational factors correctly and (2) select an appropriate leader behavior. The following exercise shows how a manager can select an appropriate leader behavior.

The Situation

You are a head nurse who supervises eight registered nurses and three nurse's aides. Although there are a few nonroutinized tasks, such as special patient care, most tasks are fairly well structured. Most nurses have at least two years of training in nursing school, but they are not well prepared to deal with all areas of nursing care. The head nurse is in charge of all aspects of administration, including selection, placement, and performance evaluation of the nurses.

The Procedure

1. Analyze the situational factors. You may use the leadership selection model shown in Figure 12.3. Note your assessments below.
   a. Task structure:
   b. Leader–member relations:
   c. Members' job knowledge:
   d. Leader's position power:
   e. Leader's job knowledge:
   f. Time element:

2. What kind of leader behavior should you use? Why?

EXERCISE 12.2. LEADERSHIP DEVELOPMENT EXERCISE

This exercise is designed to show how a manager behaves in a problem-solving situation and how the manager can improve his or her leadership behavior. You may wish to strive for participative leadership in this exercise.

The Situation

Put yourself in the shoes of Ron Engelberg who supervises Pat Jones. You have received several complaints from project engineers about her, and you talked to her about these complaints once before. Since you have not noticed any improvement, you have decided to invite her in for another consultation. You consider her to be one of your most technically competent managers, and you do not want to lose her.

The Procedure

1. Two of you should play the roles of the supervisor and the subordinate. You should play these roles for about five minutes.

2. The rest of you should observe the role players and take notes on their behaviors, especially the behavior of the supervisor. You may use the leader behavior observation guide that follows.

3. The observers provide feedback to the role players. Their comments should include whether the supervisor was showing a directive, supportive, or participative leadership style.

4. The class should then discuss how the supervisor can improve his or her leadership effectiveness without causing defensive behavior on the part of the subordinate and without yielding to the subordinate's demands.

Leader Behavior Observation Guide

Instructions: Respond to each of the following items with Y (yes) or N (no).

_____ 1. The leader dominates the group discussion.

_____ 2. The leader blames employees for the problems.

_____ 3. The leader sandwiches criticism between praise.

_____ 4. The leader lectures and instructs the employee.

_____ 5. The leader demands performance improvement.

_____ 6. The leader demands loyalty from the employee.

_____ 7. The leader allows employees to explain the problem.

_____ 8. The leader shares the responsibility for the problem.

_____ 9. The leader participates in problem-solving efforts.

_____ 10. The leader freely and openly discusses job-related problems.

_____ 11. The leader deals with anger, conflict, and feelings without suppressing them.

_____ 12. The leader shares managerial information with subordinates.

_____ 13. The leader avoids touchy issues.

_____ 14. The leader gives in easily to employees' demands.

_____ 15. The leader tries hard to please employees.

_____ 16. The leader is wishy-washy in dealing with job-related problems.

_____ 17. The leader promises to solve the employee's problems.

_____ 18. The leader plays favorites or patronizes the employee.

Providing feedback: Count the number of Y's for each group of leader behaviors and provide the participants with your observation.

_____ Directive behavior (items 1 through 6)

_____ Participative behavior (items 7 through 12)

_____ Supportive behavior (items 13 through 18)

Footnotes

1. F. E. Fiedler and M. M. Chemers, *Leadership and Effective Management* (Glenview, IL: Scott, Foresman, 1974), p. 145.

2. Theodore Levitt, "The Managerial Merry-Go-Round," *Harvard Business Review,* July–August 1974, 120–128; and F. E. Fiedler, M. M. Chemers, and Linda Mahar, *Improving Leadership Effectiveness* (New York: Wiley, 1976), pp. 152–154.

3. See Fiedler, Chemers, and Mahar, *Improving Leadership Effectiveness,* pp. 152–158.

4. J. R. Hackman and E. E. Lawler, "Employee Reactions to Job Characteristics," *Journal of Applied Psychology* 1971, **55,** 259–286.

5. R. M. Kanter, "Power Failure in Management Circuits," *Harvard Business Review,* July–August 1979, 65–75.

6. David Kipnis, *The Powerholders* (Chicago: University of Chicago Press, 1976).

7. J. P. Kotter, "Power, Dependence, and Effective Management," *Harvard Business Review,* July–August 1977, 135.

8. Dian Hosking and Chester Schriescheim, "Review of Fiedler et al., Improving Leadership Effectiveness: The Leader Match Concept," *Administrative Science Quarterly,* 1978, **23,** 496–504.

9. P. S. Goodman, Max Bazerman, and Edward Conlon, "Institutionalization of Planned Organizational Change," in *Research in Organizational Behavior,* Vol. 2, ed. B. Staw and M. Bazerman (Greenwich, CT: JAI Press, 1980), pp. 215–246.

10. W. J. Heisler, "Patterns of Organizational Development," *Business Horizons,* February 1975, 77–84.

11. T. O. Jacobs, *Leadership and Exchange in Formal Organizations* (Alexandria, VA: Human Resources Organization, 1970).

12. George Graen and J. F. Cashman, "A Role Making Model of Leadership in Formal Organizations: A Developmental Approach," in *Leadership Frontiers* ed. J. G. Hunt and L. L. Larson (Kent, OH: Kent State University, 1977), pp. 143–166.

13. J. F. Cashman, Fred Dansereau, George Graen, and W. J. Haga, "Organizational Understructure and Leadership: A Longitudinal Investigation of the Managerial Role-Making Process," *Organizational Behavior and Human Behavior,* 1976, **15,** 278–296; and George Graen, J. F. Cashman, Steven Ginsberg, and William Schiemann, "Effects of Linking-pin Quality on the Quality of Working Life of Lower Participants," *Administrative Science Quarterly,* 1977, **22,** 491–504.

14. R. J. House and T. R. Mitchell, "Path–Goal Theory of Leadership," *Journal of Contemporary Business,* Autumn 1974, 81–87.

15. See R. R. Blake and J. S. Mouton, *The New Managerial Grid* (Houston: Gulf Publishing, 1978).

16. See L. P. Bradford, J. R. Gibb, and K. D. Benne, *T-Group Theory and Laboratory Method* (New York: Wiley, 1964).

17. Chris Argyris, *Interpersonal Competence and Organizational Effectiveness* (Homewood, IL: Irwin, 1962), pp. 15–37.

18. W. L. French and C. H. Bell, *Organizational Development* (Englewood Cliffs, NJ: Prentice-Hall, 1973), pp. 112–117.

19. V. H. Vroom and P. W. Yetton, *Leadership and Decision Making* (Pittsburgh: University of Pittsburgh Press, 1973); and V. H. Vroom and A. Jago, "On the Validity of the Vroom-Yetton Model," *Journal of Applied Psychology,* 1978, **63,** 151–162.

20. R. H. G. Field, "A Critique of the Vroom-Yetton Contingency Model of Leader Behavior," *Academy of Management Review,* April 1979, 249–257.

LEARNING OBJECTIVES

1. To understand the characteristics of power.
2. To understand the types of power used in organizations.
3. To know how people acquire and use power in organizations.
4. To develop the skills of acquiring and using power.

CHAPTER OUTLINE

The Nature of Power and Politics

Power and Authority
Power and Politics
Politics and Organizational Controls
Power and Leadership
Characteristics of Power

Sources of a Manager's Power

Position Power
Reward Power
Coercive Power
Expert Power
Charismatic Power
Association Power
Relative Importance of Power Bases

Modes of Political Tactics

Attacking or Blaming Others
Controlling Information
Managing Impression
Developing a Base of Support
Forming Political Coalitions
Empire Building
Evaluating Political Tactics

How to Acquire and Use Power Effectively

Basic Motivational Patterns
Modes of Power Acquisition
Modes of Exercising Power
Legitimatizing the Use of Power

Summary and Conclusion

13 ACQUIRING AND USING POWER IN ORGANIZATIONS

Any prince who relies on his word alone, without any other preparation, is ruined. For friendships acquired through money rather than through greatness and nobility of character may be bought, but they are not owned: they cannot be drawn upon in times of need.

Niccolo Machiavelli, The Prince[1]

Power is an essential element for exercising leadership. Organizations cannot function without people exercising power to influence others. Power is like fuel. It provides the energy to run the organizational machinery. Managers cannot function without power because without it they are merely figureheads. Managers use power to influence their subordinates and to obtain the resources they need to accomplish tasks and achieve objectives. Nonmanagers also use power as a means of survival in organizations. Power in this case means some control over their work environment. Without it, they are susceptible to the power manipulation of others.

Although power is so important, it is often considered a dangerous element. It is viewed negatively because it is often associated with undesirable human actions such as corruption, domination, exploitation, political scandals, and suppression. People are suspicious of anyone who seeks power, even if it is used to help others. And some people do abuse power to benefit themselves at the expense of others.

This chapter emphasizes the importance of power that is used positively in managing organizations and shows how it can be acquired and used. The chapter discusses (1) the nature of power, (2) the sources of a manager's power, (3) the modes of organizational politics, (4) the characteristics of powerholders, and (5) the methods of acquiring and using power.

THE NATURE OF POWER AND POLITICS

Power is the ability to get what one wants. Politics refers to activities directed at obtaining power. To some people an organization is a system of political coalitions that bargain for power with each other.

In recent years, there has been a growing interest in the nature of power and its importance in performing managerial functions and activities, such as decision making, leading, and making changes. Unlike traditional organizational theories that emphasize rationality in organizational processes,[2] contemporary behavioral theories emphasize power and politics as major determinants of organizational behavior. For example, Tushman views an organizational process as a political process in which power holders try to influence goals, directions, and other major parameters of an organization.[3] Similarly, Pfeffer views organizational structure as the outcome of a contest for power between coalitions in the organization.[4] The dominant coalition uses its power to impose its will on the rest of the organization. In order to understand the dynamics of power in organizations, one must understand the concept of power and its relationship to authority, politics, and leadership.

Power and Authority

The terms *authority* and *power* are often used interchangeably in management literature, but the distinction between them is important if you want to understand the dynamics of power. As shown in Figure 13.1, *authority* is usually defined as the right to ask other people to do some-

FIGURE 13.1
Distinction Between Authority and Power.

Bases for distinction	Authority	Power
Definition	The right	The ability
Source	Position	Individual characteristics
Target	Collective interests	Individual or group interests
Exerciser	Manager	Leader
Behavioral mode	Compliance	Dependency

thing, while *power* is defined as the ability to make other people do something. Now, let us explore some implications of these distinctions.

A manager may have the authority to demand high performance from his or her subordinates, but may lack the ability to carry out this right. Since the manager lacks power to induce or force them to work, productivity goals cannot be achieved. On the other hand, an informal leader may not have the authority to demand high performance from co-workers, but he or she may have some power to influence them to produce. Managerial effectiveness can increase when the manager possesses both ability and power. Failure to have both can result in powerlessness or power abuse and can cause instability in organizations. A manager without power can lead to managerial ineffectiveness; an informal leader with power can be a threat to the formal leader.

A second distinction is that the core of authority is vested in a position, while power is a personal trait or quality. Thus, even if two persons hold positions at the same level, with the same amount of authority, they may differ in their exercise of power. One manager may have easy access to organizational resources, and so, can easily obtain necessary cooperation from other organization members; the other manager may have problems obtaining the necessary resources and, thus, cooperation.

A third distinction is that authority abides in a collective context. What legitimates authority is the pursuit of collective goals that result from collective decisions. For example, Congress passed the tax law giving the Internal Revenue Service the authority to collect taxes from citizens, for the good of the people. In contrast, power can be exercised for the pursuit of individual or small group goals rather than for the organization as a whole.[5]

A final implication is that power is associated with leadership, while authority is closely associated with managership. A manager has the right to demand behavioral compliance from other people within a specified legitimate boundary. People comply with managerial authority as a duty. On the other hand, while a leader may not have the legal right to do so, he or she may exert undue influence on other people by creating a dependency relationship. When a person depends on another for something, the latter can exert power over the former.

Power and Politics

Organizations exist for many reasons. From an economic standpoint, they exist to create surplus value over costs. From an individual standpoint, organizations are political instruments by which individuals pursue their personal interests.[6] The pursuit of individual goals, particularly at high managerial and professional levels, depends on how much power has been accumulated and can influence organizational decisions to enhance or protect one's own interests.

The fact that most organizations are structured like pyramids means that power positions become fewer as one moves up in the organizational hierarchy. This fact, coupled with a scarcity of economic resources, forces people to compete for power in an organization. They cannot achieve higher positions without power. Likewise, powerless managers are not able to acquire the necessary resources for themselves and their subordinates. Consequently, failure to acquire power or form political coalitions can easily result in personal and managerial failure.

When people compete for power, they tend to "play politics." *Politics* refers to those activities that are intended to increase one's power. For example, managers may form coalitions to serve and protect their own interests or control information flow to help or hinder other people. Not all activities that increase power, however, can be called politics. For example, gaining expertise increases one's power, but it is not considered to be "playing politics." Politics usually involves intentional acts of influencing other people for the purpose of enhancing or protecting the self-interests of individuals or groups.

Politics and Organizational Controls

The necessity of politics or power tactics becomes more evident in situations where organizational tasks are loosely structured and the number of hierarchical controls is low. In the absence of any agreement on what should be accomplished, how resources should be allocated, and how members are supposed to behave, people tend to resort to politics to gain power and more resources for themselves. For example, in the absence of an objective performance appraisal, managers may reward those employees who are loyal to them regardless of performance. In this case, winning the approval of superiors, through ingratiation or "apple polishing," may become a more important reward criterion than task performance. If management wants to minimize the amount of office politics in the organization, it may structure organizational tasks and increase hierarchical controls.

Figure 13.2 shows the extent to which politics becomes a means of controlling behavior in organizations.[7] In Cell A politics becomes the dominant source of organizational control. Behavior in organizations is controlled by political activities. In the process of formulating organizational goals, resource allocation, and reward distribution, members form coalitions to serve and protect their interests. Persuasion, bargaining, and pressure are another part of political tactics.

In Cell B, there is some agreement as to what is expected of members in their jobs but there is a lack of hierarchical controls. Many professional organizations such as those of engineers, lawyers, and professors are in this category. The members usually act collectively to formulate codes of conduct. These become group norms, and the members are ruled by them. The legitimacy of political behaviors is judged by these norms. When

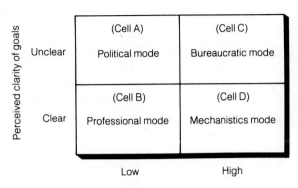

FIGURE   13.2
Control Modes in
Organizations.

conflict arises, it is usually resolved by the members rather than through
the hierarchical rule.

In Cell C, organizational controls are exercised by rules, regulations,
and policies. Such control systems are called *bureaucratic systems.* These
bureaucratic systems are created and maintained by dominant power
holders to control the remaining organizational members. These systems
are also used in the process of formulating organizational goals, allocating
resources, and distributing rewards. In response to them, the controlled
parties tend to follow rules, regulations, and policies to the letter, regardless of whether doing so contributes to the attainment of organizational
goals. They may behave in this manner to avoid any blame for not following the rules and regulations.

In Cell D, there is little room for politics. All aspects of organizational
behavior are so structured that there is no room for bargaining and negotiating. The dominant behavioral mode involves defining rules and performance measurements to guide the behavior of organizational members.
Such a control system can be found in assembly line operations.

Power and Leadership

The core of leadership is power. Without it, leadership does not exist.
What makes a leader different from a nonleader is that the leader has the
ability to influence other people—that is, has power. A manager may
exercise formal authority to produce voluntary, or nonvoluntary, compliance from subordinates, but a leader relies on informal power in the form
of persuasion and inducement to generate voluntary support.

Kanter points out that power is an essential element in exercising
managerial leadership.[8] Powerful managers are more likely to delegate and
share their authority with subordinates, to reward subordinates' accomplishments, and to promote teamwork, which enhances the power of
subordinates. Conversely, powerless managers tend to become "bossy"
instead of relying on the voluntary cooperation of subordinates. They may

find their subordinates resisting their authority, and so rely on bossiness and punishment as their means of control.

Graen and his associates also point out that powerful managers are those who have developed "in-group" relationships with their bosses; these relationships allow them to commit more resources to their subordinates.[9] Conversely, less powerful managers are considered to be "hired hands," and are given little latitude. They are often perceived as less effective managers by their subordinates. Furthermore, while in-group relationships are controlled by informal power (such as friendship and expertise), out-group relationships are controlled by formal hierarchical controls—rules, regulations, and policies.

Characteristics of Power

Certain characteristics of power influence the behavior of power users. Understanding these characteristics can help individuals acquire and use power wisely. Among the important characteristics are: (1) dependency relationships, (2) power expansion, and (3) the paradox of power.

Dependency Relationships. Power implies a dependency relationship.[10] We gain power over another because that person depends on us for something. The dependent person allows us to influence his or her behavior. In organizations, managers have power over employees because employees depend on them for organizational rewards. The dependency relationship is not one-sided, however: Employees may have less power than their superiors, but they do have some power over superiors because the superiors depend on their subordinates for productivity, cooperation, and emotional support.

Power Expansion. Power can expand. The more power a person has, the wider the range of behavioral options. Powerful people can do more things, good or bad, than their less powerful peers can. Since they can cause other people to respond positively to their wishes, they feel more secure in taking risks. Thus they can accomplish more than less influential individuals. However, as their power increases, there is more opportunity and temptation for them to abuse their power. The possibility of abusing power is great because dependent persons usually do not challenge the power abuser. They may fear reprisal or may not have the means to challenge the despot. This phenomenon is seen in the rise of dictators. Dictators increase their behavioral options, positive as well as negative, by making other people increasingly dependent on them for survival while reducing their dependency on other people.

The Paradox of Power. In order to acquire power, one may need the desire to have power and be in a position where that power can be exercised. But, in many instances, the more power a manager attempts to exert over other people, the less power the manager actually has.[11] That is, one person's effort to increase power is often perceived as a reduction in another person's power. The perceived threat produces conflict and resistance, which works against power expansion. The net result is that both parties lose the power to influence each other. On the other hand, a manager can increase power by sharing it with subordinates. When the manager is willing to share power, the subordinates are more likely to acquiesce in the manager's wishes.[12] A person who receives something from another person usually wants to give something in return. The net result is that both parties increase the amount of influence they can exert on each other.

SOURCES OF A MANAGER'S POWER

> *A manager can derive power from a variety of sources—position, reward, coercion, expertise, charisma, and association. The first three power bases are considered to be more formal than the last three.*

All managers have power, but some managers have more than others. Managers who can satisfy the needs of others or who can deprive need satisfaction can exert more influence than managers who cannot. People become dependent on certain managers because the managers have something they want. The *perceived* ability to give or withhold something other people want is the source of power.

In a business, managerial power results from ownership of material or financial resources. Society gives property owners the right to manage their businesses as they wish, within limits set up by the law. However, most managers do not own their businesses; so they are in no position to exercise ownership power. Therefore, they have to derive their power from sources other than ownership. Managerial power can be derived from holding official position, controlling rewards, using punishments, gaining expertise, having personal charm, and associating with power sources.[13] Figure 13-3 outlines the characteristics of various power bases.

Position Power

Position power is derived from the office that a manager occupies. The formal authority granted to the office does not constitute actual power, but the manager can derive power from the office. There are two reasons for

Types of Power	Behaviors	Advantages	Disadvantages
Position	Makes decisions and demands compliance.	Quick, reliable, and cost free.	Some people may resent it. Not set well with professional personnel.
Reward	Gives and withholds resources for compliance.	Quick and reliable.	Can be very costly.
Coercive	Punishes or uses threat to deal with noncompliance.	Quick, reliable, and can be used when other powers fail.	Invites retaliation, destroys relationships, and does not produce a permanent change.
Expert	Provides expertise to others.	Quick, reliable, and no costs involved.	Some may resent their dependency on experts.
Charismatic	Maintains attractive personal qualities.	No costs involved and intrinsically motivating.	No tangible rewards.
Association	Uses personal connections with powerful persons to influence other people.	No costs involved.	Increased dependency on the power source reduces the user's independency.

FIGURE 13.3
The Characteristics of
Various Power Bases.

this. First, people are culturally conditioned to accept the authority of managers. They believe that their superiors have the right to lead them. Second, because of their positions, managers have control over the distribution of organizational rewards and punishments. Some may not have direct control, but they can influence the distribution process by having access to the power center.

Within certain limits, some managers can exert more position power than others. The amount of position power that a manager exercises depends on the nature of the task and his or her willingness to use the power.

1. Managers in business, military, and government organizations generally have greater position power than managers in educational, religious, service, and other professional organizations. Even in the same organization, managers in revenue-producing departments tend to have more power than those in advisory positions.

2. Managers who are willing to exercise authority to reward and punish others command more position power than those who are not. This willingness increases the power user's credibility.

Reward Power

The ability to grant or withhold rewards is a major source of power. Anyone who has or controls resources that others value can exert power over those individuals. Managers have power because they control the distribution of organizational rewards such as pay increases, promotions, and task assignments. Reward power, however, is not limited to managers. An informal leader may have the power to accept or reject another person's membership in a desired group. The informal leader can provide emotional support and personal assistance in return for the member's compliance with group norms. Subordinates also have the power to reward or punish their superiors by accepting or rejecting the superior's authority.

Managers can gain reward power by being in managerial positions that control organizational resources. Line managers who serve the major functions of the organization tend to exert more reward power than staff managers. Since the survival of an organization largely depends on the effectiveness of these line functions, such as production and sales, most organizational resources are directed to serve these functions. Auxiliary functions are often treated as stepchildren, and, when a crunch comes, they are the first ones to go.

Coercive Power

Coercive power is the ability to force other people to act against their wishes. The ability to coerce is derived from fear of punishment. People may unwillingly comply with the power agent because they are afraid of losing their jobs, being rejected, or not receiving desired rewards. Coercive power usually produces immediate responses from the target person. Managers frequently use coercive power to terminate immediately the annoying behavior of others.

There are two kinds of coercive power: legitimate and illegitimate. A manager may illegally dismiss or discriminate against some employees because of a personal grudge. Or the manager may legally use negative sanctions, such as dismissal, reprimand, and transfer, as a means of discouraging low performance. The legitimate use of coercive power, however, can increase a manager's credibility and respect. In fact, when managers do not use coercive power against unproductive or disturbing persons, they tend to lose control and the respect of subordinates. If appropriately used, coercive power can show strong leadership.

The use of coercive power can, however, produce a number of dysfunctional consequences.[14] First, it tends to cause some damage to the leader–member relationship. Second, it may only frustrate the punished person, especially when the person does not know how to improve his or her behavior. Third, it may cause people to become defensive about criticism. Finally, it may produce aggressive responses from the punished, such as retaliation. This retaliation can sometimes be very costly. The following example illustrates the problem of using coercive power.

> *Pat Jones had been a project manager for nine months. As the pressure mounted to meet the target date, she demanded that the engineers in her project group work 60 hours a week until the job was completed. They were told that if they did not like the long hours, they could find jobs elsewhere. The engineers didn't like the job-related pressures, but they nevertheless complied with her wish because they needed the income.*
>
> *As the economy improved, jobs became more plentiful. Four key engineers left the company within a few months. Other engineers requested internal transfers. Management began wondering about the managerial competency of Jones. Management did not mind seeing her being hard-nosed in getting the job done, but it worried about whether she could last.*

How can Jones avoid such negative consequences? As pointed out in Chapter 12, she needs to develop and use informal power bases (such as expertise and personal charm) in dealing with professional employees.

Expert Power

People with expert knowledge and information that other people need can exert substantial power in organizations. Certain experts, such as tax accountants, lawyers, and computer specialists, can wield a great deal of power over others because these experts provide information that managers need. Technological and organizational complexity and specialization have increased the expert power of these professionals. The changing technological environment continuously creates demands for the services of various professional groups.

Managers can generally exercise expert power because they have more job experience and knowledge than their subordinates. In many cases, they are promoted to managerial positions because of their technical expertise. But even if they lack such expertise, they have managerial information that flows through the organizational hierarchy. Subordinates need their supervisors' experience and information to achieve their task and personal goals. By the same token, subordinates who have expert knowledge and skills can exert expert power over their superiors, with the superiors becoming dependent.

Charismatic Power

Some people have special personal qualities that give them some power over a large number of people. These qualities may include public speaking ability, interpersonal style, or high moral standards. Other people are attracted to them because of these qualities. Such personal attraction is often called *referent* or *charismatic power.* This power is derived from the feelings of individuals who want to be identified with someone with such qualities. Charismatic individuals may have no position power but they do have the ability to satisfy other people's needs for identification, approval, or emotional support.

Personal attraction elicits imitative behavior from followers. People are attracted to the charismatic person so strongly that they want to be like the person and therefore imitate his or her behavior. Charismatic people tend to be highly successful in their professions and have a dynamic lifestyle that is envied by others. However, not all successful people have referent or charismatic power. In order to be charismatic, people must have a style or flair that is unusual and pleasing. Examples of charismatic people include Winston Churchill, John F. Kennedy, Billy Graham, or John Paul II.

Association Power

Some people acquire power by being associated with someone who has power. They may have little position power, expert power, or personal attraction, but they exert power because they have direct access to the power source, or they can influence the people with power. For example, the boss's wife and secretary have association power because they are situated close to the boss and can exert influence in favor of their friends. Some staff members of key congressional leaders have more power even than other congressional representatives because they control access to these powerful representatives and their committees.

Association is an important source of power, and its use is common in complex organizations. Because of the complexity of organizational relationships and informational webs, many people find it difficult to gain access to the power source. Even if they know the source of power, they have to go through formal communication channels and time-consuming rituals to get to it. By knowing someone close to the power agent, they can cut through the complex organizational webs and rituals. Being associated with power sources is a power in itself.

Relative Importance of Power Bases

Sources of power are interrelated, and a person possesses them to varying degrees. Thus, how a person uses a certain type of power affects the effectiveness of the other powers. For example, position power is enhanced by the use of expert, charismatic, association, and reward powers. In fact, people obtain certain leadership positions through their expertise, personal charm, and association with powerful persons.

Reward power is increased by position power. Managerial position gives managers the legitimate power to reward and punish others. The possession of position power and expert power can increase charismatic power: People are attracted to successful individuals with power and status. The use of coercive power may increase position power, but it tends to reduce the effectiveness of charismatic power: People have a tendency to avoid a person who punishes them; punishment therefore goes against personal charm.

Is one form of power more potent than others? Although it is difficult to generalize about their relative effectiveness, the following observations can be made.[15]

First, the use of informal power bases (expertise, association, and charisma) can very positively influence the satisfaction and performance of employees. Informal power does not depend on the possession of formal authority; yet it tends to be more consistent and durable than position, reward, and coercive power. While informal power rests in the person, other powers are separable from the individual. For example, managers can easily lose position, reward, and coercive powers when they leave a managerial position.

Second, the use of formal power (position, reward, and coercive) tends to result in an immediate response from employees. It provides an important basis for complying with the superior's wishes. However, it is not consistently correlated with the satisfaction and performance of subordinates. People may resent the fact that they have to comply with a superior's wishes simply because they need the rewards that the superior controls—and not because he or she has personal or professional qualities. The use of formal power is often resented by subordinates, but without it managers would find it difficult to influence them. Machiavelli, in *The Prince,* contended that feared (respected) leaders with formal power could last longer than loved leaders with informal power.

Finally, the use of coercive power is the least effective method of positively influencing satisfaction and performance. It may reduce the frequency of undesirable behavior, but it does not necessarily increase the frequency or intensity of desirable behavior. People usually resort to coercive power when they are not able to wield other sources of power effectively. To be effective, coercive power must be used so that it does not openly arouse the antagonism of the punished.

MODES OF POLITICAL TACTICS

> *Managers use a variety of power tactics to serve and protect their interests in organizations. While some tactics enhance managerial effectiveness, others seem to hinder it.*

Although most managers hesitate to admit it, they frequently use political tactics to gain and protect their power in organizations. A study by Allen and his associates shed some light on the kinds of political tactics used by managers at all levels, including chief executives, high-level staff managers, and first-line supervisors.[16] The study lists eight categories of political tactics mentioned most frequently by these managers:

1. Attacking or blaming others
2. Use of information
3. Impression management
4. Development of support base
5. Ingratiation
6. Power coalitions
7. Development of association power
8. Creation of obligations

Attacking or Blaming Others

This tactic, which is seemingly unethical, was most frequently mentioned by the managers in the Allen study. More than half the managers identified it as the most frequently used political tactic. This tactic involves two approaches—reactive and proactive. Reactive behavior centers around "scapegoating." Managers try to avoid being associated with any undesirable situation or outcome. Proactive tactics are far more personal and are geared toward reducing competition for scarce resources or rewards. These behaviors involve making the rival look bad in the eyes of influential organizational members. The political actor may blame the rival for failures or degrade the accomplishment of the rival. Usually, a reactive tactic is intended to protect self-interest, while proactive behavior is intended to promote it.

Controlling Information

This tactic is the second most popular political tool. Almost half of the supervisors and over half of the chief executives and staff managers identified it as an important political tool. Few managers believed in outright lying, but they would withhold information that might be detrimental to their self-interest or that might help the rival. Information overload is a similar strategy. It is the opposite of information withholding, and is used to overwhelm the target person with data that are not particularly pertinent. This strategy is used to obscure an important issue that can be politically damaging to the political actor. Another strategy may be to control the information flow so that other people rely on the actor for information dissemination.

Managing Impression

This tactic is the third kind of political tool mentioned by the managers. It is predominantly proactive behavior designed to promote self-interest. Image building includes general appearance, dress and hair style, adhering to organizational norms, association with success, and being a part of important activities. Another strategy is to build a reputation as likable, enthusiastic, honest, and thoughtful. These personal attributes are thought to be desired by influential individuals of an organization.

Developing a Base of Support

High-level managers were more interested in building a base of support for their ideas and programs than were lower-level managers. High-level managers spend a great deal of time and effort communicating their ideas to others before final decisions are made, building a support base before a meeting is called, and having other people contribute their ideas in order to ensure the commitment.

Forming Political Coalitions

Several other tactics are used to form political coalitions. For example, ingratiation is a tactic used by lower-level managers to gain favors from their superiors. This behavior is associated with expressions such as "apple polishing" or "buttering up the boss." The tone of such behavior changes as one moves up in the hierarchy. Higher-level managers tend to speak in terms of praising others and establishing good rapport. Other tactics are developing strong ties with allies and associating with influential persons in and out of the organization. These coalitions are developed to establish exchange relationships among the participants. The participants accommodate each other's needs and expectations, provide each other with special favors and privileges, and enhance in-group relationships.[17]

Empire Building

Another political tactic, not mentioned in the Allen study, is the empire-building behavior of managers. Some managers try to gather as much authority as possible. They may view themselves indispensable decision makers whom the organization depends on. So they get involved in as many activities as they can and attempt to influence organizational decisions. They do this by filling the gap created by other managers who avoid responsibility, or by increasing the size of their office and number of subordinates. They are interested in empire building because amount of status, power, and pay is often associated with it.

Evaluating Political Tactics

Managers often use political tactics to gain and protect their power. To the extent that these tactics are used to achieve organizational goals, such politics can be seen as desirable. However, when these tactics are used to benefit the individuals or groups at the expense of the organization, organizational politics becomes dysfunctional. For example, from an organizational standpoint, withholding information and empire building may help the manager, but they are detrimental to organizational goals. Another problem is the possibility that political tactics may protect the personal and task-oriented interests of in-group managers but cripple the performance of other managers. The success of an organization may depend on the adequate performance of all managers, but the performance of some can be crippled by the uneven treatment of management.

HOW TO ACQUIRE AND USE POWER EFFECTIVELY

> *Influential managers tend to acquire and use all types of power. They tend to have a good understanding of various power types and know how to acquire and use them effectively.*

Some managers are successful in both acquiring and exercising power, while others are not. Some people may be able to acquire power but have difficulty maintaining it because they do not exercise it effectively. By observing the behavior of successful managers, you can learn the skills of acquiring, exercising, and maintaining power. You can use the following observations to guide you in behavior modeling.

Basic Motivational Patterns

Some personality factors distinguish managers who can successfully use power from those who cannot.

1. **Influential managers tend to have a strong power motive.**[18]
    They see management as a power game by which they can influence

other people in achieving their own personal and task-related goals. They are concerned with having an impact on other people through their leadership. However, they tend not to be authoritarian leaders who dominate others or make them feel weak and powerless. On the contrary, successful managers share their authority and power with subordinates to make them feel powerful.

2. **Influential managers are less motivated by affiliation needs.**[19] While they are sensitive to the needs of employees, they do not make decisions on the basis of whether employees will like them or not. Affiliation-motivated managers have a greater need for fellowship than for power or achievement. Their desire to be liked often causes them to be indecisive. Because they want to be accepted by others, they will do favors for those who satisfy their affiliation needs. When managers play favorites to the benefit of a select few, they often alienate other employees.

3. **Influential managers seem to be motivated by the socialized power motive.**[20] They are more organization-minded than less successful managers. Successful managers are motivated by a desire to influence the behavior of others for the good of the organization and its members *(socialized power)*. These managers create an organizational climate in which organization members have a sense of responsibility, organizational clarity, and team spirit. Managers who are motivated by *personalized power* are also able to create a sense of responsibility and team spirit. However, they demand that their subordinates be more loyal to them personally than to the organization they serve.

4. **Influential leaders tend to be emotionally stable and well-adjusted.** According to a study by Vaillant, successful managers are easy to get along with, are able to enjoy friends and games, and take imaginative and relaxing vacations away from their work.[21] It is a common myth that successful managers have family problems due to overinvolvement with their work. In fact, such managers tend to enjoy enduring marriages and good relationships with their spouses and children. In contrast, managers who have troubles with their spouses and children were found to be less successful than their well-integrated peers. Peace at home may help successful managers devote their energies to organizational endeavors.

Modes of Power Acquisition

Kotter suggested the first three of the following as methods of power acquisition used by influential managers.[22]

1. **Influential managers tend to acquire and use all types of power.** Unlike managers who are limited in power, effective managers ac-

quire all types. They usually feel that any power can be used under certain circumstances to produce positive results with few negative consequences. As suggested before, they may start by acquiring expert power and then seek position, reward, and coercive power.

2. **Influential managers tend to use their power to gain more power.** They invest their resources and power in ventures that might produce more power for them. They do favors for those who might feel obligated in return. These managers often undertake to do major organizational activities that are highly visible in order to demonstrate their abilities and be recognized. They may even change the organizational structure so their own people are put in positions where they can protect their interests.

3. **Influential managers tend to plan their movements in organizations.** They do not get where they are by chance or pure luck. They look for jobs that require their qualifications and move ahead into managerial positions where they can exert power and make other people depend on them. Since their moves are carefully planned and executed, they minimize errors and failures, and their successes reinforce their drive to move ahead and gain power. They take risks, but the risks are calculated. They avoid any undertaking that has a high percentage of possibility of failure.

4. **Influential managers develop coalitions with others.**[23] A manager gains power when others are willing to comply with his or her wishes. Other people comply with the manager's wishes because they believe the manager can satisfy their needs. To strengthen these interdependency relationships with others, the manager may help them achieve their goals while creating a sense of obligation in them. Important coalitions involve superiors, subordinates, peers, and influential persons outside of their organizations.

Modes of Exercising Power

The following list shows how influential managers exercise their power.[24]

1. **Influential managers feel comfortable using power.** They recognize and accept the importance of power in managing people, and they feel comfortable in using it to influence others to get the job done. To these managers, power is simply a tool with which they can get the necessary resources and cooperation from others. They do not feel immoral about gaining and using power.

2. **Influential managers intuitively understand various types of power.** They understand the strengths and limitations of various power sources and recognize the specific situations in which a particular power can be acquired and used effectively. For example, they recognize that professionals value expert power more than

position power, but they also understand that in order to exercise expert power they need to get the approval of those who have position power.

3. **Influential managers are sensitive to the legitimacy of power usage.**   They recognize the importance of the image they project to others inside and out of their organizations. They seldom exercise power impulsively. Instead, they use it cautiously and with self-control. They seldom promise more than they can deliver. Credibility usually means demonstrated, not perceived, ability in getting results. Managers with credibility are well respected for their integrity, and other people are willing to listen to them.

4. **Influential managers are sensitive to their dependency on others.**   They cope with their dependency on other people by being sensitive to it, by avoiding unnecessary dependence, and by establishing power over others. They may actively try to satisfy the needs of those they depend on because, by doing so, they also create a sense of obligation that they can collect on later. They also minimize their dependency on others by not asking for favors if they can help it.

5. **Influential managers represent the mainstream of their constituents.**[25]   They are the members in good standing of their organizational units. They represent the norms, values, and ideologies of these home units. Their strong ties with internal power coalitions gives them power to deal with external forces, such as unions, rival units, and others. Managers who do not have such ties are less likely to exert power internally as well as externally.

Legitimatizing the Use of Power

Pfeffer has suggested a number of ways managers can legitimatize the use of power.[26] Although these suggestions are Machiavellian in nature, they provide some insight into the use of power in organizations.

1. **Use performance criteria selectively.**   Managers can strengthen their power positions by adopting performance criteria selectively. Organizations use performance criteria to measure individual performance and to allocate their resources. Among the frequently used criteria are sales volume, profits, costs, market size, the number of employees, education, job skills, seniority, and others. Depending on how these criteria are selected and used, some managers benefit more than others. Successful managers influence the selection of performance criteria to favor their own power positions.

2. **Use a legitimate decision procedure.**   Committees are often used to legitimatize the decision process. The use of committees has several advantages. First, it diffuses the responsibility for the decision or

the use of power to all participants. This is especially desirable when the use of power involves unpopular actions. Second, the use of committees increases the likelihood that the use of power will be accepted. Since the committee members are involved in the decision process, they may feel that they have some influence in the use of power. Third, committee decisions usually do not deviate from the wishes of the manager. In most cases, committee members operate with the information provided and with rules specified by the manager. Finally, decisions made by committees are perceived as more legitimate than those made by a single person.

3. **Use a participative decision process.**   Managers may use a participative decision process to legitimatize their use of power. When employees participate in the decision process, they are more likely to accept and comply with the wishes of their superiors. For this reason, managers can use a participative approach as a way of expanding their power. Ironically, as we noted, there is a paradox of power—that is, some managers seem to lose their power by not sharing it with employees.

4. **Control the information flow.**   Managers can control the information flow to safeguard their power. Like other resources, information is an important source of power because people need it to do their jobs. Individuals who control the information flow exert power over those who depend on them for information. Managers can strategically control the information flow and its contents to enhance their power in the organization. They can disseminate favorable information while minimizing the impact of unfavorable information.

SUMMARY AND CONCLUSION

While power has some negative connotations, it is essential in running organizations. Organizations cannot function without people who can influence others to work toward achieving organizational goals. Managers need power to influence other people, and they have to be skillful in acquiring and maintaining it. They can acquire managerial power through professional expertise, formal position, personal attraction, association with the power agent, and/or the ability to reward and punish others.

Potential managers can learn the skills needed to acquire and exercise power by observing and imitating the behavior of successful managers and political leaders. Several behavioral examples can be used as a guide for acquiring and using power:

1. Possess the desire for power. This desire seems to motivate people to acquire the necessary power bases.

2. Acquire professional skills to gain entry into an organization. Gaining expert power is the first step toward gaining other kinds of power.

3. Gain power with others, including superiors, peers, and subordinates. Doing so requires some knowledge about people in organizations.

4. Gain and use the types of power needed to get the job done. However, be aware of the strengths and limitations of different power bases in order to use them effectively.

5. Use power to develop more power. By controlling the distribution of organizational power and resources, managers can make other people dependent on them.

6. Make the acquisition and maintenance of power an integral part of a career development plan. Managers plan and work hard to acquire and maintain it.

7. Learn to use power unobtrusively. Managers can do so by using legitimate criteria selectively and by relying on the legitimate procedure of power use.

KEY CONCEPTS AND WORDS

Authority	*Paradox of power*	*Expert power*
Power	*Political coalition*	*Charismatic power*
Socialized power	*Political tactic*	*Association power*
Personalized power	*Position power*	*Power legitimacy*
Politics	*Reward power*	*Power abuse*
Power expansion	*Coercive power*	*Scapegoating*

Questions for Review and Discussion

1. a. What is power?
   b. Why is it important for understanding organizational behavior?

2. a. How is power different from authority?
   b. How is it related to office politics?
   c. How is it related to leadership?

3. a. What kinds of power do you think you have?
   b. What kinds of power do you think you can use most effectively?
   c. What are the types of power that you cannot use effectively?

4. What are the primary power bases of the following individuals?
   a. Secretary of state
   b. A research and development engineer
   c. A U.S. senator
   d. A police officer

e. A sales manager

f. A supervisor in a union shop

5. Machiavelli concluded that "with regard to being feared and loved, men love at their own free will, but fear at the will of the prince. Therefore, a wise prince must rely on what is in his power and not on what is in the power of others." Respond to this statement by:

a. Indicating how managers can be feared or loved

b. Discussing some implications for managers

6. How does a person with a socialized power motive differ from a person with a personalized power motive? Describe how they are different in:

a. Acquiring and exercising power

b. Influencing organizational effectiveness

7. People view the use of power with suspicion. Managers should learn to use it unobtrusively. What are some possible ways of using power unobtrusively?

CASES

CASE 13.1. THE DELTA CHEMICAL CORPORATION

This exercise is designed to show you the political reality in organizations and to help you to cope with such reality. The case describes an imbalance in status and power among department heads. One manager exerts more influence on the managerial decision process than other managers, and they are bothered by it. Look at the political reality from the powerless managers' standpoint.

The Situation

Ken Dawson, executive vice-president of Delta Chemical Corporation, was distressed by personal squabbles among the department heads of marketing, production, and research and development. He was particularly concerned about the director of research and development, Dr. Arthur Bundy. Ron Jenkins, director of marketing and sales, and Dale Holovich, the production superintendent, had complained that Dr. Bundy frequently ignored operational procedures and encroached upon areas considered to be under their jurisdiction.

The firm manufactured a variety of chemicals for the pharmaceutical, medical, pest control, food, and beverage industries. As shown in the organizational chart (see Figure 13.4), the organization was divided into three major areas—production, sales, and research and development—along with other support groups. The R & D department was responsible for conducting applied research, experimentation, and product development. The production department was responsible for manufacturing products upon completion of the product development stage. The sales department was responsible for marketing research, promotion, sales, and customer services.

The activities involving product development and customer services caused

FIGURE   13.4
The Delta Chemical
Corporation.

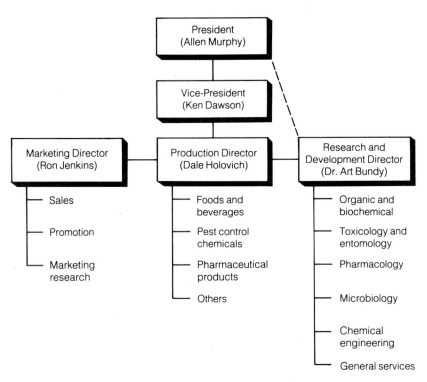

most of the conflicts between departments. Dr. Bundy had a habit of getting involved with customers in the stages of feasibility study and customer services. He often talked to these customers without consulting the marketing department. Dealing with the production department, he frequently interfered with pilot production runs, which were the responsibility of the production superintendent.

Dr. Bundy had been with the company for 15 years and was a close associate of the president, Allen Murphy. He was well respected and admired by many people in the company for his amiable and easy-going personality and for his accomplishments. He had been instrumental in the development of many fine chemical products. Dr. Bundy was a good scientist, but not an effective administrator. He kept sloppy records and did not usually follow the operational procedures when consulting with other departments.

Dawson was bothered by the R & D director's behavior and by his impact on other people, but he did not know how to approach and solve the problem. He had been with the company only two years, replacing Murphy when he was promoted to his present position as president. Although he was Dr. Bundy's superior, he often felt that Dr. Bundy had more influence on various managerial decisions than he had.

Discussion Questions

1. What do you see as problems facing the company?

2. What kinds of power does Dr. Bundy have?

3. What kinds of power does Dawson have?

4.   What would you suggest Dawson do to deal with such a problem?

5.   Outline the political tactics that Dawson may need to rely on.

CASE 13.2. THE MAKING OF A COLLEGE DEAN

Political behavior differs from one organization to another. Managers in some organizations rely heavily on their position and coercive power bases, while managers in other organizations rely primarily on informal power bases, such as expertise and internal power coalitions. When a manager does not understand the inner workings of political behavior, he or she may become powerless. This case gives you the opportunity to study the political behavior of an academic organization—a university—and discuss how one can function effectively in such organizations.

The Situation

Dr. Donald Singleton was newly appointed dean at an eastern university. After serving as program director for an educational foundation for five years, he had decided to return to academia. Since he was an articulate individual, he made a good impression on the people he met. He was therefore well received by the faculty and the community leaders.

Within a few months of his arrival, Dr. Singleton recruited several of his old acquaintances as full professors without much consultation with the faculty. When he did consult with some, he selected a few individuals who would support his views. The faculty protested this practice, but nothing changed.

Dr. Singleton was highly sensitive to external politics. He participated actively in community affairs and engaged in activities that would give him noticeable recognition and news coverage. He promised several educational programs at the university that would please local professional and trade groups. In the past, these programs had been resisted by the faculty for being nonacademic. The faculty learned of these promises through the local newspaper and the university's press releases.

The faculty moaned and grumbled but did not know how to handle the dean. They complained about his insensitivity to the collegial form of university governance, but nothing happened until they learned through the news media that he was raising funds by selling honorary professorships. The price would range from $500 to $20,000 depending on the rank. This angered the faculty, and they called a series of meetings to discuss the issues ranging from honorary professorships to recruiting. The fund-raising project was immediately dropped, and the faculty began to legislate new procedures for recruiting and for instituting new academic programs.

In the months following, a series of meetings were held to negotiate the procedures for recruiting and instituting new programs. Once these procedures were developed, the dean and the faculty were able to work together again in the process of serving the college.

Discussion Questions

1.   What were the dean's assumptions about his job?

2.   What are the nature and reality of a college dean's job? What kinds of power does the dean have?

3. What kinds of power do university professors have?

4. What could the dean do to gain power with the faculty?

5. What should he do to avoid this kind of problem in the future?

Footnotes

1. Niccolo Machiavelli, *The Prince,* trans. James B. Atkinson (Indianapolis: Bobbs-Merrill, 1976), p. 273.

2. J. D. Thompson, *Organizations in Action* (New York: McGraw-Hill, 1967), pp. 14–24.

3. M. L. Tushman, "A Political Approach to Organizations: A Review and Rationale," *Academy of Management Review,* April 1977, 206–216.

4. Jeffrey Pfeffer, *Organizational Design* (Berkeley: University of California Press, 1978).

5. A. J. Grimes, "Authority, Power, Influence and Social Control: A Theoretical Synthesis," *Academy of Management Review,* October 1978, 724–735.

6. Abraham Zaleznik, "Power and Politics in Organizational Life," *Harvard Business Review,* May-June 1970, 47–60; and V. E. Schein, "Individual Power and Political Behaviors in Organizations: An Inadequately Explored Reality," *Academy of Management Review,* January 1977, 64–72.

7. B. H. Drake, "Normative Constraints on Power Tactics Within Organizations," *Academy of Management Proceedings—1979,* Atlanta, Georgia, August 1979, pp. 176–179; and Tushman, "A Political Approach to Organizations," 210–212.

8. R. M. Kanter, "Power Failure in Management Circuits," *Harvard Business Review,* July-August 1979, 65–75.

9. George Graen and J. F. Cashman, "A Role-Making Model of Leadership in Formal Organizations: A Developmental Approach," in *Leadership Frontiers* ed. J. G. Hunt and L. L. Larson (Kent, OH: Kent State University Press, 1975), pp. 143–166.

10. J. P. Kotter, "Power, Dependence, and Effective Management," *Harvard Business Review,* July-August 1977, 125–136.

11. G. W. Dalton, "Motivation and Control in Organizations," in *Motivation and Control in Organizations,* ed. G. W. Dalton and P. R. Lawrence (Homewood, IL: Irwin, 1971), pp. 4–9.

12. A. S. Tannenbaum, *Control in Organizations* (New York: McGraw-Hill, 1968), pp. 8–19.

13. See J. R. P. French, Jr., and Bertram Raven, "The Bases of Social Power," in *Studies in Social Power,* ed. D. Cartwright (Ann Arbor, MI: Institute for Social Research, 1959).

14. Fred Luthans and Robert Kreitner, *Organizational Behavior Modification* (Glenview, IL: Scott, Foresman, 1975), pp. 117–123.

15. See J. G. Bachman, D. G. Bowers, and P. M. Marcus, "Bases of Supervisory Power: A Comparative Study in Five Organizational Settings," in Tannenbaum, *Control in Organizations,* pp. 229–239; and John M. Ivancevich, "An Analysis of Control, Bases of Control, and Satisfaction in an Organizational Setting," *Academy of Management Journal,* December 1970, 427–436.

16. R. W. Allen, D. L. Madison, L. W. Porter, P. A. Renwick, and B. T. Mayes, "Organizational Politics: Tactics and Characteristics of Its Actors," *California Management Review,* Fall 1979, 77–83.

17. G. Peters, "Insiders and Outsiders: The Politics of Pressure Group Influence on Bureaucracy," *Administrative Science Quarterly,* 1977, **7,** 191–217.

18. D. C. McClelland and D. H. Burnham, "Power Is the Great Motivator," *Harvard Business Review,* March-April 1976, 100–110.

19. D. C. McClelland and D. H. Burnham, "Power-Driven Managers: Good Guys Make Bum Bosses," *Psychology Today,* December 1975, 69–71.

20. McClelland and Burnham, "Power Is the Great Motivator," pp. 105–107.

21. G. E. Vaillant, "The Climb to Maturity: How the Best and the Brightest Came of Age," *Psychology Today,* September 1977, 34–49.

22. Kotter, "Power, Dependence, and Effective Management," 135–136.

23. N. McMurry, "Power and the Ambitious Executive," *Harvard Business Review,* November-December 1973, 140–145.

24. The first three suggestions are reported in Kotter, "Power, Dependence, and Effective Management," pp. 135–136.

25. John Bryson and George Kelley, "A Political Perspective on Leadership Emergence, Stability, and Change in Organizational Networks," *Academy of Management Review,* October 1978, 713–723.

26. Jeffrey Pfeffer, "Power and Resource Allocation in Organizations," in *Psychological Foundations of Organizational Behavior,* ed. B. M. Staw (Pacific Palisades, CA: Goodyear, 1977), pp. 278–301.

LEARNING OBJECTIVES

1. To understand the functions and types of organizational rewards.
2. To understand the differences in performance appraisal systems.
3. To know how to tie organizational rewards to performance.

CHAPTER OUTLINE

Functions of Rewards

Rewards and Satisfaction
Rewards and Performance

Types of Organizational Rewards

Extrinsic Rewards
Intrinsic Rewards
Effect of Extrinsic Rewards on Intrinsic Motivation

Performance Appraisal Systems

Requirements for Effective Performance Appraisal
Job Analysis and Evaluation
Result-Based Performance Criteria
Behavior-Based Performance Criteria
Judgment-Based Performance Criteria
Improving the Effectiveness of Performance Appraisal

Matching Rewards to Performance

Difficulties in Relating Rewards to Performance
Methods of Relating Rewards to Performance
Improving the Effectiveness of Reward Systems

Summary and Conclusion

14 MANAGING REWARD SYSTEMS

When extrinsic rewards are related to performance, the result is higher motivation and the tendency for turnover to be centered among the poorer performers. Despite the obvious advantages of organizations tying rewards to performance, rewards often are not tied to performance in many organizations. There are some situations in which tying rewards to performance is dysfunctional; however, organizations often do not relate rewards to performance even when doing so would be highly functional.

Edward E. Lawler, Motivation in Work Organizations[1]

Organizations can use a variety of rewards to attract and maintain people and to motivate them to achieve their personal and organizational goals. Pay, job security, employee benefits, promotions, congenial co-workers, supportive supervisors, status systems, challenging task assignments, and provision for professional growth are just a few examples. Managing these rewards is an important task of managers. Not only do they control the distribution of these rewards, but they can also influence how the employees perceive the value of rewards and the relationship between rewards and performance. As pointed out in Chapter 6, employees make motivational decisions based on how they perceive the value of rewards, the instrumental relationship between performance and rewards, and the expectancy of getting the job done. This chapter focuses on (1) the function of rewards, (2) the types of rewards, and (3) the methods of distributing them.

FUNCTIONS OF REWARDS

> *Organizational rewards serve two major functions: (1) satisfying employee needs and (2) motivating employees to produce. These two functions can be effectively achieved only if the rewards are tied to performance.*

People join and work in organizations to satisfy their needs. Because organizational rewards can satisfy these needs, they have a significant effect on employee behavior. Consequently, the distribution of these rewards has a significant effect on both employee satisfaction and work motivation.

Rewards and Satisfaction

Considerable research has been conducted on the relationship between rewards and satisfaction. Based on the research evidence, Lawler has summarized the following five points.[2]

1. **Satisfaction with rewards is a function of how much is received relative to how much the individual feels should be received.** When employees receive less than they believe they deserve, they are dissatisfied. When they receive more than they believe they deserve, they may feel uncomfortable.

2. **Satisfaction with rewards is a function of social comparison.** People compare what they do for and receive from the organization with other employees. If they feel that others are receiving more than they do for the same amount of effort, they may feel dissatisfied.

3. **Employee satisfaction is influenced by both intrinsic and extrinsic rewards.** Since different needs are satisfied by different rewards, employees should be provided with a variety of rewards.

4. **People differ in the rewards they desire and in how they evaluate different rewards.** Employees want different things from their jobs, and these differences in reward preference change over a period of time.

5. **Some extrinsic rewards are important only because they lead to other rewards.** For example, the size of a desk or an office is of no inherent value, but it is considered an important reward because it symbolizes the officeholder's power and status.

Knowing what rewards satisfy employees helps managers formulate reward systems that can better satisfy employee needs. Three conditions must be met before a reward system can be effective.[3]

1. **The magnitude of a reward must be large enough to satisfy a person's needs.**   For example, the size of a pay increase must be large enough to make the reward meaningful. A nominal pay increase may be considered an insult rather than a reward.

2. **The reward must compare favorably with those received by others performing similar jobs.**   When rewards are contingent upon performance, employees are more likely to perceive the reward system as equitable.

3. **The reward system should recognize individual differences in reward preference.**   Since people want different things from their jobs, these differences must be reflected in the reward system.

Rewards and Performance

Rewards may satisfy employee needs, but unless they are tied to performance, they may not cause high performance. If rewards are to motivate employees' job performance, they must be valued by the employees (have perceived value), and they must be contingent upon performance (have perceived equity). If the valued rewards are given to workers independently of their performance, poor performers will be better satisfied than higher performers. In such a case, satisfied poor performers are not motivated to improve their performance, and dissatisfied higher performers may actually reduce their performance levels. Thus, unless they are tied to performance, even valued rewards lose motivational power.

 ## TYPES OF ORGANIZATIONAL REWARDS

> *Organizational rewards can be classified into two categories—extrinsic and intrinsic. Extrinsic rewards are external to task performance, whereas intrinsic rewards are associated directly with it.*

When a task is exciting, interesting, and challenging, people tend to perform it for sheer enjoyment. They may enjoy having responsibility, using their skills and knowledge, knowing how well they perform, and feeling a sense of accomplishment when the task is completed. These reasons for enjoying the task are called *intrinsic rewards,* and they are derived directly from performing it.

Extrinsic rewards are external to the task performance, and they can be given to employees either when the task is accomplished or independently of their performance. Organizations use both types of reward to attract and motivate people to achieve organizational goals. As Figure 14.1 suggests, the connection between rewards and performance is closer for intrinsic rewards than for extrinsic rewards.

Extrinsic Rewards

There are two kinds of extrinsic reward—substantive and interactive. *Substantive rewards* are tangible reinforcers that satisfy existence needs (biological, safety, and security) and some relatedness needs (power, status, and competition). Money, job security, and promotion are prime examples. *Interactive rewards* are social reinforcers derived from interpersonal interactions. These rewards satisfy such relatedness needs as affiliation, companionship, emotional security, power, and influence.

Monetary Incentives.   Monetary incentives are the most powerful extrinsic incentives there are; they can satisfy a number of needs. They are valued because they not only can satisfy existence needs but also can symbolize a number of things employees value, such as material possessions, status, and independence. Money is a versatile reinforcer, for, with it, one can acquire other reinforcers such as food, homes, insurance, economic status, and power.

Money can have a strong incentive value for high productivity if its application is contingent upon job performance. Pay systems lose their effectiveness when monetary rewards are given to employees independently of their performance. Performance-contingent pay systems are far more powerful in arousing work motivation than non-performance-contingent pay systems. For example, productivity under a piece-rate system tends to be higher than that under an hourly-rate system.[4]

Job Security.   Job security guarantees a continuous flow of income. It reduces the anxieties associated with possible need deprivation that result

FIGURE   14.1
The Relationship Between Performance, Rewards, and Satisfaction.
(After Edward E. Lawler and Lyman W. Porter, "The Effect of Performance on Job Satisfaction, *Industrial Relations,* 1967, **7,** 20–28. Used with permission.)

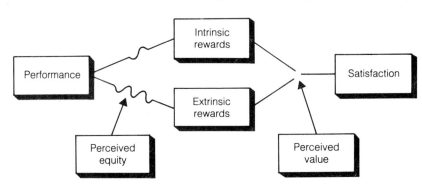

in problems such as mental illness, alcoholism, and suicide.[5] When jobs are taken away, people lose not only their economic means but also their sense of identity and self-esteem. By reducing the unproductive fear that needs will not be satisfied, employers can free employees to use their energies in productive endeavors. However, job security should be contingent upon the employees' value and contributions to the organization. When job security is granted to all employees, regardless of their contributions, the organization will be flooded with freeloaders of its own creation.

Promotion.   Like money, promotion can be given to employees independently of job performance although it will have a stronger motivational value if it is based on performance. It is also an important reward because it can satisfy a variety of needs, including increased pay, self-esteem, and recognition. However, it is limited, since frequent use of promotion is not possible and, even if it were possible, frequency would dilute its value.

Social Reinforcers.   Attention, praise, and a pat on the back are social reinforcers that satisfy the needs for affection, approval, and self-esteem. These social expressions can be used to encourage desirable behaviors while discouraging undesirable ones. For example, research indicates that the study behavior of students is improved by the use of praise, while the incidence of disruptive behavior is decreased by lack of praise.[6]

In work organizations, co-workers—including superiors, subordinates, and peers—can produce social reinforcers, and consequently they can influence the behavior of others. To the extent that social reinforcers are valued by employees and are connected to performance, they can have a positive impact on employee job performance.[7]

Intrinsic Rewards

Intrinsic rewards are the direct result of task performance. They satisfy such growth needs as competence, achievement, and self-actualization. When a task is intrinsically motivating, people exert their energies to experience a sense of doing something worthwhile and to realize their potential. Interesting job content, an achieving climate, and growth opportunity are the prime sources of intrinsic rewards.

Job Content.   People enjoy performing interesting jobs. If the job is intrinsically motivating, they may perform it without extrinsic rewards. What makes a job intrinsically motivating? A motivating job has a number of task attributes—such as being interesting and offering individual responsibility—that stimulate work motivation.[8] That is, a job becomes intrinsically motivating when it requires a variety of responses and skills, leads to a whole unit or a major portion of a product, provides performance feedback, and allows employees control over their work environment (see Chapter 15 on job design).

An Achieving Climate.   An achievement-oriented climate not only satisfies the need to achieve but also motivates people to achieve. People with high achievement needs tend to set realistic goals, take moderate risks and personal responsibility, and be task-oriented.[9] These people's needs are better satisfied in an achievement-oriented climate than in a non-achievement-oriented climate. Stringer points out that the level of achievement motive can be increased in an organization where (1) goal-setting behavior is encouraged, (2) personal responsibility for accomplishment is demanded, (3) performance feedback is provided, (4) employees are allowed to take moderate risks, and (5) rewards are based on performance.[10]

Autonomy.   Autonomy refers to the privilege given to employees of controlling their own work environment without close supervision. It satisfies the need to be free and independent. Some people seek managerial and professional positions simply because these jobs provide them with more autonomy than other jobs.[11] Promotion is sought by many people for the same reason.

Growth Opportunity.   People with growth needs search for opportunities to develop and advance in their professions. Professional growth and advancement allow these individuals to engage continuously in challenging and interesting jobs. A job that is intrinsically motivating at one time may not be so in the future. As a person gains more experience and job skills, he or she may find the same job less challenging. Unless employees are allowed to grow and advance in their jobs, they may become dissatisfied. In essence, growth opportunity creates an expectation that the job will continue to be challenging and motivating.

Effect of Extrinsic Rewards on Intrinsic Motivation

Common sense indicates that motivation should increase when both intrinsic and extrinsic rewards increase. However, Deci indicates that emphasis on extrinsic rewards can reduce intrinsic motivation. In his experiments with students performing intrinsically motivating tasks (matching puzzle pieces and writing headlines), he found that paying the subjects on a performance-contingency basis tended to reduce the amount of time they spent on the tasks.[12]

Deci interprets this research to mean that when a person performs an intrinsically motivating task, the locus of control is within the person. That is, the person performs the task because he or she enjoys it. However, when a performance-contingent reward is introduced, the locus of control becomes external. In other words, the person may feel that he or she is performing the task for money or other extrinsic rewards rather than for sheer enjoyment.

Deci's findings are plausible in situations where a small-sized reward and a moderately motivating task are involved. However, if the reward size is significant and the task is truly motivating, it is doubtful whether the reward will reduce intrinsic motivation.[13] When the task is truly interesting and intrinsically motivating, the employee may perform it regardless of extrinsic rewards. But if extrinsic rewards follow in addition to intrinsic motivation, they may add to the performer's satisfaction.

PERFORMANCE APPRAISAL SYSTEMS

> *Since the motivational value of rewards increases when they are tied to performance, performance appraisal is needed to determine the level of individual contributions or performance.*

Successful task performance automatically produces intrinsic rewards but not extrinsic rewards. A conscientious effort must be made to relate extrinsic rewards to performance. It has been pointed out several times that when a reward system fails to tie extrinsic rewards to performance, it can cause various employee problems such as a feeling of inequity, dissatisfaction, and low productivity. In order to tie rewards to performance, management must be able to measure an employee's contributions to the organization—job performance.

Performance appraisal is a way of measuring the contributions of individuals to their organizations. The objectives of performance appraisal are twofold: (1) to reward past performance and (2) to motivate future performance improvement. The information obtained from this performance appraisal can be used in granting pay increases, promotions, and task assignments. Since appraisal is closely related to the most sensitive area of human relationships—determining the worth of an individual—it should be handled with great care.

Requirements for Effective Performance Appraisal

There are two major requirements for an effective performance appraisal system: (1) objectively measurable performance criteria and (2) objectivity in the evaluation process. When an appraisal system lacks these requirements, there may be ineffective utilization of its reward system.

Performance Measurability.   Three qualifications are essential for developing objectively measurable performance criteria—relevancy, reliability, and discrimination.

Relevancy refers to the degree to which the selected criteria are related to performance goals. For example, production speed can be a more relevant performance measure than a person's appearance.

Reliability refers to the degree to which the criteria produce consistent results. Quantifiable measures such as production units and sales volumes produce relatively consistent measurements, while various subjective criteria such as attitudes, creativity, and cooperativeness produce inconsistent measurements that depend on who evaluates them and how they are evaluated.

Discrimination measures the degree to which a performance criterion can tell differences in performance. If the ratings tend to be all "good" or "poor," the performance measure is not discriminating.

When performance criteria possess these essential qualifications, employees are likely to be less defensive and more receptive to performance appraisal. Conversely, when employees are evaluated on vague and unspecific performance criteria, they tend to become defensive and even feel threatened.[14]

However, many jobs in organizations, especially those in service industries, do not lend themselves to objective performance measurement. Except for some jobs in the production and sales departments, most jobs in areas such as accounting, law, medicine, and government cannot be quantitatively defined and measured. In the absence of quantifiable measurement, the use of subjective performance criteria often becomes inevitable.

Judgmental Integrity. Even with objectively measurable criteria, perceptual and judgmental error in performance appraisal still remains a problem. As indicated in Chapter 5, a number of perceptual elements can distort the evaluation process. A few examples are:

Selective perception. The manager may selectively perceive certain performance criteria as more important than others and use these as a basis for evaluating employee performance.

Halo effect. The manager may use a single performance dimension to determine an employee's worth to the organization.

Similarity effect. The manager may rate the employees who have values similar to his or her own more highly than those who do not.

Stereotyping. The manager may evaluate a person in a particular social group on the basis of the general characteristics of the group rather than on the person's unique characteristics or contributions.

In addition to these perceptual distortions, judgmental errors can stem from the rater's personality and motivation. Some raters are harsher or more lenient than others; so the same employee's performance can be rated higher or lower depending on who does the evaluation.[15] The rater's motivation also affects the evaluation process. A self-serving rater is more likely to value personal loyalty than an institution-minded rater. The rater's motivation to be accurate and objective determines the quality of performance appraisals.

Thus, managers may consciously or unconsciously distort the evaluation process. Hamner and his associates point out that, even when objective performance criteria are clearly defined, white supervisors tend to rate blacks differently from whites, and females differently from males, even when their performance levels are the same.[16] Unless the raters show integrity in their judgments and those rated perceive these judgments to be fair, the evaluative system tends to be ineffective.

Questions of subjectivity and judgmental error often discourage or even prevent some employers from using formal performance appraisal. Instead, they informally evaluate their employees, or evaluate their worth on the basis of seniority or loyalty rather than on their performance contributions. Since most organizations use performance appraisal in one form or another for a variety of reasons, it is important to develop evaluation procedures that are reliable and acceptable to the people involved.

A systematic way of conducting performance appraisal includes: (1) job analysis, (2) performance criteria, and (3) performance appraisal.

Job Analysis and Evaluation

Job analysis is the process of studying job content or job-related behaviors that are crucial to task performance. It records data about training, skills, required efforts, experiences, responsibilities and so forth, that are needed to perform the job. In essence, it shows the job requirements.

The first part of job analysis is to provide a *description* of a job's contents and essential requirements. This information is used for recruitment, placement, job classification, and so forth. For example, if the job requires a high level of technical skill, a person with such a skill will be sought. If it requires a high level of interaction among employees, cooperative behavior can be promoted in lieu of competition. Job description also describes the kinds of employee behavior desired by management. It shows the amount of authority and responsibility the job carries and indicates the necessary relationships with other members.

Job analysis is also important in determining the value of a job to an organization. This process is called *job evaluation*. Job value is usually determined by (1) the importance of a job to the organization, (2) the degree of skill required, and (3) the availability of labor in a particular field. Job evaluation provides information for determining pay scales for various jobs. That is, once a job's value and the labor availability are determined, management can set pay scales. Once pay scales are set, managers need to evaluate the performance of their employees to determine individual pay levels. There are basically three different types of performance criteria: (1) result-based, (2) behavior-based, and (3) judgment-based.[17]

Result-Based Performance Criteria

Result-based performance evaluation defines job performance in terms of accomplishing organizational goals, such as product units, profits, costs, market share, and so forth. Instead of evaluating job-related behaviors, which are the *means* of achieving performance goals, it measures the end results—the goal attainment. These performance measures are defined in specific and quantifiable terms, such as increasing profits by 10 percent or reducing costs by 5 percent.

Performance goals can be set either by management or by the work group. Researchers suggest that when employees participate in goal-setting processes, they tend to set higher goals and show higher productivity than when they are told to do their best or their goals are assigned.[18] Participative goal-setting practice is called *management by objectives* (MBO), which is considered a motivational tool because the participants become ego-involved in decisions they have made. They tend to accept the decisions as their own and feel personally responsible for implementing them.

Management by objectives is designed to be a motivational program that encourages employee participation and goal attainment, but it can also be used as a basis for evaluating employee performance. An MBO performance evaluation program focuses on what employees have achieved. The key features of an MBO program are as follows:

1. Performance goals are set jointly by superior and subordinate. This participative goal setting tends to increase employee acceptance of the goals.

2. Since jointly set goals tend to be more realistic and challenging, they appeal to both individual and organizational needs.

3. Task responsibilities are assigned to individuals or work groups. The participants know what is expected of them in the goal-attainment process.

4. Periodic progress review is conducted to see how well employees are progressing on their jobs. This review is designed to provide performance feedback so that any necessary corrective actions can be taken.

5. Since performance goals and responsibilities are clearly specified in advance, subordinates usually know where they stand.

6. Employees' performance is evaluated on the basis of what they have accomplished rather than on their personal characteristics. This approach tends to minimize judgmental errors.

The advantages of using result-based performance measures are that they (1) provide performance targets, (2) are specific and measurable, (3) tend to minimize judgmental errors, and (4) are directly related to achieving organizational goals.

The main disadvantages are that (1) many jobs do not lend themselves to quantifiable measurement, (2) employees tend to ignore non-quantifiable performance areas such as exercising leadership and helping others, and (3) when the measures are used on an individual basis, it may discourage cooperation among organization members.

Objective performance measures can be effectively used for jobs that can be expressed in specific, quantifiable terms, such as in sales and production departments. These measures can be developed and used on an individual or group basis. Individualized measurement increases individual motivation. But if the task requires a high degree of cooperation among work group members, or if its performance is achieved through joint effort, individualized performance evaluation should be discouraged.

Behavior-Based Performance Criteria

Most jobs in organizations do not lend themselves to the use of objective-based performance measures. For example, it is difficult to develop and use such measures for jobs in public relations, the controller's office, research and development, educational institutions, and government agencies. If objective-based performance measures cannot be used, then management may develop and use behavior-based performance measures. These performance criteria measure the *means* of achieving goals rather than the *end results*.

Behavior-based performance measures, which are often called *behaviorally anchored rating scales* (BARS), are derived from a list of "critical incidents" related to various performance dimensions. The usual steps in developing and using these scales are:[19]

1. A group of supervisors and subordinates identifies *key performance dimensions*—that is, job-related behaviors that tend to improve task performance. For project managers, meeting deadlines, helping co-workers, and solving technical problems can be key performance dimensions.

2. The same group identifies a set of *behavioral incidents* related to each of the key performance dimensions. For example, in the case of meeting project deadlines, some managers may always meet the deadlines, while others do not.

3. These behavioral incidents are rated in order of their desirability or importance, and *rating scales* are assigned to them. As shown in Figure 14.2, meeting deadlines all the time may be assigned nine

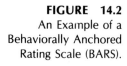

FIGURE 14.2
An Example of a
Behaviorally Anchored
Rating Scale (BARS).

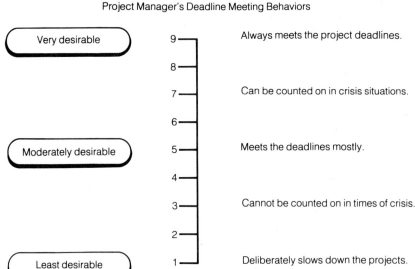

Project Manager's Deadline Meeting Behaviors

Very desirable	9	Always meets the project deadlines.
	8	
	7	Can be counted on in crisis situations.
	6	
Moderately desirable	5	Meets the deadlines mostly.
	4	
	3	Cannot be counted on in times of crisis.
	2	
Least desirable	1	Deliberately slows down the projects.

points on a nine-point scale, while slowing down the project is assigned one point.

4. Rating scales are developed for all performance dimensions. The resulting rating scales are called BARS.

5. The evaluator uses these rating scales to rate an employee's behaviors on the job.

The advantages of using behavior-based performance measures are that (1) behaviors can be observed and measured objectively, and (2) BARS measure specific and relevant job-related behaviors. Since they are specific and observable, judgmental errors can be minimized.

The potential disadvantages are that (1) BARS do not directly measure the end results—goal attainment—and (2) developing the rating scales for various jobs in organizations is very time-consuming. Organization members may argue that their jobs are different from others and therefore require different kinds of behaviors.

Behavior-based performance measures can be used in job situations where critical job behaviors can be observed and measured. Meeting deadlines, finishing reports, opening new accounts for customers, handling customer complaints successfully, and solving technical problems are examples of critical job-related behaviors. But these measures cannot be used in situations where job performance involves nonobservable activities—leadership, creativity, and intelligence. Many jobs in managerial and professional fields involve cognitive and mental processes that cannot be observed or objectively measured.

Judgment-Based Performance Criteria

Judgment-based appraisals evaluate employee job performance in terms of less specific behavioral descriptions—quantity of work, quality of work, job knowledge, cooperation, initiative, reliability, interpersonal competence, loyalty, and so forth. Judgment-based appraisal is often called the *traditional method* because it has traditionally been used in many organizations. Figure 14.3 is an example of judgment-based performance evaluation.

FIGURE 14.3

An Example of a Judgment-Based Performance Appraisal Form.

Performance Appraisal Form

Employee Name: _____   Date: _____

Title: _____   Length of Service: _____

Division: _____   Rater: _____

Instruction: Evaluate the employee on the following criteria.

Performance Criteria	Unsatisfactory 1	2	Average 3	4	Excellent 5
1. *Quantity of Work:* The amount of work done within a given period of time.					
2. *Quality of Work:* The quality of work done in terms of its accuracy and completeness.					
3. *Job Knowledge:* The amount of job knowledge and skill.					
4. *Creativeness:* Originality of ideas and problem-solving behavior.					
5. *Cooperation:* Willingness to work with and for others.					
6. *Dependability:* Conscientiousness and reliability in regard to attendance and work completion.					
7. *Initiative:* Eagerness in undertaking new tasks and in seeking increased responsibilities.					
8. *Personal Qualities:* Personality, sociability, leadership, and integrity.					

There are two types of judgment-based performance appraisal: rating and ranking.

Rating Method.   The *rating method* is the oldest and most widely used form of performance appraisal. It usually includes a number of job-related behaviors that are broadly defined, and the rater is asked to respond to each of these behavioral dimensions on some type of rating scale. These scales may range from "very good" to "very poor," or from "most desirable" to "least desirable."

A major problem with this method is that performance measures are so loosely defined that they are vulnerable to a variety of judgmental errors —selective perception, halo effect, similarity effect, stereotyping, and leniency or harshness, for example. These judgmental errors reduce the relevancy, reliability, and discriminability of the performance measures. As indicated earlier, the same person's performance can be rated very positively or negatively depending on who does the evaluating.

Ranking Method.   In order to overcome the limitations of the rating method, some companies use an alternative form called the *ranking method.* Although there are many variations of this method, a common feature is that the rater is forced to rank-order the ratees on single or multiple performance dimensions. All employees are ranked from "best" down to "poorest."

This method has several defects. First, it forces a manager to rank employees as high or low performers even if they are all about the same. It is not fair for some employees to be ranked as "poor" performers, and rewarded accordingly, when they may be as good as those who are ranked higher. When people are arbitrarily ranked, they feel threatened and become defensive.[20] Second, it is difficult to rank a large number of people. When many employees are ranked, ranking becomes more arbitrary.

Although judgment-based performance appraisal has some deficiencies, it is widely used in situations where job behaviors cannot be clearly defined and measured. With proper training and experience, managers or raters may improve the accuracy of their appraisals. Various rating errors can be minimized if raters are aware of the possibility of perceptual and judgmental errors, and if they deal with a smaller number of employees.[21]

Improving the Effectiveness of Performance Appraisal

Although performance appraisals are widely used in most organizations, their effectiveness varies greatly. In many organizations, they are poorly used and fail to achieve their objectives. Factors leading to their ineffective use include:

1. The selection of irrelevant performance criteria such as personality, mannerisms, and impression.
2. The rater's perceptual and judgmental errors.
3. The rater's inability to evaluate the ratee's behavior.
4. The rater's self-serving motive—office politics.
5. The ratee's resistance to performance appraisal.

If we view these factors in reverse, we can conclude that the effectiveness of a performance appraisal system depends on (1) the relevancy of the selected performance criteria, (2) the rater's ability to evaluate the ratee's performance correctly, (3) the rater's motivation to evaluate accurately, and (4) the ratee's acceptance of the appraisal process.[22] The following suggestions should help improve the effectiveness of performance appraisal.

1. **Match performance criteria to job situations.**   As indicated earlier, since jobs differ in their characteristics, performance criteria should also differ. Objective-based performance criteria can be used in job situations where performance goals can be clearly defined and measured. Behavior-based criteria are recommended in job situations where job behaviors can be expressed in terms of the means of achieving performance goals rather than the *end results.* Judgment-based criteria must be used in job situations where job behaviors cannot be expressed in observable, measurable terms.

2. **Use a participative appraisal approach.**   Participation in the appraisal process is likely to increase employees' acceptance of the system. Employees can influence the selection of the performance criteria, know what is expected of them, and discover their own strengths and limitations. Even in nonparticipatory appraisal systems, such as judgment-based appraisal, open dialogues between superiors and subordinates can enhance mutual understanding of each other's expectations.

3. **Focus on specific behaviors or goal attainment.**   It was pointed out earlier that people become defensive when they are evaluated on nonspecific performance criteria or on personality traits such as appearance, cooperativeness, creativity, initiative, potentiality, and loyalty. Using these criteria is threatening because it involves an evaluation of what the person *is* rather than of what he or she *does.* People can change or improve what they do, but it is often difficult for them to change what they are. When evaluation involves a suggested change in areas the person is not able, or does not know how to change, it only frustrates the person and generates defensive-

ness. For this reason, the evaluation must place emphasis on specific behaviors that can be changed.

4. **Focus on problem solving rather than on judgment.**   Performance appraisal interviews should focus on setting and achieving performance goals rather than on judging personality traits. Frequent performance reviews allow discussions of problem areas as they occur and help employees solve problems before they become serious. These reviews reduce the need for negative feedback later and are far less threatening than annual performance appraisals. When a manager exhibits such supportive appraisal behavior, it tends to increase subordinates' acceptance of the appraisal system and their willingness to improve performance.[23]

5. **Separate pay discussion from performance appraisal.**   One of the major objectives of performance appraisal is to decide the pay level of the employees. Yet, if performance appraisal is mixed with pay discussion, people will be preoccupied with the issue of money, and the issue of performance improvement will become secondary. Experts suggest that pay discussions be held later, or that they not be held at all, since some people are so emotional about money that it may lead to a no-win situation.[24]

6. **Train the performance evaluators.**   The value of performance appraisals can be improved by training the evaluators. A study by Latham and his associates demonstrated that managers in a large corporation can be trained to minimize a variety of perceptual and judgmental errors that often occur in performance appraisals, such as selective perception, halo effect, and similarity effect.[25] This training involves role-playing and observation. The trainees (1) have an opportunity to see how other managers make various rating errors, (2) actively participate in role-playing sessions (usually videotaped), (3) learn to what extent they are prone to make such errors, (4) learn to minimize such errors, and (5) receive feedback about their accuracy from the observers—both the trainer and the other trainees.

MATCHING REWARDS TO PERFORMANCE

Organizational rewards can be related to the performance of (1) individuals, (2) groups, or (3) the entire company. The selection of a particular reward system should be based on differences in task situations and the purpose of rewarding.

Much emphasis has been placed on the importance of matching rewards to performance. From a theoretical standpoint, the matching principle is an essential part of both reinforcement and expectancy theories: Reinforcement theory sees it as the key to reinforcing desirable behaviors; expectancy theory sees it as a way of improving the reward–performance instrumentality.

Difficulties in Relating Rewards to Performance

If the impact of rewards on work motivation is to be maximized, employee performance must be equitably and fairly measured and rewarded. However, tying rewards to individual performance is a complex task, and in some cases it may even have dysfunctional consequences for organizational performance. This caution is based on the following limitations.

Inability to Identify Individual Performance.   Most jobs in organizations either do not have objective performance criteria or are jointly performed. These limitations make it difficult to identify individual performance.

Increased Competition.   Individualized rewards may encourage individual work motivation, but the emphasis on individual motivation may cause excessive competition among work group members. Competition can be harmful to performance in job situations requiring a high degree of cooperation among group members.

Shift in Behavioral Cause.   As discussed earlier, when extrinsic rewards are tied to performance, one's locus of causality or control may shift from internal to external. If too much emphasis is given to extrinsic rewards, some people may feel they are performing the job for extrinsic rewards rather than for intrinsic reasons. Thus, if a task is intrinsically motivating, there is no need to emphasize the tie between rewards and performance. Doing so only risks the possibility that intrinsic motivation will be lost.

In spite of these difficulties, the idea of tying rewards to performance is so crucial to organizational success that it should not be abandoned without a conscious effort being made to improve and implement it. What makes a capitalistic society economically more viable than other societies is that it rewards good performance. If rewards cannot be tied in any way to individual performance, an attempt should be made to relate them to group performance.

Methods of Relating Rewards to Performance

There are three bases on which rewards can be related to performance—individual, group, and companywide. Each of these reward systems can have a different impact on employee behavior and motivation. The following discussion focuses on the effects of various reward systems on three organizational concerns—individual motivation, group effort, and institutional loyalty (see Figure 14.4).

Individual-based Reward Systems.   Examples of individualized reward systems are piece-rate incentives, sales commissions, sales contests, and promotions. They are called individualized systems because rewards are based on individual performance. These systems have considerable impact on individual motivation, but they encourage competition and so can have detrimental effects on group effort. Their effect on institutional loyalty is likely to be neutral or low because they neither encourage nor discourage employees' long-term commitment to the organization. Since they are effective in arousing individual work motivation, they can be applied in job situations where the tasks can be performed and measured individually.

Group-based Reward Systems.   Group incentives and group performance bonuses are given to workers on the basis of group performance. Since rewards are given to employees on a group basis, it can encourage cooperation. However, the effects of such systems on individual motivation and institutional loyalty are likely to be moderate. Rewards are not directly tied to individual performance, but everyone's reward depends on how much he or she contributed to the group's productivity. Also, the work group represents the organization, so any group loyalty can be positively related to it.

Group-based systems can be effectively applied to job situations

FIGURE 14.4
Relative Effectiveness of Pay Systems. (After K. H. Chung, *Motivational Theories and Practices.* Columbus, Ohio: Grid Publishing, 1977, p. 157. Used with permission.)

Pay Plans		Performance Measurement	Individual Motivation	Group Effort	Institutional Loyalty
Individual	Piece-rate	Productivity	H	L	N
	Commission	Productivity	H	L	N
	Production bonus	Productivity	H	L	N
	Merit-rate	Supervisor rating	M	L	N
Group	Piece-rate	Productivity	M	H	M
	Sconlon plan	Labor cost saving	M	H	M
	Production bonus	Productivity	M	H	M
	Merit-rate	Supervisor rating	M	H	M
Companywide	Profit-sharing	Profit	M	M	H
	Stock option	Profit, stock price	L	M	H
	Fringe benefits	Nonperformance contingent	N	L	M

High (H), medium (M), low (L), and neutral (N)

requiring a high degree of cooperation among group members and to situations where job performance cannot be measured on an individual basis. The Scanlon Plan, for example, is often adopted to encourage group effort in such a situation. Joseph Scanlon, after many years of observing the weakness of individual incentive systems, proposed a system that encourages cooperation. Under this system, any profits derived from labor and cost-saving ideas are shared with the contributing work group.[26]

Companywide Reward Systems.   Companywide reward systems include profit-sharing, stock options, and fringe benefits. These systems may be used to encourage long-term personal commitment to the organization. But, since rewards are given to employees on the basis of their membership rather than their performance, they tend to have little impact on individual motivation. If the rewards are based on the overall success of the company, however, they may encourage individual motivation and group efforts to some extent. On the other hand, non-performance-contingent rewards (most fringe benefits) have little impact on individual motivation and group effort.

The Lincoln Electric Company uses a profit-sharing plan that encourages both individual motivation and institutional loyalty.[27] Under this plan, the total amount of bonus distributed is determined by the size of the company profit, but the amount each individual receives is based on individual performance. It is thus possible for management to reward employees according to their performance. Since individual bonus is tied to individual performance, it can encourage individual motivation. At the same time, such a companywide bonus plan can foster institutional loyalty.

Use of Mixed Systems.   No one system is effective in meeting all organizational needs—individual motivation, group effort, and institutional loyalty. Selection of reward systems should reflect differences in task characteristics and organizational concerns. Since most organizations have a variety of tasks and are concerned with both individual and group effort, they will probably need diversified reward systems.

Improving the Effectiveness of Reward Systems

Designing and administering a reward system that is satisfactory to both management and employees is difficult. The following suggestions will help overcome some of the difficulties in relating rewards to performance.[28]

1. **Tailor the reward systems to meet the needs of the organization and its members.**   As indicated earlier, jobs differ in their interactional requirements and performance measurability. Some can be performed, measured, and rewarded individually; others need to be

performed, measured, and rewarded collectively. The selection of reward systems should be differentiated to reflect these distinctions.

2. **Clarify the relationship between rewards and performance.** When employees know how and why they are rewarded, they can direct their energies to job-related behaviors that lead to performance and rewards. Even in job situations that do not lend themselves to objective measurement, dialogues between superiors and subordinates regarding performance expectations can help clarify this relationship.

3. **Maintain fairness and integrity in managing reward systems.** Although "fairness" and "integrity" are elusive ideas, managers should try to apply them, for it is important that employees perceive that their rewards are fair and equitable. Managers who make an effort to relate rewards to performance, and communicate this fact to employees, will be *perceived* as fair and will probably be respected. Those who reward employees arbitrarily, capriciously, or on the basis of friendship or politics will destroy the perceived equity in the reward systems and discourage high performance.

4. **Train managers in motivational techniques—especially reinforcement theories and practices.** Managers do not have direct control over employee needs and perceptions, but they can influence employee behavior through organizational rewards. Their understanding of motivational theories and practices, therefore, can greatly enhance the effectiveness of organizational reward systems.

5. **Emphasize the importance of intrinsic rewards.** Extrinsic rewards are only a part of the reward package, but they are important rewards, especially in job situations where intrinsic rewards are lacking. In job situations where intrinsic rewards can be developed and used, however, more emphasis should be placed on their use. The satisfaction of intrinsic rewards is more closely related to performance and has more enduring effects on work motivation than that of extrinsic rewards.

 ## SUMMARY AND CONCLUSION

This chapter presented various ways of managing extrinsic reward systems. The motivational value of rewards increases as (1) the rewards become large enough to satisfy employees' needs, (2) the reward system recognizes individual differences in reward preference, and (3) the rewards are tied to performance. Since Chapter 6 dealt with the first two requirements, this chapter focused on tying rewards to performance.

Matching rewards and performance starts with performance appraisal. Performance appraisal to assess individual contributions to organizational goals can serve as the basis for rewarding employees. There are three ways in which individual contributions can be evaluated—on the basis of (1) objectives achieved, (2) behaviors that contribute to achieving an objective, and (3) personal judgments of an employee's contribution to the achievement of company objectives. Selection of certain performance criteria should be based on differences in job characteristics—interactional requirements and performance measurability.

Once individual contributions are assessed, management can relate rewards to performance. Basing rewards on performance is not always desirable, however, for while it may encourage individual work motivation, it can cause excessive competition among work group members. And when jobs demand a high degree of cooperation, competition can be harmful to overall organizational performance. Depending on the needs of the organization, then, management should differentiate its reward systems—on an individual, group, or companywide basis.

KEY CONCEPTS AND WORDS

*Performance
  appraisal*
Extrinsic rewards
Intrinsic rewards
Job analysis
Job evaluation
*Management by
  objectives (MBO)*
*Result-based
  criteria*

*Behavior-based
  criteria*
The Scanlon Plan
*Judgment-based
  criteria*
*Behaviorally
  anchored rating
  scales (BARS)*
*Individual-based
  rewards*

Group-based rewards
*Companywide
  rewards*
Judgmental errors
Rating errors
*The Lincoln Electric
  Plan*

Questions for Review and Discussion

1. a. What determines employee satisfaction with rewards?
    b. What are the conditions under which both satisfaction and performance can be increased?
2. a. What is performance appraisal?
    b. What are the purposes of performance appraisal?
    c. What are some common problems or difficulties in conducting performance appraisal?
3. a. What is a behaviorally anchored rating scale (BARS)?
    b. How is it different from the performance appraisal rating method?

4. a.   What is an MBO performance appraisal?
    b.   What are some strengths of an MBO performance appraisal?
    c.   What are some limitations of using MBO as a performance appraisal tool?

5. a.   What are the major differences between extrinsic and intrinsic rewards?
    b.   Does the use of extrinsic rewards reduce intrinsic motivation?

6. a.   What are the differences between individual-based, group-based, and companywide reward systems?
    b.   Describe situations in which each of these reward systems can be effectively utilized.

7. Government regulations and union contracts often demand that performance appraisals be based on objective performance criteria.
    a.   How feasible is it to develop objective performance criteria for jobs in organizations?
    b.   Can management develop objective performance criteria for an office worker, an accountant, or a public relations officer?
    c.   What kinds of performance criteria should be used to assess the performance of such employees?

CASES AND EXERCISE

CASE 14.1. DEVELOPING AN APPRAISAL SYSTEM

This case should help you understand some problems associated with performance appraisals and allow you to design a more appropriate appraisal system. You should discuss the advantages and disadvantages of various appraisal systems.

The Situation

Pat Jones had been on the job as a project manager for about a year. During the year she had been able to complete most of the scheduled projects, but the human cost had been high. The engineers often had to work 60 hours a week. Some left to find jobs with "better pay" and "more decent hours"; others requested internal transfers.

Ron Engelberg, the plant manager, called Jones in to discuss her annual performance appraisal. She had been rated high on all the task-oriented performance criteria (quantity of work, project quality, technical competence, and the like) but only "average" or "poor" on some relation-oriented criteria (supervision, interpersonal skills, and personality).

Managers know that a low rating on the relation-oriented criteria usually means the end of a person's managerial career. Faced with this predicament, Jones became very angry and defensive about her performance rating. She demanded that Engelberg explain why she was rated poor in supervision and personality. She insisted that her project group was one of the most productive groups.

Engelberg felt uncomfortable about the performance appraisal session. He agreed that Jones had achieved her performance goals during the year, but he still felt that she should be more skillful in dealing with her subordinates.

As he was experiencing some problems with the current performance appraisal method, the plant manager instructed the personnel manager to come up with a more satisfactory appraisal method.

Discussion Questions

1. What kind of performance appraisal system does the company use at the present time?

2. Why does Engelberg feel uncomfortable about the performance appraisal system?

3. What kind of performance appraisal system would you suggest? Show your proposal.

4. How would you evaluate Jones's managerial competence?

CASE 14.2. THE YANG AIRCRAFT COMPANY

When pay increases are not tied to performance, they lose motivational power. However, tying pay to performance is often difficult to do. This case illustrates such a problem.

The Situation

Yang Aircraft is a medium-sized company manufacturing light airplanes. It employs approximately 5,000 workers. About 10 percent are professional engineers, who are engaged in a variety of research and development activities. Most of them have either B.S. or M.S. degrees; some even have Ph.D.s. Most of their activities are on a project basis, and they have pioneered many fine products in aviation. Their salaries rank high in the industry. Except during years of general depression in the industry, employees receive healthy pay increases.

The company recently hired Dr. Sam Jones, a son of the chairman of the board of directors, as its personnel director. He has a degree in management and specialized in wage and salary administration. As he reviewed the compensation practice, he wondered whether such a practice is an effective motivational tool. It seemed to him that employees considered their pay increases to be an entitlement and/or a cost-of-living increase. He felt that some changes should be made to recognize the contributions of high performers while motivating low performers to improve their performance.

Discussion Question

Suppose you are asked to propose a performance appraisal and pay system. What kind of system would you recommend? Explain why and show your proposal.

EXERCISE 14.1. PERFORMANCE APPRAISAL AND PAY INCREASE

Many jobs in organizations do not lend themselves to objective performance measurement. In the absence of objectively measurable criteria, management uses judgment-based performance measures to evaluate employees. This exercise allows you to develop a set of judgment-based performance criteria and use them to evaluate employee performance. It also allows you to use the evaluative information to determine pay increases.

The Situation

You are the general manager and supervise six managers. You need to conduct an annual performance appraisal for the managers and make pay increase decisions for each one. The company does not have any formal performance appraisal program or a policy governing pay decisions. The total size of pay increments you can give to these managers depends on the year's profit. Since this year has been a good one, you should be able to spend between $14,000 and $16,000 on the pay increases.

Employee Profiles

Gene Shriver. Gene, 28 years old and married, with two children, currently earns $24,000 annually. He has a B.A. from a midwestern state university and has been with the company for four years. He started as a management trainee and moved up to his current position as accounting manager two years ago. He is easygoing and personable and gets along well with his subordinates and peers. He does not impress others as being bright, but he is a hard worker. You have checked with others, and they feel he is an average performer.

Marjorie Taylor. Marjorie, 30 years old and single, currently earns an annual salary of $23,000. She is a graduate of a prestigious private eastern college and has been with the company for five years. She worked as an executive secretary for the first two years, before becoming the administrative services manager. She is considered very bright, but temperamental and impatient with mediocre employees. Turnover in her department is high, but departmental productivity is considered excellent. You are concerned about her personality.

Fred Lopez. Fred, 26 years old and married, with no children, currently earns an annual salary of $29,500. He has an M.B.A. from a state university and has been with the company for two years. He supervises five technicians in the production laboratory, and his earlier experience as a production foreman suits the job. You rate him highly as a manager and a person, but other people do not share your enthusiasm.

Henry Parker. Henry, 45 years old and divorced, with two children in college, earns $26,000 annually. He has been with the company for 15 years and has been in his current position as production manager for the last five. He is well liked by his employees and other managers, especially old-timers. He has done a good job as production manager, but you sense that he is relatively unhappy now because young people are entering the company in managerial positions with high starting salaries. His resentment is shown in his antagonistic attitudes toward other managers, especially young ones.

Gary Littleton. Gary, 40 years old and married, with three children, currently earns $32,000. He came to the company two years ago as the sales manager. While the sales department is the most important in the company, it is considered the most difficult one to manage. Turnover rate is high among competent sales personnel, as many companies pay premiums for competent salespeople. Gary has improved the situation a little, but the turnover problem is still one of your major concerns.

John Chandler. John, 35 years old and married, with no children, earns $28,000 a year. He has been with the company for seven years. He has been in his current position as personnel manager for the past three years. You have known him as a personal friend, and you consider him one of your best subordinates. But, for some reason, your judgment is not shared by other managers, who consider him a "paper pusher."

The Procedure

1. Divide yourselves into small groups.

2. Each group prepares a performance appraisal form and evaluates the managers on it. (Evaluate each manager on the performance criteria you have developed.)

3. Each group recommends pay increases for the six managers.

4. Reassemble as a class and compare the pay increases for each employee. Each group may give its justification for individual pay increases.

5. Discuss cases where major differences are found in the size of the pay increase recommended. Each group may defend its position and criticize others by pointing out the consequences of each pay decision.

6. The class as a group then summarizes the exercise by discussing various factors that influence pay decisions. This discussion may include pay level, performance criteria and their relative importance, reasons for individual pay increases, and the effects on employee work motivation.

Footnotes

1. E. E. Lawler, *Motivation in Work Organizations* (Monterey, CA: Brooks/Cole, 1973), p. 145.

2. E. E. Lawler, "Reward Systems," in *Improving Life at Work,* ed. J. R. Hackman and J. L. Suttle (Pacific Palisades, CA: Goodyear, 1977), pp. 164–166.

3. Ibid., pp. 167–168.

4. Lawler, *Motivation in Work Organizations,* pp. 114–119; and K. H. Chung and W. D. Vickery, "Relative Effectiveness and Joint Effects of Three Selected Reinforcements in a Repetitive Task Situation," *Organizational Behavior and Human Performance,* 1976, **16,** 114–142.

5. Berkely Rice, "The Worry Epidemic: Mental Stress in the Economic Crunch," *Monthly Labor Review,* August 1975, 74–76; and A. W.

Kornhauser, *Mental Health of the Industrial Worker* (New York: Wiley, 1964).

6. C. H. Madsen, W. C. Becker, and D. R. Thomas, "Rules, Praise, and Ignoring: Elements of Elementary Classroom Control," *Journal of Applied Behavior Analysis,* 1968, **1,** 139–150.

7. L. W. Porter, "Turning Work into Nonwork: The Rewarding Environment," in *Work and Nonwork in the Year 2001,* ed. M. D. Dunnette (Belmont, CA: Wadsworth, 1973), p. 113.

8. K. H. Chung and M. F. Ross, "Differences in Motivational Properties Between Job Enlargement and Job Enrichment," *Academy of Management Review,* January 1977, 113–122.

9. D. C. McClelland, *The Achieving Society* (New York: Van Nostrand, 1961); and D. C. McClelland, *Assessing Human Motivation* (Morristown, NJ: General Learning Press, 1971).

10. R. A. Stringer, "Achievement Motivation and Management Control," *Personnel Administration,* November–December 1966, 4–6.

11. T. W. Harrell and B. Alpert, "The Need for Autonomy Among Managers," *Academy of Management Review,* April 1979, 259–268.

12. Edward Deci, *Intrinsic Motivation* (New York: Plenum, 1975); and Edward Deci, "The Hidden Costs of Rewards," *Organizational Dynamics,* 1976, **4,** 61–72.

13. H. J. Arnold, "Effects of Performance Feedback and Extrinsic Reward upon High Intrinsic Motivation," *Organizational Performance and Human Behavior,* 1976, **17,** 275–288.

14. H. H. Meyer, E. Kay, and J. R. P. French, "Split Roles in Performance Appraisal," *Harvard Business Review,* January–February 1965, 123–129; and P. H. Thompson and G. W. Dalton, "Performance Appraisal: Managers Beware," *Harvard Business Review,* January–February 1970, 149–157.

15. R. G. Burnaska and T. D. Hollman, "An Empirical Comparison of the Relative Effects of Rater Response Bias on Three Rating Scale Formats," *Journal of Applied Psychology,* 1974, **59,** 307–312.

16. W. C. Hamner, J. Kim, L. Baird, and W. Bigoness, "Race and Sex as Determinants of Ratings by 'Potential' Employees in a Simulated Work Sampling Task," *Journal of Applied Psychology,* 1974, **59,** 705–711.

17. Michael Keeley, "A Contingency Framework for Performance Evaluation," *Academy of Management Review,* July 1978, 428–438.

18. G. P. Latham and G. A. Yukl, "The Effects of Assigned and Participative Goal Setting on Performance and Job Satisfaction," *Journal of Applied Psychology,* 1976, **61,** 166–171; and G. P. Latham, T. R. Mitchell, and D. L. Dossett, "Importance of Participative Goal Setting and Anticipative Rewards on Goal Difficulty and Job Performance," *Journal of Applied Psychology,* 1978, **13,** 163–171.

19. R. S. Atkin and E. J. Conlon, "Behaviorally Anchored Rating Scales: Some Theoretical Issues," *Academy of Management Review,* January 1978, 119–128.

20. K. N. Wexley and G. A. Yukl, *Organizational Behavior and Personnel Psychology* (Homewood, IL: Irwin, 1977), pp. 213–218.

21. H. J. Bernardin and C. S. Walter, "The Effects of Rater Training and Diary Keeping on Psychometric Error in Ratings," *Journal of Applied Psychology,* 1977, **62,** 64–69.

22. Thomas Decotiis and Andre Petit, "The Performance Appraisal Process: A Model and Some Testable Propositions," *Academy of Management Review,* July 1978, 635–646.

23. W. F. Nemeroff and K. N. Wexley, "Relationships between Performance Feedback Interview Characteristics and Interview Outcomes as Perceived by Managers and Subordinates," *Proceedings of the 37th Annual Meeting,* Academy of Management, Orlando, Florida, August 1977, pp. 30–34.

24. Steven Kerr, "Overcoming the Dysfunctions of MBO," *Management-by-Objectives,* 1976, **5,** 13–19; and Meyer, Kay, and French, "Split Roles in Performance Appraisal," 128.

25. G. P. Latham, K. N. Wexley, and E. D. Pursell, "Training Managers to Minimize Rating Errors in the Observation of Behavior," *Journal of Applied Psychology,* 1975, **60,** 550–555.

26. See F. G. Lesieur (ed.), *The Scanlon Plan: A Frontier in Labor Management Cooperation* (New York: Wiley, 1958).

27. J. F. Lincoln, *Incentive Management* (Cleveland: Lincoln Electric Company, 1951).

28. See W. C. Hamner, "How to Ruin Motivation with Pay," *Compensation Review,* Third Quarter 1975, 17–27.

MANAGEMENT AND ORGANIZATIONAL BEHAVIOR

1. Understanding the Job of Managing

2. Studying Organizational Behavior

INDIVIDUAL BEHAVIOR

3. Satisfying Human Needs

4. Learning and Reinforcing

5. Understanding the Perceptual Process

6. Understanding the Motivational Process

SUPERVISORY BEHAVIOR

11. Understanding the Leadership Process

12. Developing Leadership Skills

13. Acquiring and Using Power in Organizations

14. Managing Reward Systems

INTERPERSONAL AND GROUP BEHAVIOR

7. Understanding Interpersonal Dynamics

8. Improving Communication Effectiveness

9. Understanding Group Dynamics

10. Dealing with Intergroup Conflicts

ENVIRONMENTAL ADAPTATION

15. Task Design—Matching Jobs to People

16. Designing Organizational Structure

17. Making Managerial Decisions

18. Managing Organizational Change

ORGANIZATIONAL EFFECTIVENESS

19. Developing Effective Organizations

APPENDIX

Developing Careers in Organizations

Micro-organizational analysis

Macro-organizational analysis

PART

V ENVIRONMENTAL ADAPTATION

*P*art V is primarily concerned with the relationships between task, people, structure, technology, and environment. The contingency view of an organization, discussed in Chapter 2, suggests that various organizational components (such as task, people, and structure) interact with each other, and at the same time interact with external environmental factors (such as technology, labor, market, economics, and politics). Because of these multiple influences, an organization needs to find workable fits among various internal components that are, at the same time, congruent with external environments.

 Chapter 15 focuses on the relationships between people and their jobs. The major issue is task design, which aims at meeting employee needs and technological demands. Chapter 16 focuses on organizational design. It contends that organizational structure must be designed to meet the information processing needs created by internal and external environments. Chapter 17 is primarily concerned with managerial decision making under uncertainty. It reviews several modes of managerial decisions. Chapter 18 deals with various ways of adapting to and coping with environmental changes.

LEARNING OBJECTIVES

1. To recognize the importance of matching jobs to people.
2. To develop the skills of diagnosing the characteristics of tasks and people.
3. To acquire the skills of matching jobs to people—the technology of job enrichment.

CHAPTER OUTLINE

The Concept of Job Enrichment

Job Simplification
Job Enlargement
Job Enrichment
The Matching Concept
Job Involvement
A Job Involvement Model

Motivational Characteristics of a Job

Task Attributes of Enlarged Jobs
Task Attributes of Enriched Jobs
Do Job Enlargement and Enrichment Pay Off?
Constraints on Implementing These Programs

Individual and Organizational Characteristics

Individual Characteristics
Organizational Characteristics

How to Enrich Jobs in Organizations

Diagnosing Organizational Components
Action Steps for Job Expansion
Improving Employee–Organization Fits

Summary and Conclusion

15 TASK DESIGN—MATCHING JOBS TO PEOPLE

The emerging confrontation between the worker and his job is more than a psychic demand. It is an issue of major economic significance to the individual firm, to entire industries, and to the economy as a whole. Worker attitudes and adjustments to the workplace have a direct bearing upon productivity, costs, quality of product, profitability, and competitiveness in the world market.

Jerome M. Rosow, The Worker and the Job [1]

Work is the central life interest for many adults. It is the primary institution through which people satisfy their diverse needs. They earn a living by working, they socialize in work organizations, and they realize their potentialities through work. Work is also a primary means of achieving social goals—economic, political, and cultural. People spend a considerable amount of time working. In fact, work seems to be the only thing that people can do eight hours or more, day after day without much interruption. All the other activities we enjoy, such as eating, playing, and sex—no matter how much we enjoy them—are easily satiable.

Because work is such an important element in our civilized lives, it remains a serious subject for social scientists and practicing managers. It has become an issue for many workers because it has been losing intrinsic value. Some workers express dissatisfaction with their jobs, and this dissatisfaction seems to have an adverse effect on productivity and the quality of life in general.

This chapter is primarily concerned with ways of making work more satisfying to employees. To this end, it studies the motivational characteristics of jobs, employees, and organizational practices. It asserts that employee job satisfaction and performance are likely to increase only when these three organizational components are matched. After examining these motivational characteristics, the chapter proposes a way of finding a fit or match between them.

THE CONCEPT OF JOB ENRICHMENT

The effort to make a job more satisfying to workers can be broadly defined as job enrichment, *and it is related to several job design concepts—job simplification, horizontal job loading, vertical job loading, and matching jobs to people.*

The concept of job enrichment is related to a number of job design strategies that have developed over a period of time. A brief review of this development can help us better understand the movement behind the job enrichment effort.

Job Simplification

During the period of rapid industrialization (1880–1950), job design meant job simplification and specialization. As industrialization progressed, jobs became so large and complex that they had to be divided into small parts to make them manageable. Instead of performing an entire job, workers were now asked to perform only a portion of it. Job simplification made it possible to introduce task specialization so workers could be easily trained and replaced.[2]

Task specialization and small, interchangeable units of labor characterized the era of mass production systems, which greatly expanded the volume of consumer goods for mass consumption. Better pay and a high standard of living were realized during this period. The very success of the mass production era, however, brought new problems that demanded changes in production methods. As people satisfied their economic needs, they demanded greater job satisfaction. But jobs were becoming less responsive to this demand.

Job Enlargement

In the 1950s, there was a growing awareness of workers' reactions to their fragmented jobs. Production methods were criticized by management scholars as inconsistent with human needs. Mass production systems did not provide workers with opportunities to socialize on the job or to satisfy their needs for achievement, self-expression, creativity, and control. Such employee problems as absenteeism, turnover, low morale, and low productivity were said to be partially related to the boredom and monotony created by these highly specialized and routinized jobs.[3]

An early reaction to this situation by practicing managers and scholars was to introduce job rotation and job enlargement. *Job rotation* means rotating individual workers among different jobs; *job enlargement* is a job design strategy that increases task elements on a horizontal level. That is, the content of a job is increased, and the worker thus performs a major work unit rather than a fragmented job. The purpose of job rotation and job enlargement is to reduce the boredom and monotony that arise from performing a fragmented job repetitively.

Job Enrichment

In the 1960s, some critics argued that when meaningless task elements are added to a meaningless job, the job remains as boring and meaningless as before. For example, dishwashers may wash pots, pans, and silverware in addition to dishes, but they may not find the added job elements more meaningful than just washing dishes. To increase the motivational potential of a job, these critics suggested, a job should be expanded vertically to include managerial functions.[4] A popular notion during this period was that employees should be given the authority to manage their own jobs.

The Matching Concept

Job enrichment increases the motivational potential of a job. In the 1970s, however, some managers and scholars, found that not all employees and/or organizations wanted or were ready to implement job enrichment programs.[5] They found that some workers prefer demanding tasks, but others do not. Likewise, while some organizations can function well with job enrichment, others are not even able to satisfy the lower-order needs of pay and job security. When employees are struggling to satisfy these needs, they are not likely to respond positively to job enrichment aimed at satisfying higher-order needs. Since tasks, individuals, and organizations differ in their motivational characteristics, these variables should be matched to yield the maximum motivational result. The matching concept is the dominant theme of this chapter.

Job Involvement

We are interested in studying task design because it is related to the degree to which employees are involved in their work. But, although task design is an important determinant of job involvement, other factors influence the worker's work motivation. A literature review by Rabinowitz and Hall, and a subsequent empirical study by Saal, have identified a number of task, individual, organizational, and outcome factors that are related to job involvement.[6] The correlates of job involvement, shown in Figure 15.1, are drawn from these two sources.

A Job Involvement Model

A number of job design models promise a high level of employee motivation. For example, Herzberg and his associates suggest that jobs must be designed to allow a greater amount of personal achievement, recognition, responsibility, advancement, and growth.[7] Although Herzberg's approach to job design is intuitively appealing, his work has been criticized by several researchers for not taking individual differences into account in predicting the outcomes of such a strategy.[8]

Another popular model is the job characteristics model proposed by Hackman and Oldham.[9] This model considers not only the motivational characteristics of a job but also individual differences in motivational characteristics. Hackman and his associates indicate that motivational outcomes (satisfaction, performance, and work involvement) are derived from the critical psychological states (meaningfulness of work, responsibil-

FIGURE 15.1
Approximate Correlates of Job Involvement.

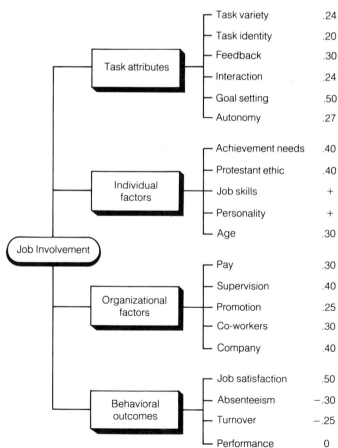

Task attributes	
Task variety	.24
Task identity	.20
Feedback	.30
Interaction	.24
Goal setting	.50
Autonomy	.27

Individual factors	
Achievement needs	.40
Protestant ethic	.40
Job skills	+
Personality	+
Age	.30

Organizational factors	
Pay	.30
Supervision	.40
Promotion	.25
Co-workers	.30
Company	.40

Behavioral outcomes	
Job satisfaction	.50
Absenteeism	−.30
Turnover	−.25
Performance	0

ity for work outcomes, and knowledge of results). These psychological states are created by the presence of five core job dimensions (skill variety, task identity, task significance, autonomy, and performance feedback). These dimensions possess the motivational potential of a job. When the motivational potential of a job is matched with the motivational characteristics of an employee (technical and psychological readiness), the outcome levels are likely to be high.

Although the Hackman and Oldham model has made an important contribution to the field of job design, it has not been fully supported by empirical studies. One reason for this lack of support may be that the model fails to consider a number of organizational factors, such as pay, supervision, company policy, and structure, that moderate employee reactions to their jobs.[10] The job involvement model, shown in Figure 15.2, suggests that when a job design effort is made, it should be done in conjunction with any development that has occurred in individual and organizational factors. Therefore, it is important to consider individual and organizational factors in addition to the characteristics of a job.

MOTIVATIONAL CHARACTERISTICS OF A JOB

> *A number of job characteristics or task attributes can increase the motivational potential of a job. These attributes can be divided into two major categories—enlarged and enriched.*

Although the terms *enlarged jobs* and *enriched jobs* are often used interchangeably, we can make a distinction between them. The distinction is that an enlarged job is horizontally expanded on a technical dimension, while an enriched job is vertically expanded on a managerial dimension.[11]

FIGURE 15.2
A Job Involvement Model.

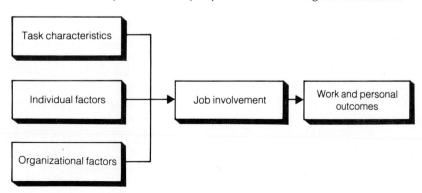

The distinction is important from a job design standpoint because people differ in their job preference. Some people prefer technically expanded jobs; others may prefer vertically expanded jobs requiring managerial responsibilities.

Task Attributes of Enlarged Jobs

Job enlargement is often called "horizontal job loading" because it simply adds more task elements to an existing job. When a job is enlarged, workers perform a larger work unit involving a variety of task elements rather than a fragmented job. An enlarged job has the following task attributes:

Task Variety.   A fragmented job requiring a limited number of unchanging responses can easily lead to boredom. When the number of task elements is increased, the job requires a greater variety of responses; these, in turn, can cause an array of mental arousals. These arousals can reduce the feeling of boredom.

Technically enlarged jobs require additional abilities and skills from the performers. People derive job satisfaction when they are able to use their mental and physical abilities and skills on their jobs. A job gains motivational value when its performance depends on the effort a worker exerts. Simplified jobs are not motivating because they do not require many of the worker's abilities or much effort. Jobs that are too large or complex are also not motivating because they require more skills and abilities than the worker possesses.

Task Identity.   When related task elements are combined, a job becomes larger and closer to a whole production unit. Workers performing such work units begin to see their own contribution to the completion of a product or project. When the major work unit is finished, a worker can identify his or her work with the product. Consequently, the job becomes psychologically more meaningful and significant to the performer than a fragmented job.

The time period required to complete a work unit needs to be psychologically meaningful also; it may range from half an hour to a few days. However, if the job is overenlarged, requiring a long production cycle, the worker will be frustrated because it takes too long to receive reinforcement induced by task completion. Such a large work unit must be divided into smaller work units that are psychologically meaningful and provide some reinforcement before the whole project is completed.

Performance Feedback.   People want to know how well they are doing on their jobs. Fragmented jobs do not provide them with meaningful performance feedback. Any worker can count the number of metal pins or nuts he or she has produced (say 15,950 units per hour), but this information has little psychological meaning. If the worker assembles ten units of radios or motor engines, however, he or she may feel a sense of accomplishment.

Performance feedback serves three motivational functions.[12] First, it serves as an external stimulus to mental activation or arousal. Second, task-induced performance feedback is more meaningful than externally induced feedback, such as supervisory performance appraisal. The worker is more likely to use internally generated feedback for setting performance goals. Finally, the worker can use performance feedback to take corrective actions.

Worker-Paced Control.   People want to have some control over their work methods. Instead of being subservient to machines, they want to be the masters who control and use these machines. Mechanized production systems make it difficult for workers to control production speeds and methods, however. Such systems require workers to operate at a monotonous rate, using work methods that are standardized, regardless of individual differences in skills, abilities, and work habits. Enlarged jobs allow workers some degree of control over their work paces and methods.

It may seem that worker-controlled production systems would be less efficient than machine-controlled systems. And it is true that, as production volume increases, a machine-paced operation can be faster and more efficient. However, this increase in productivity can be offset by the costs of low morale, absenteeism, turnover, sabotage, and labor strife. Furthermore, worker-controlled systems are more flexible and can be adjusted to reflect changes in technology.

Task Attributes of Enriched Jobs

Enriched jobs give workers the opportunity to interact with other people —co-workers, superiors, and clients. Workers participate in decisions affecting their work environment and exercise some autonomy in managing their own jobs. These task attributes—interactional opportunity, participation, goal-setting, and managerial autonomy—can satisfy the needs for socialization, self-esteem, and self-actualization.

Interactional Opportunity.   The opportunity to interact with other people on the job not only satisfies workers' needs for socialization but also makes them feel responsible for helping others achieve their goals. The job becomes more meaningful when people know that their actions affect the lives of other people. When a job is performed jointly by group members, it can stimulate a sense of mutual responsibility that helps them coordinate their activities.

When the job involves interaction with people outside the immediate work group, it assumes a new meaning because employees can influence the satisfaction of clients. When workers can see how their work affects clients, they feel personally responsible for it. A job enrichment study at AT&T showed that when employees had direct contact with clients, their feeling of personal responsibility for their work increased.[13]

Employee Participation. Participation in managerial decisions can influence both employee job satisfaction and performance by satisfying the need for socialization and self-esteem. Also, when employees participate in making decisions that affect their work environment, they tend to feel the decisions are their own and feel personally responsible for carrying them out.[14] They become "ego-involved" in the decisions, and the success or failure of those decisions and subsequent actions becomes their own success or failure.

Through participation, workers learn the kinds of effort and job skill needed to perform their tasks and discover how these efforts and skills should be used to achieve performance goals. As pointed out earlier, when workers know how their efforts and skills are related to task performance, their work motivation is likely to increase. Participation also helps to clarify the roles that each worker has to play in the process of getting the group tasks accomplished. When people know how their efforts are related to task performance and understand their roles, they are more likely to be effective on their jobs than when they are confused.

Goal-Setting Opportunity. Goal setting is the process by which an employee establishes performance goals for himself or herself, or performance goals for the group. Goal setting can influence work motivation in a number of ways. First, performance goals are a target an employee strives to achieve. Once the target is identified, the employee can channel his or her energies toward it. Second, when a person has participated in goal setting, he or she tends to internalize the established goals. Third, as pointed out in Chapter 14, performance goals produced by participation tend to be higher than assigned goals. Finally, employees are generally more satisfied with their work when they are able to participate as well as set performance goals than when they engage in participation or goal setting alone.[15]

Managerial Autonomy. The core of job enrichment is the autonomy and control exercised by employees over their own jobs. Under this managerial system, work group members are given some latitude and freedom in managing resources and in dealing with day-to-day problems. Their responsibilities may even include hiring co-workers, assigning individual tasks, selecting their own supervisor, and deciding daily production quotas.

Managerial autonomy not only satisfies workers' needs for self-esteem and independence but also increases their sense of personal responsibility for performance outcomes. When people have control over their work environment, their *locus of control* is more likely to be internal than external. People who have an internal locus of control—that is, the feeling that whatever happens to them is due to their own actions—are more likely to feel responsible for their performance outcomes than those with an external locus of control.[16]

Do Job Enlargement and Enrichment Pay Off?

Job enlargement usually involves worker-paced production systems. Such systems may reduce production speed, or create a situation in which workers have to exert more energy to produce at the same rate as before the jobs were enlarged. However, people may draw more job satisfaction from using their skills and energy to produce high-quality products than from producing a large quantity of low-quality products. Several studies of the effects of job enlargement (primarily horizontal job loading) on employee work motivation tend to confirm these concepts.[17] Thus, job enlargement is more likely to improve employee job satisfaction and product quality than to increase productivity.

Job enrichment seems to gain motivational power when combined with job enlargement. It is doubtful whether enriching a job without technically enlarging it can have a strong motivational impact. Employee satisfaction and productivity will generally be high when both job enlargement and job enrichment are *jointly applied* to redesigning work systems. The HEW report *Work in America* advocates that job design include both job enlargement and job enrichment, and it indicates that such a combined approach resulted in increased productivity ranging from 5 to 40 percent.[18] The companies included in this report were AT&T, Banker's Trust, Corning Glass, General Foods, Motorola, Texas Instruments, Lufthansa (Germany), Norsk Hydro Fertilizer (Norway), Saab (Sweden), and Volvo (Sweden).

The following example illustrates how the manager at the General Motors Tarrytown plant utilized the job enrichment concept to solve labor and operational problems.[19]

> GM's Tarrytown plant had one of the worst labor and production records of the late 1960s and early 1970s. It suffered from high absenteeism and turnover. Operating costs were high. Mistrust and disputes characterized the relations between management and labor. The number of grievances mounted to an intolerable level.
>
> Faced with these problems, the general manager approached union officers and suggested some changes in labor–management relations and work systems. Union officers were initially suspicious

of management's intentions, but at last they decided to give the changes a try. In reality, union leaders were as frustrated as management in dealing with employees, for they had little control over them. Young workers did not have much respect for authority— management's or the union's.

As a start, the workers in the hard- and soft-trim departments were asked to participate in redesigning their production facilities and in solving operational problems. Traditionally, management called on labor and workers to cooperate in increasing productivity. In the new system, however, management would cooperate with labor in solving operational problems and in enhancing the quality of work life at the plant.

Things did not work out very smoothly. The layoffs in 1974, due to the oil crisis, created a setback in the job enrichment movement. Nevertheless, management and labor determined to keep the practice, and by 1977 it had spread companywide. It was a costly program, but its payoffs were substantial. Absenteeism went down from 7.25 percent to about 2.5 percent. There were only 32 grievances on the docket in December 1978, as compared to about 2,000 in 1971. Furthermore, management indicated that the increase in productivity was substantial, though it would be difficult to measure exactly.

Constraints on Implementing These Programs

Although job enlargement and enrichment can increase the motivational potential of a job, they do not automatically increase work motivation. In addition, a number of constraints hinder a widespread application of these programs.[20]

1. **Workers differ significantly in their needs and job skills.** Some workers want to and can perform complex and demanding tasks; others prefer simple tasks that do not require making decisions or learning new skills.[21] Workers who prefer more demanding jobs can satisfy their needs by moving into technical, managerial, and professional positions. Others may choose unskilled jobs.

2. **Organizations differ in their ability to satisfy the needs of their employees.** Some organizations are able to satisfy the higher-order needs of employees, but others must struggle just to meet their lower-order needs. When employees are dissatisfied with pay, job security, social interaction, supervision, and company policy, they are less likely to respond positively to job enrichment, which promises only high-order need satisfaction. In times of economic recession, people are more concerned with their jobs and paychecks than

with job content. Furthermore, supervisory personnel who have been accustomed to giving orders and pushing for high productivity are likely to resist job enrichment because it means sharing power with subordinates, and it requires lengthy training to acquire a new set of leadership skills.

3. **In spite of the favorable reports on job enrichment outcomes, there is no concrete evidence that job enrichment will invariably result in increased productivity.** In fact, there is some disturbing evidence that job enrichment efforts often fail to produce positive results if they are not properly implemented.[22] Since negative results are rarely reported, it is difficult to estimate the percentage of failure. But even just a few failing experiences are enough to discourage other employers from trying.

4. Except for a few cases, such as GM's Tarrytown plant, **labor unions have not been supportive of job enrichment efforts.**[23] First, they seem to suspect that such programs exploit workers—that they give workers more responsibility for the same pay. Second, they seem to be afraid that an increase in productivity by such programs will lead to layoffs of some of their members. Finally, such programs are a threat to their existence; that is, a successful job enrichment program may reduce the workers' need for union protection.

 ## INDIVIDUAL AND ORGANIZATIONAL CHARACTERISTICS

> *A number of individual and organizational factors moderate the effects of task attributes on employee behavior—needs, job skills, work ethic, pay, job security, and others. These factors must be considered in designing jobs.*

Organizational tasks differ in their motivational characteristics; so do the individual attributes of employees and their work environment. Unless these factors are taken into account in designing jobs, enlargement and enrichment programs are not likely to produce positive results. In this section we examine some of the factors that moderate employee reactions to jobs and explain some of the reasons why the motivational characteristics of the job, the individual, and the organization should be integrated.

Individual Characteristics

A number of individual factors influence workers' reactions to their jobs. Among the most influential ones are (1) higher-order needs, (2) job skills and knowledge, (3) Protestant work ethic, (4) personality dimensions, and (5) demographic factors.

Higher-Order Needs.   A number of studies report that people with higher-order needs (such as self-esteem, achievement, and autonomy) prefer to perform enlarged and enriched jobs.[24] Such task attributes as task variety, task identity, feedback, and autonomy help them satisfy these higher-order needs. Other studies suggest that some blue-collar workers, striving to satisfy lower-order needs, can easily tolerate or may even prefer simple jobs that pay well and/or routinized jobs with ample opportunities for socialization.[25]

However, a few researchers found no significant relationship between higher-order needs and worker reactions to enriched jobs.[26] A possible reason for this finding is that non-work environmental factors such as pay, job security, supervision, and organizational structure might have interfered with worker reactions to their jobs. Thus, if workers are dissatisfied with these non-work factors, they may not exert their efforts fully, even though they enjoy the enriched jobs.

Job Skills and Knowledge.   An important managerial function is staffing organizational tasks with employees who have the necessary skills and knowledge to perform those tasks. When people are assigned to jobs for which they are not qualified, they tend to become frustrated with the jobs and unable to meet their employer's performance expectations. Overqualified employees are also frustrated with their jobs because their abilities, skills, and knowledge are underutilized and unappreciated. Jobs become meaningful only when they require a variety of job skills and efforts at the level at which the workers are able and willing to work. At that level, workers feel that their efforts and skills are being effectively utilized.

Protestant Work Ethic.   The Protestant work ethic, or the work ethic in general, is based on the belief that work has moral and/or spiritual value. The work ethic originated in the religious belief that hard work is a way of glorifying God. For people with this belief, hard work and their personal responsibility for working are inherent.

In contemporary society, the meaning of the work ethic is less an article of religious faith than a work norm shared by the middle-class working population. Studies suggest that possession of the Protestant work ethic is one of the most reliable predictors of job involvement or work motivation available.[27] Workers with the work ethic are more likely to respond positively to demanding jobs requiring hard work and personal responsibility than those without it. Also, these studies argue, people living in rural areas are more likely to be guided by this ethic than those who live in urban areas.

Personality Dimensions.   Two personality dimensions are frequently mentioned as affecting worker reactions to their jobs: *locus of control* and *personality type.* Mitchell and his associates point out that people with an internal locus of control tend to be better satisfied with their jobs and more receptive to participative management than those with an external locus of control.[28] They are also more likely to be attracted to job situations that offer opportunities for individual achievement than those with external controls.

People also differ in their ways of dealing with stressful situations. As pointed out in Chapter 3, people who have a high level of anxiety or neuroticism (Type A personalities) may do well in well-structured job situations, but they may experience unmanageable stress in ambiguous and unstructured task situations. People with a low level of anxiety (Type B personalities) seem to function well in ambiguous and less structured task situations.[29]

Demographic Factors.   Whether or not people prefer demanding jobs seems to depend on their age, education, and occupation. As people mature and gain more job experience, they become more willing and ready to assume more responsibility and to deal with complex tasks. Since these attributes are often associated with job success, most adults seem to be interested in acquiring them. Thus, successful people seem to show more interest in demanding jobs than less successful people. People who are better educated and trained prefer to engage in technical and professional occupations where they can utilize their skills and knowledge.

Organizational Characteristics

Some industrial psychologists tend to play down the importance of non-work factors such as pay, job security, social interaction, supervision, and company policy as motivators.[30] They argue that these non-work factors do not stimulate intrinsic motivation, and that most people are reasonably well satisfied with them. However, although these factors may become less critical as society becomes more affluent and managers become more sophisticated in dealing with employees, the need for them will never be fully satisfied because of recurring economic difficulties and organizational conflicts among and between work group members. Unless they are reasonably well satisfied, though, workers will be less concerned with the satisfaction of higher-order needs that is promised by job enrichment.

The following are several important organizational factors that influence the success of job enrichment efforts.

Pay and Job Security.   Only when workers are reasonably satisfied with pay and job security are they likely to respond to the concept of job enrichment. When these needs are not satisfied, workers will be preoccupied with the means of satisfying them. Further, when workers are paid less than other workers in the same industry and in the same community, or when they do not have job security, it is difficult for management to convince them that they will benefit from job enrichment.

Even in a company where job security is provided and reward systems are adequately managed, managers often find it difficult to resolve conflicts concerning differential salaries. Pay differences are needed to recognize individual merit, but such a competitive pay method can destroy the cooperative spirit. Maintaining the delicate balance between individual motivation and group cooperation can significantly influence the success or failure of a job enrichment program.

Supportive Climate.   Job enrichment programs require a high degree of trust and openness among organization members. Thus, the relationship between the task attributes and work motivation is affected by employees' satisfaction with supervisors and co-workers.[31] When people distrust their supervisors or co-workers, they are not likely to cooperate with them in exchanging needed job-related information or setting high performance goals. Conversely, supervisors who neither trust nor have confidence in their subordinates are unlikely to share their managerial prerogatives.

Under enrichment programs, the role of supervisors changes from giving orders and supervising workers' activities to developing productive work groups and supporting them in carrying out their activities. Since the participative leadership style is unknown to many supervisors in traditional organizations, they must develop this skill before job enrichment is attempted. This kind of participative climate should be present at all organizational levels, including top managers and union officials. Without such a supportive climate, any effort to enrich jobs is likely to fail.

Organizational Flexibility.   Job enrichment requires flexibility in structuring organizational relationships. When workers are given authority and responsibility to manage their own jobs, they should also be given autonomy and flexibility in defining task goals, in selecting the means of achieving these goals, and in assuming appropriate goals in the goal-attainment process. Yet most traditional organizations rigidly define and structure organizational relationships, duties and responsibilities, and work procedures. In order to increase the effectiveness of a job enrichment program, management should go beyond the mere technical expansion of a job by providing for organizational flexibility.

Porter and his associates and Pierce and his associates show how important organizational flexibility is in affecting worker reactions to their jobs.[32] Although there are some differences in their findings, these two studies generally agree that when employees with higher-order needs are assigned to complex tasks in a flexible organizational environment, their satisfaction and performance are the highest. When the same employees perform simple tasks in a rigid organizational environment, their satisfaction and performance are the lowest. High performance is usually attributable to organizational flexibility and task complexity.

HOW TO ENRICH JOBS IN ORGANIZATIONS

> *Job enrichment involves finding a match between the job, the employee, and the organization. When these organizational components are matched, employees find their jobs more challenging and meaningful.*

So far we have identified a number of factors that influence workers' reactions to their jobs. In this section, we are concerned with ways of finding a match among these factors. We are concerned with such a match because it increases work motivation for several reasons. First, when the job fits the worker's skill level, the worker will feel that he or she can perform the job (the expectancy). Second, the worker will feel that job performance will result in task accomplishment accompanied by some rewards (the instrumentality). Third, the feeling of task accomplishment and its accompanying rewards should satisfy the worker's needs (the valence). As pointed out in Chapter 6, when a worker perceives the expectancy, instrumentality, and valence of the work environment, his or her motivational effort is likely to increase.

Figure 15.3 shows some potential consequences of match and mismatch between employees and their jobs in an organization. For example, people with professional skills and higher-order needs should be matched with highly enriched jobs such as managerial, professional, and scientific professions. People who have job skills but do not have the desire to exercise managerial authority and responsibility may be assigned to enlarged jobs that do not require managerial functions. Unskilled workers can be matched with simplified tasks, for they derive motivation from pay and job security rather than from the job itself.

Finding such a match is not simple. It requires an involved process that identifies the problem areas and changes the motivational attributes of the organizational components causing the problem. The process begins

FIGURE 15.3
Potential Consequences of
Matching or Mismatching
Jobs and Employees.

Jobs \ Employees	Professional	Skilled	Unskilled
Enriched	High level of job satisfaction and performance	←——→	Overwhelmed by job complexity and responsibility
Enlarged	↕	Experiencing meaningfulness in the job	↕
Simplified	Frustrated, feel powerless and useless	←——→	Motivated by monetary incentives

with an analysis of various organizational components—tasks, individuals, groups, and managerial practices. Information obtained from this analysis will show which organizational components need to be changed to arrive at a workable match.

Diagnosing Organizational Components

Job enrichment efforts will fail to produce positive results if management fails to identify the real causes of employee problems. Employee problems have a number of causes other than job challenge. When the problem does not lie in the job itself, it cannot be solved by changing job components. Therefore, management must diagnose the specific causes of problems before any remedies can be prescribed.

A diagnostic survey can help managers identify the sources of employee problems. An example of such a survey can be found in Exercise 15.1. Note that the survey instrument is composed of two parts: (1) the task attribute survey and (2) the individual and organizational readiness survey. The first part studies the task attributes of a job—task variety, task identity, ability utilization, performance feedback, work-pace control, interactional opportunity, participation, goal setting, and managerial autonomy. In essence, it identifies the motivational potential of the job.

The second part investigates the motivational characteristics of employees and organizational practices—job skills, interpersonal competence, work ethic, higher-order needs, pay satisfaction, job security, trusting relationship, leadership style, top management support, union support, and organizational flexibility. The results indicate whether the employees and the organization are ready to undertake a job enrichment program.

Survey results can be used as shown in Figure 15.4. If the responses to the employee and organizational readiness part of the survey are more favorable than the responses to the task attribute survey, it means that the job can be enlarged or enriched. For example, if the job lacks task variety, related task elements can be combined to increase this variety.

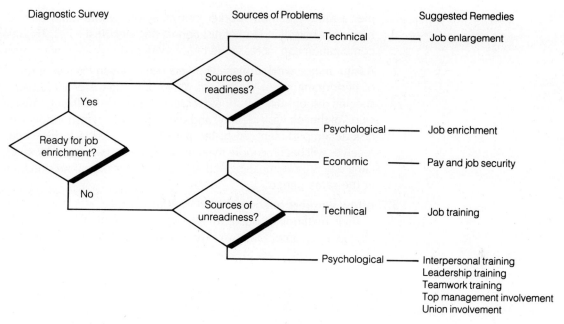

Diagnostic Survey   Sources of Problems   Suggested Remedies

FIGURE 15.4
Decision Process for
Enriching Jobs or
Employees.

If the responses to the first part are more favorable than the responses to the second part, then employees and/or the organization are not ready to undertake job enlargement or enrichment. Here again, an analysis of the second part will show the problem areas. Depending on the sources of the problems, management can undertake either *employee enrichment programs* (pay, job security, and skill training) or *organizational enrichment programs* (leadership training, trust building, teamwork training, top management support, and union support).

Even if the employees and the organization are not ready to undertake a job enrichment program, management can still enlarge the job if it is extremely fragmented. A minimum-to-moderate level of job enlargement—a technical expansion—can help workers reduce boredom and monotony. Such job enlargement, however, should not go beyond the employees' technical comprehension.

Action Steps for Job Expansion

If the job lacks motivational potential compared to employees' motivational demands, it should be expanded to meet these demands. The following actions are suggested to increase the motivational potential of a job.[33] The extent to which each of these suggestions should be carried out depends on the workers' technical and psychological readiness.

1. **Combine related task elements.** A number of related task elements can be combined to form a meaningful work unit. For exam-

ple, a radio assembly worker can assemble whole radio units by himself or herself instead of just connecting electrical wires. This task combination can increase the task variety and task identity of a job.

2. **Assign major work units.** Workers can be given the responsibility of performing major work units. When a worker is charged with a specific responsibility, it should increase his or her feeling of "owner-ship" of the job (task identity) and sense of personal responsibility for task accomplishment. Also, the performance feedback the worker receives will become more meaningful. For example, assembling one car a day is more meaningful than putting thousands of nuts on bolts in the same period.

3. **Allow workers to control work method and pace.** People differ in their methods of doing things, and their psychological rhythms change over time. Once workers have obtained the necessary job skills and knowledge, they should be given some latitude in control-ling work methods and production speed.

4. **Form work groups.** When a job is large and composed of various work units, it is often desirable to assign a group of workers to perform the interrelated work units. This action increases opportuni-ties for the workers to interact with each other on the job. Such interactional opportunities satisfy their need for socialization. Work-ing in a group also allows for job rotation, which gives workers an opportunity to learn and perform different tasks requiring a variety of skills.

5. **Encourage workers to establish cliental relationships.** Workers who have little contact with the users of their products or services are less concerned with the customers' reactions to them than are workers who have such personal contacts. Personal contact allows employees to satisfy their socialization needs and get performance feedback directly from the clients.

6. **Allow workers to manage their own jobs.** Traditionally, manag-ers are responsible for performing the managerial functions, while workers are responsible for carrying out organizational tasks assigned to them. When a job is enriched, employees are allowed to perform some managerial functions previously restricted to managerial per-sonnel. They now plan, organize, perform, coordinate, and control their own jobs. This action should have a positive impact on such task attributes as participation and managerial autonomy.

Improving Employee–Organization Fits

If the diagnostic survey indicates that the organization and its employees are not ready for job enrichment, management should concentrate on improving employment conditions and employee–employer relationships rather than on changing task components. The following actions are suggested as a way of achieving this goal.

1. **Match people to jobs.**   Instead of fitting jobs to people, management can hire and place people whose technical and psychological qualifications match the job's task attributes. One of the most common mistakes in employee selection and placement is hiring the best people in the labor market without considering how they will fit with given jobs. These "best" people are often overqualified for the jobs and hence become frustrated. Another problem, in terms of cost and time, is to hire underqualified people and train them to fit the jobs. This practice is sometimes inevitable because of labor market conditions and constant changes in technology, but it can be minimized if employees are carefully selected.

2. **Train employees.**   Since technology changes so rapidly, employee training becomes necessary to maintain the fit between people and their jobs. When enlargement or enrichment programs are considered, employees need to be trained to cope with the job's changing requirements. If employees lack the necessary job skills, increasing task components or managerial responsibility will only add to their frustration.

3. **Satisfy existence needs.**   As pointed out earlier, when people's existence needs are not satisfied, they are less likely to respond positively to job enrichment. Workers should be given some degree of job security, and their pay level should be at least competitive with, if not higher than, the pay level of other workers in the same industry in the same community. Also, changing the pay method from an hourly wage to a salary schedule should make the status of these employees comparable to that of supervisory personnel.

4. **Do away with status symbols.**   Since workers are becoming the managers of their own jobs, it seems reasonable to treat them like managers. This can be done by removing various status symbols—such as executive parking lots, cafeterias, and dress codes—that separate workers from managerial personnel. Removing these symbols should confirm to employees the sincerity of management's intention to enrich their jobs.

5. **Create a supportive climate.**   Job enrichment will be fruitless unless it is accompanied by a change in organizational climate toward more cooperation and partnership among members. To this end, management should do away with competitive reward systems that encourage competition, aid employees in solving operational prob-

lems, serve as teachers and consultants rather than act as bosses, and act as supporter and catalyst of such organizational change.

6. **Promote organizational flexibility.** Management can promote organizational flexibility by adopting selected practices such as flextime and flexible organizational design. Under *flextime,* workers schedule their own work hours. They do so in consultation with the supervisor or the work group so they can meet personal and organizational needs, but without conforming to rigid schedules. Organizational structure can also be changed to improve organizational interactions among and between work groups. Linking-pin organization, project management, and matrix organization are some examples of flexible organizational designs (see Chapter 16).

SUMMARY AND CONCLUSION

Various ways of making jobs more meaningful—job enlargement, job enrichment, and matching jobs to people—have been presented in this chapter. *Job enlargement* involves technical changes in a job. When task elements are added to an existing job, the job becomes more meaningful because it uses the worker's skills and allows the worker to identify his or her efforts with the final product. *Job enrichment* involves changes in behavioral aspects of a job. Workers are given the managerial authority and responsibility to manage their own jobs.

Job enlargement and enrichment increase the motivational potential of a job. However, they will not produce positive results unless employees are willing and ready to perform these enlarged and enriched jobs. Since people differ in their needs and job skills, not all people will respond positively to complex jobs. In order to produce an optimum level of work motivation, the characteristics of a job need to be matched with those of an employee.

Matching jobs to people is essential for increasing work motivation. However, many organizational factors moderate workers' reactions to their jobs. Even with a match, therefore, workers are not likely to perform better unless they are reasonably well satisfied with such factors as pay, job security, supervision, and management support. These organizational factors should be adequately provided for before any job enrichment effort is made.

KEY CONCEPTS AND WORDS

Job simplification
Job enlargement
Job enrichment
Matching concept
Task attribute
Task variety
Task identity

Psychological state
Job involvement
Diagnostic survey
Employment
  enrichment
Organizational
  enrichment

Locus of control
Managerial
  autonomy
Protestant work ethic
Flextime

Questions for Review and Discussion

1.   a.   What is job enlargement?
     b.   What is job enrichment?
     c.   What are the major differences between job enlargement and job enrichment?

2. How do job enlargement and enrichment affect employee work motivation? Explain the psychological process by which a job's task attributes influence work motivation.

3. "Despite considerable enthusiasm, job enlargement and enrichment are not widely practiced in organizations." Explain why.

4.   a.   How do individual differences among workers affect the ways they react to their jobs?
     b.   What implications do these differences have for designing jobs?

5. What role do non-work organizational factors play in worker reactions to their jobs? Give some specific examples in answering this question.

6. Assume that you are the manager of a television manufacturing company and are responsible for enriching jobs. What major steps do you need to follow in the process of enriching the jobs?

CASE AND EXERCISE

CASE 15.1. THE UNITED TELEPHONE COMPANY

This case allows you to diagnose the causes of employee problems in an organization. You may start with an analysis of the situation and propose a specific course of action to deal with the problems you have identified.

The Situation

The United Telephone Company is an independent telephone operator in a metropolitan area. Its service department is responsible for installation and repair services to residential and commercial customers. Processing a service request is a complicated business. A typical service request is received by telephone by a service representative. A handwritten order is sent to a supervisor for review, and the reviewed order is sent to a typist in the typing pool. The typed order then goes to the service order center, where a supervisor verifies the order before it is sent to the field service department. The field service personnel complete the service order, and a completion work report is sent to the service department. The completion report is then reviewed by a supervisor before it is sent to the service order center. The business representative at the service order center reviews the completion report and prepares the service order completion reports to be sent to the client and the billing and order departments.

Business volume has increased substantially in recent years because of a general upsurge in the economic prosperity of the region. The increased business volume has brought an increase in customer complaints. Customers complain that their service orders are delayed and/or that they receive inadequate service. If they call the office for an explanation of these problems, nobody seems to know what happened. Internally, the department has a number of personnel problems. Tardiness, absenteeism, and turnover are high among typists and service representatives. In order to combat these problems, management has stepped up the control procedure by increasing the number of reviews and verifications of service orders; they have also increased the pay and fringe benefits for employees.

Discussion Questions

1.   What are the main causes of the problems?
2.   What would you suggest the company do to solve the problems?
3.   Should they introduce job enlargement and/or job enrichment programs? Explain why or why not.

EXERCISE 15.1. CONDUCTING A DIAGNOSTIC SURVEY

Many well-intended job enrichment programs fail to produce positive results because management has failed to diagnose the real causes of employee problems. This exercise is to help you identify the critical factors that should be considered in designing or redesigning a job. The survey instrument used in this exercise is divided into two parts: (1) the task attribute questionnaire and (2) the individual and organizational readiness questionnaire.

The Procedure

1.   Conduct a job enrichment diagnostic survey of a job you have held or now hold. If you have not worked where this is feasible, select the job of someone you know.

2. Compute the motivational potential index (task attributes) from part A of the survey.

3. Compute the individual and organizational readiness (individual and organizational characteristics) from part B of the survey.

4. Interpret the survey results and discuss their implications.

A. The Task Attribute Questionnaire

Instructions: Each questionnaire item measures the motivational potential of a job. Respond to each item by checking the column that best describes your assessment of the job.

Items	Very Little 1 2 3	Somewhat 4 5 6 7	Very Much 8 9
1. To what extent does the worker perform different activities requiring a variety of job skills?			
2. To what extent does the worker perform the whole unit or a major portion of a product?			
3. Does the job provide meaningful performance feedback?			
4. To what extent does the worker have control over his or her work method and pace?			
5. To what extent does the job provide the worker with opportunities to interact with co-workers or clients?			
6. To what extent does the job allow employees to participate in the managerial process?			
7. To what extent does the worker have autonomy in utilizing his or her own time and other resources?			

Motivational potential index = sum of the responses /7

B. The Individual and Organizational Readiness Questionnaire

Instructions: Each of the survey questions concerns an aspect of individual and organizational readiness to job enrichment. Respond to each item by checking the column that best describes your assessment of the individual and organization you have selected.

Items	Very Little		Somewhat					Very Much
	1 **2**	**3**	**4**	**5**	**6**	**7**	**8**	**9**
1. To what extent is the worker satisfied with his or her pay?								
2. To what extent does the worker have job security in the organization?								
3. How well is the worker technically prepared to perform the job?								
4. How well can the worker interact with his or her co-workers or clients?								
5. How well can the worker perform his or her job with a minimum level of supervision?								
6. Does the worker want responsibility for the task accomplishment?								
7. To what extent is the worker committed to the organization?								
8. Can supervisors function as participative managers?								
9. Do the employees trust management?								
10. Does top management support job enrichment?								
11. Is the union supportive of job enrichment, if it is a unionized company?								
12. How flexible is your organization?								

Individual and organizational readiness index = sum of the responses /12

Footnotes

1. Jerome M. Rosow, *The Worker and the Job* (Englewood Cliffs, NJ: Prentice-Hall, 1974), p. 7.

2. F. W. Taylor, *The Principles of Scientific Management* (New York: Harper & Row, 1911).

3. R. H. Guest, "Job Enlargement: A Revolution in Job Design," *Personnel Administration,* 1957, **20,** 9–16; C. R. Walker, "The Problem

of the Repetitive Job," *Harvard Business Review,* 1950, **28,** 54–59; and C. R. Walker and R. H. Guest, *The Man on the Assembly Line* (Cambridge, MA: Harvard University Press, 1952).

4. F. Herzberg, B. Mausner, and B. Snyderman, *The Motivation to Work* (New York: Wiley, 1959); and L. E. Lewis, "The Design of Jobs," *Industrial Relations,* January 1966, 21–45.

5. J. R. Hackman, G. Oldham, R. Jansen, and K. Purdy, "A New Strategy for Job Enrichment," *California Management Review,* Summer 1975, 57–71; and L. W. Porter, E. E. Lawler, III, and J. R. Hackman, *Behavior in Organization* (New York: McGraw-Hill, 1975).

6. Samuel Rabinowitz and D. T. Hall, "Organizational Research on Job Involvement," *Psychological Bulletin,* 1977, **84,** 265–288; and F. E. Saal, "Job Involvement: A Multivariate Approach," *Journal of Applied Psychology,* 1978, **63,** 53–61.

7. Frederick Herzberg, "One More Time: How Do You Motivate Employees?" *Harvard Business Review,* January–February 1968, 53–62.

8. J. R. Hackman, "Is Job Enrichment Just a Fad?" *Harvard Business Review,* September–October 1975, 129–138; and C. L. Hulin and M. R. Blood, "Job Enlargement, Individual Differences, and Worker Responses," *Psychological Bulletin,* 1968, **69,** 41–55.

9. J. R. Hackman and G. R. Oldham, "Development of the Job Diagnostic Survey," *Journal of Applied Psychology,* 1975, **60,** 159–170.

10. See R. B. Dunham, "Reactions to Job Characteristics: Moderating Effects of the Organization," *Academy of Management Journal,* 1977, **20,** 42–65; and H. P. Sims and A. D. Szilagyi, "Job Characteristics Relationships: Individual and Structural Moderators," *Organizational Behavior and Human Performance,* 1976, **17,** 211–230.

11. K. H. Chung and M. F. Ross, "Differences in Motivational Properties Between Job Enlargement and Job Enrichment," *Academy of Management Review,* January 1977, pp. 113–122.

12. M. M. Greller and D. M. Harold, "Sources of Feedback: A Preliminary Investigation," *Organizational Behavior and Human Performance,* 1979, **23,** 309–338.

13. R. N. Ford, "Job Enrichment Lessons from AT&T," *Harvard Business Review,* January–February 1973, 96–106.

14. V. H. Vroom, "Ego-Involvement, Job Satisfaction and Job Performance," *Personnel Psychology,* 1962, **15,** 157–177.

15. R. S. Schuler and J. S. Kim, "Interactive Effects of Participation in Decision Making, the Goal Setting Process and Feedback on Em-

ployee Satisfaction and Performance," *Academy of Management Proceedings,* 1976, 114–117.

16. T. R. Mitchell, C. M. Smyser, and S. E. Weed, "Locus of Control: Supervision and Work Satisfaction," *Academy of Management Journal,* September 1975, pp. 623–631.

17. E. H. Conant and M. D. Kilbridge, "An Interdisciplinary Analysis of Job Enlargement: Technology, Costs, and Behavioral Implications," *Industrial and Labor Relations Review,* 1965, **18,** 377–395; and Guest, "Job Enlargement," 9–16.

18. United States, Department of Health, Education, and Welfare, *Work in America* (Cambridge, MA: MIT Press, 1973); and see R. E. Walton, "Work Innovations in the United States," *Harvard Business Review,* July–August 1979, 88–98.

19. R. H. Guest, "Quality of Work Life—Learning from Tarrytown," *Harvard Business Review,* July–August 1979, 76–87.

20. See Mitchell Fein, "Job Enrichment: A Reevaluation," *Sloan Management Review,* Winter 1974, 69–88.

21. J. P. Wanous, "Individual Differences and Reactions to Job Characteristics," *Journal of Applied Psychology,* 1974, **59,** 616–622; J. M. Ivancevich and J. T. McMahon, "A Study of Task-Goal Attributes, High Order Need Strength, and Performance," *Academy of Management Journal,* 1977, **20,** 552–563.

22. David Sirota and A. D. Wolfson, "Pragmatic Approach to People Problems," *Harvard Business Review,* January–February 1973, 120–128; and E. R. Gray, "The Non Linear Systems Experience: A Requiem," *Business Horizons,* February 1978, 31–36.

23. George Strauss, "Quality of Work Life and the Union," in *Perspectives on Behavior in Organizations,* ed. J. R. Hackman, E. E. Lawler, and L. W. Porter (New York: McGraw-Hill, 1977), pp. 479–486.

24. Hulin and Blood, "Job Enlargement"; Wanous, "Individual Differences"; and Ivancevich and McMahon, "A Study of Task-Goal Attributes."

25. M. S. Myers, "Who Are Your Motivated Workers?" *Harvard Business Review,* January–February 1964, 73–88; and Fred Luthans and W. E. Reif, "Job Enrichment: Long on Theory, Short on Practice," *Organizational Dynamics,* Winter 1974, 30–43.

26. J. K. White, "Individual Differences and the Job Quality-Worker Response Relationships: Review, Integration, and Comments," *Academy of Management Review,* April 1978, 267–280; and E. F. Stone, R. T. Mowday, and L. W. Porter, "Higher Order Need

Strengths as Moderators of the Job Scope–Job Satisfaction Relationship,'' *Journal of Applied Psychology,* 1977, **62,** 466–471.

27. See Rabinowitz and Hall, ''Organizational Research on Job Involvement,'' p. 275; and Saal, ''Job Involvement,'' p. 57.

28. Mitchell, Smyser, and Weed, ''Locus of Control,'' p. 629.

29. D. W. Organ, ''Effects of Pressure and Individual Neuroticism on Emotional Responses to Task-Role Ambiguity,'' *Journal of Applied Psychology,* 1975, **60,** 397–400.

30. Herzberg, ''One More Time''; and M. S. Myers, *Every Employee a Manager* (New York: McGraw-Hill, 1970), pp. 11–13.

31. G. R. Oldham, ''Job Characteristics and Internal Motivation: The Moderating Effect of Interpersonal and Individual Variables,'' *Human Relations,* 1976, **29,** 559–569.

32. Porter, Lawler, and Hackman, *Behavior in Organizations;* and J. L. Pierce, R. B. Dunham, and R. C. Blackburn, ''Social Structure, Job Design, and Growth Need Strength: A Test of a Contingency Model,'' *Academy of Management Review,* June 1979, 223–240.

33. J. R. Hackman, ''Work Design,'' in *Improving Life at Work,* ed. J. R. Hackman and J. L. Suttle (Pacific Palisades, CA: Goodyear, 1977), pp. 96–162; and K. H. Chung, *Motivational Theories and Practices* (Columbus, OH: Grid Publishing, 1977), pp. 204–212.

LEARNING OBJECTIVES

1. To understand the impact of environment and technology on organizational structure.
2. To learn various ways of designing organizational structure.
3. To acquire the skills of selecting an appropriate organizational structure.

16 DESIGNING ORGANIZATIONAL STRUCTURE

In order to coordinate interdependent roles, organizations have invented mechanisms for collecting information, deciding, and disseminating information to resolve conflicts and guide interdependent actions. The collection of mechanisms used constitutes the organizing mode of the organization.

Jay R. Galbraith, Organization Design[1]

Organizational structures come in many forms. Some are quite simple; others are very complex. Some are rigidly structured; others are loosely structured. The type of structure shows how an organization deals with the forces in the environment—that is, with the market and technology—and how it processes information internally.

This chapter is based on the concept that environmental forces determine the type of organizational structure. It investigates the effects of the environment on organizational design. An underlying theme is that organizational structure should reflect the effects of environmental forces. Specifically, the following topics are discussed in the chapter: (1) the reasons for organizational design, (2) the impact of environment and technology on structure, (3) types of organizational design, and (4) the selection of organizational structure.

WHY DESIGN ORGANIZATIONAL STRUCTURE?

> *Organizational design refers to the process by which organizational activities are structured. Its main objective is to develop an organizational structure that can help management achieve its goals effectively and efficiently.*

In Chapter 2 an organization was defined as a sociotechnical system composed of individuals, groups, tasks, and managerial controls. These organizational components interact with each other in the process of achieving organizational goals. The chapter also pointed out that organizational effectiveness increases when the organizational components are compatible not only among themselves but with environmental forces. The concept of organizational design can be best understood within the context of our definition of organization and the concept of organizational fit. Organizational design is the process of structuring organizational activities so the structure is compatible with other organizational components as well as with environmental demands.

Among the important functions served by organizational design are: (1) the hierarchy of organizational objectives, (2) the concept of division of labor, and (3) a system of coordination and control. The hierarchy of objectives is the basis for structuring organizational activities in terms of means-ends chains. The concept of division of labor provides the basis for organizational grouping. Organizational design is also intended to provide a system for coordinating the activities of various organizational units.

Means-Ends Chains

An organization is a goal-pursuing entity, and its structure shows how organizational activities are organized to best achieve its goals. In complex organizations, objectives are structured in terms of means-ends chains, in which the objectives of a subunit are the means of achieving the goals of the next higher unit. The following example illustrates such a hierarchy of objectives.

> *The Delta Corporation is a small producer of electronic gadgets, and its main objective is to make a decent profit. In order to achieve this goal, the president feels that the company has to produce its products at low costs, expand its market, and continuously update its products. The president assigns these operational responsibilities to three departments—production, sales, and research.*

The production department is primarily responsible for producing a certain number and type of electronic gadgets at low cost per unit. The sales department is responsible for marketing the products to increase sales volume as well as the market share. The research department is responsible for generating innovative products. As shown in Figure 16.1, achieving departmental goals becomes the means of achieving the corporate profit goal.

Departmental goals can be further divided and assigned to sections. For example, the sales department's activities can be divided into selling, marketing research, product feasibility study, and promotion. Performing these subunits' activities becomes the means of achieving the marketing department's goals.

This hierarchy of objectives provides an organization with a logical basis for determining what activities are needed to achieve their goals and how these activities are structured. The corporate goal becomes the basis for developing the objectives of each organizational subunit. Such a hierarchical arrangement of organizational objectives enables management to evaluate the contributions of its subunits to the organization. Failure to design a structure in terms of means-ends chains can mean a failure of subunits to contribute to the organization. Without such a hierarchical structure, it would be difficult to tell how a subunit's activities are related to the attainment of the corporate goal. For example, the research department of the Delta Corporation can actively engage in a number of research activities that do not contribute to the corporate goal.

Division of Labor

Organizational design involves dividing organizational activities into various groups. The concept of division of labor provides a basis for this organizational division. It is concerned with the extent to which jobs are divided to permit some degree of specialization.[2] Rather than performing

FIGURE 16.1
A Structure of Means-Ends Chains.

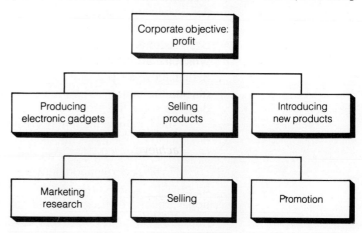

an infinite number of tasks, a worker is specialized in a limited number. There are several reasons for division of labor. First, in complex job situations, no one person can perform all the required activities. These activities need to be divided so each worker can perform a manageable number of tasks.

Second, with a limited number of tasks to be performed, the employee becomes proficient in performing them. By performing them over and over, the worker can gain expertise and increase production efficiency. Finally, division of labor allows differentiation in professional groups. Since some tasks require a high degree of job skills, while others can be done by untrained personnel, management can staff complex tasks with skilled personnel and simple tasks with untrained personnel.

There are a number of ways in which people and tasks can be divided into groups. The first approach is to group them by their functional specializations, such as production, sales, and research. The second approach is to group them by project. People who are associated with a particular project are grouped together. The third approach is to develop a matrix structure, in which people are assigned to both functional and project groups.

A System of Coordination

Organizational design provides a system of coordination.[3] A coordinating system is essential for managing an organization because it ensures the concerted effort of organizational subunits toward the attainment of organizational goals. Without this coordination there is no way of knowing how subunits' activities are related to overall goals. In complex organizations, since the activities are divided into a large number of subunits, the need for coordination becomes greater.

Organizational activities are coordinated in a number of ways. First, the *organizational hierarchy* serves as a coordinating mechanism. The manager who supervises the organizational units coordinates their activities. When subordinates have coordinating problems, the manager helps work them out.

Second, *rules and procedures* can be used to resolve coordinating problems among organizational units. The virtue of rules and procedures is that they are prepared in advance. Thus, when a problem actually occurs, the concerned parties can refer easily to these rules and procedures to solve the problem.

Third, management may create a *coordinating agent,* such as coordinator or coordinating committee, to deal with various coordinating problems. A coordinating agent mediates the differences between groups.

Finally, coordination between functional specialists can be achieved by creating a *self-contained project group.* People from different functional groups are brought together to carry out the assigned project. In this case, coordination is done through face-to-face interactions on an informal basis.

The selection of an appropriate coordinating system depends on several factors, such as the nature of task and the environment in which the organization functions. If the task requires a high degree of interaction between various functional specializations within a specified time period, the creation of a project structure is highly appropriate. If the coordinating problem involves conflict over a judicial boundary between groups, the use of hierarchical systems, or rules and procedures, is appropriate.

The notion of organizational design suggests that organizations have choices in structuring the hierarchy of goals, in structuring organizational activities, and in devising a system of coordination and control. The strategic choices to a large extent depend on the *interactional* or *informational processing requirement* of a task. Some tasks require a high degree of interaction among functional group members; others require interaction among functional specialists.

In addition, the nature of the external environment seems to influence the information processing requirement of an organization. Galbraith argues that an organization is an information processing system and that uncertainty in the environment increases the need for greater information exchange among various functional specialists.[4] Differences in information processing requirements necessitates differences in organizational design.

ENVIRONMENT, TECHNOLOGY, AND STRUCTURE

> *Organizational size, technology, and environment have a significant influence on organizational structure. However, the selection of a structure ultimately rests in the hands of the decision maker.*

If you visit a McDonald's hamburger shop, you will notice that one group of employees serves customers and another group of employees cooks. This is a simple organizational structure. However, if you visit an office of the Boeing Aircraft Company, it will be difficult to tell who is doing what for whom. Because the organizational relationships are so complex, even the employees themselves may find it difficult to delineate their authority and responsibility relationships. What causes such a difference in organizational structure? A literature review reveals that three factors influence the shape of organizational structure: organizational size, technology, and environment.[5]

Size and Structure

The size-structure relationship is easy to understand. An increase in size (number of employees) is likely to increase the number of work groups, which in turn increases organizational complexity. The increase in size will demand greater administrative control and coordination. However, whether or not it increases the number of administrative personnel proportionally has not been determined.[6]

Technology and Structure

The process of transforming organizational inputs (such as materials, capital, equipment, and labor) into outputs (goods and services) is called *technology,* and the type of technology influences the way an organization is structured. For example, Woodward found that there were distinctive relationships between technology and structure.[7] She identified three types of technology: (1) unit or batch production, (2) mass production, and (3) process production. As one moved from unit toward process production systems, the number of management levels and the executive span of control increased, but the ratio of administrative staff decreased. She also found that firms that relied on mass production systems were more highly structured than those that relied on unit or process technology.

Perrow was more general in classifying the types of technology.[8] He proposed that technology could be viewed in terms of (1) whether or not problems are analyzable and (2) whether or not problems are familiar. Based on these two dimensions, he identified four types of technologies: routine, engineering, craft, and nonroutine. Drawing on Perrow and others, we may establish the following typology describing the relationship between technology and structure.

Mass Production Technology.   Mass production refers to a production process in which a large volume of a standardized product is produced in a standardized manner. Producing standardized nuts and bolts involves mass production technology. Since the products are standardized and the production methods are mechanized, such a system requires a low level of information processing among the specialized functions. Any required coordination among functional groups can be achieved with a hierarchical structure. A simple structure is sufficient to maintain the necessary coordination.

Long-linked Technology.   Long-linked technology is characterized by a production system requiring a long series of operations before the end product is completed. Most construction projects involve a long-linked technology. Building a house, for example, requires a series of activities (such as preparing foundation, construction, and furnishing). Since long-linked technology needs the cooperation of various organizational subunits, coordination is necessary to integrate the activities of these subunits. An effective coordination mechanism is the key to success in long-linked technology.

Unit Production Technology.   When the company produces goods and services based on customer specifications, its production system cannot be standardized or structured. A loose functional organization, with a low level of specialization, is more suitable than a highly specialized functional structure in such an environment. For example, TV repair technicians should be able to fix all types of television sets and not just specialize in one kind. However, if volume of business is sufficient, they may decide to specialize in a particular type of television set.

Intensive Technology.   Intensive technology requires an organizational structure in which information flows freely—both internally and externally. Since the tasks are substantially different, there is a greater need for task integration. Most tasks or projects are unique, so the selection of technology and structure must be decided on in specific situations. A flexible and complex form of organizational structure is likely to be more suitable to such technology than a simple organizational structure.

Environment and Structure

The environment in which an organization operates seems to influence organizational structure. A study by Burns and Stalker finds that a mechanistic organizational structure is suitable to organizations operating in a stable environment, while a flexible or organic structure is suitable to those operating in a dynamic environment.[9] A mechanistic organization has characteristics that can be identified with bureaucracy—specialization, formalization, and centralization. It is also characterized by routinized activities and programmed decisions. An organic organization, on the other hand, has a relatively flexible and adaptive structure. It places emphasis on lateral rather than vertical communications and on exchanges of information rather than on giving orders.

A more general model of environmental typology is proposed by Duncan.[10] According to him, types of environment are determined by two environmental dimensions—stability and complexity. *Stability* refers to predictability in the environmental forces—that is, in resources, market, technological development, economic conditions, and so forth. *Complexity* refers to the variability of environmental forces that an organization has to deal with.

Duncan argues that the lowest perceived uncertainty occurs in a simple-static environment in which only a few factors are unpredictable and changing. He suggests a functional organizational structure to deal with such an environment. The highest perceived uncertainty is experienced by organizations operating in a complex-dynamic environment, in which a large number of factors are constantly changing and are thus unpredictable. Duncan suggests an organic organizational structure, which emphasizes flexibility and adaptability, to cope with environmental uncertainty. A moderately perceived uncertainty is then found in organizations operating in a simple-dynamic or a complex-static environment.

Relationship Between Environment, Technology, and Structure

Based on the environmental and technological typologies just discussed, we may establish an organizational taxonomy that describes the relationship between environment, technology, and structure. Figure 16.2 summarizes this relationship.

Simple-Static Environment. In a simple-static environment, technology is simple and the market environment is stable. Inputs from the environment are relatively constant, and technology is simple and relatively unchanging. A factory that produces nuts and bolts operates in such a simple-static environment. Once the production facility is established, producing nuts and bolts becomes a routine operation and can easily be mechanized. Mass production systems are usually developed in such an environment. Organizational structure in production systems like this are likely to be simple and mechanistic.

Complex-Static Environment. In a complex-static environment, environmental inputs are relatively stable, but the technology employed is

FIGURE 16.2
An Organizational Taxonomy—Relationships Among Environment, Technology, and Structure.

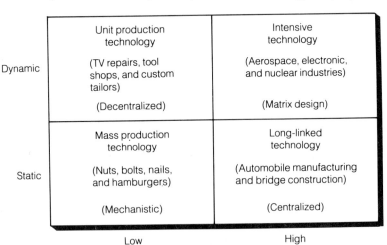

	Low	High
Dynamic	Unit production technology (TV repairs, tool shops, and custom tailors) (Decentralized)	Intensive technology (Aerospace, electronic, and nuclear industries) (Matrix design)
Static	Mass production technology (Nuts, bolts, nails, and hamburgers) (Mechanistic)	Long-linked technology (Automobile manufacturing and bridge construction) (Centralized)

Degree of Stability

Degree of Complexity

relatively complex. A bridge construction company and an auto manufacturing company operate in such a complex-static environment. Since the technology is complex, it requires the cooperation of people with various technical abilities. Thus, to function effectively, the production systems must be well coordinated. Long-linked technology is associated with such production systems. A flexible but centralized organizational structure is likely to be used to achieve the necessary coordination.

Simple-Dynamic Environment.   A crafts worker producing goods on a customer-order basis (such as a repair technician, custom cabinetmaker, machinist, printer, or tailor) operates in a simple but dynamic environment. The technology may be simple, but the kinds of problems or tasks the workers perform are not predictable. Each job is different from the others, so the production system cannot be standardized. Craftsmanship is essential in such batch or unit production systems. Since managerial decisions need to be made at the operational levels, a decentralized organizational structure, such as a project group and group management, is more appropriate than a centralized structure.

Complex-Dynamic Environment.   A company that relies on intensive technology, such as one that develops nuclear propulsion or weapons systems, deals with a complex and dynamic environment. Managers make decisions under uncertain conditions, while workers require diverse job skills and knowledge. The problems confronting management cannot be solved by standard and routine decision procedures. Organizations employing such intensive technology need to have an organizational structure that is capable of processing information from and to the environment and between various functional and project work groups. A matrix structure is often used in such organizations.

Evaluating the Organizational Taxonomy

The proposed organizational taxonomy presents a logical and systematic way of studying the relationship between environment, technology, and structure. However, whether or not a manager will choose a structure based on the suggested taxonomy largely depends on the manager's cognitive and motivational orientation.[11] Managers differ in their cognitive capacities. Some managers may not perceive environmental complexity and uncertainty as others do. Some managers may have a low tolerance for ambiguity and thus avoid complex organizational designs. The manager's motivation also may dictate the choice of organizational structure. Authoritarian managers are more likely to structure organizational activities than nonauthoritarian managers. Because of such managerial discretion, it is difficult to find a simple and consistent correlationship between environment, technology, and structure.[12]

TYPES OF ORGANIZATIONAL STRUCTURE

> *Organizational structure shows a pattern of interactions among organization members. An organization structures its activities to conform to its environmental demands.*

Organizational structure is more than an array of boxes on a chart. Such structure shows (1) the pattern of authority and responsibility relationships among organization members, (2) the communication flow within the organization, and (3) the system of task differentiation and integration. Conventional wisdom is to divide organizational activities into groups with similar task responsibilities. As organizations grow, their activities are further differentiated in the form of projects or products. A complex form of organization is developed to help the firm collect the necessary information from the environment and use it for decision making. Generally, the greater the task complexity and uncertainty, the greater the amount of information that must be collected and processed among various functional specialists. This requirement has a significant impact on the selection of organizational structure.[13]

It was pointed out earlier that there are basically three types of organizational structure: functional, project, and matrix. Depending on how a functional organization is managed, it can be further classified into a classical or a linking-pin structure. This section deals with these four types of organizational structure and shows how they are related to the environment. It is important to point out that many organizational designs in use are a composite of various forms and that they are an outgrowth of the functional organizational structure.

Classical Form of Organization

The classical organizational structure is often called *bureaucratic* or *mechanistic*. It is the most common form of organizational design. A typical form of classical design is shown in Figure 16.3. With this design organizational activities are divided into various functions that are internally homogeneous but externally heterogeneous. These functional groups may include production, sales, and research, and each function is further divided into different processes. For example, the production function is divided into such processes as stamping, plating, assembly, and painting. The classical model of organization has the following organizational char-

FIGURE 16.3
Classical Form of
Organization.

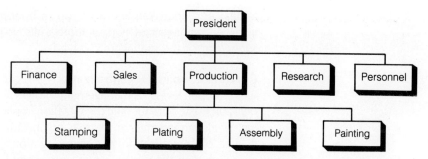

acteristics: (1) functional departmentalization, (2) line and staff functions, (3) hierarchy of authority, (4) span of control, (5) flat or tall organization, and (6) bureaucratic rules.

Functional Departmentalization.   As shown in Figure 16.3, organizational activities are divided into various functional groups. This form of labor division is most commonly used in structuring organizational activities because it has a commonsense appeal. It provides in-depth task specialization and a simple communications network.

Line and Staff Division.   In functional organizations, there is a distinction between line and staff activities. Line functions are directly involved in achieving the fundamental purpose of the organization, whereas staff functions support the line functions.

Authority Relationship.   In order to carry out managerial responsibilities, managers are given two types of authority—line and staff. Line authority is the right that a manager has over the subordinates in his or her jurisdiction. This authority includes the right to give instructions and to ensure productivity. Staff authority is the right to give advice or suggestions to people in other departments. This authority does not carry the right to reprimand others formally when the advice or suggestions are not followed.

Hierarchy of Authority.   In functional organizations, authority is exercised through a hierarchical structure. Two management principles ensure the authority structure. First, the *unity of command principle* indicates that no subordinate should receive orders about the same activity from more than one boss. The cost analyst receives orders from the accounting manager about how financial records should be kept, but it is done with the understanding of the production manager. Second, the *scalar principle* arranges the authority-responsibility relationships along hierarchical lines. This principle implies that managerial authority and responsibility flow in a clear and unbroken line from top to bottom. When there is a dispute between managers of two or more units, it is referred to the common supervisor of the managers involved.

Centralization vs. Decentralization.   These terms refer to the degree to which upper levels of management allow lower-level managers to make decisions. The bureaucratic organization implies centralized decision making, while an organic or flexible organization implies decentralization. Degree of centralization or decentralization, however, is a relative concept. Between the two extremes, upper and lower levels of management share decision-making responsibilities to varying degrees. The impact of centralization on behavior is that it increases uniformity of actions, but it tends to create among lower-level employees the feeling of becoming "cogs in the machine."

Span of Control.   Span of control refers to the number of employees a supervisor oversees. Researchers argue that span of control should vary with the nature of the task, the people being supervised, and the manager's experience.[14] For example, while a platoon sergeant in the army has about nine soldiers to supervise, the Roman Catholic Church has about 750 bishops and other officials reporting directly to the pope. The difference is that the tasks and people in the army need close supervision, while those in the Catholic Church need only general guidance.

Flat or Tall Organization.   The span of control used has an impact on the shape of an organization. For a given size, a wide span of control means a flat organization; a narrow span of control means a tall organizational structure. A flat organization has fewer management levels between the top and the bottom, while a tall organization has many managerial levels. Although it is difficult to generalize, bureaucratic organizations are likely to have a tall organizational structure because their managers tend to exercise close supervision.

Bureaucratic Rules.   One prominent aspect of bureaucratic organizations is their reliance on impersonal rules, procedures, and policies as a way of managing their members and activities. These control mechanisms are developed and used to ensure uniformity in the behavior of organizational members and to do away with personalization of organizational practices. In addition, these control mechanisms are designed to achieve the logical and scientific way of managing complex organizations.[15]

Evaluating the Classical Model.   The classical form of organization has both strengths and limitations. On the positive side, it permits task specialization, clear task assignments, a streamlined chain of command, and organizational predictability, and it is easily understood. Because of its clarity, simplicity, and predictability, it is widely used in managing complex and large organizations. Despite those who criticize bureaucratic organizations for their rigidity, many managers seem to prefer this form because it brings order and clarity to organizational activities.[16] This is a reason why so many organizations take the bureaucratic form of organizational design. The form is useful for organizations operating in a simple-stable environment or for managers who are primarily concerned with organizational predictability.

On the negative side, the classical form of organization is relatively slow to respond to changes in the environment. Since it divides organizations into various functional groups, it needs time to coordinate the groups' activities. Coordination becomes more difficult when these functional groups develop their own group goals, which may conflict with those of other groups. In addition, the classical organization produces a number of dysfunctional behaviors that may work against organizational efficiency. Among these behaviors are: (1) Rules become ends in themselves; so people adhere to these rules even when they do not serve the intended purpose. (2) Decision making becomes so routinized that it becomes difficult to search for viable alternatives. (3) Relationships may become so impersonalized that organizations may exist to support the hierarchical structure rather than to serve people.[17]

Linking-Pin Form of Organization

Linking-pin organizations also follow the functional organizational design. However, unlike the classical organization, this type is composed of interlocking groups that make managerial decisions concerning their work-related activities. An organization using employee participation at all levels characterizes the linking-pin organization structure. As shown in Figure 16.4, the linking-pin organization allows group members to make managerial decisions and to have these decisions carried to either the next higher or the next lower managerial groups by supervisors who have dual membership—in their own group and in a group at the next higher level. This overlapping group structure, combined with group decision-making practices, can help to achieve an optimum integration of the needs of both the organization and its members.[18] Furthermore, it is considered to be an effective method of achieving intergroup coordination and cooperation.

The linking-pin organization is often called *System 4 management* because it represents the fourth of Likert's managerial systems. These four are: (1) exploitative authoritarian, (2) benevolent authoritarian, (3) consultative, and (4) participative.[19] To realize the ideal of System 4 management, the manager must rely on three principles: (1) the principle of supportive relationships, (2) the use of group decision making, and (3) the establishment of high performance goals.

Underlying Assumptions.   The linking-pin organizational structure is based on the following assumptions:

1. Organizational tasks require a high degree of interaction among group members. Task interdependence—both sequential and reciprocal—forces organization members to cooperate and coordinate.

2. Organization members have the desire, ability, knowledge, and skill to participate in the decision process and to manage their own group activities.

3. Organization members are capable of responding to organizational demands in a responsible manner. When the members' personal goals are congruent with organizational goals, participative management is likely to succeed.

Where Best Utilized.   The linking-pin structure can be best utilized in organizations operating in a complex-static environment. Such organizations include automobile manufacturers, universities, and banking industries. For example, General Motors is known as an effective user of System 4 management.[20] The rationale for this system is that most tasks in such industries require a high degree of interaction among organizational members, and that a growing number of people in our society demand some control and influence over their work.

FIGURE 16.4
Linking-Pin Organization.

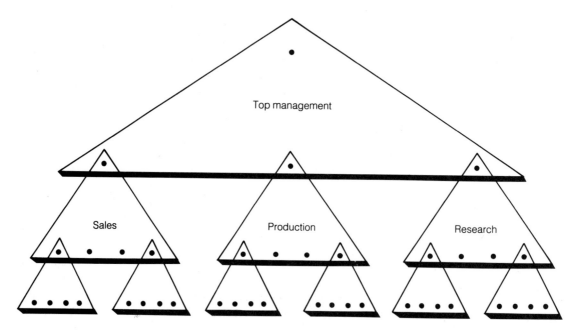

Strengths and Weaknesses. The linking-pin form of organization has both strengths and limitations. On the positive side, it encourages cooperation and coordination among work group members. It encourages employee participation, and thus also satisfies needs for autonomy and self-control. Furthermore, through the linking-pin process, the organization is able to link lower-level activities to high levels of management more effectively.

On the negative side, linking-pin organization is criticized for slow decision making. Participative management, as stated previously, is a time-consuming process; it should not be used in task situations requiring timely responses. However, participation can result in high-quality decisions, enhance acceptance by the employees, and facilitate the implementation process. Another problem is the difficulty of coordinating the activities of various functional groups. Although conflicts among functional groups can be resolved by supervisors at the next higher managerial level, there still remains the problem of members' loyalty to their own subgroups.

Project Form of Organization

The need to adapt to a changing environment calls for a flexible organizational design. In order to respond quickly to environmental changes, work groups can be organized around particular projects or products and allowed to make day-by-day operational decisions (see Figure 16.5).[21] Members of these self-contained groups are brought in from various functional departments. Since the project or product group collects relevant information and monitors its own activities, this form of organization allows large amounts of information and activity to be managed without overloading the hierarchical structure. Galbraith thus perceives it to be a strategy for coping with environmental complexity.[22]

FIGURE 16.5
Project Form of
Organization.

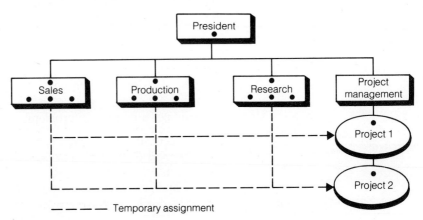

– – – – – Temporary assignment

When to Use the Project Design.   This form of organization is desirable when the organization has identifiable projects or products that are large enough to justify special attention. Since establishing a self-contained managing unit composed of various functional specialists is expensive, there must be sufficient business volume to justify its existence. Otherwise this structure is not desirable.

While the underlying rationale for using project and product forms of organization is the same, *project structure* exists only temporarily (until a project is completed), whereas *product structure* is created and exists to deal with a product that may remain profitable for a long time. For example, aircraft industries such as Boeing and McDonald Douglas usually work on government contracts on a project basis, while they maintain their product divisions to produce commercial jetliners. When product divisions are large enough, they may be managed as distinct profit centers, almost as if they were separate companies. General Motors is a good example; it is organized by product lines.

Advantages of Using This Design.   Following are some of the advantages of using the project or product form of organization.

1. It reduces environmental complexity to a manageable level. Relevant information is collected and used at the project or product group level, thereby reducing top management's burden of information processing.

2. It facilitates interaction among functional specialists; information processing usually occurs within the group on a face-to-face basis.

3. It can respond rapidly to changes in the environment, making possible rapid collection and digestion of new information.

4. It fosters goal congruence among group members, as shared goals reduce potential conflicts among functional specialists.

5. It provides the members with opportunities to participate in the decision processes, since the decisions are made at the project or product group level.

Disadvantages of Using This Design.   Despite its many potential advantages, the users of this organizational form, especially in a project structure, encounter a number of problems.

1. Many projects are not large enough to be self-sufficient. They must receive support from functional departments or share available resources with other projects, and this often creates confusion and conflict with the functional departments and other project groups. It may also cause frustration for project managers, who have the re-

sponsibility for completing the tasks without the authority to command the resources needed.

2.   Project structure often creates feelings of insecurity and uncertainty among members, as it does not provide permanent employment. Also, employees may be uncertain about their relationship with functional departments. The problem of loyalty being divided between project and functional affiliations often creates a feeling of anxiety and uneasiness.

3.   Since a project or product group operates independently of functional departments, the chance of duplication of effort, facilities, and resources is increased.

4.   When a person is assigned to a particular project or product group, questions often arise as to what is an effective use of his or her time. If the project or product group requires only part of a person's time, how should the remaining hours be spent?

These problems, with the exception of the second one, are relevant to both project and product structures. Product organization, however, can better overcome them. The environmental certainty and structural permanence of product organization allows this structure to better plan and use the organization's resources. Once organized, product groups become "little companies" or "self-contained work units," composed of various functional specialists who work on a permanent basis.

Matrix Form of Organization

A matrix organization is often suggested to overcome some of the problems associated with project structure. Instead of separating project groups from the functional structure, the matrix organization superimposes the former on the latter.[23] This structural arrangement is shown in Figure 16.6.

FIGURE   16.6
Matrix Form of
Organization.

A College of Business Administration

Departments / Programs	Accounting	Finance	Management	Marketing	Economics
Undergraduate					
Master's					
Ph.d.					
Executive development					

Features of This Structure.   The main features of a matrix organization are found in dual membership and authority-responsibility relationships. As organization members are assigned to both functional and project groups, they report to two managers, one in their functional department and one in the project or product group.

Authority and responsibility are shared by both functional and project managers, and their relationships flow both vertically and horizontally throughout the organization. Functional managers usually have line authority over functional group members in such functions as task assignment, promotion, and salary adjustment. The project or product managers have task-related authority over their project group members in carrying out their project or product activities.

Where Used.   Matrix structures are found in organizations that operate in a highly complex-dynamic environment. Such organizations have to gather and digest information constantly and respond quickly to any change in the environment. Lateral and vertical flows of information in the matrix organization meet such an information processing requirement. This form of organizational structure is widely used in aerospace, automobile, chemical, electronic, and pharmaceutical firms. General Electric, General Motors, Monsanto, National Cash Register, Texas Instruments, and TRW are just a few of the users of matrix organization.

As the market and technological environments become more complex and dynamic, organizations in relatively stable industries, such as banking, insurance, government agencies, and universities, are employing the matrix structure to a limited extent.

Strengths of This Organizational Form.   The matrix organization has the following characteristics that can be identified as strengths.[24] (These characteristics also differentiate the matrix from the other forms of organization—functional, linking-pin, and project.)

Matrix organization promotes *adaptability and flexibility* in organizational structure. Not only do project and product groups form and dissolve; so do functional groups. This flexibility gives the organization the ability to cope with changes in the market and technological environments.

Matrix organization facilitates *effective use of project and functional managers.* It facilitates information flow between project and functional groups. In addition, since many decisions are made at low levels of management, chief executive officers have more time to interact with the environment.

Matrix organization provides managers with *dual career paths or ladders.* Project or product managers who are successful in dealing with various functional specialists become prime candidates for divisional and general manager positions. Functional managers can become specialists in their particular function or serve different projects before they advance to higher managerial positions.

Disadvantages of This Organizational Form.   These same advantageous characteristics can be detrimental to some organizations. First, the complexity in organizational relationships (that is, dual membership, authority relationship, and reporting systems) can create confusion and conflict among various functional and project groups. This confusion and conflict is created because the matrix structure violates the principle of unity of command.

Second, the power struggle between functional and project managers can lead to organizational instability. As you will see in Case 16.2, some organizations abandon the matrix structure because of such power struggles. Functional managers often form coalitions to undermine the power of project managers.

Finally, a substantial amount of time and resources is required to develop a smoothly functioning matrix organization. Organization members must be trained to function in such a complex organizational environment. This training should be aimed at developing a set of interpersonal, leadership, group process, and conflict resolution skills.

 ## ORGANIZATIONAL DESIGN STRATEGIES

> *Organizational design involves a strategic choice of organizational structure and an active cultivation of an existing structure.*

In designing organizational structure, managers should be conscious of the following points. First, organizational design can be seen as an evolutionary process that moves from a simple to a complex structure. Second, it is essential to match structure to environment. Finally, it is important to develop and promote boundary-spanning roles within and outside of the organization.

Evolution Toward Matrix Organization

Organizational structure evolves through several stages. Kolodny argued that a firm's organizational structure moves from a simple to a complex form. He took the position that environmental forces determine the progression toward a matrix design.[25] The following scenario illustrates this evolutionary process.

> *A company may start by producing a single product. As business increases, the company's activities are divided into various func-tions such as production, sales, and research. As business further increases, the market and technological environments become more complex, for competition stimulates advances in the indus-try, and better service and prices are demanded. These environ-mental demands force the company to rely on marketing, production, and research experts for better managerial decisions and daily operations. Coordination among these functional groups is achieved through the managerial hierarchy or the linking-pin pro-cess.*
>
> *The company diversifies its product lines and even satisfies customer demands on a project basis. As the market diversifies, the traditional means of coordination become less responsive to envi-ronmental changes. Variations in the product lines, uncertainty in the marketplace, and technological changes all threaten the com-pany's main products with obsolescence. In order to meet this challenge, the company establishes project and product groups, which enhance the organization's capacity to deal with the exter-nal environment. But those groups tend to lose contact with the internal environment—especially with functional groups—and so a matrix structure is created to facilitate information flow between project groups and functional departments.*

This scenario is a simplified version of the organizational evolution that can occur over several decades. The many uncertainties in today's industrial world seem to hasten the evolutionary process. Rapid technolog-ical developments, the energy crisis, and instability in world politics all contribute to environmental uncertainty. Not many industries are immune from the whims of environmental uncertainty. So-called stable industries such as food processing, beverages, banking, insurance, and education now rely on matrix systems to cope with rapidly changing environmental demands.

Matching Structure to Environment

The success of a given design depends on the organization's ability to delimit and delineate the environmental forces and match them with a compatible structure. Failure to do this often results in an environment–organization mismatch that causes a number of dysfunctional behaviors.[26] For example, when an organization maintains a highly centralized func-tional structure in a highly complex and dynamic environment, it will have difficulty gathering and digesting information from the environment. This difficulty will be reflected in the company's adverse performance.

Matching structure to environment is not easy, for a number of internal and external factors, including tasks, employees, leadership, group climate, technological complexity, and market uncertainty, must be considered. Although any attempt to find a match involving a large number of contingencies runs the risk of oversimplification, such an attempt will give you some insight into designing organizational structure. The organizational taxonomy presented in Figure 16.2 can serve as a starting point for matching structure to technology and environment.

Developing Boundary Spanners

Organizational structure provides a means of getting needed information to appropriate decision makers. Individuals who are in charge of information processing activities are called *boundary spanners,* because they are the ones who gather, filter, and process information passing through organizational boundaries.[27] Since boundary spanners are exposed to large amounts of information, they need to be adept at judging and processing relevant information. They must determine what information is important and who gets what items of information.

As shown in Figure 16.7, there are two kinds of boundary spanners: internal and external. *Internal boundary spanners* exchange information among organizational subunits. Tushman argues that internal boundary spanners play an important role in facilitating the innovative process since

FIGURE 16.7
Internal and External
Boundary-Spanning
Activities.

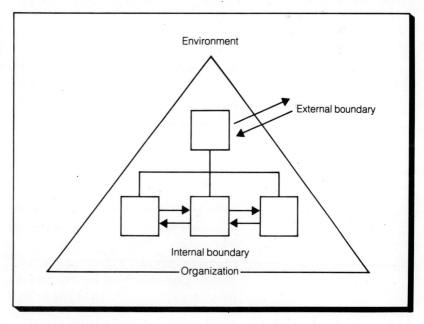

they process information through several phases—idea generation, problem solving, and implementation.[28] These innovative phases are performed by various functional and/or project groups; thus, boundary spanners need to be skillful in processing information between them. Supervisors, coordinators, group representatives, and liaison personnel usually perform this service.

External boundary spanners gather information and exchange it between the organization and its environment. They interact with external agents, such as customers, suppliers, competitors, and the general public. Thus, it is they who project the organization's image to outsiders. Public relations people, project personnel, company representatives, innovators, market researchers, and lobbyists serve as external boundary spanners.

All organizations need to perform boundary spanning activities. But the extent to which organizations engage in these activities varies greatly. Leifer and Delbecq indicate that, the greater the environmental uncertainty and complexity, the greater the amount of boundary spanning activity.[29] Organizations operating in a complex and dynamic environment need to process more information in a timely manner than those operating in a simple and stable environment.

Some Symptoms of Poor Design

What happens when a structure is poorly designed? Poor structural design can lead to a number of dysfunctional behaviors that can result in organizational ineffectiveness. Duncan lists the following potential problems of structural deficiency:[30]

1. Managers may be alerted to problems too late to develop contingency plans. An organization loses touch with the external environment without adequate information-gathering mechanisms.

2. Information may not be distributed to the right person or place, and valuable data may become useless.

3. Management may have difficulty coordinating the activities of various information users and thereby lose control over information flow.

4. With all the above problems, the organization will not be able to react to environmental changes, thus preventing corrective actions.

5. Individual managers may experience the role conflict that occurs when decision makers act as reactors rather than as planners.

6. Managers may also experience role ambiguity because they are expected to do something, but they do not know what or they lack the necessary structural mechanisms to do it.

These are some of the symptoms of a poorly designed organizational structure. Managers should be aware of these symptoms and take corrective action. While a structural mismatch may not have a direct effect on the organization's ability to achieve its immediate goals, it will restrict the firm's ability to respond to environmental and technological demands. As organizational design is a major tool for adapting to these demands, organizations should develop a systematic way of monitoring the relationship among environment, technology, and structure.

SUMMARY AND CONCLUSION

Organizations differ in their structure. There are basically four types of structure—bureaucratic, linking-pin, project, and matrix. The *bureaucratic structure* is the most common form of organizational design, and it can be effectively used in a simple-static environment. The needed coordination among work groups can be achieved through the hierarchical structure. From this structure, other forms of organization can emerge.

As the environment becomes more complex and dynamic, organizational structures take more complex forms. The *linking-pin structure* encourages the participation of functional specialists in the decision process. As the task becomes more complex, it demands inputs from these specialists.

The *project* or *product structure* is used in organizations that have identifiable projects or products requiring special attention. When the projects or products require timely responses from functional specialists, these are taken out of functional departments and assigned to particular project/product groups.

The *matrix organization* superimposes project or product structure on the functional structure. This structure is designed to facilitate the flow of information within project or product groups and between project/product groups and functional departments. Matrix structures are usually found in organizations that operate in a complex and dynamic environment. These structures permit the processing of information between an organization and its environment in a timely manner.

KEY CONCEPTS AND WORDS

Boundary spanner
Centralization
Decentralizaton
Environmental
  influence
Environmental
  stability
Flat organization
System 4
  management
Functional
  structure

Information
  processing
  requirement
Line authority
Linking-pin structure
Long-linked
  technology
Mass production
  system
Matrix structure
Bureaucratic
  structure

Project structure
Scalar principle
Span of control
Staff authority
Tall organization
Technological
  complexity
Unit production
  system
Unity of command
  principle

Questions for Review and Discussion

1. Discuss the manner in which environmental certainty and complexity interact to determine the type of technology used in organizations.

2. Describe the environmental characteristics of a university, and show how it should be organized.

3. The conventional wisdom of organizational design is to divide organizational activities into various functional groups.
   a. What are the reasons for such a design?
   b. What are some potential problems?

4. A new trend in organizational design is to study the information processing requirement of an organization and then design a suitable structure. Discuss the types of information processing requirements, and explain how they are related to organizational structure.

5. a. What is a line function?
   b. What is a staff function?
   c. What kinds of authority does a staff manager have? A line manager?

6. What are the advantages and disadvantages of the project organizational structure?

7. What are the advantages and disadvantages of the matrix organizational structure?

8. What are some potential consequences of using an improper organizational design?

CASES

CASE 16.1 A & J INSTRUMENTS

This case allows you to analyze the environmental characteristics in which a company operates and to design or redesign the organizational structure. You are encouraged to look into other related problems such as employee motivation and organizational change.

The Situation

A & J Instruments produces a wide range of measuring instruments. The company's main product lines include barometers, electric gauges, lie detectors, radiometers, speedmeters and thermostats. In the past, about 60 percent of the company's business was derived from government contracts, and the rest was from the private sector. The company bid on government contracts and produced the required instruments based on their specifications. However, the industry in general has been experiencing a setback in recent years due to a substantial reduction in defense industrial production.

In order to counteract the reduction in business volume, the company has been actively but unsuccessfully seeking business in the private sector. More instrument manufacturers are competing in the market, and products are becoming increasingly complex and sophisticated. Thus, A & J Instruments has experienced difficulties in securing major contracts. The company's bid costs are usually higher than those of other competitors, and its quality is not equal to theirs. Unlike government contracts, which require production of instruments based on the clients' specifications, private contracts require substantial amounts of development and marketing activity.

The general manager of the firm has indicated that the company is revising its managerial strategy to cope with the changing technological environment. He is responsible for developing a managerial strategy that will involve several changes in manufacturing, research and development, and marketing. He has expressed interest in inviting a management consulting team to help him formulate a plan. At least a part of the plan involves organizational design.

Discussion Questions

1. Analyze the changes in the environmental characteristics and information processing requirements of the company.

2. What kind of organizational structure would you recommend? Explain why.

3. What are some other problems that have not been discussed?

CASE 16.2. THE BEACON AIRCRAFT COMPANY, PART 1

This case shows you the advantages and disadvantages of functional and matrix organizational designs. Also, it should help you understand the political problems associated with organizational design. The case allows you to redesign an existing organizational structure.

The Situation

The Beacon Aircraft Company manufactures and sells three types of aircraft—single-engine, twin-engine, and jet. Before 1979 the marketing division was divided into contract administration, customer services, marketing research, and sales. The sales department was further divided into three markets—domestic, international, and government. As business volume increased, it became increasingly difficult to provide well-coordinated services to customers, for each product line and market segment required different kinds of customer service.

Since the functional structure was inadequate, the marketing division was reorganized. The new structure took the form of matrix organization. In this structure, the domestic sales group was divided into three product lines—single-engine, twin-engine, and jet engine. In addition, personnel from other departments were assigned to particular market or product groups. Initially, this matrix structure caused some confusion, but people soon learned to function under it. In fact, they began to identify more closely with a particular product line or market segment than with their own functional departments (see Figure 16.8).

The matrix structure provided satisfactory customer services, but there began to be some strain in organizational relationships. Since people were more closely identified with product or market groups, the managers in functional departments began to lose influence over their own department members. At the same time, they noticed a substantial increase in power in the hands of the sales department.

FIGURE 16.8
The Beacon Aircraft Company—Marketing.

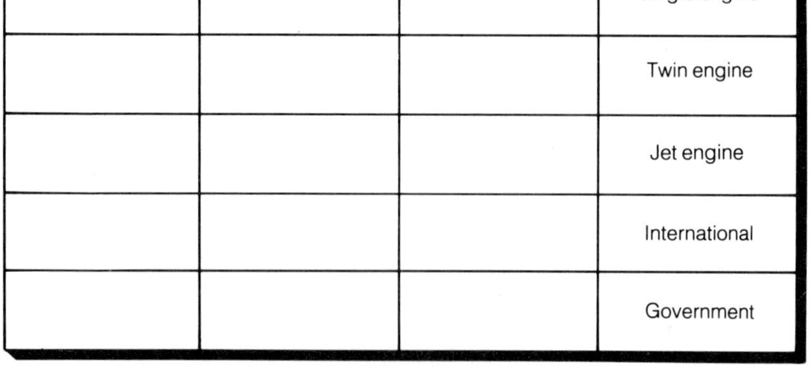

	Vice-President Marketing		
Contract Administration	Marketing Research	Customer Services	Sales Groups
			Single engine
			Twin engine
			Jet engine
			International
			Government

The functional managers complained that they could not adequately control the activities of their departments.

In response to these complaints, the vice-president in charge of marketing quietly dissolved the matrix structure and returned to the functional structure. The new structure still maintained the product groups, but no personnel from other departments were formally assigned to these groups.

Discussion Questions

1. What do you see as major problems facing the company?
2. What could the divisional manager have done to avoid such problems?
3. What kind of organizational structure would you recommend? Explain why and how it can be implemented.

Footnotes

1. J. R. Galbraith, *Organizational Design* (Reading, MA: Addison-Wesley, 1977), p. 40.
2. Adam Smith recognized the value of specialization in his book, *The Wealth of Nations* (London: Methuen, 1976).
3. See J. D. Thompson, *Organizations in Action* (New York: McGraw-Hill, 1967), pp. 55–59.
4. Galbraith, *Organizational Design,* pp. 35–39.
5. J. D. Ford and J. W. Slocum, "Size, Technology, Environment and the Structure of Organizations," *Academy of Management Review,* October 1977, 561–575; and J. R. Montanari, "Managerial Discretion: An Expanded Model of Organizational Choice," *Academy of Management Review,* April 1978, 231–241.
6. See T. Anderson and S. Warkov, "Organization Size and Functional Complexity: A Study of Administration in Hospitals," *American Sociological Review,* 1961, **26,** 23–28; and J. Child and R. Mansfield, "Technology, Size and Organizational Structure," *Sociology,* 1962, **6,** 369–393.
7. Joan Woodward, *Industrial Organization: Theory and Practice* (New York: Oxford University Press, 1965).
8. Charles Perrow, *Organizational Analysis: A Sociological View* (Belmont, CA: Brooks/Cole, 1970), pp. 75–85.
9. T. Burns and G. W. Stalker, *The Management of Innovation* (London: Tavistock Publications, 1961).
10. Robert Duncan, "Characteristics of Organizational Environments and Perceived Environmental Uncertainty," *Administrative Science*

Quarterly, 1972, **17,** 313–327; and Robert Duncan, "What Is the Right Organizational Structure?" *Organizational Dynamics,* Winter 1979, 59–79.

11. H. R. Bobbitt and J. D. Ford, "Decision-Maker Choice As a Determinant of Organizational Structure," *Academy of Management Review,* January 1980, 13–24.

12. Montanari, "Managerial Discretion," pp. 231–241; and Ford and Slocum, "Size, Technology, Environment," pp. 561–575.

13. Galbraith, *Organizational Design,* pp. 35–39.

14. See W. G. Ouchi and J. B. Dowling, "Defining the Span of Control," *Administrative Science Quarterly,* September 1974, 357–375; and D. D. Van Fleet and A. G. Bedian, "A History of the Span of Management," *Academy of Management,* July 1977, 356–373.

15. See Max Weber, *The Theory of Social and Economic Organization,* trans. A. M. Henderson and T. Parsons. (New York, Oxford University Press, 1947).

16. Charles Perrow, "The Short and Glorious History of Organizational Theory," *Organizational Dynamics,* Summer 1973, 2–16.

17. See V. A. Thompson, *Modern Organization* (New York: Knopf, 1964), pp. 152–177.

18. Rensis Likert, *The Human Organization* (New York: McGraw-Hill, 1967), pp. 51–52.

19. Ibid., pp. 3–12.

20. W. F. Dowling, "At General Motors: System 4 Build Performance and Profits," *Organizational Dynamics,* Winter 1975, 23–38.

21. D. I. Cleland and W. R. King, *Systems Analysis and Project Management* (New York: McGraw-Hill, 1968).

22. Galbraith, *Organizational Design,* pp. 81–95.

23. S. M. Davis and P. R. Lawrence, *Matrix* (Reading, MA: Addison-Wesley, 1977), chap. 3.

24. H. F. Kolodny, "Evolution to a Matrix Organization," *Academy of Management Review,* October 1979, 543–553.

25. Ibid., pp. 544–550.

26. L. E. Greiner, "Evolution and Revolution as Organizations Grow," *Harvard Business Review,* July–August 1972, 37–46.

27. Howard Aldrich and Diane Herker, "Boundary Spanning Roles and Organization Structure," *Academy of Management Journal,* 1977, **20,** 217–230.

28. M. L. Tushman, "Special Boundary Roles in the Innovation Process," *Administrative Science Quarterly,* December 1977, 587–605.

29. Richard Leifer and Andre Delbecq, "Organizational/Environmental Interchange: A Model of Boundary Spanning Activity," *Academy of Management Review,* January 1978, 40–50.

30. Duncan, "What Is the Right Organizational Structure?" pp. 77–78.

LEARNING OBJECTIVES

1. To learn the process by which managers make decisions.
2. To learn the different types of decision-making modes that can be used in varying situations.
3. To acquire the skills of managerial decision making.

17 MAKING MANAGERIAL DECISIONS

Insight, understanding, ranking of priorities, and a "feel" for the complexity of an area are as important as precise, beautifully elegant mathematical models—and in fact usually infinitely more useful and indeed more "scientific." They reflect the reality of the manager's universe and of his tasks.

Peter F. Drucker, Management [1]

Managers in organizations are constantly making decisions about topics ranging from major investments to minor work schedules. In this chapter, we study how managerial decisions are made in organizations. First, we look at the process of making managerial decisions. Then we discuss the types of decision making used in organizations. Since the subjects of individual motivational decisions and group decision processes are discussed in Chapters 6 and 9 respectively, this chapter focuses on managerial decisions.

The decision process involves the formulation of objectives, evaluation of alternatives, and execution of decisions. At each stage, the decision maker deals with a number of decision variables, such as economic considerations, value systems, political coalitions, and environmental influences. Depending on how much emphasis is given to each of these variables, the mode of decision making changes.

ELEMENTS OF MANAGERIAL DECISIONS

Managerial decision making involves several stages, including: (1) goal formulation, (2) problem identification, (3) search for alternatives, (4) analysis, (5) choice, and (6) execution.

Managers differ in the ways they make decisions. Some spend considerable time, effort, and resources searching for information, analyzing it, and making choices based on the analysis. Others may spend little time searching for information and make decisions based on intuition. Whatever the decision style, a decision involves knowing the objectives, evaluating alternatives, and making a choice.

The Decision Process Model

Decision making is defined as the process by which we make a choice among various alternatives to achieve our goals. This process, as shown in Figure 17.1, includes: (1) establishing objectives, (2) defining the problem, (3) searching for available alternatives, (4) evaluating the alternatives, (5) selecting an alternative, and (6) implementing the decision.[2]

Establishing Objectives.   Organizations exist to achieve certain objectives, such as maximizing profits, creating innovative products, educating

FIGURE   17.1
The Managerial Decision
Process.

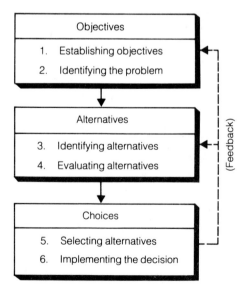

students, or providing health care. Within the organization, each subunit has goals, such as increasing sales volume, reducing production costs, increasing the market share, and/or developing new products. Understanding these goals is important, because it is the basis for formulating operational goals and for selecting specific alternative courses of action.

Defining the Problem.   In order to make any intelligent decision, one must be aware of the problem. When an intended goal is not achieved as expected, the decision maker becomes aware of a problem. An apparently troublesome situation may be a problem for some but not for others, depending on whether or not it hinders the goal-attainment effort. For example, when a union strikes in an expansionary period, management sees it as a problem and searches for a solution. But if the strike occurs during a recessionary period, management may not perceive it as a problem and may be slow to try to end it.

Searching for Available Alternatives.   If there is only one viable alternative, the only decision to be made is either to accept it or reject it. Usually one alternative is to do nothing. In reality, though, the decision maker usually has a number of alternatives from which to choose. These alternatives and their consequences should be identified before a decision is made. If the existing alternatives are not satisfactory, then the search process goes on until a viable alternative is found. This step becomes important when an organization operates in a dynamic and complex environment that requires constant changes in products and production methods.

Evaluating the Alternatives.   Once the alternatives are identified, they must be evaluated. Evaluation may be a simple process if the decision maker has knowledge about the decision outcomes. But in most situations, such knowledge is limited or unavailable. When the decision maker does not have such knowledge, he or she is likely to rely on judgment or intuition to evaluate the merit of each alternative.

Selecting an Alternative.   A given alternative is selected because it is believed to be the best, or at least an acceptable, solution to the problem. Finding such a solution, however, is not simple. Because it is not always possible to know what the best solution is, a less-than-perfect alternative is often accepted instead. Further, when the decision involves multiple goals, the optimal solution to a problem involving one goal can have a negative impact on the achievement of other goals. For example, the introduction of a new machine may solve a production problem, but it may mean eliminating employees—or a decline in employee morale.

Implementing the Decision.   A decision is of little value unless it is implemented. Yet it is possible for a good decision to become useless because of poor execution. Implementing a decision usually involves what is the very essence of management, that is, managing people. Since a decision is implemented through people, they need to be properly supervised and motivated. Also, the decision maker should be aware of the impact the decision will have on other people and make the adjustments needed to minimize any negative impact. This final stage also involves monitoring the progress of the decision. If the decision does not produce the intended result, some changes must be made in the decision process.

Types of Managerial Decisions

Types of managerial decisions differ, reflecting differences in organizational problems and situations in which decisions are made.[3] There is no single and satisfactory way of classifying decision situations. However, the organizational taxonomy presented in Chapter 16, can be used as a basis for developing a typology of managerial decisions. This typology is based on two problem-related dimensions: (1) complexity of decision variables and (2) uncertainty of decision outcomes. Figure 17.2 shows the basic typology and identifies four kinds of decision modes: programmed, analytical, judgmental, and adaptive.

1.   **Programmed Decisions.**   A programmed decision is one that is routine and repetitive in nature. It usually occurs in a situation involving a limited number of decision variables where the outcomes of each alternative are known. For example, the manager of a fast-food hamburger shop may know from experience when and how many hamburger patties and buns are to be ordered. Or the decision may have been reached already, so the delivery is made routinely. Most programmed decision problems are solved by habitual responses, standard operating procedures, or clerical routines.

FIGURE 17.2
Types of Managerial Decisions.

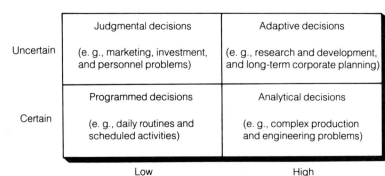

2. **Analytical Decisions.** An analytical decision involves a complex problem with a large number of decision variables, where the outcomes of each decision alternative can be computed. Many complex production and engineering problems are like this. They may be complex, but solutions can be found. Management science and operations research provide a variety of computational techniques that can be used to help find optimal solutions. These techniques include linear programming, network analysis, inventory reorder model, queuing theory, statistical analysis, and so forth.

3. **Judgmental Decisions.** A judgmental decision involves a problem with a limited number of decision variables, but the outcomes of decision alternatives are unknown. Many marketing, investment, and resource allocation problems are in this category. For example, the marketing manager may have several alternative ways of promoting a product, but he or she may not be sure of their outcomes. Good judgment is needed to increase the possibility of desired outcomes and minimize the possibility of undesired outcomes. Tools are available to help managers make rational decisions under conditions of uncertainty; some of these tools are discussed later in the chapter.

4. **Adaptive Decisions.** An adaptive decision involves a problem with a large number of decision variables, where outcomes are not predictable. Because of the complexity and uncertainty of such problems, decision makers are not able to agree on their nature or on decision strategies. Such ill-structured problems usually require the contributions of many people with diverse technical backgrounds. In such a case, decision and implementation strategies have to be frequently modified to accommodate new developments in technology and the environment.

Although we have classified the types of managerial decisions into four distinctive categories, they are not necessarily independent and exclusive. In reality, many managerial problems have both analytical and judgmental characteristics or other combinations of characteristics. The following example illustrates the complex nature of managerial problems.

The Southern Paper Company produces and distributes a variety of paper products throughout the southern states. The company's headquarters and plants are located in a small town near Atlanta, Georgia. Its distribution centers include Atlanta, Birmingham, Montgomery, Jacksonville, Miami, New Orleans, and Dallas.

In the late 1960s and early 1970s, the company's business expanded so rapidly that production approached the plant capacity, and the company planned to expand. In 1978, a team of management scientists from a local university was called in to conduct an economic analysis of alternative plant locations at various distribution centers.

After several months of analyzing production and distribution costs using a management science tool called the "transportation method," the consulting team recommended that the new plant be located near New Orleans. They felt that at this location, the new plant could best serve market demands in Louisiana, Mississippi, Texas, and part of Alabama.

To the consultants' surprise, however, management decided to expand existing plant capacity rather than construct the new plant at the recommended site. Management could find no fault with the cost benefits of the consultants' recommendation, but it argued that these benefits were not great enough to justify the risks associated with the uncertainty of local politics, taxation, and the labor market at the proposed site. Moreover, several of the managers preferred to stay in Georgia.

In this example, management used an analytical decision model to determine the economic payoffs of proposed alternatives. The analysis provided management with data on how much it could save or would give up when a particular alternative was adopted. The decision, however, involved more than an economic issue. It involved a judgment about political and tax-related issues and the welfare of the employees. Once all of these economic, political, tax, and labor-related issues were adequately considered, management was in a position to make a satisfactory decision.

Decision Problems in Organizations

Organizations encounter all types of managerial problems. However, the types of decision problems they frequently encounter generally vary depending on the kind of environment in which they operate. For example, firms operating in a simple-static environment are more likely to encounter routine decision problems than adaptive decision problems. However, it would be incorrect to say that such firms never encounter ill-structured problems that demand adaptive decisions. A major change in the environment, such as the energy crisis, can create problems that cannot be solved by conventional wisdom or an operational procedure. It is only correct to say that these firms encounter fewer ill-structured problems than firms operating in a complex-dynamic environment.

Furthermore, even in the same organization, some functions encounter more ill-structured problems than others. For example, people in research and development are more likely to deal with ill-defined problems than people in production. From a hierarchical standpoint, top management tends to be involved with judgmental and adaptive decisions, while lower levels of management are more likely to be involved with pro-grammed and analytical decisions.

Since we are primarily concerned with managerial behavior adapting to environmental uncertainty, we will focus our attention on solving judg-mental and adaptive decision problems. In the remainder of this chapter, then, we discuss three decision-making models: (1) judgmental, (2) adap-tive, and (3) creative. The creative decision model is added to help deci-sion makers to search for new ways of solving organizational problems.

 ## JUDGMENTAL DECISION MAKING

> *When the decision maker does not have complete knowledge about decision alternatives and/or their outcomes, he or she is likely to rely on intuition or judgment to arrive at a decision.*

Economists seem to assume that (1) the objective of a business firm is to maximize profits, (2) the manager will behave rationally in attempting to achieve this goal, and (3) he or she has complete knowledge about the decision alternatives and their potential consequences.[4] In reality, these assumptions are erroneous because a firm tends to have multiple goals reflecting the different interests of various groups comprising the entity, and the decision maker usually does not have such complete knowledge. Only the assumption that the decision maker tends to behave rationally has a certain validity.

Within this context, how does a rational decision maker behave? To answer this question, we need to know how much information or knowl-edge the decision maker has regarding the decision alternatives and their potential outcomes. The state of knowledge possessed by the decision maker may range from certainty to uncertainty on a continuum. For conve-nience, however, this continuum can be divided into three separate states: (1) certainty, (2) risk, and (3) uncertainty.[5]

Decision Making Under Certainty

Under the condition of certainty, the decision maker has complete knowl-edge about the availability of viable alternatives and their potential out-comes. When the decision maker has such knowledge, he or she has no problem finding an optimal solution. The only action that must be taken is to compare the potential outcomes of each alternative and select the one that promises the highest payoff. For example, when you look for a job, you will take the job offer that promises the best employment conditions. If the decision involves a large number of decision variables, the decision maker may rely on management science or operations research techniques to compute the outcomes of various alternatives.

In reality, however, the decision maker usually does not have such complete knowledge. Because of the cognitive limitations of knowing all viable alternatives and their potential consequences, we tend to settle for a solution that is "good enough." Herbert Simon calls it "satisficing behavior," and this concept will be further discussed later in the chapter.[6] When the decision maker has complete knowledge, the only judgment he or she needs concerns the results of computation. However, as the state of uncertainty or lack of information increases, the amount of judgment needed to make a decision increases.

Decision Making Under Risk

Under the condition of risk, the decision maker has some knowledge about the availability of viable alternatives and the outcomes of each alternative. However, unlike the condition of certainty, each alternative has several possible outcomes that change as the state of nature (or external condition) changes. The decision maker may select an alternative based on an assumption that a certain state of nature or condition will prevail. For example, you may buy a speculative stock with an assumption that the economy will be congenial for such stock. If the expected condition prevails, the decision maker will achieve the goal being sought. Otherwise, he or she will fail to achieve the intended goal. The selection of an alternative involves the risk of failure.

How does a person make a decision under the condition of risk? The condition of risk assumes that the decision maker has some knowledge as to the probability that each state or condition will occur. The decision maker can use this knowledge to maximize his or her expected payoffs or outcomes. The expected payoffs are often called the *expected value.* It is defined as the arithmetic mean of the potential payoffs under various conditions associated with a particular alternative. For example, you buy 100 shares of a company's stock at $10 per share. If you are lucky, the price goes up to $20 within a year. If you are not lucky, it may go down to $5. Assume that the probability of being lucky or unlucky is 50 percent. The expected value *(EV)* of your investment will thus be $250, or

$$EV = [(\$20 - \$10) \times 0.50] + [(\$5 - \$10) \times 0.50]$$
$$= \$2.50 \text{ per share}$$

The following example illustrates how managers use their judgment in making managerial decisions under risk. Note that the judgment is made in estimating potential payoffs for various alternatives under various conditions and in relying on the economic forecasters' predictions of economic conditions.

> *The Belmont Construction Company has two alternative projects: building residential units or building an office complex. The sale of residential units is highly sensitive to economic conditions, and the payoff can vary greatly, depending on these conditions. The office complex is for the government, and the contract is on a cost-plus basis. Economic forecasters predict that the probabilities of having good, normal, and poor economic conditions are 0.25, 0.25, and 0.50, respectively. Figure 17.3 is a payoff matrix presenting the payoffs under the various conditions. The expected values of the two projects are found as follows:*

$$EV(R) = (70,000 \times 0.25) + (38,000 \times 0.25) + (12,000 \times 0.50)$$
$$= \$33,000$$
$$EV(O) = (40,000 \times 0.25) + (40,000 \times 0.25) + (40,000 \times 0.50)$$
$$= \$40,000$$

Figure 17.4 shows how the same problem can be expressed by a decision tree. A decision tree is a simple graphic device that enables the decision maker to visualize the courses of action (alternatives) available, the kinds of risk involved, and the payoffs associated with each alternative. For example, it shows the expected values of the two projects, the three states of nature and their associated probabilities, and the payoffs for each alternative under the three states of nature.

The expected value analysis shows that the office complex project is preferrable to the residential building project. The former has greater expected payoffs than the latter. The kind of risk involved in this decision is that the decision maker will lose the opportunity to make $70,000 if economic conditions turn out to be good. Once again, you are reminded that all the figures used in this decision process are judgmental in nature —they represent educated guesses at best.

FIGURE   17.3
The Payoff Matrix for Alternative Construction Projects.

Decision Making Under Uncertainty

Under conditions of uncertainty, the decision maker has very limited knowledge about the potential payoffs of various alternatives and the

Alternative strategy \ Probability of economic condition	Good 0.25	Normal 0.25	Poor 0.50
Residential building	$70,000	$38,000	$12,000
Office complex	$40,000	$40,000	$40,000

FIGURE 17.4
The Decision Tree for
Alternative Construction
Projects.

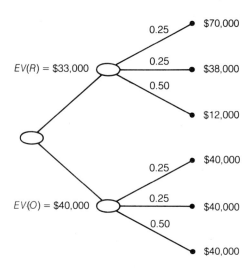

probabilities associated with various states of nature. In the absence of such information, the decision maker reflects his or her own personality, intuition, judgment, and motivation in making a choice. A number of decision rules, however, can help the decision maker under conditions of uncertainty. These decision rules will be examined in conjunction with the payoff matrix shown in Figure 17.3.

The Equality Rule.   This rule assumes that each economic state has an equal chance of occurring. Since the decision maker has no knowledge about the probabilities associated with the economic states, it seems logical to assume them to be equal. This argument is based on the notion of "the principle of insufficient reason." When equal probabilities are assumed, the expected values of the two projects will turn out to be the same, and the choice becomes indifferent. The expected values are found as follows.

$$EV(R) = (70,000 + 38,000 + 12,000)/3 = \$40,000$$
$$EV(O) = (40,000 + 40,000 + 40,000)/3 = \$40,000$$

The Pessimistic Rule.   This rule assumes that the decision maker is a pessimist who thinks and acts as if nature will be malevolent. Consequently, he or she will select the decision alternative that produces the maximum payoff under the least favorable state of nature. This strategy is called the *maximin criterion.* In our example, the maximin payoff will be $40,000, which is associated with the office complex project.

The Optimistic Rule.   This rule assumes that the decision maker is an optimist who thinks nature will treat him or her kindly. Consequently, the decision maker will select an alternative that produces the maximum payoffs under the most favorable condition. This strategy is called the *maximax criterion.* In the case example, the maximax payoff is $70,000, and it is associated with the residential building project.

The Coefficient of Optimism.   Hurwicz has tried to provide a decision rule lying between the pessimistic and optimistic rules.[7] He suggests that the decision maker should take the largest and the smallest payoffs into account when making a decision. The decision maker can do this by finding the *coefficient of optimism,* which lies somewhere between the two extremes, ranging from 1 to 0 on a scale. The coefficient can be found graphically by charting the payoffs of the two alternative projects, as shown in Figure 17.5. It is found at the point where the payoff lines of the two alternatives intersect. At this point the decision maker is indifferent between the two alternatives. However, if the decision maker feels that the future will be brighter than the coefficient of optimism, then he or she is likely to select the optimistic alternative, which promises larger payoffs than the conservative alternative. In our case example, the coefficient of optimism is about .48.

The Regret Rule.   This rule describes the decision behavior of a poor loser. The decision maker attempts to minimize the amount of regret that would occur should unexpected states of nature prevail. For example, the Belmont Construction Company may undertake the office complex project, assuming that the future economic state will be less than favorable. However, if the economic condition turns out to be good, the company

FIGURE 17.5
The Coefficient of
Optimism.

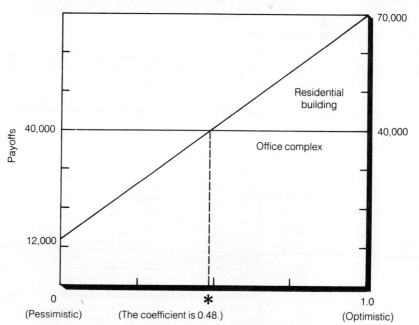

will lose the opportunity profit of $30,000. The difference between the payoff realized and the opportunity profit that could have been realized if other alternatives had been selected is the amount of regret.

The amounts of regret under various conditions are shown in Figure 17.6. Provided with this information, the decision maker will select the residential building project because it produces lesser amounts of regret ($2,000 and $28,000) than the office complex project. If the office complex project is selected, the amount of regret that the decision maker may experience amounts to $30,000.

Which Decision Rule is Better?   These decision rules all assume that the decision maker behaves rationally to optimize the outcome of a decision. Note, however, that these rules produce inconsistent results. The optimistic and regret rules recommend the residential project; the pessimistic rule suggests the office complex project; and the equality rule is neutral in its recommendation.

Which decision rule should one follow? The answer to this question depends largely on the decision maker's personality, motivation, and financial situation.[8] For example, an optimist with financial means would probably prefer a speculative alternative, while a cautious individual with limited financial means would prefer a conservative alternative. Between these two extremes are people with varying personality and situational makeups.

ADAPTIVE DECISION MAKING

> *Adaptive decision making is characterized by incremental adjustments in planning and action in the face of environmental complexity and uncertainty. It also involves a heuristic decision mode.*

Judgmental decision making deals with decision problems under the conditions of risk and uncertainty. Although the decision maker makes

FIGURE 17.6
The Amounts of Regret Under Various Economic Conditions.

Economic condition / Alternative strategy	Good	Normal	Poor
Residential building	0	2,000	28,000
Office complex	30,000	0	0

decisions with limited information, most problems he or she deals with are relatively simple and well-structured. In complex and dynamic environments, however, many organizational problems are relatively ill-defined and ill-structured.[9] A problem is ill-defined in the sense that (1) the decision makers cannot agree on a clear formulation of their goals, (2) they cannot agree on an appropriate strategy for a solution, and (3) the nature of the problem changes as time passes.

According to Mintzberg, there are three modes of managerial strategy making: (1) the entrepreneurial, (2) the planning, and (3) the adaptive.[10] In the *entrepreneurial mode,* the decision maker forcefully makes bold, risk-taking decisions more or less intuitively. He or she may rely on personal judgment based on personal conviction and experience.

In the *planning mode,* the decision maker collects and analyzes a vast amount of information concerning decision alternatives, variables, and outcomes in order to formulate the overall strategic plan of the organization. The development of such a plan is, however, extremely difficult for a number of reasons: (1) the inability of the decision maker to concentrate on more than a few things at a time, (2) his or her limited awareness of the environment, (3) limited knowledge about decision alternatives and their consequences, (4) limited reasoning and analytical capacities, and (5) incomplete and inconsistent preference systems.[11]

Because of these difficulties, Mintzberg has suggested that an *adaptive decision mode* be used in dealing with ill-defined problems occuring in a complex-dynamic environment.[12] Whereas the strategy of the entrepreneurial and planning modes consists of forceful leaps forward in the face of uncertainty, the adaptive mode suggests a series of small and disjointed steps. Caught in a web of conflicting forces involving a large number of people with a stake in an organization (such as stockholders, management, employees, unions, government, and others), management is often unable to formulate a clear statement of objectives. In addition, with a constantly changing environment, it is difficult to formulate a comprehensive plan of action. Thus, the decision maker needs an adaptive planning approach that enables him or her to be flexible.

Two kinds of decision strategies can be utilized in an adaptive decision process—incremental and heuristic. The incremental strategy describes a series of steps to be taken by the decision maker, while the heuristic strategy provides the criteria or rules with which the decision maker guides his or her actions.

Incremental Decision Strategy

The incremental concept was introduced by Lindblom as "a science of muddling through."[13] Faced with the problem of defining a clear-cut goal and the inability to formulate a comprehensive plan to achieve this goal, the decision maker needs to take a step at a time in formulating decision alternatives and in taking actions toward a certain desirable end that is related to the overall goal. These steps may be selected because they are expected to improve the status quo. The effectiveness of an incremental adjustment alternative is evaluated in light of its overall effect on the system—that is, on an organization or society. If the effect is judged to be generally favorable, or if it, at least, does not produce resistance from any segment of the system, the alternative can be continuously adopted. If it is judged to be unfavorable, or if it produces resistance, another incremental step can be taken.

The concept of incremental decision uses the concepts of bounded rationality and satisficing behavior. As Herbert Simon has argued, people are limited in their ability to know all the viable alternatives and their consequences, and this limitation makes it impossible to make perfectly rational decisions. When the decision maker makes a decision based on limited information, it is called *bounded rationality*. [14] Under this condition, the decision maker attempts to *satisfice* rather than *maximize* his or her decision outcomes. In other words, the decision maker selects an alternative, or achieves a goal, that is "good enough." It may not be optimal, but it is at least satisfactory. The incremental decision maker tries to achieve a series of satisfactory goals rather than to maximize the goals each time he or she makes a decision.

Fred Wu describes the incremental decision steps as follows:[15]

1. Identify a set of problems and incremental goals.
2. Assess the current situation and identify incremental adjustments that must be made to cope with the problems.
3. Assess the potential consequences of the incremental adjustments.
4. If the potential consequences are judged satisfactory, take the necessary action. Otherwise, go back to step 2 and identify a new set of incremental adjustments.
5. Evaluate the effects of the incremental adjustments implemented and go back to step 1 to make the next round of incremental adjustments.

This five-step process has the following characteristics. First, the decision maker selects a few incremental adjustments that are considered to be satisfactory. Not all possible alternatives are searched and evaluated. Second, these incremental adjustments are chosen not because they lead to the attainment of some remote goal, but because they can improve the current condition and are consistent with the decision maker's aspirations. Third, the impact of making incremental adjustments is evaluated so that new problems may be identified. Finally, the process represents a chain of loops, each loop containing the completion of one round of incremental adjustments. The incremental goals may be revised, reflecting the outcome of incremental adjustments that have been implemented.

In the incremental approach, long-term goals are elusively defined, and toward these ends a number of small and large incremental changes and adjustments are made. For example, the nation has the elusive goal of achieving energy independence. To this end, the government and its people are making a number of small and large incremental adjustments or changes in their way of using and developing energy. Energy conservation, the development of nuclear energy, reliance on coal, development of synthetic energy, and utilization of solar energy are all parts of such incremental plans and actions. There are two reasons why a comprehensive energy plan could not be easily formulated for sometime.

First, the state of technology involved with the use and development of alternative sources of energy is constantly changing. What seems to be promising at one time soon becomes questionable. For example, the development of nuclear energy was highly promising until the Three-Mile Island accident clouded its future.

Second, caught in the web of conflicting interests between various economic groups and between various regions of the country, Congress was unable to develop a comprehensive energy plan. Furthermore, the changes in leadership in the Administration and the Congress make it difficult to develop such a plan.

Faced with these technological and political problems, policy makers have to rely on the incremental approach to cope with the energy problem. As shown in Figure 17.7, they undertake a series of incremental adjustments toward the elusive goal of energy independence. They make each round of incremental adjustments—one round at a time—and evaluate the impact of these adjustments before another round is undertaken.

FIGURE 17.7
Goal Attainment Through
Incremental Adjustments.

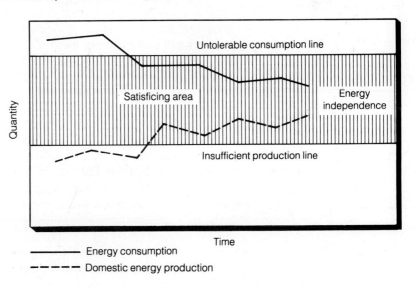

The adjustments they make are usually reactive, fragmented, and disjointed.

The incremental decision process provides a way of thinking about and coping with ill-defined problems occurring in a complex-dynamic environment, but it does not provide rules by which the decision maker can guide his or her actions. To overcome this limitation, we suggest the decision maker use a set of heuristic decision rules.

Heuristic Decision Strategy

The term *heuristic* is derived from the Greek "heuriskein" which means "serving to discover." The aim of heuristic strategy is not to suggest any specific solution to a problem but to suggest a cue or rule that can help the decision maker find a solution.[16] A heuristic tool reduces complexity to a manageable level, thus enabling the decision maker to find a plausible solution. For example, "when in doubt, punt" is a heuristic saying for football players. This saying may help the player make a decision in a confusing situation.

When faced with ill-defined problems in a complex, uncertain environment, the decision maker can rely on a limited number of decision variables to guide his or her decisions. A study by Rockart found that business executives define their own information needs and collect the information relevant to these needs. In doing so, they usually focus on a few key performance areas, such as profit, technological reputation, financial stability, and employee morale.[17] The information collected on these performance areas then guides their decisions and subsequent actions.

Most contingency models, presented throughout this book, are heuristic in nature. For example, the motivational principles examined in Chapter 6 are heuristic tools that enable managers to formulate specific motivational programs. These principles do not provide managers with specific solutions to employee motivation problems but with a conceptual framework for understanding and finding solutions to these problems. Managers can use this framework as a guide for formulating specific motivational programs suitable to their own unique situations. Leadership models, reward systems, organizational designs, and task design strategies are all heuristic tools, or "walking sticks," that can guide managers along complex decision paths.[18]

Evaluating Adaptive Decision Making

The adaptive decision mode describes the decision process involving ill-structured, messy problems in a complex-dynamic environment. It also suggests how decision makers can improve their effectiveness in dealing with such decision problems. On the negative side, one can argue that the adaptive decision strategy lacks a sense of direction and forcefulness. In the same vein, one can argue that it does not propose a proactive action that can cause changes in the environment. Such criticism is unjust, however, because the adaptive strategy is not intended as a proactive tool.

 CREATIVE DECISION MAKING

> *The creative decision-making process is used to discover or invent new ways of solving organizational problems. Brainstorming is commonly used to stimulate creativity in organizations.*

Many organizational problems, such as hiring new employees or adding a new manufacturing facility, can be solved with conventional decision tools, such as economic and behavioral decision analyses. But when conventional wisdom cannot find adequate solutions to problems, a creative decision process is needed. A creative decision process is an effort to discover or invent new ways of solving problems. Its main function is to increase the number of viable alternatives for solving problems.

The creative decision process has become increasingly important in recent years. The accelerating rate of technological change calls for a constant flow of new ideas for new products and production methods. Also, the dwindling supply of conventional energy sources calls for the development of new energy sources, as well as for creative ways of conserving the existing energy supply.

What can management do to stimulate creative behavior in organizations? Organizational creativity can be increased by (1) using creative individuals, (2) encouraging the use of creative decision processes, and (3) developing a creative organizational climate.

Using Creative Individuals
Creative individuals are said to have certain characteristics that distinguish them from noncreative individuals. The research findings of MacKinnon and Steiner have produced the following list of personal characteristics of creative individuals. They tend to:[19]

1. Be bright rather than brilliant. While they are not necessarily geniuses, they are good at generating many ideas in a short period of time.

2. Have a positive self-image and feel good about themselves.

3. Be emotionally expressive and sensitive to the world around them.

4. Be stimulated by the nature of the problem.

5. Suspend judgment until they have the opportunity to review the relevant facts of the problem.

6. Show originality in their thinking.

7. Be nonconformists who value their independence and require less social approval.

8. Be rich in fantasy but have a clear view of reality.

9. Be less authoritarian and dogmatic on issues.

10. Be more concerned with meanings and implications of a problem than with its details.

This list is tentative and limited, but it does provide an idea of how creative individuals can be identified. A creative organization is one that has a number of creative individuals and encourages their creative activities. Creativity can be increased to some extent by using creative decision processes.[20]

Encouraging the Use of Creative Decision Processes

A number of techniques can be used to stimulate creative behavior. In applying these techniques, two basic rules must be followed: (1) Evaluative judgment must be suspended during the idea-generating stage, and (2) all ideas, regardless of their merit, must be considered during the idea-evaluating stage. The most popular techniques are brainstorming, grid analysis, and the catalogue technique.

Brainstorming.   *Brainstorming* is used to generate a free flow of ideas by encouraging participants to express their ideas without having them evaluated by others in the group. Evaluative comments are discouraged by the group leader. A typical brainstorming session consists of six to nine people who spontaneously produce ideas related to a specific problem. The key objective is to produce a large number of creative ideas.

A variation of this technique is the *Gordon technique,* developed by W. J. Gordon.[21] In the Gordon technique, however, no one but the group leader knows the exact nature of the problem. This keeps members from arriving at any hasty conclusions. When the members do not know the exact nature of the problem, they may generate a wide range of ideas without focusing on any one solution. It may take more time than the brainstorming session, but it can generate a wider range of ideas.

Grid Analysis.   *In grid analysis* a number of ideas, concepts, materials, and tools that may be related to a particular problem are listed on both sides of a two-dimensional grid and potential uses for all possible combinations are studied. For example, assume that a construction company is interested in building a low-cost housing development without sacrificing size or quality. In their attempt to do this, the product development group may list a variety of construction materials and methods horizontally and vertically on a two-dimensional grid. The group then brainstorms each of the combinations to discover a number of ways in which the materials and methods can be creatively used. For example, the group may find a way of producing building blocks from soil.

Catalogue Technique.   The *catalogue technique* is a simple way of making people consider the relationship between apparently unrelated things. A picture, a word, or some item of merchandise is randomly selected from the page of a catalogue. Then a second item is randomly selected from another page. The two items are brainstormed to produce some ideas or potential uses for them in combination. This process may be continued for an hour or two so that a sufficient number of ideas is generated.

Developing a Creative Organization

In order to achieve creative goals, an organization needs more than creative people and creative techniques. It needs an organizational climate that encourages creativity. Organizations that hire people with similar personal characteristics, stress conformity, and rely on authoritarian leadership can easily inhibit creativity. Like creative individuals, creative organizations tend to possess certain characteristics. They tend to:[22]

1.   Allow employees to exercise self-control.
2.   Encourage open communication at all levels of management.
3.   Encourage boundary-spanning activities with the external environment.
4.   Hire people with a variety of personal backgrounds and experience.
5.   Evaluate ideas on their merits, rather than according to the status of the originators.
6.   Encourage research activities.
7.   Allow organization members to take risks.
8.   Use the techniques available for increasing creativity.
9.   Separate creative from productive functions.

Converting Creative Ideas into Action

Once ideas are generated, they have to be evaluated according to economic and behavioral decision criteria. Since the ideas are produced in brainstorming sessions without judgmental evaluation, they need, at this point, to be tested for practical application.[23] The following questions can be asked for this purpose:

1. Is the idea technically feasible?
2. Does the organization have the resources necessary to implement the idea?
3. Is the idea economically profitable?
4. Is the idea socially acceptable?

If the idea survives the test of these criteria, it can be processed for practical application. Many innovative ideas are not implemented, even if they are technically feasible, for economic and social reasons. For example, nuclear energy has not been widely used because of its costs and social resistance to its use.

 ## SUMMARY AND CONCLUSION

Managers are paid to make decisions. They are expected to be professional in making decisions, and yet all managers are not necessarily good decision makers. What makes managerial decisions so difficult is that so many factors influence the decision outcomes. This chapter has examined the complex process of decision making, and presented three types of decision models.

The decision process model involves three basic elements—*objectives, alternatives,* and *choices.* The decision maker must be aware of the decision objectives and the problems involved in achieving them. This knowledge serves as a basis for identifying and evaluating a set of viable alternatives. On the basis of this evaluation, the decision maker selects an alternative that offers satisfactory payoffs.

Depending on the nature of the decision objectives and the situations in which decisions are made, the modes of decision can vary. *Programmed* and *analytical* decision modes are frequently used in organizations or functional units that deal with well-defined problems. *Judgmental* and *adaptive* decision modes are used in organizations or organizational units that deal with ill-defined problems. A creative decision-making process is suggested as a method of stimulating innovative ways of solving problems.

KEY CONCEPTS AND WORDS

Decision making	Judgmental	The coefficient of
The state of nature	decisions	optimism
Certainty	Adaptive decisions	Bounded rationality
Risk	Expected value	Satisficing behavior
Uncertainty	Equality rule	Incremental decision
Programmed	Maximax rule	Heuristic decision
decisions	Maximin rule	Brainstorming
Analytical decisions	Regret rule	Grid technique

Questions for Review and Discussion

1. Think of a major decision you have made recently.
   a. What were some major factors or problems involved in making the decision?
   b. Describe the process by which you made the decision.
   c. Did you use one of the models described in this chapter?

2. a. How important is one's subjective judgment, or intuition, in making managerial decisions?
   b. To what extent do managers rely on their intuitive judgment?

3. What is the role of analytical decision models or management science tools in managerial decisions?

4. C. Jackson Grayson, Jr., has argued that management science tools are almost useless for helping managers make better decisions.[24] Do you agree or disagree with his assertion? Explain why or why not.

5. Some managers complain that they cannot make decisions because of a lack of information. How much information is necessary to make good decisions?

6. What are some major decision models that can be used in organizations? Explain how these models can be used.

7. What is the importance of the adaptive decision process in organizations?

8. What is the importance of the creative decision process in organizations?

EXERCISES

EXERCISE 17.1. THE TALLEY INVESTING COMPANY

This exercise shows how management can use economic decision models to select an investment opportunity. It involves decision making under conditions of uncertainty. In addition, the decision maker should consider a variety of factors other than economic ones.

The Situation

The Talley Investing Company is a conglomerate that aggressively tries to acquire small companies. Three possible acquisitions are under consideration—an aircraft company, a fast-food chain, and a gambling casino. A quarter of a billion dollars will be committed to this acquisition. The payoffs for each alternative under three economic conditions have been prepared by the acquisition department. The payoff matrix is shown in Figure 17.8.

The Procedure

1. Divide yourselves into groups of five to seven.
2. Each group should analyze the payoff matrix and select an investment alternative.
3. When the class reassembles, each group is to present its choice and explain the rationale for its decision.
4. The class should then discuss the factors that influenced the investment decisions.

EXERCISE 17.2. THE IDEA LIGHTNING COMPANY

This exercise will help you learn to use a creative decision process to produce innovative ideas. The brainstorming approach should be applied.

FIGURE 17.8
Payoff Matrix for
Alternative Investments.

Economic condition / Alternative strategy	Good	Normal	Poor
Aircraft	60	50	30
Fast foods	50	45	40
Casino	65	50	35

(Unit: in million dollars)

The Situation

The Idea Lightning Company is a consulting firm specializing in producing creative ideas. The company receives a variety of requests ranging from finding an innovative way of using coat hangers to solving the air pollution problem. Current projects involve the following problems:

1.   People are born with an extra thumb on both hands. It will be located between the old thumb and the index finger.

2.   People are born with x-ray vision.

3.   People will be blinded within three years by a nonremovable chemical in the polluted air.

4.   Creative uses of coat hangers.

The Procedure

1.   Divide yourselves into groups of five to seven.

2.   Each group is to select a problem from the list and brainstorm it for about 15 minutes.

3.   Each group should appoint a secretary to record the ideas produced.

4.   When the class reassembles, the secretary of each group will present the ideas the group has produced.

5.   If some of these ideas are judged realistic, evaluate them on the following criteria:
     a.   Is the idea technically feasible?
     b.   Is it economically feasible?
     c.   Is it socially acceptable?

Footnotes

1.   Peter Drucker, *Management: Tasks, Responsibilities, and Practices* (New York: Harper & Row, 1973), p. 516.

2.   See J. R. Lang, J. E. Dittrich, and S. E. White, "Managerial Problem Solving Models," *Academy of Management Review,* October 1978, 854–866.

3.   See L. R. Beach and T. R. Mitchell, "A Contingency Model for the Selection of Decision Strategies," *Academy of Management Review,* July 1978, 439–449; and J. D. Thompson, *Organizations in Action* (New York: McGraw-Hill, 1967), pp. 134–135.

4.   J. W. McGuire, *Theories of Business Behavior* (Englewood Cliffs, NJ: Prentice-Hall, 1964), chap. 3.

5. J. G. March and H. A. Simon, *Organizations* (New York: Wiley, 1958), p. 137.

6. H. A. Simon, *Administrative Behavior* (New York: Free Press, 1957), p. xxv.

7. Leonid Hurwicz, *Optimality Criteria for Decision Making Under Ignorance* (Cowles Commission discussion paper, *Statistics,* 1951), No. 370.

8. See D. W. Miller and M. K. Starr, *The Structure of Human Decisions* (Englewood Cliffs, NJ: Prentice-Hall, 1967), pp. 124–126.

9. R. L. Ackoff, *Redesigning the Future* (New York: Wiley, 1974); and I. I. Mitroff and J. R. Emshoff, "On Strategic Assumption-Making: A Dialectical Approach to Policy and Planning," *Academy of Management Review,* January 1979, 1–12.

10. Henry Mintzberg, "Strategy-Making in Three Modes," *California Management Review,* Winter 1973, 44–53.

11. E. H. Caplan, "Behavioral Assumptions of Managerial Accounting," *Accounting Review,* July 1966, 496–509.

12. Henry Mintzberg, *The Nature of Managerial Work* (New York: Harper & Row, 1973), pp. 159–160.

13. C. E. Lindblom, "The Science of 'Muddling Through,' " *Public Administration Review,* 1959, **19,** 79–88.

14. Simon, *Administrative Behavior,* pp. 61–78.

15. Fred Wu, "Incrementalism in Planning and Control," *Academy of Management Review,* forthcoming.

16. F. A. Shull, A. L. Delbecq, and L. L. Cummings, *Organizational Decision Making* (New York: McGraw-Hill, 1970), pp. 88–90.

17. J. F. Rockart, "Chief Executives Define Their Own Data Needs," *Harvard Business Review,* March–April 1979, 81–93.

18. J. W. Lorsch, "Making Behavioral Science More Useful," *Harvard Business Review,* March–April 1979, 171–180.

19. D. W. MacKinnon, "The Nature and Nurture of Creative Talent," in *Readings in Managerial Psychology,* ed. H. J. Leavitt (Chicago: University of Chicago Press, 1964), pp. 90–109; and G. A. Steiner, *The Creative Organization* (Chicago: University of Chicago Press, 1965), pp. 22–23.

20. Niles Howard, "Business Probes the Creative Spark," *Dun's Review,* January 1980, 32–38.

21. W. J. Gordon, "Operational Approach to Creativity," *Harvard Business Review,* November–December 1956, 41–51.

22. Steiner, *The Creative Organization,* pp. 22–23.

23. H. G. Hicks, *The Management of Organizations* (New York: McGraw-Hill, 1972), pp. 230–231.

24. C. J. Grayson, "Management Science and Business Practice," *Harvard Business Review,* July–August 1973, 41–48.

18 MANAGING ORGANIZATIONAL CHANGE

To understand what is happening to us as we move into the age of super-industrialism, we must analyze the process of acceleration and confront the concept of transience. If acceleration is a new social force, transience is its psychological counterpart, and without an understanding of the role it plays in contemporary human behavior, all our theories of psychology . . . must remain pre-modern.

Alvin Toffler, Future Shock [1]

Things change constantly. Technological development changes the methods of producing goods and services. Jobs become increasingly complex and technologically more interdependent. People receive more education and demand more control over their work environment. Concerns over energy shortages, full employment, and the environment call for an increased role for government. All these changes present challenges for organizations and their managers, and require them to adapt. Organizations that can adjust to these changes will prosper, while those that cannot will fail.

This chapter deals with organizational change. More specifically, it discusses (1) the importance of organizational change, (2) forces in the environment, (3) modes of environmental adaptation, and (4) methods of introducing organizational change.

IMPORTANCE OF ORGANIZATIONAL CHANGE

> *An organization is a living organism. Its survival depends on its ability to adapt to the changes in its environment, and its adaptive strategy can be either "proactive" or "reactive."*

Organizations exist in cultural systems that provide opportunities while also imposing constraints. The environment provides the resources and opportunities for the organizations' existence. At the same time, it determines what organizations can and cannot do. If they are to remain prosperous, organizations must adapt to the demands of the environment. Since these demands are constantly changing, organizations must also change. Not adapting is a major cause of organizational failure.

Organizational Adaptation

The following examples show how three auto makers coped or failed to cope with the oil crises of the 1970s.

American Motors. American Motors was once known as the sickly child in the American automobile industry.[2] Besieged by competition from other auto makers, the company decided to rely on Jeeps, postal vehicles, and military trucks for its survival. Not any more. For fiscal year 1979, the company posted a profit of $84 million on sales of $3.1 billion. American Motors' car sales were surging while the industry as a whole was losing sales. What was the reason for American Motors' success?

Before 1974, American Motors was not able to satisfy customers' demand for large and luxurious cars because it produced small cars. The small car market was then dominated by foreign manufacturers. When the energy crisis stimulated the small car market, however, the company was able to capitalize on the opportunity. Its product line has shrunk from six models to three and has focused on small cars—Concord, Spirit, and Pacer. The introduction in 1979 of the Eagle, with four-wheel drive, and its alignment with the Renault company should help American Motors secure a major portion of the small car market.

General Motors. In 1974, General Motors had the worst record for gasoline mileage among U.S. auto makers—about 12 miles per gallon. GM's market share went down to about 45 percent, which was its lowest level since 1952. Three years later, the average mileage of GM cars was about 18 miles per gallon—the best among the major auto makers—and its market share was back up to about 55 percent.[3]

How did GM turn the situation around? Faced with the energy crisis of 1974, the managers of its five divisions decided to "downsize" most of their cars. Rather than pursue this strategy independently, they decided to adopt the project center concept in order to meet the demands created by the downsizing strategy on a cooperative basis. Project members were brought in from several divisions to work on various problems common to all divisions. These problems ranged from chassis to electrical systems design.

The costs of adapting to environmental change have been enormous, running at an annual rate of around $1 billion—about a third of GM's 1976 net income. Expenditures are expected to increase further in the 1980s as the company attempts to meet the demands for emission controls, safety standards, and downsizing. However, the project center concept has eliminated much redundancy and has accelerated the implementation process.

Chrysler Corporation.   Chrysler Corporation was the third largest auto maker in the United States. With a full line of cars, vans, and trucks, it had competed directly with other auto makers. Its market share was about 15 percent in 1976, but it declined to about 9 percent in 1979. The company reported a loss of more than $1 billion on revenue of $12 billion in 1979, and it had to rely on a loan guarantee of $1.5 billion from the government, and loans of $2 billion from other sources, just to stay in business.[4]

What went wrong with Chrysler? Lee Iacocca, chairman of the corporation, blamed the heavy costs of meeting government regulations for the company's problems. Although the regulations placed a heavy burden on all the auto makers, he argued that Chrysler suffered more than others because of its limited resources.[5] This argument had some merit, but the major problem was the company's failure to downsize its product line. The company's small cars, Omni and Horizon, were doing well in the market, but they were introduced too late, and the supply was too limited.

These examples illustrate the need to adapt to environmental changes. Many once-successful companies have ceased to exist or have had problems because of their failure to adapt to environmental changes in a timely manner. The Great Atlantic and Pacific Tea Company (A & P), Robert Hall, Penn Central, Continental Mortgage, Rolls Royce, and many of the major airlines, auto makers, steel makers, and textile firms share the common problem of environmental adaptation.

Individual Adaptation

Organizations introduce changes through people. Unless the people are willing to accept the need and responsibility for organizational change, these intended changes cannot occur. In addition, individuals have to learn to adapt their attitudes and behavioral patterns to constantly changing environments. In a frequently changing environment, organization members should be able to adopt new patterns of behavior. A flexible organizational structure encourages such adaptation. Conversely, rigidly controlled organizational relationships between and within work groups will hinder the information processing activities needed to make timely decisions.

As we shall see later in the chapter, technological changes usually cause organizational tasks to become more complex and interdependent. Task complexity requires that people be trained in their jobs for the future as well as for the present. Task interdependency demands that people work together in groups rather than as individuals. In order to perform complex and interdependent tasks effectively, organization members should be technically as well as psychologically prepared to adapt. Managers especially must be more skilled in dealing with people in such an environment.

CHANGING FORCES IN THE ENVIRONMENT

> *Many environmental forces influence work and people in organizations. These include economic conditions, technology, market competition, labor market, unions, and government influences.*

Organizations do not exist in a vacuum; they exist in an environment that provides them with opportunities as well as threats to their existence. Since they depend on this environment, organizations are influenced by the forces within it. Many environmental forces influence organizations; these forces can be classified into two major environmental categories—general and specific.[6] The *general environment* contains forces that influence all organizations in a given society. These forces may include the technological, market, labor, government, and value systems. The *specific environment* contains factors unique to a given organization. These may include specific industry competitors, suppliers, particular resources, unions, and government regulations that directly affect the operations of the organization. Since we cannot deal with all the specific environmental factors affecting individual firms, we will focus our attention on a few general environmental factors.

Changing Economic Conditions

Organizations need economic resources to perform their functions. These resources include land, labor, capital, raw materials, energy, technology, and management. Any change in these resources will greatly affect the organizational capacity to produce goods and services. We may expect some positive changes in certain resources (such as labor, management, and technology), but other resources can cause problems for organizations. For example, the problems of the energy crisis and dwindling resources are likely to be with us for some time, and these problems will cause economic uncertainty. Unless we can find ways of coping with these problems, the economy as a whole will experience a period of stagnation.

Technological Development

The rate of technological change is greater than it has been in the past. The introduction of computers in production systems, the development of nuclear energy, and the use of satellites in communication have all contributed to the acceleration of technological change. Further developments in technology are seen in other areas. For example, IBM is developing a silicon memory chip small enough to pass through the eye of a needle, yet able to store 64,000 bits of information. Within five years, the memory storage capacity is expected to increase to 250,000 bits with no increase in cost. Bell Labs is developing fiber optics, which will be used to transmit telephone messages on rays of light.

The nation faces an even greater challenge. Its production systems rely heavily on petroleum-based technology. As energy sources become scarce, alternative sources of energy—coal, thermal, solar, and nuclear—need to be developed. Technologies for harnessing these alternative sources, however, have yet to be perfected. Not only will it take time to convert production systems from one type of technology to another, but many jobs will become even more complex than they are now. These technological factors imply the need for technological change and development, and such changes will ultimately have an impact on individual organizations.

Increasing Market Competition

The market environment changes constantly, and these changes have profound effects on organizations. Among the important factors are consumer preference, competition, and product innovation.

Anyone who is sensitive to fashion will notice that *consumer preferences* change constantly. In the 1970s, disco dancing, tennis, long hair, and large cars were fashionable, but their popularity has declined in recent years. In the early 1980s, gold and silver, small cars, videotapes, big bands, and wood-burning stoves have become popular among consumers. Some of these items will undoubtedly become less fashionable in the near future.

Competition forces many producers out of the market. Unless a firm continues to improve existing products or introduces new ones, another firm will take over its share of the market. In addition to domestic competition, firms are now facing increased competition from abroad. Many firms in the automobile, electronics, steel, and textile industries are facing severe competition from international companies. For example, the market share of foreign cars was only about 10 percent in 1959, but it rose to 27 percent by early 1980.[7] In fact, more cars are now sold in the United States by foreign manufacturers than are sold by Ford, the second largest domestic auto company.

Labor Market Environment

The labor market environment in the current decade will be quite different from that of the 1970s.[8] A dominant aspect of the 1960s and 1970s was the inroads made by new job seekers—young people, minorities, and women. These workers are now entering the prime years of their career, and causing severe competition for desirable jobs. Another development is that the people who were born during the baby boom in the late 1940s and the 1950s are now moving into the prime age bracket. These workers are expected to be more productive than people in other age groups because of their maturity and job experience, but there may be severe competition among them for desirable jobs. These two developments, coupled with the increasing level of education, may create increasing pressure to make organizational tasks more challenging and intrinsically motivating.

Changing Characteristics of Unions

Contrary to the recent trend, the 1980s may prove to be an expansion period for the labor movement. In 1953, 34 percent of the nonagricultural sector was organized; but now the percentage has dropped to around 25 percent. The public image of the labor movement has also declined. Most people agree that unions are needed to protect the interests of workers, but their image as a socially constructive force has nevertheless been declining.[9]

The labor movement has an opportunity to expand its membership in the 1980s.[10] The very group that is increasing its union membership is the one that has resisted unions in the past. The class stigma attached to unionism has been diminishing because of the participation of white-collar workers, including teachers, nurses, social workers, and government employees. In addition, the people who are entering into their prime age bracket and face severe competition for desirable jobs may look to unions to protect their interests.

Growing Government Influence

The role of government has changed over the years from passive to active participation in the economy. It originally participated to protect the public interest from the power of business, but now government itself is a power bloc in the economy, along with labor and management. The passage of federal laws and regulations, such as the Fair Labor Standards Acts, the National Labor Relations Act, the Civil Rights Act, and the Occupational Safety and Health Act, which are designed to protect the interests of the public and employees, tend to restrict the power of managers.

In addition, the government is taking an active role in planning the nation's economic activities so that the economic system can better serve the public welfare. It serves as the "employer of last resort" in order to maintain "full employment." It also plays the role of a power balancer among various interest groups. It has become a provider of services that cannot be provided by profit-oriented enterprises. It conducts and finances basic research that can direct technological changes in the economy.

Although it is difficult to predict what lies ahead, it appears that the 1980s are likely to be more turbulent and unpredictable than past decades. An implication of this trend is that managers have to cope with more frequent changes in an increasingly complex and uncertain environment than ever before. In order to function in such a turbulent environment, managers need to develop strategies for coping with various environmental and organizational changes.

COPING WITH ENVIRONMENTAL CHANGES

There are basically three ways in which organizations can cope with environmental changes. These strategies—adaptation, avoidance, and control—range on a continuum from reactive to proactive.

Since organizations depend on the environment for their survival, they need to manage their external dependence actively. There are three ways in which organizations can manage their external dependence: adaptation, avoidance, and control.[11] The *adaptive strategy* is to change or adapt an organization's internal components to fit external changes. The *avoidance strategy* is to reduce external dependence through self-sufficiency or dependency diversification. The *control strategy* is to change the external forces to fit an organization's internal characteristics.

Adapting to External Changes

The adaptive strategy takes the marketing approach to environmental demands. It usually starts with an assessment of the needs of the marketplace and then produces goods and services to meet these needs. More specifically, it involves the following sequence of activities:[12]

1. **Sensing the needs or changes in the environment.** It may involve studying the changes in consumer preference, income distribution, or competitors' behavior. Or it may involve organizational sensitivity to economic, political, and technological developments. For example, if a competitor comes out with a technologically advanced product, the organization should be aware of this development and be prepared to deal with it.

2. **Processing the relevant information to users.** Once information is collected, it needs to be channelled to people who can use it. For example, a salesperson may know what competitors are doing in the market. This information must be channelled to those who can act upon it. Potential users may include people in product research and design and marketing promotion.

3. **Changing the firm's internal components.** The obtained information may provide some clues as to what and how certain internal components should be changed. For example, if the information involves technological development, it implies that the organization needs to change the task component. In order to change the task component, the organization may need people with advanced technological skills. The changing nature of the task and people may necessitate changes in the organizational structure and reward systems. One valuable piece of information can evoke a series of organizational changes.

4. **Facilitating organizations through people.** Organizational changes may not occur unless people involved are willing to change. Task and structural changes often pose threats to people. Because changes can cause technical displacement or a reduction in status, people may resist changes that are perceived to be threats. Many behavioral scientists find this problem to be a major obstacle to organizational change.

5. **Exporting organizational outputs.** Once organizational changes are carried out, the organization should be able to produce new kinds of (or improved) goods and services. These new products may require improved or modified distribution channels or strategies. If so, the necessary changes should be made in order to market and sell these products.

6. **Obtaining performance feedback.** In order to ensure the success of organizational changes, the organization must assess the performance of new systems. This information will reveal whether a change was successful or if it needs additional adjustments. This step can be combined with the first step—sensing environmental changes—in order to continuously provide relevant information for organizational change and improvement.

The adaptive strategy basically involves successful changes in an organization's internal components—tasks, individuals, groups, and organizational controls. In order to be successful, when a change occurs in any particular component, the organization should be able to concurrently change other components. Failure to maintain such changes can lead to organizational ineffectiveness. Since the adaptive strategy involves complex changes in various organizational components, these changes must be well planned and executed. (The strategy for planned organization change is discussed in the last section of this chapter.)

Avoiding External Dependence

An organization can reduce external dependence in a number of ways. These strategies include: (1) finding an environmental niche, (2) diversifying dependence, and (3) developing mutual interdependence.[13]

1. **Finding an environmental niche.** An organization can avoid external dependence by carving out environmental niches where external dependence is easy to manage. This can be done by selecting specific environmental domains with little or no competition, no restrictive regulations, but plenty of suppliers and customers. Indeed, this is too ideal to be realistic, but some innovative companies keep other organizations out of competition and maintain monopolistic positions in the market. IBM, Polaroid, Xerox, Kodak, and Texas Instrument can be considered to be such organizations.

2. **Reducing dependence through diversification.** To the extent that an organization depends on a limited number of outsiders for its needed resources and outputs, the degree of its dependence on them increases. The organization can reduce this dependence through diversification. Diversification can take several different forms. First, the organization may cultivate alternative sources of suppliers or may depend on many small suppliers rather than on a few major ones. Second, the organization may expand vertically by acquiring the sources of supply and distribution. Some major oil companies and automobile manufacturers have taken this approach. Finally, the organization may expand its domain in the market by diversifying its product lines. It may do so to reduce its dependence on a few products. Large conglomerates such as City Investing, W. R. Grace, Raytheon, and Transamerica Corporation are just a few examples of such companies.

3. **Developing mutual dependence.** When people or organizations depend on each other for survival or for positive exchange relationships, one party may not take an arbitrary action against the other because of fears of repercussion. However, when one party is more dependent on the other, an imbalance in their exchange relationship is created. The stronger party can take an action against the depen-

dent one without being challenged. In order to avoid such one-sided dependence, the dependent party may have to diversify its dependence or increase the other party's dependence on it. Such a necessity for mutual dependence is vividly demonstrated in international power politics.

Controlling Environmental Forces

Organizations can reduce their external dependence by controlling the forces in the environment that, in turn, control their behaviors. These forces may include competitors, suppliers, customers, legislative bodies, and unions. Many tactics can be employed to control the environment. Some are as follows:[14]

1. Create an organizational structure with a large number of boundary spanners, who interact with the environmental forces. Creating a public relations department or project group is an example.

2. Hire individuals from external elements who can establish personal linkages to those who control the environment. For example, companies that rely on defense contracts may hire ex-generals to provide such personal linkages.

3. Create or participate in trade associations. They reduce competition among their members and allow them to control their environments jointly. Many professional organizations protect their members' interests through such organized efforts.

4. Lobby the legislative and/or regulatory agencies to create favorable environments for an industry or organization. This is a reason why an army of lobbyists operates in Washington and in state capitals.

Other devices can be used to control the environment as well. These include such tactics as price fixing, forcing out competitors, false advertising, and bribes. However, these methods are mostly illegal or against contemporary social norms and values. For this reason, not many respectable organizations use such tactics explicitly or extensively.

Pervasiveness of Organizational Adaptation

Organizations use a variety of strategies to cope with external dependence. Although these strategies are available to all organizations, some are more likely to use proactive strategies (avoidance and control) than others. Large and powerful organizations are more likely to have the resources to rely on such strategies than smaller organizations. However, large organizations are not immune from the need for adaptive changes. No organizations are large and powerful enough to avoid external dependence totally. For example, even the Congress is forced to change its behavior to respond to voters' pressures. Big and powerful companies such as AT&T, General Motors, and IBM have to cope with such environmental forces as the energy crisis, competition, and government regulations.

With external dependence comes the need for organizational change. Organizations need to change their internal components to adapt to changes in the environment. Organizational change can be a natural or a planned process. If a change occurs in a stable environment, as a part of organizational growth, the change can be a natural one. However, when an organization changes its behavior in response to external changes, it tends to become a planned process. Because such change involves a large number of organizational components, adequate planning and execution are needed to ensure its success.

 PLANNED ORGANIZATIONAL CHANGE

> *Some organizational changes may occur naturally, but most require careful planning and execution. A successful change takes place in three stages—unfreezing, change, and refreezing.*

Changes in the environment require changes within organizations. A technological change necessitates a change in production systems. A change in consumer demands calls for modification of a company's products. A change in any part of the organization will have a ripple effect on other parts. Because of this ripple effect, organizational change is a complex process. One way for managers to understand this complexity is to use a conceptual framework for the change process. This can help them plan for large-scale changes in organizations.

The Process of Organizational Change

People change their customs, habits, and institutions when they become dissatisfied with the status quo or when there is a more desirable substitute. A successful change involves (1) recognizing the need for it, (2) learning a new behavior or substitute, and (3) feeling comfortable with the new situation.

This change process was best expressed by Kurt Lewin when he described three stages of change—unfreezing, change, and refreezing (see Figure 18.1).[15]

1. **Unfreezing.** The first stage creates the need for change. It involves unfreezing existing attitudes and value systems, managerial behaviors, or organizational structures.

2. **Change.** This is the action-oriented stage. Actual changes occur in current value systems, managerial behaviors, or structures.

3. **Refreezing.** The third stage involves the refreezing of the newly acquired values, behaviors, and structures. A new status quo is established at this stage.

Lewin's model of change can serve as the foundation for developing the strategy for organizational change. As shown in Figure 18.1, the first step toward organizational change is to *recognize the need or pressure for change.* The need may arise because of changes in the external environment or from problems within the organization. Once the need is identified, the status quo in organizational behaviors or structures needs to be changed. This can be changed by increasing the pressure for change and by reducing any forces resisting change.

The second stage of the model involves *knowing what and how to change.* As pointed out in Chapter 2, an organization is composed of four major components or subsystems, namely, tasks, individuals, social groups, and management controls. One must know which component needs to be changed and understand how the change will affect other components. According to the systems concept, a change in one component necessitates change(s) in the other components to make them compatible.

The third stage involves *maintaining the new found compatibility.* This can be done by correcting any existing or potential misfits among organizational components before they become unmanageable.

Institutionalizing Organizational Change

Goodman and his associates argue that this process of change should be institutionalized.[16] Unless it is, it will be difficult to initiate behavioral changes and sustain them. The process of institutionalization has two phases—individual and organizational. The individual phase involves two kinds of decision: (1) decision to adopt and (2) decision to maintain.

FIGURE 18.1
A Model of Organizational
Change.

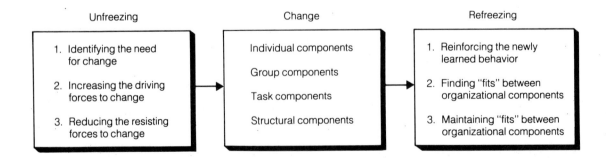

Unfreezing	Change	Refreezing
1. Identifying the need for change	Individual components	1. Reinforcing the newly learned behavior
2. Increasing the driving forces to change	Group components	2. Finding "fits" between organizational components
	Task components	
3. Reducing the resisting forces to change	Structural components	3. Maintaining "fits" between organizational components

Decision to Adopt a Change.   The decision to learn a new behavior is a motivational decision. It depends on how the person perceives (1) his or her ability to adopt the new behavior, (2) the relationship between the new behavior and its outcomes, and (3) the value of these outcomes. Notice that this decision is based on the expectancy theory of motivation, which was discussed in Chapter 6.

Decision to Maintain a Behavior.   The decision to maintain a newly acquired behavior will be based on whether the behavior produces expected results. If it produces desired outcomes, it will be continued. Otherwise, it will be discontinued. In addition to this necessary reinforcement, the level of commitment to a change made by a person can be an important factor in maintaining it. Uncommitted changes can be easily discarded.

In addition to these individual decisions, the organization is responsible for facilitating and maintaining the newly learned behavior. The organization needs to create the reward and social systems that are supportive of the change. People need to perceive that the new behavior is appropriate to the overall norms and values of the organization and that their behavior leads to desirable outcomes, including organizational rewards.

Recognizing the Driving Forces

Pressures for organizational change come from external and internal sources. *External* pressures are generated by changes in the environment —technology, market structure, labor, government, or people. Any major change in the environment necessitates changes in organizational components—that is, in tasks, individuals, groups, and managerial practices. Some of these pressures may involve technological innovation, employee training, organizational restructuring, behavior modification, power equalization, and so forth.

Internal factors forcing change stem from a number of sources. Low employee morale, high turnover and absenteeism, and low productivity signal the need for change in reward systems, supervisory styles, or task designs. For example, organizational rewards may not satisfy the needs of employees; tasks may not be intrinsically motivating; or employees may lack necessary job skills. Another major source of problems is structural deficiency. For example, organization members may have difficulty obtaining the information needed to make decisions. People may not know who is responsible for doing what, and thus be unable to coordinate their activities with others. Decisions may be postponed or made too late.

Recognizing major changes in the environment and problems within the organization is the first step toward organizational change. Intuitive managers may recognize these pressures for change and take corrective action. In many organizations, however, the need for change may go unnoticed until a major problem arises. By the time the problem strikes, however, it may be too late to solve it. It is important for managers to develop a keen sensitivity toward their external as well as internal environments.

Increasing the Driving Forces

Once the need for change is identified, it has to be communicated to people who will be involved in the changing process. As noted earlier, if organizational members know why the change is needed and how it will help them, they are more likely to adopt it. Managers can do several things to increase members' acceptance of a change. Some of the strategies are as follows:

1. **Express the need for change.** People who will be affected by the change have to know why the change is needed. If they do not, they will hesitate to cooperate in the change process. Threats from outside, such as competition, technological change, and political uncertainty, can be conveyed as the major reasons for change. Internal problems, such as high turnover and absenteeism, low morale, and low productivity, are other good reasons for change.

2. **Communicate the potential benefits.** People have a tendency to ask, "What's in it for me?" Unless they feel that the change will benefit them—or that failure to change will hurt them—substantially, they are less likely to cooperate. If no benefits can be identified, the costs of not changing must at least be understood.

3. **Protect the interests of concerned people.** People fear change because it may cause them to lose their jobs, income, or status. Assurances of job security, income protection, and maintenance of status can increase the acceptance of change. That is not to say that people's interests must be protected at all costs—sometimes management must infringe upon the interests of some people in order to ensure or improve the positions of all. However, it is important to protect the interests of individuals whose services are continuously needed.

4. **Get people involved in the process.** Participation can help people accept change. Some individuals have a positive outlook on change, and when they participate, the progress of change is facilitated. Generally, individuals who are capable, intelligent, mobile, and self-confident are more likely to welcome change than those who are less capable and more immobile.

5. **Communicate the progress of change.** In order to minimize fear of the unknown, the content and progress of change must be com-

municated to employees. It is often difficult to know all the potential consequences and influences of a given change, but, by keeping employees informed of its progress, management can at least maintain a climate of trust.

6. **Use a respected change agent.**   The credibility and power of the change agent can facilitate the process of change. The change agent must be familiar with the technical and behavioral aspects of a given change and must be someone with an influence on organizational functioning. In this regard, top management involvement in an organizational change, with the assistance of behavioral scientists, can be most desirable.

7. **Reinforce earlier changes.**   When an organization undertakes a large-scale change involving a series of continual modifications, it is important for people to see that earlier changes have been successful. In order to succeed from the beginning, management may start with changes that have a better chance of quick success and then gradually move into more complex areas.

Managing the Resisting Forces

Most of the strategies designed to increase the driving forces are equally applicable for reducing the resisting forces to change. People resist change because they perceive that it can be harmful to them; thus, it is essential that they be made aware of its need and benefit. Understanding the reasons why people resist change can help managers formulate a plan to reduce the resistance. Some of these reasons are:

Lack of Resources.   People or organizations may resist change because they lack the necessary resources. For example, most Americans and their leaders are aware of the need to develop alternative sources of energy, but the costs of doing this are so high that they resist needed changes. Problems in the auto and steel industries fall into this category: They need huge investments to upgrade their production facilities.

Institutional Inertia.   The noted scholar C. N. Parkinson wrote: "Work expands so as to fill the time available for its completion."[17] This is called *Parkinson's Law,* and it is illustrated by students who are "too busy" to write their term papers until the last minute. It was also demonstrated by the U.S. Congress in dealing with energy programs. As late as 1980, Congress had not been able to produce a comprehensive energy program. There were no fewer than 80 committees with a hand in energy policy. Because of this proliferation of competing committees, no one seemed to know how and where the energy policy was progressing.

Fear of the Unknown.   Organizational changes bring about elements of uncertainty. People tend to resist change because they are not sure how it will affect them. The introduction of new machinery may eliminate their jobs. An organizational change may relocate them to new places or new positions. People resist new developments in science and technology, such as DNA molecule research and nuclear energy, because they are uncertain about the impact these developments will have on human lives. Uncertainty causes anxiety—and people want to avoid it.

Economic Reasons.   People resist changes when they feel that these changes may lower their incomes. Medical doctors resist a change in the admission policy of medical schools, fearing that an increase in admissions will lead to an increase in the supply of doctors, which could reduce income levels. Unions may resist technological innovation because they fear displacement. Lawyers resist the introduction of legal service clinics because these clinics reduce the demand for their services. Both lawyers and doctors resist advertising of legal or medical services, fearing that competitors will undercut their fees and lure away their clients or patients.

Disturbance of Social Relationships.   Organizational changes usually bring about changes in existing social relationships. Changes in organizational structure usually mean redistribution of authority and power among managers. Managers who fear losing such authority and power tend to resist proposed changes. Changes in machinery also bring about personnel shifts that create new working relationships. If people feel comfortable with existing social relationships, they will resist changes that may disturb them.

Unfreezing the Status Quo

Change means doing away with the status quo. The status quo, or equilibrium, is maintained because there is a balance between the driving forces (or pressures) for change and the forces resisting change. If change is to be introduced successfully, this status quo must be broken or unfrozen. The status quo can be unfrozen by:[18]

1.   Increasing the driving forces for change
2.   Reducing the forces resisting change

A study by Billings, Klimoski, and Breaugh demonstrates how management can introduce a change in production systems without creating adverse effects on employee behavior.[19] The study involved a change in technology in a hospital dietary department. Before the change, meals were prepared in batches by individual dieticians on large delivery carts. Each dietician prepared individual meals including main dishes, beverages, rolls, and salads according to the menu. Once meals were prepared, the cart was taken to the appropriate floor.

Later, this batch production system was changed to a mass production system. In this system, foods were prepared in large quantity and individual dishes were prepared by an assembly line method. To this end, a conveyer was installed, with food stations set up along both sides of the belt. Trays were fed into the conveyer belt with patients' orders attached. The dietician at each station placed on the tray the food requested on the order. The assembled meals were then taken to the floor on a small cart.

It was expected that the change in production systems would generate some resistance and job dissatisfaction among the people involved because the jobs had become less intrinsically motivating. Motivational attributes such as task variety, skill requirement, interactional opportunity, and mobility were reduced by the change. Yet the expected resistance and job dissatisfaction did not occur. The technological change had an effect on the nature of the job, but it had little adverse effect on employee behavior.

Figure 18.2 explains how the hospital administrator introduced the technological change without adverse effect. The actual changeover took less than 12 hours, but the planning and preparation took more than six months. As shown in the figure, management was aware of the driving forces for change and the forces resisting change and dealt with them effectively. The driving forces for change, such as frequent breakdowns of delivery carts, high repair costs, and unnecessary movements in the kitchen, were well communicated and understood by both management and workers. The forces resisting change, such as fear of layoffs, technical unfamiliarity, disturbed social interactions, and lower professional status, were reduced by providing job security, simulated training, and opportunities to participate in the change process.

Changing Organizational Components

Traditionally, organizational change was thought to mean modifying only one subsystem of an organization. For example, if there was a change in technology, modifying a task was thought to be sufficient. In recent years, however, more attention has been paid to large-scale organizational changes involving several organizational components. This approach is based on the systems view that an organization is composed of four major components—tasks, individuals, groups, and managerial controls—and that a change in any one of them requires changing the others (see Figure 2.2). Failure to do so is expected to have negative effects on organizational outputs—such as job satisfaction, morale, and productivity.[20]

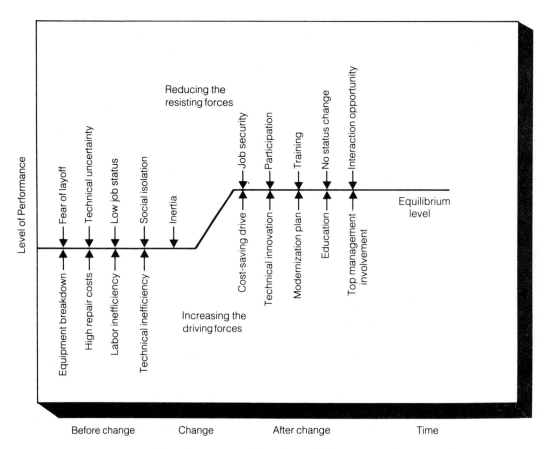

Before change   Change   After change   Time

FIGURE 18.2
A Planned Change in an
Organization.

The theories and practices of changing organizational components are discussed throughout this book. Particularly, the method of identifying the sources of organizational problems and their corresponding components was discussed in Chapter 2. Part II dealt with issues related to individual behavior and components. Part III presented ways of improving and changing the performance of group components—that is, interpersonal and group effectiveness. Parts IV and V were primarily concerned with managerial components—leadership, reward systems, structure, decision making, and organizational change. Methods of changing task components were discussed in Chapter 15. A summary of these tools will be presented in Chapter 19.

Reinforcing Newly Acquired Behavior

The process of refreezing a newly acquired behavior involves reinforcement at both individual and institutional levels. The individual must feel that the change has produced positive outcomes. If individuals find that the outcomes do not meet their expectations, they are likely to search for other alternatives. For example, a manager who changes his or her leader behavior may expect an improved leader–member relationship or improved group performance. If the manager's new behavior does not produce such a result, he or she may revert back to the old behavior.

Reinforcement also should take place at the organizational level. In order to accomplish this, there must be concurrent changes in reward, social, and other managerial systems. For example, if a cooperative behavior is desired and maintained, the reward systems should be designed to encourage cooperation rather than competition. The newly acquired behavior must be compatible with organizational norms and values. For example, when a manager practices cooperative behavior, it has to be reciprocated by other managers. If the existing organizational norms do not support cooperative behavior, the manager will soon modify his or her behavior.

Maintaining Organizational Fits

In order to continuously reinforce the newly acquired behavior, the organization needs to maintain the organizational fits among various organizational components that are supportive of such behavior. Without such organizational compatibility, the organization will encounter instability. Since the newfound behavior cannot be adequately reinforced in an unstable organizational climate, it may soon be discontinued.

Remember, however, that an organization operating in a complex-dynamic environment may not be able to maintain a level of organizational fits for long. Since both internal and external components change constantly, organizational fits cannot exist at one level for a long time. Under this environment, managers need to search for organizational fits at different levels. For these managers, the task of performing organizational change becomes a continuous process—finding a moving equilibrium.

SUMMARY AND CONCLUSION

Changes in the environment present organizations with opportunities as well as threats. If an organization understands the meanings of these changes and prepares for them, it should survive and prosper. If not, the organization may stagnate and ultimately fail. The necessity for environmental adaptation is more critical in the 1980s than in previous decades because of the accelerating rate and magnitude of environmental changes. Among the most important conditions affecting organizations are energy and technological development. These two factors will most likely dictate the economic, political, and social environments, which in turn will affect the fate of organizations.

The change model presented in this chapter provides managers with a conceptual tool for understanding the process of organizational change. This model can also be useful for helping them determine an effective way of managing change. The model suggests several steps. First, managers must be aware of the need for change—the driving forces. Second, they must be aware of the reasons for resisting change —the resisting forces. Third, managers must increase the driving forces and, at the same time, reduce the resisting forces. Fourth, managers introduce the necessary changes in organizational components. Finally, managers must maintain compatibility or fit among various organizational components.

KEY CONCEPTS AND WORDS

Organizational change	*Parkinson's Law*	*Institutional inertia*
External dependence	*General environment*	*Adaptive strategy*
Planned change	*Specific environment*	*Avoidance strategy*
Environmental adaptation	*Freezing*	*Control strategy*
	Unfreezing	
	Resistance to change	

Questions for Review and Discussion

1. Identify several environmental factors that greatly affect organizations. Explain how these factors influence these organizations.

2. Are some organizations more sensitive to environmental changes than others? Give some examples of organizations that effectively manage their dependence on the environment.

3. Discuss various ways of dealing with environmental demands.

4. Why do people resist change? List some reasons.

5. How does Lewin's model of change deal with the forces resisting change?

6. Can an organization introduce a change in one subsystem without affecting other subsystems? Explain.

7. Identify some major characteristics found in successful organizational changes.

CASE AND EXERCISE

CASE 18.1. THE CITY AGENCY CONSOLIDATION PLAN

This case shows how difficult it is to introduce an organizational change. Because of diverse interests in an organization, not all parties would welcome a change. While a change may benefit some, it may pose some threats to others. The managerial challenge lies in introducing a change that can benefit all parties concerned.

The Situation

Metro City has about 260,000 people. Its emergency service department provides all types of emergency medical services, including ambulances, cardiac treatments, and other first aids. The service personnel treat the patients before they are taken to hospitals. The department hires about 50 employees, and its operating costs run around $1.6 million annually. Although the department charges the service users, the bulk of operating costs are from tax dollars.

As the tide of Proposition 13, which helped Californians reduce their tax burdens, spread all over the country, city officials have become interested in economizing city agencies' operations. Among the cost-cutting efforts is the idea to merge the emergency service department with the fire department. The fire department has about 230 firefighters. In order to achieve this goal, the city manager has created a committee, composed of officials from the two departments, to formulate a consolidation plan.

As the committee's work started, members began to see the pros and cons of the plan. Some of the reasons for consolidating the two departments are as follows:

1. The firefighters are currently providing some emergency services. In fact, since the fire stations are conveniently located all over the city, they are able to get to the scene before the ambulance arrives.

2. By providing a cross-the-line training, the employees will be equipped to handle both firefighting and emergency services. The employees' idle time

can be best utilized by this training. This plan can help ease the tax burden by at least $500,000 annually.

3.   If an acceptable plan cannot be worked out, the departments should prepare alternative cost-cutting plans. The city is determined to reduce tax burdens.

Although the majority of city officials and firefighters seem to approve of the consolidation effort, emergency service personnel do not share the same sentiment. They view the proposed plan as a step backward. They argue that the change will reduce the quality and sophistication of emergency services. This view is shared by the city medical society, which was instrumental in establishing the emergency service department five years ago. The city board of supervisors are responsible for making the decision, and they welcome citizens' inputs into the matter.

Discussion Questions

1.   Why do some city officials and firefighters prefer the consolidation plan?
2.   Why do the emergency service personnel and the medical society resist the proposed change?
3.   Should the city consolidate the two departments? Explain why or why not.
4.   What can the city manager do to introduce a successful change that is acceptable to all parties concerned?

EXERCISE 18.1. THE BEACON AIRCRAFT COMPANY, PART 2

This exercise will help show how the process model of change can help managers develop a set of strategies for organizational change. By understanding the driving and resisting forces in a change situation, managers can systematically attempt to unfreeze the status quo, introduce the necessary change, and refreeze the new status quo.

The Situation

The marketing division of the Beacon Aircraft Company has gone through two reorganizations in the past two years. In 1979, its structure changed from a functional to a matrix form. But the matrix structure did not satisfy some functional managers. They complained that the structure confused the authority and responsibility relationships. In reaction to these complaints, the marketing manager revised the structure back to the functional form. This new structure maintained market and project groups, which were managed by project managers with a few general staff personnel. But no functional specialists were assigned to these groups.

After the change, some problems began to surface. Project managers complained that they could not obtain adequate assistance from functional staffs. It not only took more time to obtain necessary assistance, but it also created problems in establishing stable relationships with functional staff members. Since these problems affected their services to customers, project managers demanded a change in the organizational structure—probably again toward a matrix structure. Faced with these complaints and demands from project managers, the vice-president is pondering another reorganization. He has requested an outside consultant to help him in the reorganization plan.

The Procedure

1. Divide yourselves into groups of five to seven and take the role of consultants.

2. Each group identifies the driving and resisting forces found in the firm. List these forces below.

The driving forces	The resisting forces
_____	_____
_____	_____
_____	_____
_____	_____
_____	_____
_____	_____

3. Each group develops a set of strategies for increasing the driving forces and another set for reducing the resisting forces.

4. Each group prepares a list of changes it wants to introduce.

5. The class reassembles and hears each group's recommendations.

6. Compare these recommendations with those made in Case 16.2: the Beacon Aircraft Company, Part 1. The class may discuss the usefulness of the process model of change in dealing with the case.

Footnotes

1. Alvin Toffler, _Future Shock_ (New York: Random House, 1970), p. 86.

2. "AMC's Charge," _Time,_ November 19, 1979, 86.

3. C. G. Burck, "How G.M. Turned Itself Around," _Fortune,_ January 16, 1978, 87–100.

4. "Driving for a Rescue Deal," _Time,_ September 24, 1979, 70.

5. Lee Iacocca, "Chrysler Deserves Federal Help," *Wall Street Journal,* December 3, 1979, p. 26.

6. R. N. Osborn, J. G. Hunt, and L. R. Jauch, *Organization Theory* (New York: Wiley, 1980), pp. 124–126.

7. See "Detroit Hits a Roadblock," *Time,* June 2, 1980, 56–58.

8. See Richard B. Freeman, "The Work Force of the Future: An Overview," in *Work in America: The Decade Ahead,* ed. Clark Kerr and J. M. Rosow (New York: Van Nostrand, 1979), pp. 58–79.

9. Irving Bluestone, "Emerging Trend in Collective Bargaining," in *Work in America,* Kerr and Rosow, pp. 231–242.

10. Arnold Weber, "Conflict and Compression: The Labor Market Environment," in *Work in America,* Kerr and Rosow, pp. 268–280.

11. See Jeffrey Pfeffer and G. R. Salancik, *The External Control of Organizations: A Resource Dependence Perspective* (New York: Harper & Row, 1978), pp. 92–112; and J. P. Kotter, "Managing External Dependence," *Academy of Management Review,* January 1979, 87–92.

12. E. H. Schein, *Organizational Psychology* (Englewood Cliffs, NJ: Prentice-Hall, 1980), pp. 233–238.

13. See Kotter, "Managing External Dependence," p. 88–89.

14. See Pfeffer and Salancik, *The External Control of Organizations,* pp. 106–110 and 278–281.

15. Kurt Lewin, "Group Decision and Social Change," in *Readings in Social Psychology,* ed. G. E. Swanson, T. M. Newcomb, and E. L. Hartley (New York: Holt, Rinehart and Winston, 1952), pp. 459–473.

16. P. S. Goodman, Max Bazerman, and Edward Conlon, "Institutionalization of Planned Organizational Change," in *Research in Organizational Behavior,* ed. B. Staw and M. Bazerman (Greenwich, CT: JAI Press, 1980), pp. 215–246.

17. C. N. Parkinson, *Parkinson's Law* (Boston: Houghton Mifflin, 1957).

18. K. D. Benne, "Changes in Institutions and the Role of the Change Agent," in *Organizational Behavior and Administration,* ed. P. R. Lawrence and J. A. Seiler (Homewood, IL: Irwin and Dorsey, 1965), pp. 952–959; also see J. P. Kotter and L. A. Schlesinger, "Choosing Strategies for Change," *Harvard Business Review,* March–April 1979, 106–114.

19. R. S. Billings, R. J. Klimoski, and J. A. Breaugh, "The Impact of a Change in Technology on Job Characteristics: A Quasi-Experiment," *Administrative Science Quarterly,* June 1977, 318–339.

20. D. A. Nadler and M. Tushman, "A Congruence Model for Diagnosing Organizational Behavior," in *Organizational Psychology,* ed. D. A. Kolb, I. M. Rubin, and J. M. McIntyre (Englewood Cliffs, NJ: Prentice-Hall, 1979), pp. 442–458.

MANAGEMENT AND ORGANIZATIONAL BEHAVIOR

1. Understanding the Job of Managing

2. Studying Organizational Behavior

INDIVIDUAL BEHAVIOR

3. Satisfying Human Needs

4. Learning and Reinforcing

5. Understanding the Perceptual Process

6. Understanding the Motivational Process

SUPERVISORY BEHAVIOR

11. Understanding the Leadership Process

12. Developing Leadership Skills

13. Acquiring and Using Power in Organizations

14. Managing Reward Systems

INTERPERSONAL AND GROUP BEHAVIOR

7. Understanding Interpersonal Dynamics

8. Improving Communication Effectiveness

9. Understanding Group Dynamics

10. Dealing with Intergroup Conflicts

ENVIRONMENTAL ADAPTATION

15. Task Design—Matching Jobs to People

16. Designing Organizational Structure

17. Making Managerial Decisions

18. Managing Organizational Change

Micro-organizational analysis

Macro-organizational analysis

ORGANIZATIONAL EFFECTIVENESS

19. Developing Effective Organizations

APPENDIX

Developing Careers in Organizations

PART

ORGANIZATIONAL EFFECTIVENESS

This book has been about behavior in organizations. We are interested in studying organizational behavior because it is related to organizational effectiveness. In this final chapter, we summarize a set of organizational conditions that need to be present to make an organization effective. These conditions are reviewed from three different perspectives: theoretical, developmental, and managerial. The theoretical perspective describes the ideal state in which various organizational components are compatible with each other. The developmental perspective concerns the organization's effort to enhance organizational capacity in order to reach the ideal state. The managerial perspective is primarily concerned with solving immediate managerial problems.

LEARNING OBJECTIVES

1. To understand the concept of organizational effectiveness.
2. To learn ways of improving organizational effectiveness.
3. To understand the importance of learning managerial skills.

CHAPTER OUTLINE

The Theoretical Perspective

What Is Organizational Effectiveness?
Internal Organizational Fits
External Organizational Fits
An Integrative Contingency Model
Assessment of Contingency Theory

The Developmental Perspective

Diagnosing Organizational Components
Identifying the Sources of Misfits
Undertaking OD Programs
Assessment of Organizational Development

The Managerial Perspective

Human Relations Skills
Conceptual Skills
Administrative Skills
Technical Skills
Personal Qualities
Need for the Contingency Approach
Assessment of the Managerial Perspective

Summary and Conclusion

19 DEVELOPING EFFECTIVE ORGANIZATIONS

Given the ever-changing . . . goals that are pursued by many organizations, managers have a continual responsibility to restructure available resources, alter technologies, modify climates, develop employees . . . in an effort . . . to attain such goals. Hence, the manager emerges as the primary facilitator of organizational effectiveness through his or her actions and behavior.

Richard M. Steers, Organizational Effectiveness [1]

Managers are responsible for developing and maintaining effective organizations. To do this, they must not only reach the organization's objectives, such as productivity, efficiency, financial stability, and survival, but also satisfy employees' personal needs, such as job security, social acceptance, emotional support, and personal growth. The ways in which managers can successfully achieve these objectives have been discussed throughout this book.

In this chapter, we discuss the concept of organizational effectiveness from three different but interrelated perspectives: theoretical, developmental, and managerial. We do this by summarizing the main themes of theories, concepts, and tools presented in previous chapters. In addition, we try to synthesize the theories and tools when it is feasible.

THE THEORETICAL PERSPECTIVE

> *Organizational effectiveness can be achieved (1) when there exists a fit between the organization and its environment, and (2) when there are fits among various organizational components—tasks, individuals, groups, and managerial controls.*

What is an effective organization? What makes an organization effective? These questions are discussed in this section from a theoretical perspective. The theoretical perspective describes conditions under which an organization can be effective.

What Is Organizational Effectiveness?

Organizational effectiveness means different things to different people. To some it means profit or return on investment, while to others it may mean an organization's ability to satisfy its members, including employees, managers, and stockholders. To some it means an organization's ability to achieve its goals currently; to others it means a firm's ability to adapt continuously to changes and survive in the changing environment.

Although the concept of organizational effectiveness varies depending on one's frame of reference, all of these different perspectives are important in understanding its meaning. Reflecting the diversity of these concerns, we define organizational effectiveness as:

> *An organization's ability to realize its multiple goals (such as profit, productivity, employee satisfaction, social responsibility, financial stability, and so forth) and its ability to adapt and survive in a changing environment (through adaptability, environmental control, survival, and so forth).*

This definition encompasses not only the current but the future state of organizational effectiveness, and it also takes a multidimensional approach to achieving organizational goals.[2] Once the concept is defined, we can describe the conditions under which organizational effectiveness can be achieved.

The theoretical perspective of organizational effectiveness is based on the contingency view of an organization. This view hypothesizes (1) that an organization is composed of several components, and (2) that it is a part of the environment in which it functions. The organization receives inputs, such as capital, technology, raw materials, personnel, and customer demands, from the environment and transforms them into outputs, including goods and services. How well the organization transforms the inputs into outputs depends on how well it organizes the internal components and responds to changing conditions in the environment. The contingency view suggests that there should be two types of "fit." First, there must be fits among the various internal organizational components themselves. Second, there must be fits between the organization and its external environment.

Internal Organizational Fits

The contingency view tends to stress the internal consistencies, or fits, among organizational components at the microlevel. Several internal consistencies have been investigated and discussed in this book. The following organizational fits among internal components must be maintained to achieve the current state of effectiveness:

1. **Task–individual fit.** Since jobs and people differ in their motivational characteristics, they have to be matched if they are to produce the most satisfactory motivational results. When they are not matched, employees will probably be frustrated, as they will be either overqualified or underqualified for their jobs.

2. **Task–group fit.** Group effectiveness tends to increase when the type of group process used matches the group task. For example, when the task requires knowledge inputs from functional specialists, management should use the participative group process with multiple communication channels.

3. **Task–structure fit.** Organizational structure should be designed to meet the information processing requirements of the task. For example, a matrix form of organizational structure can be used in a task situation requiring timely information processing within and outside of the organization.

4. **Task–leader fit.** Organizational effectiveness increases when the manager's leadership style matches the nature of the group task. For example, a directive leadership style is suggested for managing unstructured tasks, while a supportive style is recommended for managing structured tasks.

5. **Leader–group fit.** It is also important to match leadership style with people. Directive leadership is more effective for managing other-directed people, while the participative style is more suitable for managing inner-directed people.

6. **Reward–group fit.** The way in which reward systems are managed can either encourage cooperation or promote competition. While individualized reward systems stimulate individual work moti-

vation, they discourage group effort. Group-oriented systems yield the opposite results.

7. **Reward–task fit.** Tasks differ in their interactional requirements. Some tasks require a high degree of interaction, others do not. Competitive reward systems should be matched with tasks requiring no interaction, while noncompetitive systems are best matched with tasks requiring a high degree of interdependence.

External Organizational Fits

In recent years there has been increased emphasis on the importance of environmental influences on organizational effectiveness and survival. Perrow has suggested that the impact of good internal management by itself on organizational effectiveness is limited, because so much depends on the impact of environmental elements, such as the market, competition, the labor force, legislation, technological developments, and others.[3] An organization exists in a turbulent environment that changes rapidly and that imposes an increasing number of constraints upon it. Within such an environment, managers must be able to recognize major environmental changes and respond quickly by restructuring internal organizational components.

Environmental forces also have a major impact on the nature of organizational tasks, information processing requirements, and structure. Some of the more important of these relationships are as follows:

1. **Environment–task fit.** Organizations operating in a simple-static environment tend to rely on mass production systems; those operating in a complex-dynamic environment rely on intensive technological systems. A misfit will occur when a mass production technology is attempted in a complex-dynamic environment.

2. **Environment–information fit.** Organizations operating in a simple-static environment may require only a low level of information processing; those operating in a complex-dynamic environment require higher levels of information processing. Organizations need to provide mechanisms by which the required information can be adequately processed.

3. **Information–structure fit.** Organizational structure plays an important role in information processing. A functional form of structure may be suitable for organizations operating in a simple-static environment, but a matrix form is more suitable for those operating in a complex-dynamic environment.

These organizational fits are partial contingency models in the sense that they deal only with parts of an organization. When these models are studied independently, they may produce inconsistent results in predicting organizational success.[4] For example, assume that two firms have adopted a matrix organizational structure in response to changes in a complex-dynamic environment. Assume further that one firm has trained its people to function effectively within such a flexible organizational structure, while the other firm has not. In this example, although the two firms have achieved organizational fit at the macrolevel, the former will probably be successful, and the latter will not. The latter has failed to achieve the organizational fit at the microlevel; that is, there is no match between the task and the people.

An Integrative Contingency Model

It was suggested earlier that an organization can become more effective if it realizes organizational fits at all levels of the organization. Figure 19.1 shows the essence of such an integrative contingency model.

FIGURE 19.1
An Integrative Contingency Model.

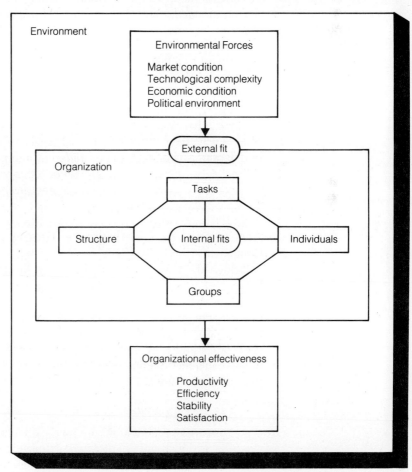

This model has three important implications for management. First, an organization must remain congruent at both the macrolevel and the microlevel. It must respond to changes in the environment and bring about concurrent changes in organizational components. Only as these changes occur can one expect the organization to perform effectively. To quote Nadler and Tushman:

> *Other things being equal, the greater the total degree of congruence or fit between the various components, the more effective will be organizational behavior at multiple levels. Effective organizational behavior is defined as behavior which leads to higher levels of goal attainment, utilization of resources, and adaptation.* [5]

Second, the directions of predominant influence tend to be (1) *from* the environment *to* the internal structure, in order to achieve external organizational fits, and (2) *from* internal structure *to* individual and group behavior, in order to achieve internal organizational fits. While organizations and their environment can influence each other, environmental forces tend to influence organizations more than organizations influence the external forces. Except for a few powerful individuals, most people and organizations have little significant impact on their external environment. This observation implies that they have to adapt to the environment rather than the other way around.

Finally, the contingency model suggests that organizations operating in different environments need different internal organizational fits. The internal subsystems of an organization operating in a complex-dynamic environment should probably be different from those of one operating in a simple-static environment.

Assessment of Contingency Theory

Contingency theory has received increased attention in the past decade and now has a well-established position in management literature. Few books and articles fail to mention the necessity of maintaining organizational fits as a way of improving organizational effectiveness. They suggest that the effectiveness of individual and organizational performance is contingent upon how well various organizational components match with each other and how well these components match environmental demands. This theory concludes that the most important managerial task is to find organizational fits at all levels of the organization.

THE DEVELOPMENTAL PERSPECTIVE

> *An organization is most effective when it is able to recognize environmental changes and to change its internal components accordingly. Efforts to increase this ability represent the developmental perspective.*

How does an organization become most effective? How can it develop the ability to adapt to the changing environment? In the preceding section we saw that organizational effectiveness increases when there are fits among organizational components at both the macro- and microlevels. This integrative contingency model provides some clues as to what should be done to find such organizational fits. It implies that the sources of organizational misfits need to be found and corrected. The managerial effort to find the sources of misfits and to correct them is defined here as *organizational development* (OD). A comprehensive OD effort involves (1) diagnosing organizational components, (2) identifying the sources of misfits, and (3) undertaking corrective actions, that is, OD programs.

Diagnosing Organizational Components

The environmental conditions that organizations face change constantly. Effective managers are aware of these changes and continually engage in problem identification and problem-solving activities. Several studies have suggested that OD efforts have failed to produce positive results because of management's failure to understand the real causes of organizational problems.[6] When management does not understand the real causes of the problem, it may prescribe the wrong remedies.

The process of diagnosing organizational components is an analytical process. It requires an investigation of the characteristics of various organizational components. The contingency theory provides a conceptual framework for diagnosing internal and external organizational components.

Some of the more important organizational components are the following:

1. **Environmental forces**—the market, competition, technological development, the labor force, and economic and political conditions. The degree of environmental complexity and uncertainty should also be included in the diagnosis.

2. **Task components**—technical complexity, skill requirements, interaction requirements, programmability, and the performance cycle.

3. **Individual components**—job skill and experience, personality, need structure, interpersonal competence, and managerial competence.

4. **Group components**—group norms, group cohesiveness, roles and status, intergroup behavior, group processes, and social rewards.

5. **Managerial components**—leadership style, reward systems, organizational structure, decision processes, and change strategies.

Identifying the Sources of Misfits

The analysis of organizational components provides the information needed to identify and isolate the sources of misfits. The sources of misfits can be found by studying the relationships between various combinations of organizational components. Since these components impose certain demands on each other, their characteristics must be matched if they are to be compatible. It was pointed out earlier that when all pairs of major organizational components are matched, the organization will function most effectively.

The most common misfits and their characteristics are:

1. **Environment–task misfit.** The organization does not have the technological capacity to cope with changing technological developments.

2. **Environment–structure misfit.** The structure is not able to process information needed to function in a fast-changing environment.

3. **Individual–structure misfit.** The structure is too restrictive to meet individual employees' need for independence.

4. **Task–individual misfit.** The individual's needs are not adequately met by the task, or the individual does not have the necessary job skills.

5. **Individual–group misfit.** The individual does not receive the necessary support from his or her work group.

6. **Task–group misfit.** Group norms hinder the process of meeting the demands of the tasks—cooperation and performance standards are lacking.

7. **Leader–member misfit.** Leadership style does not match the characteristics of employees.

8. **Reward–task misfit.** The reward systems encourage competition at the expense of the cooperation needed to accomplish interdependent tasks.

Undertaking OD Problems

Once the sources of organizational misfits are identified, management can undertake developmental activities to try to correct them. Such developmental programs are divided into two major categories: behavioral and structural. Behavior-focused programs have as their target the development of individuals and groups; structure-focused programs seek to change the task, structural, and managerial components (see Figure 19.2). Although some developmental activities are related to several target behaviors, the activities are classified according to what they emphasize.

Behavior-Focused Programs. Behavior-focused programs are directed at changing the attitudes, behavior, and interactional patterns of individuals and groups. Their main purpose is to increase the individual's or group's ability to solve problems by having the individual or group engage in authentic and cooperative behavior.[7] Some of the more popular developmental programs are career planning and development, assertiveness

FIGURE 19.2
A Topology of OD
Programs.

Target Behaviors	Types of OD Techniques
Individual behavior	Career development Assertiveness training Sensitivity training Transactional analysis
Group behavior	Team building Intergroup team building Process consultation Managerial grid
Task and structure	Job enlargement Job enrichment Linking-pin organization Matrix organization
Managerial practice	Behavior modification Flextime Survey feedback Management-by-objectives

training, sensitivity training, transactional analysis, process consultation, team building, intergroup team building, and the managerial grid.

1. **Career planning and development.** Career development activities consist of (a) helping organization members decide what they want to do with their professional lives, (b) improving individuals' capacities to function productively in organizations, (c) matching individuals with organizations at different stages of their lives, and (d) planning human resources utilization in organizations.

2. **Assertiveness training.** This training is given to employees to help them express themselves in a constructive manner. It is designed to help people satisfy their needs without encroaching on the rights of other people.

3. **Sensitivity training.** This training is a method of changing people's attitudes and behavior through unstructured group interactions. By interacting with others in an open and unthreatening environment, people can learn more about the effect of their behavior on others.

4. **Transactional analysis.** This is a conceptual tool for analyzing the pattern of interpersonal communication. When a person communicates with another, the pattern of interaction can be either complementary or conflicting. Understanding this pattern can help people interact in a constructive manner.

5. **Process consultation.** A trained observer makes an observation on group processes—for example, on communication, decision making, individual roles, and group climate—and provides feedback to the group. The purpose is to give the group members some insight into what is going on around them in the group process. The observer can also provide some generalizations on how the group can improve its effectiveness.

6. **Team building.** While team building is, in reality, group-oriented sensitivity training, it focuses more on solving task-related problems than on improving interpersonal sensitivity. It is often called the *family T-group*. Its goal is to improve group effectiveness through better management of the interactional patterns of group members. It can be combined with process consultation.

7. **Intergroup team building.** This method focuses on helping groups interact better with each other. It identifies the sources of conflict and common interests among groups, helps them resolve conflicts, and encourages them to develop cooperative relationships.

8. **Managerial grid.** The managerial grid program is aimed at helping managers develop a leadership style that is both people- and production-oriented. This style is used in developing productive

groups, promoting cooperative intergroup relations, and managing the organization as a unit. The entire program consists of six phases: (a) laboratory seminar, (b) team building, (c) intergroup development, (d) organizational goal setting, (e) goal attainment, and (f) stabilization.[8]

Structure-Focused Programs.   These programs attempt to improve organizational effectiveness by changing tasks, structural relationships, and other managerial practices. By changing these organizational components, managers not only can influence the attitudes and behaviors of organization members but can also respond to the changing environment. These programs include behavior modification, job enlargement, job enrichment, flextime, linking-pin organization, matrix organization, management-by-objectives (MBO), and survey feedback.

1. **Behavior modification.**   This method, which is often called *behavior mod* (or even *B Mod*), integrates the reinforcement theory with managing organizational rewards. The effectiveness of reward systems increases when the rewards are matched to employee needs and directly related to performance.

2. **Job enlargement.**   This method is often called *horizontal job loading,* as the job is expanded horizontally when task elements are added to an existing job. It makes the job more meaningful by adding task variety and using the worker's job skills more fully.

3. **Job enrichment.**   This is often called *vertical job loading,* for the job is expanded vertically when managerial responsibilities are added to it. Workers tend to feel more responsible for accomplishing their jobs when they are given the managerial responsibility for them.

4. **Flextime.**   This is a system of work scheduling whereby employees set their own working hours—within certain limits—with the approval of the supervisor. Employees can set their own starting and stopping times, provided that they work a full day and are present during the core working hours (say, between 10 A.M. and 3 P.M.).

5. **Linking-pin organization.**   This is an organizational design that uses participative work groups at all management levels. It is called the *linking-pin organization* because one group's activities are connected to other groups by supervisors who serve as the linking-pins between them. This approach is also called *System 4,* because it represents the fourth of Likert's four managerial systems: (a) exploitative authoritarian, (b) benevolent authoritarian, (c) consultative, and (d) participative.[9]

6. **Matrix organization.**   This form of organization facilitates the flow of information within the organization and between the organization

and its environment. It is probably best suited to organizations that operate in a complex-dynamic environment.

7. **Management-by-objectives (MBO).**   MBO is a managerial process in which managers and subordinates jointly establish performance objectives for the subordinates and evaluate the latter group's performance using them. This management tool can be used effectively in organizations operating in a relatively stable environment.

8. **Survey feedback.**   This method consists of three activities: (a) collecting data about various organizational components from the organization or its subunits, (b) analyzing the collected data, and (c) disseminating the results to concerned parties. Attitude surveys, climate surveys, and systems analyses are examples of this technique. Management may use this information to improve the effectiveness of its managerial practices. Management can also use it to determine the types of organizational development activity to use.

Assessment of Organizational Development

Organizational development (OD) has also gained increased attention from management theorists and practitioners in the past two decades. It has emerged as a tool for introducing changes in organizations. In relation to the contingency theory, OD can be regarded as the tool for achieving congruence or fit among various organizational components.

Most progressive organizations have used some type of OD program. Among them are AT&T, Owens-Corning, Exxon, General Electric, General Foods, General Motors, Procter & Gamble, Texas Instruments, TRW, and Union Carbide. A study by Heisler indicates that about half of the companies responding to his survey reported that their organizations were involved in an OD program.[10] The most frequently mentioned OD programs were: (1) team building, (2) MBO, (3) systems analysis, and (4) job enrichment and enlargement. The least-used programs were managerial grid and sensitivity training.

How effective are these OD programs? Although many companies report that they are satisfied with them, there is no concrete evidence that these programs result in increased organizational effectiveness.[11] They tend to have a more positive impact on personal outcomes, including attitudes and personal sensitivity, than on organizational outcomes like profit and productivity. This tendency is more evident in behavior-focused OD programs, such as sensitivity training, transactional analysis, and managerial grid, than in structure-focused programs like job design, organizational design, and MBO.

OD is based on the assumptions that people are capable of developing genuine, open, and trusting relationships in work organizations, and that they will be fully committed to each other and to the organization if they are treated with respect, dignity, and consideration. These assumptions may be valid among some employees, but they are found to be unrealistic in many industrial and government organizations.[12] When OD efforts are pursued in organizations that do not support such assumptions, the efforts are unlikely to produce positive results.

THE MANAGERIAL PERSPECTIVE

Managers need to have certain skills in order to carry out their managerial responsibilities most effectively. These skills can be classified as human relations, conceptual, administrative, and technical.

A major problem with OD programs is that they often fail to recognize the organizational pressures and realities managers face in their jobs. Many managers struggle to achieve and maintain "bottom-line performance," or to hold onto the job and power. For them, OD programs may seem far removed from reality. Unless they are able to cope with day-to-day pressures effectively, they are unlikely to be interested in those OD programs that demand humanization of the organization to please employees.[13] This is one reason why so many OD tools are "long on theory but short on practice."

An implication of this observation is that OD efforts must begin by helping managers deal with their immediate problems, such as maintaining a network of personal contacts, holding onto power in their organizations, and becoming assertive in meeting their own needs.[14] Only when these problems have been dealt with should efforts be directed toward humanizing the organization for other members.

The managerial perspective requires a set of skills that are needed if the managerial activities are to be performed most successfully. These include (1) human relations, (2) conceptual, (3) administrative, and (4) technical skills.[15]

Human Relations Skills

Human relations skills include interpersonal, leadership, and group process skills. Interpersonal skills are needed to create and maintain a network of contacts with people outside the chain of command. Leadership skills are important in supervising, motivating, and leading employees. Group process skills are the ability to work through and with various work groups.

Interpersonal skills enable managers to get the information and support they need from people outside their chain of command. These skills also enable managers to gain support from employees without relying on the formal authority they usually use to obtain compliance. Formal authority may be available, but it should be used sparingly. Instead, in nonauthoritarian organizations, and in dealing with people outside their chain of command, managers should rely on interpersonal skills to obtain needed information and support.

A number of abilities are classified as interpersonal skills. First, managers are expected to be *assertive* in expressing their ideas, feelings, and opinions, while at the same time remaining *sensitive* to the needs of other people. Second, they must learn to *communicate* both formally and informally by carrying on conversations and being attentive listeners. Third, managers must be able to *negotiate* with peers and develop mutual support systems. Finally, managers should acquire *power bases*—including position, reward, expertise, and association—to cope with interpersonal conflicts or "office politics."

Leadership skills are required by managers to supervise subordinates and effectively lead them to achieve organizational goals. Leadership skills include the ability to: (1) match people with jobs, (2) motivate and lead employees, and (3) apply appropriate incentives to satisfy employee needs. Managers are effective leaders when their subordinates willingly comply with their wishes. This compliance is most likely when the manager's leadership style is compatible with the subordinates' characteristics.

In general, leadership skills involve the ability (1) to know what is expected from a leader in a given leadership situation, (2) to meet this expectation, and (3) to function effectively in various situations and with varying tasks and followers.

Group process skills are needed because organizations consist of small groups, which are the basic work units carrying out most organizational activities. Managers need to acquire these skills if they are to use these groups effectively to solve organizational problems and achieve their goals.

Two kinds of group skill are required in the group processes: *developing teamwork* and *achieving intergroup cooperation.* Team-building skills involve the ability to (1) develop cohesive work groups, (2) use the groups to solve organizational problems, and (3) lead group members to achieve organizational goals. The skills involved in achieving intergroup cooperation include the ability to (1) secure cooperation among work groups and (2) resolve conflicts among them.

A variety of group processes—such as majority rule, compromise, consensus, and consultation—are available to help managers solve organizational problems.

Conceptual Skills

Conceptual skills include the mental abilities to acquire, analyze, and interpret information received from various sources. Effective managers are able to obtain meaning from inadequate—and often conflicting—data. Managers who are unable to do that tend to respond alike to all inputs without recognizing their relative importance. Consequently, they lose a sense of control and direction. Managers need to develop the conceptual skills that will enable them to perceive what goes on in their work environment and permit them to react appropriately. These conceptual skills include analytical, entrepreneurial, decision-making, and allocation skills.

Analytical skills include the ability to divide a complex situation into its component parts and study their characteristics in order to understand the characteristics of the whole. As shown in Chapter 2, the systems theory provides a systematic way of thinking through complex managerial problems so a framework for improving managerial effectiveness can be developed.

Entrepreneurial skills include the ability to search for opportunities and the willingness to take calculated risks. These skills help make managers sensitive to the changing environment so they can find opportunities in problems stemming from it. The ability to take advantage of opportunities before others do and to prevent problems before they arise is the essential quality that sets successful managers apart from unsuccessful ones. Creativity, innovation, and risk-taking behavior need to be encouraged and rewarded if entrepreneurial skills are to be developed.

Decision-making skills are an extension of analytical and entrepreneurial activities. Managers operate in an uncertain world in which decision outcomes are usually not known. Yet managers are expected to make decisions and take actions that will maximize positive results while minimizing undesirable or dysfunctional consequences. A number of analytical tools can help managers to achieve such goals. The contingency theory and some decision-making models can enhance the chances of making more profitable decisions under conditions of uncertainty.

Allocation skills are required of managers because organizations have limited resources available to achieve their goals. Therefore, they are required to choose from among competing resource demands. In so doing, managers must decide what projects are to be carried out, by whom, and with how much of which resources. Analytical skills help managers make these decisions most effectively.

Administrative Skills

Administrative skills include the ability to establish and follow policies and procedures, process paperwork in an orderly manner, and manage expenditures within a budget. These skills are an extension of the other skills, especially the conceptual abilities. Managers arrive at decisions by using their conceptual skills; they implement these decisions by using administrative skills.

Managers seem to dislike performing administrative duties. Yet the effective performance of these activities is what sets them apart from nonmanagers. In addition, as a society becomes more legalistic, there is an increasing demand for administrative activities. The increasing number of laws and regulations, and the increased readiness of employees to sue their employers, call for the skillful execution of administrative duties.

Technical Skills

Technical skills include the ability to use the knowledge, tools, and techniques of a specific functional field, such as accounting, engineering, manufacturing, personnel, or sales. Although the amount of time managers spend performing technical activities decreases as they move up the organizational ladder, they still need to understand the technical functions they are supervising. They also need to acquire some technical knowledge about other functions with which they are involved. If they are general managers, or in top-level management positions, they need to understand all phases of the technical functions of the organization.

Personal Qualities

In addition to these managerial skills, managers need to possess certain personal qualities that may help them be better managers. There is no definite list of personal qualities an individual requires to manage all types of organizations, but certain qualities are found more frequently among successful managers than among less successful managers and nonmanagerial personnel.

Some desirable personal attributes that have been identified by behavioral scientists are: (1) intelligence, (2) physical health, energy, and drive, (3) emotional and mental health, (4) empathy, (5) the desire to manage and influence people, (6) the ability to tolerate ambiguity, frustration, and pressure, and (7) the willingness to take risks.[16]

Some of these personal qualities can usually be acquired by individual managers through education, training, and experience. Since these qualities are personal matters, each individual must deal with and develop them personally.

Need for the Contingency Approach

Do all managers need all of the managerial characteristics and personal qualities mentioned in the preceding sections? On the basis of the contingency theory, the answer would be no. Instead, however, the answer has to be, "It all depends." Managers may need most of these skills and qualities to manage people and complex organizations, but they will place a different emphasis on each of them depending on (1) the function or task being supervised, (2) the type of organization in which the managers operate, and (3) the managers' rank and position in the organizational structure.

For example, managers in accounting, engineering, and finance usually require skills different from those used by sales and production managers. The technical aspects of their work require the use of analytical and technical skills. Conversely, managers in line functions tend to rely more on interpersonal and resource allocation skills. Also, as managers progress upward through managerial levels, their need for technical skills decreases, while the significance of conceptual skills increases.

Assessment of the Managerial Perspective

The managerial perspective is primarily concerned with handling day-to-day managerial responsibilities. It presents a set of managerial skills needed to perform the various managerial activities effectively, including interpersonal, informational, and decision roles. When managers are able to discharge these responsibilities successfully, they are more willing to experiment with OD programs aimed at creating ideal organizations. Some OD programs, such as sensitivity training, the managerial grid, and System 4, can help managers humanize their managerial practices in relation to employees. However, since these tools are often perceived as being far removed from managerial realities, managers tend to feel less enthusiastic about applying them. The managerial perspective requires that OD programs be more practical in dealing with day-to-day managerial problems.

SUMMARY AND CONCLUSION

This chapter has summarized the major theme of the book from three different but interrelated perspectives—theoretical, developmental, and managerial. The theoretical perspective emphasizes the need for a contingency approach to management. It suggests that organizational effectiveness increases (1) when there are fits among the internal organizational components—tasks, individuals, groups, and managerial practices—and (2) when there is a fit between the organization and its external environment. The greater the total degree of organizational fits at both micro- and macrolevels, the more effective the organization should be.

The developmental perspective (OD) provides a means of achieving organizational fits by changing various organizational components. Such developmental programs are divided into two major categories—behavioral and structural. Behavior-focused programs are directed at changing individual and group behavior; structure-focused programs are aimed at changing the task, structure, and managerial components. These OD programs are essentially off-the-job activities aimed at improving the organization's capacity to deal with change.

OD programs strive to create "ideal organizations," but they often fail to provide managers with the tools they need to acquire the managerial skills to cope with the demands and pressures managers face from the real world of managing. These include human relations, conceptual, administrative, and technical skills. When managers are able to cope successfully with day-to-day managerial responsibilities, they are more likely to appreciate the ideals of OD efforts.

The three different perspectives projected throughout this book are highly complementary. The contingency theory specifies a set of conditions under which an organization becomes effective. The OD concept provides the tool for achieving these conditions. OD tends to be concerned with the long-term objective of improving organizational effectiveness; the managerial perspective is primarily concerned with discharging day-to-day managerial responsibilities.

When these three perspectives are integrated into managerial education, they will have a significant impact on managerial practice.

KEY CONCEPTS AND WORDS

Internal organizational fit
External organization fit
Micro-macro contingency
Integrative contingency model
Organizational development
Behavior-focused OD program

Personal quality
Structure-focused OD program
Transactional analysis
Assertiveness training
Sensitivity training
Team building
The managerial grid
Career development
Flextime
Matrix organization
Job enrichment

Behavior modification
System 4
Survey feedback
Management-by-objectives (MBO)
Human relations skill
Conceptual skill
Administrative skill
Technical skill

Questions for Review and Discussion

1. "Each managerial situation is unique; so the manager must use the contingency model to diagnose it." What does this statement mean to you?

2. "The concept of organizational development (OD) is based on the notion that people are capable of developing open, trusting, and

supportive relationships in work organizations." How realistic is this assumption for managerial situations with which you are familiar?

3. What are some conditions under which OD efforts can be implemented effectively?

4. a.   What are the behavior-focused OD programs?
    b.   What are the structure-focused OD programs?

5. What can managers do to improve the effectiveness of OD programs?

6. a.   What kinds of skill do managers need to perform their jobs?
    b.   Why do they need each of these skills?
    c.   Can these skills be taught? Explain.

7. Many successful managers never attended college or participated in management development programs. What can account for their success? Does it mean that managers are born rather than made? Explain.

CASE AND EXERCISE

CASE 19.1. NON LINEAR SYSTEMS*

This case is presented to help you understand some of the problems involved in applying behavioral science theories to a specific organization. Although the experiment at Non Linear Systems was a failure, you can make some generalizations about it that should then help you in applying behavioral theories in organizations.

The Situation

Non Linear Systems, a small manufacturer and marketer of electronic measuring instruments, was a pioneer in experimenting with the application of behavioral theories on a large scale. In the early part of the 1960s, the company introduced several organizational changes, including the following:

1. **Flat organization.**   The structure was designed to consist of three levels: (1) an executive council, (2) departments, projects, and marketing regions, and (3) work groups. The executive council was composed of the president and seven vice-presidents. This council functioned as a planning and policy-making body. In addition, it was responsible for formulating the company's multiple objectives, which included market standing, innovation, productivity, financial resources, profitability, manager performance, worker performance, and public responsibility.

*This case is derived from E. R. Gray, "The Non Linear Systems Experience: A Requiem," *Business Horizons,* February 1978, 31–36. Used with permission.

Department and project managers reported to the council members as a body, rather than to individual members. They were delegated almost complete authority over operational matters. Prior to this change, the company had had a traditional functional structure.

2. **Group management.** Assembly line operations were eliminated and replaced by assembly teams. These teams were responsible for planning, assembling, and checking their own work.

3. **Straight salary.** All workers were placed on straight salary. Time clocks were eliminated and workers were not penalized for absences. Moreover, no layoff policy was announced.

4. **No accounting control.** The accounting department was eliminated. The record-keeping function was reduced to a minimum and made the responsibility of each individual department.

These organizational changes reflected the theories of Maslow (need hierarchy) and McGregor (Theory X and Theory Y). The new managerial practices were introduced to satisfy the higher-order needs of employees—to give them autonomy, recognition, a sense of achievement, responsibility, and creative and challenging work.

These practices were based on McGregor's Theory Y assumptions that workers like their jobs, seek responsibility, and are able and willing to manage their own work.

In the early years of these changes, the company's management was praised by scholars, teachers, writers, and practitioners for applying behavioral science theories to an actual operating, profit-oriented business. But in 1965, with diminishing sales and deteriorating competitive position, the company abandoned some of the new managerial practices. In 1970, additional changes were made, and management returned to the original organizational structure that existed before the experiment. When this happened, some critics said behavioral theory was not applicable to industrial settings.

Discussion Questions

1. What do you see as the reasons for failure?

2. If you were the manager of the company, what kinds of OD programs would you have proposed?

3. What would you have done to overcome the problems the company was experiencing?

EXERCISE 19.1. TAKING A MANAGERIAL SKILL INVENTORY

If you expect to be a manager in the future, you may have already begun to ask yourself how well qualified you are to be a manager and how you can become qualified for such a position while you are still in school. This exercise is designed to help you take stock of your current qualifications and to show you what managerial qualifications you need to acquire in the years ahead.

The Procedure

1. Take an inventory of your managerial qualifications, using the checklist that follows.

2. Prepare a profile of your qualification inventory. It will reveal your areas of weakness.

3. Think about how you are going to remedy any weaknesses in your qualifications. This may be the starting point for your concern about your career development.

4. Although you may not be interested in a managerial career, remember that most of the managerial qualifications listed in the checklist are applicable to most professional jobs.

The Managerial Qualification Checklist

Instructions: Each of the following items concerns managerial qualifications. Respond to each item by placing an X in the column that indicates your assessment.

Items	Low 1	2	3	4	High 5
Personal Qualities:					
1. *Motivation to Manage:* The desire to manage an organizational unit.					
2. *Motivation to Lead:* The desire to have an influence on other people.					
3. *Capacity for Empathy:* The capacity to put oneself in another person's shoes.					
4. *Tolerance for Ambiguity:* The capacity to tolerate ambiguity.					
5. *Emotional Strength:* The emotional strength to function under pressure.					
6. *Risk-Taking Behavior:* The capacity to take risks.					
Managerial Skills:					
7. *Interpersonal Skills:* The ability to create and maintain personal contacts.					
8. *Leadership Skills:* The ability to motivate and lead other people.					

Items	Low 1	2	3	4	High 5
9. *Communication Skills:* The ability to collect and disseminate information.					
10. *Group Process Skills:* The ability to use work groups to solve problems.					
11. *Entrepreneurial Skills:* The ability to take advantage of business opportunities.					
12. *Analytical Skills:* The ability to understand what goes on in the organization.					
13. *Resource Decision Skills:* The ability to make correct resource decisions.					
14. *Negotiation Skills:* The ability to negotiate differences with others.					
15. *Administrative Skills:* The ability to plan, organize, and execute activities.					
16. *Technical Skills.* The ability to solve technical problems.					

Footnotes

1. R. M. Steers, *Organizational Effectiveness* (Pacific Palisades, CA: Goodyear, 1977), p. 183.

2. Ibid., pp. 38–56; and B. A. Kirchhoff, "Organizational Effectiveness Measurement and Policy Research," *Academy of Management Review,* July 1977, 347–355.

3. Charles Perrow, "The Short and Glorious History of Organizational Theory," *Organizational Dynamics,* Summer 1973, 2–15.

4. L. W. Mealiea and Dennis Lee, "An Alternative to Macro-Micro Contingency Theories: An Alternative Model," *Academy of Management Review,* July 1979, 333–345.

5. D. A. Nadler and M. Tushman, "A Congruence Model for Diagnosing Organizational Behavior," in *Organizational Psychology,* ed. D. A. Kolb, I. M. Rubin, and J. M. McIntyre (Englewood Cliffs, NJ: Prentice-Hall, 1979), pp. 451–452; the same sentiment was ex-

pressed by J. W. Lorsch, "Making Behavioral Science More Useful," *Harvard Business Review,* March–April 1979, 171–180.

6.   L. E. Greiner, "Red Flags in Organizational Development," *Business Horizons,* June 1972, 17–24; and D. Sirota and A. D. Wolfson, "Pragmatic Approach to People Problems," *Harvard Business Review,* January–February 1973, 120–128.

7.   See Newton Margulies and A. P. Raia, *Organizational Development* (New York: McGraw-Hill, 1972); and W. L. French and C. H. Bell, *Organizational Development* (Englewood Cliffs, NJ: Prentice-Hall, 1973).

8.   R. R. Blake and J. S. Mouton, *The New Managerial Grid* (Houston: Gulf Publishing, 1978).

9.   Rensis Likert, *The Human Organization* (New York: McGraw-Hill, 1967).

10.   W. J. Heisler, "Patterns of OD in Practice," *Business Horizons,* February 1975, 77–84.

11.   J. I. Porras and P. O. Berg, "The Impact of Organizational Development," *Academy of Management Review,* April 1978, 249–266; and also see R. E. Walton, "Work Innovations in the United States," *Harvard Business Review,* July–August 1979, 88–98.

12.   P. E. Conner, "A Critical Inquiry into Some Assumptions and Values Characterizing OD," *Academy of Management Review,* October 1977, 635–644; and W. R. Nord and D. E. Durand, "What's Wrong with the Human Resources Approach to Management?" *Organizational Dynamics,* Winter 1978, 13–25.

13.   W. R. Nord, "Dream of Humanization and the Realities of Power," *Academy of Management Review,* July 1978, 674–679; and M. E. Shaw, "The Behavioral Sciences: A New Image," *Training and Development Journal,* February 1977, 26–31.

14.   C. P. Bowen, "Let's Put Realism into Management Development," *Harvard Business Review,* July–August 1973, 80–87.

15.   This list of managerial skills is derived from R. L. Katz, "Skills of an Effective Administrator," *Harvard Business Review,* September–December 1974, 90–102; and Henry Mintzberg, *The Nature of Managerial Work* (New York: Harper & Row, 1973), pp. 188–193.

16.   This list of personal qualities is derived from J. Sterling, "The Myth of the Well-Educated Manager," *Harvard Business Review,* January–February 1971, 79–89; E. H. Schein, *Career Dynamics* (Reading, MA: Addison-Wesley, 1978), pp. 235–239; and L. C. Megginson, *Personnel and Human Resources Administration* (Homewood, IL: Irwin, 1977), pp. 256–258.

MANAGEMENT AND ORGANIZATIONAL BEHAVIOR

1. Understanding the Job of Managing

2. Studying Organizational Behavior

INDIVIDUAL BEHAVIOR

3. Satisfying Human Needs

4. Learning and Reinforcing

5. Understanding the Perceptual Process

6. Understanding the Motivational Process

SUPERVISORY BEHAVIOR

11. Understanding the Leadership Process

12. Developing Leadership Skills

13. Acquiring and Using Power in Organizations

14. Managing Reward Systems

INTERPERSONAL AND GROUP BEHAVIOR

7. Understanding Interpersonal Dynamics

8. Improving Communication Effectiveness

9. Understanding Group Dynamics

10. Dealing with Intergroup Conflicts

ENVIRONMENTAL ADAPTATION

15. Task Design—Matching Jobs to People

16. Designing Organizational Structure

17. Making Managerial Decisions

18. Managing Organizational Change

ORGANIZATIONAL EFFECTIVENESS

19. Developing Effective Organizations

APPENDIX

Developing Careers in Organizations

Micro-organizational analysis

Macro-organizational analysis

DEVELOPING CAREERS IN ORGANIZATIONS

Developing a career is a continuous process. It does not start when a person accepts employment, nor does it end when a person leaves a job. It is a lifelong endeavor in which one undertakes a series of activities and occupations and meets many challenges and problems. The individual must undergo many years of formal education, receive job instruction and training, perform loyally and capably as an employee, and cope with personal, interpersonal, and organizational problems. Becoming a manager adds even more complexity and responsibility to one's life, because that involves dealing with other people's careers and problems.

Career development can be a random process in which people stumble into something or somebody and their careers take off. A study by March and March found that the career choices for Wisconsin school superintendents could be characterized as a random process that occurred as a result of an almost casual selection process.[1] In this process, if someone is perceived to be competent, and if a position is available at the time, he or she is promoted. If the person is perceived to be incompetent, he or she is demoted or fired. This judgmental and selection processes take place casually without concrete or reliable information.

Although some people may consider career choices as random events that depend on job availability, career sponsors, and competitors, most of us are able to predict these events—at least to a reasonable degree —and prepare to deal with them. We can develop career goals, for example, and prepare the necessary qualifications. We can also search for career opportunities and cultivate career sponsors.

Career development is a selection and developmental process which takes place between individuals and their employers. It can be seen as a process of matching individual and organizational needs over time. When we take this career developmental perspective, career development is no longer a random process. It involves a conscious effort on the part of both the individual and the organization to develop individual careers and match them with organizational needs.

This appendix is aimed at providing some guides that can be useful in developing individual careers and matching them with organizational needs. To this end, it discusses (1) a general pattern of career development, (2) career paths in organizations, and (3) individual and organizational responsibilities in the developmental process.

CAREER DEVELOPMENT STAGES

A career is what a person does for a living. It is represented by a series of work-related experiences over the person's working life. For most managers, their career is of central interest, as it influences their material well-being, circle of friends, place of residence, and overall satisfaction with life. As careers become the central life interest, managers as well as would-be managers become increasingly interested in career development in organizations.

Although people differ in their career development experiences, they generally progress through an orderly sequence of developmental stages. Donald Super and his associate propose a model of career stages that includes (1) growth, (2) exploration, (3) establishment, (4) maintenance, and (5) decline.[2] Douglas Hall suggests that Super's model generally corresponds to Erikson's life cycle and Maslow's hierarchy of needs.[3]

Erikson's life cycle model comprises five stages: (1) childhood, (2) identity, (3) intimacy, (4) generativity, and (5) ego identity.[4] Maslow, as pointed out in Chapter 3, arranged human needs in a hierarchy in the order of (1) biological, (2) safety, (3) social, (4) self-esteem, and (5) self-actualization.[5] Figure A.1 shows the relationships between these models at different stages of career development.

Growth Stage (Birth–14).
This stage represents the period during which children depend on their parents for existence. They grow physically, mentally, and emotionally during this period and learn most of what they will ever know, including their value systems and religious and political beliefs, as well as how to walk, talk, and so forth.

Exploration Stage (Age 15–24).
This period is the first real career stage, for young people try out different roles in school, family, and leisure activities and perform "experiments" in the form of part-time or regular employment. In this stage, individuals

FIGURE A.1
Stages in Career
Development. (From
Careers in Organizations
by Douglas T. Hall, p. 57.
Copyright © 1975 by
Goodyear Publishing Co.
Reprinted by permission.)

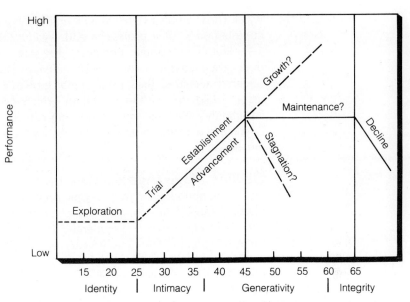

display a need for self-examination and identity formation. Also, pressure is often quite intense during this period, as people must satisfy their lower-order needs while preparing to satisfy their higher-order needs in the future.

Establishment Stage (Age 25–44).

Having found an appropriate occupation, people now strive to establish a place in it. The early part of this stage is characterized by a concern for security, with primary emphasis on obtaining acceptance and recognition.[6] Socialization takes place during this period as a means of obtaining acceptance.

Having established their place, people begin to display a need for intimacy, and this intimacy leads them to make commitments to both their organization and their co-workers. When security and intimacy needs have been gratified, individuals tend to channel their productive energy into making a major impact on their profession and organization. During this period, the need for achievement and autonomy can be the prime motivator of behavior.

Maintenance Stage (Age 45–64).

Having made their place in the world of work, some people may direct their energy to producing something meaningful to leave to the next generation. This is what Erikson called "generativity" and what Maslow meant by the need for self-actualization. This need can be met in a number of ways. Those who strive to satisfy it on the job will likely make a significant contribution to their profession and organization (professional growth).

For many people, however, this stage poses a dilemma. If they direct their energy to off-the-job activities such as hobbies or family-oriented activities, their professional growth may stagnate (career plateau).[7] Also, this is the period in which people experience what is commonly called the "mid-life (or mid-career) crisis." It is created by the conflicting demands of the self, family, and work that are imposed on the individual.

Decline Stage (Age 65–Death).

This is the period when most people prepare for and enter retirement. As physical and mental capacities begin to decline, work activity slows down and ultimately ceases. Consequently, this stage is characterized by a need for ego integrity. After many years of serving other people—including family members, superiors, subordinates, the company, and society—people finally seek time to fully serve themselves.

Evaluation of Career Stage Model

There are, of course, people who do not follow this career development route. Some people may never go beyond the stage of exploration, while others may change careers in the middle of their lives. The model, however, does represent the general pattern of career development for most working people. The stages in the model also seem to coincide with the process of satisfying the dominant needs of human beings. In the earlier stages of their lives, people are concerned with establishing the means of survival, such as getting education, training, and job experience. This concern is then followed by a need for intimacy and socialization. Once economically and socially secure, they can pursue the need satisfaction of generativity and self-actualization.

CAREER PATHS IN ORGANIZATIONS

As indicated earlier, career development can be seen as a series of matching individual and organizational needs. As individuals have different needs and qualifications, so do organizations. Organizations have different career paths, that require different psychological makeups and career preparations. These differences should be reflected in career choice and development.

Career opportunities available in organizations can be classified into three catagories: (1) technical and professional, (2) managerial, and (3) entrepreneurial. This section deals with the demands, opportunities, and costs involved in pursuing each of these career paths.

Technical and Professional Careers

A variety of technical and professional careers are available in most organizations. These include accounting, engineering, financial analysis, law, marketing, systems analysis, personnel, production, and other functional specializations. Although there are some differences among these specializations, they have some common elements. For example, they generally require analytical abilities, specific technical skills, and the general knowledge associated with particular fields. These qualifications are usually acquired through long years of formal education and training.

A study by Schein indicates that people who pursue careers in technical and professional fields are motivated by the *content of their work,* a feeling of *being competent in their profession,* and sense of *task accomplishment.* [8] Also, they have a tendency to avoid managerial positions that will prevent them from performing their specialized activities. If they accept managerial responsibility, it will be within their area of technical competence. They are rooted in the analytical work, and actively disdain managerial work, viewing it as a "political jungle" and a "professional graveyard."

There is considerable justification for this view. One's professional and managerial activities are frequently incompatible due to differences in orientation. When professional/technical people are employed by an organization at the entry level, they are usually competent in their area of expertise and are oriented toward—and committed to—their professional associations. They have current knowledge of their field, they attend conventions and other data-providing meetings, and they do research—or whatever is necessary to progress—in their field. Their orientation is horizontal and directed toward other professionals, either inside or outside the organization.

However, as they move up the managerial ladder, their orientation progressively shifts upward and inward toward managerial colleagues within the organization. They have less time for—and interest in—their profession. The same is true of technical personnel so far as their skills and expertise are concerned. Both groups, unless they are very dedicated and exert great effort to overcome the tendency, will become obsolete as they move up the managerial ladder and become increasingly involved with solving other people's problems.

In some organizations, technical and professional personnel can climb to the top of the ladder without having to leave the technical/professional path. In universities, for example, faculty members can advance through professorial ranks—instructor, assistant professor, associate professor, full professor, chaired professor or distinguished professorship—without ever having to give up the teaching or research they love. Some industrial firms have "dual promotion ladders," whereby they reward good technical or professional performance with salary increases, titles, and other evidences of recognition, instead of always "promoting" them to management positions.

The key to advancement in these situations includes keeping current in your field of specialization through research, study, reading, attending learning sessions, and other methods. This is not easy! For example, it has been estimated that about 20 to 25 percent of an engineer's time will be spent in educational experiences on the job or on company time,[9] and that graduate engineers must spend 10 percent of their time each year just to keep up with current graduates and 20 percent if they want to remain of equal value to their employers and society.[10] In summary, one key to advancement and success is to remain up to date in your particular field of specialization. This is critical in the face of rapidly changing knowledge and competition from well-trained newcomers in the organization. Those who cannot keep up with this demand will be better off moving into administrative positions where more generalized knowledge and experience are rewarded.

Managerial Careers

Managerial careers focus on managing people. Unlike managers in technical groups, who see management as secondary to their professional interests, managers who pursue managerial careers perceive it as their ultimate career goal.[11] Professional, technical, and functional jobs are seen as necessary interim steps on the way to higher managerial positions. People see the necessity of becoming competent in one or more of the functional areas, but they do not commit themselves to any specific area. Instead, they are more interested in developing managerial qualifications such as human relations skills, conceptual skills, and personal qualities.

Why do people pursue managerial careers? The payoffs for managerial careers are usually *money, status, power, control,* and the *challenge* of solving problems through and with other people. The very things that technical people dislike, or even deplore, as a "political jungle," "playing God," and "management disarray" are seen by these managerially oriented people as challenging and stimulating. These are the very things they want and can get excited about in their work.

There are many and varied options and paths for those who wish to pursue managerial careers up the organizational ladder. People with strong conceptual skills should do well as managers in technical and functional work groups. If they combine conceptual skills with human relations skills and personal qualities (or emotional competencies), they could do well as senior functional managers or even move into general management positions. The job of managing the whole organization requires a combination of human relations and conceptual skills along with relevant personal qualifications. People who have human relations skills but lack conceptual skills and emotional strength tend to do better at lower levels than at higher levels of management.

Entrepreneurial Careers

Another career path available in organizations is the entrepreneurial career. Entrepreneurs are different from those who pursue technical and managerial careers. While technicians and managers are motivated by technical and managerial competence, task accomplishment, money, power, status, or security, entrepreneurs are primarily motivated by the desire to create and achieve something that is their own. Several studies have pointed out that the achievement motive is associated with entrepreneurial behavior—that is, with business venture and risk-taking.[12]

Entrepreneurial individuals can satisfy their high achievement needs in organizations that encourage entrepreneurial behavior. They may prefer to work in research and development departments where they can get involved in new products, or in sales departments where they have a good opportunity to achieve and to be rewarded for their accomplishment.

So far, we have discussed career options available in organizations. This discussion has been concerned with the kinds of tasks requirements and personal qualifications, along with payoffs and costs, associated with different careers. Pursuing careers, however, involves more than selecting a career field. As the task requirements and personal qualifications change, one must prepare to take on different task responsibilities at different levels and/or in different areas of specialization. The following section deals with the direction of career movements in organizations.

DIRECTION OF CAREER MOVEMENTS

People move in many directions while pursuing career options in organizations. These movements, which occur for various reasons, such as a promotion or job rotation or more power, involve crossing career boundaries. According to Schein, there are three types, or directions, of movement: vertical, radical, and circumferential; and each of these is associated with one or more of the three boundaries: hierarchical (rank), inclusion (centrality), and functional.[13] Figure A.2 shows a model of an organization illustrating these career movements and boundaries.

Vertical Movement

Vertical movement requires crossing a *hierarchical boundary,* which separates nonmanagerial technical and professional positions from the managerial ranks in the same specialty area. This usually means a promo-

FIGURE A.2
Career Boundaries in an
Organization. (Reproduced
by special permission from
*The Journal of Applied
Behavioral Science,* "The
Individual, the
Organization, and the
Career: A Conceptual
Scheme," by Edgar H.
Schein, **7,** 4, 404,
copyright 1971, NTL
Institute.)

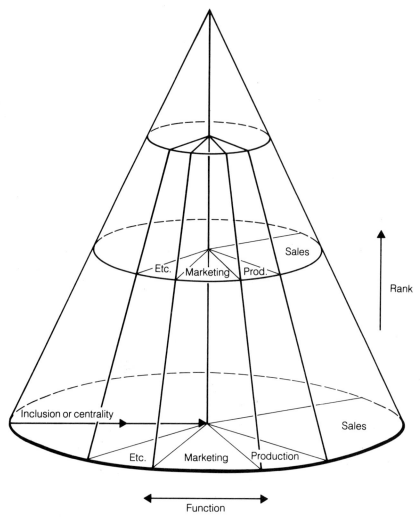

tion or demotion. Some people successfully aspire to and pass a number of hierarchical boundaries in their progression to higher levels of leadership. Others level off early in their careers, either from lack of ambition or from inadequate initiative, ability, opportunity, or luck.

Radial Movement

Radial movement involves gaining power or moving toward the center of power. In order to move into an "inner circle" of power, one must pass through an *inclusion* (membership) *boundary,* which separates people in the inner circle from those "on the outside looking in." One can gain admission to power positions formally, with a formal title, or informally, through charisma, manipulation, or some other method.

Circumferential Movement

Circumferential movement is passage through a *functional boundary,* which separates one technical, functional, or professional work group from another. One reason for this type of change in position is to broaden one's technical competence. Also, people who aspire to be general managers or higher-level executives may make such a move to gain a broader perspective of the organization.

> One of the largest energy corporations in the United States had a policy of job rotation as part of its executive development program. Potential managers were moved horizontally into almost all departments, jobs, and areas.
>
> Initially, new technical and professional graduates worked on drilling sites and in service stations. After entering the managerial ranks, they were moved from one functional specialty (such as economic planning, engineering, electronic data processing, or marketing) to another and immediately begin making decisions and performing other managerial functions. After mastering that function or job, they moved to another technical area.
>
> This policy created a short-term loss of efficiency, but it was more than compensated for by long-range effectiveness due to broader perspective, understanding of different specialized problems, and a sense of confidence in decision making.
>
> The firm's current chief executive officer is a product of this system.

Hybrid Movement

Hybrid movement, a combination of vertical and circumferential, involves a transfer from a nonmanagerial technical or professional position to a managerial position in another area of expertise. This type of motion often creates conflict in people who, because of it, have to make a painful career decision. They want to stay in their specialized area, where they feel "nice and comfortable working with things they know"; yet this opportunity, which will take them away from their chosen field, is difficult to pass up. Becoming a manager means movement toward the top of the organization, but it takes away the intrinsic rewards that technical people value—technical competence, task accomplishment, and concrete performance feedback. This loss, however, is compensated for by such rewards as having control over others, increased pay and responsibility, and higher status.

Socialization and Influence

As shown, career movement involves a series of passages through various organizational boundaries. When a person crosses a boundary, the individual and the organization (or the work group) both attempt to influence the other. Usually, however, the organization influences the individual before the individual can have any significant influence on the organization.[14]

Before a person can influence the group process, he or she must be accepted socially. Newcomers are usually considered "outsiders"; they have not yet formed political alliances with other group members, so they cannot influence any decision that requires the approval of others. Hence, influence is most likely to occur at the mid-point of a career stage and continue until the person is about to move to another position. Once a person's imminent departure becomes known to others, he or she is considered a "lame duck" and has only minimal influence.

The processes of socialization and influence continue throughout people's work lives. The need for socialization occurs during the early career stages, and the ability to make some impact on the organization occurs during later stages. The ability to influence the organization can be acquired with increased job experience and status. The concepts of socialization and innovation are particularly important for individuals who aspire to move radially and/or circumferentially in an organization. They have to be technically and psychologically prepared to be noticed and accepted by the members of the group they wish to join.

CAREER PLANNING AND DEVELOPMENT

People have satisfactory careers when their vocational needs match the organization's task requirements. This compatibility can occur only when the employee and the organization know each other's needs and expectations. Yet the common assumption in many organizations has been that the decision makers are the ones who best understand the needs of their employees. This assumption often leads to people being moved to satisfy the organization's needs rather than individuals' needs. Such a practice can have negative consequences because the affected employees are often dissatisfied with the new assignments and perform less than satisfactorily. In this section we present various ways employers can improve the career developmental process.

How Career Planning and Development Works

A number of organizations are sensitive to the needs of their employees and provide them with career planning and guidance, as well as developmental aids. For example, the American Telephone and Telegraph Company (AT&T) was a pioneer in introducing a systematic career planning and development program.[15] The first industrial assessment center was founded in 1956 at AT&T, where it was used to identify talented managers. AT&T is now using the assessment method for career development as well as for selection. The program involves: (1) the assessment of managerial potentials, (2) the establishment of career goals and plans, (3) the establishment of development objectives, and (4) career development counseling.

The 3M Company has a similar career development program called the Management Assessment Program (MAP), which emphasizes the determination of (1) career goals, (2) developmental needs, and (3) placement opportunities.[16] Employees can either volunteer for participation in the program or be nominated. Participants complete various tests, exercises, and interviews, and then each has an interview with a personnel research staffer to receive the assessment feedback. The assessment information is used by the participants to determine their career goals and developmental needs. It is also used by management for personnel decisions such as transfer and promotion.

How To Make Career Planning More Effective

The following actions are suggested to make career planning and development more effective in meeting the needs of both employees and their employers.[17]

Establish a Human Resource Plan.   The organization should institute coherent and comprehensive human resource planning. If the company has overall corporate planning, it should be reflected in the human resource planning. When corporate planning involves a new kind of work, management cannot safely expect the necessary talents to be somehow available to do that work. An active planning and development program is needed, then, to meet the organization's personnel requirements and employees' development needs.

Take a Human Resource Inventory.   In order to plan effectively, management should take an inventory of the skills possessed by its employees. This information should include (1) the quantity and quality of the present levels of skill and talent, (2) the present levels of performance, (3) the potential for growth in technical, managerial, and entrepreneurial skills among individual workers, and (4) the career stages of present employees. Such information can be collected through assessment and performance appraisal systems.

Establish Developmental Objectives.   Only after the human resource needs are determined can management establish its developmental needs and initiate specific plans to meet them. Management may launch development programs for certain employees or recruit new employees where new skills are needed. And if developmental efforts are to be responsive to the needs of employees, the career goals and aspirations to these employees should be reflected in the plans.

Maintain a Dialogue Between Managers and Employees. Dialogue between managers and their subordinates is an important tool for matching individual needs with organizational requirements. Instead of guessing what the career goals of their subordinates are, managers can have meaningful dialogues with them to increase their own understanding of the subordinates' career goals,—as well as their own—developmental needs, career paths, and personal interests. This process involves creating an organizational climate in which subordinates feel free to exchange their views and feelings on various issues with their superiors.

Inaugurate Developmental Activities. After identifying developmental needs, management should inaugurate developmental activities to help match jobs with employees' abilities. These activities may include recruiting, selecting, training, job rotation, placement, career counseling, job enrichment, and performance appraisal. The organization may create a personnel development or human resource development committee to coordinate these activities.

Monitor the Progress of Developmental Activities. The career planning and development cycle should end with activities that monitor the progress of developmental activities and measure and evaluate their impact on developmental objectives. This feedback can be used to assess the effectiveness of various developmental activities, estimate future developmental needs, and establish developmental goals and plans for the future. Personnel experts—or those in the human resource development committee created by the organization—should be involved in the monitoring process.

How Organizations Develop Managers

Although there is no best way to develop managers, certain features seem to be common in many programs. Digman found the following to be common in several development programs he surveyed:[18]

1. Companies usually hire people at the entry level, except for some specialists.

2. After a period of successful performance, the managerial potential of the employees is assessed.

3. The employees with managerial potential are promoted to supervisory positions and take part in supervisory training programs.

4. The new supervisors receive on-the-job coaching from their superiors. This coaching involves skills building in a weak area.

5. After mastering this job, they are rotated to another assignment to learn new supervisory skills in another environment.

6. The supervisors then participate in a middle-management program designed to develop human relations and conceptual skills.

7. After successful performance at supervisory levels, they may move up to the middle-management positions.

8. Either before or after they move into the executive level, they usually participate in an advanced management program designed to develop decision-making skills.

MANAGING YOUR OWN CAREER

Although employers are partly responsible for developing their employees' careers, you are ultimately responsible for developing your own career. You need to know what you want for your life and prepare to achieve your lifetime goals. In planning and developing your career there are certain things you can do. Although they do not guarantee success, they can enhance your chances of succeeding. These career developmental strategies include: (1) establishing career goals, (2) performing a personal self-analysis, (3) formulating a long-term developmental plan, and (4) progressing within and between organizations.

Establishing Career Goals
Establishing career goals involves knowing what you want for your life. Career goals are those that can be satisfied through working in organizations. In order to achieve these goals more effectively, you may take the following steps.

First, Set Personal Goals.   Knowing or deciding what you want to do with your life is the starting point for establishing your career goals. It is an important step because you cannot separate your vocational goals from other personal goals. You may achieve your personal goals through work, or your work-related goals may positively or negatively affect your other goals. For example, if you are not able to obtain job satisfaction, you may spend more time off the job in order to compensate for your job dissatisfaction.[19]

Other people cannot help you choose or decide your career goals, because they are a mixture of (1) your own values, which are based on your cultural heritage,[20] your early home life,[21] your religious upbringing, and your schooling; (2) your needs, which are influenced by your past and present physical, economic, and mental and emotional environments; and (3) your dreams and aspirations.

However, most people have some idea about what they want to do in work organizations. A young person who admires a baseball player may say, "I want to be a baseball player when I grow up." A sales representative may say, "I would like to be the sales manager some day, become wealthy by middle age, and retire sometime before the age of 65." Sometimes the search for life goals begins with just the knowledge of what one does or does not want to be or accomplish. Having such knowledge, even though it may be imprecise, is better than saying, "I am 45 years old, but I still don't know what I want to do." The more precise, definite, distinct, and accurate your goals are, the better your career planning will be. Therefore, you need to explore career opportunities in greater detail.

Obtain Information on Career Opportunities.   Your career dreams and aspirations must be translated into career opportunities before you can set clear goals. So once your personal goals and career interests are identified, the next step is to find out the opportunities and requirements of the jobs that may suit your interests and talents. There are several ways of getting such information.

1. Obtain data on job opportunities from career-oriented publications, such as:
    a. The U.S. Department of Labor's *Occupational Outlook Handbook,* which can be obtained from the U.S. Government Printing Office in Washington, D.C. This book is published every other year and contains up-to-date information on job duties, educational requirements, employment outlook, and earnings for 300 occupations and 35 industries.
    b. The College Placement Council's *College Placement Annual* (available from the Council at P.O. Box 2263, Bethlehem, PA 18001) contains career information from approximately 1,000 employers.

2. Consult your campus career planning centers. Most universities have career planning or placement centers that provide information on job opportunities. They also provide job search workshops and arrange job interviews with prospective employers.

3. Consult your professors. Most professors have some contacts among employers and knowledge about career opportunities in their fields. They can also advise you on how best to prepare yourself to pursue your career in the field.

Select Career Goals That Promise Satisfaction. On the basis of your personal goals and the opportunities available, you can now choose a career that will satisfy your own interests as well as those of your family and your professional growth. There are situations in which you may consider one particular interest more important than others. For example, professional interest can be the most important one when you are striving to establish a place for yourself in an organization at an early stage of career development. In the long run, however, if your work interest does not match your other interests, you will experience job dissatisfaction that will reduce your work involvement. So you must ultimately consider your personal and family interests in choosing a career.

Select Your Academic Major. Closely related to career selection is the choice of an academic major. People generally enter academic fields that appear to have good employment prospects. For example, accounting, engineering, and computer science are currently popular subjects and will probably continue to be so through the mid-1980s. Some students go into these fields because they like them and have the necessary aptitudes. These students will find that their career goals match their personal interests. Many other students, however, go into these academic fields not because they like them but because they expect better job opportunities. Upon graduation, many of these students may find that their jobs do not match their personal interests and taste. Others may be disappointed to find that there are no jobs in these areas, as there are too many graduates seeking the popular positions.

Students commonly enter academic fields that promise jobs at the moment. Remember, though, that job opportunities fluctuate over the years. For example, majors in the liberal and fine arts were in oversupply during the past decade. Now, however, some of these majors are being recruited by business and governmental organizations to staff their marketing, advertising, international, and administrative positions. These graduates may offer some specific skills that business or engineering graduates lack.

Performing a Personal Self-Analysis

This stage is best summed up by the motto, "Know thyself." Do a self-analysis to see what you can and cannot do, and why you cannot do it. There are a number of practical things you can do to know yourself better.

1. List all the major projects, hobbies, and other things you have done in the past few years. Identify the activities that gave you the most

personal satisfaction and most nearly match your talents and interests.

2. List all of your favorite activities in order of preference. Relate them to specific skills you have. This list will reveal the kinds of talent and interest you possess.

3. Consult your campus career counselors. Most schools have counseling services involving career planning. They may administer some tests (such as the Strong Interest Inventory and the Kuder Occupational Interest Survey) to assess your career aptitudes and interests.

4. Get advice from your professors and/or superiors at work. Ask for their honest assessment of your strengths and limitations. (Be prepared not to be defensive when you receive such an assessment.)

    Knowing your personal and vocational interests and talents will help you determine the type of work that fits you best. Although this information will give you only a rough idea of yourself, it does provide a concrete basis for locating a specific career option or options in the labor market.

Formulating Long-Range Developmental Plans

You cannot achieve your career goals without years of hard preparation. This period includes your formal education, job training, and job experience. To this end, you must identify your developmental needs at various stages of career development.

Educational Stage.   This stage corresponds to the exploration stage of the career cycle. At this stage, you should follow a well-rounded academic curriculum that provides both general and specific educational experience. *Ford's Insider,* a supplement to college newspapers, indicates that most employers prefer college graduates with both general and specific education.[22] General education usually includes communication and interpersonal skills, while specific education deals with the more technical knowledge needed in your anticipated vocation. A "well-rounded" education will provide you with the breadth of general education and the depth of specialized skills. College graduates with such backgrounds have the best chance in the labor market because they can be easily groomed for both technical and managerial positions.

Early Career Stage.   This is the beginning of the establishment stage in your career cycle, for you develop action skills that allow you to apply the concepts and theories you learned in school. Your efforts should be directed toward the technical and functional field you have chosen. These are the formative years when you can be creative, innovative, and competitive in your professional development. With this need for growth in your technical or functional field is the need for cultivating political alliances—the need for social development. You need to be assimilated into the organization's social system so that you feel emotionally secure and have influence with other people.

Middle Career Stage.   This stage represents the latter part of the establishment stage and the early part of the maintenance stage in the career cycle. At this stage, you may want to redefine your career role or at least adapt to changes. Faced with the problem of technical obsolescence and competition from newcomers, you may either update your technical and functional skills through education and training, or you may rely on interpersonal and political skills to function effectively in the organization.[23] By this time, you should have the "wisdom" and political skills to be able—that is, to be in a managerial or professional position—to develop and coach other people.

Later Career Stage.   This stage represents the latter part of the maintenance career stage. You should now gradually prepare to withdraw from work involvement and get involved in activities outside of the organization. You may even have to switch your role from that of an active "power player" to one of reactive counselor.

At this stage, you may try to do some of the things that you missed doing in the past. For example, some successful top executives or professionals such as doctors, lawyers, and engineers may quit their jobs and move to rural or smaller urban areas to engage in manual vocations, such as farming and woodworking.

Progressing Within and Between Organizations

The fourth and final stage of your own career management is charting the treacherous course vertically within an organization and horizontally between institutions.

Selecting an Organization to Work For.   Your career actually begins with your first "permanent" job. Therefore, selecting an organization to work for is as important as selecting a career. Just as a mismatch between an individual's abilities and his or her career goals leads to job dissatisfaction, so does a mismatch between individuals and their organizations. After all, the organization provides the jobs, the supervisors, and the rewards that affect your career development, and it can either facilitate or hinder your vocational progress.

The problem of mismatch is most critical during your first job experience. A study by Schein reported that about 75 percent of MBA (Master of Business Administration) graduates in the sample changed their employment during the first five-year period, and most companies lost over half of their college graduate employees within five years.[24] An earlier study indicated that only about 20 percent of college graduates stay with their first employers more than two years.[25] This high turnover can be attributed to the mismatch between the graduates' expectations and the realities of organizational life, which has been called "reality shock."[26] Such a shock often occurs because the employers promise newcomers something that they cannot deliver, or because students have overestimated their worth to the employer.

Organizations have personalities just like people. People will enjoy their jobs more and be more productive if their personalities are compatible with that of the institution they work for. Such compatibility is called the "psychological contract."[27] Downey and his associates found evidence to support this hypothesis in the significant correlation they established between individual needs, organizational climate, and job satisfaction.[28] It follows, then, that people who are aggressive and achievement-oriented will be happier in aggressive and performance-conscious organizations; people who are power- and status-conscious will be happier in prestigious and politically oriented organizations; and people who have strong socialization needs may prefer a warm, friendly, and supportive organizational climate.

How can you determine whether your personality fits that of a given organization? A number of signs you can look for are revealed in the ways the organization rewards and treats its employees.[29] Specifically, you can look for these signs:

1. **The kinds of people who are rewarded in the organization.** Are they high performers? Are they team players or independent achievers? This information will provide a clue as to whether this organization will reward you for performance or for cooperation.

2. **The meanings of status symbols and rituals.** People communicate their acceptance and rejection through these symbols and rituals. They include club membership, a reserved parking space, a private office, access to confidential information, acceptance in informal social gatherings, and so forth. In order to predict whether or not you will be accepted by other members, you need to understand what these symbols and rituals mean and determine whether or not you will be or have been granted such privileges.

3. **The extent to which the covert and overt rewards satisfy your needs.** Are the status symbols important to you? Does pay increase reflect your performance? Are the task assignments challenging enough for you? Your answers to these questions will determine your commitment to the organization.

Increasing Career Mobility. An important key to success in career development is mobility. The more mobile you are, the greater are your chances of moving around within and outside of the organization at will. Career mobility stems from several sources, including (1) technical and professional competence, (2) interpersonal and political competence, and (3) psychological, mental, and emotional flexibility.

The following suggestions for increasing your mobility are derived from several sources, including DuBrin, Hall, Jennings, and Schoonmaker.[30]

1. **Gain broader job experience.** People who hope to reach top management must have a broad perspective of the organization and its environment. Therefore, movement within the organization—cutting across various functional boundaries—is highly desirable. If you become overspecialized, it will be difficult to move around inside or out of the organization. Mobility increases when you have a variety of job skills and experience.

2. **Be professional, be successful.** People cannot argue with performance and success. Performance and success attract people's attention, and these qualities help you cross various organizational boundaries—hierarchical, radical, and functional. In order to move ahead continuously, you must demonstrate success and performance on each of your successive jobs.

3. **Help your "boss" succeed.** One major role that a subordinate plays is helping his or her superior to function effectively. The more valuable you are to your "boss," ideally, the greater approval and support you will get from him or her. Becoming a crucial subordinate to a mobile superior is one way of advancing, since you can move ahead with a mobile superior.

4. **Develop supportive relationships.** Developing good relationships with subordinates, peers, and clients is as important as maintaining good relationships with superiors. These people directly affect your day-to-day operations and indirectly affect your career progression. They may not directly promote you to a higher position, but they can affect your performance—or reported performance—and this has a bearing on your chance of promotion.

5. **Blow your own horn.** Many people contribute a great deal to their organizations without anyone's ever knowing it. If you are truly interested in career mobility, you should make other people aware of your accomplishments and qualifications. There are several ways you can make your achievements known to others, especially superiors. You can send memos to them whenever important projects are

completed, document your accomplishments in the personnel file, and let the boss know how much other people value your work. Job offer letters and "To Whom It May Concern" letters praising your work can be tactfully used for this purpose.

6. **Find a career sponsor.** Your immediate superior can be a career sponsor at a given career development stage. But usually a "career sponsor," "mentor," or "patron" is the person who coaches, teaches, counsels, and sponsors another person for an extended period of time. A study by Roche found that more than two-thirds of top-level executives in his survey had a mentor, and that those who had such a mentor were more successful and happier with their career progress than those who had not.[31]

SUMMARY AND CONCLUSION

A career is a person's vocation, profession, or life work; it comprises a series of work experiences that stretch over the individual's life span. As it is such an integral part of our lives, it affects our work, family, and self-interests. Career development involves the process of matching vocational requirements and demands with family and self-interests and personal abilities. When these are matched, a person can experience a rewarding career.

People go through several stages in developing their careers: (1) growth, (2) exploration, (3) establishment, (4) maintenance, and (5) decline. At the early stage of their life, (growth, exploration, and establishment), people are primarily concerned with security, survival, and accomplishment. This concern is followed by a need for socialization and intimacy at the mid-point of their lives. Once established in their careers, they are concerned with leaving something concrete to the next generation —generativity.

There are several career paths in organizations: (1) technical and/or professional, (2) managerial, and (3) entrepreneurial. In the process of pursuing their careers, individuals move through various parts of the organization through promotion, job change, and a gain in power. These movements involve crossing hierarchical (rank), inclusion (power), and/or functional boundaries. After crossing a boundary, people must be accepted by the existing members (socialization). Once accepted, an individual can have an influence on the organization.

Both the individual and the organization are responsible for career development. The individual, of course, is ultimately responsible, but the organization can assist its employees' development by identifying their career needs and by providing opportunities for growth.

Footnotes

1. See J. C. March and J. G. March, "Performance Sampling in Social Matches," *Administrative Science Quarterly,* September 1978, 434–453; and J. C. March and J. G. March, "Almost Random Careers: The Wisconsin School Superintendents, 1940–1972," *Administrative Science Quarterly,* September 1977, 377–409.

2. D. E. Super and M. J. Bon, *Occupational Psychology* (Belmont, CA: Wadsworth, 1970).

3. D. T. Hall, *Careers in Organizations* (Pacific Palisades, CA: Goodyear, 1976), pp. 47–64.

4. E. H. Erikson, *Childhood and Society* (New York: Norton, 1963).

5. A. H. Maslow, *Motivation and Personality* (New York: Harper & Row, 1954 and 1970).

6. D. T. Hall and Khalil Nougaim, "An Examination of Maslow's Need Hierarchy in an Organizational Setting," *Organizational Behavior and Human Performance,* 1968, **3,** 12–35.

7. T. P. Ference, J. A. F. Stoner, and E. K. Warren, "Managing the Career Plateau," *Academy of Management Review,* October 1977, 602–612.

8. E. H. Schein, *Career Dynamics: Managing Individual and Organizational Needs* (Reading, MA: Addison-Wesley, 1978), p. 17.

9. See W. M. Tate (President of Southern Methodist University), "Things Aren't Like They Used to Be," *Proceedings of the 26th University Personnel and Management Conference* (Austin: University of Texas, 1964), p. 35.

10. See a comment by Dr. Steison (Department of Civil Engineering, Carnegie Institute of Technology), quoted in "The Rising Crisis in Skills: More Jobs Than Skills," *Steel,* September 7, 1964, p. 41.

11. Schein, *Career Dynamics,* pp. 134–146.

12. See D.C. McClelland, *The Achieving Society* (New York: Free Press, 1961); David C. McClelland, "That Urge to Achieve," *Think Magazine,* November–December 1966, 19–23; D. C. McClelland and D. G. Winter, *Motivating Economic Achievement* (New York: Free Press, 1969); and Satvir Singh, "Achievement Motivation and Entrepreneurial Success: A Follow-up Study," *Journal of Research in Personality,* 1978, **12,** 500–503.

13. Schein, *Career Dynamics,* pp. 36–48.

14. E. H. Schein, "The Individual, the Organization, and the Career: A Conceptual Scheme," *Journal of Applied Behavioral Science,* 1971, **4,** 401–426.

15. D. W. Bray, R. J. Campbell, and D. L. Grant, *Formative Years in Business* (New York: Wiley, 1974); and J. P. Campbell, M. D. Dunnette, E. E. Lawler, and K. E. Weick, *Managerial Behavior, Performance, and Effectiveness* (New York: McGraw-Hill, 1970), pp. 213–231.

16. Hall, *Careers in Organizations,* pp. 165–166.

17. See Schein, *Career Dynamics,* pp. 189–199.

18. L. A. Digman, "How Well-Managed Organizations Develop Their Executives," *Organizational Dynamics,* Autumnn 1978, 63–80.

19. Robert Rapoport and Rhonda Rapoport, "Work and Family in Contemporary Society," *American Sociological Review,* June 1965, 381–394.

20. A. L. Kroeber, *Anthropology,* new ed. (New York: Harcourt, Brace & World, 1948), pp. 7–8.

21. J. F. Kinnane and M. W. Pable, "Family Background and Work Value Orientation," *Journal of Counseling Psychology,* Winter 1962, 320–325.

22. The Ford Motor Company, *Insider: A Continuing Series of College Newspaper Supplements* (Knoxville, Tenn.: 13–30 Corp., 1978), pp. 9–11.

23. Harry Levinson, "On Being a Middle–Aged Manager," *Harvard Business Review,* January–February 1969, 51–60.

24. E. H. Schein, "The First Job Dilemma," *Psychology Today,* March 1968, 22–37.

25. "Hanging on to Talent," *The Manager's Letter* (American Management Association), November 20, 1963, 1, quoting W. B. Murphy, President of the Campbell Soup Company.

26. Hall, *Careers in Organizations,* p. 66.

27. Roosevelt Thomas, "Managing the Psychological Contract," in *Organizational Behavior and Administration,* ed. P. R. Lawrence, L. B. Barnes, and J. W. Lorsch (Homewood, IL: Irwin, 1976), pp. 465–480.

28. H. K. Downey, Don Hellriegel, and J. W. Slocum, "Congruence Between Individual Needs, Organizational Climate, Job Satisfaction, and Performance," *Academy of Management Journal,* March 1975, 149–154.

29. See R. R. Ritti and G. R. Funkhouser, *The Ropes to Skip and the Ropes to Know* (Columbus, OH: Grid, 1977).

30. See A. J. DuBrin, *Fundamentals of Organizational Behavior* (Elmsford, NY: Pergamon Press, 1978), pp. 159–170; E. E. Jennings,

Routes to the Executive Suite (New York: McGraw-Hill, 1971); Hall, *Careers in Organizations,* pp. 181–189; A. N. Schoonmaker, *Executive Career Strategy* (New York: American Management Association, 1971); and Laurence Peter and Raymond Hull, *The Peter Principle* (New York: Morrow, 1969).

31. G. R. Roche, "Much Ado About Mentors," *Harvard Business Review,* January–February 1979, 13–28.

NAME INDEX

SUBJECT INDEX

80 81 82 83 84 9 8 7 6 5 4 3 2 1